C0-AVN-570

C

A HISTORY OF LATVIA

Alfred Bilmanis

A HISTORY
OF
LATVIA

BY

ALFRED BILMANIS

1951

PRINCETON, NEW JERSEY

PRINCETON UNIVERSITY PRESS

PRINTED IN THE UNITED STATES OF AMERICA BY
PRINCETON UNIVERSITY PRESS AT PRINCETON, NEW JERSEY

TO THE

LATVIAN PEOPLE

To many people in the Western world the identity of the Baltic peoples is at best very vague. Before the end of the First World War there was, it is true, some realization that the "Baltic provinces" of Russia were inhabited by some minor tribes of peasant folk, but the element which counted for anything were Germans who were known to be influential at the court of the Tsar. The native Baltic peoples of the eastern littoral of the Baltic seacoast had had no spokesmen in the West to present their case for independence. Yet they won, within a short eighteen months after the signing of the Versailles Treaty, almost universal *de jure* recognition. The free states of Estonia, Latvia, and Lithuania, small, intelligent, sturdy, without previous experience in politics, conducted their internal and external affairs with dignity and efficiency for the two decades they were left in peace by their powerful neighbors. But since 1940, their long history of forced subjection to rapacious conquerors has been repeated. The waves of conquest from the West, then from the East, have surged over their land, and they have had to bow their heads in bitter and helpless humiliation.

It is perhaps the proudest tradition of our Western Christian heritage that any people has a right to a hearing, that justice and truth may prevail. Yet it is passing strange that, even after the Latvian nation won their freedom and proved their national cohesiveness and economic viability, there has not appeared in any Western language a serious, full-length study of their history. It was to remedy this omission that Dr. Bilmanis devoted his energies the last years of his life, firm in the conviction that if the democratic world had before its eyes the simple truth of the long history of his people's sufferings and strivings there was no doubt that justice would be done.

By the time of his death, on July 26, 1948, Alfred Bilmanis had had a distinguished career as scholar, journalist, editor, and diplomat. Educated at the Universities of Moscow and Strasbourg, he taught school in the Caucasus and Krasnostav, served with distinction as a junior officer in the Imperial Guard, and after 1917 became inspector of a commercial college in the Polish Ukraine until 1920. Then, returning to Latvia, he became head of the press section of the Latvian Foreign Office. He accompanied his official duties by scholarly writing and academic practice, and became Professor Extraordinary of History at the Riga College of Commerce. He was Latvian delegate to the League of Nations from 1929 to 1932, when he went to Moscow as Minister. In 1935 he was transferred to Washington as Minister. During the trying years of German and Russian occupation and absorption of his native land, he continued to hope for her ultimate liberation. He was confident that he could best serve that end by presenting to the Anglo-Saxon world the facts of Latvia's historical development through the ages, her indisputable accomplishments in self-government, the injustice and brutality to which she was currently being subjected. There issued from his pen in the years from 1936 to his death a great number of scholarly articles, brochures, and books, in all of which he emphasized the importance of an understanding of the Baltic area for European and consequently world peace, and specifically the constructive role Latvia had played and could play in the future for a democratic world. The culmination of all his scholarly endeavors was to be this *History of Latvia*, upon which he was working at the time of his death.

The organization of the book follows, in the post-tribal times, the course of the successive periods of foreign conquest. At times it is clear that the native Letts have only the scanty history of a slave population. The German settlement in the Middle Ages, the growth of the Teutonic Knights—these are well recorded by the Germans themselves. Their conflict with a westward-looking Muscovy in the thirteenth century is also thoroughly chronicled on both sides. But for the story of the Letts, over whose prostrate body the Teuton-Slav conflict raged, our sources are few. The expansion of feudal Poland in the fifteenth and sixteenth centuries brought a new element of partition and confusion into Latvian history, to be further confounded by the entry of Sweden under the Vasas into east Baltic problems. Yet the Swedish era was, for the native Balts, an improvement upon any of the preceding conquests. The Swedes were either liberal or indulgent, and the Latvians sensed some of the hopefulness of having some weight in their own land. The decline of Sweden after the defeat of Charles XII at Poltava meant a return to subjection to a determined conqueror, and throughout the eighteenth and nineteenth centuries, under Tsarist Russian control, the native Latvians saw the "Baltic barons," who had survived the changes of administration by maintaining a class solidarity and an urbane adaptability to each new conqueror, still the virtual lords of the land. Yet, miraculously, the spirit and cohesiveness of the native Latvians remained unbroken and survived political and economic discrimination.

It might be useful to point to some salient features in this work which are original contributions to Baltic history. The essential nature of Latvian tribal society as a native peasant democracy has not been previously so clearly delineated. The serious work of Latvian archeologists, folklorists, and philologists of the past generation has here been thoroughly assimilated. It was this early and deep-rooted traditionalism which enabled the native Balts to survive the ebb and flow of successive foreign invasion and conquest. The book also reveals how, though their first contact with Western civilization when mediated by German colonizers and feudal crusading orders was unfavorable, yet, when faced with a choice between Muscovite easternism and the westernism they knew from the Hansa merchants, the Lutheran clergy, and the German landed gentry, the Latvian people accepted the West, and thereafter never wavered in that loyalty. They came to regard themselves as a key outpost of Western culture against the westward push of Moscow, a feeling which even the arrogance of the German squirearchy was unable to eradicate. One finds current in Latvia, albeit somewhat retarded by reactionary German or Polish mediation, the major intellectual, political, and social movements that have turmoiled Europe since the thirteenth century.

Dr. Bilmanis has given particular attention to the growth of national consciousness in these centuries, relating it to the whole European movement for national recognition, yet emphasizing its peculiarly Latvian characteristics. But he also had in view, at this point, as throughout the book, the great significance of Latvia, with of course her two neighboring small states, in the perennial struggle for dominance of the Baltic and, by logical extension, of the "heartland" of Europe. The dramatic if confused story told in Chapter 16 of the conflict between Russian and German imperialisms in 1918 and 1919 is no more than a modern version of the struggle of which this Baltic coastal area has been the scene through all its recorded history. Careful attention to the course of this conflict, seen in the light of events of just twenty years later in this same region, will be very rewarding.

The treatment of the post-1914 period becomes at times almost a primary source. Not only was the author personally active in the

changes that took place, and acquainted with the principal partic-
ipants, but in his capacity as a responsible official of the Latvian
Foreign Office he had access to all the documents. Writing many
years after the events, using the available material in many languages,
with a high sense of historical responsibility, Dr. Bilmanis has composed a lasting monument to the enduring capacities and aspirations
of his people. One should not, perhaps, use the word "objective" of
such a work. The term has come into a certain disrepute by reason of
its appropriation by German scholarship until it has come to mean
"pro-German." This *History of Latvia* is written with love and hon-
esty. More could hardly be demanded of any national historian.

The work as the author left it required some editing and retouching,
some condensation and very occasional amplification. The author's
widow, Mme. Halina Bilmanis, has been most generous and helpful
in suggesting details and approving the editorial redaction that seemed
necessary. It was my high privilege to have known Dr. Bilmanis well
during these latter years, and to have discussed with him on frequent
occasions plans and progress in the composition of the work. I can
only join my hope to his that the cause for which he so faithfully
labored may be substantially furthered by this definitive history of
his native land.

                                       S. HARRISON THOMSON
Boulder, Colorado

Contents

FOREWORD — vii

PART I: TRIBAL LATVIA — 1
1 A Sea, a Land, and a People — 3
2 Amberland — 26
3 Early Latvian Customs and Culture — 38

PART II: GERMAN DOMINANCE — 51
4 Establishment of the Principality of Livonia — 53
5 Conquest of Southern Livonia — 70
6 Ascendancy of the Teutonic Knights — 86
7 Muscovite Wars and Partition of Livonia in the
Sixteenth Century — 113

PART III: POLISH AND SWEDISH CONTROL — 135
8 Polish Suzerainty — 137
9 Swedish Dominion — 160
10 The Duchy of Kurland — 182

PART IV: RUSSIAN RULE — 195
11 The Rise of Russian Hegemony in the Baltic — 197
12 Russian Rule and German Influence — 214
13 The Birth of a National Consciousness — 231
14 Revolution, Reaction, and War: 1905-1917 — 258

PART V: INDEPENDENCE — 283
15 The Shaping of a Modern State — 285
16 The Struggle for National Survival — 300
17 Self-Rule: Trial and Error. 1920-1934 — 332
18 National Unity — 357

PART VI: AGAIN THE PREDATORY POWERS — 379
19 Betrayals and Invasions — 381

BIBLIOGRAPHY — 409

INDEX — 415

PART I
TRIBAL LATVIA

Chapter 1

A Sea, a Land, and a People

WHILE the upheavals of the Russian Revolution were shaking loose large border fragments of the Slav Empire and the chaos of the First World War lingered in the bitter contest and confusion which flared in the seceded Russian Baltic Provinces, three small nations were being painfully born. By 1920 the succession states of Estonia, Latvia, and Lithuania found themselves finally free of German and Russian depredations. For the first time since their medieval tribal age they fully possessed their venerated soil and breathed unchallenged the clear, cool Baltic air. After seven centuries of foreign dominations—German, Swedish, Polish, and Russian—they were eager to take their place as accredited democracies in that Western European community of nations to which they had so long but unwaveringly aspired.*

Sisters in geography, in a shared history of subjection and exploitation, and in common aspirations toward a peaceful, progressive future, they yet exhibited cultural and national distinctions long cherished as a legacy from a remote era of liberty. These national idiosyncrasies were founded on early tribal variations, and were expressed through the ages in either unequivocal differences, or in more subtle shadings in language, biological stock, folklore, temperament, customs, and tastes. These differences could now be nourished contentedly, since the massive alien oppressions which had ignored or punished these separate manifestations of national consciousness had been overcome. Latvia, together with her neighbors to the north and south, plunged into an era of intensive self-realization and development. Self-contained but internationally-minded, comfortable yet faithful to her tragic past, conservative in customs, experimental in politics, economics, and culture, she hoped against hope to endure as a valuable and respected bridge between East and West, and as one of the devoted guardians of a free Baltic Sea.

This sea had played no small part in determining the character, the habits, and the expectations of the peoples of the Baltic lands since

* For a comprehensive bibliography on Latvian history, geography, politics, sociology, and economics, the reader is referred to the author's work, *Baltic Essays* (Washington, 1945), pp. 222-256.

their settlement on its shores in prehistoric times. It was the limit set to their expansion; it was their element, their provider, their poetry, and, in so far as it brought in some of their conquerors, their betrayer. This great inland gulf of the Atlantic Ocean, with which it was connected by the narrow outlet of the Danish Straits during the Ice Age, was essentially a large lake, with no great depths, small tides, a low salt content, frequent storms, and a tendency to freeze in some of its reaches during long periods of the winter. This "Mediterranean of the north," instead of separating continents and races, had served rather to unite all the Baltic peoples within a single Nordic-Baltic cultural cycle.

Several theories have been advanced in explanation of the term Baltic, as applied to both a sea and a land region. A few Scandinavian and German historians favor a derivation from the strings of Danish isles, or "belts"; while Latvian scholars are convinced that the word springs from the Latvian-Lithuanian root *balt-*, meaning white. Poetic fancies have seen the source of this name in the wind-swept, shining white waters of the Baltic Sea. More probably that body of water got its name from its southeastern and eastern shores, an area settled by blond, blue-eyed tribes who contrasted with the darker Finno-Ugric peoples to the north. These light-skinned prehistoric settlers were called *Balts*, or Whites, whence *Baltia*, the name which the Roman geographer Pliny the Elder, who wrote of his journey to the north of Europe in the first century A.D., uses to describe the land which he affirmed was similarly denominated by the Phoenician merchant Pytheas of Massilia, who had visited it in the fourth century B.C. Wolfstan, the geographer of Alfred the Great, called this country "Whitland," an obvious translation of *Baltia*. This latter term, then, appears to be much older than the name of the Baltic Sea, which was first used, in the form *mare balteum*, by the eleventh century chronicler Adam of Bremen.[1]

The Latvians today sometimes refer to their country as *Baltija*, but they call themselves by the ancient name of *Latviji* (pronounced *Latweeschi*). The derivation of this name is somewhat obscure. Many authorities see its origin in a river Lata, Late, or Latve, allegedly to

[1] F. Beyer, *Coniectura de nomine Balthis maris* (*Commentaria* of St. Petersburg Academy of Science V), p. 350ff. The work of Friedrich Kruse, *Ur-Geschichte des Esthnischen Volkstammes und der Kaiserlich Russischen Ostseeprovinzen Liv-, Esth- und Curland* (Moscow, 1846), in spite of its age is extremely rich in archeological, linguistic, and ethnographical data.

be found in the region of Latgale. Support for this theory was afforded by the discovery of a few rivers once named Late, Latupe, and
Latva in the basin of the upper Pripet, a region which the ancient
Baltic tribes may well have traversed on their way to the Baltic coast.
It is presumable that the small tribal enclave of the Livs, settled
among the Latvian tribes but speaking a Finno-Ugric language, de-
formed *Latviji* to *Latvis*, and gave it the new meaning of "forest-
clearers," as descriptive of the early, pioneering Latvian cultivators.
It was as "forest-clearers" that these people were known to the medieval German merchants and missionaries who further transformed the
"heathen" name to *Lette*. The first small portion of Baltic land which
the Germans controlled they called *Liefland* (*Liffland*, *Livland*) after
the small colony of Livs. This name, in its Latin form of *Livonia*,
was later extended to the much larger region which fell to the German
conquest. *Lettland* continued in use, through later centuries, with
reference to the heart of greater Livonia (which, for a period, included southern Estonia) i.e., the Latvian provinces north of the
Daugava.[2]

Ancient *Baltia*, also widely known as Amberland, stretched along
the southeastern shores of the Baltic from the mouth of the Vistula
to the *Kurisches Haff*, or Gulf of the Kurs, and on to the northern
shores of the Gulf of Riga. Over this coast and its hinterlands, the
Baltic Sea exerted, in ancient as in modern times, an inestimable
climatic and cultural influence.

A fair portion of credit for the rich cultural development manifest
even in medieval tribal times has been given to the good fortune
which the Baltic peoples enjoyed in their relatively moderate climate,
by comparison with other societies at that latitude. Modern Latvia
lies in the north-central sector of Europe, in a region protected from
the Arctic winds by the Norwegian mountain range, and warmed by
the Gulf Stream through the Baltic Sea. The Latvian climate is mildly
damp, with a durable snow cover, rainfalls, mostly in the summer,
averaging annually 27.9 inches, prevailing southwest winds, stormy
autumns and winters, and misty springs. In general, the temperature
will average about two degrees centigrade lower than that of Denmark.

While, by transmitting the influence of the Gulf Stream, the Baltic
Sea made possible a varied agriculture in the Baltic lands, it offered

[2] J. Endzelīns and K. Mühlenbach, *Latviešu valodas vārdnīca*, II ([Latvian
Dictionary], Riga, 1927), 425.

further wealth in its heavy runs of fish and, along its swampy shores especially in earlier times, in its deposits of amber, long known as the "northern gold." The Baltic Sea was the breeder of a hardy strain of fishermen and sailors who set out in all weathers save the winter freezes, which locked the Gulf of Riga from December until, sometimes, as late as April. The modern harbors of Liepāja (Libau) and Ventspils (Windau) in the province of Kurzeme (formerly Kurland), and of Ainaži in Vidzeme are ice-free; while Riga can now be kept open with ice-breakers.

For all its difficulties of navigation, it was by way of the Baltic Sea that Western European and even Mediterranean influences reached the Baltic tribes in ancient and medieval times. During the greater part of the Middle Ages the Baltic remained a free sea, since no nation was sufficiently strong to impose effective restrictions on shipping passing through the Danish Straits. Frisians, Anglo-Saxons, Icelanders, and Norwegians entered its waters. Scandinavian marauders and, later, German Hanseatic merchants descended on its south, southeastern, and northeastern shores. The island of Gotland, 95 miles from the Kuronian coast and called *Eystrasalts Auga,* or "the Eye of the Baltic," became an important Viking depot and a station on the *Austrvaegr,* the leading Viking trade route to the East, over the Baltic and down the Daugava River. It was the importance of this route which led to the use of the German name *Ostsee* for the Baltic Sea. It was over the *Ostsee* that the Germans brought commerce and Christianity, the two faces of the medieval colonizing urge, to be offered to or imposed upon the heathen fishermen, amber-gatherers, bee-raisers, horse-breeders, and "forest-clearers" who formed a tribal society on its southeastern and eastern shores.

Almost as important in their effect upon Latvia's commerce and culture were the long, straight watercourses which linked the Baltic seaways with the Slavic hinterlands and, in medieval times, with the trade of the Orient. The largest and most navigable is the Daugava (Duna, Dvina), with a total length of 627 miles and a basin of 34,000 square miles. It takes its rise near the Valdai Mountains in Russia, flows for 230 of its miles through central Latvia, and empties into the Gulf of Riga, where it attains a width of a full mile. Half a million tons of Latvian goods are transported on this river annually, of which 98.5 per cent (1938) is timber.

Latvia's second largest waterway, the 275-mile-long Gauja, runs

through the province of Vidzeme, north of the Daugava, the core of
ancient Livonia. Because of its rapids it is only partly navigable. The
chief river of the province of Zemgale, the Lielupe, has an inland port
at Jelgava (Mitau), accessible to medium-sized sea-going vessels
through the Daugava-Lielupe canal. The Venta, main river of the
province of Kurzeme, is used chiefly for floating logs; while its deep
mouth offers the valuable ice-free harbor of Ventspils.

These rivers serve the modern Latvian economy, both as means of
transport and as sources of power. It has been estimated that their
rapids are capable of supplying 3,260 billion kilowatt hours of electric
energy annually. One of the biggest Baltic dams has been constructed
on the Daugava at Kegums, near Riga, where 240,000 HP of energy
are generated yearly.

But the role of these waterways was even more significant in the
early history of the Latvian people. It was most probably by the Gauja
and Daugava routes that the Baltic tribes, traveling up the Dnieper
basin from the Black Sea region and finding good interfluvial connections and portages on the Russian plains, descended to their final
point of settlement on the Baltic shores. From the fifth to the tenth
centuries A.D. the Vikings out of Gotland took the Gauja, Daugava,
and Lielupe routes to Novgorod, Lithuania, and Byzantium. Thus was
the rich trade of the Volga and the Dnieper routes drawn up to the
north, where the German merchants were to succeed the adventurous
Vikings. When German missionaries settled around the mouth of
the Daugava, the "northern Hellespont," they were the spearhead of
that German pressure from the West which was to meet, in the un-
lucky land of "Livonia," the Slavic pressure from the Russian East,
which grew increasingly greedy for "windows" on the Baltic. Vast
struggles for the Baltic dominium were to arise from the encounters
of these two thrusts. During the later Middle Ages enterprising German merchants and Russian fur traders floated goods on the Latvian
rivers and stored them in *riji*, or barns, where the Vikings before
them had stored hides, honey, furs, flax, corn, and other treasures of
the Baltic region and its hinterlands. These trading activities, which
brought the wealth of the Novgorod marts into the Western European
Hanseatic cities, gave to early Latvia, then no more than a loose
group of tribal provinces, that character of a transit territory which
was to make her the prey of foreign exploitation down the centuries.
Even after gaining her independence in the twentieth century, Latvia

adopted the policy of placing transit facilities at the service of Soviet Russia and Germany. But up until 1918, and again in 1940 and 1941, geography and hydrography largely determined the fate of "the key to the Baltic," as Latvia, because of her commercially and militarily strategic position, has been called.

The prehistoric settlers found themselves amply provided with fish, not only from the Baltic, where the low salt content and the absence of plankton to encourage larger fish favored quantities of the smaller species, but also from the many rivers and streams and the innumerable lakes of this land of glacial origin. Latvia has 2,980 lakes, covering about 1.64 per cent of her total area. The largest are Lake Rāzna, in Latgale; and Lakes Engure, Usma, and Liepāja in Kurzeme. Lake Burtnieks in Vidzeme figured in some of the early myths and legends of the tribes.

Marshes and bogs cover about seven per cent of Latvia's area. Though modern drainage projects have reclaimed part of them for agriculture, many of them still furnish peat as a valuable export. Peat and bog iron-ore were among the earliest natural resources to be exploited by the Latvian tribes. From earliest times the marshes of the Rītupe, Ludza, and Zilupe rivers, together with the swampy virgin forests of Rosica-Crissa, watered by the tributaries of the Daugava and by a large number of lakes, have formed a natural boundary between the Latvian lands and the swampy Russian plains which rise to the Valdai Mountains.

This natural barrier is the basis of the Latvian-Soviet Russian frontier, which is 211 miles long. Latvia's longest border is the Lithuanian, with an extent of 350.6 miles; while the Estonian and Polish borders measure 234.1 and 66 miles respectively, making a total of 862 miles of frontier. Latvia's coastline has an extent of 310 miles.

Modern Latvia covers an area of 25,700 square miles, approximating the combined areas of Massachusetts, Vermont, Connecticut, and Rhode Island. In size she ranked nineteenth of the 35 independent European states in existence in 1932. Rising from a coastal plain, her central rolling hills subside, eastwards, into the marshlands bordering the Russian plains. The highest altitude is that of Mount Gaisina (1,023 feet), and the commonest altitude of the hills in central Latvia, in northeastern Vidzeme, in Latgale, and in parts of Kurzeme is 400 feet above sea level, only one fourth of Latvia's total area being above that level. Her morainal topography places Latvia, together with Estonia and Lithuania, in that region of northern Europe which the

Swedish geographer, Sten de Geer, has named *Balto-Scandia*, a geographical unit clearly separated from the Great Russian plains.

L. Slaucītājs, an eminent geologist at the Latvian State University in Riga, has established Latvia's geological origin as a platform of sedimentation, generally of Devonian formation, interrupted by a few vertical dislocations. Middle Devonian red sandstone is found in the northern section, whence it was moved onto other parts of the country, in the form of fine sand, by the crushing pressures of the two Ice Ages. The glacial period, which fixed Latvia's surface formations, left large deposits of gypsum, clay, limestone, chalk, lignite, and brown coal, as well as numerous peat bogs, and some sulphuric springs and mud. The coastal bogs and large stretches of sand dunes were produced by changes in the Baltic Sea during the Alluvial Age.

Latvia's rocky terminal moraines, her sandy areas, and her marshes detract from her agricultural value. The diluvian soil of her ground moraines has been rendered fertile through centuries of fidelity to its demands, since only in Zemgale can naturally rich soil be found. The early "forest-clearers" were determined to make their laboriously acquired farms yield; and so persistent were their efforts that much of medieval Europe sought rye, red clover, and flax seeds as well as a variety of medical herbs in the Baltic lands. About 60 per cent of modern Latvia is under cultivation, thanks to extensive drainage projects and an intensive program of fertilization. Rye, wheat, barley, oats, flax, hemp, and clover are all successfully produced, many of them for export. Sugar beets and potatoes are the chief vegetable crops, though most of the other northern European vegetables are grown for domestic consumption or for seed, quality seeds being a specialty of Latvia's agricultural program. Fruit trees and a variety of berry vines, in spite of the short summers, produce well and, together with the blazing flower gardens, support one of the earliest Latvian industries, the production of honey, which served the ancient tribes as a sweet, a preserver, the basis of the potent Baltic mead, and a profitable export commodity. The Thracians had reported to Herodotus that penetration of the Baltic lands was rendered almost impossible by the great swarms of bees which possessed the flowery meadows and orchards.

Animal husbandry was an art which the migrating tribes may have brought with them from more southern regions. At least we know that the horse figured prominently in their primitive culture. The cool, well-watered meadows of the Baltic lands permitted the development of excellent strains of horses, as well as the raising of milk cattle, and sheep. The production of fatted pigs and quality poultry, in modern times, has opened a wide foreign market for bacon and eggs, which rank close to the famous Latvian dairy products, particularly butter, on the export list.

The gently rolling, glowing landscape of the farming areas contrasts richly with the dark and silvery greens of the thick forests which have always furnished one of Latvia's most reliable natural resources. Thirty per cent of her area is covered by dense growths of white pine and fir (constituting respectively 52 and 29 per cent of the total forest area); and by birch, aspen, black alder, maple, ash, elm, chestnut, walnut, linden, and oak. Several huge oaks have been preserved from pagan times, when these trees, believed to house the souls of ancestors, were the center of religious rites. The linden, long the symbol of womanly grace, appeared among the poetic imagery of ancient songs. Latvian timber, in addition to supporting a shipbuilding industry dating back to the seventeenth century, has been a valuable export since Duke Jacob spurred on the economy of his cherished Duchy of Kurland. The British Isles, under the Stuarts, came to appreciate the virtues of Kuronian oak for shipbuilding purposes. Construction timber was one of Great Britain's leading Latvian imports in the period between the World Wars.

Latvia does not have the sort of natural resources that fosters heavy industry. Iron-ore, coal, and oil are almost nonexistent, though there are indications that the first of these may yet be found in certain areas. Her bog iron-ore was the basis of a brisk iron and steel industry in Kurland during the seventeenth century. Latvia's chief industrial resource is her hydro-electric power, together with the power potential of her peat. Her considerable reserves of gypsum, limestone, and chalk provide raw materials for the lime and Portland cement industries which, in addition to supporting an intensive domestic building program, supplied the British and Scandinavian markets. Large deposits of red and blue clay are the basis of the highly-developed brick and ceramics industries. Zechstein, found in southern Kurzeme, is used in the fabrication of paints.

But Latvia's chief resources, in addition to her forests, remain those of her diligently cultivated soil and of her abundantly populated waters. Her Baltic fisheries have provided her with export commodities of international reputation. Her well-stocked lakes and rivers contribute considerably to the attractions of her tourist trade.

Latvia's Baltic seaports have long formed an essential part of her natural wealth. Fully equipped with the most modern storage and transit facilities, serving a well-developed Latvian merchant marine, and open to the trading nations of the world, Riga, and to a lesser extent Liepāja and Ventspils, have done more than anything else to bring the Latvian flag before the eyes of the world. These ports are served by railways built during the industrial phase of the Russian Tsarist régime and intended to link the Baltic ports to the Russian economic centers, as well as to connect the German with the Imperial Russian railroads. During her period of independence Latvia rounded out her claim to excellent transit facilities by building and maintaining first class roads for through traffic between East and West.

Latvia's climate and her gentle landscape have also contributed to her national wealth, in so far as they have attracted the more discriminating type of tourist to her quiet and comfortable resorts. A number of sea and lake resorts, as well as health spas had a regular clientele, highly appreciative of the cool summers, the bracing sea air, and the peculiar silvery light which bathes the Baltic lands.

A journey through Latvia's four provinces, which correspond roughly to medieval tribal kingdoms, reveals variations in landscape, climate, and agricultural conditions which, over the centuries, have developed in their inhabitants differences in customs, occupations, and temperament. The fertile plains of Zemgale, south of the Daugava, have nurtured Latvia's most prosperous agricultural communities, with solid, comfortable, well-ordered farms and a race of farmers noted for their spirit of independence and somewhat stubborn individualism. The coastal province of Kurzeme, with its relative isolation from the international struggles which raged over the rest of Livonia, and with its long periods of prosperity under the Dukes of Kurland, has bred equable peasants, growers of potatoes and cereals, and a hardy strain of seafarers. Old Latvian customs have lingered longest in this peaceful area. Vidzeme, north of the Daugava, is more hilly and has a poorer soil and a harsher climate than the two southern provinces. Stock-breeding has been the chief pursuit of its agricultural population, in whom hard labor and a resistant environment have developed endurance and adaptability, together with a marked tendency toward association and cooperation. Latgale, the southeastern province, has a raw climate and a large number of lakes and rivers in the long valleys carved out by the Ice Age. Proximity to Russia and a long period of Polish domination retarded Latgale's economic and social growth, introduced a few Slavic customs, but at the same time intensified the peasants' loyalty to ancient Latvian fears and faiths.

Only in Latgale could one find, up until the Agrarian Reform of 1920, the characteristic Russian collective village, or *mir*. In general, since their liberation from serfdom at the beginning of the nineteenth century (though not until 1861 in Latgale), the Latvian farmers have preferred the isolated, privately owned holding which recalled the self-sufficient farms of early medieval times. Many of the Latvian farms combine the conveniences of rural electrification and modern dairy and cultivating equipment with certain traditional features. The farmhouse, usually two-storied, is nestled among flower gardens and orchards with their inevitable beehives. Next to the house is the *klēts*, a combined storehouse and cold cellar, under whose roof the body of the *saimnieks* (head of the household) passes its last night before burial. The *rija*, or barn, possesses a threshing floor made of clay and a big oven built of clay bricks. Near it are cowsheds, a huge fodder shed, and perhaps a windmill. Beside a brook or a lake will be the *pirts*, or steambath house, an institution dating back to ancient times. Steam, produced by pouring water on big, heated stones, circulates over the bathers who lie on benches, beating themselves with bundles of birch branches.

Married children are encouraged to build their farms close to the parental holdings. Farmhands can usually obtain some private property and livestock for their personal use during the period of their contract. In conformity with the time-honored tradition of self-sufficiency, most Latvian farms during the period of independence were cultivated by the owner, his immediate family and relatives, so that hired agricultural labor did not loom large in his economy.

Of Latvia's total population of 1,950,502 in 1935, about 64 per cent inhabited rural areas, but only 169,844 were hired farmhands. There were at that time 237,350 individual farm units, 83.4 per cent of which were of 30 hectares or less; 50 hectares (124 acres) being the limit allowed by law, except for model or experimental farms. Latvia's predominantly agricultural character strongly marked the smaller provincial towns, since even those with industries usually depended on the farmers for their raw materials.

Latvia's towns and cities developed over a long period from medieval hamlets, conveniently situated for commerce, or surrounding the fortified seats of tribal rulers. Twenty-six of her fifty-nine cities are situated on rivers, ten of them on the Daugava. All Latvian cities have their historical coats of arms. Municipal self-government was general during the period of independence, when this crystallization of the traditional independent spirit of the old rural communities formed the basis of the state.

Hundreds of early medieval castle-mounds dot the rolling Latvian countryside and trace the course of early commerce and conflict along her rivers. Shells or fragments of the massive fortified castles of the Teutonic Knights crown many of Latvia's towns, testifying to the wars which were her scourge. Almost all her towns and cities possess such ruins, the lingering signs of the destruction brought upon Livonia in the Polish-Russian, Polish-Swedish, and Swedish-Russian struggles for dominion of the Baltic lands and the sea which they guarded.

Both early and late medieval ruins are found in all the Latvian provinces. In Kurzeme, Kuldīga (the Livonian Jesusburg), was a capital of the Kuronian tribal kings; Piltene was the seat of the early bishops of Kurzeme; and Talsi has rewarded the archeologists with its traces of tribal civilization. Also rich in archeological material are the Zemgallian towns of Dobele, Mežotne, and Tērvete, all strongholds of the powerful thirteenth century tribal King Viesturs. Dobele possesses, in addition to the remains of an ancient castle-mound, the ruins of a castle of the Livonian Order. In Vidzeme lies Lielvārde, home of the legendary Latvian hero Lāčplēsis the Bear-slayer. On the right bank of the Daugava are Koknese, seat of the tribal dynast Vetseke (1205), and Jersika, residence of the thirteenth century King Vissevald, now the site of important archeological excavations. Sigulda, on the Gauja, was an old Viking stronghold and became the summer residence of the Prince-Bishop of Riga, whose splendid castle with its chapel lies in ruins. Cēsis, or Wenden, after Riga the oldest and largest city in Vidzeme (population 8,748)[3] was a stubborn stronghold through many wars, displaying the Latvian flag as early as the thirteenth century. In 1577, its garrison chose to blow up the castle rather than surrender to the Muscovites. North of Cēsis lie Valmiera, also in existence in the thirteenth century, and Valka, site of the original convocation of the Livonian Diet in 1419, and of the Latvian National Council's proclamation of Latvia's independence in November 1917. Through the center of Valka runs the Latvian-Estonian frontier, established by arbitration in 1920.

In Latgale are the traces of many ancient castles and fortresses

[3] Population statistics, unless otherwise indicated, are taken from the census of 1935.

along the thousand-year-old Latvian-Russian border. This province's largest city, Daugavpils (population 45,160), in modern times an important railroad junction for lines into Russia, Poland, Lithuania, the Ukraine, and White Russia, was a tribal stronghold and a busy station on the Viking *Austrvaegr*. Many Latgallian towns contain monuments to the Roman Catholic and Greek Orthodox faiths which, for historical reasons, had larger followings here than in the rest of predominantly Evangelical Lutheran Latvia.

Many of Latvia's leading cities combine the attractions of historical patina with pronouncedly modern architecture and improvements. The Kuronian port of Liepāja, Latvia's second largest city (population 57,098), named after its linden trees (*liepa*), closely neighbors the site of the inland port of Jurpils or Seeburg, mentioned as early as the ninth century. Liepāja flourished under the Dukes of Kurland, was captured from the Russians by the English in 1854, and was subsequently developed as a naval base by the Russians, whose entire Baltic Fleet sailed from there to Japan in 1904. Liepāja, however, proved itself essentially indefensible when it fell to the Germans in 1915. After the First World War it was revived, given a navy yard and drydocks as well as some local industries, while preserving its ancient amber industry and its important fisheries. It is connected by rail- and highway with Ventspils, Kurzeme's second largest ice-free port and Latvia's fifth largest city (population 15,671) and chief timber port. Like Liepāja, Ventspils lies opposite southern Sweden, at a distance of 275 miles.

Latvia's fourth city, Jelgava (population 34,099), called by the Germans Mitau, from the Latvian *Mitava*, meaning market place, lies on the Lielupe River (also called the Aa). In existence by the thirteenth century, Jelgava became the capital of the Duchy of Kurland, whose Dukes adorned it with Italian architecture, and, seeking to create a small Versailles, introduced opera and a ballet. Its famous buildings have been badly damaged in both World Wars.

Relatively undamaged in the First World War, Latvia's capital city, Riga, suffered considerable harm during the second. The House of the Blackheads (dating from 1335), the City Hall (1750), and the churches of St. Gertrude and St. Peter, among other historical buildings, were destroyed. St. Peter's, built in 1491, and its 440 foot wooden spire, the highest in the world, had already been burned and rebuilt several times. Fortunately the ancient castle of the Teutonic Order, the churches of St. John and St. James, the latter dating back to the thirteenth century, the President's Palace, the Parliament building, and the Palace of Justice all survived, so that Riga still preserves its blend of Gothic and twentieth century architecture. During their twenty-two years of independence the Latvians lavished modern improvements on their beloved capital, while at the same time cherishing its many quaint traces of an old Hanseatic town. Populous port and lively political and cultural center, yet distinguished by the somewhat conservative atmosphere of a traditionally independent city; self-governing and jealous of its privileges and its caste-system all through the upheavals which beset the rest of Livonia, Riga is one of the mellowest and at the same time one of the most modern cities of the Baltic.

In the second century A.D. a settlement twelve miles from the mouth of the Daugava was known to chroniclers as the *Duna urbs*. In the early Middle Ages the site was occupied by a Viking factory, consisting of a number of storehouses or *riji, rija* being the Latvian for barn. The medieval German merchants substituted the hard g for the softer Latvian pronunciation; but Richard Hakluyt uses the form *Rie* in his *Principal Navigations*.[4] In 1207, Riga became the capital of the Livonian principality, seat of the Archbishopric under direct papal suzerainty. In 1225, it was made a free city of the Empire, and subsequently became a prominent Hanseatic town. The mid-seventeenth century, following the Swedish conquest of Livonia, saw Riga become Sweden's most important city, the granary of the realm. During the final phase of the Tsarist régime this leading port of the Baltic Provinces was heavily industrialized and connected with the Russian hinterland by excellent railways.

Greater Riga, including several suburbs on both sides of the river, covers 210 square kilometers. Her population had grown from 35,000 in 1700, to 400,000 in 1939; and her industries from 51 (factories with more than 50 employees) in 1884 to 349 in 1937.

Latvia's cities all enjoyed self-government during the period of independence, Riga, Liepāja, Ventspils, and Daugavpils forming prefectures with district rights. The nineteen districts into which the four provinces were divided by the law of 1924 were centered around leading cities whose names they bore. These districts were in turn divided into *pagasti* (from the Latin *pagus*), corresponding to the historical rural communities, the last strongholds of Latvian independence during the centuries of foreign dominion and, properly, the

---

[4] *The Principal Navigations . . .* , III (London, 1589), 253.

basic unit of modern Latvia's system of administrative decentralization. The size of each of the 517 *pagasti* varied with the size of its
component parts, those privately-owned separate farms, which constituted the ultimate social and economic units upon which the structure
of the republic rested.

Although several of Latvia's cities showed a steady industrial development during the period of independence, the rate of migration
from the rural areas was not greatly accelerated. The figures on rural
population show a decrease from 70.63 per cent in 1897 to 65.38
per cent in 1935, revealing a degree of stability reassuring in a predominantly agricultural country. Between 1800 and 1914 the Latvian
population had trebled, growing from 725,000 to 2,552,000. Death
and evacuation to Central Russia during the First World War
diminished the figure to 1,596,931 in 1920. With the return of refugees, improved living conditions, and the natural rate of growth, the
population had reached two million by 1939. In that year, of Europe's
35 nations Latvia stood fifteenth in birth rate, twelfth in death rate,
and nineteenth in rate of growth. Her population was homogeneous,
containing (in 1935) 1,472,612 Latvians or 77 per cent, 93,479 Jews,
62,144 Germans (all of whom left the country in 1939), 48,949 Poles,
206,499 Great Russians (a remarkable increase, largely due to immigration, over the 1920 figure of 124,764), 26,867 White Russians,
22,913 Lithuanians, 7,014 Estonians, and 944 Livians.

Anthropologists group the Finns, the Estonians, the Latvians, and
the Lithuanians together in the east Baltic racial division, wherein
they are classified as a sub-Nordic type, closely related to the Scandinavian. This grouping rests on the fact that all these Baltic strains
differ less among themselves than they do from the Russian peoples.
However, the Latvians and Lithuanians are distinguished ethnographically, as descendants of the aboriginal Balts, from the Finns and
Estonians, who are of Finno-Ugrian extraction. To this latter group
belonged the ancient Livs, who sought better fishing on the more
southerly Latvian shores in very early times, and who have been
almost entirely assimilated. These Livs contributed their grey eyes and
brown hair to a minority of the Latvians, the majority of whom (60
per cent) have grey-blue or blue eyes, and soft, straight dark-blond
hair. Clearly distinguishable from neighboring ancient Slavic remains,
Latvian skeletons, from the second up to the twelfth centuries, reveal
a tall, powerful build. The Latvians remain one of the tallest peoples
of Europe. They are also superior in weight of brain.

Coinciding with the natural geographic and ethnographic frontier which separated the ancient Slavic and Baltic peoples is an unmistakable linguistic boundary. Comparative philology has established the Latvian and Lithuanian languages, together with Borussian, or Ancient Prussian (extinct in the seventeenth century), as a distinct Baltic branch of the Satem division of the Indo-European family. These languages, rich in ancient roots and forms, are sometimes called the European Sanskrit, being akin to but older than the Sanskritic group. The theory that the Baltic tongues may have developed from a primitive Balto-Slavic language, shared by the Balts and Slavs in some remote era when they might have lived united near the Carpathian Mountains, has recently been discarded by some of its originators. Slavicisms in the Baltic languages can be explained by the process of cultural osmosis. Lithuania, with wider and more intimate Slavic connections in the late Middle Ages and early modern times, contains a larger number of Slavic words than Latvian, more isolated from Slavic cultural influence by a natural barrier of impassable swamps. Within the Baltic region a clear line is drawn between the properly Balt Latvian and Lithuanian languages and those of the Finns, Ingrians, Estonians, and Livs, all belonging to the Finno-Ugrian group of the Ural-Altaic family of languages.[5]

Latvian is in some respects even more archaic than the kindred Lithuanian, preserving the s of the original Satem group, a short o, and the first syllable stress. Long relegated to the unofficial vernacular during successive foreign dominations, its formal preservation, from the seventeenth to the beginning of the nineteenth century, lay in the hands of German Lutheran pastors who compiled dictionaries and handbooks for their own use in dealing with their Latvian flocks. The purification of the language, inevitably distorted by this German interpretation, began in the middle of the nineteenth century. Latvian philology came into its own after the establishment of a Department of Philology at the Latvian State University when this institution was opened in 1919. Philologists have since shared the limelight with folklorists, archeologists and historians in a nation which accords honor and gratitude to the restorers of its remote past.

The tenacity of the ancient Latvian tongue is revealed in the immense number of folksongs and tales carried down by word of mouth,

[5] Leon Dominian, *The Frontiers of Language and Nationality in Europe* (New York, 1917), pp. 104-107. See also H. Rosen, *Die ethnographische Verhältnisse in den baltischen Provinzen und in Litauen* (St. Petersburg, 1915), pp. 329-333.

in innumerable elaborations, from the earliest days of Balt culture. Other evidence is found in the survival of geographical and place names over Latin, German, and Russian transmutations.

We have already indicated that the Latvians never used the German *Liv-* or *Liefland,* or the Latin *Livonia.* Closest to their chosen *Latvija* was the *Lothavia,* mentioned by Dionysius Fabricius in 1610.[6] Fabricius also called the *Latviji Lothavi,* a close approximation of the vernacular. The thirteenth century chronicler Henricus de Lettis derived his term *Letti* (which he applied to the inhabitants of Latgale, called by him *Lettia* or *Lettigallia*) from the German *Lette,* discussed above. The German *Letten* appears on a Gerardus Mercator 1616 map of Livonia, to distinguish the inhabitants of Liefland from the northern *Esten.*

The names of the old tribal kingdoms suffered transformations or disappeared until officially restored as modern provinces after the First World War. Kurzeme (meaning land of the Kurs) became the Latin *Curonia,* the German *Curland* (Courland) or *Kurland,* and under Russian rule, the *Kurlyandskaya Gubernya.* Zemgale, Latinized to *Semigallia* and Germanized to *Semgallen,* was incorporated into the Duchy of Kurland and lost its tribal name altogether. Vidzeme (meaning midland) was called *Iduma* by Henricus de Lettis, evidently a Livian distortion. This provincial name was also officially lost when the region was incorporated into Livonia proper, or the region north of the Daugava and south of the Estonian lands, in contrast to the greater Livonia which included part of Estonia and lands south of the Daugava. The smaller Livonia, or Liefland (also *Lettland*) was rechristened by the Russians (as one of their Baltic Provinces) *Liflyandskaya Gubernya.* Latgale, the *Lettigallia* of Henricus de Lettis, was separated from the rest of Livonia in the seventeenth century when it became the Polish *Inflantes,* a corruption of Liefland.

Just as they cherished the old titles of their early tribal kingdoms, the subjugated Latvians clung to the original names for their towns and rivers. They refused the German *Düna* (or *Duena*) and the Russian *Dvina* for their main river; and *Dünaburg* or *Dvinsk* for Daugavpils. They preferred Jelgava to *Mitau,* Ventspils to *Windau,* or *Vindava,* Liepāja to *Libau* or *Libava,* Cēsis to *Wenden,* Kuldīga to *Goldingen,* Alūksne to *Marienburg,* Rēzekne to *Rositten;* and the

---

[6] Dionysius Fabricius, *Livonicae historiae compendiosa series,* in *Scriptores rerum livonicarum,* II (Riga, 1848), 439f.

river names Gauja and Lielupe to *Liflyandskaya Aa* and *Kurlyand-skaya Aa.*

During the German Ostland satrapy (1941-1945) the Nazis, in imitation of the German-Balt squires, resumed Germanization of Latvian geographical names. This was followed by Russification when the Soviet Union annexed Latvia in 1945. But the Latvians are no more likely to relinquish their stubborn hold on their ancient names now than they were under the subjugations of the past.

This tenacity evidenced in the preservation of their officially slighted language the Latvians also exhibited in the retention of much of their culture patterns established during their early days of liberty in a land they could call their own. This land, its climate, its soil, its beauties, and its demands, as well as its strategic commercial and defenseless military position, in large part determined the character of the tribal Latvians, their manner of life, and their subsequent devotion to what they knew to be a distinct, substantial, and historical national heritage.

A difficult land to tame, soil demanding ceaseless care, short delightful summers contrasting with long grey winters, the challenge of the boisterous Baltic and the tonic of its bracing air, the vistas opening down the long rivers leading to wealth but admitting foreign interference, the legends of the somber forests—all these bred in the early Balts a complex of character traits which set them apart from the passive, mystical, fatalistic Slavs. Judging from the powerful skeletons which have been disinterred, as well as from the traces of a well-developed early medieval agricultural culture, physical strength and vigor must have marked the tribal Latvians as they do their descendants. A nation of strong, tall men, and handsome, agile women bears witness to an active contest with the elements severe enough to beget healthy endurance yet sufficiently heartening to establish a practical optimism and the love of labor as typically Latvian attitudes. A nice balance of challenge to and rewards for continuous effort produced just those characteristics which were to determine the survival, spiritual as well as physical, of a people with the luck of history against them. The Latvians who so proudly sailed their recaptured nation into the sea of peace, freedom, and prosperity following the First World War, had their ancient forebears to thank for the spirit of endurance, perseverance, laboriousness, adaptability, resourcefulness, and self-reliance which had brought success to their struggle for liberation.

The sterner qualities, which have welded the Latvians into an enduring nation of realists and enterprising individualists, are tempered by softer traits which have found expression in their legends and lyric poetry, in their passion for music, and in the traditional designs which are cherished in their many crafts. The Latvian arts, which have long enjoyed the intimate support and interest of the whole nation, reflect an intense love of nature in its subdued and delicate northern mood; a loyalty to the national tradition, and devotion to the family, Latvia's strongest institution. The lyric melancholy of the music and poetry is derived partly from the northern poetic temper, determined by the contrast of harshness with sudden exquisite moments in nature; and partly from centuries of suffering in whose darkness was called up the remembrance of past dignity and peace.

This lyric melancholy is lightened by a sense of proportion and by a vein of humor, whose keen irony the Latvians used as a weapon, sometimes their only one, against their oppressors. Particularly provocative of this form of attack were the German-Balts, so obviously dependent upon Latvian agricultural skill and natural energy for their survival as a squirearchy. The confirmed ignorance and idleness of this master class at its feudal worst gave rise to a bitterly mocking strain of folk humor in their victims; as did, though in a lighter vein, the inefficiency and venality of Russian bureaucrats at the end of the nineteenth century. Among their successive sovereigns, the Swedes alone inspired the Latvians' respect.

The core of Latvian self-respect and self-preservation as a people was the family. The independent, isolated, self-sufficient farm of early tribal times, cultivated and defended by the head of the household and his clan, survived as an ideal throughout the centuries of dispossession, and as an incitation, when serfdom was officially ended, to acquire land at any cost. Restored to their position of independence, the Latvian families, whether remaining on the land or joining a prosperous business and professional class, upheld the early respect for private property, independence of action, regard for tradition, kinship loyalty, and a high degree of devotion to the central figure of the mother.

The large amount of freedom and prestige which the Latvians accord their women seems to be historically deeply rooted, if one may judge from the remarks of early chroniclers regarding the privileges enjoyed by the females of the Baltic tribes. In contrast to the Slavs, the Latvians have never placed their heaviest forms of labor on the backs of their women, though the latter have taken their share of work on the farms willingly and with marked vigor. While from earliest times women achieved the status of companions to their mates, it is as a mother that the Latvian woman has always attained her most honored position, receiving into her hands the basic education of her children in religion, in the preservation of the national tradition in its moral and artistic manifestations, and in the love of a healthy, orderly, zestful existence. In the agricultural communities the influence of the women has been particularly evident, inspiring the essential neatness of Latvian husbandry, the colorful comfort of the farmhouses, and the traditional flavor of the village festivals with their splendid national costumes and their great variety of folksongs and dances. These Baltic women have also preserved, despite the youthful optimism and practical outlook of their men in modern times, some of that ancient sadness which is a sort of pride with defenseless yet highly self-conscious small nations.

As a proper reward for her comradely sharing of her men's age-old vicissitudes and burdens, for her thriftiness, and her courage, the Latvian woman received, during the period of independence, all the privileges of democracy. The vote, higher education, positions in the professions, and a full share in her nation's economic and cultural life were freely accorded her. Her motherhood was protected by progressive maternal and child welfare measures and by numerous public or private institutions devoted to the care of the children of working mothers. These progressive standards have contributed not a little to that wholeness which distinguishes this Baltic nation whether in liberty or thralldom.

This assessment of the qualities of the Latvian people should suggest their peculiar fitness to survive the succession of foreign dominations which has been their historical lot. Further, it should indicate their temperamental affinity with the institutions and ideas of Western Europe to whose community, as a vigorous and one of the earliest surviving branches of the Indo-European race, they have always belonged, geographically, ethnographically, culturally, and historically. All of Western Europe's major cultural trends reached the eastern shores of the Baltic, though with some natural retardation and a certain modulation inevitable under the static conditions of German squirearchy and Russian satrapy. Feudalism, humanism, protestantism, mercantilism, liberalism, and the more recent fashions in economics, politics, sociology, and the arts, have all left their more or less lasting traces in Livonia, the Baltic Provinces, or the succession states. If feudalism lingered far beyond its natural term, the hindrance lay in the nature of the German-Balt gentry, an essentially foreign ruling class who dared not liberalize their institutions lest they lose their hold on their disaffected subjects and their valuable lands.

But the very obsolescence and extreme harshness of the German-Balt yoke only served to stimulate the basically democratic tendencies of the Latvians, and their yearning for the honors and rewards of Western liberalism. The established European Powers were astonished and sometimes tolerantly amused by the piety with which the new nations of the Baltic practiced what their leaders had preached during the struggle for independence. That they were in their proper element at last did not always occur to those who had thought of them as Junker soil or Tsarist dependency. The reactionaries among the German-Balts and White Russians, who must suffer the benefits of democracy, hastened to point out that radicalism was grounded in the character of the Baltic peoples, basing this accusation on the inevitably "revolutionary" spirit of the leaders of the late nineteenth century National Revival, on the incessant demands of the Estonians, Latvians, and Lithuanians for their own land, and on their fondness for cooperative and associative organizations. This radicalism, a natural result of alien domination, had served the Latvians well as a cultural defense-mechanism; and, in more fortunate times, had played its part in restoring a war-ruined economy and developing a high degree of agricultural prosperity.

But even more marked than the group-mindedness of the Latvians, or than their rationalism and tolerance of economic and political experiments, is their respect for private property, civil rights, and the liberty of the individual—predilections which have made them resistant to Marxian socialism and drawn them unequivocally into the fold of Western democracy. Indeed, in the twenties they were prone, out of sheer enthusiasm, to romanticize parliamentarism and carry it to extremes.

Though neophytes in the practice of political liberalism, they had long nurtured the concepts of democracy; one of their most cherished convictions being that of the equality of the individual before the law. The ancient Latvian common law had developed a noticeable parallelism to the Roman law, which was later introduced in Livonia and became the basis of modern Latvian jurisprudence. Equality of opportunity, another Latvian aspiration which was sharpened by centuries of foreign privilege, was balanced by that sense of individual responsibility which has produced a strongly civic-minded and law-abiding nation with a high regard for public opinion and its correlative, a free press. An active press and an excellent public education were two of the most popular manifestations of a finally established democratic way of life, which broadened into a liberal national culture demanding the participation of all classes and eager for acceptance into the larger European stream. Latvia's intelligentsia, stemming in its early, mid-nineteenth century period from peasant stock, never lost sight of this vital matrix, nor of the pride which all Latvians took in the prosperity of their land and the skill of their workers. Centuries of diligent husbandry, combined with a natural mechanical ability, had enabled the Latvian people to contribute their share to Western European technical civilization. Their fidelity to the agrarian outlook and the opportunities offered the smaller interests to participate in a moderate industrial and commercial development reflect a deep conviction of the moral value of labor and responsible enterprise, for which individual and national prosperity were considered a morally valid reward.

Although convinced of the virtues of peaceful intentions and self-reliance, the Latvians have not been devoid of an international outlook. True, their impressive fighting spirit, not the less reliable for being essentially antimilitaristic, has been chiefly aroused in the cause of self-defense. It is likewise true that the perennial pressures of over-weening neighboring Powers have inclined the Baltic nations to hold hard to small gains and look on war as disproportionately disastrous to themselves. But these viewpoints, conducive to isolationism, have been balanced by these nations' commercial dependence on the rest of the Western community, and on their sense of solidarity with other democratic states, as evidenced in their intense interest in the League of Nations. More particularly, their sense of international responsibility has been focused on the question of the freedom of the Baltic Sea, an issue which has inspired considerable constructive planning in the strategically located Latvian nation.

History has amply demonstrated that the area comprised in "Livonia" is the key to the *dominium maris Baltici*,[7] and that upon the control of this region and of the Baltic Sea hinged the power politics of the Germanic and Russian Empires and, to a large extent, the peace of northern Europe. Whereas the Germans have habitually

[7] This expression was first used by the Polish queen Bona Sforza, mother of King Sigismund II.

cloaked their aggressions in this area under such concepts as "Christianizers," *Kulturtraeger*, "protectors," and even "peacemakers," the ancient Muscovites and their heirs have been franker in their claim to Livonia as a gateway to Western Europe, maintaining, in the words of one of their governors-general of the Baltic Provinces, that "the historical mission of the Baltic Provinces is to serve as a battlefield for the problems of the highest politics in Europe."[8]

The Baltic peoples have a different interpretation of their historical mission. Viewing the question of the freedom of the Baltic as inseparable from that of the freedom of all seas, and placing it on a strategic footing with that of the Mediterranean, they have seen their greatest contribution to peace to lie in their guardianship of a free Baltic. Many authorities in international relations have agreed with them unreservedly.

Convinced of the validity of their role not only as guardians of a free Baltic but also as a cultural-economic bridge between Western Europe and European Russia, Latvia and Estonia diverted a large proportion of their energies and resources to the development of their ports, harbors, and other transit facilities. While these developments contributed greatly to the prosperity of peace time, they could only stimulate the aggressiveness of powerful neighbors who might again choose the policy of expansionism. Still more dangerous to the eastern Baltic area and to that part of Europe for which it might serve as a spring-board, were the air bases which it might afford, in as much as the growth of air power has diminished the purely strategic significance of the Baltic Sea.

The continued military vulnerability of the Baltic States, which in the past had repeatedly exposed them to German and Russian aggression and counter-aggression, favored the emergence of the concept of a Baltic Union, some advocates of close cooperation going so far as to support the formation of a United States of the Baltic. In addition to regulating its own regional affairs, and functioning organically within a larger framework of European collective security, the United States of the Baltic should, because of its peculiar geographical position, be neutralized, and have its independence internationally guaranteed. Only under these conditions could the three democratic nations of this fatally contested region attain the ethnographically and culturally valid dimensions of their individual nationhoods, fulfill

[8] Quoted by Arveds Schwabe (Švābe), *The Story of Latvia and her Neighbors* (Edinburgh, n.d.), p. 11.

their proper function of a militarily undisturbed and essential bridge between East and West, and contribute organically to the collective security of the rest of Western Europe. To play such a constructive part in establishing the equilibrium of peace can be the only destiny acceptable to the people who, out of centuries of chaos, so painfully and persistently forged the Latvian nation.

Chapter 2

Amberland

THE peoples who came to lead a primitive tribal existence on the swampy and heavily forested southeastern and eastern shores of the Baltic, though scarcely known to recorded history before Tacitus, may well have possessed the heritage of a brilliant past in more temperate climes. Though the origin of the Latvians is somewhat veiled, recent studies of their impressive folklore have yielded clues to a surmisable ancient civilization.

One of the most suggestive sources for a tentative understanding of this legendary past is the *Dainas*, a massive collection of folksongs, some 36,000 (650,000 including variations) in all. This body of fairy-tales, epics, proverbs, and sorcery formulas[1] offers a rich fabric of myth, imagery, fantasy, and epic, wherein may be distinguished certain motifs and allusions, certain sturdy tales which seem the solid warp of history.

The *Dainas* claim that the ancient Latvians were descended from the sun, which they worshipped, and that they adhered to a religious dualism, recognizing male and female deities and good and evil genii in nature. Although there may not be sufficient grounds for believing that the Latvians were one of the peoples afflicted by the Flood (among these tales is a Latvian legend of this catastrophe); or that. since their religion was akin to the pre-ethic Indo-European sun mythology, their cradle must have been India or Iran, there is some suggestion of an ancient southern homeland which some cataclysm forced these people to leave in search of more peaceful conditions farther to the north.

The reflection of an ancient civilization is also to be found in the numerous allusions to rich cities and castles, to kings and heroes in fine armor, and to princesses laden with gold and jewels. A study of Latvian popular arts, peculiarly luxurious in design and fantasy, also

[1] There are several collections of these *Dainas*: by A. Bielenstein, A. Lerčis-Puškaitis, P. Šmits, and K. Barons; the latter in 6 vols., published by the St. Petersburg Academy of Science, 1908ff. See also the group of Latvian *Dainas* in English translation in U. Katzenellenbogen, *The Dainas. An Anthology of Lithuanian and Latvian Folksongs, With a Critical Study* (Chicago, 1935).

reveals a rich inheritance, both in imagination and technique.[2] The most current of the popular motifs is the swastika, the symbolic image of the instrument with which peoples of ancient technical civilizations produced fire, and common to the folk designs of many ancient races. It is a striking fact that numerous decorative motifs from excavated Troya are suggestive of and sometimes similar to the modern Latvian popular designs, which have been handed down from earliest times.

These hints of a far from primitive remote past for this Baltic people are borne out by recent archeological discoveries, which have established the skill of the early settlers in agriculture, animal husbandry, boatbuilding, the making of jewelry and weapons, the tanning of hides, working of wood and clay, and the weaving of clothes. The *Dainas*, too, in their detailed descriptions of daily life, present a picture of manual skill and relative comfort.

We have alluded to a possible natural catastrophe which drove the early Balts from some southern, perhaps a Mediterranean place of origin. What was their route to the northern shores where they finally settled? Geography, ethnography, philology, and archeology provide the clues to this trek.

There are grounds for believing that before moving farther north the Balts may have settled for a while somewhere north of the Black Sea.[3] The route from there on would lie up the long Russian and Baltic rivers and would fan out into White Ruthenia, Pomerania, and East Prussia. The long, navigable rivers with points of portage, linking the Black Sea Basin to the Baltic, would certainly have played a determining role in the direction of the migration. Here philology offers its testimony. A study of the White Russian region reveals more than a hundred rivers bearing names which appear also in the Baltic lands, presumably introduced there by the migrating tribes descending the Daugava and the Gauja to the Baltic shore.[4]

Such vast distances could not have been covered in boats alone. Horses and horse-drawn vehicles must have been an essential means of transportation. Both archeology and folklore prove the preeminence of the horse in early Latvian, Lithuanian, and Ancient Prussian culture. Horse crania have been found embedded in key points of buildings and under main gates; many of the ships' bows of the Kurs bore

[2] See in general A. Bielenstein, *Die Holzbauten und Holzgeräte der Letten* (St. Petersburg, 1907), 2 vols.

[3] F. Zālītis, *Latvijas vēsture* (Riga, 1947), p. 16.

[4] K. Būga, *Tauta ir Žodis*, 1 (Kaunas, 1923), 17-30.

the horse for figurehead; and this animal even figured in religious ceremonies. The Baltic horse was no heavy charger, but a small and active pony whose coat grew shaggy in winter.

We may safely assume close kinship among the tribes which, in prehistoric times, reached the south and southeastern shores of the Baltic and settled there in contiguous areas: the Ancient Prussians or Boro Russians, and the Latvian Kurs, all along the coast from the Vistula estuary north to the Gulf of Riga; other Latvian tribes, the Zemgallians, Selonians, Latgallians, and Talavians, spreading out north and south of the Daugava River; the Yadvingi, southeast of the Ancient Prussians on the upper Narev and Bug rivers; and the Lithuanians, only one of whose tribes, the Samogithians, reached the Baltic at the mouth of the Niemen, while the rest of that people occupied the upper Niemen basin. All these peoples, near kin to the now extinct Aryans, may be considered autocthons of the area extending, coastwise, from Danzig northwards as far as Aināži on the Estonian border, and inland over the basins of the Vistula, Nemunas, Venta, Lielupe, Daugava and Gauja rivers, on to the upper basins of the Pripet, Dnieper, Daugava and Oka rivers to the south and southeast.[5]

The philologists have assisted the anthropologists in establishing this kinship. Just as these peoples can be classified in one East-Baltic racial group, so can the Latvian-Lithuanian language, which is older than Sanskrit, be grouped in the Baltic branch of the Indo-European family of languages. More specifically, the language of the Kurs, which was the same as that of the Ancient Prussians, has been established as a purely Latvian dialect.[6]

For all the weight of argument provided by the latest researches of archeology, anthropology, ethnology, and philology, the thesis that these tribes were the original settlers of the south and southeastern Baltic regions has not gone unchallenged in certain quarters. Various scholars have claimed priority for the Goths, the Finnish Livs, and even the Slavs.

The Gothic theory, resting as it does on slender philological grounds, is easily disposed of. Except for a few migrating Goths from the island of Gotland who, in the fifth century A.D., moved across Latvia to Russia, no other Goths appeared in Latvia. The so-called Western Goths came the nearest to the Ancient Prussians when they

---

[5] P. Einhorn, *Historia Lettica* (Dorpat, 1649), in *Scriptores rerum livonicarum*, II (Riga, 1848), 577.

[6] See in general J. Endzelīns, *Ueber die Nationalität und Sprache der Kuren* (Leipzig, 1912).

paused for a short while on the estuary of the Vistula on their way from southern Scandinavia to the Black Sea region. One of their tribes was known as the Wakia-Goths and it was from this name that the Ancient Prussians and the Kurs derived their name for Germans: *Vatci*, or *Vatzi*, which has endured in modern Latvian.[7]

The Livian theory, promoted by the German philologist Doering[8] and supported by the Finnish philologist and historian Koskinnen,[9] claims for the Livs of Karelia the original settlement of Latvian territory. Archeology has never substantiated such an assumption, while anthropology and ethnography have tended to disprove it. From earliest times the Latvians were distinct from, though in friendly relations with, the neighboring Finnish Livs. The latter were predominantly sailors and fishermen, exchanging their fish for the agricultural surplus of the "forest-clearers," as they called their Latvian neighbors. The two peoples shared certain settlements, and intermingled in Riga and in the regions both north and south of the Daugava River. The Livs adopted from the Latvians many of the latter's agricultural methods and other skills. Eventually, the smaller group (the Livs) became assimilated to the larger, bringing to the common stock their distinctively Finnish grey eyes.

The Slavs have no more claim to original settlement of the Baltic lands than do the Germans or the Finns, in spite of Tsar Ivan IV's pretensions in the sixteenth century. Historical research has proved that the Slavs of Novgorod first appeared near the Latvian-inhabited lands in the eighth century, when some enterprising merchants from Novgorod managed to establish a spearhead in the originally Latvian fortress of Pleskava, a name which the Slavs changed to Pskov. A similar salient appeared in Estonia, where the Slavs occupied Izborsk (Eastborg). These were the farthest penetrations of the Slavs into the Baltic lands, where the basin of the river Velikaya has continued into modern times as the traditional frontier between the Slavs and the northern Latvians.

There are indications that, immediately following the Ice Age, or about 9000 B.C., primitive tribes of hunters, perhaps of Finno-Ugric

[7] A. Schwabe, *Latvijas tiesību vēsture*, I, (Riga, 1932), 23-28. This is the definitive history of Latvian law.

[8] J. Doering, *Ueber die Herkunft der Kurländischen Liven in Sitzungsberichte der Kurländischen Gesellschaft für Litteratur und Kunst* (Mitau, 1880), p. 28.

[9] Y. Koskinnen, *Sur l'antiquité des Livs en Lettonie* (*Acta Societatis Scientiarum Fennicae*), VIII (Helsinki), 102.

origin, roved the Baltic lands, but left no conclusive cultural traces. After examining all the evidence, eminent anthropologists, a German among them,[10] have concluded that about the middle of the Neolithic Age (2000 B.C.), and on into the Bronze Age (1500-500 B.C.) and the older Iron Age (500-1 B.C.) the ancient Balts, direct ancestors of the modern Latvians and Lithuanians, settled permanently in their northern homelands, thus constituting themselves one of the earliest established of European ethnic groups. By the beginning of the Christian era, the original Balt peasant culture had divided into a western (Ancient Prussian) and an eastern (later Lithuanian and Latvian) branch. Philology and archeology indicate that at this time close cultural and trade relationships existed between the Baltic and the Finno-Ugric tribes.[11]

The Balts first appeared on the scene of Western civilization when they were discovered to be the fortunate possessors of a most rare and precious natural resource: amber. The *Dainas* glorified ancient Latvia as Amberland and paid justifiable tribute to the product which brought the blessings of the Mediterranean Bronze Age to Baltia.

Amber is the fossilized gum of an extinct species of pine tree native to low-lying swampy ground such as that formed by lignite deposits in the Baltic regions after the glacial period. In early times it was found and mined, as it is today, along the shores of East Prussia, Kurland, and the southern coast of the Gulf of Riga. The ancient Mediterranean civilizations prized it more highly than gold. They used it as a medicine, as incense, in jewelry and dress, and even saw occult powers in its magnetic qualities. Baltic amber beads have been found in the graves of the Pharaohs; and Baltic amber has appeared in Italy, Greece, the Caucasian regions, and Turkestan. The American historian of the Vikings, B. Bie Ravndal, maintains that "in prehistoric times perhaps no single factor more fundamentally affected the international affairs of the north, which intimately concerned not only its economic, but also its cultural relations with the outside world, than the trade in amber. In antiquity it had served as the main spearhead of Mediterranean civilization, and its repercussions were felt even down to the Viking times."[12]

Possibly the Frisian merchants were the oldest intermediaries between the Balts and their earliest Mediterranean customers, the Phoe-

[10] A. Bielenstein, *Die Holzbauten u. Holzgeräte der Letten*, II, 348-375.
[11] A. Schwabe, *Latvia and her Neighbors*, p. 5.
[12] G. Bie Ravndal, *Stories of the East Vikings* (Minneapolis, 1938), p. 39.

nicians, who sailed through the Gibraltar Straits north for amber. Most probably the later Etruscan merchants maintained direct trade relations with the inhabitants of Amberland by a continental route through Germany. Another ancient route ran from the Black Sea, over the Dniester, the San and the Vistula rivers to the East Prussian coast. Pliny the Elder mentions a Phoenician merchant, Pytheas of Massilia (Marseilles), who made a journey in 330 B.C. to the "island of Baltia" to acquire amber.

But the earliest detailed description of amber, of the amber coast, and the "amber fishers" is left us by Tacitus who, at the end of the first century A.D., in his *Germania* (chapter 71), took notice of the peoples on the frontiers of Germany proper, at the outer limits of the known world.[13]

Of amber, Tacitus reported, ". . . this substance lay long neglected until Roman luxury gave it a name and brought it into demand. . . . The Aestii gather amber into rude heaps and offer it for sale without any form of polish, astonished at the price they receive for it."

Of these *Aestii*, or *Aestyorum gentes*, perhaps so named by Tacitus after the amber estuaries, the Roman historian made some fairly precise observations. He thought that their language was akin to that spoken in the British Isles, while their clothes and customs resembled those of the Suevi (Swedes). They were skilled in agriculture; carried the image of a boar's head on their shields; used the formidable battle axe, suitable only to big men; and worshipped "the Mother of gods." He also remarked that these people called amber *glese*, which was the Ancient Prussian and Kuronian name for that product, and seems to indicate that the *Aestyorum gentes* were no other than the Ancient Prussians and the Kurs, who were, indeed, the only amber gatherers of those days.

It was chiefly due to the amber trade, supplemented by the traffic in furs, that the Baltic peoples were able to share in the luxuries of the Roman Bronze and Iron Ages. Amber itself could be used as money to purchase gold, silver, bronze, and copper, or weapons and ornaments made from these metals; or the "Baltic gold" might be bartered against these imports. Archeological excavations have revealed a wealth of objects made from these metals, stone and iron work similar to the Etruscan, as well as a quantity of Roman silver and gold coins. A major find of Roman coins was made at Liepāja (Libau) in Kurzeme. The Latvians frequently melted these down and wrought

[13] Tacitus, *De Origine et situ germanorum,* cap. 45.

jewelry from the metals. They called the gold coins *austini*, from the Latin *aurum*.

It was during the Roman Iron Age (1-400 A.D.) that the Baltic peasant culture, stimulated to rapid development by brisk commercial relations with the Roman Empire, particularly the Danube Basin, effected the further split into the Latvian and Lithuanian branches; while, to the north, the Finno-Ugrians became more clearly differentiated into Finns and Estonians. At this time also, a distinct ethnic and cultural frontier, coinciding with a natural geographic border, is distinguishable between the Baltic peoples and the sparsely settled territories to the east.[14]

The fortunate economic position of the ancient Latvian tribes did not fail to attract the attention of their neighbors. According to the Gothic historian Jordanes,[15] Hermanric, a king of the Ostrogoths, held the Baltic lands under his sway for a certain period in the late fourth century. Jordanes also records that in 523-526 the *Aestii* sent ambassadors with amber and a message to the Ostrogoth emperor Theodoric, who returned a message in Latin together with a gift of gold coins. This correspondence would presume some considerable distance. There is no evidence that the Ostrogoths claimed effective dominion over the *Aestii*. We have already mentioned the brief appearance of the Goths from Gotland around the year 475.

In early times the real disturbers of Ancient Prussian and Kuronian peace and plenty were the Scandinavian seafaring peoples. The most successful penetrators of Latvia were the Vikings, who, from the end of the fifth to the ninth centuries, took over the largest Latvian rivers as their roads to fortune. Large marauding bands from Gotland would foregather at Riga, which became a Viking factory, whence they split up into three expeditions: one pursuing the *via Semigallorum*, down the Zemgallian river Lielupe into Lithuania; another taking the Gauja route to Estonia and thence, by way of Pskov and over Lake Ladoga on to Novgorod, where they met merchants up from Persia, Byzantium, and Central Asia by way of the Volga; and a third choosing the most famous of the Viking trade routes, the *Austrvaegr* (East Way), which followed the Daugava from its mouth to the point of portage to the Berezina, a tributary of the Dnieper, then on down the latter to Byzantium.[16]

---

[14] G. Vernadsky, *Ancient Russia* (New Haven, 1943), p. 228ff.
[15] Jordanes, *De Rebus geticis*, cap. 23.
[16] G. Vernadsky, *op.cit.*, p. 261ff.

At one time the Slavicized Vikings combined with the Russians in attacking Baltic settlements, on the whole unsuccessfully, since the Baltic peoples had acquired improved methods of warfare and techniques of organization from the Scandinavians. A fleeting tribal overlordship established by the Viking-Russian forces was soon overthrown. The Chronicles report that in 1106 the Slavs of Polotzk, attacking the Zemgali, were defeated with a loss of 9,000 men. The fact that the Viking trading posts on Latvian territory were mostly situated on the right bank of the Daugava River suggests that the tribes living north of that river, the Tālavi and the Latgali, were the friendliest towards the Norsemen, in whose exploits they may conceivably have participated.

In the tenth century the Dnieper route to Constantinople was completely cut off by Asiatic nomads from the Ukrainian steppes. Subsequently the voyages of the later Vikings, called Varangians by the Slavonic chroniclers, were limited to the Baltic area and adjacent Slavic lands. At that time Novgorod in Rysaland (Russia) and Visby on the island of Gotland became the chief staple depots for goods coming from the Baltic and Slavic lands as well as from the Orient. Oriental merchants, journeying by the Volga route to Novgorod and Pskov, continued down the Gauja to Visby and other Baltic trading centers. The Novgorodian merchants, whose fortunes were founded on Baltic commerce, built a church as well as a factory at Visby, and ventured as far west as Lübeck and Denmark.[17]

These far-northern voyages of the Eastern traders explain the fact that Arabian geographers were able to describe the wonders of the Latvian tribal kingdom of Tholova (Tālava). Their accounts were no doubt based on the tales related by returning Persian merchant venturers to the perilous lands of amber, hides, and luxurious furs.[18]

The extent of Baltic commerce with the Orient is amply attested by the large stores of oriental silver coins which recent excavations have brought to light. Such coins, struck in Baghdad, Damascus, Basra, Kufa, and Isphagan have been found at the old Zemgallian port of Daugmale, fourteen miles south of Riga, which had existed since the second century A.D. The shallows around the island of Dole, near Riga, have corroborated this evidence. Byzantine gold has been

[17] See for Viking expansion T. D. Kendrick, A History of the Vikings (London, 1931).
[18] See the recent study of Tadeusz Lewicki, Polska i kraje sąsiednie w świetle "Księgi Rogera" geografa arabskiego z XII w. Al-Idrīsīego (Cracow, 1945).

found in Latvia, as well as Byzantine coins of the time of the Emperors Basilius II (976-1025) and his brother Constantine VIII.

These vestiges of early medieval trade, revealing as they are, do not point exclusively to the Orient. An abundance of English, German, Danish, Polish, and Swedish coins indicate the ever-widening spheres of Latvian commercial relations in the early Middle Ages.[19]

Naturally these relations were most profuse in the Baltic area proper, more especially with the seafaring Scandinavians. The pattern of Baltic rivalry, which was to dominate the foreign relations of the riparian states down into modern times, had already emerged in the earliest centuries of the Christian era. However, before we turn to the testimony of the chroniclers, whose business it was to record the feats and defeats of contesting kings, we must realize that, in these early times, long periods of stabilized commercial relations, punctuated by local and easily compromised conflicts, may have been the rule.

Latvian language and culture show a marked Scandinavian influence, which could only have resulted from an intimate relationship over an extended period of time. Archeological excavations indicate that just such an economic-cultural relationship existed between the Scandinavian and the Baltic regions for at least 2,000 years. The Latvians adopted from the Swedes their measures and weights; their accounting system as used at Birka, the Swedish central staple depot for East-Viking trade; and perhaps their monetary system, since the Latvian word for money, *nauda*, is derived from the Old Swedish *naut*. Riga took over some of the laws of Swedish Visby. The Latvians adopted the Scandinavian runic letters. The Vikings offered salt and superior metals and weapons in exchange for the produce of the eastern Baltic lands. Finally, the Scandinavians were the first to introduce Western Christianity in Latvian territory, sending missionaries and even building a church in Kurland in the eleventh century, a hundred years before the loudly self-acclaimed arrival of the German christianizers.

But a certain combination of circumstances in the Latvian lands, together with the overweening ambition of a few of the Danish and Swedish rulers, inevitably led to repeated conflict. The Latvians had their amber, which in turn brought them enviable quantities of gold and silver; they were the holders of strategic river routes which led to further wealth; and one of their tribes, the Kurs, were belligerent

[19] F. Balodis, *Die Burgberge Lettlands* (Rome, 1940), p. 18.

seafarers, quite willing to take on all comers whose greed seemed threatening. Furthermore, the Kurs frequently found a willing ally in the Estonians, who also suffered from Scandinavian depredations.

In these early times the Kurs inhabited not only the apex of the Kurzeme peninsula, south of Riga and opposite Sweden, but extended their settlements south along the coast as far as Danzig. Seafarers and fishers par excellence, they roamed the Baltic, probably sailed into the North Sea, and possibly even ventured along the coasts of France and Spain into the Mediterranean. Such initiative must early have attracted the notice of the Danes, through whose waters they must pass to reach the Western seas, and whose own unmistakable ambitions in the Baltic both preceded and outlasted the Viking tumult.

Our first glimpse of conflict comes from the *Hadinga Saga*, which relates that in the second century A.D. King Lokher of Kurland captured the invading Danish Prince Hading who, after his wounds were healed, was permitted to return home.[20] A century later, the Danish chronicler Saxo Grammaticus relates in his *Gesta Danorum*[21] that another Kuronian king, Dorno, defended his people against a Danish invasion at the *Duna urbs,* presumably Riga. The lines were not always so clearly drawn. This same Danish chronicler also takes occasion to praise the Kurs as brave fighters when they allied themselves with the Danes at Brawalla *ca.* 750 to fight the Swedes who in the seventh century had acquired a tribute-paying dependency in Kurland.

Our next source of information on Kuronian-Scandinavian relations is Archbishop Rimbert of Bremen who, in his biography of Bishop Anscarius written in 870,[22] gives the following account of events in the years 853 and 854. In 853 the Kurs, after freeing themselves from Swedish overlordship, repulsed the invading Danes, who left at least half their dead on the battlefield and a considerable booty, as well as half their warships, in the hands of the victors. The next year the Swedish King Olaf broke into Kurzeme to recapture the Danish booty which had evidently been originally collected in Sweden. After taking Seeburg, he passed on to Apule which was forced after eight days to sue for peace. The Swedes neither occupied nor plundered this city, being content to demand only the Danish booty. They even

---

[20] O. von Rutenberg, *Geschichte der Ostseeprovinzen,* 1 (Leipzig, 1859), 10ff.

[21] *Saxonis Grammatici Gesta Danorum* (Strassburg, 1886), p. 39.

[22] *Vita Anskarii auctore Rimberto* (ed. G. Waitz), in *Scriptores rerum germanicarum* (Hannover, 1884), pp. 60-62.

signed a treaty with the Kurs which left the latter masters of their
own land.

Particularly interesting is Bishop Rimbert's description of the
Kuronian cities of Apule and Seeburg (which became Grobina).
Archeology has located the latter on the shore of Lake Liepāja. Apule,
with its garrison of 15,000, must have been larger than Seeburg, with
only 7,000. It appears also, according to the Bishop, to have been the
storage place for important booty. Apule, then, may be fairly safely
designated as the capital city of the tribal kingdom of Kurland in the
ninth century.

The next chronicler to mention the Kurs seems to have been Bishop
Adam of Bremen who presents the following description: "The people . . . are extremely uncouth and because of their excess of idolatry
all their neighbors avoid traffic with them. Courland is rich in gold
and the horses are excellent."[23]

The bishop also mentions that the Danish King Sweyn Astrittson
subsidized the building of a church in 1048 at Domesnaes on the
apex of Kurzeme, where the Danes evidently had a foothold at that
time. But in this century the Kurs seem to have taken the offensive,
so frequently ravaging the Danish coast that in the Danish churches
arose the prayer: *"För Kurerna bevare oss, milde Herre Gudi."*[24]

In 1161 the Danish Prince Abel landed at Palanga in southern
Kurland. There his chaplain Ernemordus, after baptizing the local
Kurs, was appointed by Abel as Bishop of Kurland. In 1169 he set
out for Rome to obtain consecration, and rather abruptly vanished
from history. A year later, the Danish King Olaf II landed in Kurzeme
but was forced to retreat. In 1171, the Kuronian stronghold on the
island of Oeland was destroyed by a Danish prince. This seems to
have promoted a Kuronian-Estonian alliance directed against both
the Danes and the Swedes, resulting in the destruction of the Swedish
depot of Sigtuna, which had replaced ancient Birka on Lake Maelar.
The Scandinavians were so dismayed that in 1191 they even organized an unsuccessful crusade against the Kurs and the Estonians.[25]
The Danes invaded Kurzeme for the last time in 1219, when they
ransacked Piltene, the future residence of the Bishop of Kurland.

At the turn of the century other forces appeared on the scene

[23] *Magistri Adami Gesta Hammaburgensis ecclesiae pontificum* in *Monumenta germaniae historica*, VII (Hannover, 1846), 374 (IV, 16).
[24] F. Balodis, *Det Äldsta Lettland* (Stockholm, 1940), p. 163.
[25] Henricus de Lettis, *Origines Livoniae sacrae et civilis* in *Scriptores rerum
livonicarum*, II (Riga, 1848), *sub anno* 1191.

which were to prove more than a match for the skirmishing Danes. The Germans, entrenched in Visby by 1163, were about to make their first bid for predominance in the trade-laden Baltic. In the guise of merchants and missionaries they proposed to bring civilization to a land which they claimed to have found empty of anything save a few barbarians, and which they named after the Livian fishermen they encountered in the Gulf of Riga, *Liefland* or *Livonia*.

Chapter 3

Early Latvian Customs and Culture

THE claim of saving and civilizing uncultured, enslaved, wrong-headed, or simply inferior peoples has certainly not been a monopoly of the Germans. That nation, however, has shown a singular tenacity in revitalizing and tempering this naïve state of mind into a perennial weapon of expansionism. The historian is continually challenged by this recurring *idée fixe* whose prime manifestation is the distortion or denial of the evidence of history.

One of the earliest examples of a phenomenon which has rather gained than lost impetus in modern times may be fruitfully reexamined in the light of the comparatively recent auxiliary sciences which greatly reinforce the case of the *bona fide* historian against the *homme-à-thèse* or the outright propagandist. Certain German-Balt historians have persistently restated the pretensions of the Hansa merchants and Teutonic crusaders to having "discovered" on the southeast shores of the Baltic at the mouths of the Daugava and Gauja rivers an entirely new land suffering from general uncouthness and a spiritual void. These enterprising saviors ignored the autochthonous culture whose traces were to be carefully disclosed and assessed centuries later by ethnologists, philologists, and archeologists. The medieval merchants and missionaries out of Lübeck and Bremen found what they needed to find in a future colony: a few dangerous heathen living primitively at the source of wealth.

Even the sparse testimony of the chroniclers which we have already consulted indicates that this wealth was indeed more than a promise. We receive the impression of luxury goods in transit, of rich war booty and the ability to pay tribute, of fortified castles and garrisons capable of protecting a people's treasure, of arms and warships, excellent horses, silver and gold. Evidently the Balts were rich enough to be envied and sufficiently organized to defend themselves. Their extended commerce naturally entailed far-flung cultural relations, with Rome, with Byzantium, and with Persia. The technicalities of the market, including a monetary system and a system of weights and measures, were well developed. It may logically be deduced that their standard of living must have corresponded to such advanced economic conditions.

Ample archeological excavations have revealed that the amber trade, so fortunately fostered by a geographic position which opened the discovered world to the Balts, brought them a fair share of the material benefits of the Roman Bronze and Iron Ages. Considering in addition that an ancient heritage, carefully bequeathed from generation to generation, may have nurtured the imagination and inspired inventiveness and manual skill, and that ample resources provided both by imported metals and locally mined bog-ore, we are not surprised to find that Latvian technical culture was on a par with that of medieval Scandinavia. A certain lag behind Western Europe is indicated by the establishment of three Iron Ages: the first, from the first to the fourth centuries A.D., the second, from the fifth to the eighth, and the third, from the ninth to the twelfth centuries, corresponding to the Middle Ages in Western Europe. A closer examination of the archeological evidence will permit at least a partial reconstruction of the Latvian tribes' means of existence during this period.

From the time of the establishment of the Latvian Board of Monuments in 1923 archeological excavations were carried on somewhat sporadically at various sites of ancient settlements, castle-mounds and burial grounds, some of which had attracted the attention of scientists as early as the eighteenth century. In 1933 archeological research was systematized and concentrated on a few important castle-mounds: among them Daugmale, on the left bank of the Daugava some sixteen miles south of Riga, at the site of an ancient Zemgallian port, in existence since the second century A.D.; Talsi, one of the ancient capitals of Kurzeme; Tērvete and Mežotne, residences of the medieval rulers of Zemgale; and, particularly, Jersika (Guersike), capital of the tribal kingdom of Latgale, with its nearby castle-mounds of Klangi and Dignaja.

In general, the Latvian castle-mounds, which protected settlements and the castles of rulers, were fortified by rows of huge horizontally laid beams, piled one on top of another and closely fitting a steep hillside, thereby forming a protective wall which was usually topped by wooden tower-like superstructures. In the center of the wall was a large stockade. All these fortifications, occasionally supplemented by projecting eave-like constructions, were roofed with bark, which was in turn spread with a layer of clay for protection against fire-arrows.[1]

The major excavations at Jersika have yielded rich returns.[2] The name Guersike, derived from *Gretzky*, meaning "a trader with the Greeks," suggests that this may originally have been a settlement of the Vikings in the time of their *Austrvaegr*. Later it became the capital of Latgale. When the streets were uncovered, the clay-covered pavement of small cobblestones, somewhat resembling our modern hard roads, was found to be well-preserved. A network of streets and an arrangement of regular blocks and open squares was disclosed; the main street led from the entrance gate to the open space in front of the principal building of the castle, and other streets and alleys were laid out parallel or at right angles to the main street. Characteristic of Jersika is a separate artisans' quarter, with small workshops grouped around an open space which probably served as a marketplace. Together with its two castle-mounds, one on the north and one on the south bank of the Daugava, this capital city covered an area of some 18,000 square meters. Its situation strongly suggests that it may have served as a toll-gate for the collection of taxes from the Daugava river traffic.

At Talsi, Daugmale, and Mežotne, traces of ancient settlements at the base of the castle-mounds can still be found. Like Jersika, Mežotne covered a considerable area and was protected by twin castle-mounds.

In all the explored Latvian castle-mound settlements large stores of grain have been discovered in what must have been the basements and barns of former buildings. Barley, wheat, rye, oats, linseed, and peas, preserved in loose heaps, special bins or sacks, have come to light, testifying to the prominence of agriculture in the life of ancient Latvia. A fortifying diet is further suggested by the uncovering of the bones of cows, pigs, goats, sheep, and chickens. The numerous traces of horses have already been mentioned.

Particularly revealing are the workshops with their tools and variegated products. It has been established that by the end of the early Iron Age, between the eighth and twelfth centuries, the Latvians

[1] E. Brastins has published a catalogue of Latvian castle-mounds: vol. I (Riga, 1923), *Kurzeme*; vol. II (Riga, 1926), *Zemgale*; vol. III (Riga, 1929), *Latgale*; vol. IV (Riga, 1930), *Vidzeme*.

[2] F. Balodis, *Jersika* (Riga, 1940). See also F. Balodis, *Det Äldsta Lettland* (Stockholm, 1940), the authoritative study for all archeological matters, with copious illustrations.

were expert fashioners of bronze, silver, and gold ornaments, skilled coppersmiths and blacksmiths, leather-workers, wood-carvers, and bone-cutters. At Jersika have been recovered crucibles, founder's moulds, many bronze pincers and blacksmith's iron tongs, iron fittings for wooden chests, keys and locks. Daugmale and Talsi have also yielded iron objects made out of the locally produced bog-ore. Jersika further appears to have been the center of a flourishing pottery trade, if we may judge from the number and variety of clay objects exhumed.

The exploration of graves has uncovered further evidence of advanced artisanship, particularly in articles of personal adornment. Fine jewelry and rich embroideries, most of them with motifs which have survived into modern times, attired the dead. The buried weapons, iron-covered shields, long and short swords, spears with iron spikes, and battle axes, were locally made and could not compete with the steel mail, helmets, cross-bows, and military engines of the Western European armor-smiths, many of whose inspirations were of Saracen origin.

Not only were the early Latvians safe in their fortified settlements, but their living quarters appear to have been far from primitive, assuring their inhabitants warmth, roominess, and self-sufficiency. The rulers resided in large castles called *pils* (cf. Greek *polis*) which were well protected by castle-mounds and often fostered clustering settlements capable of developing into tribal capital cities. Skilled artisans, often in quarters of their own, sold or bartered their goods at the market place. This exchange permitted the importation of such luxuries as spices, salt, and rich apparel and contributed to the relatively high standard of living in the settlements.

The manors of the lords were usually situated on hills and as elaborately laid out as Roman *villae*. In the living quarters themselves large basements provided for storage and concealment in time of war. Adjoining kitchens, cowsheds, stables, storage houses, threshing houses and mills formed a unit of self-sufficiency further augmented by surrounding orchards, gardens, and lakes or streams for fishing. Timber stood at hand. A characteristic feature of Latvian homes was the steambath, or *pirts*, located near brook or pond. It was found not only in the wealthy villas, but even in the humbler *villulas* or *majas* of the yeomen.

The Latvian yeomen lived on independent farms whose dwellings suggest the Western European rather than the north Baltic or the

Russian type of peasant dwelling. On their own land, solitary and independent, the farm families were perforce diligent and self-reliant, skilled in the various crafts which provided tools, utensils, and clothing. A fair degree of inventiveness is revealed in the machines which they contrived for weaving, churning, milling, and other necessary farm processes. In the fields, the yeoman had the use of ploughs with iron shares or wooden shares shod with iron, iron harrows, scythes, and sickles, and oxen or horses to draw his plough. The three-year crop system prevailed: rye or wheat followed by oats or barley, with the fields lying fallow every third year.

Archeological research has established the medieval Latvians as possessors of a fully adequate technical civilization, wherein the keen sense of self-preservation, through cunning adaptation to the land and climate and by the provision of weapons and fortresses, was supplemented by a sense of beauty and tradition. The folklorist has much material at hand to prove the feeling for design, the prolific imagination, the love of continuity which governed the highly developed artistic sense of the early Latvians. Their folksongs, the *Dainas*, show numberless variations within a typical pattern, being at once multiple and, in their spirit and essential style, uniform. National costumes, excavated after a thousand years, reveal in their brilliant embroideries the same motifs and color schemes which are still treasured today. Particularly striking in the arts and crafts is the almost total absence of seepage from the adjoining Russian and German cultures. Further proof of the age of this culture can be deduced from the diversity of its forms and the exuberant variety of its designs.

Not only are the objects brought to light and the art forms studied impressive by reason of their richness, but their spread over a certain well-defined area is of major significance to the historian of cultures. It becomes evident that as early as the Roman Iron Age (the first Latvian Iron Age, from the first to the fourth centuries), an eastern cultural border had been established which corresponded closely to the ethnic and the later political frontiers. That this was the natural limitation of a specific cultural area is suggested by the absence of any particular pressure at that time from the sparsely populated eastern regions. Only in the succeeding period of the barbarian invasions (*ca.* 400-*ca.* 800) did the eastern Slavs (Russians), in their turn pressed by the sub-Black Sea Goths, overflow into the territory of the extreme eastern Balt tribes, who at that time were spread out as far as the source region of the Volga, Oka, Dnieper, and Daugava rivers. One of these tribes, the Latgali, now moved farther down the Daugava to join their kinsfolk in eastern Latvia, at the same time pressing the Estonians farther to the north.[3]

A full sense of the cultural and political definition of Latvia's eastern frontier came to the archeologists when they discovered that out of 320 excavated fortified castles, 158 formed a planned defense system directed against the eastern Slavs. Further testimony was offered by grave excavation on either side of the natural frontier of swamps, which offered a sharp contrast between the Latvian graves, containing richly embroidered garments, jewels, arms, and coins, and the Slavic graves which hold none of these objects. The philologists added conclusive evidence when they established an ancient linguistic dividing line corresponding to the anthropological and geographical frontier.

The *Dainas* are never far from the mind of the student of origins and early development. Most significant is their revelation of a sense of nationhood, and their stress on unity and independence: unity once known and then lost, freedom and union to be restored someday to the "sons and daughters of the Sun." The legends taught that the Ancient Prussians, Lithuanians, and Latvians were all descended from a common patriarch, Videvuds, from whose sons sprang the various tribes. Among these tribes arose folk heroes who, for their time, united tribal loyalties around their particularly strong, clever, or daring personalities. Such were Kurbads, a sort of pioneering Hercules of the Kurs, Caunis the Wizard, Ojars the Tiller, and, pre-eminently, Lāčplēsis the Ruler.

The most popular tale among the Latvians appears to have been the Lāčplēsis or Bearslayer legend, which relates the finding by a tribal ruler of a she-bear's human nursling whom the prince brought to his castle and reared into an immensely strong and cunning boy who inherited the throne and became an exemplary ruler of the Latvian land. Lāčplēsis proclaimed laws, established tribunals, created a sound administration and a strong military organization. In addition to his military household, he constituted a council of the *burtnieki*, wise men who could read and write, were versed in the common law, and probably composed the priesthood. They were also the guardians of certain sacred scrolls which were kept in the "Castle of Light" on the shore of Lake Burtnieks. According to legend the castle sank

[3] A. Schwabe, *The Story of Latvia and her Neighbors*, p. 6.

back into the waters when the key was treacherously stolen from Lāčplēsis by the Black Knight.

Lāčplēsis has always been the most cherished national hero of the Latvians, representing as he does the epoch of the establishment of a tribal state in the new homeland, and belonging to all Latvians, regardless of tribal differences. Through centuries of subjugation the people have believed that Lāčplēsis will return from the depths of the Daugava, where he continues his struggle with the Black Knight, and will restore the Castle of Light, symbol of national independence.

The account of Lāčplēsis' administrative talents emphasizes the respect which the Latvians, from the earliest times, had for the common law, which was based on ancient ethical concepts. These concepts are illustrated throughout the *Dainas*,[4] by allegory, moral tales, and sacral formulas. Every soul, they taught, possessed the notion of right and wrong. The idea of wrong-doing is represented by the left hand, *kreisā*, whence is derived in Lithuanian (which is closely akin to Latvian) the term *kreisva* for wrong, with which one may compare the relationship between Latin (*manus*) *sinistra* and English *sinister*. According to the *Dainas*, any human being is free to choose in his life the straight or the winding road. In Latvian the right road is called the *tiešais celš*; by derivation *tiesa* is the term for court, *tiesibas* for rights, and *tiesnesis* for judge.

The basic concepts of right and wrong, freedom of choice, and retribution, together with the ancient Latvian belief in a primary divine source of all law and justice, nurtured the development of a common law which had certain parallels to old Roman law, and was essentially like that of Western Europe. The early Latvians appear to have been law-conscious and law-creative to the point of regulating legally most of their mutual relations. An elaborate system arose which distinguished family rights, contract and property rights, authority and law, and was interpreted by proper tribunals where offenders were tried and punished according to the ancient tribal law.[5]

As an example of the development of this law, we see in early medieval times the primitive custom of blood revenge giving way to a system of monetary fines. The considerable sum of forty marks silver as the price for a slain man suggests that the clan was the col-

---

[4] A. Schwabe, *Latvijas tiesību vēsture* (Riga, 1932), 2 vols. *passim*.

[5] L. Arbusov, *Die Altlivländischen Bauernrechte* in *Mitteilungen aus der livländischen Geschichte* (Riga, 1924-1926).

lective respondent in such cases. Parallels with concepts dominant in early Frankish law are obvious. A group of the concepts of international law is shown in the treaties which the tribal kings of the twelfth and thirteenth centuries concluded with their allies or conquerors.

The ethical sense of the early Latvians, set forth in their folklore and realized in their solid and respected common law, found further expression in the bases of their religion, which recognized good and evil, though not with any high degree of abstraction. As we have seen, the Latvians believed themselves to be descended from the sun, whose cool northern light they continued to worship, presumably as their remote ancestors adored some more powerful southern luminary. This god was presented in the *Dainas* as a wealthy chieftain and warrior clad in a wide glittering mantle, riding a horse with a golden saddle. Strong, kind, and wise, he defended moral and legal principles. The sun-god was the source of goodness, but other deities ruled in nature and received a share of worship. In time the god of thunder tended to become supreme in the popular mind, which also lent itself to a proliferation of the good and evil spirits in nature 'till a universal animism ruled the folk imagination. Particular localities had individual divinities; each household, indeed, might boast of familiar spirits.[6] Protective deities and spirits on an intimate scale were the natural creation of a people who must wrest a living from a difficult land and threatening elements. Practical propitiation seemed more effective than abstract worship.

Into this nexus of highly personal cults handed down from generation to generation much in the nature of prized recipes, cozy and useful and defended as a valuable property would be, the austere mystery of Christianity must at first have struck cold. Its universalism could scarcely appeal to scattered and toughly individualistic localities. Certainly tact was needed to convey its strange beauty and peculiar demands to the devotees of an entrenched pantheism which fully satisfied a society of hunters and farmers. The scattered missionaries, both Roman Catholic and Greek Orthodox, who had some success in this region in pre-German times, must have been gifted with tact and suppleness in dealing with this people. For the German claim to have discovered a stubborn heathen people in "Livonia," though no doubt accurate in its choice of the first adjective, is substantially invalidated by traces of Christian influence centuries before the German pene-

[6] J. Meuvret, *Histoire des pays baltiques* (Paris, 1934), pp. 35-41.

tration. The Byzantine chronicles of Amartolo testify that the Apostle Andrew had preached Christianity in the Baltic region. Olaf of Sweden, who ravaged Kurzeme in the ninth century, had in his expedition merchants who stayed on to evangelize and pave the way for priests. In the eleventh century a Scandinavian missionary, Hiltuin, had preached among the Balts. As we have seen in the chronicles of Rimbert and of Adam of Bremen, in 1048 a Roman Catholic church was built in Kurzeme through the bounty of a Danish king;[7] while in 1161 another Danish prince established a bishopric in that tribal kingdom.[8] In the old Scandinavian trading port of Riga excavation has uncovered the site of a Roman Catholic chapel, which must have been built long before the arrival of Bishop Albert who claimed to have founded that city in the year 1200. Greek Orthodoxy had also made a number of converts by the end of the twelfth century.

The great number of crosses found in eleventh and twelfth century graves is further evidence of the spread of the Christian faith in these early times. Certainly we must grant that a goodly amount of native superstition may have been grafted onto the Christian symbol. Judging from the folktales, the figures of Christ and the Virgin had to be shrunk to the size of familiar deities before they were acceptable to the folk imagination.

The tolerance of the tribal rulers towards these new divinities and their priests was notable. Due in good measure to this attitude of the rulers, both the Greek Orthodox (in Tālava and Latgale) and Roman Catholic expressions of Christianity were known among the 250,000 odd Latvians of the twelfth and early thirteenth centuries.

One manifestation of the Latvian pagan religion of the early Middle Ages had been a form of ancestor worship. This was a phenomenon inherent in a culture centered around family life. From earliest times the family as a social unit and the peasants as a class formed the social framework of an emergent peasant democracy. The medieval Latvian yeoman had none of the serf about him, since sufficient slave labor was provided by Slavic and Scandinavian prisoners of war as well as by purchased slaves. The peasant lived virtually as a freeman on his own land, owing only certain military services and fixed labor corvées to the lords and rulers in return for their protection

[7] *Adami Gesta Hammaburgensis* in *Mon. germ. hist.*, VII (Hannover, 1846), 17. See further K. Kruse, *Ur-Geschichte des Esthnischen Volkstammes* (Moscow, 1896), p. 506f.

[8] *Libellus gestorum* in *Mon. germ. hist.* (Hannover, 1888), 246.

in time of war. The closely-knit farm families were self-reliant, jealous of their independence, and governed by a set of mores which assured the security of family property and self-respect. Betrothals and marriages were regulated by contracts and subject to the approval of the elders. Women were accorded the sort of freedom which accompanies true regard. In their hands rested the preservation of the valued family, clan, and tribal traditions. The patriarchs were revered, even after death, and from this veneration of the elders sprang the institution of chieftaincy.

The entire Latvian social organization rested exactly on the small peasant family unit. Several closely related units formed the greater family (*saime*), which recalls the Roman *familia*. A union of kindred *saimes* formed the clan (*gints*) (cf. Latin *gens*) whose territory (*pagasts*) formed an administrative unit governed by the oldest of the clan (called in the *Dainas kundzins*, diminutive of *kungs*, meaning lord or seigneur), who was chieftain, high priest, and president of the local tribunal of justice (*runa*). The *kundzins* lived in a castle surrounded by a stockade to which, in time of danger, flocked the yeomen with their families and movable possessions. The members of the chieftain's proper household were called *draugi* (cf. Gothic *driugan* and the Latin *drungus*), and formed the *draudze* or bodyguard. The *draudze* gradually evolved into an administrative unit, in much the same way as the *comites palatii* of Charlemagne became his officials. The term eventually came to mean parish or, in the Duchy of Kurland, county.

A territory occupied by several clans was called the *novads*, translated by the Latin chroniclers as *terra*. The *novads* was ruled by the *kungs* (*princeps*) who was the senior of the genealogically oldest family in the territory. Within this pattern of family patriarchs, clan chiefs, and territorial princes, the evolution of tribal kingships was inevitable. In time of war some particularly powerful or able *kungs* would assume leadership over several *terrae* and thus become a *lielkungs*, or tribal king, called in the chronicles *dux*, *princeps*, or *rex*.

To obtain and maintain such a position, the tribal king must have exhibited many of the traits which characterized the prototype of all such rulers, the strong, wise, and excellent Lāčplēsis. In addition, he must have possessed unusual wealth, since he had to equip his yeoman militia with horses and weapons, as well as lead them in battle. The king required a large military household and often maintained considerable armies, as did that ninth century king of the Kurs who held

15,000 warriors concentrated in his capital city of Apule. In addition
to his initial fortune which may have gained him his position, a tribal
king could levy tolls on river commerce, and taxes on the lords of
manors. He received military services from both the lords and the
yeomen, hospitality from the lords, and labor services from the
peasants. War booty and ransoms were a further source of wealth,
while war prisoners replenished the supply of serfs. Thus a tribal king
was in a position to live fairly largely in his castle which often displayed a tempting show of wealth, well worth ransacking.

The functions of the tribal kings were by no means exclusively military. They represented their kingdoms abroad, signed treaties, and dispatched envoys. The defeat or submission of a king meant defeat and
submission for all his tribe. They administered justice, making journeys through their assembled *terrae* two or three times a year for
this purpose. According to the *Dainas*, the kings had advisers who
could read and write, the *burtnieki* of the Lāčplēsis legend, to assist
them in their administrative and diplomatic functions. Probably the
embassy which the *Aestii* sent to Theoderic consisted of such "wise
men" who could interpret the Latin message returned by the Gothic
emperor.

The principle of hereditary rule and of primogeniture appears to
have been recognized if not formalized in certain of the Latvian tribal
kingdoms towards the end of the Middle Ages. King Vissevald of
Latgale, at the beginning of the thirteenth century, looked upon his
kingdom as his inherited patrimony, referring to his capital city of
Jersika as *hereditas patrum meorum.*[9] It became customary for the
eldest son to succeed his father, while other sons, though remaining
subject to the eldest, became the masters of separate *terrae*, semi-
independent lords and founders of minor dynasties who, together
with the branching families of the clan chiefs, formed a somewhat
amorphous native aristocracy known more for its enthusiastic independence than for any *esprit de corps.*

The land ruled by a tribal king was called the *valsts* (Latin *regnum*).
The root *vald-*, meaning rule, appears in the names of many of the
tribal rulers; as, for instance, in Vissevald (all-ruler), Tālivald (far-
ruler) and Vienvald (one-ruler). During the course of the Middle
Ages there emerged five tribal kingdoms: those of the Talavians and
Latgallians north of the Daugava River (Latgale was called Lettia by

[9] Henricus de Lettis, *op.cit., sub anno* 1209.

the Germans, who gave the name of Letts to these Latvians); and those of the Kurs, Selonians, and Zemgallians south of the river. The Livs, after whom the Germans were to name the whole country, formed only a few scattered fishing settlements along the Gulf of Riga and at the mouths of the Gauja and the Daugava.

This loose political organization did not differ in nature from that of medieval Sweden, with her twelve tribes, Poland or Lithuania. A further consolidation, wherein one dynasty of peculiar power and prestige, under favorable circumstances, could have united all the tribes, might have eventuated, as it did in Sweden in 1222, under the family of the Folkjunger jarls, and as it did in Poland under the Piasts.

Latvia may not have been far from a similar unification in the thirteenth century, when such a ruler as Vissevald of Latgale possessed considerable wealth and authority, and stood forth as a champion against the marauding Russians. But at this time the natural course of development was interrupted by the first of a series of determined foreign bids for domination which stunted the native political growth for centuries to come. With the luck of history on their side, the experienced German colonizers were able to drive in their shattering wedge, barbed with the formidable weapon of militant Christianity, before the Latvian tribes, too long guilty of particularism, had seen the wisdom of hardening into a solid peasant nation which might have offered infrangible resistance to an invasion of petty German nobles, their mercenaries and their priests. Unification was, instead, to be imposed from without. Tribes were pitted against each other, by baffling and subjugating one at a time the often too trusting rulers, and by the threats and bribes of politicious churchmen. Even so, for all the force and cunning which confronted them, the Latvians, together with the equally outraged Estonians and Lithuanians, showed a remarkably ardent and resilient century-long opposition both to the intruders and to their once acceptable but now inimical religion.

PART II
GERMAN DOMINANCE

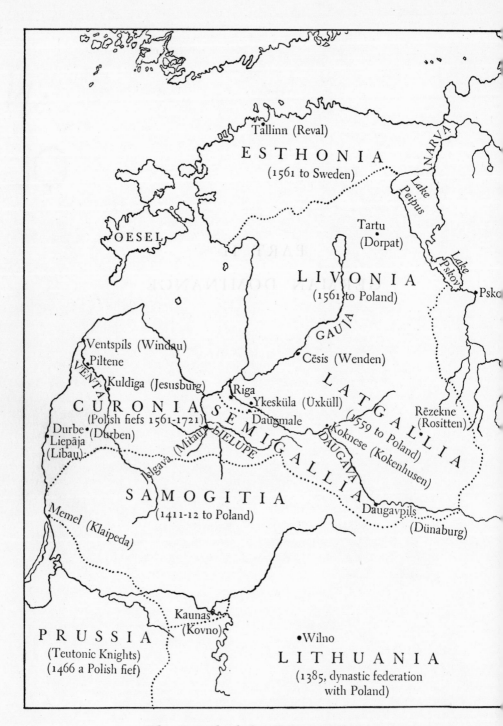

The Period of the Teutonic Knights

Chapter 4

Establishment of the Principality
of Livonia

DURING the High Middle Ages the Baltic lands were considered an unfailing source of many of the foodstuffs and raw materials needed by the growing cities of Germany, Holland, Flanders, and France. The rye and linseed, the smoked meats and fish, cheeses and honey, flax, medicinal plants, and beeswax of these regions were much sought after, as were the oak timber, rope, and sailcloth which were, after amber, the chief exports of the Kurs. The rising class of north German merchants, eager for a corner on these rich resources as well as for a dominant position in the Russian trade to which control of Gotland and the eastern Baltic was the key, systematically set about eliminating Scandinavian competition from this area.

The aggressive commercial element among the north Germans must rank first, in time, among the forces which were to shape from the Latvian tribal kingdoms the beginning of a westernized political community. The north German merchants, the Baltic thrown open to them by the founding of Lübeck in 1158, wasted no time in penetrating, exploiting, and colonizing this tempting new territory.[1]

As early as the tenth and eleventh centuries the north Germans pushed from Bremen eastwards along the Baltic shores into the territories of the northern Slavs, considered at that time to be the special sphere of influence of Denmark. In the eventual and decisive clash the powerful north German Hanseatic cities emerged victorious. After the subjugation of the local Slavs and the second founding of Lübeck by Henry the Lion in 1158 on the site of an ancient Slavonic town, they planned the commercial conquest of the eastern Baltic shores, inhabited by the Ancient Prussians, Latvians, and Estonians, for the exploitation of their rich agricultural lands, and the control of their ports and river settlements—"way stations" to the trade centers of the East.

Around the middle of the twelfth century, German merchants from Lübeck and Bremen appeared more often on the estuary of the

[1] C. Schiemann, *Russland, Polen, und Livland*, II (Berlin, 1887), 1-14.

Daugava. In 1163, Visby, some eighty nautical miles from the shores of Kurzeme and the foremost staple depot for the Baltic trade, had become preponderantly German; and from then on the German penetration of the Baltic lands became more intensive and systematic.[2] By 1195 Novgorod had concluded a commercial treaty with the Gotlanders and the Germans.[3]

The prospective colonizers realized that their best chance lay in dealing with the Livs, kinsfolk of the Finns, who had come to the Latvian shores in search of better fishing, and had settled, as a national minority, between the mouths of the Daugava and the Salace rivers in Vidzeme (Iduma). The Germans rightly judged that these Livs, strangers in Latvia and with only four castle-mounds defending their small area, rather than oppose them would prefer to accept their protection against the tribe of the Latgallians, with whom the Livs were in a constant state of feud. The Germans also knew that the Livian settlements on the Daugava and Gauja rivers separated the southern from the northern Latvians. They could sign treaties with the Livs and then, in turn, with every one of the sovereign Latvian tribes; and eventually, by pitting one tribe against the other, they could subdue all these peoples, as had already been done with the northern Slavs on the southern Baltic shores.[4]

As the plan developed it became apparent that the Daugava must be secured upstream as far as possible to create a German-dominated trade route to the Slavic principality of Polotzk and to Smolensk, by then the chief Russian center for German trade. In order to control a trade route to Pskov and Novgorod, the Gauja River and Estonia had also to be secured. But for the time being, treaties of friendship were to be signed with the tribal rulers south of the Daugava in Kurzeme and Zemgale, and Estonia was to be left alone. Visby, as a naval base, was chosen as a springboard, and the first strategical assault was planned against the Livs.[5]

This national minority had played no particular part in the early history of Latvia. The name *Lifland* appears on a Scandinavian runic stone about the middle of the eleventh century. The first chronicler

[2] F. Nyenstedt, *Chronicae* (1604), in *Monumenta Livoniae antiquae*, v (Riga, 1839), *sub anno* 1163.

[3] G. Vernadsky, *Kievan Russia* (New Haven, 1948), p. 336.

[4] E. Seraphim, *Grundriss der baltischen Geschichte* (Reval, 1908), p. 9. For the whole German campaign, see Arnold of Lübeck's *Chronica Slavorum*, lib. v, cap. 30, suggestively entitled *De conversione Livoniae*.

[5] G. Vernadsky, *op.cit.*, p. 232ff.

to mention the Livs is the Russian monk Nestor, writing in the early twelfth century. Arnold of Lübeck related the conversion of *Livonia*, in the fifth book of *Chronica slavorum*, entitled *De conversione Livoniae, sub anno* 1207. The name Livonia, originally given by the Germans to the coast settlements of the Livs, was eventually to be extended to the hinterland, inhabited by the Latvian tribes and, to the north, by the Estonians.

On the heels of the invading merchants, the financiers of Christian conversion, trod their indispensable allies the missionaries, who must secure by primitive threats and bribes, sometimes by masterly diplomacy, the loyalty of the peoples who might otherwise turn on the greedy traders. For a remarkably detailed account of this intensive penetration of an autochthonous culture by the vanguard of the expanding West we turn to the notable chronicler Henricus de Lettis, whose chronicles, composed in 1225, are considered the most important historical account of the establishment of the Livonian principality.

Henricus was of Latvian birth, possibly the son of a converted Latvian nobleman, and probably one of the Latvian hostages taken by one of the missionary bishops to be sent to Rome or Bremen for an education. The high quality of Henricus' Latin proves him a cultivated man. Latin became the official language of Livonia, used in all official decrees, treaties, and state correspondence. From a parish priest, Henricus became the secretary of Bishop Albert. In 1214, he introduced Roman Catholicism in subjugated Tālava, and gave religious instruction to the sons of King Tālivald. He also made several journeys to Rome, where he was present at the Lateran Council of 1215. In 1225, he composed his report on Livonia for the Papal Legate, Bishop William of Modena, who had arrived to foster the organization of a papal state in the Baltic, and whom Henricus accompanied on his visit to Latvia. This report, which became known as the Livonian Chronicles (*Chronicon Livonicum Vetus*) was later multiplied by copyists. One of the oldest texts, dating around 1300 and called the Codex Zamoyski, is still considered one of the closest to the archetype. The original may still lie in the Vatican archives, where it was probably filed among the scores of thousands of reports from the papal legates to various countries.[6]

In the year 1186 one Meinard, whom Henricus de Lettis described as a friar of the Augustinian Order originally from Holstein, founded

---

[6] *Latviešu biogrāfiskā vārdnīca* (Riga, 1937), p. 207f.

a bishopric in Riga.[7] For some reason he soon transferred his residence farther south to Ykesküla (Ikšķile), where he bribed the Livs with delicacies to obtain their permission to stay. At that time Greek Orthodox missionaries, escorted by armed men, would come by ship from Polotzk to proselytize among the Livs, assuring them the protection of the Knyaz (Prince) of Polotzk against the Zemgallians, the Latgallians, and the Lithuanians.

Bishop Meinard appeared as a new protector, also with an armed escort. Preferring to avoid trouble with the Greek Orthodox priests, he paid the Knyaz of Polotzk a certain sum for the right to baptize the Livs. Meinard then proceeded to build a fortress of stone, purportedly to protect his Livs against the Lithuanians who, according to Henricus, frequently ravaged the Livian communities. The Zemgallians, dwelling on the south bank of the Daugava, with their port of Daugmale almost opposite Ykesküla, considered themselves the overlords of the Livs and, resenting a German stronghold, stormed but could not destroy the fortress of Ykesküla.[8] They were repulsed by a garrison of German soldiers with crossbows.

From Ykesküla Meinard dispatched the Cistercian friar Theoderic as a missionary to the Estonians, kinsfolk of the Livs, who welcomed him with imprisonment and the threat of death. Meanwhile some difficulties had arisen with the Kurs, who, perhaps in conformity with the wishes of the Zemgallians, were attacking German merchant ships entering the Gulf of Riga and the Daugava estuary. After his escape, in 1191, Theoderic appeared in Rome, where he personally obtained from Pope Celestine III permission to promote a crusade against both the Estonians and the Kurs. Although in this enterprise Theoderic was supported by the Danes, the Swedes, and the Germans from Bremen, the crusade failed. The well-prepared expedition was dispersed by the Kuronians. The Swedish Duke Jarl Birger, after accepting a tribute of silver from the Estonians, returned home, thus disrupting the plans of his allies.

Upon the death of Meinard in 1196 the young Livonian diocese was considered of such importance that the Archbishop of Bremen proposed to Pope Celestine III that the Cistercian friar Berthold of Hannover be appointed to succeed Meinard. Berthold, arriving in

[7] The account given by Henricus is not much different from, though more detailed than, that provided by Arnold.

[8] F. Balodis, *Det Äldsta Lettland*, pp. 89-90, based largely on Henricus, as is indeed the present account.

Ykesküla in 1197, followed Meinard's example and sought, by offering rich gifts and sweet wines, to establish friendly relations with the Livian Elders. But he made the mistake of demanding a tithe from the Livs, and from the Elders—their sons as hostages. The Livs became suspicious and truculent. Berthold, fearing for his life, fled to Gotland. From there he returned to Germany whence he proceeded to Rome to report on his discouraging experience.

In response to his plea for help, Pope Celestine granted him a bull permitting him to preach a crusade against the "treacherous Livs," all of whom were promised absolution of their sins and pardon for criminal offenses if they accepted the Cross. Proceeding in several ships from Lübeck and Visby the crusaders, mostly Saxons, arrived before Ykesküla in July 1198. Here the Livian Elders resisted so stubbornly that Bishop Berthold retreated to nearby Riga where a bloody battle was fought. Berthold was killed, but eventually the Livs, who had no allies, suffered defeat at the hands of the better-armed German crusaders. The defeated Livs were forced to surrender Ykesküla, to agree to baptism, to pay the tithe, and to become subjects of the successor to Berthold.

After the crusaders had left Ykesküla, together with a delegation of Livs who were to beg pardon of the Archbishop of Bremen and request the appointment of a new bishop, the remaining Livs again revolted. They washed themselves clean of baptism in the Daugava, and then compelled the few remaining German priests to leave the country under threat of death. The German merchants hurried after them.

Meanwhile a nephew of the Archbishop of Bremen and canon of the cathedral, Albert, had been consecrated Bishop of Livonia. He was one of the shrewdest German colonizers and diplomats of his time. True to his political instincts, he consulted with the Kings of Denmark and Germany, as well as with several German princes and church dignitaries. The Baltic Crusade had been proclaimed the equivalent of a crusade to Palestine. With a well-equipped army of more than 500 crusaders (Westphalians this time), on twenty-three ships, Bishop Albert finally left Visby and arrived in Riga in March 1200. Here he soon succeeded in "pacifying" the Livs. No longer trusting them, he decided to transfer his residence back to Riga, nearer to the mouth of the Daugava and safer from unexpected Slavic, Livian and, Zemgallian assaults.

According to Henricus de Lettis, Bishop Albert invited some thirty of the local Elders to a banquet in a large house in Riga. The house was promptly surrounded by German warriors who took the Elders prisoner. Thus did the new bishop force from the Elders the surrender of their sons as hostages. With the situation now well in hand, Albert, employing the forced labor of captured Livs, began to build a cathedral, houses for himself and his priests, barracks for the military household, stone warehouses, and surrounded the whole stronghold with a wall and moat. This was the German "foundation" of Riga. Reassured, the German merchants came scuttling back.

Albert now felt free to report his successes to Pope Innocent III; and, anxious to secure them, petitioned the Pontiff to establish in the Livonian bishopric a permanent military order. He also suggested the issuing of a bull proclaiming the blockade of Daugmale, a Zemgallian port some sixteen miles south of Riga, a heathen stronghold and a threat to the concentration of German commerce in Riga. Under the authority granted by the Pope in 1201, Bishop Albert was empowered to capture blockade runners and confiscate their ships. Eventually, excavations prove, the ancient *portus Semigallorum* was burned.[9] The Germans were seemingly firmly entrenched in Riga.

The next year Albert obtained from the same Pope the coveted bull permitting him to establish in still unconverted Livonia the crusading Order of the *Fratres Militiae Christi*.[10] It was the Bishop's hope that such an Order might stabilize the Church's difficult conquest of Livonia far better than the German bands of adventurers hitherto employed who generally refused winter garrison in so somber a land, where the howling wolves and the wind seemed to echo the hatred of the humiliated "heathen." Two years later the Pope consecrated the Order, and gave it the statute of the Knights Templar. Like the Templars, the Order had a Grand Master; their costume consisted of a white cloak with a red cross on the shoulders, and a sword, whence their popular designation as Knights of the Sword. Toughened by their experiences in Palestine, these bearers of the Sword and Cross were to prove exemplary followers of the early German colonial policy which had borne the bloody slogan "he who does not wish to be christened shall die."

The Livonian Order, like other military crusading orders of that

[9] F. Balodis, *op.cit.*, pp. 90, 153-154, 164-165.
[10] O. von Rutenberg, *Geschichte der Ostseeprovinzen*, I (Leipzig, 1859), 70, 122. See also Schiemann, *op.cit.*, 15ff. The German literature on the Order is extensive.

time, had a combined military-ecclesiastical organization. The Knights of the Order took the vows of poverty, celibacy, and obedience, and undertook as a sacred duty to convert with arms the heathen and to defend the Church. Members of the Order were of three grades: the Knights, who had to be of noble origin, clerics (the *fratres capellani*), and the *fratres servientes*, rank and file soldiers and artisans.

The Knights were stationed in district castles, usually built next to the castle-mound of a conquered Latvian noble. Each such castle had a council of its own, presided over by the *commendator* or *comtur* of the castle, who was nominated by the Master of the Order as military chief of the country region adjacent to the district castle. The Master also appointed the *vogts* (*advocati*), or civil administrators of the district.

The General Assembly of the Knights, or Chapter, convened annually in September. All the officials of the Order had to present to the Master their seals and reports, after which they were relieved *in corpore* of their duties. New dignitaries, elected by the Chapter and confirmed by the Master, obtained the respective seals and papers from the Master. As a matter of custom, former dignitaries were usually reelected.

The Master of the Order was customarily elected for life by this same General Assembly, which first elected an "election marshal," who chose from the Knights another elector; the two electors then coopting a third; the three, a fourth, until they reached the number thirteen, the number for Christ and his Twelve. Since the Livonian Order had been subordinated by the Pope directly to the Bishop of Riga, the elected Master theoretically must be confirmed by the Prince-Bishop of Livonia, before whom he knelt and whose hand he kissed in token of obedience. In fact, the elections of the General Chapter were considered final. During its existence, from 1202 until its merger with the Teutonic Knights in 1237, the Order of the Livonian Templars had only three Masters. The last, Volquin, was killed in battle in 1236 when the Order suffered a defeat at the hands of the Zemgallians, then allied with the Lithuanian Samogithians.

By 1206 all the land of the Livs was strongly dominated by the Order, which, in those early days, faithfully protected and supported the Bishop and his works. The Diocese of Livonia now came actually into being.[11] Albert could widen his horizon. Having obtained control

[11] See H. K. Mann, *Lives of the Popes*, XII: *Innocent III* (St. Louis, 1925), 209-213.

over the Livian enclave in Vidzeme (Iduma), the Bishop fixed his
ambitious will on the rest of Latvian Vidzeme and on the neighboring
tribal kingdoms of Latgale and Tālava. For the time being he scrupulously avoided a clash with the kingdoms of Zemgale and Kurzeme
south of the Daugava, and even went so far as to establish friendly
relations with King Viesturs of Zemgale, who became the ally of the
Bishop against the ravaging Lithuanians menacing Riga in 1205.

In that same year the Knights of the Order, assured of Viesturs'
friendship, provoked the tribal dynast of Koknese, south of Ykesküla,
and invaded his land, which was probably a dependency of the Kingdom of Latgale (Lettia). When the Order obtained control of Koknese, the Livs dwelling on the lower Daugava were cut off from
communication with the Slavs of Polotzk, with whom they had
political and economic relations. Here was cause for tension between
the Bishop and the Knyaz of Polotzk, to whom the Livs paid tribute.
Albert hastened to pay the Prince a substantial sum of money and to
establish commercial relations between Polotzk and Riga.

After these military and diplomatic successes, Albert sailed to
Germany in 1207, where he obtained from Philip (of Suabia) the
rank of Margrave and the recognition of the Livonian Bishopric as
feudum oblatum, a principality under the suzerainty of the German
king. Albert became the ninety-fourth ruling Prince-Bishop of the
Holy Roman Empire.

When Albert returned in 1207, his political ambitions nourished
but his purse empty, the Knights of the Order, garrisoned in the castle
of Koknese, provoked another quarrel with the household of the
Latvian dynast, suffered some loss of life, and subsequently com-
plained of the ruler of Koknese, who fled for his life and was killed in
battle in 1224, fighting with the Estonians against the Germans. His
possessions were confiscated by Margrave Bishop Albert, and the
district of Koknese was incorporated into the Livonian Bishopric.

In 1208, the Knights of the Order occupied Sēlpils (Selburg), a
stronghold of the Latvian minor tribe of the Sēliji or Selonians, and
an important fortification situated at a ford of the middle Daugava.
And now Albert, controlling the middle bank of the Daugava with
the castles of Koknese and Sēlpils, could more easily extend his power
over the Latvian tribal kingdom of Latgale, situated northeast of the
middle Daugava.

The following year the Knights of the Order accused King Vissevald
of Latgale, who was of the Greek Orthodox faith, of "unfriendliness"

to the "Latins." Further suspicion was attached to him because of his marriage to a Samogithian princess and his close relations with this heathen tribe. In the absence of Vissevald the Knights sacked Guersike (Jersika), his residence, and the capital of Latgale. They plundered heavily, took women and children prisoners, and seized the Queen. In return for the release of his consort, Albert demanded of Vissevald his submission as a vassal, his conversion from Greek Orthodoxy to the Roman Catholic faith, and two-thirds of his domain. The document of the treaty of King Vissevald's submission was discovered in the Warsaw archives, and is reproduced in facsimile in F. Balodis' study of the excavations at Guersike. According to this document, after his submission in 1209 Vissevald obtained a part of his own patrimony *in beneficio* as a fief and enjoyed the *defensio* or *tuitio* of the Bishop, whom he calls "father" in the treaty and the Knights of the Order "brethren." This time Albert limited his aggressive demands to the feudal submission of a tribal king.

This leniency can be explained by the fact that in 1210 the Kurs had signed an alliance with the Samogithians and with the Knyaz of Polotzk against the Order. In due time the Kurs appeared before Riga, but neither the Slavs of Polotzk nor the Samogithians kept their promise to attack neighboring strongholds. The Kurs left after an unsuccessful three-day siege, and the Bishop hastened to renew his treaty with the Prince of Polotzk.

With the Daugava under his control to the Russian border, Albert now busied himself with the submission of the Latvian tribal kingdom of Tālava, in northern Latvia, his goal being control over the Gauja River, the road to Slavic Pskov. Once more "diplomacy" was employed.

In 1214 the sons of the Tālavian King Tālivald requested help from the Master of the Order in liberating their father, who had been captured by ravaging Lithuanians. The request was granted in return for a promise of submission to the Bishopric. Meantime Tālivald had escaped without any help from the Order and returned safely home. But the princes were held to their promise, and King Tālivald became a vassal, ceding two-thirds of his domains, paying tithe and tribute, and renouncing the Greek Orthodox faith for the Roman Catholic. His sons, converted to Roman Catholicism with Henricus de Lettis for their instructor, also became simply feudal *viri* of the Prince-Bishop, with only small sustenance holdings for which they had to render an annual tribute.

In this same year of Tālivald's submission the final blow came to Latgale. The Order again ransacked and burned King Vissevald's capital of Guersike, this time accusing the King of conspiracy with the Samogithians and the Slavs of Novgorod against the Bishop. Guersike was never rebuilt, and over the next ten years Vissevald was divested of his remaining possessions.[12] His complaint to the papal legate, William of Modena, had no effect.

Albert excelled at manipulating the personal ambitions of the smaller Latvian nobility to create mutual distrust. He would then step in with the offer of episcopal protection in return for the cession of two-thirds of the lands of these tribal lords, leaving for their sustenance the remaining third, and that for their lifetime only. Eventually all Latvian rulers and nobles became simple freemen granted a small holding. They were thankful even for this much bounty from the sovereign Bishop.

But in the north, where the Estonian tribes, manifesting from early times a remarkable solidarity, were in ceaseless conflict with the Latvians, Albert and the Order found a more seasoned enemy. According to Henricus de Lettis, it was by request of the Latvians that the Germans intervened, as a simple police measure, in 1208. In 1217 Albert did achieve the subjugation of southern Estonia, after the death in battle of the courageous King Lembit. But northern Estonia, as well as the Estonian Islands, remained free, and soon the whole nation, supported by the Russian princes of Pskov and Novgorod, was again seething with opposition. The Russians themselves further harassed the Germans incessantly by invading the confines of Livonia.

In view of the growing danger, Albert in 1218 undertook a voyage to Denmark to petition King Valdemar II for military cooperation. The following spring, Valdemar with a force of 60,000 landed in the islands and northern Estonia. He conquered Reval, which henceforth was called Daani-linn or the fortress of the Danes, whence the name Tallinn, soon to become the second port of Livonia. Valdemar also defeated the Russians. But there were not permanent victories. In 1222, after an eviction of the Danes from the island of Oesel (Saaremaa), a general uprising threatened. The King of Denmark had returned to his own country, where he was being held captive by a vassal of the Empire. Once more the Russians were called in by the Estonians, given half the booty taken from the Knights of the Order and

[12] F. Balodis, *Jersika*, pp. 14, 17, 21.

the German merchants, and stationed in garrisons throughout the land.[13]

The Estonians now made the tactical error of taking the offensive in the Latvian lands. The Livonians promptly joined the Knights of the Order in self-defense and the Estonians were defeated on the Seda; while the Russians, after a four-week siege of Tallinn, were forced to withdraw. Recapturing the offensive in 1224, the Crusaders successfully besieged the fortress of Tartu (Dorpat). Three years later the island of Oesel was occupied. After some dissension it was agreed that the Danes should retain northern Estonia; independent bishops should rule over districts in the southeast and the west; and the dominion of the Order should extend over the intermediate region.

The exploits of the Danes in Estonia, by releasing the German forces, had opened up to Albert the long-awaited opportunity of invading Zemgale. In 1219, there appeared in Riga some envoys from the Zemgallian fortress of Mežotne, seeking Albert's protection against an expected Lithuanian assault. Promptly the Bishop promised his aid in exchange for their acceptance of baptism.

A year earlier, Albert had appointed Count Bernhard, the Bishop of Selonia, as titular bishop for still unconquered Zemgale. He had also brought back with him from Germany new crusaders, among them the Duke of Saxony and Anhalt together with his military engines and numerous troops. With these troops Albert, disregarding his earlier treaty of friendship with King Viesturs, appeared in person before Mežotne and "baptized" the inhabitants. Leaving a garrison, he returned to Riga, perhaps assuming that King Viesturs would accept a *fait accompli*. Viesturs did not comply. Hurrying from his residence with a great force, he surrounded Mežotne and went himself with the bulk of his army to meet the German troops ascending the Daugava. These he crushed, leaving only a few to escape to Riga, where they were soon joined by the abandoned garrison at Mežotne.

The Germans organized a second attempt on the fortress in February 1220. Henricus de Lettis gives a long and gruesome account of the attacks and counterattacks which ensued: Albert and his crusaders, the Duke of Saxony and his huge war engines, the Master of the Order and his Knights with four thousand Germans and another four thousand Livs stormed the fortress fearsomely, opposed a large gathering of Zemgallians and Lithuanians, and wrought such havoc among

[13] C. Schiemann, *op.cit.*, p. 30ff.

the defenders that these sued for peace. Finally: "The Bishop and the Duke together with the rest of the force took pity upon them and sent the sign of the Holy Cross into the castle; and they believed them and promised that in future they would never break the Holy Christian Sacrament. And they came down from the castle with their women and children and departed for their villages. The army, however, went up into the castle and looted the money and all the goods and horses and cattle. And the Livs and Lettgallians left nothing there, but took everything, and, having set the castle afire, returned with their booty to Livonia, praising God for the vengeance that was taken against this nation that had broken its obligations, forgotten its promises, cast away the faith of Christ, derided Christian grace, and did not fear once again to soil themselves with pagan rituals."[14]

The reports of the brutalities of the crusaders traveled far over the lands of the Latvians. But the Zemgallians do not seem to have been decisively defeated, since the Germans now returned to Riga, relinquishing voluntarily their hold on Mežotne.

Still dependent upon outside powers for supplies and soldiers and having been refused these by the Emperor Frederick who had other interests in Palestine, Albert now once more approached the King of Denmark, offering him feudal homage in return for military assistance. The Bishop was also eager to obtain the consent of Valdemar to the appointment of his brother Hermann as Bishop of Estonia, then under Danish control.

According to Henricus de Lettis, Albert made the final acceptance of Denmark's suzerainty over Livonia contingent upon the consent of the Riga burghers, the Knights of the Order, and the Elders of the baptized Livs and Latvians. The seniors categorically refused. When the Danish Burggraf for Riga arrived in the town in 1221, the whole population forced him to leave. The voice of the people of Riga, particularly the Elders, was decisive. Even the Order had to submit to this popular decision, although it sought to intimidate the Livian Elders by arresting them. The Danes had lost out decisively, and did not try again to obtain dominion over Riga.

In consequence of this revolt, relations between Albert and the King of Denmark became strained. Some merchants of Riga were arrested in Reval. Only in 1222, during Valdemar's above-mentioned campaign in the island of Oesel, when the Bishop sent assistance, did

---

[14] Henricus de Lettis, *op.cit., sub anno* 1220.

he and the King become reconciled. Only then did the King of Denmark agree that Albert's brother, already appointed and consecrated in 1220, could now be installed in Dorpat (Tartu) as Bishop of Estonia.

In 1225, the papal legate, Bishop William of Modena, for whom Henricus de Lettis composed his report, arrived in Riga. He found himself adjudicating the dispute which had broken out between the Danes and the Riga Germans over northern Estonia. He must also endeavor to settle matters between the Order and the Zemgallian King Viesturs. Following the invitation of the legate, Viesturs appeared in Riga for a conference. Viesturs there agreed that Christianity might be freely preached, as, indeed, it already had been, in Zemgale; but refused to become a vassal of the Bishop of Riga, probably bearing in mind the fate of the Kings of Latgale and Tālava. His distrust was not unfounded. After the legate's departure the Order renewed its raids into Zemgale. In retaliation the Zemgallians, in 1227, joined the Kurs in an attack upon the fortified monastery of the Cistercians at the mouth of the Daugava, doubtless intending to sever the German overseas supply line. Owing to a diversionary invasion of Zemgale by the Order this operation failed. Viesturs hurried home to repulse his ruthless enemy. He died in 1229, still king of a free Zemgale.

In that same year Albert died, after almost thirty years of rule in a principality which was in good part his own creation. Only in the regions south of the Daugava had he failed to extend his control. No mere account of his military and diplomatic successes, reverses, compromises, and ultimate victories can do full justice to the accomplishment of this determined expansionist, or suggest the nature of the forces which sometimes aided, and sometimes hampered his career of conquest.

Not all the opposition which the Bishop encountered came from revolting tribes, betrayed rulers, outraged local allies or from enemies rising on the borders of his domain. There were times when Albert found that those elements which he had imported for his own purposes were out of hand. The German soldier adventurers, brought in to threaten or subdue certain obstinate native points of resistance, sacked and pillaged beyond all the bounds of good policy, and aroused more widespread disaffection than their particular conquests justified. The Knights of the Livonian Order, for the most part German fortune-seekers, sought to establish a feudal domain of their own, and by their excesses often brought down the disapproval of the Papacy and the

Emperor, both upon themselves and their by now grudging ally, the Bishop.

Thus, a study of Albert's "reign" in the Baltic lands, as it may properly be called, reveals a curious pattern of external ambition and power overlying and adumbrating the internal tribal turmoil of this newly exploited region. Three separate but necessarily cooperative forces sought the upper hand in "christianizing" so choice a potential state: the Prince-Bishop, the Livonian Order, and, from a distance, discreetly but undeniably, the Papacy itself. Nor must we overlook, in this conflict of spiritual powers, the first-comers, the most tenacious settlers, and the ultimate real victors, since they assimilated themselves with the native rising class of burghers—the German traders.

Albert, expert in juggling the fears and designs of the native rulers, sought to prevail over the Order by stirring up the benevolent interest now of the Empire, now of the Papacy. Occasionally he received more attention than he had bargained for. But he could not have kept any check on the rampant and never-surfeited Knights of the Sword without outside pressure. In 1224, the Emperor Frederick II, perturbed by the atrocities committed by the Order, issued his Baltic Manifesto in which he informed kings, dukes, princes, margraves, and all subjects of the Holy Roman Empire that he had obtained reliable reports of the molestation of the converted inhabitants of Prussia, Samblandia, Livonia, Estonia, and the other Baltic lands.[15] The Emperor condemned such action and categorically forbade all kings, dukes, princes, counts, and other magnates to molest these free citizens of the Holy Roman Empire, whom he had taken, together with their children, under his high protection, assuring them their freedom and possessions, and confirming "to them and to their heirs in perpetuity liberty and all their privileges," making them "subject only to Holy Mother church and the Roman Empire, just as other free men. . . ." This *sui generis* Magna Charta of the Balts has been consistently ignored by German-Balt historians.

Albert either could not or would not restrain the Order or lend his own loyalty to this decree. In 1225, he saw fit to submit to Henry, the son of Emperor Frederick II, and at that time King of the Romans. In order to achieve complete dominion over the converted Baltic lands, both the Bishop and the Order were seeking some *titulus justus* or juridical basis. Pursuant to Albert's application, Henry issued a

[15] *Les sources de l'histoire de Lettonie*, II (Riga, 1937), 78f.

decree by which the lands of Latvia and Estonia were united in one Livonian Mark, whose recognized prince was the Bishop. This was a confirmation of the title of Margrave bestowed by Philip, and a final recognition of a new German Mark, or frontier province, in the East.[16]

Albert also obtained the right to strike coins, to grant city rights, to the possession of all metals, mines, and all discovered treasure. Himself the nephew of the Archbishop of Bremen, Albert seems to have been a confirmed nepotist. The brother whom he had promoted to the Bishopric of Estonia with a seat in Dorpat, also by the grace of Henry became a prince of the Holy Roman Empire. Another brother, Engelbrecht, died as *Canonicus praepositus* of Riga; a third became the presiding *canonicus* of Dorpat; and the fourth was given a title of nobility and married the daughter of a deposed Russian prince and was appointed as the Bishop's civil lieutenant in Vidzeme.

Though Albert had always sought close ties with the Empire, he had never failed to realize that papal protection and approval was necessary to him if he was to maintain even an equal footing with the growing power of the Order. As early as 1210, he had obtained the right to appoint and consecrate bishops in the newly baptized Baltic lands. In 1213, he had been made directly dependent upon the Pope and hence exempt from the power of the Archbishop of Bremen or any other metropolitan.

The rights of the Livonian Bishop, both temporal and spiritual, were impressive. As a prince of the Holy Roman Empire, he could grant the rights of citizenship of the Empire. As a bishop, he was the apostolic representative in his diocese endowed with all the religious prerogatives of that office: in the purely ecclesiastical sphere, with the right to appoint priests and consecrate bishops; more widely, with the right of adjudications in civil and criminal cases, according to canon law.

Next to the Bishop, the highest clerical authority in the diocese was the Cathedral Chapter of Riga, composed of twelve canons of the Cathedral. This virtual State Council had some powers of its own, among them the right to elect a candidate for a vacant bishopric. This right was introduced by the Lateran Council of 1215 in order to counteract the tendency of secular princes to nominate bishops. Before his election the prospective bishop had to sign the so-called "capitulation" or program of his future activities. The name of the

---

[16] As related by Henricus de Lettis, *op.cit.*, *sub anno* 1225.

candidate was then presented by the chapter to the Pope for confirmation. After confirmation the new bishop obtained from the Pope
the *jus in officia* and *jus in re.*

The Riga Canons, in contrast with the more aristocratic tradition
of Germany, stemmed from burgher families of the north German
cities. It is perhaps significant that the twenty-four ruling Prince-
Archbishops of the Riga diocese from 1254 to 1561 were, with the
exception of the last one (a Margrave), either of urban middle class
origin or of the petty nobility. This social background of the church
dignitaries had a strong influence on the state policy of the Livonian
principality, which came to be, in general, friendly to the natives.

After the death of his political patron, Philip of Germany, Albert
turned again to the Pope, Innocent III, now the supreme temporal as
well as spiritual power in Western Europe. At the Fourth Lateran
Council, in 1215, the Pope proclaimed the new Livonian Bishopric
Terra Mariana, under the special protection of the Holy See.

In the diplomacy of Innocent III, whose protection Albert had
been forced to seek in a difficult time, the ambitious Bishop was to
meet more than his match. Innocent fostered no less ambitious a plan
than the building of a strong papal state on the Baltic, facing the
schismatic Greek Orthodox Slavs.

The *Terra Mariana,* the germ of this state, had a promising future.
To this "Land of the Virgin Mary" belonged not only the land of the
Livs, or Livonia proper, situated along the northern shores of the Gulf
of Riga and forming an enclave in the Latvian province of Vidzeme
(Iduma); but also the latter itself, together with the three vassal
Latvian principalities of Koknese, Latgale, and Tālava. Thus this
embryonic papal state occupied practically all the territory of present-
day Latvia north of the Daugava; and its importance was enhanced
by its geographical situation on the approaches to the Slavic and
Lithuanian hinterlands, rich with the raw materials so necessary to
the West.[17]

The continuity of the Holy See's policy in the Baltic is seen from
the fact that the successor of Pope Innocent III, Honorius III, did not
deviate from it. In 1220, in condemning the murder of the surrendered
Zemgallian nobles in Mežotne, Honorius proclaimed the converted
Zemgallians "children of God," entitled to the same rights as other

[17] H. K. Mann, *Lives of the Popes in the Middle Ages,* Vol. xii, *Innocent III*
(London, 1925), p. 209ff. and literature there cited.

Christians of the Occident. Both the Order and the Bishop were alarmed by this protective measure.

Once more Albert veered toward temporal patronage. In 1220, as we have seen, he endeavored to submit Livonia to King Valdemar II of Denmark, who at that time had close ties with the Bishop's home town of Bremen. By this extravagant démarche, taken, presumably, to obtain Valdemar's confirmation of Albert's brother as Bishop of southern Estonia, the Bishop defied the supremacy of both the Pope and the Emperor Frederick II, newly crowned by Honorius in September 1220.

But the burghers of Riga and the Livian and Latvian Elders chose to remain under the protection of the Holy See and the Emperor. They were rewarded by the latter's Baltic Manifesto and, in the same year (1224), by the papal bull *libertas imperii*, granting the converted Latvians full rights of citizenship in the Holy Roman Empire. In that same year, Albert, in violation of the Manifesto, granted half of the annexed kingdom of Vissevald of Latgale to one of his vassals, Meiendorf, in fief. The following year saw the arrival of the papal legate, William of Modena, to investigate the activities of the Bishop, who had committed yet another breach in submitting to Henry (VII) and accepting from him the rank of Margrave of Livonia.

While Albert at times felt powerful enough to defy both his Emperor and his Pope, he apparently paid for this independence by failing to attain archiepiscopal rank. The conflict between him and the Papacy seems to have resulted in a draw. In the following chapter we shall study the convolutions of the struggle between the Papacy and an opponent more unruly and rapacious than any single man: the Order of the Teutonic Knights in Livonia.

Chapter 5

Conquest of Southern Livonia

THROUGHOUT the thirteenth century the Papacy maintained both the political ambitions and the conciliatory attitude toward native populations which had characterized the Baltic policy of Innocent III. Between 1198 and 1303 (the date of Boniface VIII's death), some 204 papal bulls were issued dealing with Baltic problems. Upon the death of Honorius III in 1227, his successor, Gregory IX, issued a protective bull addressed to the converted Balts. Two years later, when the Archbishop of Bremen tried to impose his own candidate for the bishopric vacated by Albert's death, the Pope supported the right of the Riga Cathedral Chapter, as decreed by the Fourth Lateran Council in 1215, to elect a candidate; and recognized their choice of Nicholas, who was consecrated in 1229 by the second papal legate to Livonia, Bishop Baldwin of Aune.

The Pope conferred upon Baldwin ample powers, among them the right to consecrate bishops, discipline and remove priests and abbots, and sign treaties. These prerogatives were intended to support far-reaching political schemes; for the papal vision now embraced no less a goal than the creation of an independent Prusso-Livonian state. The emphasis was shifted from the expansion of the Livonian conquest under the aegis of the irresponsible Brethren of the Sword, to the union of Livonia, by christianizing Kurzeme, Zemgale, and Lithuanian Samogithia, with Prussia, currently being won for the Holy Virgin by one of the Papacy's more powerful weapons against European heresy, the Teutonic Knights.

This Order had been founded in 1190, at the time of the Third Crusade, by certain burghers of Bremen and Lübeck as the *Fratres Hospitalis Sanctae Marie Teutonicorum per Jerosolemitam*, a charitable organization much on the order of the early Templars and Hospitallers. In 1198 it was raised to the rank of a military Order of Crusading Knights. Its membership from the first was to be exclusively German.

As the Eastern Crusades grew increasingly futile, the Papacy saw fit to transfer the activities of the still vigorous Teutonic Order to the spiritually unstable realms of Central Europe, particularly Hungary, where the Knights zealously harried the Moldavians and Wallachians. But by 1226 the Hungarians, feeling that they had had a sufficiency both of the Order's services and its appetites, invited the Germans to move on. This they did promptly enough, having received an invitation from Duke Conrad of Mazovia, a Polish Duchy, to join him in a war against his redoubtable neighbors, the heathen Boro-Russians (Borussians) or Prussians.

This was not the first attempt to convert the isolated and deeply pagan inhabitants of that stretch of the southern Baltic coast between the Niemen and the Vistula rivers; a region particularly inaccessible to conquest, or even to external influence, because of the dunes, lagoons, and swamps which defended it both coastwise and to the interior. Here dwelt those *Aestii*, those amber-gatherers of Roman times, the Ancient Prussians, close kin to the adjacent Kurs. In the tenth century Bishop Adalbert of Prague had attacked the challenge of their aloofness with fire and sword, and had perished for his pains in 997. The equally bold Bohemian Bishop Bruno met the same fate in 1009. In 1167, the Polish King Bolesław invaded the Prussian land and destroyed the sanctuary in the sacred wood of Romove. Ten years later, the Prussians succeeded in expelling the Poles, thereby winning the right to be left alone until the beginning of the following century.

In 1208, at Dobrzyn in Polish Mazovia, which bordered upon Prussian territory, a Cistercian friar founded an order similar to that of the Livonian *Fratres Militiae Christi*.[1] This renewed attempt to baptize the Prussians appears to have been concerted with the work of that other Cistercian Theoderic, who being much beset in Livonia, was anxious to divert the attention of the Prussians from rendering assistance to their cousins the Kurs. The Duke of Mazovia, Conrad, who had just failed in an attempt of his own to persuade the Prussians, encouraged the foundation of the Order of Dobrzyn by building them a castle which might serve as an outpost of conquest. Four years later, the Papacy addressed a warning to this branch of the *Fratres Militiae Christi*, whose brutalities kept pace with those of the Order in Livonia.

The Prussians, far from defeated, felt indeed somewhat encouraged both by the increasing weakness of the Order, which received few new pilgrims, and by the attitude of the Emperor Frederick II as revealed in his Manifesto of 1224, wherein he condemned the misdeeds of the Polish Mazovians and the Knights of Dobrzyn and at the same time

---

[1] P. von Duisburg, *Chronicon Prussiae* (Jena, 1679), p. 2, c. 4.

extended his high protection to all Christian converts of Prussia, Samblandia (a district between Prussia and Samogithia), Semigallia (Zemgale), Livonia, and Estonia. In 1225, Pope Honorius III issued a bull which took all Baltic converts under the papal wing.

That same year, Conrad promised the Teutonic Knights a grant of land at Kulm (near Thorn), and the right to whatever conquests they made at the expense of the Prussians, in return for their help in subduing the heathen.[2] A year later, Frederick II, always a strong supporter of this Order and now particularly in need of their benevolence towards his personal aspirations in Jerusalem, promised his friend Hermann von Salza, the Grand Master, this same land of Kulm as a sovereign domain of the Order. With the Emperor's backing, von Salza insisted that Conrad sign a treaty guaranteeing the rights of the Order, which the Duke finally did in 1230, thereby recognizing the sovereignty of the Teutonic Knights over the land of Kulm. At the same time the Emperor, disregarding his previous Baltic Manifesto, acted on the feudal principle of *nulle terre sans seigneur*, which maintained that a land "belonging to none" might rightfully be given away by the Emperor. He granted Prussia, which certainly did not belong to the Empire, to the Grand Master of the Teutonic Knights as a *feudum oblatum* of the Holy Roman Empire.[3] The prospect of rich land greatly stimulated the enlistment of the German aristocracy's younger sons in the ranks of the Order.

The Teutonic Order now proceeded to a conquest which took them sixty years of bloody struggles to achieve. Not until 1308 did the fortress of Marienburg in Prussia become the residence of the Grand Master, who had remained in Venice since the fall of Acre in 1291. Unlike the Order of the Templars which was disbanded in 1312 by Pope Clement V under heavy pressure from the King of France, the Teutonic Knights were left alone to develop further their always strongly national character, achieve high political power, and establish in Prussia the prototype of modern Prussian bureaucracy and Junkerdom.

As early as 1229, the papal legate Baldwin, had approached the Teutonic Order on the subject of a merger with the Brethren of the Sword in Livonia; but the time was not ripe, the Teutonic Knights not yet being securely enough ensconced in embattled Prussia. Nor

[2] For a consistent account of this hotly debated incident and its sequel, see K. Górski, *Państwo Krzyżackie w Prusach* (Gdańsk, 1946).

[3] A. de Wahl, *Histoire de l'Ordre Teutonique*, 1 (Paris, 1784), 298.

was the powerful von Salza disposed to hurry a union with the small and, in Western Europe, unpopular Order of the Brethren.

In the meantime, it seemed expedient that Kurzeme should be secured for a future union with Prussia, Baldwin quite correctly insisting that the Kurs were the same people as the Prussians. Finally, Zemgale and its neighbor, Lithuanian Samogithia, must be brought into the fold to complete the Baltic papal dominion.

Volquin, the Master of the Brethren of the Sword, was in complete accord with these plans, as far as the subjection of the native tribes was concerned. The question of ultimate control would be another matter. Nor was he much concerned with the more diplomatic methods of the Papacy. Bold rather than wise, spurred on by the love of a fight and the greed for land and booty which ruled his Order, Volquin turned to the frontal attack of the Kurs and the Zemgallians, seemingly careless of the growing Lithuanian sympathy for these oppressed peoples. Nor, apparently, did he realize the superior strategic position of the southern tribes, secured as they were by the Daugava, the Baltic, and the increasingly cooperative Lithuanians to the south. This favorable situation of the Kurs and Zemgallians was in contrast to that of northern Latvia, where the Livs had opposed the Latgallians and Talavians, who had also been attacked by Estonians, Slavs, and Lithuanians, and therefore had called on the Order for help.

An example of the Order's obtuseness, hasty greed, and outright insubordination to papal policy was their treacherous behavior in regard to Lamikis (Lammekinus), King of the Kurs. Shortly after the death of Bishop Albert, Lamikis, impressed by the Danish conquest of Oesel and by the unfortunate issue of the Estonian struggles, was in a frame of mind to fall in with papal ambitions. He was ready to become a Catholic and a direct vassal of the Pope, if by so doing he could save his kingdom from invasion either by the Danes or by the dreaded Order. On December 28, 1230, Lamikis concluded with Gregory IX, through the legate Baldwin, a perpetual treaty of peace,[4] according to which the Kurish king accepted baptism, agreed to the establishment of a bishopric in Kurzeme, and became a direct vassal of the Pope, who in return preserved Lamikis' title of king, and assured to his subjects the possession of their lands and property. This treaty, an act of pacification between equals, was ratified by the Pope

[4] The texts of the Kuronian treaties are found in Les sources de l'histoire de Lettonie, II, 141-146.

in February 1232. Lamikis was to have appeared in Rome the following year for his coronation.

The Kurish king never received his crown from the Pope. In 1230,
the Brethren of the Sword, loath to see so rich a land pass from their
future control, defied both the treaty and its promulgator, the papal
legate. They charged into Kurzeme, ransacked and burnt the castles
of the *seniores*, massacred a great number of the latter, and probably
killed their king. The few remaining Elders had to sign a treaty of full
submission to the Order. The Kurs then appealed directly to the Pope
for justice. Their ambassadors, intercepted in the Netherlands at the
instigation of Volquin, were released under papal pressure and finally
appeared in Rome. Though nothing further was heard of them, it
seems probable that it was as a result of their complaints that the
papal legate Baldwin of Aune was recalled. In 1234, Bishop William
of Modena, by now a prominent Roman canonical jurist, inquisitor,
and member of the Dominican Order, returned to Riga for his second
term as papal legate. In accordance with the treaty signed by the
luckless Lamikis, William of Modena was now appointed the first
Bishop of Kurzeme. He proceeded to found a Dominican monastery
in Riga, and undertook several inspection journeys through the land.
In 1234, with the aim of bringing the domain of the Livonian Knights
closer to that of the Teutonic Order in Prussia, Bishop William
granted the *Fratres Militiae Christi* two-thirds of still rebellious
Kurzeme with the right of *dominium*. Henceforth the Bishop of
Kurzeme was to be chosen from among the chaplains of the Order.

In the meanwhile, Volquin, unshakeable in his pride and daring,
kept up a reckless pace of conquest with bloody encounters in Kurzeme
and raids far afield into Zemgale and its southern neighbor, Lithuanian
Samogithia. For all the outrage of the tribes, resulting from reports of
the treachery in Kurzeme, there was no unified opposition to the forays
of the Order, each stronghold depending on its own limited resources,
if boundless determination and wrath. One by one the castles fell to
superior forces. But the defense line of the Germans was growing more
and more tenuous. Finally in September 1236 two tribes set aside feuds
and jealousies and together trapped the forces of the Order under
Volquin, on their way home after a particularly rewarding raid into
Samogithia.[5] Laden with booty and off their guard, the troops camped
on the bank of a brook in Zemgale, at a place called Saule, near Bauska.

[5] The *Rhyme Chronicles*, written in 1246, are an unusually valuable source
for this struggle. Vol. II, *Script. rer. livon.* (Riga, 1848).

A following force of vengeful Samogithians had allied themselves with the equally resentful Zemgallians, through whose territory the Order was riding home. During the night these new allies encircled the victors, and at dawn they attacked. Taken by surprise, the Order's numerous troops, including auxiliaries supplied by Pskov, milled around helplessly. The heavily armored Knights were unable to maneuver their equally encumbered mounts on the swampy terrain. Volquin was killed. The Slav auxiliaries were decimated, "the godless heathen defeated them and only one out of every ten returned home."[6] Goods and weapons, cattle and horses, women and children and prisoners of war seized in Samogithia were liberated and sent back to their own country. The armor and weapons of the Knights fell into enemy hands to be immediately used against them. The Brethren of the Sword had suffered an almost final defeat.

Had the Samogithians, Zemgallians, and Kurs now firmly united their aims and endeavors, they could have capitalized upon the decisive advantage they had won. They were in a position to fall upon the panic-ridden Germans in Riga, and drive the remaining invaders into the sea, thus liberating the land. But leadership and a sense of organization were still lacking to the native tribes, and the Germans, though virtually defenseless, hung on.

Far from censoring the Baltic tribes, Pope Gregory IX, by the Bull *Non obstantibus,* condemned the brutalities of the *Fratres Militiae Christi,* which had provoked the Order's doom. For after Saule this crusading organization was indeed reduced to a powerless remnant which only prompt and decisive papal action could now save.

This action took the form of forcing the merger with the Teutonic Knights which up until now had been hanging fire. The crusaders in Prussia had been scandalized by the reports of a Slav menace, indifferently met, in Livonia. In 1234, the Russian Grand Duke Jaroslav had appeared before the castle of the Order in Dorpat (Tartu) and, after devastating the environs, had received the submission of the Bishop of Dorpat. Appalled by this news, Hermann von Salza, perhaps with the possibility of a merger in mind, had in 1235 dispatched an investigatory commission to Livonia. The unfavorable report of this commission upon the attitude of the Livonian Knights cooled any interest which the Teutonic Knights might have had in their brethren-at-arms, since it revealed that the Livonian Knights had formed with the Slavs of Pskov against the Estonians a military alliance which

---

[6] *Les sources de l'hist. de Lett.,* II, 185-188.

actually permitted the admission of Russian auxiliaries into the army of the Order.[7]

But after Saule there was no time for such minor scruples. The Catholic mission in Livonia must be rescued, and a suzerain papal state saved from a threatening Muscovy. The Teutonic Knights, for their part, had suffered a loss of prestige because of defeats inflicted by the unbreakable Prussians. They were in no position to oppose the dictates of their greatest protector, the Pope, who in 1237 summoned Hermann von Salza to Rome for the purpose of uniting the Livonian Brethren of the Sword to the Order of the Teutonic Knights. The Order of the Teutonic Knights in Livonia, or the Livonian Order as we may conveniently call it, though theoretically a subdivision of the Teutonic Order in Prussia, retained a certain degree of independence from the latter, being under the rule of a Provincial Master who was appointed by the Grand Master in Marienburg. The constitution, rules, and statutes of the Teutonic Order were adopted entire by the Livonian branch.

This crusading Order, like the Templars before them, had accepted the rule of the Augustinian monastic Order. In the early days, unflinching obedience had been required to the vows of chastity, obedience, and poverty. A set of customs and regulations in accord with these vows was evolved, whose infringement had, in the days of some genuine crusading ardor, been severely punished. A knight might not receive letters, possess personal wealth, hunt for pleasure, eat as he pleased, or sleep away from the castle of the Order. What the individual knight lost in personal privileges, the Order as a whole gained back: the right to possess great collective wealth, immunity from secular justice, the protection and comfort of magnificent fortress-castles, and a very free life indeed in the field. The Order was divided into three classes: the Knights proper, who must be exclusively of noble birth; the clerics, consisting of chaplains, usually of noble family, and learned professionals—physicians, architects, jurists, artists, etc.; and the lay brothers who were the soldiers and artisans. Most useful to the order was a separate class of noble vassals, the *Adelsfahne*, who provided auxiliaries and general unruly valor in military exploits for no reward other than the roistering, and the presumptive gratitude of the Blessed Virgin in whose honor they rode forth.

The Grand Master of the Order exercised almost unlimited control

[7] C. Schiemann, *Geschichte Russlands, Polen u. Livland*, II (Berlin, 1887), 46ff.; and *Rhyme Chronicles*, 1905-1970.

over the government of the Order. His direct representative through-out the country was the Landmaster, who traveled for purposes of inspection and administration. A Council of five, all of whom were heads of administrative departments of the Order, was chosen by the Grand Master and the Chapter to assist the Grand Master. The Chapter, foregathering annually in a General Assembly, held the supreme power which could overrule both the Grand Master and the Council. In 1237, Hermann von Salza appointed Hermann Balke, the Provincial or Landmaster of the Teutonic Knights in Prussia, as Provincial Master of the new branch in Livonia. With an escort of fifty Teutonic Knights, Balke rode from Marienburg to Riga. The few remaining *Fratres Militiae Christi* in Livonia now donned the white mantle with a black cross of the Teutonic Order, though they con-tinued to wear the black tunic underneath which earned them the Latvian nickname of the "Black Knights."

In the first decades of its new existence the reorganized Livonian Order was to suffer from isolation and a degree of military weakness. Little help could be expected from Prussia, where the Teutonic Knights were themselves in difficulties. In 1241, their neighbor to the west, the Duke of Slavic Pomerania, a territory which separated the new colonial east Germany from the western motherland, attacked the Knights, simultaneously stirring up the Prussians to another rebellion. That same year the Mongols penetrated as far as Silesia and defeated a combined Polish-German force at Wahlstatt.

This Mongolian diversion, which prevented the Prussian Knights from contributing any effort to conquering the still unchristianized territories which separated them from Livonia, did enable the Livonian Order to take a decisive stand against the ever recurring Russian menace. With the Mongols menacing Muscovy itself, as well as the White Russian and Ukrainian feudal principalities, Novgorod, Pskov, and Lithuania, the latter kingdom was open to a friendly approach on the part of the Order, who now suggested that they make a common front against the Great Russian marauding expeditions out of Pskov. This diplomatic move yielded the Order large returns.

In rapid succession the Germans liberated Dorpat from Russian overlordship, occupied Pskov, and even appeared to menace Novgorod. Thoroughly alarmed, the Republic of Novgorod recalled Prince Alexander Nevsky, who had led them victoriously from 1230 to 1240, when he had defeated Jarl Birger on the Neva. In 1242, Prince Alexander rescued Pskov from the Livonian Order. But a further

Russian advance into Livonian territory proved ill-advised, since the Latvian and Estonian militia rallied to the support of the Germans, and chased the Muscovites back to Pskov. Prince Alexander now employed a maneuver learned from the Tartars. Widely circling the rear of the Order's forces, who were crossing frozen Lake Peipus in the early spring of 1242, he trapped their heavy cavalry which could not fight on the ice, and captured sixty of the skidding Knights.

But Nevsky did not feel himself sufficiently strong to pursue this accidental advantage. Instead, he signed a peace treaty with the Order. That same year, the Knights defeated and routed the Slavs of Pskov; and soon Pskov itself became a patrimony of the Lithuanian princes, thus serving to cement the Lithuanian-German alliance against further Muscovite attacks. The Livonian Order had now expanded as far as the natural boundary of swampland which separated northern Latvia from Russia, thus securing its defensive position in the north and liberating its energies for the long-impending southern conquest.[8]

To this purpose the newly refounded Livonian Order seemed disposed to make a sager use of diplomacy than did the old Order under the impetuous Volquin. The time-honored tactics which had yielded such good results in the north in the days of the wily Albert, the precepts of divide and rule, of bribe, deceive, and coerce, were now to be applied in the tribal kingdoms of Kurzeme and Zemgale.

The opening move of the Livonian Order was to promise certain of the Kuronian nobles protection against possible Lithuanian ravages in return for permission to erect German fortifications near the castle-mounds of these nobles. The chosen protégés found themselves forced to give up the greater part of their lands to the Order, while the yeomen, besides paying tithe and tribute after baptism, were inducted into the auxiliary militia of the Order and obliged to participate in exploits directed against their still unbaptized kinsfolk.

Not all of Kurzeme, however, yielded to this softening-up treatment. That faction of the Kurs who refused to accept such subjugation were supported by the Zemgallians and Samogithians. Furthermore, in the region between Kurzeme and Samogithia, there still remained several threatening Kuronian-Samogithian strongholds. Indeed, the whole tribal Lithuanian kingdom of Samogithia, which blocked any German coastal advance from the Kurish boundary to the mouth of the Niemen and covered the southern Latvian border, had to be dealt with either by force or diplomacy before the Livonian Order could

[8] C. Schiemann, op.cit., II, 54ff.

compass the long-desired junction with Prussia. Large-scale diplomacy carried the day.[9]

About 1240, one of the Lithuanian tribal kings, Mindaugas, had gained sufficient preeminence to be regarded as the military chief of the whole nation. Thus empowered, he took the offensive against the Livonian Order, who, from their bases in Kurland, threatened his coastal kingdom. Into Kurland he marched and there laid siege to a stronghold of the Order. Although he did not take the fortress, he did succeed in establishing himself as the champion of Baltic resistance, and as such was in a position to deal with the Order. In 1250, Mindaugas approached the Master with an offer of an alliance, which was accepted. The Order agreed to recognize Mindaugas as king of all Lithuania in return for his acceptance of baptism and the cession of the northern part of Samogithia to the Germans. Since the Samogithians were at that time engaged in a feud with Mindaugas, the Lithuanian chief saw no objection to surrendering their territory.[10]

In 1252, at the castle of Varute, Mindaugas received a brilliant procession of the Knights of the Order, accompanied by the Bishop of Kulm, who bore the crown of a Grand Duke which they duly set on the brow of the ambitious Lithuanian. A year later, the first Lithuanian Roman Catholic diocese was founded.

Most opportunely, Lithuania, under the leadership of a converted conqueror, promised to be the much needed buffer state which might save the Christian West from the Tartars who had already greatly weakened Muscovy. For a short while, indeed, Mindaugas fulfilled these expectations, occupying Pskov and Novgorod, but by a reverse of fortune he later had to submit to a Tartar invasion of his own kingdom. However, his word to the Livonian Order had proved good. After his baptism and coronation, Mindaugas released all German prisoners of war, confirmed the grant of Samogithia, and conceded trade privileges to the burghers of Riga, besides permitting the establishment of the bishopric and the free preaching of Christianity among his subjects. In 1260, the complacent king even made a will granting the Order, upon his demise, not only Samogithia and parts of Kurzeme, but also the Latvian province of Selonia, south of the middle Daugava.[11] It is interesting to note that this latter territory was not his property. Disposal of it was therefore easy.

[9] *Rhyme Chronicles*, 5720ff.   [10] *op.cit.*, 3543ff.
[11] Text of will in F. G. von Bunge, *Liv-, Est-, und Curländisches Urkundenbuch*, II (Reval, 1853), 271f., 383.

But before the Livonian Order could rejoice in a definitive junction with Prussia, which seemed assured by the foundation of Memel by the Teutonic Knights in 1253 at the strategic mouth of the Niemen on the site of Lithuanian Klapeja, victory had to be further secured in irreconcilable Kurland; and Zemgale, the last of the free tribal kingdoms, must be overrun. For a vivid account of the campaigns in Zemgale we turn to the Rhyme Chronicles of the Teutonic Order, which were disposed to give a grudging credit to the valiant resistance of the tribe.

During the fifties under the leadership of their King Schabe, the Zemgallians, who had been reduced to paying tribute to the Order, succeeded in clearing their land of Germans. To the amazement of the latter, King Schabe (whom the Rhyme Chronicles call "ein tapferer Held") permitted the expelled agents of the Order (*vogts*) to take along all their personal belongings. Such conduct, the Chronicles granted, was no less than "ritterlich,"[12] a term the Germans seldom applied to an enemy. But occasional knightly behavior did not appease the Master of the Order, who immediately mobilized his forces and appeared before Tērvete, the capital of Zemgale and residence of King Schabe. This fortress the Germans were unable to take. Leaving garrisons in their newly built castle near the old Latvian stronghold Dobele, as well as in Samogithian Karšava, the Order retired to Riga to gather reinforcements.

The Master of the Order now hurried to Prussia to solicit help against the Zemgallians. The King of Denmark came forward with the offer of a Danish contingent from Reval. Estonian auxiliaries and Kuronian militia were put into the field. All these forces were rallied in the northern, subjugated part of Kurzeme. From here they marched unopposed through southern Kurzeme as far as Durbe, where they stood poised to invade Zemgale. At this point, the scouts of the Order brought word that a Samogithian detachment, having refused to accept Mindaugas' deal with the Order, had invaded Kurzeme and was now returning home with heavy booty and many captured Christian Kuronian women and children. This victorious force was due to cross the path of the German forces at Durbe. The German commanders, in spite of the treaty of alliance with Mindaugas, decided to attack these Lithuanians who had so rudely invaded a territory protected by the Order.

The commanders of the Kuronian militia now requested of the

---

[12] *Rhyme Chronicles*, 5247.

German commanders that any Kuronian women and children taken from the Samogithians be returned to their own people. To this the German commanders agreed; but the rank and file of the Order's army (to whom these prisoners had been distributed as booty) categorically refused, insisting that by military law all that they might capture from the Samogithians should be theirs. The enraged Kuronian commanders promptly renounced their baptism, and during the engagement with the Samogithians assaulted the German forces from the rear.[13]

On July 13, 1260, the army of the Livonian Order, with its 150 Knights and several thousand foot soldiers, encountered the Samogithians and met decisive defeat at their hands. Both high commanders of the Order were killed. The armored knights on horseback were driven into a swamp, surrounded, and completely annihilated. The rank and file fled in panic, harried and cut down by the enemy.[14] Once more native tactics, agility, and vengeful spirit had proved too much for the heavily accoutred, slow-moving, and over-confident Germans.

For a few years the Kurs and the Zemgallians, entrenched in their fortified castles, were to enjoy an illusion of freedom. Throughout Lithuania a strong pagan reaction set in, and in 1261 the Samogithians, penetrating to the heart of Livonia, defeated the Germans once more at Lielvārde, on the Daugava. Even King Mindaugas was inspired to revolt against the Order, but his old sin of compromise found him out, and in 1263 he was murdered by another Samogithian ruler who had not forgiven him his appeasement of the Order. Unfortunately for these Baltic tribes, the Russians chose this time to seek peaceful relations with the Germans, lured by the irresistible promises of the Hansa which, eventually, in 1279, did open a factory at Novgorod. The Livonian Order was thus left free to rally its forces in the south. It now bent all its effort to a final conquest of Kurzeme.

The Kuronian castle of Sintelin, near Piltene, was stormed and ransacked, its garrison burned alive, and only women and children under eleven years of age spared to become slaves and hostages.[15] Aizpute was taken under similar circumstances; and finally Kuldīga, the old capital of Kurzeme, fell to the Order who renamed it Jesusburg. Unable to rally from these successive blows, the Kuronians signed, under heavy conditions, a peace treaty with the Order in 1269. The

[13] P. von Duisburg, op.cit., p. 185.
[14] Dionysius Fabricius, Livonicae historiae . . . series, cap. 43.
[15] Rhyme Chronicles, 5966-5968.

subjection of these irreconcilables was technically accomplished, though they never yielded in spirit to their new masters.

Only one independent Latvian tribal kingdom now confronted expanding Livonia, that of Zemgale. As an offensive measure, the Order, in 1265, had built the castle of Mitau across from Zemgallian Jelgava, on the Lielupe River. In 1272, the Germans, who had on their hands a feud with the Riga burghers, signed a peace treaty with this tribe. They then exhibited such a degree of misconduct that the Zemgallians rose under their vigorous King Nameitis, who in a short time liberated a number of strongholds from German control. Twice in 1279 Nameitis inflicted crushing defeats on the German Knights. The following year, he appeared before Riga and captured the Marshal of the Order, and sent him as a gift to the Samogithian King Troiden, who was supporting Riga's resistance to the Order.

In 1281, the forces of the Order, now freshly reinforced from Germany, appeared before Tērvete, the foremost stronghold of King Nameitis. Unable to take the castle, the Germans offered a peace treaty, which was accepted. That same year, Nameitis fell in battle against the Teutonic Knights somewhere in Prussia. In revenge for Nameitis' gesture of help to the Prussians,[16] the Order, as late as 1286, invited the eminent nobles of Zemgale to a "peace conference," and thereupon murdered them all.

The Germans now concentrated their military activities upon the chief fortress of Zemgale and the residence of her kings, Tērvete. Since they could not storm this castle, they erected, in close proximity to it, a fort of their own which they called Heiligenberg, from which they subjected the Zemgallians to a relentless crossbow fire. The defenders then decided to burn Tērvete and retire to other forts, at the same time dispatching a cavalry detachment over the Daugava to counterattack the Germans in Riga and Ykesküla. In 1287, the Zemgallians managed one more victory, at the river Garoza, in which thirty-three Knights, including the Master of the Order, were killed.

But this proved to be only a short respite. Balked by the impregnability of the Zemgallian strongholds, the Germans, once more reinforced, resorted to scorched-earth tactics. They attacked with fire and sword the lonely settlements of the yeomen, cut down the farmers in their fields, drove away the cattle, ravaged even the ripening corn.

[16] P. Olins, *The Teutonic Knights in Latvia* (Riga, 1928), pp. 43-45.

Now indeed "the defenders of the faith in Livonia and Prussia turned into Christian pious tigers."[17]

Starved, powerless, and desperate, the Zemgallians burned their remaining castles, and, in 1290, about 100,000 of them migrated to Samogithia,[18] where they joined the Lithuanian militia, thus contributing considerably to the greater success of the Samogithian Grand Dukes in their renewed struggles against the Teutonic Order. To fill the void and cultivate the fallow fields, the Livonian Order now transferred to Zemgale several thousand Latvians from the northern part of Livonia.

The Zemgallians, firmly united in spirit and deed with the Lithuanian Samogithians, carried on their war with the Germans into the fourteenth century. In 1323, Prince Gediminas of Lithuania, using the title of Duke of Zemgale, claimed this land as his patrimony.[19] There are some grounds for the belief that he was the grandson of Nameitis, the last king of the Zemgallians. In 1345, Gediminas' son, Grand Duke Algirdas, at the head of the united Zemgallians and Samogithians, ravaged the castles of the Order, reoccupied Tērvete and Mitau, assaulted Riga, and marched as far as Cēsis (Wenden). Such skirmishes continued throughout the century. As late as 1372, the Order was still meeting the Zemgallians in numerous battles.

According to a report prepared by a Master of the Livonian Order in 1351, by that time the Order had lost in battle against the Zemgallians and Kurs a total of 117,000 men, among them six Masters of the Order, 28 dukes and counts, 49 barons, 11,000 knights and gentry, 4,000 armed burgher militiamen, and 23,000 hired soldiers. Thus the Order paid dearly for the territory south of the Daugava and the permanently resentful subjection of the Kurs and the Zemgallians. Furthermore, their more or less definitive victories in Kurland, Zemgale, and East Prussia were offset by a corresponding strengthening of resistance in Lithuania, whose military might was considerably reinforced by influxes of fugitive Prussians as well as the 100,000 Zemgallians, mostly cavalrymen and experienced warriors, mentioned above.

The difficulties which the Livonian Order had experienced in subduing the last vestiges of Latvian independence were paralleled by the

---

[17] O. von Rutenberg, op.cit., I, 146.

[18] F. G. von Bunge, Liv-, Est-, und Curländische Urkunden. Regesten bis zum Jahre 1300, II (Leipzig, 1881), 25.

[19] K. E. Napiersky, Russisch- livländische Urkunden (St. Petersburg, 1868), p. 46.

ten years of reverses suffered by the Crusaders west of the Niemen, which followed the 1261 uprising of the Prussians. Eventually, the tremendous losses inflicted on the desperate Prussians turned the tide, so that in the next decade the Teutonic Knights were able to claim final victory in this territory, and reduce those Prussians who had not fled or been killed to a state of serfdom. The propagation of the gospel had long fallen into a state of desuetude in this dark land.

As the Livonian Order consolidated its position in the Baltic and created that sovereign papal state for which it had been preserved and protected by the Papacy, the latter came to look upon the blandishments of the Order with an increasingly jaundiced eye. At the time of the merger in 1237 Pope Gregory IX had by decree subjected the refounded Livonian Order directly to the Prince-Bishop of Livonia, who was to remain the feudal and spiritual suzerain of this branch of the Teutonic Knights. It then became imperative that the Riga bishopric should be powerful enough to rule the increasingly intractable Crusaders, whose ranks were being swelled by many of the most spirited princes in Europe, a number of whom felt the need of adventure at all costs.

In 1239, Bishop William was appointed legate to Prussia, where he resided until 1242. Two years later he was elevated to the cardinalate, and in 1245 he advised Innocent IV to appoint as his successor in the Baltic Archbishop Albert Suerbeer, the former primate of Armagh. In 1254 Riga, raised to an archbishopric, received Albert Suerbeer as its first metropolitan. Upon his investiture, Albert II was granted by the Pope both the *jura spiritualia* and the *jura temporalia*, an act concurred in by the Holy Roman Emperor who customarily reserved for himself the granting of the *jura temporalia*. This was *de facto* recognition of the Baltic conquests as the *jus ac proprietas* of the Holy See, and of Prince-Archbishop Albert II as titular ruler of all the Baltic.

To all intents and purposes the papal state in the Baltic was now solidly founded. The dioceses of Livonia, Kurzeme, Zemgale, and Selonia became closely connected with the diocese of Prussia. In 1255, King Mindaugas received his crown from the Archbishop of Riga. The Archbishop himself came to have considerable local prestige, especially with the burghers of Riga, whose rights the prelates consistently supported against the claims of the Order. So influential did the Roman Church feel itself in Livonia that at one point it had hoped to effect a union with the Greek Orthodox church, which appeared threatened by the Mongol-Tartar invasions of Muscovy. But the Mongols failed to provide the persecution which might have turned the Eastern Church to Rome for protection, and the Catholic hopes were not fulfilled.

For all its perfected machinery of control, the Papacy, worn out by its contests with the Holy Roman Emperors over the question of temporal powers, and, under Boniface VIII (1294-1303), dealt a staggering blow by the rising spirit of nationalism, could not ultimately hold its own with those confirmed nationalists, the Teutonic Knights in Prussia and in Livonia. These organizations gobbled up all the lands and properties which came their way, remembering their suzerainty to the Pope only when questions of papal privilege or protection arose. When, in 1299, two envoys of the still hopeful Zemgallians personally presented to Boniface VIII a long list of accusations against the Livonian Order, it was to little avail. From then on the Popes could only hope to gather a few revenues in the Baltic lands.

An outward sign of the Order's increasing lack of respect for papal control was the insubordination they showed to the Riga archbishops, from whose suzerainty the Knights systematically emancipated themselves. Under persecution and even imprisonment the local prestige of the archbishops steadily declined, to the point where Archbishop Isarus, in 1302, was forced to flee the country. His successor, Frederick, preferred to reside at Avignon, as did almost all of the successive archbishops until the defeat of the Teutonic Order at Tannenberg in 1410 once more rendered Riga salubrious to the princes of the Church.

What the Papacy had not reckoned with when it threw its weight behind the Livonian Order and gave full support to the colonizing activities of the Teutonic Knights in Prussia was that the members of this Order, of German aristocratic origin, would soon develop the unshakeable purpose of founding a Baltic state of their own. "The Land of the Holy Virgin" was, in a few generations, to take on the aspect of a feudal wilderness; where law was what the land-grabbing knights chose to make it, war and starvation were all the dispossessed peasantry might expect, and hatred was the black seed bursting in the breast of Latvians as they slaved to gather the great grain crops for the insatiable Germans.

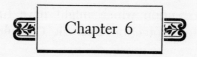

Chapter 6

Ascendancy of the Teutonic Knights

THE two powers—the Papacy and its fighting force, the German Crusaders—which had worked together for nearly a century to effect this notable subjugation of a resistant people in a rugged land were not destined to share equally in the victory. The papal *Terra Mariana* had been born of a lofty concept implemented by a protective attitude toward the converts, the appointment of astute clerical diplomats to guard both the papal interests and those of the natives, and a firm hand on the militant Order. Such measures were possible while the German Knights were still grimly hewing out their conquest, and the papal prestige was at its peak. But at the turn of the century, after the defeat of the Zemgallians had put a term to the period of aggressive conquest, the Papacy, shaken by scandal and schism, lacked the requisite power and authority to strengthen or even adequately maintain its influence in so remote an area.

The papal policy which had planned, directed, and sustained the conversion of Latvia was on a different plane from and doomed to give way to the ambitions of the German Knights. The Livonian Order, once its crusading was done, was not to remain satisfied with certain fixed revenues and the cure of souls, being under the far keener imperative of personal greed. The immediate acquisitiveness of those who had done the hard fighting and then chosen to remain on the prostrate land was bound to carry the day over a distant spiritual power, unmotivated by land-hunger and constrained to delegate its authority to a few militarily helpless and understandably nervous prelates.

That same deeply nationalistic colonizing impetus which had prompted the Teutonic Knights in Prussia and Pomerania to settle the land, as their conquest progressed, with imported German peasants, moved the Germans to secure their control over the lands of Livonia. But here actual colonization proved impractical, since western Germans could not be prevailed upon to leave their comfortable country for an unfriendly region which must be reached by sea. Thus the Teutonic Knights in Livonia perforce depended upon the Latvian peasants to cultivate the land for ultimate German profit. This basic condition of the Livonian occupation determined the peculiar inversion of feudalism as it developed in that land during the three centuries of German ascendancy following the century of conquest.

During this period, when feudalism was melting away in Western Europe under the combined stresses of nationalism and the rise of a money economy operating through all the strata of society, this already obsolete social system was tightening its grasp on the Baltic peasants till it became a stranglehold. Whereas in the West the peasants were breaking free from thralldom, in Livonia under foreign masters they were losing at an accelerated tempo all vestiges of independence. German feudalism, as seen here in its last and most exaggerated manifestation, forged a caste system which was to prove more fatal to the Baltic yeoman than all the bloody battles gone before.

The secret of the German success, for success of a limited kind it may be called, lay in the gradual evolution of mastery, through feudal and, later, Roman law, rather than in an immediate imposition of serfdom upon the native landholders. By a steadily increasing abuse of those impositions which feudalism had created to assure the general welfare of mutually dependent liege-lords, vassals, and freemen; by deception and timely violence, the German squires continued the conquest in social and economic rather than military and political terms. Their leisurely victory over the defenseless peasants proved even more profitable than the original humiliation and despoilment of the pagan leaders.

Since the basis of feudalism is land, the first stages of the subjugation saw the Crusaders seeking to consolidate their domains, which had been acquired by pursuing, from earliest times, a consistent policy of obtaining large grants from the Church. The first Bishop Albert, being in constant need of their assistance, had granted the Brethren of the Sword, for sustenance, one-third of the conquered lands of northern Latvia. In 1224, the Crusaders obtained from Bishop Hermann of Dorpat, in southern Estonia, one-half of the territory of that bishopric; while four years later they demanded from the Bishop of the Estonian island of Oesel one-half of his domain. In 1234, the Brethren acquired two-thirds of the Kurzeme bishopric, together with the right to appoint the bishop. Although, in 1251, the merely nominal bishopric of Zemgale was merged with the archbishopric of Riga, the Order of the Teutonic Knights in Livonia retained one-half of Zemgale, with the rest of that province coming under its control at the end of the century.[1]

A further aggrandizement of their domains occurred in the middle of the fourteenth century when the rest of Estonia fell into their hands. The tyranny of the Danish and German feudal overlords, who had in turn received their fiefs from the Danish king with unlimited rights over the property and persons of their peasants, whose necks and hands they might sever at will, finally precipitated a desperate uprising of the Estonian peasantry. On April 23, 1343, more than 1800 German and Danish nobles were killed. Ten thousand Estonians now besieged Reval, while revolts broke out on Oesel and in Zemgale. The Grand Master of the Teutonic Order in Prussia undertook to quell this insurgence with due severity. In August 1346, he negotiated the purchase of northern Estonia by the Teutonic Order from King Valdemar IV of Denmark for 19,000 marks silver. The control of the territory was then handed over to the Teutonic Knights in Livonia.

By 1347, the Livonian Order had under its rule 67,000 square kilometers, whereas the domains of the Church, including the archbishopric of Riga-Zemgallia, the bishopric of Kurzeme and the Estonian bishoprics of Oesel, Dorpat, and Reval, comprised hardly more than 40,000 square kilometers.[2] The domains of the two powers were intermingled geographically, a fact which contributed to the constant tension between them. A further source of irritation to the Order was the conditions under which it held some of its domains. For in contrast to the omnipotent Prussian branch, the Livonian Order had received its land, with the exception of Kurzeme, Zemgallia, and Estonia, as a *feudum datum* of the Church; that is, for sustenance only, albeit with power to administer justice. In actuality, however, the Order, with the fixed intent of building up large estates, paid scant attention to feudal niceties where the Church was concerned, and tolerated no interference from the supreme suzerains, the archbishops, who were militarily powerless and, after the middle of the fourteenth century, preferred residence at the papal courts of Avignon or Rome to insult and actual molestation at the hands of the intractable Order.

The former Crusaders, transformed into squires, were not inclined to be respectful of the more grandiose aspects of feudalism which

[1] The classic discussion of the social and legal aspects of Livonian feudalism is to be found in A. Schwabe's *Latvijas tiesību vēsture*, I (Riga, 1932), which forms the basis of the present sketch.

[2] A. Schwabe, *op.cit.*, I, 721.

would entrammel them in a hierarchy of loyalties leading up to the Pope himself. Their interests lay in the functioning of feudalism at their own level and beneath them. The most they would do for the Church was to let it and its immediate vassals alone, and even this much could not be looked for when there was anything material to be gained by interfering with the bishoprics. Thus it was that two separate feudal systems, that of the Church and that of the Livonian Order, were fastened upon the divided Baltic lands. From this dual control sprang immediate rivalries, which further trampled upon the rights and welfare of the Latvians and Estonians, as well as legal and administrative complexities and conflicting loyalties which were to plague future generations.

The chief distinction between the feudal rule of the bishoprics and that of the Livonian Order was the early propensity which the Order exhibited for keeping sovereignty in its own hands. Whereas the Prince-Archbishop often granted his German vassals even small fiefs "with justice and all rights," the Master of the Order bestowed no such privileges, as witnessed by the nearly one hundred extant diplomas of enfeoffment issued up to 1500, not one of which allowed any vassal any degree of judiciary power. Furthermore, the Master of the Order established a bureaucracy in his territories which freed him from the necessity of delegating any of his sovereign powers to his fief-holders. His entire domain was divided into commanderies, defended by great castles and ruled by the castle commanders or comturs together with administrative agents (vogts), both functionaries being directly responsible to the Master of the Order. These commanderies were in turn composed of districts whose officials must answer to the comturs. The latter were usually impressive and dreaded men of noted ability and proven loyalty.

This administrative centralization was particularly effective in the early days of the Order's ascendancy, during the first two centuries of Christianity, when the Germans were content to limit themselves to a purely administrative and political control, leaving the workers of the land in actual possession of their property and personal rights. The vassals of both the Church and the Order were few and obedient, while the number of the free smallholders was still large enough to determine the complexion of the social structure.

The most favored vassals of both the liege-lords, Archbishop and Landmaster, were naturally the German Knights, who were granted large fiefs (with judicial rights, by the Church) from which they were privileged to collect the feudal impositions of tithe, tribute, and labor-duty, and for which they owed only personal military service of the most knightly kind. These vassals were, for the most part, of the West-phalian nobility and, consequently, inclined to resent the somewhat overweening attitude of the Prussian branch, whose members came largely from the Rhineland.

The second group of noble vassals were the Latvian *seniores terrae* who, through suasion or self-conviction, had surrendered their terri-tories to the Order for protection, receiving them back as fiefs for which they owed such feudal services, military and sometimes ad-ministrative, as were considered beneath the dignity of the fighting German Knights. These Latvian feudatories did not receive marked discriminatory treatment, beyond the fact that their fiefs were smaller than those of the German vassals, and that they were not permitted to collect feudal dues on their domains. The investitures of both groups were frequently identical; their protection was equally guar-anteed; and both were largely tax-exempt. It was this last advantage which enabled the Livonian Order gradually to enlarge a third group of feudatories whose growth meant the passing of independent native land tenure.

This third group were the small fief-holders. To it belonged a few non-noble Germans in the ranks of the Order; but for the greater part, and to an ever-increasing extent, it consisted of Latvian and Estonian smallholders who, to avoid the cumulative burden of tribute and service which was the yeoman's lot, surrendered their hereditary rights to their lands and received them back as fiefs. In this position they owed only limited feudal services and a moderate Church or Order tax. The inexorable workings of the feudal system had brought about the paradoxical situation where, in order to preserve some personal freedom and a fair subsistence, the small freeholder must yield his property rights and place his welfare in the hands of an overlord.

Those yeomen who held on to their valued hereditary right to the land of their ancestors found themselves left with little else. For it was on this group that, in the course of time, the feudal yoke fell heaviest. Whereas, in time of war, the vassals bore the chief burden of feudalism, in a period of peace and exploitation not the Knight and his militia but the peasant and his land and cattle must pay for the maintenance of a feudal structure inclined to ease and magnificence. When the Germans no longer needed to be concerned with the loyalty of the Latvians in time of strife, they began to tighten the reins of tribute and labor-duty which had lain slack on the freemen during the conquest.

Since, even in their holier days, the end had ever justified the means for the Teutonic Knights, it should occasion no surprise that, as they increased in worldliness, they resorted once more to their time-honored policy of treachery. Theoretically, German dominance in the Baltic lands was based on a series of treaties, concluded with those natives who supported the Christian cause during the course of the conquest, which consistently guaranteed both property and personal rights to the subjugated people. A treaty of 1272 with the Zemgallians even went so far as to affirm that, should a peasant not wish to cultivate his land, he might sell it. These treaties were reinforced by papal decrees, among them Gregory IX's bull of 1236, which specifically forbade the requirement of any personal service which was not connected with "participation in military expeditions and the defense of the country." For the first two centuries of their control both Church and Order were content to exercise only the power of dominion in Livonia, limiting their sovereignty to administrative and political powers employed, in general, for the public welfare. Such a state of affairs, guaranteeing as it did the military protection of the state, while allowing the peasants to cultivate, in relative freedom, their still hereditary lands and thus heal the ravages of war, could scarcely have been called oppressive. Had the Master of the Order and the Prince-Archbishop resolved their conflicts and at the same time kept a firm hand on their German vassals, Livonia might have flourished and become a well-knit and wealthy state. But, while mutual jealousies absorbed the best energies of the two liege-lords, their respective vassals cynically switched sides, tended to ignore their duties to their suzerains, knew no responsibility to their own subjects, and seized every occasion to grasp more land. Treaty-breaking was of little consequence to these votaries of the *fait accompli*.

It was under these amoral conditions that the manorial system was developed in Livonia (which we must now think of as including Estonia). This form of social organization, characteristic of an advanced stage of feudalism, was originally introduced by the Livonian Order when it felt itself in need of the goods and services, the general self-sufficiency which such a system could guarantee. Foreshadowings of the later manors are found as early as the thirteenth century, when certain Livonian documents contained the word *allodium*, designating a piece of land, together with its buildings, just outside a castle of the

Order. This *Vorwerk*, as it was then called in German, often consisted of a mill and granaries, indicating that it existed primarily for the purpose of gathering and grinding the grain tithe brought in by tribute-payers. Soon these *Vorwerke* were extended to include the adjacent fields which were cultivated by the yeomen bound directly to the Order by labor-duty. The Livonian Order acquired the land neces-sary for the establishment of its manors sometimes by free agreement with its subjects, sometimes by forcible means, but most frequently by annexing the land belonging to the members of rural communities who were missing in the wars. In the latter instance, instead of allow-ing the community to divide the land among its surviving members, the administrator of the Order, by invoking the Sachsenspiegel law on escheats and heirless properties, reverted the land to the liege-lord (*dominus terrae*). The latter might then have it cultivated directly for the Order; but, with increasing frequency, was most likely to turn it over to the nearest vassal as a fief, which, in the natural process of crystallization into permanency of temporary relationships, tended to become the hereditary possession of the vassal's family.

The new landlord sometimes placed artisans or tenants on these vacant smallholdings, but more often converted them into manor fields to be cultivated by labor-duty supplied by the nearest rural community (*draudze*) which was now subjected to the manor-lord, who became the feudal intermediary between the community and the sovereign.

Thus, in the neighborhood of the free Latvian and Estonian land, and for the most part at its expense, there arose a new kind of landed property, the manor, which was separated by a district boundary from the old, historically developed rural community, or *draudze*, which now came to be called a *pagasts*. For some time yet the farmsteaders of the *pagasti*, though bound by tribute and labor-duty charges to the manor-lords, were allowed to preserve their keenly valued property rights, which they considered God-given. At the investiture of a new vassal, the farmsteaders of the *pagasti* often assisted at the marking off of the manor boundaries, the better to secure their own properties. The *pagasti* were self-ruling territories whose local courts, administer-ing the common law, were permitted to uphold the farmers' rights to their property. These decisions were confirmed by the feudal courts, since neither the Archbishop nor the Landmaster had granted more than public rights to the manor-lords. But these legal rights of the farmers did not restrain the increasingly greedy vassals, who resorted more and more to expropriation of the *pagasti* lands, as the control of the sovereigns of Church and Order weakened. The Masters of the Order seem to have had neither the inclination nor the power to uphold the thirteenth century treaties; and the right of *dominium* shaded into and was superseded by the right of *proprietas*. At the same time, as the Baltic yeoman finally lost his hereditary rights, either submitting to enfeoffment or expropriation, some of the more powerful vassals succeeded in obtaining the right of inheritance to their fiefs, thus further liberating themselves from their suzerains.

The direct control of the land did not suffice the German squires, whose love of luxury demanded that this land be exploited to the limit, an enterprise which required control of the labor supply. It was at this juncture that the personal rights of the yeomen were threatened. The three-fold feudal imposition of tithe, tribute, and labor-duty, which lay lightly on the freemen in the thirteenth and fourteenth centuries, was a formidable threat in the hands of the insatiable vassals of both Church and Order in the latter half of the fifteenth century. Abuse of the labor-duty imposition led to the increase of this charge from the three or four days a year required of the yeoman in the thirteenth century, to five or six days a week in the late fifteenth century, so that if he cultivated his own holdings at all it had to be at night.[3]

At the same time, the indebtedness of the farmer to the squire took on alarming proportions. This was due chiefly to bad harvests, drought, and disease, which had forced the peasants to borrow from their overlords seed, cattle, or horses to tide them over and enable them to raise enough produce to pay their tribute. The cattle and horses were usually loaned out by the Germans at a usurious rate, which further increased the indebtedness of the farmers. By the fifteenth century these farmer debts had reached such proportions and were so common that in most of the transactions relative to the manors they were listed as assets of the manor. Since it was not to the advantage of the manorlords to sell out insolvent farmers, they forced them to discharge their debts by installments, thus making them lifelong debtors.

But even thralldom did not insure the manor-lords, since the peasants, in increasing numbers, abandoned their goods and lands and fled to the towns or to the domains of another liege-lord, where they were treated as new settlers. By the second half of the fifteenth

---

[3] See Schwabe, *Grundriss der Agrargeschichte Lettlands* (Riga, 1928) for the whole manorial system and the conditions of the peasantry.

century, the presumption was established that, in general, the farmers
were the debtors of the manors, and hence they could not leave without the permission of their squire. The first statute to this effect appeared in 1458, in the bishopric of Dorpat; similar laws were soon
passed in the remainder of the feudal estates. Thus the peasants were
irrevocably attached to the land (*ad glebum adscripti*). But, since the
feudal law did not grant to the squirearchy the rights of detention,
trial, or punishment of the farmer, or even of extradition of fugitives,
the manor-lords had recourse to the subtleties of the Roman law,
introduced in Livonia in the sixteenth century. The peasant was now
placed in the category of the Roman *servi*, in contrast to that of the
liberi (freemen). He was no longer an individual, but a mere "thing"
of the manors. Yet still he broke his bonds and escaped, and still the
squires fell into extradition disputes with each other and bitter
quarrels with the towns who received the fugitives.

The Baltic yeomen did not take their plunge into servitude without
protest. Bloody revolts flared up through the centuries, the worst of
which was the above-mentioned Estonian uprising of 1343. But
famine, disease, and oppression had weakened this class beyond the
point of effective resistance, and every revolt only served to push the
peasant further down into misery. However, peasant memory is always
tenacious, and through generations of enslavement the Latvian and
Estonian yeomen nursed the knowledge that they had been betrayed.

Yet there had been little likelihood from the first that the fair
treaties concluded by the Order while still at war would be observed
after final victory. The responsible aspects of suzerainty were of little
interest to knights who had put aside their crusading life, together
with whatever degree of austerity and fealty such a life entailed, to
lead the riotous existence of coarsening squires. The most ruthlessly
oppressive of the vassals were those of the Archbishop, who from the
beginning had been granted full judiciary powers.

The assumption of such powers became the goal of the emancipated
manor-lords throughout Livonia, a goal the more easily attained since
the political anarchy which obtained during the German ascendancy
was mirrored in the complexities of the judicial system. Theoretically,
the supreme sovereign (*dominus terrae*), the Prince-Archbishop, was
also the supreme judge (*judex supremus*). In practice, the Livonian
Order did not acknowledge the judicial supremacy of the Archbishop.
The latter had his own courts, but their function was limited to accepting appeals from the Archbishop's direct vassals who, since they

had been granted judiciary powers, were inclined to keep such matters in their own hands. In 1403 the Livonian Order became officially exempt from the Archbishop's jurisdiction. It would soon be the turn of the vassals to elude the control of the Master of the Order who, in the earlier stages of feudalism, exercised judicial powers through his appointed *vogts*, whose duty it was to bring disputes before the comtur. The latter's sentences, in turn, could be revised by the Master.[4]

As the power and independence of the vassals of the Church and the Order grew, developing a corporative spirit, they organized themselves into feudal parliaments, the *Manntage*, which elected their own judges, the *Mannrichter*, whose decisions were considered final in disputes between the vassals themselves and between the vassals and the liege-lords. Here was another step in the process of decentralization which was leading Livonia into social chaos.

The feudal principle that a man should be tried and sentenced by his peers was for a time applied to the yeomen, allowing them their own rural courts and judges who, both in criminal and civil cases, were free to apply the ancient common law. Sentence was executed by the *vogts* of the suzerain. Cases could be appealed from these rural courts up through the courts of the *vogts* to the tribunal of either one of the liege-lords.[5]

Theoretically, all the laws and statutes of the Holy Roman Empire and of Canon Law were in force in Livonia. In actuality, the Prince-Archbishop and the Master of the Order, the *Manntage* of the vassals and some of the vassals independently, and the autonomous city of Riga, all could and did issue their own ordinances or import statutes from abroad.

Thus, while the Archbishop had introduced in his domains the so-called Bishop's Code, his vassals chose to adopt the *Sachsenspiegel*, which they renamed the Livonian Spiegel. The Livonian noble vassals were subject to the *Ritterrecht*, based on the Danish code issued in 1314 to regulate the relations of the Estonian vassals and the Danish king. The City of Riga, after adopting the Gotland code of law in 1228, exchanged it in 1280 for the Hamburg code; in addition to this Riga issued its own regulations for its burghers. The Latvian common law obtained in the rural communities, where it was handed down by word of mouth.

[4] See in general F. G. von Bunge, *Geschichte des Gerichtswesens* (Reval, 1814) for legal aspects.

[5] A. Schwabe, *Latvijas tiesību vēsture*, I, 165-206.

Confusion was worse confounded by the tendency developed among the manor-lords to create their own laws and ordinances. This was part and parcel of their rising insubordination to the centralizing aspects of feudalism. In the sixteenth century, when the German squires were permanently settled on their estates, which by this time had become hereditary, they arbitrarily assumed the judicial prerogatives which had pertained to the *vogts* of the bishops and the Order. Courts (*Schlossgerichte*) were now instituted on the manors, with the lord acting as accuser, investigating judge, judge, and constabulary. Against such unlimited powers lodged in foreign hands, the people of the *pagasti*, which were legally still connected with the manor only by tax-paying and labor-duty obligations, had no recourse. Slavery was at hand. In the Latvian folklore the German squire and judge came to be recognized as every bit the equal of the Devil.

During the course of this systematic reduction of the Baltic peasant to serfdom, the squires, who sought by every means to attach the yeoman to the land, found themselves in opposition to the towns, whose interests demanded that the farmer be allowed to raise and trade his produce freely. The asylum afforded by the towns to the escaped peasants further aggravated the resentment of the squires.

The squires individually and the Livonian Order corporatively were in turn regarded as commercial rivals by the towns, since they chose to set themselves up in the business of exporting grain and amber, in direct competition with the towns. In 1263, the Teutonic Order as a whole had obtained from Pope Urban IV the privilege of buying and selling, provided such business was not carried on for profit. When it found that no further advantages could be expected from the unsympathetic French Popes, the Order contrived a false bull (under the date 1257), which permitted the Knights to engage in commerce "on account of their poverty." As the price of grain rose in Western Europe, and as their taste for high living could no longer be sustained by the taxes in kind of the peasantry, the Knights, both in Prussia and in Livonia, made a determined bid for the Baltic trade.

Such a venture naturally brought them into competition with that string of north German and Baltic towns which were to form the aggressive and autocratic Hanseatic League. As early as 1157, the north German cities had collectively defied the Emperor Frederick Barbarossa who sought to violate their self-government by imposing his burgraves upon them. This resistance was the seed of the Hansa

movement.[6] The solidarity of the later Hanseatic League was successfully put to the test during the course of its systematic opposition to
Danish domination of the Baltic.

In the second half of the twelfth century there sprang into being,
modeled on the north German Hansa, the equally Germanic Hansa of
Visby, especially concerned with the fostering of the Baltic trade. The
most prominent members of this organization were Lübeck, Münster,
Dortmund, Bremen, and later, Reval and Riga. During the thirteenth
century the Hanseatics, using Visby as their base, penetrated the
Baltic hinterland, along the old Viking routes. With the active cooperation of Riga, trade with the Russian hinterland was secured to
the Hansa,[7] a commercial treaty being concluded in 1229 between
Riga, together with most of the above-mentioned German cities, and
Smolensk.[8] The importance of this trade is indicated by the existence
in the middle of the fourteenth century of a Riga suburb of Russian
merchants with their own churches and trading centers.

Characteristic of the League were its strictly monopolistic practices,
highly favorable to the member cities. The Baltic centers enjoyed a
profitable export trade of amber, grain, wax, honey, hides, furs, and
smoked fish and meats; in return for these they obtained Western
European cloth, metal instruments, wines, spices, and salt. The Hansa
dictated that all trade abroad should be on a cash basis; while goods
should be shipped only in bottoms belonging to the League. This
assured the Hansa absolute control both of prices and freight rates.
Bremen, Lübeck, and Hamburg were given the exclusive privilege of
building the Hansa ships, which were of a peculiarly shallow draught
suitable to river and harbor traffic.

A Hanseatic factory or Komtor was opened in Riga in 1279,[9] and
that city became an official member of the League in 1282. Shortly
thereafter Visby, menaced by the Danes, lost her preeminence to
Lübeck which, at the turn of the century, became the supreme
Hanseatic Komtor for the Baltic trade, and the ultimate tribunal in
jurisdictional matters. The Riga Komtor was itself considered to be
next in importance to that of Novgorod, since it controlled the
Daugava trade flowing down from Lithuania, Smolensk, Polotzk,
Vitebsk, and Livonia proper. The Hanseatic towns of Limbaži

[6] E. G. Nash, *The Hansa* (London, 1929), p. 10.
[7] A. Winkler, *Die deutsche Hanse in Russland* (Berlin, 1886), pp. 5-7.
[8] G. Vernadsky, *Kievan Russia*, p. 338f.
[9] K. von Schlözer, *Livland*, 1 (Berlin, 1850), 165.

(Lemsal) and Koknese (Kokenhusen), in Latvia, served as inland storage points in the Russian trade with Riga. Next to Riga ranked the Estonian Komtors of Dorpat and Reval, important for the trade with Pskov and Novgorod.

With its great wealth, strong navy, and far-flung political power, the Hansa was in a position to take over full control of the Baltic, which it did in 1370 when it finally overcame the resistance of Denmark and occupied the four Danish fortresses dominating the Sound. Such a position could not have been attained without first establishing a *modus vivendi* with the Teutonic Knights.

When the latter first began to put the surplus of their manors on the market in competition with the north German Hansa, the towns protested. However, in view of the Teutonic Order's military might and its strong political influence in the West, where the Hansa was fighting for its rights, the League soon saw the wisdom of working with rather than against the Knights, who, both in Prussia and Livonia, came to be looked upon as protectors of the Hansa. In Prussia the grain trade became the monopoly of the Teutonic Knights, converted from outright rivals to sponsors of the Hansa; while in Livonia the Order, as the biggest landowner, became the chief supplier of grain to the Hanseatic trade. The Teutonic Order gave further evidence of its good will by intervening for the Hansa at the courts of Western Europe and by preserving a benevolent neutrality at the time of the Danish war with the League (1362-1370).[10]

One of the major attributes of the Hanseatic towns was their jealously guarded autonomous government. In the nature of things, this principle of autonomy, embodied in the flourishing city of Riga, was anathema to the Livonian Order, whose aristocratic Westphalian Knights could not tolerate the free airs of the burghers, and whose vassals desired a closer control of the mouth of the Daugava for their own commercial purposes. In addition, as the metropolis of all Livonia, Riga was the residence of the archbishops, and hence fated to become the storm center of the undying antagonism between the Church and the Livonian Order. Indeed, this "Venice of the North" was to keep the Knights armored through a century of civil war.

Such a destiny was determined by the accident of geographical position. Though Riga's origin is too remote for recovery, the name, derived from the Latvian *rija*, meaning storehouse, indicates that the

[10] L. Koczy, *The Baltic Policy of the Teutonic Order* (Toruń, 1936), pp. 22-32.

site was early occupied by those oaken storehouses which composed the factories of the most ancient Baltic trade routes. There is evidence that such a factory existed at the site of an ancient ferry over the Daugava, a little to the south of modern Riga.[11] During the early Middle Ages Riga was called the *Duna urbs*, or the city on the Duna (Daugava). By the eighth century, the *Duna urbs* had become an important Viking trading post on the *Austrvaegr*. In the eleventh and twelfth centuries merchants, first from Visby and then from Lübeck and Bremen, began to settle in Riga, transforming it from a staple-depot to a commercial port.

The German settlers of Riga were particularly favored by the first Bishop Albert for the part they played in defending the Livonian bishopric. After their spirited defense of the city against a Kuronian assault in 1210, the Bishop, the following year, rewarded the citizens of Riga, by according them the so-called Visby rights, among which were tax-exempt trade, the right to elect their own judges, and the right to found merchant and trade guilds with the permission of the Bishop. The privilege of tax-free trade attracted still further settlers to Riga, and greatly stimulated her commerce. In 1225 Albert, to win the sympathies of the burghers, granted Riga the rights of a *civitas*, among which was the privilege of striking coins. This led Riga to build up its own monetary system, though other valid monies were still accepted.

The most valuable privilege of a medieval *civitas* was autonomous government. Albert signed two treaties on this subject with the burghers of Riga, wherein the Bishop renounced his *dominium directum* over the city, while preserving the right to confirm the elected chief justice. The city government henceforth consisted of an elected council of consuls, who in turn chose the proconsul, or burgomaster.

As a reward for its assistance in the Livonian crusades, Riga had a share in the Bishop's territorial acquisitions, obtaining land in the newly acquired districts of Livonia proper and Kurzeme, adjacent to the city. This territory formed the nucleus of what eventually was a large suburb, the *Statmark*, whose farmsteaders paid the city council tribute and labor-duty, in return for which they were allowed to own their land and enjoy a separate suburban self-government. Riga underwent a further aggrandizement of her domains when she obtained in fief one-third of the large Estonian island of Oesel.

In 1290, Riga adopted the city statutes of Hamburg, at that time

[11] Dionysius Fabricius, *Livon. hist. comp. ser.*, cap. 17.

the most liberal in regard to self-government, approximating those of a republic. The Hamburg statutes provided for a city council consisting of sixteen councilors, of whom four were annually replaced by cooptation. The council nominated two burgomasters who, together with a group of councilors, elected the city judge and two treasurers. Two of the councilors also became members of the city high court. The city council itself functioned as the highest court of appeal.[12]

In the time of the first Bishop Albert, the Latvian and Liv burghers of Riga had been accorded the same rights and privileges as the German settlers. Their Elders participated in the signing of treaties, while their craftsmen and traders were allowed to organize independent guilds. But after Riga joined the Hanseatic League matters changed for the worse for the native Rigans. For the Hansa, which had originated in a spirit of independence, soon sought to quell any such spirit in its foreign members on the Baltic. The privilege of being a wholesale merchant in these Baltic cities was reserved to the German members of the Great Merchants' Guild. The candidate for such a privilege must have served an eight-year apprenticeship under an accepted Hanseatic merchant, which entailed a strict indoctrination in Hanseatic ideals, and the development of blind devotion to the interests of the organization and obedience to the Hansa superiors.

Once subjected to this exponent of Germanism, the Latvians and Livs in Riga found their rights considerably curtailed. Administrative positions were closed to them, as were the major merchant and trade guilds. To the members of the powerful German guilds was reserved the privilege of serving in the cavalry of the city militia, while the native burghers were reduced to the status of foot soldiers. After 1469, Latvians were no longer permitted to acquire real estate in the city.

The resident archbishops were disposed to pamper the susceptibilities of the burghers as a class and defend the autonomy of Riga. These tendencies further inflamed the ill will of the Livonian Order toward both the natives and the arrogant German merchants of the city. Riga was a tinder box which might be expected to kindle as soon as the Crusaders were freed from external wars and able and willing to embark on civil strife.

The spark was provided in 1297,[13] when the Riga burghers decided

[12] J. G. L. Napiersky, Die Quellen des Rigischen Stadtrechts (Riga, 1876), pp. 53-130.
[13] P. Olins, The Teutonic Knights in Latvia, pp. 50-54.

to build a bridge across the Daugava in the vicinity of the Order's Castle of St. George. Although this was a purely civilian measure, the Knights chose to look upon it as a military threat and in retaliation declared many of the city's privileges canceled. Whereupon war broke out and the Knights seized Archbishop Isarus, who had sided with the Rigans, and imprisoned him. This high-handedness cooled the ardor of the other bishops, who had also supported the burghers. Lübeck, to whom Riga appealed for help, turned a deaf ear to her sister-in-the-Hansa. Promised Danish help was not forthcoming. The Papacy did not intervene. Under these circumstances the Rigans turned to the Lithuanians, who had once before been appealed to by the Archbishop for assistance against his enemies, the Knights. In the summer of 1298, King Vitenis of Lithuania-Samogithia, reinforced by the citizens of Riga, defeated the Order's army at Treiden, on the Gauja, killing the Master and sixty of his Knights. But a few weeks later, the Livonian Order received the inevitable assistance from the Teutonic Knights in Prussia, and Vitenis went down to defeat. This was followed by a truce, during which the Archbishop, at the insistence of Boniface, was released from prison and went to Italy to die.

The Rigans now addressed the Pope in the following terms: "The knights, having excluded citizens and other Christians, made agreements for commercial purposes with the pagans [probably the un-baptized Lithuanians] and invited them to take their goods to certain places occupied by the Order, where commercial transactions which are detrimental to the whole country are made. Whereas they are knights, and wish to be treated as such, they deal in every trade un-becoming to knighthood . . . selling fruit, cabbage, radishes, onions, and other such commodities."[14]

But Boniface was dying, and the Knights, for all their deplorable peddling, were still capable diplomats. In 1304, at Dorpat, they con-cluded with the bishops of Dorpat and Oesel, as well as with the vassals of the Danish King in Estonia, an alliance which, though ostensibly concerned with the protection of Christianity in Livonia, was aimed directly at the Archbishop and the city of Riga. This isolation of the archbishopric was further strengthened when, in 1305, the Order bought and converted into a fort a cloister and abbey at the mouth of the Daugava, thus cutting off the harbor of Riga from the Baltic. Riga countered with a new alliance with Lithuania and the Slavs of Pskov and Novgorod.

[14] Quoted in J. Straubergs, *Rigas vēsture* (Riga, 1937), p. 123f.

The successor to Isarus, Archbishop Frederick, in 1312 personally presented to Pope Clement V in Avignon 230 articles of complaint against the Teutonic Knights in Livonia. In its turn, the Order accused the Archbishop and the Rigans of conspiring with the pagan Lithuanians. In 1313, Pope Clement V excommunicated the Livonian Order, which was again denounced, in 1318, by John XXII. In 1325, Archbishop Frederick's interdict was ignored by the Order. Five years later, the Antipope Nicholas V recognized the supremacy of the Livonian Order over the archbishops.

Eventually, in 1330, the Master of the Order, Eberhard von Monheim, after a siege of six months, achieved the surrender of starving Riga. The burghers were forced to break a special gate into the city walls for the entrance of the victorious Master and his retinue. This gate was held open for more than a hundred years as a symbol of defeat.

That same year, Riga signed a peace agreement with the Livonian Order by which the Knights of the Order were reaffirmed as citizens with the right to own houses and enter into commerce. The city council had to swear fealty to the Master of the Order instead of to the ruling archbishop. To crown the triumph, the Emperor Louis IV, in 1332, recognized the juridical supremacy of the Livonian Order over Riga, although the city defied this decree as having no juridical basis.

The supremacy of the Order, however, was not definitely established, for in 1356 the Golden Bull issued by the Emperor Charles IV granting sovereign judicial rights to the princes in their dominions strengthened the cause of the Archbishop of Riga.[15] Ten years later, under menace of excommunication by Pope Urban V, the Order and the city council of Riga were forced to return to the sovereignty of the Archbishop. Indeed, the internecine war was to endure for some two hundred years more, with the Riga burghers steadily refusing to submit to the Order, and the latter attempting various combinations of force to humble the city.

In spite of the fact that Riga's position in the Hansa was an important one, the League persistently refused to acknowledge the repeated calls for aid which Riga sent out to her sister towns during her long-drawn-out contest with the Knights. Two reasons may be adduced for this singular neutrality. The first is the jealousy with which the Livonian cities guarded their rights to act as intermediaries in the rich Russian trade, thereby enriching themselves at the expense

[15] See H. Reineke, *Kaiser Karl IV und die deutsche Hanse* (Lübeck, 1931).

of the German towns, which could more profitably have dealt directly with the Slavs. The second reason lay in the delicately balanced relationships, already detailed, of the Hansa with the Teutonic Order. At the beginning of their struggle with Riga the Livonian Knights opened negotiations with Lübeck which seem to have assured the effective passivity of the Hansa in this quarrel.

During the course of the fourteenth and fifteenth centuries, the Order and its vassals became ever more firmly entrenched in divided and confused Livonia. For all their skirmishes with Riga and the Church, their domains continued to grow and their wealth to accrue. They had made a successful bid for a share of the Baltic trade. They had found the means of extracting the last ear of grain from their lands and the last drop of sweat from their serfs. They were in a position to ignore or molest their suzerain, the Archbishop, as they saw fit, and to flout the Pope himself.

As the self-confidence of the Livonian Order grew, so did its oligarchical nature. While the number of minor vassals, mercenaries and officials was continually on the increase, the ruling body of full-fledged Knights shrank to the point where there was not a sufficient number of them to fill the already reduced quotas of the castles. By the end of the fourteenth century, the number of German Knights had decreased to three hundred and it continued to diminish. The Master and the twenty-eight comturs took on in increasing measure the character of high-ranking state officials and bureaucrats. At the same time the Order grew more aristocratic in its nature, demanding of any new aspirant to knighthood that he present proofs of at least a dozen noble ancestors.

During the entire German occupation the foreign policy of Livonia was directed not by the archbishops but by the real chief of state, the Master of the Livonian Order. Despite the shrinking body of fighting Knights, the Order's military might remained sufficient to guard the frontiers of Livonia against the minor threats which arose during the fourteenth century. These, for the most part, were sporadic incursions from the principalities of Pskov and Novgorod. The Tartar domination effectively held back the Russians from any further efforts to expand toward the Baltic. The Danes, as we have seen, after giving up their interest in Estonia, were too involved with the aggressive Hansa to concern themselves with the southeastern Baltic regions.

There did remain one imponderable threat to German hegemony in Prussia and Livonia: a rapidly expanding and still pagan Lithuania.

And it was from this direction that the blow came which finally staggered German military might. The policy of the Livonian Order in regard to this threatening state on its southern border cannot be considered separately from the diplomacy and overt acts of the Teutonic Order in Prussia.

The latter's final claim to any crusading purpose lay in the presence of a pagan state, and that a mighty one, on its borders. In 1323, the Lithuanian Grand Duke Gediminas, explaining that his country's revolt from the Christianity of Mindaugas had been brought about by "the injustices and treacheries"[16] of the Teutonic Order, expressed to the Pope his willingness to accept anew Christianity for himself and his people. To show his good faith, Gediminas invited representatives of the Archbishop of Riga, the Livonian bishops, the Livonian Order and the Danish vassals of Estonia to meet him at Vilna where, in October 1323, a general treaty of peace was signed. This was far from welcome news to the Grand Master in Prussia, who saw the ground cut from under his crusading Knights by this inconvenient conversion of the last pagan nation. His servants, the Prussian bishops, sharply reprimanded the Livonian Knights and bishops for dealing with "these cunning and false sons of Satan who would destroy first Prussia . . . and then Livonia."[17]

The accommodating Livonian Knights accordingly violated the peace treaty, forcing the Livonian bishops to do likewise, and exerted themselves to the utmost to revive paganism in Samogithia by making Christianity both unattractive and difficult. They also took every occasion to provoke hostilities with the Lithuanians. Reports of these perversities led Pope John XXII to send his nuncios to Riga, whence they addressed a letter to the Grand Master in Prussia, ordering him, under threat of excommunication, to respect the treaty of Vilna. This threat availing nothing, and the Knights persisting in their encouragement of paganism, the Archbishop of Riga, in 1325, excommunicated the whole Teutonic Order with all its vassals. This extreme measure was blandly ignored.

In the face of such treachery, Gediminas appears to have suffered a revulsion from Christianity. He expressed his outrage by sending two punitive expeditions into Prussia and Livonia. Under these conditions, the position of the Germans in Samogithia did not seem likely to improve over what it had been in the late thirteenth century, when certain districts and strongholds fell to the Knights, but not the terri-

[16] P. Olins, op.cit., p. 59.   [17] P. Olins, op.cit., p. 60.

tory as a whole, which continued to be the coveted corridor which would connect the two branches of the Teutonic Knights. Indeed, to the determination of the Lithuanians to hold their Lowlands may be attributed the fortunate isolation of Livonia. For had this barrier fallen, both Latvia and Estonia would probably have suffered the same infiltration and ultimate denationalization by the masses of Germans who had successfully annihilated, both ethnographically and culturally, the more exposed Ancient Prussians.

Had Lithuania, in this century of her greatest leaders, responded to the constant irritation from the Germans on her boundaries with a determined and sustained effort to defeat them, she might have swept them from the Baltic littoral. Certainly her might and her conquering spirit would have been adequate for the task, but the ambitions of the grand dukes were deflected from the Baltic to the south and south-east Slavic lands, now softening under the Tartar flagellations. Gediminas built up in these regions an astonishing empire, which his sons extended from the Black Sea to the Baltic, including White Ruthenia and the Ukraine. The control of such an exotic state demanded the best energies of the grand dukes, whose policy became more keyed to Byzantium than it ever had been to Rome. Ruthenian was now the official language of greater Lithuania. War with the Germans became necessarily localized and sporadic, so that the Teutonic Knights in Prussia grew harsher in their border raids, and the Livonian Order accelerated its push in Samogithia, erecting a new castle at Kovno.

Actually, the precarious independence which Samogithia managed to maintain into the fifteenth century was due more to the stubborn resistance which the Samogithians themselves offered the predatory Germans than to their defense by the Lithuanian leaders, who, between 1382 and 1398, surrendered this territory four times to the Teutonic Order. These diplomatic successes achieved by the Germans resulted from the division of power in the unwieldy Lithuanian Empire among mutually jealous brothers and cousins.

Gediminas had unwisely divided up his vast dominions among seven sons, of whom two, Algirdas and Kestutis, eventually became co-rulers of Lithuania. The sons of these two, Jagiełło and Vitold (Vytautas) respectively, did not inherit the fortunate harmony of their fathers. Jagiełło, by enlisting the help of the Teutonic Order with whom his uncle, Kestutis, was at war, and ultimately by murdering this uncle, established himself as supreme ruler of Lithuania. Whereupon the Germans received the son of Kestutis, Vitold, into the Christian faith and then supported him, in 1383, in an invasion of Lithuania. However, the following year the two cousins were reconciled. Vitold now joined Jagieło's forces after burning down several German strongholds on his own initiative.[18]

In the meantime, Jagieło's position had been greatly strengthened by a momentous dynastic union with Poland, whose lords had offered him both the Polish throne and their young queen Jadwiga in marriage. By the act of Krewo, in 1385, Jagieło agreed to the union of the Grand Duchy of Lithuania with the Kingdom of Poland, under one ruler, and to the christianization of Lithuania. In February of the following year, Jagieło was baptized and married at Cracow, and in March he was crowned King Władysław II of Poland.

The Teutonic Knights, who had resented and questioned Jagieło's conversion and roundly denounced the Polish alliance, welcomed the once more rebellious Vitold and reinforced him in another civil war. In 1392, occurred another reconciliation whereby Vitold was made Jagieło's viceroy in Lithuania, where he became the actual and highly energetic ruler.

The fate of the much-abused Samogithians now hung on the will of this same Vitold who, in the past, had been willing to make alliances with their German enemy. In the winter of 1403, combined Livonian and Prussian troops invaded the Lithuanian Lowlands, and the following year, Vitold, concerned with recovering the strayed province of Smolensk, once more ceded Samogithia. In 1407, the Lowlanders called upon the princes of Western Europe to intercede between them and their Teutonic oppressors who, they claimed, were doing little to christianize the province. Vitold, irked by German interference in the grain trade with Poland, now definitively espoused the Samogithian cause, thus bringing about a final rupture with the Teutonic Order.[19]

At this point, the Poles, having, for a century, nourished their resentment over the seizure of Danzig, which had shut them from the sea, lost all patience with the international bad manners of the Teutonic Order and, following the leadership of Jagieło, who preserved an interest in his Lithuanian domains, joined the Lithuanians in a crucial opposition to the Knights of the Cross. In July 1410, Vitold led a large composite force of Poles, with Czech and Silesian mercenaries, of

[18] On Vitold's policies see J. Pfitzner, *Witold von Litauen* (Brünn, 1930), chaps. 6-8.

[19] T. G. Chase, *The Story of Lithuania* (New York, 1946), chaps. 4-6.

Lithuanians proper, of Ruthenians and even some Tartars, across the Prussian border toward Marienburg. He was met, between the towns of Tannenberg and Grunwald, by the Teutonic Order's army of 83,000 volunteers and mercenaries. On the fifteenth of July, the battle was engaged which was to leave 100,000 dead of both sides on the field, with Grand Master Ulrich von Jungingen among the slain. After this tremendous carnage, what was left of the Order's forces fled. Fifty-one of their standards had fallen to the enemy.

This spectacular defeat toppled, in one day, the military might, the prestige, and the expansionist hopes of the Teutonic Order. That the Knights held Marienburg and remained dominant in Prussia for another hundred years was due to the extraordinary misuse of victory by the Lithuanians and the Poles, whose increasing disunity was to serve the Germans well. In 1411, the latter may be said to have won the peace of Thorn, which stipulated merely the payment of an indemnity, the renunciation of German claims to Mazovian Dobrzyn and to Samogithia for the lifetime of Jagiełło and Vitold. The mouths of the Vistula and the Niemen stayed in German hands. Vitold proceeded to christianize Samogithia and plan a revival of Lithuanian glory which Poland tended to overshadow. It was part of his plan to preserve the state of the Teutonic Order as a factor favorable to himself in the delicate balance of power.

Part of Vitold's diplomacy, during the crisis which culminated at Tannenberg, had been directed at dividing the forces of the enemy. By May 1410, the Livonian branch of the Teutonic Order had been persuaded to sign with Lithuania a treaty of friendship which gained the Order the northern part of Samogithia in return for Livonian neutrality in the coming conflict. Consequently, only a few Livonian volunteers under the flag, not of the Order but of an unknown vassal, went to the assistance of the Prussian forces.

Shortly after Tannenberg, the Livonian Order was forced to release its reward to the victorious Vitold. Samogithia slipped from German control, and Livonia and Prussia were irrevocably sundered. This fact, combined with the decline in power and prestige of the Prussian Order, served to loosen the bonds which had bound the Livonian branch to headquarters at Marienburg. A further defeat suffered by the Teutonic Order at the hands of the Poles in 1435 accelerated the political independence of the Livonian Knights.

Up to this time the Grand Master in Prussia had customarily chosen and appointed the Landmaster of Livonia, who made, in writing, cer-

tain promises of financial and military aid to the Prussian branch. Part
of the Landmaster's absolutism in his own domains had been due to
the fact that he was the direct appointee of the Grand Master and
owed nothing to his Livonian vassals. But in 1413 the Assembly of
the Knights of the Livonian Order presented two candidates of its
own choosing, one of whom the Grand Master was obliged to confirm.
By 1454, the Knights presented only one candidate, with insistence
upon his confirmation. The Landmaster now came to feel himself
more dependent upon the Livonian Knights who elected him than
upon the Grand Master.

The shrinkage of the number of the Knights-electors continued
until, by 1451, the Livonian Order had only 195 Knights, of whom
161 were Westphalians, 26 Rhinelanders, two born Livonian-Germans
and six non-Germans. This oligarchy, close-knit and jealous of its
exclusiveness, chose to preserve its head (called Master rather than
Landmaster after the defeat of the Prussian Order), in princely splendor,
although in a position of decreasing political power. In 1481, Emperor
Frederick III bestowed on the Master of the Livonian Order, Bernt
von Borch, the title of Prince of the Holy Roman Empire, at the
same time conferring upon him sovereign rights over Riga and its
Archbishop. By the end of the fifteenth century the Masters of the
Order struck their own coins (combining the cross of the Order with
the coat of arms of the incumbent Master), dispatched envoys abroad,
headed a complex administration, and lorded it over a regal court.
They were still militarily powerful, for besides the nearly 200 well-
trained Knights, the Order commanded the services of about 1,200
German mercenaries, a considerable artillery, a corps of engineers,
sharpshooters, the several-hundred-strong heavy cavalry provided by
the noble vassals, the light cavalry of the smaller fief-holders, and
about 40,000 Latvian light yeoman militia, which might be mobilized
in case of emergency. These forces overwhelmingly surpassed those
of the Archbishop's militia (2,000) and the militia of Riga (5,000).[20]
However, the Order had little confidence in its yeoman militia, who
might be expected to seize any opportunity to avenge the misery of
the peasantry. In order to substitute a standing army of mercenaries,
a law was passed in 1494 whereby the tax on fifteen farmsteaders was
sufficient to support one mercenary.

Like the castle of the Master, the comturies of the larger districts,

[20] F. K. Gadebusch, Livländische Jahrbücher. 4 vols. (Riga, 1780-1783),
p. 500.

such as Jesusburg, Wenden (Cēsis), Sigulda, and Dünaburg were also staffed with high-ranking dignitaries. These comturies were divided into *castellaturas* and *villaturas*, the first being the military county, the second the rural district. Each *castellatura* had a judge (*vogt*) whose counterpart in the *villatura* was the clerk, who also served as the tax collector.

As the Livonian Order, divorced from Prussia, closely and independently organized, turned inward on itself it grew increasingly sensitive in matters of prestige. Its excitability in regard to the Archbishop and the Rigans became, if possible, even more intense. The situation was not helped by evidence of confusion in the papal policy.

Throughout their contest with the Church the Livonian Knights had been spurred on in part by their desire to obtain the coveted clerical privilege of the Order in Prussia, which appointed the bishops and chaplains from its own ranks. In 1394, this wish was partially realized when Pope Boniface VIII issued a bull limiting the ecclesiastical posts of the diocese to members of the Order. But in 1424 another papal bull released Riga from its oath to the Order and recognized the Archbishop as the one and only spiritual and temporal ruler of the city. Both these papal decrees only led to further ill will and bloodshed between the city and the Knights.

The victory of Catholic Poland and Lithuania over the Teutonic Knights had contributed to the strengthening of clerical authority in general and that of the Archbishopric of Riga in particular. In addition, the Great Schism was ended and the Papacy, restored to Rome, could hope for more influence. In 1411, Prince-Archbishop John V returned to Riga, where he took over control from the interim Regency Council. After a defeat of the Livonian Order in 1435 by Polish-Lithuanian forces, a rapprochement took place between the Order and the Archbishop, culminating in the treaty of Kirchholm of 1452, which established a condominium. The Council of Riga accepted the sovereignty of both the Archbishop and the Master of the Order. But this agreement did not end the struggle for power. Toward the end of the century the Archbishop, conniving with the City Council, broke with the Order; whereupon the Master, Prince von Borch, captured the unfortunate prelate and humiliated him to such an extent that Pope Sixtus IV, in 1486, excommunicated the Master and forced him to abdicate. In the same year, after four years of skirmishes, the City and the Order submitted to the arbitration of the Pope, who advised Riga to recognize the supremacy of the Master of the Order.

These terms proving unacceptable to the proud city, she continued to struggle. But in 1491, the forces of the Order, under the able Marshal von Plettenberg who, in 1495, was to become a distinguished Master, defeated the Riga militia and 4,000 Swedish soldiers who had been called in by the embattled city.

Humiliating terms were now imposed by the Livonian Order. Riga was forced to make considerable material reparation, to accept once more the condominium of the Order and the Archbishop, and to renounce her independent foreign policy. In conformity with this last stipulation, the city canceled a highly favorable trade agreement which she had concluded with King Henry VII of England in 1498. Pressure had been brought by the Hansa on the Livonian Master to scotch this treaty which was considered contrary to Hanseatic interests.[21]

During all this period of strife an agency had existed which, with a little more good will all around, might have resolved or at least mitigated the deplorable discord. This institution was created by an Archbishop who possessed statesmanship of a calibre otherwise fatally lacking in Livonia at this time.

Archbishop John VI Habundi, learned jurist and professor of canon law, entered upon his office in 1418. After assessing the conflicting forces in Livonia, together with the strong autonomous movement of the Hanseatic cities, he saw the advisability of getting all parties together in a diet which, like the Reichstag of the German Empire, might coordinate the divergent interests of the estates of Livonia. This proposal met with general agreement, and in 1419 the first Diet was convened under the title *Landes Herren Tage*, later shortened to *Landtag*.

The Constitution of the Livonian Diet, written by the Archbishop in 1418, created a virtual confederation which included the five Baltic bishoprics-principalities of the Holy Roman Empire: Riga, Kurzeme, Dorpat, Oesel-Viik, and Reval; the autonomous Livonian Order; the self-governing Hanseatic cities of Riga, Dorpat, and Reval; and the host of semi-independent feudal seigneurs abounding throughout Latvia and Estonia. This Constitution allowed the Diet fundamental legislative prerogatives, in accordance with the feudal traditions of the Golden Bull of 1356, which decreed that statutes and laws should be made by the princes only with the consent of the feoffees.

The Diet was to convene annually, but did not always do so since it had not been clearly determined by whom it should be convoked.

[21] P. Olins, *op.cit.*, pp. 65-67.

Each Estate of the Landtag, i.e. the representatives of the bishops, the Order, the vassals, and the cities, had only one vote, irrespective of the number of delegates.

In 1424, the Diet of Valka (Wolmar) legalized the status of bonded serfs, a social category hitherto unknown in Livonia. By this measure a defaulted farmer could be legally bonded as a serf for a period of ten years, during which he worked without wages. Ironically, he was permitted to redeem himself from serfdom by the payment of one silver mark per year; or another person might pay his debt, in which case the defaulter became the serf of his redeemer for the rest of the term. At the same time forceful rules, also hitherto unknown in this land, for the returning of fugitive farmers were introduced.

Since the farmers by feudal law could be represented in the Landtag only by the fief-holders, they had no means of opposing this new legislation. Their fate was further sealed when the 1435 Diet proclaimed itself the highest judicial tribunal in the land. At this time, the Diet also became the final arbiter in feudal disputes between the Church and the Order and their respective vassals. All appeals to Pope or Emperor were forbidden. Also in 1435, the Livonian Confederation signed a military alliance which empowered the Diet to declare war and sign peace treaties.

The Livonian-German landed noble vassals, together with the Knights of the Order, eventually emerged as the leading Estate in the Diet, whose decrees came to favor this class above the others. The opposing Estates of the clergy and the burghers were often treated as incompetent or even absent, while the decisions of the oligarchic nobility were not infrequently imposed by force. Under such conditions, there could be little political virtue in the Landtag or unity in the Livonian Confederation.

The ruling class itself was split into two groups: the *Ritterschaft*, the grandees of the old nobility, with eight or more noble ancestors, who held as fiefs the larger manors; and the *Landschaft*, consisting of the lesser nobles. Snobbery sundered these divisions, just as mutual suspicion divided the clergy and the Order, the clergy and the burghers, and the burghers and the Order in spite of the fact that one and all were German.

Thus the Livonian Confederation, contrary to the hopes of its founder, degenerated into a loose association of mutually exclusive interests. Again, in the political sphere, the German Order, while it consistently gained its own ends, was unable to create that unity which might ultimately have accepted and served the German cause in the Baltic.

It is now appropriate to qualify the term success, applied early in this chapter to German feudality in Livonia. Certainly, from the point of view of the private interests of the squirearchy, social, economic, and legal means had been found to direct the energies of the land into these channels. By the fifteenth century the German yoke sat squarely on Livonia, and the overlords were free to indulge their instincts for luxury, irresponsibility, and arbitrariness to the limit, owning as they did both the land and the people.

Yet, at the time of its fullest dominion, German rule was threatened by an inherent weakness whose roots are discernible even in this account of conquest and mastery. Certain errors of strategy are clearly perceptible. Samogithia was not secured. Riga was hopelessly alienated. Church and Order often appeared as despoilers disputing their prey rather than as the two arms of conquest and earnest reconstruction. Although moral superiority may be fully accorded to the clerical party, the irony of history had timed this missionary effort to coincide with the low ebb of Roman Catholic prestige; so that the Livonian archbishops, poorly supported from Rome and Avignon, were forced to resort to frequently undignified compromises, and to rely on ethically unsound German media to achieve an unstable supremacy.

The German effort to impose the obsolete social system of feudalism was basically unrealistic. Both Church and Order ended by losing control of this ill-chosen colonizing instrument; not, immediately, to the subjected peoples, but to the profiteering middle men, the foreign squires whose dangerous class ascendancy over an essentially democratic people could assure no manner of internal stability to Livonia.

Chapter 7

Muscovite Wars and Partition of Livonia
in the Sixteenth Century

SINCE 1237, Livonia's shadowy and amorphous statehood had lain cushioned on the might and international prestige of the Teutonic Order and its protégé, the German Hansa. After the middle of the fifteenth century and on into the sixteenth, these two powers, declining in influence, either fought against the current of the times or compromised with the trends of secularization, nationalism, and balance-of-power politics. The Teutonic Order wisely chose the latter course. Although it had rallied to a degree after Tannenberg, the Prussian Order's days were numbered. After 1410, the Order's financial position became so precarious that it increased its already considerable involvement in the grain trade, thereby damaging the interests of such Hanseatic cities as Thorn (Toruń), Danzig, Elbing, and Königsberg. Relations between the burghers and the lords became increasingly uneasy, while the Hanseatic League resented bitterly the Order's continued attempts to wean away the Prussian towns for its own purposes. In 1454, open conflict broke out between the Prussian Estates and their rulers; and during the course of this Thirteen Years' War the Danzigers inflicted a severe naval defeat both on the Teutonic Order and on its ally Denmark; while Poland won a decisive victory on land. At the end of the war in 1466, the Second Treaty of Thorn radically transformed the Teutonic Order, making half its membership Polish, and forcing the Grand Master to accept vassalage to the King of Poland.[1]

The final step in the secularization of the Teutonic Order in Prussia was taken when the Grand Master, Albert of Brandenburg, a cousin of the Hohenzollern Elector of Brandenburg, after a personal meeting with Martin Luther in 1524, accepted Protestantism and offered East Prussia as a *feudum oblatum* to Sigismund I of Poland. The Polish King then bestowed this territory on Albert as a fief, in the form of an hereditary dukedom, subject to Poland. In 1526 Duke Albert completed his achievement of a worldly status by marrying the daughter of

[1] K. Górski, *Państwo Krzyżackie w Prusach* (Gdańsk, 1946), pp. 127-154.

the King of Denmark. His Knights lost little time in following this example and becoming legally married, landed, hereditary nobles of the new dukedom. The west German branch of the Order of the Teutonic Knights, whose *Deutschmeister* resided in Mergentheim, now assumed the governance of the residual Order as a whole.

Tannenberg had put an end to the Teutonic Order's effective support of the Hanseatic League. European princes lost all respect for this "high military protector," and at the same time grew increasingly resentful toward the arrogance of the Hansa itself. In 1447, the League committed the diplomatic error of proclaiming a trade monopoly in the Baltic. England and the Flemish cities, both with growing maritime ambitions, promptly closed the Hanseatic komtors in their respective countries. The Netherland cities went so far as to declare a general boycott of the Hanseatic trade, while the Flemish navy disrupted the Norwegian herring trade with the Hansa, receiving support in this action from English ships which blockaded the Danish Straits in 1468, and captured Hanseatic vessels. This war lasted five years, and at its end the Hansa was obliged to admit English and Flemish merchants to trade freely in all Baltic ports. A virtual monopoly of two centuries in the Baltic had been broken, never to be restored.[2]

The Baltic, whose rich trade possibilities the Hansa had so effectively developed, was fast becoming the immediate interest of two riparian states whose ambitions waxed as German maritime and territorial control in these regions waned. Whereas Denmark had allied herself with the crumbling Teutonic Order and, recently, with the intransigent Hansa, Poland and Sweden chose to develop their own independent Baltic policies. Sweden, under the successful rulers of the Vasa family, set about emancipating herself from Danish-Hanseatic control, and entered the commercial field as an important customer for Baltic grain and a contestant for the Muscovite trade. Poland, after Tannenberg, intensified her Baltic program under the slogan of "freedom of the Baltic Sea." She regained control both of the indigenously Polish province of Pomerania and of Danzig which, together with other East Prussian Hanseatic cities, submitted to Polish sovereignty in 1453, thus closing the rich Vistula trade to the Hansa.

Still another emergent Power drew closer to the contested Baltic, although it could claim no historical riparian rights. The thrust of Muscovy was soon to make itself felt along the Livonian and Lithu-

---

[2] E. G. Nash, *The Hansa*, p. 187f.; W. Sobieski, *Der Kampf um die Ostsee* (Leipzig, 1933), p. 188ff.

anian frontiers, setting up currents of military and diplomatic agitation in these lands which were finally to undermine the flimsy foundations of German power in Livonia.

Muscovy had hitherto depended on the merchants of Pskov, Novgorod, Smolensk, Riga, Narva, and Reval to bring her goods into the Baltic trade, having been too preoccupied with the Tartars to make an independent bid in this field. These invasions of the Tartars, which had begun early in the thirteenth century, declined after a Muscovite victory in 1380, although the menace was not to abate completely for another hundred years. In 1328, under the determined leadership of Ivan Kalita, Moscow gained ascendancy and proceeded to consolidate a number of independent principalities, thus coming into direct competition with Gediminas of Lithuania, who also sought union and empire. The historical enmity of Poland-Lithuania and Russia had its seed in this encounter of two expanding Powers.[3]

By the second half of the fifteenth century, Muscovy regarded itself as the suzerain of Novgorod and Pskov, although in reality they remained independent republics, serving as buffers between the Livonian bishopric of Dorpat and the Muscovite expansion. In 1449, Muscovites coming from Pskov broke into Livonia, only to be repulsed. There followed the signing of a twenty-five year truce between Livonia and Pskov. Some local skirmishing persisted between the Slav principality and the Livonian Order until 1471, when Muscovy, which had finally assumed sovereignty over the republic of Novgorod, concerned itself with the "protection" of Pskov. Russian freebooters ransacked Livonian territory and, when a Livonian army sought to storm Pskov, Muscovite forces 25,000 strong invaded and ravaged Livonia with such fury that the German Knights kept to their castles, leaving the country undefended for five weeks. In 1482, the Grand Prince of Muscovy, Ivan III, was willing to sign a ten-year truce with Livonia, his interests at the time being elsewhere.

That same year, the Grand Prince erected, confronting the Hanseatic outpost of Narva, his own fortress of Ivangorod, whence the Muscovites sought to trade directly with Western Europe by way of the Swedish port of Viborg, opposite Narva. Two years later, Ivan III closed the Hanseatic komtor in Novgorod, ordering the arrest of forty leading Hanseatic merchants, apparently in reprisal for the persecution of Russian traders in Reval. Muscovy was making it clear that she had

---

[3] The classic treatment of this centuries-long enmity is by O. Halecki, *Dzieje unii jagiellońskiej*, 2 vols. (Cracow, 1919, 1920).

no further use for the services of the German middlemen who had made such enormous profits from the Russian trade.

However, the counterstress offered the Muscovite expansion by Poland-Lithuania still continued to absorb the chief energies of the Grand Prince;[4] while Livonia, whose diplomacy was erratic, bore watching at every step. Ivan III had fortified his position by an alliance with Denmark and a truce with Lithuania, whose Grand Duke had married Ivan's daughter. However, in 1501 the Master of the Livonian Order, Walter von Plettenberg, was able to secure a treaty of alliance with Grand Duke Alexander, who was already at war with his father-in-law and on the move against Pskov.[5] After a preliminary victory near Ostrov, von Plettenberg, in 1502, with only 14,000 men, defeated a Muscovite army of 90,000 near Pskov. He had not received the help promised by Alexander who, upon the death of his brother, the King of Poland, had hurried to Cracow to be chosen king, and had begun peace negotiations with Moscow to assure his election. The Livonian Order, thus abandoned by its ally and unable to profit from the victory of Pskov, signed a six year truce with Ivan III, who in that same year, 1503, agreed to an armistice with Alexander, now King of Poland as well as Grand Duke of Lithuania.

Ivan III's successor, his son Vassily, in order to prevent a Livonian-Lithuanian alliance, extended the truce with Livonia for another fourteen years. During the negotiations, the short-sighted Livonian representatives agreed to renounce the alliance with the ruler of Poland-Lithuania, with whom Muscovy was once more at war. The following year, the Grand Prince, profiting by Livonia's isolation, definitively subjugated Pskov and Novgorod. Vassily then began action against Lithuania by taking Smolensk. In 1514, he approached the Hansa with the proposition of a treaty of commerce to be signed with Novgorod, now under Muscovite auspices, with the ultimate aim of influencing all the East Prussian cities and alienating them from Poland. But the Muscovites, by their policy of violence, had already destroyed the merchant class in Novgorod, which might have supported such a move.

During the next few years, both the Pope and the German Emperor sought to bring about a reconciliation between Muscovy and Poland-Lithuania, which existed in a state of perpetual skirmishing, neither

---

[4] F. Papée, *Polska i Litwa na przełomie wieków średnich*, 1 (Cracow, 1904), 48ff.

[5] S. M. Solovyev, *Istoria Rossii*, v (St. Petersburg, 1895), 190-192.

peace nor declared war. As Muscovy's might grew, its interest in conciliation declined. This situation full of menace drifted slowly from
bad to worse, and with it drifted the perpetually confused foreign
policy of the Order in Livonia.

A new lease on life had been granted this luckless land by the
accession to power of Walter von Plettenberg, intrepid fighter, brilliant military strategist, and astute and influential statesman.[6] It was
due almost solely to this personality that Livonia was to enjoy a period
of sunset calm before the final night. His rule as Master of the Order
(1494-1531) was a remarkable maintenance of the *status quo* against
heavy odds. That it was not, in reality, a "golden age" for Livonia, as
some claimed, was due to von Plettenberg's inability to break across
the caste system which held his loyalty and consider as more than
wretched beasts the Latvians and Estonians who worked Livonia's
fields and would yet die to defend them from further conquest.

For Livonia was now seething with disruptive forces. To the internal
jealousies of the Order, and the perennial conflict between the bishoprics and the Order, was now added the Rigans' ready adoption of
Lutheranism, which set them against their traditional protector, the
Archbishop. By 1524, all the churches of Riga were taken over by the
Lutherans, who were steadily gaining influence among the vassals and
squires throughout the land. That the new faith was held in check at
all was due to the influence of von Plettenberg, a staunch Roman
Catholic. Although subjected to some pressure by foreign embassies, he
refused to follow the example of Albert of Brandenburg, secularize his
Order and turn Livonia into an hereditary duchy. He remained satis-
fied with the titles of supreme ruler of Livonia, which had been
accorded to him by the Livonian Diet of 1526; of Prince of the Holy
Roman Empire, confirmed by the Emperor in 1530; and of *Magister
Magnus*, or Grand Master, in whose name, from now on, the Livonian
Diet was convoked.

Acutely aware of the external threats to his state, von Plettenberg
made a serious effort to suspend some of the internal conflicts which
so greatly weakened the country's resistance. He respected the susceptibilities of the bishops, relaxed the oppression of the Order upon the
Rigans, and eased the situation within the Order itself by excluding
Rhinelanders from its ranks. In these endeavors he was supported by
the unusually benign and reasonable Archbishop Caspar Linde, one of
the few German statesmen who adopted an intelligent and sympa-

[6] Schiemann, *op.cit.*, II, 152ff.

thetic attitude toward his Baltic subjects.[7] His successor, in 1524, made further cooperation unlikely by intriguing with both Lithuania and Muscovy, so that von Plettenberg saw no alternative but to appeal for support to the German Empire, although he rightly suspected the Empire of being in no position to help the Livonian cause, since it had done nothing to oppose the secularization of Prussia.

Von Plettenberg's master stroke was the conclusion, in 1531, of a peace treaty with Muscovy, which was to endure for twenty years. This truce was undoubtedly due to the military exploits of von Plettenberg early in the century, which had greatly impressed the Muscovites, who otherwise might not have been inclined to keep the peace until 1551. Had his successors shown even a part of his courage and statesmanship, Livonia might have held together a little longer, or at least been spared the horrors which her bungling rulers were soon to precipitate.

In 1535, von Plettenberg died, and Hermann von Brüggeney, his coadjutor and the Comtur of Dorpat, as well as custodian of the treasure of the Livonian Order, became his successor by a *coup de force*. This action constituted the final break with the mother Order of the Teutonic Knights, which, since the treaty of Thorn, had had no practical influence in Livonia. All ties with Germany were now definitively loosened. The Grand Master of the Livonian Order ruled autonomously.

From this time on, Livonia's affairs, both internal and external, under the leadership of a succession of incompetent and discreditable Masters and prelates, became a tangled web indeed. Swayed by every wind, with personal power their only goal, these rulers set the country on the steep decline to ruin.

An almost infallible gaucherie marked Livonian diplomacy during this period. Grand Master Brüggeney and, later, Heinrich von Galen, unaccountably acceded to the wishes of Lübeck in the matter of certain Western European skilled workers and tradesmen whom Tsar Ivan IV the Terrible (1533-1584) had contracted for, with the consent of the Emperor Charles V. Passage to Muscovy was denied them, and thereby both the Tsar and the Emperor were offended. Grand Master von Galen also contrived to alienate the King of Sweden, Gustavus Vasa. He had violated a military alliance with this monarch, who, after personally leading his forces against Muscovy in Finland,

[7] O. von Rutenberg, *Geschichte der Ostseeprovinzen*, ii, 298f.

was compelled to sign an unfavorable treaty with the enemy because of von Galen's defection.

In 1554, a Livonian embassy arrived in Muscovy, hoping to obtain an extension of the truce. True to the policy of his predecessors, Ivan IV agreed to extend the armistice, this time for fifteen years, only on condition that Livonia would abstain from any alliance with Lithuania. Consistent with their customary lack of vision, the Livonian statesmen once more engaged to isolate themselves from Polish-Lithuanian support. Like von Plettenberg, von Galen, sensing his insecurity, now turned in desperation to the Germans for encouragement, ordering his ambassador to sign the peace of Augsburg of 1555, reaffirming the Livonian toleration of Lutheranism. But a year later, Charles V abdicated, and no German prince seemed disposed to bestir himself on behalf of Livonia. The indifference of the Empire and its princes has been explained both by the unpopularity of the arrogant and unmannerly Livonian Knights themselves, and by the fact that they had never paid any of the taxes due the Empire.[8]

In the meantime, internal affairs in Livonia were reaching yet a lower level of intrigue, disloyalty, and boundless ineptitude, with the German statesmen, blind with personal ambition, becoming the pawns of foreign powers. To understand this political decay, we must retrace the private diplomacy of the archbishops to the year 1529, when Archbishop Thomas Schoening had appointed as his coadjutor and successor the Elector William of Brandenburg, the cousin of Duke Albert of East Prussia and a nephew of King Sigismund I of Poland. Both the Archbishop and William of Brandenburg had hoped to see the latter assume the rule of Livonia upon the death of von Plettenberg, thus putting an end to the supremacy of the overbearing Livonian Order. Brüggeney's *coup de force* had prevented this; but William, who did attain the archbishopric, still cherished the hope of building a German principality after the East Prussian pattern in Livonia, and to that end appointed as his coadjutor Prince Christopher of Mecklenburg. A close family cabal appeared to be in the making, since Prince Christopher acknowledged kinship to the King of Denmark, the Duke of Prussia, and the King of Poland, while his protector, William of Brandenburg, was closely related to the two latter potentates.

In 1546, the Livonian Diet, under the influence of the Order, had adopted a law forbidding the appointment of foreign princes as archbishops, bishops, or coadjutors of Livonia. Riga had recognized the

[8] O. von Rutenberg, *op.cit.*, II, 475.

Elector William as Archbishop with the understanding that she would respect the new law in the future. Hence, to obtain the necessary agreement for the appointment of his protégé, Archbishop William asked Prince Christopher's cousin, King Sigismund II of Poland, to intervene. Grand Master von Galen, who was well aware of the Archbishop's plan to establish his coadjutor as the hereditary ruler of Livonia, dispatched the Comtur of Dünaburg (Daugavpils), Gothard Kettler, to Germany to engage mercenaries against all eventualities. In 1556, a new Diet was convoked which, upon the evidence of an intercepted correspondence between the Duke of Prussia and the King of Poland on the one side and the Archbishop on the other, accused the latter of high treason and proclaimed him an enemy of Livonia. The following year, upon the sudden death of von Galen, his successor, von Fürstenberg, seized and imprisoned both Archbishop William and Prince Christopher.[9]

Sigismund II, offended by the treatment accorded his cousins, in 1557 sent his naked sword and an ultimatum to the Grand Master, demanding the liberation of the prisoners and the reinstitution of William as the head of the archbishopric of Riga, which was henceforth to be regarded as an independent principality friendly to Poland. One hundred thousand of Sigismund's troops waited at Posvol, poised for attack. Since the Livonian Order could count on no more than 7,000 Livonian Germans, six companies of German mercenary *Lansknechte*, and some thousands of mobilized Latvian militia,[10] only the timely intervention of the German Emperor Ferdinand I saved it from defeat. The Grand Master was persuaded to free the Archbishop and the Prince, pay 60,000 thalers to the King of Poland to cover his military expenses, and personally apologize to the aggrieved prelate in the presence of Sigismund II.

Von Fürstenberg profited from the occasion in September 1557 to sign a military alliance with the King of Poland, acting in his capacity as Grand Duke of Lithuania. The agreement contained a clause promising that the Livonian truce treaty with Muscovy would not be renewed after expiration without the consent of Lithuania. By signing this treaty of Posvol,[11] the Grand Master of the Livonian Order broke

---

[9] Schiemann, *op.cit.*, II, 281ff.

[10] F. K. Gadebusch, *Livländische Jahrbücher*, I, 500.

[11] P. Dogiel, *Codex Diplomaticus regni Poloniae* . . . , Part v (Vilna, 1759), no. 128.

the pledge made to Ivan the Terrible by his predecessor not to conclude an alliance with Lithuania.

Poland and Lithuania felt secure from commitment since they had agreed in 1556 to an armistice with Ivan IV which bound them not to lend any military help to Livonia should she engage in a war with Muscovy.[12] Thus, von Fürstenberg had gained nothing from his diplomatic maneuver, but had, on the contrary, given the Tsar a pretext to denounce the truce of 1554. A nervous Livonian embassy to Muscovy did not succeed in repairing the damage. Ivan the Terrible was now prepared for war and conquest, having added to his already long list of titles the new one, "Heir of Livonia," which he derived from the fact that a remote ancestor had once ruled Dorpat. While his predecessors had been chiefly concerned with extending their control over Russian populations, Ivan felt that the time had come to put an end to unreliable Livonian policy, teach that country a fearful lesson, castigate those Germans who had insulted the Orthodox faith, and break through to the Baltic, all in one blow.

After fifty-six years of peace between Livonia and Muscovy, the latter's forces crossed the border near Pskov on January 22, 1558. Large hordes of Kirghiz, Kalmuks, and Tartars, with a sprinkling of Russians, swept across the frozen lakes and rivers and spread to the south and north, ransacking cities and manors, burning, killing and raping, and taking thousands of prisoners who were deported to Muscovy.[13] The Knights of the Order, although pledged to defend this Christian country, once more took to their castles, hoping to wait out the storm. In May, Narva fell to the Muscovites, whereupon English traders immediately appeared with supplies for Ivan the Terrible's army. Muscovy had finally established the long-coveted direct trade relations with England. When the news of the capture of Narva reached the Tsar, he accorded peremptory treatment to certain Livonian ambassadors who had come to sue for peace, demanding the unconditional surrender of their country and expelling them from Moscow after subjecting them to personal humiliations.

Livonia's situation now appeared desperate. Even the castles of the Order were no longer a refuge since the German *Lansknechte*, whose pay was in arrears, began surrendering these fortresses to the Muscovites, who had promised to make up the deficient salaries. That the

[12] L. Arbusov, *Grundriss der Geschichte Liv-, Est- und Kurlands*, p. 15.
[13] S. Solovyev, *op.cit.*, v, 294; von Rutenberg, *op.cit.*, II, 443; B. Russov, *Chronica der Provintz Lyffland* (1584), in *Script. rer. livon.*, I, 53.

Muscovites immediately slaughtered the German mercenaries did not seem to arouse their distrust. Thus, the Latvians and Estonians, in addition to bearing the brunt of a savage war, were treated to the spectacle of disloyal mercenaries and a high command devoid of spirit, dignity, or even enough intelligence to save itself.

In the spring of 1558, the Livonian Order sent a delegation to the King of Poland to remind him of his obligations under the treaty of Posvol. Sigismund replied that, bound as he was by a truce treaty with Muscovy, he could defend only Polish-Lithuanian territories. His answer amounted to an invitation to the Livonians to become Lithuanian subjects.[14]

When King Gustavus of Sweden declared himself to be equally committed to an armistice with Muscovy, von Fürstenberg followed the time-honored last-ditch policy of appealing to the German Emperor and the Reichstag, who promised a financial subsidy which never materialized. The Emperor did concern himself to the extent of sending out letters to the Kings of Denmark, Sweden, Poland, England, and Spain, soliciting help for menaced Livonia. The Western rulers were more than indifferent to the fate of the notably uncivil Livonian branch of the crumbled Teutonic Order. The Emperor's appeal to the Tsar to make peace, as well as mediation proposals from the Kings of Poland, Denmark, and Sweden, proved equally fruitless. Ivan the Terrible saw no reason to check his advance, since the weakened fabric of Livonia was giving way at every point.

In May 1558, von Fürstenberg abdicated in favor of his coadjutor Gothard Kettler. Kettler was a vigorous man, but he was not the worker of miracles that would have been necessary to stay the infectious defeatism of the forces of the Order. In July, Dorpat surrendered with its arsenal of 500 guns and the treasure of the Order. Representatives of the Bishop, the nobility, the Chapter of the Order, and the burghers, recognized Ivan the Terrible as their sovereign.[15] Reval, pressed by the Muscovites to do likewise, was otherwise minded, since that city had already been pawned by the Grand Master of the Order to the Prince Royal of Sweden, Eric Gustavson, who, upon his accession to the throne in 1560, accepted the willing surrender of Reval.[16]

Although Kettler did rally the Order's forces to the point of attacking Pskov, he lacked sufficient strength to meet the returning Mus-

---

[14] O. von Rutenberg, op.cit., II, 475; O. Halecki, op.cit., I, 141ff.
[15] O. von Rutenberg, op.cit., II, 140.
[16] E. G. Geijer, Geschichte Schwedens, II (Hamburg, 1832), 161ff.

covite hordes, which, early in 1559, after a victory at Tirsa, once more spread out over Livonia. Riga, well trained by now in stubborn resistance, repulsed a Muscovite attack. Throughout Livonia indignation ran high against the terroristic tactics of the invaders; and in July 1559, the Livonian Diet issued a decree making every third Estonian and Latvian a soldier of the Order, to be trained and commanded by noncommissioned officers of the German militia.[17] But a militia armed with pikes, forks, and axes had little hope of running the fierce, English-armed Muscovites out of Livonia.

In August, Gothard Kettler, now despairing, went to Vilna to implore the King of Poland for protection. He obtained two new treaties,[18] whereby Sigismund II, as Grand Duke of Lithuania, once more promised military help, this time for the cession in pawn of nine Livonian border districts, amounting to about one-sixth of Latvian territory. Their redemption value was set at 700,000 thalers, a sum which was supposed to cover Poland's expenses for military aid to Livonia. This aid amounted to no more than Polish-Lithuanian occupation of the castles in these districts, which extended southeast of the Daugava in the old tribal kingdom of Selonia, and north of the Daugava, along the Latgallian frontier with Polotzk and Vitebsk. Although Kettler had insisted that the treaty ceding these territories contain a clause reserving the suzerain rights of the Holy Roman Emperor over these castles, thus preventing their outright annexation by Poland or Lithuania,[19] they were never actually released by these powers, which continued to hold them without title.

For all their apparent coolness and meagre assistance to the Livonian cause, Poland and Lithuania were well aware of the direct menace to themselves of Muscovite expansion. Sigismund II, dreading to break his armistice with Muscovy, but at the same time fearing further penetration of the Baltic regions by Ivan IV, was anxious to prevent the shipping of military supplies to the Muscovite forces through the port of Narva. Since England would certainly make large profits by this trade, the Polish King entered into correspondence with Queen Elizabeth on the subject of the Baltic situation in general and the Polish blockade of Narva in particular. He assumed an anxious

[17] F. Bienemann, *Briefe und Urkunden zur Geschichte Livlands*, II (Riga, 1876), doc. no. 472.

[18] P. Dogiel, *op.cit.*, v, nos. 130, 135.

[19] S. Henning, *Liffländische-Curländische Chronica* (Leipzig, 1594), cap. 20b.

and admonitory tone, imploring that "none of the subjects of your Majesty hereafter presume to use the navigation to the Narve forbidden by us, and full of danger not only to our parts but also to the open destruction of all Christians and liberal nations. . . . For now we do foresee, except other princes take this admonition, the Muscovite puffed up in pride with those things that be brought to the Narve, and made more perfect in warlike affairs with engines of war and ships, will make assault this way on Christendom."[20]

England chose to continue the profitable traffic, often engaging in running battles with the Polish navy, which was not strong enough to blockade Narva unaided. The Fellowship of English Merchants for Discovery of New Trades, after opening trading posts in Archangel and Russian-occupied Narva, in 1566 obtained from Parliament the right to a trade monopoly with Muscovy.

In 1560, Emperor Ferdinand I, pressed by Poland, Sweden, East Prussia, and Mecklenburg, issued a manifesto forbidding all traffic over the Baltic to Narva. But, in the absence of an imperial navy to enforce this edict, several Hanseatic cities—including Danzig, now under Polish sovereignty, Riga, and Reval—lured by high profits, smuggled goods into Narva from Viborg. Besides the English, many French, Dutch, and Scottish merchants could not be dissuaded from sending goods to Muscovy. In 1562, evidently under Hanseatic pressure, the Emperor tempered his manifesto to cover only munitions; but in this form it was equally flouted.

It seems doubtful whether Ivan the Terrible any longer required vast military supplies as far as his Livonian campaign was concerned, for that country was in dissolution. Portions of this diseased state were being jettisoned in a desperate attempt to save some part of it for the Order and the German vassals and squires. In 1559, Gothard Kettler had pledged the district of Grobina in southern Kurzeme to the Duke of Prussia for a loan of 7,000 thalers. That same year, the King of Denmark had leased, for an indefinite period and the sum of 20,000 thalers, from the Bishop of Kurzeme and Oesel, the island of Oesel and the district of Piltene in northern Kurzeme opposite Danish-held Gotland.[21] Any further hopes Denmark may have had of restoring her former Estonian possessions were thwarted by Sweden, who, as we have seen, received the submission of Reval in 1561. That same

---

[20] R. Hakluyt, *The Principal Navigations . . .* , III (Edinburgh, 1886), 251-253.

[21] O. von Rutenberg, *op.cit.*, II, 478.

year the bishopric of Reval was released from its allegiance to the Livonian Confederation by the Archbishop of Riga's coadjutor, Prince Christopher of Mecklenburg.

Poland, looking with disfavor upon Sweden's success in obtaining a foothold in Livonia, tolerated some Danish pretensions in Estonia. Indeed, the time had now come for the King of Poland himself to step forward and claim the lion's share of crumbling Livonia before Muscovy or Sweden should further advance their interests in that region.

Poland's plans had been well and slowly ripened. She had watched the Order go down to repeated military defeat and embark on a desperate policy of making concession after concession in any quarter from which help might be expected. This action was supported by the German landed nobles, who saw their possessions hopelessly threatened by the Muscovite victories. Since Poland and Lithuania were still the most likely sources of military protection, it was inevitable that the German-Livonians would now agree to any arrangement which might preserve their lives and some of their property. Poland could win Livonia without going to war.

The instrument for Poland's policy was at hand in the person of Gothard Kettler, political realist, compromiser, and highly ambitious ruler. While he was still the Comtur of Dünaburg he had established close relations with the Governor-General (Voyevode) of Vilna and Prince of the Holy Roman Empire, Nicholas Radziwiłł, who was to lead a valiant but unsuccessful attack against the Muscovites in Livonia in 1551, as well as with other Polish-Lithuanian magnates. These statesmen nourished Kettler's ambitions to become Duke of Livonia, after the fashion of the Master of the Teutonic Knights in Prussia. Equally amenable to Polish overlordship in Livonia were those two polonophiles, Archbishop William of Brandenburg and his coadjutor Prince Christopher; while the Knights and vassals of the Order were easily beguiled by Polish promises of recognition of their privileges and landed possessions, as well as of observation of the Augsburg Confession.[22] Only the city of Riga stood out against Polish suasion. She had once repelled the Muscovites single-handed, and she now had every intention of preserving her independent status as a free and wealthy Baltic city.

[22] A. von Richter, *Geschichte der deutschen Ostseeprovinzen*, I (Riga, 1857), 346f.

On November 27, 1561, representatives of the Livonian vassals for-gathered at Vilna were unexpectedly served by Prince Radziwiłł's secretary with a virtual twenty-four hour ultimatum to sign their un-conditional submission to Poland or leave at once and empty-handed. In a panic, the vassals pressed the Master and the Archbishop to accede to Radziwiłł's request. The following day, Gothard Kettler, Archbishop William, Prince Christopher of Mecklenburg, representa-tives of the vassals of the Livonian Order and of some of the cities, swore fealty in written form to the King of Poland, signing a document known as the *Pacta subjectionis*.[23]

At the last moment, Kettler and the Archbishop had been urged to address their letters of submission not to the King of Poland, as had been agreed upon orally, but to Sigismund II Augustus as Grand Duke of Lithuania. This the two statesmen categorically refused to do, insisting that as Princes of the Holy Roman Empire, with the Emperor for their liege-lord, they could submit only to a king. They had de-tected the trap; for, had they submitted to Sigismund in his capacity as Grand Duke, Livonia would have become a province of Lithuania; and in case of the latter's annexation to Poland, a project which was already in the wind, Livonia would have suffered the same fate.

But, although Sigismund yielded on this point, he had his way in the matter of dividing Livonia in order to keep it under control. The Archbishop and his coadjutor who, in view of their family connections with Poland's king and the latter's former attitude of protection and encouragement, had expected a fair reward at Vilna, received only the guarantee that they might continue to fulfill their duties as church-men. Sigismund, who was having trouble with the Duke of Prussia, rather than strengthen the hand of another Hohenzollern (the Arch-bishop), preferred to promote the interests of Gothard Kettler, who was not of princely origin and could claim no connection with reigning houses. Kettler obtained from the "King of Poland and Grand-Duke of Lithuania and [now] Livonia," Kurzeme and Zemgale in fief as a Duchy, with the right of inheritance restricted to the direct male line, so that should this line fail, the Duchy of Kurland (Kurzeme) would escheat to the Polish Commonwealth, into which it would be incor-porated. This new Duchy, covering about forty-two per cent of the territory of Livonia, did not fulfill Kettler's expectations, since he had hoped to become Duke of all Livonia with Riga for his capital.[24] That

[23] P. Dogiel, *op.cit.*, no. 249; O. Halecki, *op.cit.*, II, 145f.
[24] F. Bienemann, *op.cit.*, IV, 311.

city, holding out tenaciously against Radziwiłł's urgings and promises, succeeded in preserving her independence for another twenty years.

The rest of Livonia, i.e. northern Latvia together with Estonia, except those parts occupied by Muscovy (Narva and the bishopric of Dorpat), and those ceded to other Baltic Powers, was directly incorporated into Poland. It continued, however, to be menaced by the Tsar's forces. Whereas most of Latgallia, now called the Polish *Inflanty* (perhaps a corruption of "Liefland"), was immediately united to the Polish Crown and its castles occupied; the *Ducatus ultradunensis*, or that part of Livonia north of the Daugava which was yet to be contested, Poland left temporarily under the administration of the Duke of Kurland, evidently with the hope of avoiding immediate conflict with Muscovy.

On March 5, 1562, in front of the City Hall in Riga, Gothard Kettler remitted to the envoy of the King of Poland, Prince Radziwiłł, his Grand Master's insignia of power, receiving in exchange the rank of Duke of Kurland and Semigallia (Zemgale). After this he signed his Reversal to his enfeoffment. To those Livonian (Estonian) vassals and comturs who had not been represented at Vilna and were now gathered in Riga, Prince Radziwiłł promised the same treatment accorded the other vassals, in a document which is known as the *Cautio Radziviliana*.

German-Balt historians have insisted over several centuries that, in addition to the *Pacta Subjectionis*, the *Cautio Radziviliana*, and Duke Gothard's Reversal, there was signed by King Sigismund II, on November 28, 1561, in Vilna, the so-called *Privilegium Sigismundi*, granting exceptional rights to the Livonian squires. They have quoted articles from documents which are, in reality, preliminary drafts,[25] written and signed by the Livonian squires and submitted to Prince Radziwiłł for consideration. But no final document was ever signed by Sigismund II, nor was any such document ratified by the Polish-Lithuanian parliament (*Sejm*). Indeed, the alleged privileges are of such a character that, had the King acceded to them, the squires would have immediately become autocratic hereditary barons, owning outright that eighty-two per cent of the Livonian manors which, theoretically at least, were still held as fiefs of the Archbishop or the Master of the Order.[26] Such a measure would have resulted in a good part of the Livonian territory slipping from Polish overlordship. Rather than accord such dangerous

[25] E. Seraphim, *Grundriss der baltischen Geschichte*, p. 249f.
[26] C. von Ceumern, *Theatridicum livonicum* (Riga, 1690).

privileges to his new subjects, Sigismund, at Vilna, limited himself to an oath,[27] wherein he swore to recognize and respect the already existing and legally acquired ecclesiastical and lay rights, liberties, and privileges of the Livonian dignitaries, nobles, vassals, and other persons of any estate and condition. This insistence on the principle of legality, and the inclusion of all persons in the promised protection of legal rights was later to prove a useful weapon in the hands of the Polish King Stephen Bátory when he sought to curb the Livonian squires and alleviate the plight of their peasants.

On the very day in 1562 that Gothard Kettler resigned his Grand-Mastership, the Livonian branch of the Teutonic Knights was dissolved. The German branch of the Order continued its existence in Württemberg until 1809, when it was disbanded by Napoleon who proclaimed Württemberg a kingdom. In 1840, the Teutonic Order was revived in the Roman Catholic Austrian Empire, as a spiritual-humanitarian organization with the Archduke of Austria as its Grand Master. The choice of Austria for this restitution was determined by the fact that the founder of the Austrian Empire, Rudolf of Hapsburg, himself an erstwhile Teutonic Knight, in 1275 had helped to save the Order from defeat at the hands of the Zemgallians by furnishing financial and military aid. Thus it came about that the archives of the Order of the Teutonic Knights as well as those of the Livonian Order found their final resting place in Vienna.

That the Order of the Teutonic Knights persisted as long as it did in its various branches constitutes an example of cultural lag similar in nature to the quixotic last Crusade which ended operatically at Lepanto. Its essential purpose, as an Order of militant monks, had vanished with Lithuania's acceptance of Christianity in the late fourteenth century. Like the obstinately monopolistic Hansa, such a politico-religious organization had become highly anachronistic in the era of economic, religious, and social particularism into which a laicized Western Europe had now passed. The spirit of medieval internationalism, suitable to militant religious orders and fostered by the twin powers of the Papacy and the Holy Roman Empire, had been submerged by the astonishing freshets and floods of the Renaissance and the Reformation. To these cultural currents the domains of the Teutonic Order in Livonia and Prussia had remained, in general, a backwater; although Protestantism found a ready enough reception

27 P. Dogiel, op.cit., v, no. 250.

in countries which had seen the Roman faith in a far from favorable
light.

In their private lives the members of the Teutonic Order had gone
with the tide, leading an existence which was in actuality extremely
worldly. The Prussian branch, influenced by Luther, followed this
trend to its logical conclusion. The Livonian Order, however, persisted in certain diplomatic habits of mind which, had they not involved the subjugated Baltic peoples in disaster, might well appear
ridiculous to the historian. Although they had long discouraged papal
interference, they continued to call upon the Holy Roman Emperor
as liege-lord, and other Western princes as Catholics, to rally to a
cause which the Western European rulers had long since relegated to
romance. The princes of that time were no more disposed to break a
lance in honor of the Virgin Mary than they were to bear the insolence
of the Hansa or the stupidity and notorious turpitude of her one-time
protectors, the now money-mad, land-grabbing, and thoroughly unsoldierly Knights of the Cross.

Paralyzed by fear of Muscovy, their hopes obstinately fixed upon
the West, the diplomats of the Livonian Order seemed entirely blind
to the pattern of new interests and forces which were converging on
the Baltic, where the relatively modern concept of the "sphere of influence" was to find peculiarly suitable conditions for its development.
Their diplomacy resolved itself into a series of short-sighted, short-term
settlements which, by their haste and inconsistency, aroused the suspicions of all of Livonia's neighbors. A fatal lack of political realism and
vision prevented the Livonian Germans from concluding a stable
alliance with Poland-Lithuania or Sweden, either of which ascendant
powers, had she been able to trust her ally, might have undertaken to
shelter Livonia against the encroaching Muscovites. Instead, the rule
of *sauve-qui-peut* became the order of the day, with Livonian dignitaries and vassals falling over one another in their eagerness to make a
bad bargain for fear of a worse. In very little time they found their
"state" deftly divided among Denmark, Sweden, and Poland; while
Muscovy preserved a foothold in the north. "Livonia" no longer had
a material existence.

The German-Balt historians have never ceased to deplore this loss
of what they have called the earliest German colony.[28] Certainly they
have had every reason to regret the Reich's failure to establish a stable

---

[28] E.g., A. von Engelhardt, *Die deutschen Ostseeprovinzen Russlands* (Munich, 1916), *passim*.

claim to the wealth of a land which, for over three hundred years, had provided German merchants and adventurers with easy fortunes. Such a statesman as Gothard Kettler has been harshly judged by his compatriots for his haste in selling out to Poland. The German-Baltic squires, however, cannot be said to have "lost" their properties, since the condition of their surrender to foreign suzerainty was the confirmation of their possessions and privileges. Through the successive foreign dominations which were to follow the Polish triumph of 1561, the German self-styled "Baltic barons" held on so stubbornly to their lands that, on the eve of the First World War, half of all the Latvian estates were still in the hands of a few hundred German proprietors.

The German bid for Latvian and Estonian gratitude on the grounds of having saved these people from an earlier absorption by Muscovy, which would certainly have obliterated their national character, is scarcely plausible. We have seen that the eastern Slavs had been too troubled and disorganized to begin their expansion to the Baltic any earlier than they did; and that, when they did strike out, the Germans in Livonia made a remarkably poor showing as "protectors." It is likely that, had the Latvians and Estonians been allowed the freedom to achieve political unity, they would have preserved their countries' independence far better than did their foreign overlords, to whom the stimulus of patriotism was obviously lacking.

A study of the Livonian Order's military preparedness even under the alert von Plettenberg reveals a state of negligence scarcely credible in view of the original nature of the Order and the grave danger it confronted. The castles and fortifications on the menaced eastern border were in disrepair, their defense entrusted to poorly paid and therefore unreliable mercenaries. The German squires, fearing their peasantry, preferred these *Lansknechte* to a standing army; yet they refused to spare the funds for their services, demanding instead that the farmers, already bled white, suffer yet another imposition for this purpose. In 1507, the Livonian Diet had passed a law disarming the natives, even forbidding them to carry the traditional short side-swords. The militia were expected to fight to the death with pitchforks, since no Livonian Diet, until the above-mentioned panicky assembly of 1559, would vote for any military preparations which would entail expense to the vassals of the Archbishop or the Order. These vassals had long since forgotten that the prime condition under which they had originally received their fiefs had been their assumption of certain military obligations.

The German historians' claim that Germans colonized and protected Livonia must then be restated in terms of exploitation and policing. With equal justice, the German pretension to have brought Christianity to this land, although valid in itself, must be balanced against their subsequent discrediting of this faith in the eyes of their converts. For it would be hard to find in any Christian or pagan country a higher degree of moral lawlessness than that which prevailed in German Livonia. Even in the time of von Plettenberg such cruel customs as trial by fire and immuration were common, while the oppression of the peasants grew more arbitrary and depraved with each succeeding generation of luxury-loving squires. The spectacular degeneracy of these squires has been partly explained by the fact that Livonia was generally recognized as the refuge for criminals and for bankrupt Westphalian nobles, who, after rapidly mending their fortunes under the auspices of the Church or the Order, sent for their poor relations.[29] The latter, landless nobles known as *Hofleute*, had scarcely any employment other than to drink the manors dry and wander over the land as looters and violators of women. While intermarriage was severely punished, all possible license with the native women was *de rigueur* with the German-Balts, whose predecessors, the crusading knights, had not considered the vow of chastity as consonant with feudal privilege. Small wonder that "Livonian incivility" had become a byword in the rest of Europe.

Several centuries of exposure to irresponsibility and depravity in high places were not without their effect upon the native peoples, many of whom, as their enslavement appeared hopeless, gave way to superstition, crime, and despair.[30] That the subjugated Balts did preserve not only a sense of indignation but sufficient humanity to serve as a grafting stock for a future flowering may be credited in good part to the naturally noble melancholy, blended with tonic irony, which ruled the peasant imagination, producing a fund of folklore that sustained the oppressed from generation to generation. The recollection of dignity and freedom seemed proof against the iron hand of the Germans. True, this memory was doomed to flow underground for still more centuries to come, but it was to prove powerful enough in the end to emerge as the sap of a hale and fertile national revival.

The German pretension to have fulfilled a cultural mission in

[29] E. Seraphim, *Klaus Kursell und seine Zeit* (Reval, 1897), pp. 49, 160-162.
[30] O. von Rutenberg, *op.cit.*, II, 305ff.

Livonia is quite inadmissible. This would have demanded a creative spirit which Knights and prelates alike were far from possessing. Efficient destroyers of aboriginal culture, often good policemen of their own *status quo*, their touch was a blight on artistic, intellectual, or civic activity. Their only monuments were their stern, defensive castles. The Chronicles of the Order, while detailed and at times lively, seem created in a void, as indeed they were, since no national matrix fostered the deeds recorded therein. Not a single educational enterprise was encouraged under German occupation. The squires and vassals themselves had to send their sons abroad if they wished them reared away from brutishness. While the rich German burghers might follow this example, the native citizens had too few means of acquiring enough wealth for the luxury of a foreign education. As for the yeomen, it was imperative that they should be left in darkness if they were to be reliable slaves.

Characteristic of the *Herrenvolk* complex was the increasing, uneasy intensity with which the Germans controlled their Baltic subjects. A mixture of fear and quickening greed seemed to drive them to multiply their police measures, enlarge their administrative scope, widen their monopolies, reinforce their power on all sides, and generally wind the spring to the breaking point. This was mainly the achievement of those officials and administrators of the Livonian Order who bore the marks of what was later to be known as Prussianism. It was oddly coupled with and perhaps aggravated by the carelessness and sloth of the squires, many of whom could not be brought to make any effort to protect their long-range interests but contented themselves with immediate and erratic injustice and the encouragement of vicious customs. The heavy hand of police rule and the social indifference of the squires were equally incapable of inducing any degree of respect or acquiescence in the Latvian and Estonian peoples. These never, through history, accorded to their German minority the added name of "Balts" which the squires early arrogated to themselves and the so-called "barons" persisted in with a curious pride. To their subjects, the Germans were ever the intolerable *Vatzi*, hatred for whom pervaded many of the *Dainas*, now desperately cherished by a people who had lost even the official or written use of their native tongue and must sing over their terrible history in secrecy.

Although the Baltic peoples, dismayed by the exotic, Tartar-inspired atrocities of the Muscovite invaders, had fought fiercely to preserve their homes, and in so doing had saved many German skins, they had no voice in the sudden surrender of their country to yet another foreign sovereign. However, if they had little to hope for from the overlordship of another pronouncedly feudal power, they must have felt, after three centuries of German hegemony, that they had very little to lose.

PART III

POLISH AND SWEDISH CONTROL

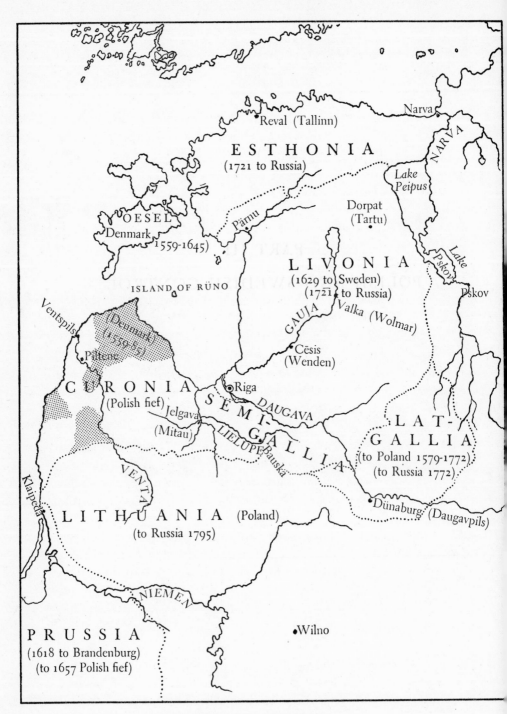

The Polish and Swedish Period

Chapter 8

Polish Suzerainty

THE tide of intrigue and bloodshed which had steadily mounted and finally overwhelmed Livonia during the ascendancy of the Teutonic Order, was to show no marked abatement under Poland's feudal dominion. The Baltic populations of a now partitioned Livonia were to continue to suffer the scourges of internal abuses and external aggression. The bewilderment of a continuous state of fluctuation appeared to be their fate. Although the Polish rulers exhibited a deeper sense of political realism than had the German Archbishops and Masters of the Order, Poland's control was subject to external vicissitudes which fatally hampered the development of any constructive statecraft in her new domains.

The new suzerain of Livonia, the Polish King Sigismund II (1548-1571), lost no time in plunging into baroque diplomatic maneuvers in order to ward off the blow that threatened him, now that he had expanded his dominion to the very confines of the Muscovite sphere. Taking advantage of the strained relations between Sweden and Denmark, the Polish King continued to urge upon the King of Sweden's brother, Duke John of Finland, a project which he had already offered Eric XIV in July 1561, that is, a dynastic alliance through the marriage of John to Sigismund's sister, Catherine Jagiełło. Eric had repudiated the match and further shown his indifference for Polish friendship by his capture of Pärnu in February 1562. But Sigismund persisted in his wooing of the hesitant John, whom he now wished to see established as the hereditary duke of a united Finland and Estonia under Polish suzerainty. Such a plan seemed feasible in view of the kinship of the Finns, the Ingrians, and the Estonians, to all of whom the Swedes were as much interlopers as were the Germans in Livonia. Certainly, it exactly suited Sigismund's own growing ambitions in the Baltic sphere, where such a new principality would naturally assume the role of buffer state, hitherto played by Livonia. Since he regarded Estonia as part of that Livonia which had submitted to his suzerainty, Sigismund granted this province to John as a ducal fief in September 1562. At the same time, he bestowed Catherine, with seven Livonian castles for dowry, upon the new Duke of Finland and Estonia, who seemed a promising ally indeed. But John's good fortune proved short-lived since, upon his return to Finland, he was seized by the troops of the furiously suspicious Eric, who had his brother charged with high treason and imprisoned. Not until Eric's own political fortunes ended in madness in 1569 did John regain his freedom.[1]

Sigismund's elaborations in the north had availed him nothing. All through 1562 the Muscovite Tsar held northern Livonia in his grip. Late in that same year, Ivan the Terrible found himself in a position to break his truce with the Polish Commonwealth, which seemed to him intolerably expanded. He sent Sigismund II a highly provocative note, signed by the title, among others, of "heir and master of Livonia since times immemorial."[2] In this threatening letter Ivan IV promised to burn and devastate the length and breadth of the land and to bring with him in his victorious train a funerary receptacle designed especially for the head of the Polish King. The stakes were down, and Lithuania was up in arms.

In 1565, the Tsar took Polotzk and ordered its entire Jewish population drowned in the Daugava.[3] The Muscovites then rapidly occupied all of Lithuania as far as Vilna. Only after a crucial struggle did the defending forces in 1564, by inflicting decisive defeats upon the enemy at Orsza and Mogilev, turn the Muscovites back into northern Livonia. Ivan IV now proposed to Sigismund that Livonia be partitioned between the two stalemated Powers along the line of the Daugava. But the Polish King turned a deaf ear, and Muscovite skirmishes were to continue in the north for another four years.

Further evidence of Sigismund's determination to maintain his country's new position as a full-fledged Baltic power was disclosed in his involvement in that phase of the continuous and ever-broadening struggle for preponderancy in the "Mediterranean of the North," generally known as the Northern Seven Years' War.

In this contest Poland's vested interest in Livonia led her inevitably to ally herself with Denmark and Lübeck, who braced themselves to defend a profitable *status quo* against the aggressive Eric and his aim to force the Danes from their Swedish coastal provinces and thereby gain control of the Sound while incidentally pursuing the Swedish

---

[1] For a succinct Polish account of these adventures, see W. Konopczyński, *Dzieje Polski nowożytnej*, I (Warsaw, 1936), 90-110.

[2] Text of note in S. Henning, *Liffländische-Curländische Chronica*, chap. 39a.

[3] S. Solovyev, *Istoria Rossii*, VI, 223.

advantage in Livonia. This alignment was somewhat unnatural since Sweden and Poland shared a grievance over Denmark's arbitrary control of Baltic shipping. The opportunistic Ivan IV, at the outbreak of the war in 1563, had given some encouragement to Denmark; but as Sweden gained ascendancy he offered Eric a treaty of alliance directed against Denmark, in the expectation that Sweden would abandon her Estonian claims in favor of Muscovy. He further suggested to Eric that the latter's brother John should grant a divorce to Catherine Jagieło in order that she might become the bride of the Tsar. By this means, Ivan IV hoped to establish a legal claim to the Polish-Lithuanian throne in case of the death of the heirless and ailing Sigismund II. Eric himself was willing to yield up his Polish sister-in-law; but the Swedish magnates, considering such an act highly dishonorable, opposed it the more vigorously when in 1566 a son was born to Catherine and John. Thus, all that the Tsar obtained from Sweden was a treaty of friendship, signed in 1567, whereby Muscovy kept Narva but renounced the rest of her claims to Estonia.

Sigismund's appearances on the larger stage of the Baltic conflict had effectively prevented him from establishing any personal overlordship in Livonia, where social and economic life continued to stagnate under the stifling influence of the German squirearchy, whom their neighbors, the Lithuanian magnates, encouraged in their idle arrogance. A few administrative changes were introduced which seemed but the shifting of a surface pattern over the deep scars of German conservatism.[4]

At the outbreak of the Polish-Muscovite war in 1562, Sigismund II chose to charge the Duke of Kurland with the administration of northern Livonia, the *Ducatus ultradunensis*, for so long as military matters should occupy Poland's energies. Gothard Kettler, being constitutionally entitled to declare his neutrality, had done so promptly upon the outbreak of hostilities since his domain was not directly threatened and in any case his suzerain, the Polish King, permitted him to keep only a token army.

After the decisive repulse of the Muscovites in 1564, Sigismund appointed his own viceroy, the Voyevode Chodkiewicz, to govern this portion of Livonia, now divided into the districts of Riga (outside the city), Wenden, Treiden, and Dünaburg. The district "senators" had the right to participate in the Polish *Sejm* (Parliament), where they enjoyed the veto privilege in matters concerning the *Ducatus ultra-*

---

[4] C. Schiemann, *op.cit.*, II, 309ff.

dunensis. Each of the Livonian districts had a court, whose judges were these same senators, and whence appeals could be carried to the viceroy as the supreme judge. The latter, as the personal representative of the Polish King, resided in the Castle of Riga, the former seat of the Grand Masters of the Order. The old Livonian Diet continued to function as a sort of general convention whose primary function was to elect as deputies to the Warsaw *Sejm* two Germans, two Poles, and two Lithuanians.

It was again military expediency which determined a further transformation in the status of the *Ducatus ultradunensis.* Late in 1564, this region, now to be known as *Livonia transdunensis,* was incorporated as an autonomous province into the Grand Duchy of Lithuania. This move followed upon repeated urgings of the Lithuanian magnates, who were eager to improve the finances of the Grand Duchy by the annexation of the Livonian income, as well as to procure the services of the highly-regarded Livonian militia. Sigismund yielded to Lithuanian pressure when he became convinced that a closer union of his Baltic domains would strengthen his defense against the Muscovites. The representatives of the Livonian squires in the Polish *Sejm,* knowing their whole class to be still in deadly terror of Tsarist attack, were easily persuaded to sign at the *Sejm* of Grodno the act of union known as the *Diploma unionis.*[5]

At the time, the Lithuanian magnates looked upon this act as a mere confirmation of an already existing state of union. This attitude, like that of some future Lithuanian historians, was based on a biased interpretation of the events of 1561. In that year, the special pleaders claim, all of Livonia, including Estonia, was incorporated into Lithuania directly, rather than into the Polish Commonwealth as a whole. But, as we have seen in a previous chapter, both Gothard Kettler and Archbishop William had particularly insisted on their subjection to the King of Poland, and the Vilna documents establish the fact that the *Pacta subjectionis* was so addressed. Prince Nicholas Radziwiłł's position as a Lithuanian magnate in no way implies that he acted for the Grand Duchy alone since he was the appointed representative of the King of Poland. In the *Cautio Radziviliana* of March 1562, also signed by Radziwiłł and considered by certain Lithuanian historians as further proof of Livonia's early incorporation into their country, the Prince merely promised in *nomine regis* to respect the legitimate rights of those Livonian landed nobles who were absent at Vilna.

[5] O. Halecki, *Dzieje unii jagiellońskiej,* II, 157ff.

Furthermore, any claim that the *Diploma unionis* brought about a reunion between the Lithuanians and their Latvian "brethren"[6] ignores the fact that this agreement between the Polish *Sejm* and the representatives of the *Ducatus ultradunensis* included certain promises addressed exclusively to the German squires in Livonia. The latter were assured that the governor-general of the new province would be German-speaking; that offices in the autonomous province should be held only by German-Balt nobles; that the official language of the courts must continue to be German; and that the existing local law codes, the Livonian *Sachsenspiegel* and the *Ritterrecht* would continue in force until a new code had been prepared. Thus, the *Diploma unionis* actually enhanced the power of the German oligarchy over the Latvians of Livonia.

Lithuania's special position in regard to Livonia did not long endure since in 1569 the Polish King, over the protest of many of the magnates, induced the Grand Duchy, which had had a common ruler with Poland ever since 1386, into a more organic union with the kingdom. By the Union of Lublin these two major component parts of the Commonwealth were drawn closer together by a single Diet, a common foreign policy, and other functional bonds.

This move on the part of Sigismund II to create a more closely-knit state, at the same time punishing the uncooperative tendencies of the Lithuanian magnates, was prompted both by his continued anxiety over Muscovy, whose incursions had penetrated as far as Kurland, and by a new confidence founded on a fortunate reversal of Sweden's attitude toward Poland. This state of affairs was brought about by the forced abdication of the mentally unsound Eric XIV early in 1569, and the succession of his brother, who ascended the Swedish throne as John III. As the brother-in-law and personal friend of Sigismund, John lost no time in concluding the unprofitable war with Denmark by the peace of Stettin in 1570. He also transformed the treaty of Kovno of 1562 into a close bond between Sweden and Poland, with the latter no longer contesting the former's possessions in Estonia, and Sweden accepting Poland's suzerainty over Livonia proper.

Just such an alliance had long been the *bête noire* of the Muscovite Tsar, whose answer to the ascendancy to the Swedish throne of a trusted ally of Poland was the breaking of the treaty of friendship concluded with Sweden in 1567. In 1570, John III found himself

---

[6] C. R. Jurgela, *History of the Lithuanian Nation* (New York, 1948), p. 222ff.

launched in what was to be a thirteen-year war with Muscovy, during which he was to lose all of his Estonian holdings save Reval. Ivan IV offset his aggression in the north by a conciliatory attitude toward Poland, whom he rightly suspected of being as weary of the Livonian tug-of-war as were the Muscovites themselves. The Tsar, after maintaining his former offer of the Daugava line as a basis for negotiation, even went so far as to volunteer the return of Lithuanian Polotzk, which he still held under occupation. As a preliminary step, a three-year armistice was signed in 1570, which left eastern Estonia, including Narva and the territory of Dorpat, under Muscovite control, while the rest of the province remained in Swedish hands.

But the slippery Ivan was far from acting in good faith, since he had up his sleeve the astonishing scheme of building up in Livonia a vassal kingdom docile to Muscovy. With this agreeable end in view, the Tsar, as early as his declaration of war on Poland in 1562, had dispatched a letter to the Duke of Kurland, promising to spare that "land of God" from Muscovite "anger." In 1570, simultaneously with the ambiguous peace overtures to Poland, Ivan again secretly approached Duke Gothard, this time to offer him the crown of Livonia, on condition that he break with Poland and become the vassal and ally of the Tsar. But this Gothard Kettler categorically refused to do.

Ivan then turned to Denmark, seeking the consent of King Frederick to the proclamation of his half brother Duke Magnus, lord of Danish Piltene and Oesel, as King of Livonia under the suzerainty of Muscovy. In 1560, Magnus had been received with honors in Livonia as the son of the Danish King, whom the nobles and burghers at that time hoped would assume control over all of Livonia and thus free them from the necessity of accepting either Polish or Muscovite dominion. Whereas the contest with Sweden otherwise engaged Denmark's attention, Duke Magnus persisted in his ambitions and accordingly, in 1570, proceeded with alacrity to Moscow to receive the crown of Livonia.[7] Subsequently, a treaty was concluded between the Tsar and his new protégé, the most important clauses of which constituted a military alliance directed against Poland and Sweden which put Magnus at the beck and call of the Tsar, forcing him to tolerate the presence of a large Muscovite army in what he was pleased to consider his Livonia.[8]

Magnus' position in his new domains was not a popular one, identified as he was with the hated Muscovites. Not only the Livonians,

---

[7] E. Seraphim, *Grundriss der baltischen Geschichte*, pp. 174-178.
[8] S. Solovyev, *op.cit.*, VI, 241f.

but the Duke of Kurland, the King of Poland, and the King of Sweden all regarded the "shadow king" as a tool of the Tsar, whose very helpless vassal he was. Since he was allowed no army of his own, Magnus advanced into Livonia with a borrowed force of Tartars, Kalmuks, Mongols, and other unruly Asiatic tribes, a course scarcely calculated to further his cause in the new "kingdom." Besides the dread aroused in the Latvian commoners by this reappearance of their ancient barbarian enemies, dismay now seized the Livonian nobility at the prospect of becoming subject to the same indignities which were the lot of the boyars in Muscovy.

In March 1571, Magnus began the siege of Reval. But that Estonian city, a strong fortress in itself, was obtaining reserves and supplies by sea both from Riga and from Sweden, and Magnus was obliged to raise the siege the following August. His position was further weakened by the fact that the 25,000 Muscovite troops which had been loaned him were now needed to stem the rising tide of the Crimean Tartars. Magnus saw no alternative but to retreat, which he did with marked vindictiveness, taking up residence, upon the order of the Tsar, in the castle of Karkus near Dorpat.

In August 1571, Sigismund II died without a male heir. Since he was the last of the Jagiellonian dynasty founded in Poland two centuries earlier, the monarchy was now declared elective, and a serious situation confronted both the Polish Commonwealth and the Baltic region as a whole.

Several notable candidates presented themselves for election to the Polish throne. Preeminent among them was the German Emperor Maximilian II, dominated by the dream of fashioning a vast Central European empire embracing Austria, Hungary, Bohemia, Poland, and the Baltic lands. In return for the Polish crown he now offered Poland union with Bohemia. The favor was refused. In turn, Ivan the Terrible presented himself as a candidate, demanding in exchange for his "protection" of Poland that he be elected hereditary king, and be ceded outright all of Livonia north of the Daugava. In case this offer should prove unacceptable, he made an alternate one to the Lithuanian magnates, to whom he proposed that he should become their grand duke, thus uniting Lithuania directly with Muscovy.[9] Although a few of the magnates saw here an opportunity to vent their spleen over their

---

[9] A. Richard, *Charles de Dançay. Ambassadeur de France en Danemark* (Poitiers, 1910), p. 119.

frustration at the time of the *Pacta subjectionis*, this second fruit of Ivan's fertile imagination was refused as categorically as the first.

A third candidate proved more fortunate. The French Henry of Valois, after duly promising to build a Polish navy with his own resources, and marry the fifty-four-year-old spinster sister of the late Sigismund, carried off the election in 1573. This constituted a diplomatic victory for France, who was at that time particularly anxious to fortify Sweden and Poland in order to weaken the Hapsburg Empire. To balance still further the Baltic situation in her favor, France also saw to it that one of the younger brothers of King Henry of Poland, François, the Duke of Alençon, was chosen prospective King of Livonia, and pledged to marry Princess Elizabeth, the sister of the Swedish monarch. It was justly surmised that by now Magnus might have his price since he could no longer expect effective help from Moscow.

All these fair schemes were blown to tatters by the wind of King Henry's scandalously sudden departure from his new realm. Crowned on January 25, at Cracow, he took his secret and speedy departure from Poland in June to ascend the throne of France as Henry III. Whatever triumph he might have felt at his attainment of the Jagiellonian crown had been adumbrated by the highhandedness of the Polish nobility (*szlachta*), who, at his election, had sought to circumscribe his royal prerogatives by a series of offensive stipulations known as the *Pacta conventa*.

With her throne once more open to international competition, Poland's situation continued precarious. The candidates remained much the same as two years previously: the Emperor Maximilian and his son Prince Ernest, yet another French Prince, John III of Sweden and his infant heir Sigismund August, Ivan the Terrible and his son, and the Transylvanian Prince Stephen Bátory.

The Hapsburg Emperor was pre-elected by the Polish Senate, under the influence of the *szlachta*. But the *Sejm* of the gentry fastened their choice upon the dazzling Bátory. This Hungarian warlord had the full support of the highly influential Jan Zamoyski, Sigismund II's brilliant chancellor, who could raise 100,000 cavalry among the devoted gentry at a moment's notice. Zamoyski was especially impressed by Bátory's splendidly trained army of professional soldiers, heavily equipped with artillery. While Maximilian dawdled over his acceptance, even seeking to have his son nominated in his stead, the fifty-year-old Prince

Stephen accepted all conditions and set out briskly for Cracow where, on May 1, 1576, he was crowned King of Poland.

After the new warrior-king had attended to the subjugation of rebellious Danzig in 1577,[10] he turned his remarkable energies to a decisive encounter with Muscovy, whose forces, during the summer offensive of 1577, held everything north of the Daugava save Riga and Reval. In spite of the meanness of the subsidies voted by the short-sighted *szlachta*, Stephen's large standing army of Hungarian musketeers and artillery, supplemented by Polish and Lithuanian cavalry, and Latvian and Estonian militia, appeared an impressive threat to the Tsar.[11]

On the diplomatic front, Muscovy also felt the impact of the fortunate Polish election. By marrying the elderly Princess Anna, Stephen had become the brother-in-law of the King of Sweden, thus further solidifying the friendship of these two Powers which, although divided by economic and religious questions, had long felt the need for union in the face of the looming and unrelenting peril of Muscovy's thrust to the Baltic. In 1577, the puppet King Magnus, sensing the shift in power and anxious to be rid of his personal bondage to Ivan, entered into secret relations with the new Polish King. Simultaneously, by manifesto, he invited the Livonian nobility to submit to his sovereignty and receive his protection against the ravaging Muscovite bands. Somewhat surprisingly, many of the nobles promptly fell in with this arrangement; whereupon the Tsar, outraged by what he chose to regard as treachery, took to sacking and burning the Livonian castles, and forced Magnus to seek refuge from his furious pursuit in the old Latvian stronghold of Cēsis (Wenden). When Ivan himself assaulted this castle, Magnus, wishing to spare the city, surrendered. None the less the Tsar, in retaliation for a shot which had been taken at him during the negotiations, ordered the city destroyed and its citizens fantastically tortured. Magnus was imprisoned until the intervention of his half brother, King Frederick of Denmark, procured his release.

Magnus now sought a haven in Piltene, where he became friendly with Duke Gothard of Kurland, to the extent of appointing the Duke's eldest son, Prince Frederick, his personal heir; although he continued to uphold the rights of his brother, the King of Denmark, to Piltene

[10] C. Lepszy, "Gdańsk et la Pologne à l'époque de Bátory" in *Etienne Bátory, Roi de Pologne, Prince de Transylvanie* (Cracow, 1935), pp. 212-241.
[11] O. Laskowski, "Les Campagnes de Bátory contre la Moscovie" in *Etienne Bátory, Roi etc.*, pp. 375-403

and Oesel. In 1578, Magnus broke openly with his overlord the Tsar by announcing his intention of abdicating from the throne of Livonia, and entering into further negotiations with Poland to that end.[12] That same year, the Latvian commander Janis Birin played a major part in routing the Muscovites from Wenden, whose fortress they had occupied since 1577. In 1579, King Stephen recaptured Polotzk and began a push in the direction of Pskov; while, simultaneously, Sweden's army advanced in northern Estonia, where they capped their victories over numerous Muscovite garrisons by taking Narva in 1581, the year that Stephen Bátory laid siege to Pskov. That same year, Magnus appeared once more in Livonia, this time fighting on the side of the Poles and the Lithuanians against the crumbling resistance of the Muscovites, whom he joyfully chased as far as the Latvian frontier.

Magnus died in 1583, after submitting to the suzerainty of King Stephen in Warsaw. Two years later, Frederick of Denmark sold Piltene to the Polish King. Since the latter was short of ready cash, he borrowed the necessary sum from the Duke of Prussia, pledging him Piltene in return. From this peculiar situation arose the subsequent status of the Kuronian district of Piltene as an autonomous, self-governing province under the direct suzerainty of the Polish King. In the seventeenth century Duke Jacob of Kurland redeemed Piltene and incorporated it into his Duchy, where it preserved its autonomous character into modern times.

With the fall of Narva, which meant the cutting off of English supplies to the Muscovites, and with Stephen's persistent siege of Pskov, Ivan the Terrible sensed the decline of his Baltic fortunes and showed a weary willingness to sue for peace. With characteristic duplicity he approached Pope Gregory XIII for mediation, leading the Pontiff to believe that he might join the Roman Catholic Church and combat the Turks. The Papal Nuncio, the Jesuit Possevino, after initial difficulties, finally obtained in January 1582 the ten-year truce of Kiwerowa Horka (near Zapoli), whereby Muscovy ceded Polotzk and the whole of Livonia to Poland, thus decisively closing her "window on the Baltic" while permitting her former enemy to achieve the furthest eastern expansion of her frontier in all Polish history to that time. Muscovy's other opponent, Sweden, was granted a three-year truce in 1583, which in 1585 was to be extended till 1590.

King Stephen, flushed with victory, now took a step whose wisdom has been warmly debated. Pressing his luck, he sought to regain

[12] S. Henning, op.cit., cap. 68a.

Estonia, even proposing to reimburse Sweden for her military expenses incurred in liberating this province from the Muscovites.[18] Stephen's anxiety had been aroused by some Swedish movements which suggested that Reval might be only a steppingstone to Riga and to Mitau, the capital of Kurland. Now that the Muscovite menace was stemmed, Sweden and Poland both realized that control of the southeastern shore of the Baltic might determine the supremacy of either Power. King John III courteously but firmly maintained his legal rights to Estonia, although he did not question his brother-in-law's annexation of the purely Estonian districts of Pärnu and Tartu (Dorpat), which had been reconquered from the Muscovites by that statesman-soldier, Jan Zamoyski. In 1583, a year before his death, Tsar Ivan IV relinquished Estonia to Sweden, thus sowing the seed of future discord between the joint victors at whose hands he had suffered conclusive defeat. Russia's first effort to reach the Baltic had failed.

From 1582 until the outbreak of war with Sweden in 1601, Poland was sufficiently at peace to turn her attention to the internal affairs of the subjugated Duchy of Livonia. King Stephen, gifted with unusual powers of civil as well as military organization, and closely assisted by the energetic and highly talented Chancellor Jan Zamoyski, began administrative reforms which might have borne fruit had he not died suddenly after only ten years of rule. His death was a severe loss both to the Joint Kingdom, where he had held in check the inordinate feuds and self-seeking of the nobility while at the same time introducing important political, legal, and social reforms; and to Livonia, where he turned his attention to the plight of the common people. His successor, the Swedish King Sigismund III Vasa (1586-1632), proved bigoted and obtuse, and quite unable to move forward in the paths which King Stephen's humanity, intelligence, and zeal had opened.

One of Stephen's notable diplomatic triumphs was his persuasion of the city of Riga to join the Polish Commonwealth. At the time of the partitioning of Livonia, this self-ruling Hanseatic city covered an area of about 77 square miles and comprised a population of some 25,000. Its high walls, with twenty-four turrets and few gates, bristling with defense weapons, overlooked a heavily patrolled and forbidding moat. The Council of this proud fortress-city had hitherto repeatedly rebuffed attempts to undermine her classic independence which, by now, had cost the citizenry, both German- and Latvian-Livonian,

[18] J. Rousset, *Les intérêts présents des puissances de l'Europe*, 1 (La Haye, 1733), 166-168.

much money and blood. During the Great Livonian War, Riga had characteristically held doggedly to an advantageous commercial position by sharing the profits of the Narva trade, while showing fight the moment the Muscovites sought to lay hands on the city itself.

The latest unsuccessful assault on Riga's civic virtue had been conducted by Prince Radziwiłł at the time of the subjugation of the city's former suzerain, the Archbishop, and of her traditional enemy, the Grand Master of the Livonian Order. Radziwiłł, proclaiming himself a Calvinist and a friend of the Protestant Rigans, in 1561 had made the City Council certain promises in the name of Poland. To gain time, the Council demanded that he procure from Sigismund II himself a formal release of Riga from her suzerainty to the German Emperor, as well as the assurance that the Polish *Sejm* would confirm the privileges enumerated in the King's letter. When no such guarantees were forthcoming, the Rigan representatives at Vilna flatly refused to sign the *Pacta subjectionis.*

Their decision was reinforced by Riga's position as a strong fortress, well-defended by militia, and by her sea communications with Sweden, whose help had sustained the burghers more than once during their perennial struggles with the Livonian Order. Nor were the Rigans as panicked by the Muscovites, whom they had actually repulsed, as were the nobles, whose outmoded and decaying castles lay open to attack. Yet Riga's claim to be under the suzerainty of the Empire must be regarded as highly unrealistic. Only indirectly, through her immediate overlord the Archbishop, had Riga ever owed allegiance to the German Emperor; and since, in 1561, before submitting to Sigismund II, both the Archbishop and the Grand Master had specifically renounced their suzerainty over the city, Riga was now actually free to choose whatever liege-lord she pleased. She elected to approach the Emperor for recognition as a free city of the Empire, hoping thus to ward off Polish annexation, which, in the case of some smaller Livonian towns who had voluntarily submitted at Vilna, had resulted in the loss of their privileges under Polish administrators. Prince Radziwiłł's further lures, including a promise of religious toleration urged upon the citizens in March 1562, only left the Rigans coolly determined to preserve that independence which the Polish envoy seemed so anxious to subvert.

For the next twenty years Riga was to know relative peace and freedom, enjoying the privileges of a free imperial city; among them, her own prize court, unrestricted jurisdiction over the Daugava waterway, the right to issue passports, to coin money, and the control of weights and measures. During this period, while still courting the Emperor, Riga maintained diplomatic relations with the King of Poland, since his declared enmity might have greatly damaged the interests of the wholesale merchants to whom Polish-Lithuanian trade relations were of the first importance. After Muscovy's defeat in 1564, Poland renewed her pressure through her newly appointed Viceroy of Livonia, Chodkiewicz, who suddenly demanded the levying of customs taxes by his collectors upon all ships entering the Daugava from the Gulf of Riga. In case of refusal, he threatened to build a fortress at the mouth of the river for the purpose of blockading the Riga shipping. The city's heated protests warded off this move until 1570, when, in order to prevent the Rigans from joining forces with King Magnus, the fort was erected and a blockade begun which ended only at the instigation of the Duke of Kurland, acting as arbitrator.

King Sigismund II to the end of his days had insisted on his sovereign rights over the city. Riga hoped for a more favorable position under Henry of Valois, whose election she had helped to secure by a financial subsidy to his partisans in the *Sejm*. Certainly French commercial interests could have been counted on to indulge this flourishing port; yet even more concessions might have been expected from such a patron as the Emperor Maximilian II. The crowning of his rival, Stephen Bátory, the brother-in-law of John III, ended Riga's expectation of any further sympathy from Sweden. The City Council was of the opinion that the time had come to attain a *modus vivendi* with powerful Poland. Against the will of the Guilds, who now feared too much might be yielded, an understanding with Cracow was reached.

In 1579, a special delegation of the Riga Council, whose moving spirit was the astute and supple Secretary of Riga, David Hilchen, began secret negotiations with the representatives of King Stephen. By early 1581, while the Tsar's forces still lingered in Livonia, the Polish King was ready to confirm Riga's rights and privileges, which he did in the *Corpus privilegiorum Stephaneum*; so that in April the city of Riga consented to swear fealty to its new sovereign, King Stephen of Poland. The following year, the Polish *Sejm* confirmed these privileges, while Stephen further declared his willingness to permit the practice of the Augsburg Confession, demanding only equal rights in Riga for the Roman Catholics. In April 1582 he passed beneath a special arch of triumph which the Rigans had erected to

honor him as their savior, by virtue of his final defeat of the Muscovites.[14]

Among the privileges which the King had agreed to concede to the
jealous city were: the right of the burghers to continue in possession
of landed properties and to acquire manors from indebted nobles; the
right of the city to coin money; to retain such fugitive peasants as had
lived two years within its limits; and the right of the City Council to
judge both its own citizens and foreigners. The royal Burgrave, chosen
from among the burghers but confirmed by the King, pronounced
sentence in legal cases, appeal being open directly to the King's High
Court. King Stephen also confirmed Riga's cherished supremacy over
the Daugava waterway, although he tempered this mercy by claiming
two parts of the incoming customs duties to repair the fortunes of
his Commonwealth. On the whole, Riga had received from Stephen
better terms than the Livonian squires had obtained from Sigismund
in 1561.

Further advantages accrued from the satisfactory settlement of the
religious problem, which had grown acute in the times of Protestant
Riga's opposition to the Catholic Livonian Order. During the sixteenth
century, the religious controversy had centered in the Livonian towns,
where alone some intellectual activity was possible, and where a few
Lutheran churchmen tried painfully to admit a gleam of Erasmian
humanism into the sinister murk that shrouded Livonia. In defiance
of an archiepiscopal veto, Riga had named two such minor luminaries,
Andreas Knopken and Sylvester Tegetmeier, to pulpits in the Protestant
churches of St. Peter and St. Jacob. To strengthen her position in
regard to the Order, Riga, in 1539, had adhered to the Schmalkaldic
Union concluded among the Lutheran princes of Germany. Although
the Reformation in Livonia assumed a predominantly German character, in Riga itself the Livs and Latvians participated earnestly in the
new movement, even obtaining, in a few cases, the preaching of the
gospel in the Latvian language.

King Stephen, a firm Roman Catholic, showed some realization of
the tenacity of the new doctrines in Riga when, instead of insisting
on the restoration of the Archbishop, he contented himself with founding a Roman Catholic bishopric in the new diocese of Wenden, and in
demanding the restitution of two churches to the Catholics of Riga.
In addition, the old castle of the Order in Riga, which was henceforth

[14] Schiemann, op.cit., II, 375ff. The details of local events in Riga during
these crises in J. Straubergs, Rigas vēsture, passim.

to be the seat of the Governor-General of Poland, was also to have a Roman Catholic chapel. Stephen's appreciation of the cultural life of the city, which was centered in the activities of a lively little group of humanists, led him, after the founding of a Jesuit College, to offer the Rigans the privilege of establishing their own university. The highly conservative City Council, fearing extraordinary expenses, publicly renounced this enlightened proposal.

Nor did the Polish King overlook the clamorings of that party which, true to its tradition of resisting all the policies of the oligarchical City Council, now opposed the latter's acceptance of Stephen's suzerainty. This party was made up primarily of members of the two chief Riga guilds; the so-called Great Guild, consisting of wholesale merchants and the members of learned professions; and the Little or Artisans' Guild, which included small retail merchants and skilled workers. This social group constituted Riga's progressive and grasping Second Estate, which was usually in conflict with the aims and interests of the First Estate, that is, those patricians who controlled the city's administration and from whose leading families came the hereditary and oligarchical City Councilors. The Third Estate, composed exclusively of Latvians and Livs, just as the first two Estates were open only to Germans, included all those engaged in the humbler occupations and possessing neither electoral nor administrative rights.

King Stephen placated the members of the Guilds by confirming their statutory privileges. Upon the King's departure from Riga, the Guilds, encouraged by his gesture of conciliation, injected a new vigor into their opposition to the oligarchic rule of the City Council. Their current accusation was that, by plotting with the newly arrived Jesuits, Riga's governing class was fostering a Roman Catholic counterreformation. The fire was fanned when, by a Royal Decree in 1584, the new Gregorian Calendar, introduced by a papal bull in Western Europe two years earlier, was made obligatory for Kurland, Livonia, and Riga. Whereas the City Council accepted the new calendar as a useful reform, the Riga Lutherans, looking upon it as piece of Catholic propaganda, stood fast against its introduction.[15]

Riots broke out between the adherents of the two faiths over the question of the celebration of Christmas. In the course of the increasingly serious disturbance, Martin Giese, a politician-lawyer and the secretary of the Great Guild, supported by members of both Guilds,

[15] Dionysius Fabricius, *Livonicae historiae* in *Script. rer. livon.*, II, 486-487.

occupied the Rathaus by force and took over the rule of Riga, assuming full military powers including control of the city gates.

The leaders of the opposition to the Calendar Reform and to its promoters, the Jesuits, now called upon the Polish Viceroy, at this time Cardinal George Radziwiłł, to declare that their chief grievance was, after all, not against the Catholics, but rather against the City Council, in which they wished to obtain more rights and an enlarged representation. Early in 1585, the malcontents prepared a program to serve as a basis of conciliation between the Council and the Guilds. The inclusion in this program of the restitution of the Julian calendar was interpreted as an open defiance of the King's decree, as well as a breach of the promise of loyalty given previously to the Viceroy. The Polish King was now disposed to listen to some members of the Riga Council who, having escaped the clutches of Giese and his associates, appeared in Warsaw to denounce the Calendar movement as revolutionary. Giese was summoned to appear for trial before King Stephen at the Supreme Court in Warsaw. His refusal to appear constituted a second outright defiance of the King, whom he further outraged by ordering the decapitation of two members of the Council, a grave offense to the King's Supreme Court, which alone was competent to judge members of the Riga Council. King Stephen now decided to restore the Council's authority by outlawing the rebel Giese.

After seeking unavailingly for help in Sweden and Germany, Martin Giese returned to Riga in 1587, after the death of King Stephen and the election of Sigismund III Vasa to the Polish throne. By 1588, he was more firmly entrenched than ever as president of the Great Guild and virtual dictator of the city. During his travels abroad Giese had been impressed by the growing power of the printing press in political and religious disputes, and through the services of the secretary of the City Council, the omnipresent David Hilchen, the consent of the Polish King was obtained for the establishment of a printing office by the Council of Riga. A number of books soon appeared, in Latin, German, and a few in Latvian, under the imprint of the first printer in Livonia, the Dutchman Nicolas Mollyn.

For all his resilience and modernity, Martin Giese's dictatorial temper eventually wearied the Riga burghers, who particularly resented the bad influence of his rule upon their trade relations with Poland. When he was deposed by the Council from his office as Elder of the Great Guild, he characteristically refused to obey. Meanwhile the news had reached Riga that the Polish *Sejm* was sending two high commissioners to investigate matters in the city. Giese's supporters, interpreting this move as a violation of Riga's rights, agitated to have the city renounce its allegiance to the Polish King and proclaim its independence. Thereupon a group of burghers, dreading the armed conflict with Poland which such a step might provoke, requested the interference of a Polish commander. He actually appeared in Riga in June of 1589, but was forced by the pro-Giesean militia to beat a hasty retreat.

A month later the Polish high commissioners arrived in the city. They summoned Giese and his close collaborator Brinken to appear before them for a hearing during the course of which the rebels assumed such an arrogant tone that their immediate arrest was ordered. The burghers, fearing a Polish punitive expedition should they make a show of resistance, raised not a hand to defend the leaders of the "Calendar Revolution," and the two men were sentenced to death and promptly executed.

By the end of 1589, the old order appeared to be restored in Riga. However, the Riga City Council, finally acknowledging the position and power of the Guilds, was ready for a certain degree of compromise. The hitherto closed oligarchy now accepted the presiding Elders of both Guilds into the Council as representatives of Riga's Second Estate. From now on the First and the Second Estates began to work in close collaboration to sustain German privilege and ascendancy in the face of the rising indignation of the purely indigenous Third Estate. Thus was initiated the centuries-long struggle between the German administrative minority and the Latvian majority population of Riga.

Less exciting than Poland's relations with the dramatic city of Riga is the history of Polish control in the rest of the Livonian domains. Here again, King Stephen's death marks a dividing point between a period of social and administrative progress and decades of stagnation under the erratic rule of Sigismund III. To King Stephen fell the urgent task of repairing the ravages of war throughout his Baltic domains. As a preliminary administrative measure, the *Ducatus trans-dunensis*, henceforth called the *Provincia Livonica*, was issued a new constitution shortly after the peace treaty with Muscovy. The administration of the province, which was now divided into the three districts (*praesidiati*) of Wenden, Dorpat, and Pernau, was to be modeled on that introduced in Prussia in 1538.

That same motivation which had prompted the orderly Stephen

Bátory to consolidate the Joint Kingdom by curbing the family feuds and general lack of respect for the laws which made of the Polish *szlachta* and the Lithuanian magnates a highly disturbing element in the body politic, governed his relations with the German squires of Livonia. In general, the Polish sovereigns, though willing enough to use the German ruling class in Livonia for their own ends, showed an open contempt for the fatted squires who had run squealing before the Muscovites. An additional motive for reducing the inflated status of these "land barons" was provided by the low state of the Polish exchequer at the end of the long-drawn-out struggle with the Tsar.

In 1582, King Stephen appointed a commission of land revision for Livonia whose task it was to examine the titles by which the German landed nobles held their manors, and to reduce all such manors as had been illegally acquired. The findings of this commission brought to light the fact that, during the absence of any effective state authority throughout the Muscovite wars, the squires had greatly enriched themselves by arbitrarily annexing many deserted farmsteads of the rural communities (*pagasti*). Furthermore, under the predominantly Lithuanian administration which obtained during the wars, little attention was paid to the complaints of the peasants since the dictatorial Lithuanian magnates had long practiced cruel means of peasant oppression on their own domains. Nor was the situation much different in Poland itself, where feudalism had gone to equal extremes; the peasants having become *adscripti glebae* in 1496, the marketable property of their lords in 1543, deprived of all property rights in 1557, and in 1573 legally the subjects of their squires.[16] King Stephen, concerned nevertheless over the abject plight of the Livonian peasantry under their foreign masters, as well as angered by the greed of their German squires, in 1583 in his "New Livonian Administrative Reform" (*Nova Livoniae gubernationis reforma*), requested the Diet of the Livonian nobles to diminish the exaggerated labor-duty and taxation which prevailed on the manors, and demanded that money fines be substituted for corporal punishment of the farmers and serfs. At the same time, the Polish authorities began collection of the outstanding taxes of the manor-lords. In 1584, the Livonian Diet of the squires protested the projected peasant reforms, declaring themselves threatened by imminent poverty. King Stephen held firm, and two years later reiterated his requests. Had he lived longer, he would probably

[16] J. Lelewel, *Histoire de Pologne*, II (Paris, 1844), 240ff.

have carried the day against the barons and, to a degree, alleviated the wretchedness of the Livonian peasants.

Under Sigismund III Vasa, Polish administrative improvements in Livonia grew half-hearted and sporadic, as the deterioration of relations with Sweden began once more to involve the Polish sovereign in questions of foreign affairs and military preparedness. Successive commissions of land revision appointed by the Warsaw Diet revealed the increasing misery and helplessness of the Latvian peasantry, now virtually abandoned to the German land barons, who had little to fear from the infirm Polish-Lithuanian governance.

The Livonian squires, under the impetus of the high price levels for grain which obtained in the second half of the sixteenth century, especially for the high quality product of the "Baltic Granary," began systematically to enlarge their manors. Not only did they annex farms deserted by their owners during the wars or by peasants fleeing the unbearable corvées, but they now made deliberate and forceful appropriations of property on the farmlands of the rural communities which adjoined the manors. In order to exploit their swollen estates to the limit, the barons followed the example of the adjoining Lithuanian magnates in reducing the yeomen to the lowest level of serfdom. To this purpose, in 1599, the same David Hilchen who had figured so prominently in Riga politics as an eminent jurist was commissioned by the landed interests to prepare a code of Livonian serfdom.[17] This code, based largely on Roman law, degraded the Latvian peasantry to virtual slavery. Hilchen, who for a term represented the Livonian squires in the Polish *Sejm*, nearly succeeded through his friendship with the still influential Chancellor Zamoyski in obtaining King Sigismund III's confirmation of this code. The Polish King's anxiety to please the Livonian landed nobles, in view of the imminent war with Sweden, prompted him in 1600 to permit the use of the Hilchen Code in Livonian courts on a provisional basis.

The actual reduction of the farmsteaders to serfdom was accomplished by converting them into permanent debtors through the number and size of the tributes levied upon them. Not content with the yield of their manors, even under maximum cultivation, the squires increased the grain levies on the rural communities, often demanding as much as twenty-five per cent of the crop, and that the best part, which the squires' inspectors selected while the grain was still in the

[17] R. Vipper, *David Hilchen, Die erste rechtliche Fixierung der Leibeigenschaft in Livland*, in *Filologu beedribas raksti*, VII (Riga, 1928), 225-240.

field. The farmers were then required to harvest, thresh, and carry to market the squires' fat portion. Delivery of flax, vegetables, wool, fruits, wax, honey, meat, and dairy products was also exacted by the manor-lords, who sold what surplus remained from their own use to the neighboring cities. Those squires who lived far from a town preferred to commute these produce levies to money taxes. Since the farmers had practically no means of acquiring money, they were declared defaulters and promptly reduced to serfdom.

Under the Polish-Lithuanian régime the farmsteaders of the rural communities, who formerly had been subject to paying tithe and tribute to their overlords only through the medium of the *pagasti*, had now become individually liable directly to their squires. The latter considered themselves local sovereigns, even to the point of passing private laws both for the manors and for the adjacent communities. All these abuses were but feebly deplored by Sigismund III, flustered as he was by the rising storm across the Baltic.

A further effect of the Swedish menace upon the Polish King's Livonian policy had been to induce him to favor Lithuania's stubborn claim to administrative control in that region. Sigismund hoped thus to obtain the assistance of the magnates in his impending attempt to conquer Estonia. In 1589, he issued the *Ordinatio Livoniae*, which granted exclusively to Lithuanian nobles of the Roman Catholic persuasion the appointment to administrative offices in Livonia. The land revision act of 1590 provided that the former domains of the Livonian Order should be assessed for the support of the newly-created Livonian districts (*praesidiati*), headed by Lithuanian intendants (*starosti*). The state revenues from Livonia were to accrue alternately and equally to Lithuania and to Poland. Thus an intensive exploitation of Livonia was launched, both for the benefit of the Lithuanian magnates and for the military preparedness of the uneasy King of Poland.

The latter also began to militarize the Livonian administration, a step which was particularly necessary, since the landed nobility, who had long forgotten their feudal obligation to military service, had reduced their efforts in that field to supervision of the local militia. By this time the peasants were bearing most of the burden of defense, every fifteen farmsteaders being required to provide and arm one trooper. In 1600, King Sigismund sought to bring some order into Livonia's military affairs by elevating the district intendants into military *palatinati*, responsible to *voyevodi*. Beneath the *palatinati* were the *capitanati* (as many as twenty in the district of Wenden). All these officials were directly appointed by the King.

The province of Latgale presented a particular case, since Polish influence had prevailed there from 1559 and was to continue until 1772. The castles of this district had been occupied by Polish garrisons during the Muscovite wars, while most of the Livonian castles had remained in German hands. The German squires had for the most part become Polonized, and their names have persisted among the Polish nobility to this day. The Latvians in this region experienced the full weight of Polish feudalism blended with German oppression, a double bondage which makes the survival of their folk culture all the more surprising.

Rather more creative than the stagnant and opportunistic Polish-Lithuanian dominance of Livonia was the reign of Duke Gothard in Kurland (1562-1587). Since he was not of royal origin, this highly ambitious statesman corrected his family status by marrying the German Princess Anna of Mecklenburg in 1566. The Duke's eldest son, Frederick, was to espouse Princess Elizabeth of Brunswick; the younger, William, took for wife Princess Sophie of Prussia, who brought the district of Grobina in her dowry; while Gothard's daughter, Anna, married Prince Radziwiłł, Duke of Olyka. Thus the newly established ruling family of Kettler took on a dynastic tinge by relating itself with powerful German and Lithuanian princely houses.

The Duke's strong position, combined with astuteness and determination, enabled him to maintain a fairly satisfactory balance among all the conflicting interests of the feudal state of Kurland. The Duchy itself was in a favorable economic position, compared to the neighboring regions which had experienced the ravages of war. The Duke's neutrality had indeed been inspired.

At the beginning of his rule Duke Gothard had to face the hostility of many of the Kuronian nobles, who resented the imposition of a sovereign by Poland. Particularly disaffected were the hundred or so large German landowners, to whom the Duke was inimical to the end of his days. They, however, formed a minority of the Kuronian nobility; to the majority, the Duke finally made considerable concessions in the *Privilegium Gothardianum* of 1570, in which he rewarded the landed nobles for their recognition of him as sovereign.

The *Privilegium Gothardianum*[18] is considered to be one of the

[18] C. S. von Ziegenhorn, *Staatsrecht der Herzogtümer Kurland und Semigallen* (Königsberg, 1772), doc. no. 76. See also C. Nettelbladt, *Fasciculus rerum curlandicarum* (Rostock, 1729), pp. 119-129.

oldest written constitutions in Europe, as well as the Magna Charta of the Kuronian nobles. Among its twelve articles were provisions for the profession of Lutheranism in accordance with the Augsburg Confession; the promise of governmental attention to schools, hospitals, and asylums; and the Duke's assumption of the obligation to codify the statutes of Kurland and create a judicial organization in conformity with the views of the nobility. Article five promised respect for the class privileges of the squires; and article six recognized the *feuda* held by the nobles from the Livonian Order and the Bishop of Kurzeme as their allods, or personal property. A further concession to the squires provided that their land titles might be established by personal affidavit rather than by documents. Thus the 359 noble fiefs of Kurland were transformed into private property, while 72 were recognized as belonging to the towns and townspeople. The Duke himself still remained the richest landowner with his 215 manors.

Among the personal privileges confirmed to the nobility were the right to duty-free imports, to preside as judges on their manors over all the non-noble inhabitants, and monopolistic brewing privileges. Thus, the farmers were directly subjugated to the squires, whose personal property they and their goods and chattels now became. They no longer had the right to leave their land, hunt, brew, or sell their surpluses in the city markets. Torture and corporal punishment rewarded all transgressions, large or small. The squire, as supreme judge, had both the power to pardon and to condemn a freeman to serfdom. No appeal was possible. Not all the Kurish farmers were serfs; but those who remained freemen were required to pay some twenty different varieties of taxes.

Somewhat easier was the situation of the farmers in the autonomous district of Piltene, where they enjoyed the right of personal property and inheritance, as well as the expectation of assistance and protection from their squires in times of famine and other disasters. Still more favorable were the conditions of peasant existence on the ducal manors, where dues and taxes, fixed in written form, could not be arbitrarily increased; where military service, as well as various trades and even clerical work were open to the peasantry; and where the stewards had special instructions to consider the welfare of the farmers who could appeal to the Duke himself in case of infringement of their recognized rights.

Both the Latvian farmers and the burghers came to look for protection to Duke Gothard, who established that tradition of benevolent despotism which his successors to the ducal throne were to develop to a high degree. The Kuronian nobility chose to stand apart from the Kettlers, against whom they passionately conspired with the Polish and Lithuanian magnates. These latter showed themselves eager to encourage any degree of dissension within Kurland which might prevent it from following the embarrassing example of insubordination set by the restive Duchy of Prussia.

The Duchy of Kurland's hope for development and eventual independence lay in whatever skill her rulers were to exhibit in detecting the trend of the times in Western Europe, where this small Baltic principality was to find her opportunity for economic advancement; and in their more or less tactful evasion of the further disruptions which another century of struggle was to bring to the turmoiled Baltic regions. For Poland's suzerainty over Livonia was to yield neither profit nor peace to that ceaselessly despoiled area, whose peculiar vulnerability was to invite yet more contestants for Baltic supremacy to ride roughshod over her tragic soil.

Chapter 9

Swedish Dominion

STRONG currents of that political-religious agitation which was to grip Europe in the spasms of the Thirty Years' War were already surging through the Baltic area during the last two decades of the sixteenth century. Protestant and Catholic coalitions, looming up over the face of Europe, were casting shadows on Baltic waters. The dwindling of the Muscovite menace had released the dangerous humors of religious intolerance which had been held in check as long as a semi-barbarous foe threatened the Christian West.

As the breach in Western Christianity widened, the deeply inter-fused Roman Catholicism of the Polish Commonwealth, together with her archaic feudalism, marked her as the inevitable challenger of Protestant Sweden, whose own young and vigorous body politic now appeared threatened by the disease of religious strife. Any condominium of the Baltic which might have been hoped for by an observer of the united front which these two Powers had for a time offered to Muscovy, became unthinkable at the very moment that the two states were, if only dynastically, joined by the election of Sigismund Vasa to the Polish throne. This election brought in its train rivalry and tension between Poland and Sweden, and eventually military action. The eastern shores of the Baltic were thus now the focus of a three-cornered struggle: Poland, Sweden, and less actively, Muscovy. It is therefore necessary to follow in some detail the story of the strife between the main protagonists, while the people of what we now call Latvia recede into the background.

The Swedish Crown Prince, son of John III and nephew of Sigismund II, with the strong support of Chancellor Zamoyski, was elected King of Poland in August 1587. The Polish nobles had been strongly influenced in their choice by the promised restoration to the Commonwealth of the Swedish possessions in Estonian Livonia. The insincerity of this lure was indicated by the Statute of Kalmar, signed by both John III and his son in September 1587. This act placed Sweden and Poland on an equal footing, against the day when they would have a joint ruler. Sweden was guaranteed independence in foreign policy and religion, and the continued control of her provinces in Livonia.[1]

Sigismund III, who, after all, came empty-handed to his new kingdom, was neither liked nor trusted in the Commonwealth. He immediately sought refuge from the coolness of his subjects in an ardently Catholic entourage, similar to that which had fostered his Polish mother's religious passions in Sweden. The new ruler of Poland and heir to the Swedish throne became the crony of Jesuits, the willing ally of the Hapsburgs, and the tool of Rome. He was to nurse unremittingly the fantastic ambition of bringing both Sweden and Muscovy into the Roman Catholic fold.

Upon the death of John III in 1592, Duke Charles Vasa, the third son of Gustavus Vasa and the uncle of Sigismund III, assumed the viceroyship in Sweden. This staunch Protestant hoped, with the support of the *Räd*, to preserve his country's independence from both the spiritual and political vassalage which threatened her from Poland. Sigismund, landing at Stockholm in 1593, immediately demanded toleration of the Catholic faith and the appointment of Catholics to official positions. When his attitude met with outraged opposition on the part of the Swedish Government, Sigismund was forced to retract his demands before his coronation as King of Sweden, which took place early in 1594. In August, he returned to the more congenial atmosphere of his coterie in Poland. Relieved of his nephew's ominous presence, Duke Charles, in 1596 and again in 1597, convoked the Swedish Estates and won their repeated approval of his regency, as well as their reaffirmation of the preeminence of the Protestant faith in Sweden.

Spain and Austria now began to court the devout Polish King who was thus being flouted in the Protestant half of his domains. Spain at this time was particularly anxious to obtain a base on the Baltic against her enemies, England and the Netherlands. Encouraged by his impressive new allies, Sigismund, with an armed force, made an unfriendly descent upon Sweden in July 1598, only to be forced back in undignified haste. In February of the following year the Swedish Government allowed him the choice of returning to Sweden without an army, of sending his son Władysław to be raised as a Protestant, or

[1] For a brilliant overview of the situation in the Baltic in the second half of the sixteenth century see the recent work of Władysław Konopczyński, *Kwestia Bałtycka do XX w.* (Gdańsk, 1947), chap. III.

of being deposed. Sigismund's disregard of these offers left the Swedish Diet no alternative but to dethrone him in July 1599.[2]

A high regard for legality prevented Charles Vasa from accepting the crown until 1607, when it became evident that Sigismund's son would not be permitted to receive a Protestant training for the throne. In the meantime, open warfare had broken out between the two powers, whom a common ruler had not been able to unite. In August 1600, Charles IX, in retaliation for the seizure of his envoys to Poland and in anticipation of a Polish move against Estonia, invaded Livonia, seizing Valka (Wolmar) and Cēsis (Wenden), and closing in on Riga. This stout city he was unable to take, and the following year the Polish forces counterattacked and recaptured a part of Livonia. During the next four years, when Livonia was a center of conflict, Zamoyski and Chodkiewicz wrested further territory from the Swedes and even penetrated into Estonia.[3]

In order to strengthen his position against Poland, Charles IX signed a treaty of alliance in 1606 with Tsar Vassily Shuisky, while at the same time he invited the Netherlands to join him in the struggle against "the foes of Protestantism" and the allies of the hated Spaniards. That same year, the death of Zamoyski apparently turned the tide of victory in northern Livonia. In the south, the Swedish forces continued to be blocked by the resistance of Riga, which Charles besieged, again unsuccessfully and for the last time, in 1609. In 1611, an armistice allowed the two warring Powers to draw breath after ten years of intensive skirmishing.

Denmark now chose to declare herself by clamping down an embargo on the shipping of Swedish military supplies through the Straits. The Danish position was a strong one, owing to her continued control of the islands of Gotland and Oesel, and of the Skäne district in southern Sweden. Upon Charles' demand that Denmark discontinue commercial relations with Riga and the ports of Kurland, Christian IV directed his navy to proceed to Riga for the protection of Danish shipping. On Charles IX's sudden death in 1611, the reins of government passed to his son Gustavus Adolphus, who gave a token of his statesmanship in the compromise reached with Denmark in 1613, whereby Sweden obtained freedom of the Sound for the shipping of

---

[2] A. A. Stomberg, *History of Sweden* (New York, 1931), p. 308ff.

[3] W. Hubert, *Wojny Bałtyckie* (Warsaw, 1937), p. 234ff.; and in detail, St. Herbst, *Wojna Inflancka* (Warsaw, 1938).

Swedish, Rigan and Kuronian ports, while Denmark was allowed un-impeded commerce with Kurland and Livonia.

This satisfactory termination of the "War of Kalmar" left Gustavus Adolphus free to turn his considerable energies to the Muscovite question. In 1610, the boyars, after deposing Vassily Shuisky, had elected as their Tsar Władysław, the son of Sigismund III, a choice scarcely reassuring to Sweden. However, a Greek Orthodox people's party in Moscow, hearing rumors of Sigismund's fanatical determination to unite the Greek Orthodox Church with the Roman Catholic, opposed the accession of a Polish prince to their throne. Their own candidate, Michael Romanov, was elected Tsar in 1613 in a spirit of national revival which boded no ultimate friendliness for either Poland or Sweden.

In view of what promised to be imminent war with Poland, Tsar Michael appeared inclined, at least temporarily, to seek Swedish support. He acquiesced in Sweden's Livonian conquests, but insisted on the liberation of Novgorod and Pskov, both of which had fallen to Swedish arms during that country's attempt to take advantage of Muscovy's internal chaos before 1613. In 1617, the mediation of the Netherlands led to the conclusion of the treaty of Stolbovo between Sweden and Muscovy, by which Sweden, in return for the release of Novgorod and the recognition of Michael Romanov as Tsar, gained Keksholm, part of Ingria, and the assurance that Muscovy would renounce all pretensions to Estonia and Latvian Livonia. Free commercial relations were now established between the two conciliated Powers.[4]

By this treaty, Sweden found herself in a more favorable position in regard to Poland, who in 1618 offered an extension of the armistice of 1611. Sweden consented to continue the truce, in spite of Muscovy's anxious attempt to prevent the ripening of any good will between the two former enemies. This attempt even went to the length of offering Gustavus Adolphus a defensive alliance against Poland. But the Tsar's fears proved groundless, since the Polish-Swedish War of Succession was already verging on its inevitable second phase.

The politico-religious blocs had acquired further substance and added menace since the Netherlands had signed a fifteen-year defensive alliance with Sweden in 1614. England stood behind these Protestant Powers, which were later to receive the added support of France and many of the German princes. While these gathering forces

[4] E. C. Geijer, *Geschichte Schwedens*, III, 97.

stood at bay, Sigismund III persisted in his hope of stamping out heresy in Livonia. He quite consistently, if unrealistically, withheld recognition of the treaty of Stolbovo; his even more farfetched religious aims in regard to Sweden herself were matters of common knowledge. Under such conditions the resumption of the Polish-Swedish struggle was a matter of course.

Gustavus Adolphus, a firm believer in defensive aggression, descended on Riga with 158 ships and 19,000 men in July 1621. After five weeks of resistance, the German burghers decided to welcome the "hero of the north" in the hope that he might become German Emperor and thus be in a position to reward them generously. According to the ancient custom, a special gate, still known as the Swedish Gate, was broken into the walls of the city.[5]

Following this triumph the Swedish forces proceeded to conquer Jelgava (Mitau), Bauska, and Birži, strongholds of the Duchy of Kurland. The exiled Duke William's refusal to become Duke of all Livonia under Swedish suzerainty had brought upon his Duchy the burden of a Swedish occupational force. The Polish army, however, succeeded in recapturing a good part of the Swedish conquests in Livonia, leaving Riga and Pärnu isolated. In 1622, a respite was afforded by the conclusion of a three-year armistice.

After another outbreak of war with Denmark had been narrowly averted, Gustavus Adolphus, realizing the fragile nature of any truce with Poland, again took the offensive by occupying most of northern Livonia and then seizing the fortress of Koknese on the Daugava, whence he crossed into Kurland and Lithuania. Although confronted by some serious enemy opposition, the Swedish King successfully terminated what he considered a hard war by the brilliant victory of Wallhof on January 7, 1626.

That same year saw the shifting of the Swedish offensive to both East and West Prussia, which Gustavus considered, together with Kurland and Livonia, as the outworks of Protestant Sweden against the menace of the Catholic League, now thrusting on to the Baltic coast, where the Hapsburgs hoped to build a bastion against Sweden, England, and the Netherlands. With this widening of the sphere of action, the Polish-Swedish conflict had become an integral part of the devastating Thirty Years' War.

The gates of the Prussian cities swung open to the Protestant forces, with the exception of Danzig, which, true to its tradition of inde-

[5] T. Korzon, *Dzieje Wojen*, II (Cracow, 1912), 228ff.

pendence, held out stubbornly. Sigismund's vassal in East Prussia, George William, Elector of Brandenburg and brother-in-law of Gustavus, after a fatal hesitation, chose to remain loyal to his Polish suzerain, only to see half of his armies go over to the Swedish side.

In 1629, French diplomacy was able to mediate the truce of Altmark, which led to the peace of Bärwalde, ratified in January 1631. By this treaty, Sweden was confirmed in her dominion over Livonia, Estonia, and Ingria, as well as the major part of the Prussian coast. Although she recalled her occupation army from Kurland, she retained control of Memel and the Kurisches Haff north of Königsberg. In order to favor Memel, she insisted on the closing of the Kuronian ports to foreign trade. All that was left to Poland of her Livonian possessions was the Catholic province of Latgale, along the Muscovite border. The Elector of Brandenburg was compensated for the loss of Memel and Marienwerder by certain acquisitions in West Prussia.[6]

Gustavus Adolphus, secure in his title of *arbiter totius septentrionis*, could now confront the Catholic League and its redoubtable Waldstejn with high hopes of victory. While Sweden's control of Pomerania held in check both Lübeck and Denmark, her predominance in the Baltic assured an uninterrupted flow of supplies from the Netherlands. In addition to possessing the best artillery and heavy cavalry of all Europe, the Swedish army was now reinforced by conscripts from Latvian Livonia and Estonia. Gustavus Adolphus felt himself fully justified in pursuing his military creed of an offensive defensive by carrying the war against the Catholic League into Germany, where he made himself the protector of the Protestant League. Here, at the heart of his victory, lay the abrupt close of his grandiose career: death in battle against Waldstejn at Lützen, on November 6, 1632.

That same year also brought death to the great Swedish monarch's life-long enemy, Sigismund III of Poland. His son and heir, Władysław (1632-1648), sought to regain the Swedish throne by winning the hand of Gustavus' infant daughter Christina, but his suit was rejected. Władysław then reaffirmed the peace treaty signed by his father, at the same time renouncing all pretensions to the Swedish throne, and agreeing that the principle of *uti possidetis* should continue to be applied in Livonia. Presumably, peace was to obtain between Poland and Sweden until 1661.

The only remaining challenger of Sweden's Baltic supremacy was

[6] W. F. Reddaway in *Cambridge Modern History*, IV (Cambridge, 1906), 187f.; W. Sobieski, in *Historia polityczna Polski*, II (Cracow, 1923), 241f.

Denmark. Behind this mistress of the Sound stood the might of Spain, now engaged in a deadly struggle with Sweden's ally, the Netherlands. The Catholic Power wooed Denmark with the promise of a fleet in case Christian IV opened hostilities with Sweden, as well as the assurance of Spain's eventual recognition of Danish supremacy in the Baltic. Besides her ruling desire to isolate and crush the Netherlands, Spain cherished the further purpose of using the Baltic Sea as a transit route to Persia by way of Muscovy. Sweden alone stood in the way of such a scheme. Spain thought to prepare defeat for this Power by concluding an alliance with Poland and the rump-Hansa, promising the return of Livonia to the first, and to the second, expanded trade facilities once Sweden and the Netherlands were overthrown. Denmark fell in with these plans by offering to sign treaties with Spain, Poland, and Muscovy.[7]

In view of this cumulative menace, the Regent of Sweden, Axel Oxenstjerna, renewed the alliance with the Netherlands in 1640, for another fifteen years. Nevertheless Denmark, thoroughly committed to war, began hostilities in 1644. The promised Spanish Armada was defeated by the Swedish navy which attacked the clumsy galleons in the narrow Straits. The Dutch fleet now closed in on Denmark from the North Sea, while the Swedes pursued their advantage in the south. Thus pincered, Denmark was forced to sue for peace, this time on harder terms than in 1569 or 1613. By the treaty of Broemsebroe, concluded late in the summer of 1645, Denmark retired definitively from Estonia, ceded the much disputed Skäne district and Gotland to Sweden, and granted free passage through the Sound to the shipping of Sweden, Finland, Ingria, Estonia, Latvia, Kurland, Prussia, and Pomerania—the entire gamut of Swedish dominance. This treaty marked the final term of Denmark's persistent competition for the *dominium maris Baltici*.

Sweden's prestige was further enhanced by the Peace of Westphalia which brought the Thirty Years' War to a close in 1648. In addition to obtaining the Baltic island of Rügen, the city of Bremen, and the provinces of Wismar and Pomerania, Sweden was awarded five million thalers of German indemnity and the right to participate in the German Reichstag.

Finally, the position of Livonia's northern master was naturally strengthened in proportion to the growing weakness of the former suzerain, Poland. The Polish monarchy, never powerful at best, was

---

[7] Konopczyński, *op.cit.*, p. 101ff.

seriously compromised, upon the death of Władysław in 1648, by the election of his politically inexperienced brother, Cardinal John Casimir, who had renounced his cardinalate to marry his brother's wife. The Queen and the magnates were now the actual rulers of the Joint Kingdom, which was once more threatened by the resuscitated ambitions of Muscovy.

The latter Power, convinced that the time had finally come to demolish the tottering might of Poland, in 1655 presented a scheme for partitioning that country among Hungary, Brandenburg, and Sweden.[8] Charles X, a cousin of and successor to the unstable Queen Christina, who had abdicated the Swedish throne in 1654, preferred to play a solitary hand in the belief that Sweden stood a fair chance of recapturing the Polish crown. As early as 1648, Prince Radziwiłł had secretly approached the Scandinavian Prince with a plan for Lithuania's secession from the Joint Kingdom and union with Sweden. Charles, offended by John Casimir's refusal to grant him recognition as King of Sweden, lent himself to the connivings of the Polish and Lithuanian magnates rather than to the plan of partition, which suggested an objectionable Russian dominance of Lithuania and renewed pressure upon Livonia.

Thus Muscovy and Sweden launched separate attacks against Poland. The well-conceived Swedish operations proved immediately successful. Charles executed a pincers attack. One army landed in Livonia and marched southwest; the other, led by Charles in person, landed in Pomerania and marched southeast. Dünaburg, which the Muscovites had stormed uselessly for weeks, fell in July 1655. Charles arrived in Warsaw on August 20, and in Cracow the following October.[9] There several members of the Polish szlachta sought to induce the Swedish monarch to accept the Polish crown, on the assumption that the vacillating John Casimir could be forced to abdicate. However, many of the gentry found the idea of either Swedish or Muscovite rule equally distasteful.

The Tsar, also a candidate for the Polish throne, now offered a military alliance to Poland, on condition that she should attack Sweden through Prussia, while the Muscovites, gathering at Vilna, began action in Livonia. The poorly defended fortresses of Dünaburg and Koknese fell an easy prey; but Riga, besieged in August 1656,

[8] N. H. Gundling, Discours über den jetzigen Zustand der Europäischen Staaten, II (Leipzig, 1733), 349.

[9] L. Kubala, Wojna Szwecka 1655-1656 (Warsaw, 1913), passim.

treated the Muscovites to her customary resistance. The burghers, co-operating with the Swedish garrison under General de la Gardie, repulsed all attacks of the large Tsarist force. Early in October, Prince Dolgoruky, to whom had been reported the approach of a strong relief detachment commanded by Charles X himself, ordered his troops to retreat. This they did in considerable panic until halted at Koknese by the Tsar, who took up residence in that fortress. Eventually, the Muscovites withdrew through Estonia, in the direction of Pskov, burning Dorpat and leaving in their wake an unforgettable sample of their terroristic retreat tactics. The rich variety of their barbarisms gave rise to sermons and prayers in the Livonian churches for the protection of Providence against any further Muscovite invasions.

The convincing success of Charles X both in Poland, which he largely occupied, and in Livonia, whence he had expelled the Tsarist armies, sufficiently impressed the Duke of Prussia and Elector of Brandenburg, Frederick William, to cause him to secede from Polish suzerainty in November 1656 and conclude an alliance with invincible Sweden. Being in no position to reclaim her fief, Poland formally ceded East Prussia to Frederick William at Wehlau in 1657, thus laying the foundations of the future Kingdom of Prussia.

Sweden's star, so long in its ascendancy, had by now attracted the unfavorable attention of Europe's jealous Powers. Muscovy's declared enmity, focused in Tsar Alexis' candidacy for the Polish throne, found echoes in the opposition of another candidate, Leopold, the Hapsburg Emperor and King of Bohemia, as well as in the discontent of Hungary, the renewed pretensions of Denmark, and the waxing jealousy of the Netherlands, now intriguing with Denmark against the "Arbiter of the North." England alone remained faithful to the old Protestant alliance.

By the end of 1659, Sweden's situation had become precarious, in spite of certain successes in Denmark and a few defeats inflicted on Muscovy. The death of Charles X in February 1660 promised well for the French and English efforts to mediate a peace. Ambassador de Besminiers achieved the considerable feat of reconciling the diverse interests of Sweden, Poland, Prussia, Denmark, and the Duchy of Kurland in the momentous treaty of Oliva, signed on May 3, 1660.

By this settlement Poland once more recognized Sweden's dominion over Estonia and Latvian Livonia (Vidzeme), including Riga and the island of Rüno in the Gulf of Riga. At the same time, Poland finally renounced the claims of her Vasa line to the crown of Sweden.

The Peace of Oliva also formalized East Prussia's independence under her Hohenzollern ruler, the Elector of Brandenburg.[10]

The following June saw the conclusion of peace between Sweden and Denmark by the treaty of Copenhagen. Peace with Muscovy had to wait another year for Alexis to retreat from Koknese, which he burnt to the ground, and to renounce all pretensions to Livonia at Kardis, in July 1661. The Polish-Muscovite war was to continue for another six years of bitter struggle over the Ukraine. This province was ultimately partitioned in 1667 by the peace of Andrussovo, which fixed the Dnieper as the boundary line between Muscovy and Poland. At the same time, the Tsar agreed to withdraw his armies from Latgale, which had been under devastating occupation for nearly ten years.

We have thus far in this chapter devoted our whole attention to the power politics and the wars for which Livonia provided the terrain. The ambitions and the anxieties of a dozen European Powers swirled over this little land, leaving her scarcely time or quiet to draw her breath in peace. Yet the final victory of Sweden ushered in a period which Latvians and Estonians have long looked back to as a golden age. The measures of reform that were instituted by successive Swedish rulers reveal a humane interest in the welfare of a hitherto cruelly subjugated people which should be clearly credited to Sweden's account.

The almost incessant wars waged on Livonian soil during the second half of the sixteenth and the first two decades of the seventeenth century had severely afflicted the entire region. Many cities were burned beyond hope of restoration; while in others only a few souls survived, as in Limbaži, where eight people remained alive, and Valka, from which there emerged three survivors.[11] Wooden churches were gutted, farmsteads were burned over the length and breadth of the land, and a great number of the stone manorial castles stood in ruins.

The extent of the impoverishment of the area was revealed in the successive land revisions, which the enterprising Swedish Government ordered made in Vidzeme in 1601, 1617, 1624, 1630, and 1638. Of the 5151 farmsteads which existed at the end of the sixteenth century, only 2416 were in operation by 1624. Cattle and horses had become so rare that frequently the peasants had to replace them at the plow. Of the mere 1331 unci (one Livonian uncus equaling 44.362 acres)

[10] See in general E. Haumant, La guerre du Nord et la paix d'Oliva (Paris, 1893).
[11] Z. Ligers, Histoire des villes de Lettonie (Paris, 1946), pp. 130, 147.

under cultivation, only about 36 per cent were actually capable of providing labor-duty for the manors.

Yet the squires continued to multiply their demands upon the decimated peasantry, increasing both the produce charges and the labor-duty beyond all reason. Failure to meet these requirements provoked such atrocious punishment that, according to an early Latvian historian, even the dogs were better treated. The serfs of Livonia, like their fellow-sufferers in Poland, Hungary, Bohemia, Prussia, and Brandenburg, were without recourse in face of the merciless impositions and vicious reprisals of their masters.

At the time of Sweden's assumption of control over Livonia, the population consisted largely of indigenous farmers, most of them *adscripti*, although a number of freeholders were still to be found in the remoter rural areas. These native Latvians and Estonians had been markedly helpful to the Swedish forces during the Swedish-Polish and Swedish-Muscovite wars. The German ruling class, on the other hand, had shown a high degree of indifference to these contests.

Gustavus Adolphus was fully aware of the temper of the Livonian Germans. He was inclined to sympathize with the contemptuous attitude of their successive Polish suzerains. Nor was he forgetful of the arrogance with which the Livonian nobles in 1601 had met his father's request, in the name of Christianity, to alleviate the situation of the peasantry, to open schools for their children, and to allow them a free choice of trades. Gustavus Adolphus' attitude toward the Baltic squirearchy was at best one of reserve, expressed in 1621 by his promise to respect only such of their rightful privileges as did not harm the interest of the Swedish state.

The Latvians were not disappointed in their expectation of some degree of protection from this Swedish monarch, who was reputedly a just man and a Christian. Although their experience with German-Balt and Polish or Lithuanian feudal masters had been a consistently cruel one, the peasants hoped for better treatment from a new group of overlords. Lacking a civil service, and anxious to strengthen the political ties between Sweden and her new dependency, Gustavus Adolphus decided to install Swedish nobles in local administrative positions, in the courts, and in the Diet. To this end, he bestowed large Latvian domains on Swedish generals and officials, particularly on those who had served him well in the wars. Thus, in 1622, the King's trusted councillor, Axel Oxenstjerna, was granted the castle of Cēsis with its surrounding lands, together with the large district of

Valmiera.[12] Ultimately, more than half of Vidzeme's taxable farm-lands (as distinguished from the non-taxable manors) came into the possession of a new group of manor-lords.

Upon his assumption of control over Vidzeme, Gustavus Adolphus had promised to restore the Lutheran churches and their pastorates, as well as to establish schools, hospitals, and poorhouses. One of the first concerns of the Swedish administration was to uphold the Lutheran faith, which had been undermined in Latvian Livonia by Polish-sponsored Roman Catholicism, and in Estonia by the Greek Orthodox influence of the Muscovites.

By 1630, the new administration of the Evangelical Lutheran Church, directed by the Consistory of Riga, had ordained forty-eight pastors as against the five in existence in 1623. Twenty-two of the fifty Livonian churches and chapels had been restored. The newly-organized parish boards were to consist of two local squires and three farmers. One of the Latvian members was allowed to act as sacristan, keeping the records and reading the hymnals in Latvian, in contrast to the pastors, who for the most part spoke only German. A few of the native-born pastors prepared Latvian textbooks for their German colleagues.

The law of 1634 which established the new church organization in Vidzeme also provided for parish schools, since the few which had been opened during the Catholic period had died of neglect. The following acute analysis of the attitude of the German squires toward education is offered by Pastor Paul Einhorn, in his *Historia Lettica*: "Most of the Germans look upon the establishment of schools as inadvisable . . . because they fear evil consequences. For they say, if the Latvians should be allowed to attend schools, and obtain the right to move around freely, and to reach the stage where they might be able to read and understand the chronicles of their land, and to discover that in ancient times the country belonged to them, and that they were the masters therein, and that the Germans had seized it from them, and had pressed them into serfdom and slavery; . . . then they would relentlessly strive to free themselves from this serfdom and to regain their land and their former status."[13]

He goes on to give an example of such possibilities in the time of the Livonian Order when "certain Germans had translated one or two pages from the Chronicles into their own (Latvian) language,

---

[12] Ligers, *op.cit.*, pp. 91, 151.
[13] P. Einhorn, *Historia Lettica*, in *Script. rer. liv.*, II, 202.

and read to them how the land had formerly belonged to them and
how the Germans had brought them to slavery and serfdom. . . .
Carefully they listened, and then, thinking that no one overheard
them, began to discuss what to do. They decided to inform other
Latvians about what they had learned so that they might gather
throughout the land, attack the Germans, and drive them out of the
country."[14]

Hermann Samson von Himmelstjerna, senior pastor of the Cathedral of Riga, in his capacity as director of the Swedish religious and
educational reforms, reported and reprimanded the indolence of the
squires in providing for the spiritual needs of the farmers; their unwillingness to pay their pastors; and their outright refusal to repair
churches or open parish schools. The incorrigible nobles persisted in
flogging their pastors and withholding their salaries. These deplorable
conditions in great part determined the low calibre of the men who
supplied the dilapidated Latvian churches. Ill-educated and supersti-
tious, they did little to correct the benighted views of their parishioners. Instead, they gave full credence to the current tales of witchcraft, which led to the victimization of so many Latvian women.
Von Himmelstjerna himself published a collection of nine sermons
against witches.[15] Nor did the Livonian-German judges show any
greater enlightenment than the pastors, whose word they accepted in
the cruel witch trials. These sermons and legal processes provided the
nobles with further justification for their oppression of the "heathen"
Latvians.

The most successful early Swedish reforms were in the legal sphere.
A promise of progress was given when Gustavus Adolphus appointed
Johann Scytte, his tutor and a pupil of Hugo Grotius, as Viceroy of
Vidzeme in 1629. The court reform which followed provided a startling contrast to the judicial anarchy which had hitherto existed in
Livonia. At one stroke the nobles were deprived of their self-assumed
right to judge and condemn the inhabitants of the manors and the
rural communities, whom they must henceforth deliver over for judgment to the new district courts in Riga, Wenden, and Koknese. The
highest court of appeals was to be the *Hofgericht* in Dorpat, where a
university, the Academia Gustaviana, was opened in 1631.

Unfortunately, the manor-lords were permitted to retain the right

[14] Einhorn, *op.cit.*, 603.
[15] Hermann Samson von Himmelstjerna, *Neun Hexenpredigten* (Riga,
1626).

to inflict "a just and moderate correction" in cases of minor transgressions for which the customary punishment was a beating with "ten
pairs of rods." Abuse soon became the rule, while complaints to the
district courts were effectively discouraged by threats. Gustavus
Adolphus did not live long enough to extirpate these abuses by which
the nobility gradually undermined his judicial reforms. Two years
after the monarch's death, his enlightened viceroy fell a victim to
intrigue and was recalled from his efforts to liberalize Livonia.

On the whole, this first period of Swedish dominance, although
strongly colored by the relatively progressive beliefs of a powerful
king, did not see any lessening of the lawless authority of the Livonian
squires, who were adept at finding ways of saving their interests from
actual interference. Livonia's particularly vulnerable geographical position in wartime obliged Sweden to compromise with the German
landed nobles in order not to alienate entirely this ruling class. Furthermore, the Swedish exchequer favored the preservation of the *status
quo*, even to the extent of farming out some of the taxes to the squires,
who gladly undertook to squeeze still more tribute out of the peasantry.
To that end, a decree of the regency, in 1634, permitted the punishment of "laziness" with "ten pairs of rods."

That same year the regency also allowed the Livonian nobles to
elect a *Landmarschall* to act as an intermediary between the Swedish
governor-general and the squires, among whom the Swedish element,
a minority, had largely succumbed to the influence of the German-Balt
nobility, with whom they shared the interests of caste. In 1642, the
landed nobles obtained the right to establish their own bank. The
following year, they were permitted to convene in their own Estonian
and Livonian Diets in which, unlike the Swedish *Riksdag*, the farmers
had no representation. At the same time, there was established in Riga
the Council of the *Landrats* (Diet), consisting of three Swedish and
three Livonian-German councilors, whose function it was to act as a
permanent advisory board to the governor-general.

In 1640, the German vice-president of the *Hofgericht* in Dorpat had
been commissioned to prepare a new civil code for Vidzeme. Three
years later, he presented to Stockholm for approval what amounted to
a revision of the sinister von Hilchen code of serfdom. This the regency
found unacceptable, and in 1648 the old *Ritterrecht* was revived until
a new *Corpus Juris Livonici* could be compounded. The Livonian
squires took umbrage at the restoration of this ancient code which
contained no provisions for serfs. The latter, however, were far from

any improvement in their actual status since the legalization of the *Zuschlagung* in 1650 allowed the Livonian nobles to pay off their own debts by loaning out serfs to creditors, who collected the maximum of labor-duty. Queen Christina sought to compensate the manor-lords for the offensive *Ritterrecht* by permitting the enlargement of the above-mentioned Riga Council to a total of twelve members, three of whom became *ex officio* assessors of the *Hofgericht*. The politically confused Swedish Queen also granted the request of the aristocratic *Landrats* to have the scrolls of the Livonian landed nobles renewed, as a means of reinforcing the oligarchical character of the squirearchy. Thus almost all the feudal privileges which the manor-lords had enjoyed in the days of the Livonian Order were gradually reestablished in accordance with the increasingly reactionary tendencies of the Swedish Government under a queen who would not oppose the pressures of the Swedish aristocracy.

Her successor, Charles X Gustavus (1654-1660), sensing the growing disgruntlement of the Swedish burghers, professional classes, and farmers, obtained from the *Riksdag* the power to reduce the state domains and liberate the farmers from the serfdom which the Swedish landed nobles, following the Central European and Baltic pattern, had sought to introduce on their estates. This same liberal measure was to have been applied in Livonia where, likewise, Swedish Crown lands had been appropriated by noble leaseholders. But the Muscovite War (1656-1661) postponed any such salutary action in the threatened dependency.

After the death of Charles X in 1660 and during the infancy of his son, the German Dowager Queen Hedwiga Eleanora assumed the regency, and another period of reaction overshadowed the liberal advances both in Sweden and her dependencies. In 1660, Queen Eleanora granted the Livonian nobles the right to retain the appropriated Crown domains until the coming of age of Charles XI in 1672.

In 1668, the Livonian squires cajoled Governor-General Tott into allowing the compulsory control of fugitive peasants. Their plea was based on the assumption that the manor-lord (*Erbherr*) possessed the *potestas privata* over the "hereditary peasant" (*Erbbauer*). Tott's *Polizei Ordnungen*, issued in 1671, not only recognized this *potestas privata* but extended it to the pursuit and recovery of fugitive peasants, on the official grounds that the manor was not a property in the private law sense but a part of the territory of the state. The further argument was advanced that, by granting the squires the right to retain on their manors every man who had settled or been born thereon, the governor-general was more sure to receive the charges due to his treasury by the Latvian farmers and collected by the manor-lords.

Certainly, Sweden's laissez-faire attitude in Livonia was partly attributable to the increasingly deplorable state of her own finances during the regency. Charles XI (1672-1697) adopted a more constructive policy toward the grave economic and financial ills which beset his country and her dependencies. In 1680, the *Riksdag* began an investigation of the misdeeds of previous regencies which resulted in the granting to Charles XI of almost unlimited authority in the restoration of the economic foundations of the state. As an essential means to this end, the *Riksdag* once more reaffirmed the reduction not only of the Crown domains in Sweden, but also of the state lands in Finland, Ingria, Estonia, and Latvian Livonia or Vidzeme.

On April 27, 1681, the King, through his Governor-General of Livonia, Lichton, who was also the chairman of the Livonian Reduction Committee, addressed the following three proposals to the Livonian Diet:

"1. In order to afford the necessary means to the State for the welfare of the country, the reduction of the public domains should be effectuated.

2. All the land should be measured and assessed.

3. For the sake of justice and Christian morals, the habits of ancient pagan times, the wretched slavery and serfdom under the yoke of which so many Christians suffer, should be abolished."[16]

The issuance of such proposals only ten years after Count Tott's Police Ordinances dumbfounded the Livonian landed nobles. The Diet, invoking its privileges, categorically rejected every point in the King's program; whereupon Major-General Lichton, by royal instruction, served a further notification, with some reassuring legal modifications, on the recalcitrant *Landrats*.

During the initial period of its activity (1681-1685), the Commission of Reduction confined itself to those domains granted as knight's fiefs by the Swedish Government. Even this activity was systematically hampered by the Livonian squires, led by the Latvian noble Johann Reinhold von Patkul. In 1688, the King appointed Jacob Johann Hastfehr, also of Livonian origin, Governor-General of Livonia. Hon-

---

[16] F. F. Carlson, *Geschichte Schwedens*, v (Gotha, 1855), 158ff.

est and energetic, possessing the full confidence of the King, he lost no time in crushing the resistance of the Livonian Germans, while at the same time extending his protection to the Latvian peasantry. Thus the reduction proceeded successfully, and five-sixths of the whole area of Vidzeme, producing an annual income of 543,000 thalers, came under state ownership, with the noble landholders becoming tenants of the Crown. All reduced properties yielding up to 1,500 thalers of revenue were let on hereditary lease to their former proprietors, whose rent was collectable beginning in 1687. In addition, the tenants must pay up all state revenues in arrears since 1681. The larger estates were leased out to the highest bidder.[17]

Upon the completion of the land reduction in Livonia, the Swedish Government faced the necessity of ascertaining the new assets of the state economy. In February 1687, and again in June 1688, Charles XI issued decrees for the written assessment of the dues, taxes, charges, and other monies paid by the Latvian farmers, and their balance against the net income which the cultivators obtained from their lands. Both the area and the productivity of the land were to be taken into account.

The results of this thorough and remarkably efficient land revision were collected into five large volumes known as the Great Livonian Cadaster. The data supplied, including the names of the landowners, description of lots, fertility of the land, size of the harvests, net surpluses, charges, dues, etc., are an invaluable source of information on this period of the Latvian agricultural economy, and present an important progressive step in this still feudal land.

Thanks to this assessment, the peasant taxation system in Vidzeme was ready for reformation on the Swedish pattern. This equitable system, introduced by King Gustav Ericson in the 1530's, was based on the actual grain income of the farmsteads, in contrast to the system obtaining in Livonia, where only the size of the holding was taken into consideration, so that the holders of poor soil became hopelessly indebted. The new tax unit was to be the Swedish "taxation uncus," an arbitrary measurement comprising that area of farmland which could produce a net surplus of sixty Swedish tons of rye, that is, could give a net income of sixty thalers, the price of a ton of rye being computed at one thaler.

In addition to the grain tithe, other produce dues and the much-abused labor-duty were now set at a certain taxation value based on

[17] Carlson, op.cit., v, 518.

fixed units. The various dues were proportioned in such a way that the farmer found himself with some surplus left, which he was free to dispose of in the market. By royal decree, the stewards of the Crown manors and the tenant squires were forbidden to exact more labor-duty or contributions than were fixed in the rural registers (*vaka* books). Extraordinary labor-duty was to be calculated in the regular dues, while the commutation of any labor-duty into any form of produce or money contributions was forbidden.

These decrees applied only to the Crown lands or leased Crown estates; but since five-sixths of all Latvian farmers actually dwelt on such domains, these reforms may be said to have profited the whole peasant class. Furthermore, since the communal pastures and meadows of the rural communities remained unestimated and unassessed, this afforded a net profit to the cattle raisers and horse breeders, and constituted an inducement to the farmers to develop these activities.

The economic emancipation of the farmers was further advanced by their acknowledged right to sell what surpluses remained to them after payment of taxes, and by their ability to free themselves from taxes by payment of a lump sum. Under unfavorable circumstances, the farmers were allowed an abatement of their liabilities. Not only were the leaseholders of Crown lands forbidden to expel their peasants, but in some cases they were obliged to grant them loans. So markedly improved was the Latvian farmer's lot during this last and most progressive period of Swedish preponderance that a few of the abler ones contrived to amass a certain degree of wealth, and even make financial loans to the Government in time of war.

Charles XI, known in his own country as the *Bondekong*, or Peasant King, had a deep appreciation of the value of a healthy peasantry to the state. It was with a full realization of the importance to Sweden of a sound agricultural economy in Livonia, the rich "Granary of the Baltic," that he forced through his land and tax reforms in this dependency. And it was with an enlightened knowledge of the importance of human welfare to the development of the land that he concerned himself ardently with the political, social, and cultural improvement of the peasant farmers. This attitude of their King was equally deplored by the landed nobility, whether Swedish or Livonian.

The latter found the protective royal decrees intolerably irksome. The abolition of serfdom alone would have been enough to alienate the squires. Coming as it did in conjunction with the drastic land reductions, it placed the landed interests in unyielding opposition to the Swedish protectorate, which had so effectively restored royal authority over the jealously autonomous Baltic oligarchies. In 1692, the Wenden Diet once more protested against the reduction, Patkul again appearing as the chief inciter to rebellion. When, in the 1693 Diet, the squires persisted in their uncooperative temper, the King ordered both the board of the Diet and Patkul to appear for trial in Stockholm, where only the intercession of the Queen saved them from death. Patkul, of whom we shall hear more later, even managed to escape from prison.

Late in 1694, the intractable Livonian Diet of the nobles was reorganized by royal decree. Henceforth it was to be convoked only by order of the King, and was to serve merely as a consultative body fully subject to the Governor-General, now its chairman, who was to appoint the new administrative committees replacing the Council of the *Landrats* which had favored the Livonian squires. The reformed Diet, convened in July 1696, no longer exercised any power over the Latvian farmers.[18]

The latter were further benefited by the statute of March 21, 1696, which, in regulating the relations between the farmers and the leaseholders of the state domains, deprived the nobles of the right of paternal correction (*Hauszucht*). Not only must the leaseholders henceforth bring all their complaints against their peasants to the rural courts but the farmers themselves had now obtained the right to carry complaints against their masters up through the rural and district courts even to the Royal Court in Stockholm where, in fact, several such complaints were received.

Finally, the Latvians received from the Swedish protectorate enough attention to their cultural famine to effect at least the beginning of their salvation from that spiritual and intellectual starvation which had been their doom since German feudalism had ended all liberty. Belatedly, the great lights kindled by the Renaissance and the Reformation were to be allowed to flicker over the east Baltic lands, whose peasant populations now received their first heady taste of schooling and of reading books in their native languages; as well as, through the use of religious handbooks in the vernacular, their first intimate knowledge of the Protestant faith, which hitherto had seemed but one more aspect of Germanism, and as such scarcely worth their attention.

In 1687, compulsory parish schools, as well as a few normal schools to prepare teachers for the parish institutions, were opened in Vid-

[18] Carlson, *op.cit.*, v, 517.

zeme. In certain of the parishes pastors of Latvian origin who had graduated from the University of Dorpat were installed. Beginning in 1685, a financial subsidy from the Crown assured the printing of a Latvian version of the Bible, while a number of didactic-religious works, as well as grammars and vocabularies, now appeared in the vernacular. Even a few of the Royal Ordinances were printed in Latvian. Thus, at the height of its power, the Swedish administration sowed the first seeds of a harvest which, though far slower to ripen than the abundant Livonian grain, was to yield its rich crop in an era when Sweden's control over Latvian Livonia was no more than a relatively grateful memory.

We have left to the last a discussion of Swedish influence in Riga, since that city has hitherto generally presented a particular aspect and a special problem. Characteristically, before her submission to Gustavus Adolphus in 1621, Riga had tried to retain the good will, at least in trading terms, of the Swedes, the Poles, and the Lithuanians. Gustavus Adolphus, eager to befriend the burghers of this important port, nine days after their capitulation granted the city councilors a code of privileges no less liberal than that obtained from Stephen Bátory. Riga was declared the sole trading port of Livonia, and her merchants acquired liberal trading rights in Sweden.[19] The city was even invited to send delegates to the *Riksdag*, a privilege of which the councilors availed themselves only once. They had thereupon decided that participation in the Stockholm Diet lowered the prestige of Riga as a former autonomous Imperial city.[20]

During the last decade of the reign of Gustavus Adolphus, Riga became the largest city in the Swedish realm, surpassing even Stockholm in population. By 1648, Riga had a thousand merchants importing goods from Russia, forty concerned with Lithuanian imports, and about thirty exporters of Livonian goods proper. The war with Muscovy proved a serious hindrance to the Riga trade in mid-century, but trading activities with the Muscovites flourished to an even greater extent after the peace. The valorous repulse of the Tsarist forces by the Riga militia in 1656 inspired Charles X to ennoble all sixteen of the city councilors and permit them to crown the lion on Riga's coat of arms.

The self-governing and self-perpetuating administration of Riga was allowed to remain unchanged all during the period of Sweden's

[19] J. Straubergs, *Rigas vēsture*, p. 330ff.
[20] Nils Ahnlund, *Gustav Adolf the Great* (Princeton, N.J., 1940), p. 204f.

dominion. This meant the continuation of German control of internal city affairs, since the Elders of the exclusively German Great Guild and Artisans' Guild held the leading role in the administration. Although Latvians came in increasing numbers to settle in the suburbs, they were still entirely dominated by the oligarchic Riga Council.

Riga's growing population and wealth were matched by developments in the cultural sphere which made this, the largest of the Baltic cities, a lively intellectual center with Sweden's benevolent approval. As early as 1621, Gustavus Adolphus had reorganized the Cathedral School, which soon opened its doors to Latvians. In 1631, this college obtained further privileges, and in 1675, gaining in importance, was renamed the Academia Carolina. It was to persist into modern times when it was called the Governmental College of Riga.[21]

In 1632, the local Swedish postmaster began publication of a Riga newspaper called *Awihses*. The city printing office and the new Royal Printing Office, while publishing most of their books in German or Latin, did produce a few in Latvian, reprinting several times the Latvian religious handbook and hymnal. We have already mentioned the 1683-1689 edition of the Bible in Latvian.

While Swedish rule in Livonia brought about a certain freeing of the economic and cultural forces so long undeveloped in that region, Sweden's preponderance in the Baltic led to the establishment of that sea as a *mare liberatum*. This was in contrast to the *mare clausum* of the Hansa era, a concept which had become obsolete sometime before the dissolution of the Hanseatic League in 1669.

Mare Balticum Liberatum was the title of an anonymous treatise published in 1649 for the purpose of justifying the preponderance of Sweden in the Baltic. The author was at pains to emphasize the thesis that the freedom of the seas, at least theoretically, is as old as Western civilization. He based his argument on that of Francisco de Vittoria who, in his *De Potestate Civili*, had maintained that any interference with all men's divinely ordained right to communicate with one another would be in violation of that "natural right" pointed out by Hugo Grotius.

Such theorizing was properly in tune with the times. On the Baltic, as on other waters, sails were set to the winds of commercial expansion. English, Dutch, Swedish, and Kuronian ships carried the goods of Muscovy, the Livonian grains, the Kuronian timber, without restrictions, in free and flourishing competition which benefited the whole

[21] Ligers, *Histoire des villes de Lettonie*, p. 72.

area of Sweden's hegemony. Soon that perennial yearner after Baltic profits, Muscovy, was to take advantage of this freedom of traffic to confront Sweden herself with an ominous threat to her reasonable and humane ascendancy.

Chapter 10

The Duchy of Kurland

THE course of events in the Duchy of Kurland form a history within a history which, for the purposes of our study, must receive the same attention as the wars and policies of the larger Livonian canvas, since each of the kingdoms which made up this small principality, Kurzeme and Zemgale, was to constitute about a fifth of modern Latvia. The fact that this area was comparatively free of the onslaughts of war and that its position as a dukedom, even though a vassal one, gave it a degree of cultural solidarity and independence, enabled this nexus of a modern state to mature more rapidly than the rest of trampled and turmoiled Livonia.

Seventeenth-century Kurland also provides a neat example of small-scale absolutism. Its history is that of its dukes, vigorous and tenacious rulers, who summoned the forces of influential family connections and marshaled the natural resources of their domains to win a place in the increasingly competitive European state system. A skillful balance of pressure and compromise had to be attained in dealing with the Kuronian nobles, who supported their sovereigns' policies only so long as their class interests were well served thereby. As for the Latvian people, whose heavy labor fattened the trade of the Duchy and manned her conspicuous navy, their opinion concerned neither the foreign monarchs who chose to patronize the hustling dukes, nor the nobility who monopolized the Diets, nor the uniformly power-conscious dukes themselves, from Gothard to the last of the Kettlers, Frederick William, whose death, in 1711, coincided with Kurland's achievement of independence.

We have seen how the Duchy of Kurland's first sovereign, Duke Gothard, founded the Kettler dynasty and stabilized the internal structure of his new state by working out a compromise with the dissident nobles. With his death in 1587, a critical period began for this Polish fief, since its rule was divided between Gothard's two sons; the elder, Frederick, becoming the Duke of Zemgale, and William, the younger, receiving the dukedom of Kurzeme proper. This weakened control was just the opportunity which the ever restless nobility awaited. With the encouragement of the Polish *Sejm*, they now elected two subversive Diets, one for Zemgale and one for Kurzeme. Further, the Kuronian landed nobles lost no time in conspiring with the Polish *szlachta* to effect the direct incorporation of Kurzeme into the Joint Kingdom, where the nobility enjoyed such enviable scope.[1] In 1615, Duke William went so far as to disband the treasonous Diet in his province and execute some of the worst offenders against his sovereignty.

The Kurzeme Diet, reconvening without the permission of its Duke, accused him of murder, and sent a delegation to Sigismund III asking for William's removal from power. The Polish King, who had fostered the opposition of the nobility, had every reason for wishing to see Duke William deposed and his son Jacob barred from the succession. Under such circumstances, and after the death of the childless Frederick of Zemgale, the whole Duchy of Kurland, in accordance with the treaty concluded with Gothard Kettler in 1561, would automatically escheat to the Polish suzerain and become a Crown province.

In November 1615, Sigismund III appointed an Extraordinary Commission to examine the case which the Kurzeme Diet had brought against its Duke. Upon William's refusal to submit to investigation, the Warsaw *Sejm* summoned him for trial. Again, he refused. On May 4, 1616, on the advice of the Extraordinary Commission, the Polish *Sejm* dethroned Duke William and deprived his son of his heritage. Whereupon William Kettler fled to Germany, taking the young Jacob with him to be reared at a German court. Duke Frederick of Zemgale was now permitted to assume the rule of the once more united Duchy of Kurland.

In 1617, Duke Frederick, under pressure from Warsaw, where the Kuronian nobility continued to exert its influence, granted his subjects a second constitution, the so-called *Formula Regiminis*. This document, elaborated by the Polish *Sejm* in conjunction with the representatives of the Kuronian landed nobles, contained what were to be the administrative and judicial statutes of the Duchy, based in general on the Roman law.[2] Although it essentially repeated the first constitution, the *Privilegium Gothardianum*, some further rights were accorded to the ruling class of the landed nobles who were now recognized as a Corporation or Estate, with the right to keep its own scrolls. Perpetuity of privilege was provided for in the stipulation that no act or

---

[1] W. Konopczyński, *Dzieje Polski nowożytnej*, 1 (Warsaw, 1936), 263ff.

[2] C. S. von Ziegenhorn, *Staatsrecht der Herzogtümer Kurland und Semigallen* (Königsberg, 1772), doc. no. 76.

statute issued either by the duke personally, or by the Kuronian Diet, should contradict that piece of class legislation which was the *Formula Regiminis*.

The new constitution provided that in case of the duke's absence from his country the regency should be assumed by the Ducal Council, consisting of the chancellor or prime minister, who was appointed by the duke, and of five councilors nominated by the Diet and confirmed by the duke. This Ducal Council was the highest administrative organ in the Duchy. Supplemented by four assessors elected by the Diet, it also formed the *Oberhofsgericht*, or the highest Ducal Court for both civil and criminal cases.

The Duchy was administratively divided into the three autonomous provinces of Kurzeme, Zemgale, and Piltene, each with its own Diet, and headed by the *Capitanus major*, a military and civil chief appointed by the duke from among the nobility. These chiefs were competent to judge cases involving non-nobles and foreigners; while the nobles were tried by the *Mannrichter*, who were elected by the Diets.

The Diet of the Duchy as a whole was usually convoked by the duke at two-year intervals. It was composed exclusively of representatives of the nobility (the *Ritterschaft*), who were elected in parish conventions where they received mandatory instructions. In general, the function of the Diet was to harmonize the demands of the duke and of the nobility, and to approve all taxes. It possessed only an advisory capacity in the economic and social development of the Duchy, and no direct influence in foreign affairs.

Neither the peasants, the bourgeoisie, nor the clergy had either representation or influence in the Kuronian Diets. The dukes, however, did not altogether neglect the interests of the two latter classes, upon whom depended both the spiritual independence and the economic progress of this emergent state. As early as 1567, Duke Gothard had urged the Diet to donate certain lands for sustenance to the projected Lutheran parishes of Kurzeme and Zemgale. His primary aim was to strengthen Lutheranism in his domains in order to toughen their resistance to the pressures of Catholic Lithuania and Poland. The landed nobility was thrown a sop in the shape of clerical patronage, a privilege they guarded jealously, appointing generations of German pastors who made little effort to understand even the language of their exclusively Latvian parishes. As for the cities, the most they could expect from a benevolent despotism which must pamper its ruling class above all others, was respect for their traditional self-government, which was in the hands of the city councils. The burgomaster, like the members of the City Council, was elected for life, and had to be confirmed by the duke. To these oligarchical city councils belonged the Elders of the guilds, whose members alone enjoyed all electoral privileges.

The first capital of the Duchy of Kurland had been Kuldīga, the leading city of the old tribal kingdom of Kurzeme, and, under the name of Jesusburg, the former seat of the powerful comtur of Kurzeme. In 1576, the capital was transferred to Jelgava (Mitau), also an ancient tribal site and a fortress of the Livonian Order, which was soon to become an important economic and cultural center. Next in importance were the ports of Liepāja (Libau) and Ventspils (Windau), the latter soon to be known all over Europe for its shipbuilding,[3] for which Duke William had managed to launch an ambitious program during his short rule.

Full economic development of the potentially rich Duchy of Kurland could not be attained until the shadow of the covetous Polish King had passed from this fief. Sigismund III, who had given his blessing to Frederick's assumption of power, expected him to administer the Duchy in strict accordance with the interests of Poland, to whom Kurland was supposed to escheat upon the death of the heirless Duke. The fifteen years before Sigismund's own death (1617-1632) was a highly critical period in the history of the Duchy, rocked by a subtle and relentless match between two unyielding powers in the diplomatic arena. Scarcely to the liking of the suzerain were Kurland's persistent neutrality during the life-and-death struggle with Sweden, and her stubborn Lutheranism which confronted a now ardently Catholic Poland, to the scandal of the King's Jesuit advisors. Sigismund's annoyance must have been capped by his ultimate failure to outlive the aging Frederick.

The latter seemed determined to draw breath as long as the wrongs of his brother William and the dispossessed Jacob remained unrighted. The two elder Dukes strove ceaselessly to rally the support of European potentates to their cause, and Sigismund and the Polish *Sejm* found themselves bombarded by letters, petitions, and embassies from almost every relative of the highly-connected Kettlers. Among the interventionists were the Kings of England, France and Denmark, as well as

---

[3] Z. Ligers, *Histoire des villes de Lettonie*, pp. 124, 156; W. Eckert, *Kurland unter dem Einfluss des Mercantilismus* (Riga, 1927), p. 140f.

a number of German potentates. Sigismund III blandly referred them all to the decisions of the Polish *Sejm*, which had consistently obliged the Polish King by repeatedly confirming the decision of the Extraordinary Commission to deprive the younger branch of the Kettler family of their claims to the Duchy of Kurland.

In 1621, Gustavus Adolphus of Sweden, thinking he had found an opportunity in the persistent discouragement of the Kuronian dukes in Warsaw, offered William the whole Duchy of Livonia on condition that he accept Swedish suzerainty. But William, convinced of the validity of his title to Kurland, took the long view and abided by his legal claim.

The Dukes' strongest support came from England, with whose royal house they were connected by blood relationship. James I, a godfather of the young Jacob, in 1620 had requested the British ambassador to Warsaw, Patrick Gordon, to make a particular effort to raise the question of William's restitution in the Polish Diet. The *Sejm*, as usual, refused to reconsider the issue. There the matter rested until the summer of 1629, when the exiles heard that Charles I was about to send an ambassador to Poland to attempt mediation between the warring Kings of Poland and Sweden. Viscount Dorchester, the Secretary of State, had persuaded his monarch that English intervention, which might result in peace and thus put a term to Catholic Poland's effort to absorb Kurland, would greatly advance the religious and economic interests of England, since a Protestant Kurland, friendly to English Baltic traders, was of prime importance to England's prosperity. Charles I was thus prevailed upon to send as a special envoy to Warsaw, Sir Thomas Roe. Among his instructions, which included a detailed analysis of Europe's political troubles and of England's intentions and plans, was a paragraph emphasizing the King of England's kinship to and close friendship with the Dukes of Kurland, in whose interest Sir Thomas Roe was entitled to act.[4]

In September 1629, the English envoy, with the support of the French ambassador, succeeded in arranging a six-year armistice between Poland and Sweden. The available correspondence and documents attest to Sir Thomas Roe's understanding of the small but significant part which Kurland would play in the great political struggles of the seventeenth century, and his conviction that the restoration of the Kettler dynasty would serve the interests of England. A letter

[4] L. Gailitis, *Anglo-Latvian Relations in the XVIIth Century* (London, 1942). Mimeographed.

to Viscount Dorchester, dated Danzig, December 21, 1629, reporting on his activities in Warsaw, explicitly states that he had given his particular and undivided attention to the restitution of the Kettlers, since the southeastern coast of the Baltic might well become the "storehouse of England's grain and shipbuilding timber."

Eventually, Sir Thomas Roe, again with the cooperation of the French ambassador, persuaded the King of Poland and the Warsaw Diet to recognize Prince Jacob as the legal heir of Duke Frederick. In 1638, Jacob accompanied his uncle to Warsaw, where Frederick obtained his investiture from King Władysław IV, Sigismund's successor. A year later, upon the death of Frederick, Prince Jacob, whose father, William, had renounced his rights in favor of his son, ascended the ducal throne. With the death of William in 1640, the flourishing reign of Duke Jacob of Kurland officially began.[5]

The forty years of this reign were to establish the Duchy of Kurland as a full-fledged member of the constellation of Western states. Under a ruler naturally astute and toughened by adversity, a state policy was fashioned which placed the Duchy in the vanguard of the rising mercantile interests of the century; while the ties of kinship with powerful princely houses were fully maintained and exploited. In the interests of his position, Duke Jacob, in 1645, acquired the rank of an hereditary prince of the Holy Roman Empire; while in 1654, he allied himself with the imposing Elector of Brandenburg by marrying his sister, the Princess Louise Charlotte.

As a highly educated man, the graduate of several German universities and the rector, *honoris causa*, of the University of Leipzig, Jacob had been thoroughly imbued with the fashionable economic doctrine of mercantilism. From the very start of his reign he sought to develop his Duchy as a maritime power, realizing fully that the Baltic Sea was the only means whereby Kurland could maintain relations with the outer world without losing any measure of her independence. During his administration, the Kurs, natural sailors though barred from navigation all during the ascendancy of the Livonian Order, saw themselves and their ships ranked among the leading navies of Western Europe.

One of the Duke's first steps was to encourage further the shipbuilding industry of Ventspils, which his father had revived. He could soon boast of a considerable fleet consisting of 44 armed men-of-war,

[5] Konopczyński, *Kwestia Bałtycka*, p. 121 calls him a "remarkable meteor of Eastern Europe." Like Peter the Great, he had worked as a laborer on the Dutch waterfront.

15 unarmed warships, 60 merchantmen, and a large number of smaller vessels; which compared favorably with the 1644 Danish fleet of 20 ships, the 1630 Swedish fleet of 30 vessels, and France's navy in 1661, which possessed no more than 18 men-of-war.[6] The importance of the Kuronian fleet is reflected in a treaty of commerce, concluded between Duke Jacob and Louis XIV late in 1643, which stipulated that the Duke of Kurland should not "assist the enemies of France with his vessels nor . . . ship goods to them under pretext of the freedom of our seas hereby granted."

Duke Jacob was able to be of considerable assistance to his erstwhile patron Charles I of England, during that country's civil war, by supplying the Stuart with as many as 62 men-of-war built of Kuronian oak and armed with artillery guns cast in Kurland.[7] By 1649, there existed an outstanding account of 74,584 pounds sterling, which Jacob never seems to have collected from the hard-pressed Royalists.[8] The change to a Puritan régime did not alienate the Duke of Kurland, who concluded a neutrality treaty with Cromwell in 1654, to be supplemented in 1657 by a treaty of navigation. The Duke also took care to negotiate treaties with France, Holland, Denmark, Sweden, Spain, Portugal, and the Holy See. Thus befriended by several of the Western Powers, some of whom owed him money for naval aid, Jacob's ships carried his flag into many waters. In time, and in spite of the keen competition of the Netherlands, one quarter of all of Kurland's foreign trade was shipped under the ducal emblem.

This impressive commerce reflected Kurland's exceptional natural wealth. For not only was the Duchy part of the rich Livonian granary, whose produce was so highly prized abroad, but timber and other ship-building materials, as well as guns and anchors cast in native foundries, were much in demand in the maritime-minded West. The Duke supplemented these already considerable exports by his economic policy of founding and fostering a variety of native industries which led to the establishment of 17 foundries, 18 saw-mills, 10 woollen mills, 85 linen mills, 14 saltpeter factories, 5 fodder mills, 100 tar refineries, 10 glassworks, 30 limekilns, 20 brickworks, and 5 paper mills. Thus, a thoroughly well-balanced economy, industrial as well as agricultural and maritime, was rooted in the fortunately situated and vigorously governed Duchy of Kurland.

[6] J. Juškevičs, Hercoga Jēkaba laikmets Kurzemē (Riga, 1931), p. 268.
[7] E. Kristlib, in Londonas Avize, no. 14, April 1943.
[8] R. O. G. Urch, Latvia. Country and People (London, 1938), p. 62.

Less realistic, though still in accord with current mercantilist thinking, was Jacob's determination to double his maritime and industrial program with a pronounced colonial policy. For although he did succeed in acquiring the island of Tobago in the Antilles and a footing in African Gambia, these far venturies cost him not only numberless men and ships captured or sunk, but the ill will of those expansionist Western nations who resented Kurland's poaching on what they pleased to think of as their preserves. Whereas Louis XIV was inclined to look with benevolence upon the exotic exploits of the Duke who had provided his nation with valuable naval aid, the Dutch, already challenged by French and English enterprise, were not of a mind to tolerate the appearance of Kuronian ships in the highly disputed West Indian waters or off the Gold Coast of Africa. As for England, her naval sympathies proved unreliable in this field.

Under Charles I, Duke Jacob received a certain degree of encouragement in his colonial endeavors. It was with the English King's approval that he purchased from the Earl of Warwick the island of Tobago in 1645, to whose exclusive trading rights he received recognition by the trade agreement signed with Cromwell in 1657. But the successive shiploads of settlers sent from Kurland to the Antilles met with insufferable difficulties, being challenged by the Dutch and even the French, who disputed Kurland's claim to Tobago, and set upon by English privateers out of Jamaica. Although the English ships of the line sometimes came to the aid of the Kuronians, and the Duke himself sent warships to protect his colonists, these expeditions were, on the whole, a failure. In 1665, Tobago fell to English privateers; two years later the island passed under the control of the Dutch.

In spite of his difficulties in establishing a settlement in the West Indies, Duke Jacob readily undertook a similar enterprise in Africa. About the middle of the century, the Duke, albeit the head of a tenaciously Protestant state, attempted to organize a joint colonizing enterprise with Pope Innocent X, wherein the Papacy would have provided financial backing, while the ruler of Kurland was to have furnished 40 warships manned with 24,000 Latvian sailors.[9] The Duke, of course, was to have garnered the commercial profits of this venture, leaving the Pope to reap a harvest of spiritual dividends in the missionary line. This project died a-borning, since Innocent X's successor in 1655 would have no part of it.

Nothing daunted, Duke Jacob proceeded to purchase from a native

[9] H. Vitols, *La mer baltique et les états baltes* (Paris, 1935), p. 198.

chief the small island of St. Andrew at the mouth of the Gambia River, where he erected a stronghold which he christened Fort Jacob. He also acquired a strip of the mainland, where his trading operations brought him into immediate conflict with the ubiquitous Dutch. Pearl fishing, the slave trade, and some prospecting for gold along the Gambia River seem to have been the only commercial pursuits carried on under Kurland's flag in this distant outpost.

After the restoration of Charles II, England's attitude toward Kurland's colonial exploits seems to have veered toward disapproval. Possibly the Stuart King resented the treaties which Duke Jacob had briskly concluded with the Commonwealth. Certainly he was ill-disposed toward a renewal of Kurland's claim to unsettled accounts incurred by the Royalist cause. In 1660, five English ships demanded and received the surrender of Fort Jacob and St. Andrew's Island. Jacob's protests went unheeded in London, and he had to remain satisfied with the treaty of 1664, which granted him a royal "lease" on the island of Tobago. When his merchant ships continued to be hampered in their efforts to trade with Gambia and Tobago, the Duke regarded this treaty as broken, and continued his useless protestations while making an ineffectual fight for his colonies. The King of Sweden, Charles Gustavus, aptly defined Kurland's enterprising ruler as "too poor for a king, too rich for a duke." In the long run, Jacob was unable to enforce his claims to distant colonies.

In the best tradition of benevolent despotism, Duke Jacob's colonial policy, although theoretically of benefit to his dominion's commercial element, was a sort of private game, pursued without calculation of the human cost, and with a personal obstinacy which foreboded only ultimate personal as well as public loss. This same tradition taught the Duke to mistrust private initiative in his domains as well as foreign competition abroad, and to keep both the domestic and foreign affairs of his Duchy in his own hands. This policy, while conducive under an intelligent and energetic ruler to a degree of constructive uniformity, did not achieve for this precariously poised state the basic solidity coupled with resilience which a broad consultation of the national interests might have afforded. Particularly in the realm of international relations in the Baltic sphere did the Duke's exclusive consideration of his own ambitions together with those of his ruling class, the landed nobles, lead the young Duchy unnecessarily into troubled waters.

For it was the interests of the Kuronian nobility which ultimately involved Kurland in the nefarious Polish-Swedish struggle which had shaken the Baltic lands for half a century. In the face of an imminent flare-up of the war with her old enemy Poland, Sweden, hitherto scrupulously observant of Kurland's neutrality treaties of 1630,[10] pressed Duke Jacob to accept her suzerainty. However, the Kuronian landed nobles dreaded any falling out with Poland, whose side in the conflict they favored, primarily because of the particularly favorable position of the Polish nobility who still dominated King and Parliament. Duke Jacob therefore confined himself to offering Charles X a loan of 50,000 thalers, hoping thus to appease the aggressive Swedish monarch.

The Duke of Kurland had felt strengthened in his resistance to the Swedish overtures by his alliance with the Elector of Brandenburg, Frederick William, whose sister shared the ducal throne. When the Elector chose to join Sweden's enemies, Charles Gustavus saw no further reason for sparing the domains of the aloof Jacob. Accordingly, in 1658 the Swedish General Douglas invaded Kurland, took Mitau by surprise, captured the Duke and his consort and sent them as prisoners first to Riga, then on to Ivangorod.[11] Only by the treaty of Oliva, signed among others, by Duke Jacob in May 1660, was the Duke restored to his Duchy, after ceding to Sweden the island of Rüno in the Gulf of Riga, the Bolderaa near the mouth of the Daugava, and some territory north of that river as far as Sloka.

During this short but intensive campaign, Kurland was disastrously devastated by the movements of Swedish, Lithuanian, and even Prussian troops across her territory. The ravages of war were followed by a major epidemic which killed at least a third of the population of the Duchy. Duke Jacob's last years were necessarily spent in seeking to reestablish the welfare of his domains which his equivocal attitude toward Sweden had so compromised. Kurland's greatest ruler died in 1682.

Jacob's heir, Frederick Casimir (1682-1698), polished, ambitious, and politically adept, followed willingly in the footsteps of his Europeanized father, and thrust his Duchy still further forward into the sphere of Western European statecraft and culture. During this reign, Mitau became a copy of Versailles, with its fêtes, ballet, opera, and concerts, costing such a pretty penny that Duke Frederick Casimir, to ease the strain on the state finances, took to selling his peasants abroad for soldiers after the fashion of the German princes. The

[10] D. S. Rydberg, *Sveriges Tracktater*, v (Stockholm, 1877), 352, 375, 379.
[11] Konopczyński, *Dzieje Polski nowożytnej*, II, 41.

Latvian six-footers fetched an especially good price from the Elector of Brandenburg.

Frederick Casimir's urbane conduct of his foreign relations resulted in open cordiality with France, as well as a comfortable degree of friendship with Poland and Sweden, both of whom respected the Duke's close connections with the ruling houses of Brandenburg and Prussia. But Frederick Casimir's greatest diplomatic triumph was his enticement of Peter the Great, whom he invited to make a visit to Mitau on his way to Königsberg in 1697. At the Kuronian capital the Tsar received a royal reception, with feasts, parades, and galas, as well as magnificent gifts for himself and his household, all of which fairly dazzled the Muscovite, who had been considerably ruffled by the humiliating treatment he had received at the hands of the Swedish Governor-General in Riga. The Duke of Kurland's well-placed hospitality was to serve his Duchy well in later years, when Peter spared this area from devastation and occupation after his victory over the Swedish forces in Livonia.

Upon the death of Frederick Casimir in 1698, his inheritance fell to his infant son Frederick William, for whom the late Duke's brother Ferdinand assumed the regency. As a staunch friend of Augustus II, the Elector of Saxony and now King of Poland, Ferdinand became a general in the Polish army and a member of the Saxon-Danish-Muscovite coalition against Sweden. Again Kurland was to pay a high price for abandoning her neutral position. In 1700, Kurland's small army took part in the battle of Spilve, where the Elector of Saxony went down to defeat before the Swedes. Ferdinand, his troops dispersed, fled to Danzig, whence the young Frederick William was convoyed to Berlin for safe keeping in the charge of the future King of Prussia.

Charles XII of Sweden crossed the Daugava in the summer of 1701, and soon all of Kurland fell into Swedish hands. By August 1701, the King had ordered the surveying of the Duchy, the composition of the tax rolls, the collection of outstanding taxes, and a redistribution of the tax levy which from now on was to fall upon the manor-lords as well as on the peasantry.[12] Kurland had been speedily transformed into a Swedish governor-generalate, subject to heavy tribute for the benefit of the Swedish exchequer in the war against Poland. The ducal archives were taken to Riga for safekeeping, while Charles built a fortress in Mitau, which was soon transformed into an arsenal for the Swedish troops, whose headquarters were now in Bauska.

[12] E. Dunsdorfs, "A Swedish Cadastral Attempt in Kurzeme," in *Contributions of the Baltic University*, no. 8 (Hamburg, 1946).

Not until their victory at Poltava in 1709 did the Russians succeed in loosening Sweden's grip on this advance base. This was done in fulfilment of a promise made by Peter the Great to Frederick I, ruler of the new Kingdom of Prussia (1701) and the grandfather of Frederick William. These two friendly Powers now decided to restore the young Duke, and to strengthen his position in the eyes of all Europe by marrying him to the Tsar's niece, Grand Duchess Anna, the future Empress of Russia. Peter paid a return visit to Mitau, this time to use it as a base from which to conduct the siege of encircled Riga, which finally fell to the Russians in 1710.

That same year, Frederick William also arrived in Mitau to take over the rule of his Duchy. Shortly thereafter he proceeded to Moscow, where his marriage to the Grand Duchess was celebrated with surpassing pomp.[13] With its Duke now allied to Russia, as well as to England, Prussia, and many other princely houses, the future of the Duchy of Kurland seemed assured. But a treacherous blow to this fair destiny was in the making. Early in January 1711, while on his way home from the nuptial festivities at St. Petersburg, Frederick William died of influenza. His uncle Ferdinand again became Regent, choosing to live in Danzig, and leaving the actual government of the Duchy to the Ducal Council.

Thus, at the very time that Kurland had achieved status as an independent state,[14] the constructive Kettler dynasty which had brought about this political triumph found itself without issue. Partly as a result of this failure of the Kettler line, Kurland was to become the unfortunate pawn of Russian and Polish politics and, ultimately, the victim of Russia's irresistible encroachments on the defenseless southeastern and eastern shores of the Baltic.

[13] A description of the marriage ceremonies appears in *Das Veränderte Russland* (Frankfurt, 1744), p. 219.

[14] The Abbé de St. Pierre included the Duchy of Kurland in his *Projet de paix perpétuelle* (1713) as an independent state. It was given nineteenth (out of 24) place, between Austria and Prussia, and was to pay a yearly contribution of 300,000 livres in support of the administration of the Union.

PART IV
RUSSIAN RULE

PART IV

RUSSIAN RULE

Chapter 11

The Rise of Russian Hegemony
in the Baltic

THE appearance of Peter the Great on the Kuronian scene was but a fragment of that Romanov's major role in the intensive struggle for the Baltic, where his expansionist and peculiarly maritime urges found their final focus. Under the harsh and dynamic guidance of her most aggressive Tsar, Russia not only regained her "window on the Baltic," but established a two-century-long dominion over that highly contested sea.

The reappearance of Muscovy, after a long period of internal instability known as the "time of troubles," as a serious contender for the *dominium maris Baltici*, was prefaced by the conciliatory action of Peter I's father, Alexis, in concluding peace treaties with Sweden and Poland in 1661 and 1667 respectively. As the son of this faintly progressive—that is to say, Western-minded—ruler, Peter the Great (1682-1725) let sleeping dogs lie in the Baltic region until he had temporarily settled his affairs with the Porte, whose forces he had actually defeated at Azov in 1696; but over whom, lacking allies, he could not achieve final victory. It was the rapidly melting dream of a Black Sea fleet which set the young Tsar, an immoderate mariner and shipbuilder, to hungering after an outlet on the eastern Baltic, with its timbered shores, its excellent harbors, and its sea lanes leading west. This yearning was given some concrete shape when, on his way home from the West to quell an insurrection of the *streltsi* (the Moscow praetorian guards) in the summer of 1698, he fell in with August II of Poland (1697-1733) at Rawa. The high-spirited, treacherous Elector and King and the ever-restless young Tsar there discussed, with an exciting combination of passion and bonhomie, no less a scheme than the undermining of Sweden's hegemony of the North.[1] The extent to which Peter's interest was engaged is revealed in a pamphlet which he published the following year, wherein he set forth Muscovy's alleged historical rights to Livonia.[2]

[1] W. Konopczyński, *Dzieje Polski nowożytnej*, II, 154.
[2] W. Gerhardi, *The Romanovs* (New York, 1938), p. 254ff. This pamphlet, printed in Russian, was available in the library of the Historical Institute of Riga.

Augustus II, who had no reason to fall out with his cousin Charles XII (1697-1718), and who was furthermore bound to observe the peace treaties concluded with Sweden by his predecessors on the Polish throne, was roused to this pitch of conspiracy by the brilliantly vindictive incitements of that Livonian squire and former officer of the Swedish Guards, Johann Reinhold Patkul. We have already learned how, in 1689, and again three years later, this representative of the German Livonian gentry had protested to the Swedish monarch against that country's land-recovery project in Livonia. Exiled for his presumptuousness and deprived of his estates, Patkul wandered for four years, nursing his rage against Sweden, and his determination to prefer any foreign domination in Livonia to hers. The new King of Poland, being a German, appeared as the most desirable suzerain to Patkul and the particular class interests which he represented. In 1698, Patkul arrived in Dresden, where he fascinated August II with his master-plan to align Saxony, Denmark, and Brandenburg against Sweden, whose domains would then be divided, with Livonia falling to August II as his highly desirable share. The Baltic squires, Patkul suggested, would expect the ruler of Poland to restore their privileges. When Brandenburg proved unavailable for this purpose, Russia was substituted, not without misgivings on the part of Patkul, who astutely foresaw that she might make off with the largest part of the winnings.[3]

Augustus II, needing some victories to mend his unpopular position in his new kingdom, acceded greedily to these schemes and appointed Patkul as Saxony's ambassador to Denmark. Frederick IV, who had succeeded the peace-loving Christian V in August 1699, was without difficulty persuaded to join Saxony in a military alliance directed against Sweden, signing the treaty in September 1699.

Augustus II now sent the officious Patkul as his personal ambassador to Moscow. Patkul's arrival in the Russian capital coincided with that of a special embassy sent by Charles XII to confirm the peace of Kardis, signed in 1661. Peter saw no impropriety in renewing this peace while giving every encouragement to Patkul, whose diplomatic endeavors, which extended to the offer of Narva and as much of Finland as Peter could take,[4] resulted in the conclusion of a secret alliance between the Tsar and the Danish and Saxon envoys on November 22, 1699. The following day, Peter gave the suspicious Swedish ambassador solemn assurance of his good intentions, with a fine show of in-

[3] R. Nisbet Bain in *Cambridge Mod. Hist.*, v, 586f.
[4] J. Hampden Jackson, *Estonia* (London, 1941), pp. 63-66.

dignation and incredulity when the designs of Augustus II were suggested.[5]

Although Peter was still too unsure of the result of his peace negotiations with the Turks to embark on a campaign in the north, the Saxons and the Danes felt sufficiently certain of their preponderance to begin the Great Northern War without Muscovy. In December 1699, Frederick IV, accusing Charles XII of conspiring with the Duke of Holstein, his brother-in-law, against Denmark, launched his troops into Sweden.[6]

The King of Sweden, still in his teens, proceeded to upset the coalition's expectations by his military skill and audacity. After signing a treaty of alliance with England and the Netherlands, who were anxious to maintain the freedom of the Danish straits, Charles XII, in 1700, under the protection of his allies' fleets, crossed the narrow channel and menaced Copenhagen, thus forcing Denmark to sign the treaty of Travendal and abandon the coalition of 1699.

Meanwhile Augustus II, with the permission of Prince Ferdinand, the Regent of the Duchy of Kurland, had concentrated his own Saxon troops under the command of Patkul in Kurzeme opposite Riga, which was to be taken by a surprise assault on the night of February 11, 1700. The commander of the Riga garrison, having got wind of the plan, met the Saxons with decisive resistance. It was on this occasion that Ferdinand, by allowing his troops to be involved, recklessly broke his country's traditional neutrality, thus causing an irremediable breach with Charles XII.

In March, the Saxon forces took Dünamunde, which they renamed Augustenburg, only to lose it again very soon. By May, Patkul and what was left of the Saxon troops were on their way out of Livonia with fresh Swedish detachments at their backs. During his short sojourn in his former country, Patkul had worked hard to enlist the support of the German-Livonian landed nobles for the Tsar of Russia, who was soon to make his appearance on the scene.

On August 8, 1700, Peter the Great received news of the final conclusion of peace with the Porte. The following day he ordered the invasion of Livonia. Urged by August II and his own fierce inner drive to reach the Baltic, Peter proceeded immediately to invade Ingria, where late in 1700 he laid siege to Narva, held dear in Muscovite memory. There, to his dismay, the Tsar received the startling news

[5] R. N. Bain, op.cit., v, 587.
[6] W. Hubert, Wojny bałtyckie, p. 382ff.

that the youthful Swedish monarch, who was supposed to have his hands full in Denmark, had put that nation out of action, and swiftly swung his forces eastwards, reached Pärnu in October, and there deflected to the north where he was now advancing upon Narva. Peter beat a hasty retreat to Novgorod, leaving his raw recruits behind him to be soundly punished by the Swedish veterans.

The Tsar now appointed Patkul, who had gone on to Moscow for further conferences on strategy, as his own personal ambassador to King Augustus II, whom he sought to persuade to bring Poland into the anti-Swedish coalition. Patkul arranged a meeting between the two rulers in Lithuania for February 1701. Here Augustus II matched Peter's promise to procure financial subsidies and troops to be trained by Saxon officers, by binding himself to persuade Poland to join the combination against Sweden. Yet, for all Peter's expressed (though insincere) willingness to renounce Livonia and Estonia for the benefit of Poland, the Polish magnates showed no eagerness to declare war on Sweden.[7]

Charles' successive victories may have had some part in the Polish *Sejm's* cautious attitude. After his defeat of the Russian forces, he had immediately turned his strength against his continental foe, Augustus II. On July 10, 1701, the Swedes inflicted a defeat on the allied Kuronian-Saxon-Russian troops which had again concentrated at Riga, this time driving them from Livonia. Charles then invaded Kurland at Koknese, captured Mitau, and occupied the entire Duchy, which he swiftly cleared of Saxons and Russians. The Swedish King gave every indication of intending to stay in Kurland, which was treated as a Swedish province and made to serve as a rallying point for the planned invasion of Lithuania.

Augustus II, deceived in his expectations of an early victory, now sought to treat with the triumphant King of Sweden. The latter promptly demanded the abdication of Augustus, with a view to keeping the peace with the Polish Commonwealth, which he wished to consider as a cooperative and reliable friendly nation, a status which Sweden could not accord her as long as she was ruled by the treacherous Elector of Saxony. Upon Augustus' refusal to retire from the Polish throne, Charles crossed into Lithuania and occupied Kovno. In May 1702, he took Warsaw and shortly thereafter, Cracow. While he continued his campaign against the harassed Saxons, the Swedish

[7] W. Konopczyński in *Cambridge History of Poland*, ii (Cambridge, 1941), 5ff.

King's Polish supporters, in 1704, formed a confederation which deposed Augustus II. Charles, in July of that year, procured the election of his personal friend and contemporary, the Wojewoda of Poznań, Stanisław Leszczyński, who immediately signed a treaty of alliance with Sweden, following the precedent of the peace of Oliva with its stipulation of Polish assistance to Sweden against Russia.

But Charles had shown faulty judgment in failing to pursue his advantage over Peter in the Baltic dominions, where he had left the Lake Ladoga-Lake Peipus-Daugava frontier poorly garrisoned while he vented his rage against his Saxon cousin to the south. Throughout 1701 and 1702, the Tsar sought to revenge Narva by a series of vicious incursions into Livonia and Ingria. In the belief that the Swedish King would shortly appear on the Livonian scene, Peter gave instructions for the devastation of that land, which were carried out to the full over an area comprising Reval, Pärnu, and the district of Riga. Peter himself prepared to supervise the conquest of Ingria. In the summer of 1703, on the north bank of the Neva, a small village was built and named St. Petersburg with the fort, which was to be known as Kronstadt, nearer the sea for its defense. In the summer of the following year, the taking of Dorpat and Narva, together with the conquest of Ingria, completed Peter's triumph in the north. While Charles XII went into winter quarters near Dorpat, the Tsar turned his attention to Poland, where he was prepared to accept the proffered loyalty of a group of Polish magnates who continued to support Augustus II, declaring the Swedish King to be the enemy of their nation. In 1704, this faction signed with Peter an alliance against Sweden, thus opening the doors of Poland to the Muscovites.

Peter now chose to carry on the war on Polish soil and in Kurland, where the Russians, after taking Mitau in 1705, went into winter quarters near Grodno. In the course of the following year, Charles' temerity and mobility in the field caused the Tsar to order a partial retreat to Kiev, while Augustus felt himself sufficiently insecure to sue for peace. By his final ratification of the treaty of Alt-Runstadt in January 1707, the Elector of Saxony recognized Stanisław as his successor in Poland. The Livonian Patkul was callously delivered to Charles XII, who broke him on the wheel and cut off his head as an example to traitors.

Peter, inspired by now with unwilling respect for the wildly courageous and cunning Swedish warrior King, began looking about him for means of concluding an armistice with Charles. Since the latter refused direct communication with the Russian Tsar, England, the Netherlands, and France were all approached for mediation by Peter, who declared himself willing to renounce all of his Baltic acquisitions with the exception of his beloved St. Petersburg. Charles, however, insisted that he must have this city on the Neva; and the European nations, now thoroughly alarmed by Russia's looming power, supported the claims of the Swedish monarch.

Peter, resigned to war to the death, was determined to make Charles pay highly for his stubbornness by luring his forces deeper and deeper into the treacherous terrain of White Russia. In January 1708, Peter left Grodno two days ahead of Charles' arrival. The Russians began a slow and tormenting retreat, leaving scorched earth and flaming villages to greet the Swedes in their wake. Charles now decided to invade the Ukraine, being encouraged therein by the Hetman Mazepa, who promised Cossack support in order to throw off the yoke of Moscow. But this help resolved itself into the already ruined Mazepa and a small personal retinue; and Sweden faced defeat in the deathly shape of the exceptionally fierce Ukrainian winter of 1708-1709. In June 1709, Peter finally made up his mind to a pitched battle at Poltava, where the Swedish forces, in a greatly weakened condition, were cruelly defeated and their leader, the King, was wounded and forced to flee for refuge to a Turkish fortress.[8]

This brilliant Russian victory galvanized the old anti-Swedish coalition. Frederick IV of Denmark, after concluding an alliance with Augustus of Saxony, was resolved upon the immediate attack of Sweden. The short Skanian campaign, though unsuccessful, allowed Peter to pursue his victorious streak in Finland, where Viborg fell to him in June 1710; and in Livonia, where Riga, starved out, plague-stricken, and bombarded, surrendered on July 15, and Pärnu and Reval were taken during the course of the summer. As for Poland, Augustus II quickly reclaimed the throne with Russian assistance, and Kurland was cleared of Swedish troops.

For another eight years the Russian Tsar, distrusted yet sorely needed by his mutually jealous and scarcely reliable allies, Saxony, Denmark, and Prussia, was to confront the almost insane belligerency of Charles XII, who clung to what he insisted were his inherited

[8] A compact and knowledgeable account of this war appears in R. N. Bain's chapter "Charles XII and the Great Northern War" in *Cambridge Mod. Hist.*, v, 584-615. See also, for English participation, J. F. Chance, *George I and the Northern War* (London, 1909).

rights to the Baltic lands. The Swedish monarch's desperate determination led him to fight on German, and even Norwegian soil, where he was killed in his trenches on December 12, 1718. The Russian fleet, after waiting unavailingly for the cooperation of the Danes, made three heavy raids on Sweden, who had resisted peace overtures in the hope of receiving aid from the English navy. When it became evident that Sweden was isolated as well as exhausted, the severe terms demanded by Peter were at last accepted. In August 1721, King Frederick I, the consort of the sister of Charles XII, who had abdicated in favor of her husband, signed the peace of Nystad. By its terms Sweden, in return for Finland west of Viborg, an indemnity, and the freedom of the Baltic Sea, ceded to Russia Ingria, the province of Keksholm, the fortress of Viborg, all of Estonia, and Latvian Livonia. From now on the term Livonia was limited to the Latvian province of Vidzeme, about 35 per cent of modern Latvia.

Thus, after twenty-one years of war, Sweden had lost not only her northern hegemony, but her position as a major Power. Peter the Great had not only won the right to the title of "Emperor of all the Russias," but had laid the foundations of Russian dominion over the Baltic.

But there was another victor to share the fruits of Nystad. An English historian[9] has claimed that the real winners of the Great Northern War were the Livonian nobles, while the losers were the Baltic farmers. A French historian[10] states that the German landed nobles had delivered Latvia and Estonia to the Russians. Certainly, the Latvian and Estonian populations were no more consulted about their transfer from Swedish to Russian sovereignty than they had been in 1561, when the Poles and Lithuanians took over the land from the Livonian Order; or in 1627, when Sweden superseded Poland in the east Baltic territories.

Of the two statesmen who negotiated the treaty of Nystad on behalf of the Russian Tsar, one was the naturalized German Heinrich von Ostermann, who saw to it that the privileges of the German landowners in the Baltic were firmly secured. To this end, article XI of the treaty read: "As regards the reduction and liquidation which took place during the preceding reign of the King of Sweden in Livonia, Estonia and Oesel to the great detriment of the subjects and inhabitants of those lands, his Imperial Majesty undertakes and promises to have

[9] J. Hampden Jackson, op.cit., p. 66.
[10] J. Meuvret, Histoire des pays baltiques, p. 102.

justice rendered to everyone, whether they remain in the country or are outside of it, who has a just claim to land in Livonia, and can duly prove it, so that they can reenter into the possession of their property or lands." Commissions of restitution were promptly set up, and without delay the reduced domains were restored to the Livonian-German nobles, whose word of honor was accepted as due proof, under the pretext that documents had been lost or destroyed during the war. The Livonian squires felt that they had every reason to congratulate themselves upon the sympathy which they had evidenced for the Russian side in the Great Northern War and for the active cooperation they had afforded the Russian administration in Livonia, which had been in effect since 1710 when the squires were charged with collecting from their subjects subsidies and supplies for the Russian forces of occupation.

This restitution of the Livonian lands to their former German possessors, together with the maintenance of Russian control, however indifferent, was a direct violation of the repeated promises made to Augustus II, who, instead of receiving Livonia as his share of the victory, had now to content himself with his restoration to the Polish throne, which he owed to Peter the Great. Poland, indeed, may be listed among the losers of the Great Northern War. The Polish King fully realized that he could take no independent action as long as the appeased German nobility virtually ran Livonia to suit themselves, and the Russians continued to occupy and supervise the currently untidy affairs of Kurland. Augustus could do little more than put in an occasional word on the choice of a ruler for his insecure Kuronian fief.

During the Great Northern War, the Duchy of Kurland had become a bone of contention among Sweden, Russia, and Poland,[11] with only the King of Prussia to lend his support to its continued independence. When the Russian occupational army stayed on after the peace of Nystad, the Diet, anxious to be rid of such a burden, proposed to elect the Regent, Prince Ferdinand, as Duke. Acting upon a fabricated rumor, Peter dispatched additional troops from neighboring Vidzeme to secure the throne for the posthumous heir which was said to be expected by the widow of Frederick William, Peter's niece, the Duchess Anna. When this rumor proved unfounded, and the Diet sought once more to elect Ferdinand as Duke, the Tsar found the

[11] On the widespread devastation of the land, see F. Balodis, "Latvia and the Latvians" in *Journal of Central European Affairs*, vi (1947), 266ff.

expedient of demanding the reimbursement of Anna's marriage dowry as well as a heavy annual pension for the Dowager Duchess, who now took up residence in the ducal castle of Mitau, surrounded by Russian guards. Since the country could not possibly pay so large a sum, Peter's plenipotentiary, Prince Menshikov, assumed autocratic airs in what the Russians considered a defaulting country.

In his search for collateral, Menshikov seized the four thousand or so rare books of the ducal library, which he sent as a personal gift to the Tsar.[12] These treasures formed the foundation of the library of the St. Petersburg Academy of Sciences, opened in 1725, the year of Peter the Great's death.

Since the Dowager Duchess and her Russians appeared to be settled for a long wait, the Diet decided to cast about for an acceptable bridegroom for Anna, with the hope that he might become the Duke of Kurland. No decision could be reached until after the death of Peter, who had raised immediate objections to the choices of the Diet, especially to the Margrave of Brandenburg, supported by the meddling King of Prussia. Peter's successor, Catherine I, favored Anna's marriage to the Prince of Hesse-Homburg, a relative of the Kettlers and a general in the Russian army. At this point, Augustus II invoked Poland's constitutional right to incorporate Kurland upon the extinction of the Kettler dynasty. Probably with the secret agreement both of the King of Poland and the Empress of Russia, the Kuronian Diet finally reached a solution by electing, in June 1726, a natural son of Augustus II, Count Maurice de Saxe, as Duke of Kurland.[13]

The choice was a colorful one. The Count, who had fought in Peter's army against the Swedes, was now in the French army, and spent his time displaying his notable charm to Parisian society. He arrived in Mitau on money borrowed from his brilliant actress mistress, Adrienne de Lecouvreure, and made an easy conquest of the Dowager Duchess, who set out for St. Petersburg to obtain the consent of Catherine I to the marriage. This was granted, together with an order for the withdrawal of Menshikov and the Russian occupational troops from Kurland.

But Menshikov, who had no desire to leave a comfortable position, saw to it that the Duchess was apprised of the scandalous amours of her affianced, who was forced to jump out of windows and swim across lakes to escape his Russian pursuers. Eventually he regained

---

[12] *Das Veränderte Russland*, p. 219.
[13] Konopczyński, *Dzieje Polski nowożytnej*, II, 189-192.

Paris, where he won high honors in the service of France. However, he never officially resigned from his dukedom, whose coat of arms he caused to be represented on his sarcophagus in the Cathedral of Strasbourg.

On August 30, 1726, the Polish *Sejm* formally deposed the disgraced Count Maurice, and a month later Polish investigatory commissioners who had arrived in Mitau forced the Kuronian Diet to accept a new constitution which provided for the incorporation of the Duchy as an autonomous Polish province after the death of the heirless Ferdinand. The Kuronian nobility were well enough satisfied, since their landed possessions and the preservation of serfdom were guaranteed under this constitution.

Upon the death of Peter II in 1730, the Duchess Anna became the Russian State Council's choice for the throne, on condition that she sign a document limiting her autocratic powers. Anxious to leave the dull life at Mitau, she obligingly set her signature to these so-called Articles of Mitau. After her coronation in Moscow and upon the advice of her favorite and Minister of State, Ernst Biron, she tore up the Articles, claiming that her "holy duty" to Russia demanded that she follow in the steps of her autocratic forebears.

Now that her horizon had so hopefully widened, the new Tsarina no longer opposed the election of Prince Ferdinand, which was duly effected by the Kuronian Diet in 1731. That same year, the new Duke of Kurland received his investiture from Augustus II, who still heeded the advice of St. Petersburg in all matters regarding the Duchy.

The Russian influence in Warsaw also brought about the election to the Polish throne in 1733 of Augustus III, the son of the deceased Frederick Augustus II. In 1735, Tsarina Anna insisted that the new Polish King permit the Kuronian Diet to elect a duke upon the death of the present incumbent who, as a bridegroom at the age of seventy-five, was without an heir. Finally, in 1736, after confirmation by the Polish *Sejm*, the continuation of the Duchy's independence after the extinction of the Kettler line was legally assured. The following year, Duke Ferdinand died in his eighty-second year.

Candidates, among them the discredited Maurice de Saxe, swarmed about the ducal throne, only to be ignored. Inevitably, the prize fell to a high favorite of the Tsarina, Ernst Johann Biron, elected unanimously in 1737 by the Diet, whose nobles would on no account offend St. Petersburg, whence rich benefits had accrued to the German-Balt ruling class across the border in Vidzeme.

Ernst Johann was the son of a lower official of the ducal forestry administration, and most probably of Latvian origin as indicated by the name Birin, which the father had germanized to Bühren. By ability, personableness, and political sagacity, he had worked his way up from the steward of a ducal manor, through secretaryships, to the rank of Chamberlain of the Tsarist court, and finally to that of Minister of State.[14] While basking in the warm favor of the Duchess Anna, who had ennobled him, he had appropriated the more stylish name of Biron, which was that of the French Duc de Périgord. In 1730, the Hapsburg Emperor Charles VI had elevated him to the rank of a Count of the Holy Roman Empire. In return for a further diploma of nobility bestowed upon him by the Kuronian nobles, Count Biron had supported the election of Prince Ferdinand, and had done his best to obtain the approval of the King of Poland in this matter.

Biron worked hard to consolidate his position both in Kurland, where he purchased large estates, and on the international scene, where he found positions of prestige for his numerous brothers and sisters. He saw to it that the Russian ambassador in Paris, by offering the decoration of St. Andrew, obtained from the French Field Marshal, Duc de Biron de Périgord, the legalization of Ernst Johann's arbitrary use of that name. In return for his influence in the election of Augustus III in Warsaw, the Polish King awarded him the high Order of the White Eagle.

So certain was the Count of his election to the Kuronian dukedom that already in 1736 he had commissioned the Italian architect Bartholomeo Rastrelli, the creator of the classical Winter Palace in St. Petersburg, to begin work on a new castle in Mitau. The painters Fontebasso, Rotari, and Romandini were engaged to adorn the walls and ceilings in their richest style.

Biron rewarded the officious Kuronian nobles for their support in his election in 1737 by bringing about the final evacuation of the offensive Russian troops from Kurland. Aside from this gesture, the new Duke showed little concern for the arrogant nobles, whom he despised, and whose position he actually attacked by ordering the reduction (expropriation without compensation would be the modern term) of about one hundred and fifty manors which had originally belonged to the Kettler family and had been illegally appropriated by the squires. He issued decrees forbidding the latter to acquire addi-

[14] See, for this bizarre career, P. J. Ruhl, *Geschichte Ernst Johan Biron Herzogs* (Frankfurt, 1764), and T. Schiemann, *Russische Köpfe* (Berlin, 1916).

tional farmsteads or to oppress their peasants with exaggerated taxes and labor-duty. He improved the ports of Liepāja and Ventspils and fostered the trade and industry of the Duchy to the benefit of the ducal state income. This revival recalled the energetic days of the great Duke Jacob.

But Duke Ernst's attitude toward the Duchy was a coldly calculating one, in no way involving any affection for the land or its people. Just as he had sent only a representative to Warsaw to receive the investiture, so he was content to rule Kurland mostly in absentia, preferring to maintain his residence at St. Petersburg, where opportunity seemed limitless.

The Tsarina, who had married her favorite to one of her ladies-in-waiting, lavished affection on the child of this union, Peter. Anna's pampering of Biron's son gave rise to rumors that the lad was the fruit of the Duchess's regard for the brilliant Biron in his Kammer-junker days. Although this surmise should remain in the realm of calumny, the fact remains that young Peter was extravagantly spoilt by Anna, both as Duchess and Tsarina, who bestowed on her godson the title of Royal Highness and Duke of Russia and planned to marry him to her niece Princess Anna, the daughter of the Tsarina's sister Catherine, the Duchess of Mecklenburg. This would have placed Duke Ernst's son in the line of inheritance to the Russian throne.

These plans were defeated when Princess Anna married instead the Duke of Brunswick, to whom she bore a son, Ivan, in 1740. In October of that year, during her last illness, the Tsarina decided to proclaim her niece's son Grand Duke of Russia and her heir. To console her dear Ernst she appointed him Regent during the infancy of Ivan VI.

Biron, who was living with his family in the Summer Palace at Peterhof, was now, by an imperial ukase, the most powerful dignitary in Russia. This scarcely suited the ambitions of the Duke and Duchess of Brunswick, the parents of the heir, or of their German entourage. After the Tsarina's death on October 17, 1740, both Ivan's mother and father, who had word of the Regent's plans to return them to Germany, began conspiring against Biron, with the able assistance of Count Ostermann, a fellow German and that same trusted adviser of Peter the Great who had negotiated the treaty of Nystad. A false ukase was prepared, purportedly by order of the infant Ivan, which removed Biron from the Regency. To it was appointed in his stead the Tsarevich's mother, Grand Duchess Anna Leopoldovna. On November 7, Duke Ernst, after a short sharp struggle with a detachment of bribed palace guards, was taken off to prison where he was accused of high treason. He and his family were then incarcerated in the fortress of Schlüsselburg. On November 19, after a mock trial, Biron and his family were deported to Siberia.

The Kuronian nobles, who resented his indifference to their rights, hastened to fall in with the jealous Russian magnates and the German faction who accused Biron of all manner of outrageous conduct in realizing his unforgivable ambitions. In June 1741, the Kuronian Diet deposed Duke Ernst Johann, electing in his stead Prince Ludwig Ernst of Brunswick, the uncle of the new Tsar. Once more Maurice de Saxe was heard protesting from a safe distance.

Meanwhile, in November 1741, Grand Duchess Elizabeth, the thirty-three-year-old daughter of Peter the Great, who had lived a life of some neglect but of keen observance of the triumph of the foreign element in St. Petersburg, by a singularly bold and economical coup d'état overthrew the regency of Anna Leopoldovna. The Brunswick element was expeditiously exiled. The young Ivan was imprisoned in the fortress of Dünamunde at the mouth of the Daugava. The hated German contingent, including Ostermann, were imprisoned or sent to Siberia; while back from that remote waste posted Biron and his family, to be restored without delay to their barony of Wartenberg in Silesia.

Elizabeth Petrovna now recommended that the Kuronian Diet elect the above-mentioned prince of Hesse-Homburg, dispatching Russian troops to Mitau to implement her suggestion. The Polish King, objecting to this choice, appointed a governor of his own for the Duchy, but he was unable to gain access to Mitau because of the surrounding Russian forces. Once more Maurice de Saxe presented his claim, this time in person in St. Petersburg, where the French, who had helped Elizabeth overthrow the German court party, were in some favor. But Maurice was not received by the Tsarina, by whom his suit had a good many years before been rejected as a mésalliance. The French themselves, who had taken an interest in the Duchy of Kurland since the seventeenth century, presented a candidate in the person of Prince François Bourbon-Conti, close kin of the ruling house of France. The election finally fell to the son of Augustus III of Poland, Prince Charles, who, in 1758, assumed the government of Kurland from the Ducal Council, which had ruled all during the interregnum.

Upon her death in 1762, Elizabeth was succeeded by the son of her sister Anna and the Duke of Holstein, who ascended the throne as

Tsar Peter III. Duke Ernst Johann, having obtained some favors for the young Tsar and his father in their early and humbler days, was now remembered by Peter, who ordered his immediate restoration as Duke of Kurland. The son of the Polish King could do nothing but resign, since his father was in no position to sustain his cause.

Duke Ernst returned to Mitau in January 1763, where he embarked on an architectural spree, finishing the ducal castle begun so confidently in 1736, and in addition building other castles in the country, as well as many schools and hospitals. For many of these projects he engaged the services of Bartholomeo Rastrelli, noted architect of the Baroque Renaissance, and Giacomo Quarenchi, one of the creators of the Empire style. Perhaps the aging Duke felt that these builders in stone might provide some durable substitute for what he had written in sand.[15]

Late in 1769, Duke Ernst, anxious for repose, decided to resign in favor of his son Peter and retire to Wartenberg with his younger son Karl Ernst, who was to found a line of Prussian princes and officers. The old Duke died on December 22, 1772. His heir, Peter, set himself whole-heartedly to developing the economy of the country, and the beauty and culture of its capital. In 1775, the Duke opened the Academia Petrina in Mitau, built by the Danish architect Jensen, endowed with a rich library, and staffed with highly qualified professors from Germany.

The political weakness which had prevented Augustus III from supporting his son's position in Kurland was symptomatic of the Polish monarchy's position all during the eighteenth century. The rule of the two Saxon Kings, Augustus II and his son Augustus III, from 1697 to 1763, could scarcely be described as rulership at all since the inorganic Joint Kingdom was run to suit its archaic aristocracy, whose social and political development had stopped short of the dynamic ideas of mercantilism and benevolent depotism which had carried the Western Powers a long step forward toward the synthesis of nationalism. Poland, groping in a medieval twilight, devoid of fortifying natural boundaries, her throne in the hands of foreign rulers who never quite knew where their interests lay, was the inevitable victim of the two iron-clad, aggressive Powers who flanked her: Russia and the Kingdom of Prussia. While the former used her as a base of operations in the Seven Years' War, Frederick II felt equally free to levy military supplies on Polish territory. Warsaw seemed never to

[15] Z. Ligers, *Hist. des villes* . . . , p. 109.

be free of the sight or rumor of Russian soldiery. We have seen how the Polish monarchs were necessarily subservient to Russian interests in the Duchy of Kurland.

The death of Augustus III in 1763 inspired Catherine II, who had come to power in Russia the preceding year, to turn king-maker by forcing the election of Stanisław Poniatowski, a member of the leading Czartoryski family, to the Polish throne. Catherine, with the support of Frederick of Prussia, proceeded to maintain the *status quo*, i.e. political anarchy, in Poland by means of increased Russian troops. Poland responded to this exaggerated pressure by reversing her time-honored anti-Turkish policy and accepting the support of the Porte. This ill-considered step which tied the Eastern question to the fate of Poland, led directly to the latter's partition.

In the summer of 1772, Russia had already signed a secret treaty with Prussia and Austria providing for the partition of Poland, on condition that Russia might take her share at whatever time proved convenient for her. In September of that year, Stanisław, having received intelligence of these machinations of his one-time patroness, dispatched heated protests to Vienna, Berlin, and St. Petersburg. After further pressure had been brought on the *Sejm*, by increasing the Russian military forces in Warsaw and threatening the senators with loss of their properties, the Polish King was forced to sign, in September 1773, treaties acceding to the annexation of Latgale by Russia, together with a strip of White Russian territory including Polotzk, Vitebsk, Minsk, and Mstislav.

This Latvian province of Latgale had been a part of the Polish Commonwealth since the sixteenth century. It had enjoyed a large degree of self-government, with a Diet of its own, convening at Daugavpils, which sent delegates to the Polish *Sejm* and senators to the Polish Senate.

The fate of Kurland was now in the balance. Catherine herself considered bestowing the Duchy on her morganatic husband, Prince Potemkin. The reigning Duke, Peter, purchased in 1786 the Duchy of Sagan and Preibus in Silesia, hoping thus to assure himself the protection of his relative, Frederick II; being unaware that the latter had secretly offered Kurland, with the extra bonus of a German princess, to Potemkin.[16]

Following upon a major insurrection against Russian control in Lithuania, armed groups of Lithuanian insurgents had fled the perse-

[16] G. Soloveytchik, *Potemkin* (New York, 1947), p. 219.

cution of Russian troops by infiltrating Kurzeme in the beginning of 1794. For a few weeks these revolutionaries occupied Liepāja and Ventspils in the hope of receiving aid from abroad. The districts of Liepāja and Grobina came under the control of the insurgents, who were joined by the local Latvian population. Some of the German squires, feeling the mob at their backs, now offered to free their peasants from serfdom. Their position was saved by the arrival of Russian troops at the urgent invitation of the Kuronian Diet. Several hundred of the liberated serfs retreated with the Lithuanian insurgents to East Prussia, ruthlessly pursued by overwhelming Russian forces.

Uneasy over the proximity of these forces, Frederick William II now acceded to the secret agreement reached between Austria and Russia in 1794 to proceed to the third and final partition of Poland.[17] This agreement was signed by the three predatory Powers in St. Petersburg on October 13, 1795.

Early in that year, the Kuronian landed nobles, eager to obtain the "rights" enjoyed by their fellow nobles in Latvia, had begun to agitate for the unconditional surrender of Kurland to Russia. Count Mirabeau, who during the previous decade, as Louis XVI's representative in Berlin, had considered how to draw Kurland into a new Baltic system which would exclude Russia, could only report that "the Kuronian nobles are engaged more or less shamefully in selling out this beautiful and unfortunate province to Russia."[18] This they did in fact on March 17, 1795, when the Diet decided to secede from Poland and submit to Russia.

A special delegation, headed by Baron Heyking, now proceeded to St. Petersburg to beg for the incorporation of Kurland. Since Potemkin had died, Catherine saw no objection to this step, but she showed a curious eagerness for "legality." The Tsarina insisted that, besides the Kuronian envoy, Duke Peter, who had sought refuge in St. Petersburg, should also submit a personal petition; while even the autonomous Diet of the province of Piltene was expected to "beg" for the boon of Russian dominance. Duke Peter, whose entire property was expropriated by the Russian Government, was paid a flat sum in in-

---

[17] Aside from the masterly study of R. H. Lord, *The Second Partition of Poland* (Cambridge, 1915), the story of the partitions has been rather neglected in Western historiography. Chapters 5, 7 and 8 of vol. II of the *Cambridge History of Poland* give the best available, if undocumented, account.

[18] H. Vitols, *La mer baltique et les états baltes*, p. 204.

demnity together with an annuity of 65,000 thalers. He then retired to his Duchy of Sagan, where he died in 1800.

The Tsarina, disregarding the oral promises of autonomy made to the Kuronian nobles, imposed on Kurland the Russian form of provincial administration, with an imperial governor who presided over the Council of the landed nobles. This Council, a mere shadow of the former powerful Diet, was allowed only such functions as were consonant with Russian law. The Russian system of taxation was introduced throughout the land.

After the death of the despotic Catherine, her successor Paul, the great-grandson of Peter the Great, on December 17, 1796, reinstated an autonomous (German) administration both in Kurland and in Vidzeme. Only the Russian taxation system remained fastened on these domains.

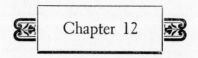

Chapter 12

Russian Rule and German Influence

THE aspiration of the Livonian-German landed nobles had at all times been in essence a simple one: actual control of the land and its people, and their own relative freedom, through effective decentralization, from any higher authority, whether local or remote. At the onset of the Great Northern War they had seen an opportunity to break the chains which bound them to Sweden, whose tutelage had grown particularly irksome during the reign of Charles XI, the *Bondekong*, when Latvian Livonia (Vidzeme) and Estonia were granted some twenty years of economic, social, and cultural progress. These too short years were to remain in the memory of the Latvians as the "good old Swedish days."

The squires, whose only loyalty was to their class, could make use of a Patkul and then claim that he had forged their written support of his treasonous plans.[1] They found no difficulty in turning first to the German on the throne of Poland, Augustus II; then, when he proved a weak reed, to Peter the Great, who promised both strength and purpose, and a proper sympathy with autocracy in any form. What they required of the conqueror of hated Sweden was territorial autonomy for Livonia and full control vested in the oligarchic Diet of the landed nobles, who had every intention of retaining the lands which they had appropriated from the Crown as their private property, to be worked by the Latvians, now once more reduced to serfdom.

The manor-lords had not, perhaps, counted on the destructive temper of Peter I. Determined to burn the ground beneath the feet of the implacable Charles XII, the Tsar had ordered the length and breadth of that perpetual battlefield, Livonia, put to the torch and sword. Contemporary testimonies insist that after the atrocities of the Russian commander Sheremetiev, at the beginning of the eighteenth century, "there was no human voice to be heard for miles, and no dogs barking or cocks crowing."[2] Valmiera, Cēsis, Valka, and many more towns were leveled. Manors and farmsteads were burned by the thou-

---

[1] F. F. Carlson, *Geschichte Schwedens*, VI, 110ff.

[2] F. Balodis, "Latvia and the Latvians" in *Journal of Central European Affairs*, VI (1947), 266f.

sands, leaving the homeless peasants to wander the land, spreading a pestilence which alone claimed about 125,000 victims. Peter further contributed to this grave depopulation by conscripting in Vidzeme for the building of his new capital, St. Petersburg, and the Ladoga canal about a thousand laborers, most of whom perished.[3]

Russian rule in Livonia, which, in actuality, dated from the fall of Riga in 1710, soon showed itself strong enough to support the German-Balt squires. The latter, shortly after the Russian victory at Poltava, had offered their submission and their services in "restoring" the ravaged land in exchange for Peter the Great's guarantee of their liberties and privileges. The Russian Government, whose interest remained focused on the Baltic ports, remained sufficiently indifferent to internal conditions in its new Baltic Provinces to allow the immediate abuse of these renewed German-Balt privileges, so that the position of the Livonian landed gentry as governors, exploiters and slave-drivers became more formidable than at any time in their history. Almost overnight, the native hopes and energies which the last decades of Swedish dominance had aroused were blotted out.

Upon the termination of his conquest of the province of Vidzeme, Peter I sent to Riga his Governor-General together with a military garrison. The Governor's Chancery was shortly crowded with Livonian-German nobles, who were to see to it that the Governors themselves were frequently chosen from among their own ranks. Of the fifteen Livonian Governors appointed during the period 1790-1885, fourteen were German nobles; while of the twelve Kuronian Governors from 1795 to 1882, ten were of this category.

The old Livonian Diet soon reconvened, and its executive, the College of Councilors, assumed the actual governance of Livonia. Referring to the support which they had given the Russian side during the war, the squires requested the Tsar's validation of the alleged *Privilegium Sigismundi* of 1561. This, in somewhat vague and general terms, they received. Peter the Great further granted the request that the estates which had been formerly in the hands of the nobles could in the future be acquired only by members of that class, while those which had been sold to the burghers could now be redeemed by the nobility. In order to protect the caste system, the ancient *matricule* of the hereditary landed nobles was reestablished. Among the 172 families on these scrolls in 1747, only 52 could claim descent from the vassals

[3] N. H. Gundling, *Discours über den jetzigen Zustand der Europäischen Staaten*, II, (Leipzig, 1733), 374f.

of the period of the Livonian Order, the rest having been ennobled during the successive Polish, Swedish, and Russian régimes.[4]

Except for several land revisions for purely statistical and assessment purposes, the Russian Government in no way interfered in the relations between the farmers and their manor-lords. The Tsars of the eighteenth century showed little concern for the welfare of their Baltic peoples, and no intention of observing either Article IX of the Treaty of Nystad, wherein Peter I had promised to "maintain all the inhabitants of the provinces of Livonia, Estonia, and Oesel, nobles and commoners, cities and magistrates, and the guilds of artisans in all their privileges, customs and prerogatives which they enjoyed under the dominion of the Kings of Sweden";[5] or Article X, which stipulated that churches and schools should be supported upon the same basis as during the final reign of the Swedish régime. None of the parish and normal schools established by Charles XI in 1687 was reopened. The peasants were surrendered to the newly invigorated despotism of their squires, who considered all the Swedish agrarian reforms, including the abolishment of serfdom, as annulled. Once more the Latvian farmer was looked upon as an outright property, to be punished, transported, dispossessed, or sold at the discretion of his owner.

An attempt to justify such arbitrariness was made by a Councilor of the Diet, Baron Rosen, who, in 1739, presented to the Department of Justice in St. Petersburg, as documentation in an appealed case, a most curious declaration[6] concerning the rights of the Livonian nobles over the land and property, labor, and lives of their farmers. These unlimited rights, Rosen claimed, were based on the Roman *jus belli*. The substance of his highly fallacious argument was that, when the *dominium* of the nobles was established at the initial conquest of the country, they acquired absolute rights over the persons and properties of the cultivators of the land, since these formed part and parcel of the *demesne*. Rosen further maintained that the nobles had at one time possessed the right of life and death over the peasants but had voluntarily renounced this privilege to the state, retaining only the power of discipline and correction. Rosen was playing upon the gullibility and ignorance of the Russian justices, who knew nothing of the original feudal conditions of the German occupation of Livonia, which

---

[4] A. Schwabe, *Agrarian History of Latvia* (Riga, 1928), p. 96.

[5] A. Bilmanis, ed., *Latvian-Russian Relations. Documents* (Washington, 1944), 20f.

[6] J. Vigrabs, *Die Rosensche Deklaration vom Jahre 1739, ein Beitrag zur Geschichte der Leibeigenschaft in Livland und Estland* (Tartu, 1937).

had in no way granted such privileges to the vassals. Certain German historians have since sought to exonerate the corporation of the Livonian nobles of culpability in this matter by insisting that Rosen acted on his own initiative.

Russia continued indifferent to the misery of the Balts and the prevarications of their masters until the Empress Catherine II, who was currently indulging a fashionable taste for liberalism, undertook a journey of inspection through Estonia and Vidzeme in 1764. The Tsarina may have been inspired in this undertaking by a personal audience with the Estonian Protestant pastor Johann Georg Eisen von Schwartzenberg, who, in his treatise against serfdom published by the Russian Academy of Sciences in 1764, had faithfully reported the horrors of peasant life in his province.[7] Catherine II was deeply impressed by the conditions which she witnessed, among them a high degree of drunkenness encouraged by the excessive distillation of alcohol by the squires, who monopolized most of the rye crop for this lucrative purpose. In 1765, she ordered the Livonian Governor-General, Count Browne, to present to the Diet of Vidzeme a project for the amelioration of the state of the farmers.

After a thorough investigation of the unbridled oppression exercised by the manor-lords, Count Browne offered the following three proposals: official recognition of the farmers' property and inheritance rights to their movable belongings; a definitive fixing of the amounts of contributions and labor-duty owed the manors in the rural registers (*vaka* books); the curtailing of the right of "paternal correction" in order to prevent its abuse in the future. Answering these moderate suggestions, the Diet asserted that the peasants were *servi* in the sense of the Roman law, and therefore, like any other property, were subject to being claimed, conveyed, and sold. In spite of the attempts of Stephen Bátory and Charles XI to change the status of the serfs, the Livonian nobility had reached the conclusion that such a step was impracticable, since "serfdom was deeply rooted in the natural genius of the nation." They alleged that the unlimited power of the squires over their serfs' persons and properties had been repeatedly confirmed by the Russian Tsars. The nobles in the Diet further maintained that, since the farmers formed the "most essential" part of the squires' property, their welfare would be of prime importance to their masters. Such as had failed to follow this "rule of economic wisdom" were merely prodigals

---

[7] Under the title *Eines liefländischen Patrioten Beschreibung der Leibeigenschaft wie solche in Liefland über die Bauern eingeführt ist.* See further R. Vipper, "Aufklärung in Livland" in the symposium *Die Letten,* ii (Riga, 1932), 26-47.

deserving of censorship. After insisting that their conduct toward their serfs had never surpassed the bounds of humanity or reason, the nobles assured Count Browne that they were possessed of "Christian feelings and a deep sense of humaneness," and that on their "word of honor," they would continue to show due kindness to the farmers in the future.

The Governor-General, recognizing not only the bald falsehoods contained in this rebuttal but also the purely declarative and therefore in no way binding nature of the promises, replied that he requested positive legal provisions for the protection of the peasants against oppression.[8] He added that the Empress had set a limit to the despotism of the nobles in this regard. Threatened by an alternative governmental measure, the Diet reluctantly produced a declaration which was essentially the proposals originally submitted by Count Browne himself, and now officially proclaimed as a "spontaneous paternal gift" of the nobility to the farmers.

Since whatever specific promises of improvement were contained in this measure were mostly canceled by other clauses and nullified by the manifest insincerity of the nobles and their long experience in terrorizing the peasants, and particularly since there was no authority to enforce the observation of these proposals, the lot of the Latvian farmer continued to deteriorate. Taxes and labor-duty requirements were doubled and sometimes tripled. Families were broken up by removal or sale of their members. The squires showed their habitual reluctance to countenance education of the Latvians, upon whom, in spite of Count Browne's insistence that the Diet introduce compulsory elementary schools, was thrown the entire burden of school support. None the less, popular education, represented by a single parish school with three pupils in 1713, made such rapid strides among the people, who bled themselves to support it, that by the end of the eighteenth century 63 per cent of the population could read and write.

The selling of persons continued quite openly. Hupel, a Protestant pastor and one of the few defenders of the oppressed Latvians, in 1777 wrote: "A man servant can be bought in Livonia for thirty to fifty rubles silver; an artisan, cook or weaver for anything up to one hundred rubles; the same price is asked for a whole family, a maidservant rarely costing more than ten rubles, while children can be bought for four rubles each. Agricultural workers and their children are sold or bartered for horses, dogs, pipes, etc."[9]

[8] A. Schwabe, op.cit., p. 101ff.
[9] Quoted in J. Hampden Jackson, Estonia, p. 72.

That same year, in the face of serious peasant revolts, Count Browne recalled to the Livonian Diet the promises of 1765. The nobles retorted by taking even more rigorous measures against the Latvians who had dared to complain or revolt. The squires, through the confidential agents they maintained in St. Petersburg and Moscow to keep on good terms with the influential officials at the Russian court, denounced the Governor-General as insane after he had ordered the physical chastisement of one of the more obnoxious of these intermediaries.

Although Catherine II continued to repose confidence in the aging Browne, her liberal fancies were drawing to an end. She was soon bent on terminating the local autonomy of Livonia. In 1783, she ordered the introduction of the Russian form of provincial administration in Vidzeme, which was now called the province of Riga, with Count Browne for its Regent, and a system of lieutenant tax-collectors. The College of the Livonian Diet was abolished, and in its stead a Provincial Administrative Commission was installed, presided over by the Regent. A further offense to the old landowning families and to the exclusive burgher oligarchies was the admission to the reorganized Diets and to the city councils of *parvenus* representing the newer strata of landed and urban gentry.

As a compensation for the loss of their political power, the Livonian-German nobles now obtained recognition of their unlimited property rights to their estates. Thus 188 manors, once fiefs, then in turn the property of the Polish, Swedish, and Russian Crowns, were now donated outright to the squires who had appropriated them during the confusion of the Great Northern War.

The introduction of the Russian poll tax led, in 1784, to widespread revolts of the peasants, who had believed that the payment of this tax to the Russian Government absolved them from the charges, dues, and labor-duty required by the manor-lords, and accordingly refused to meet these obligations. Although the Russian troops severely repressed these uprisings, deporting many of the Latvian peasants to Siberia, a government investigation was ordered which brought to light a multitude of manorial abuses. For the next decade the fear of government interference dominated the Livonian squires, and small agrarian reforms were undertaken in order to fend off investigations into the larger abuses.[10]

[10] The best testimony to the tyranny of the German squires in these years was presented by one of their number, H. von Hagemeister, *Materialen zu einer Geschichte der Landgüter Livlands* (Riga, 1836), whose judgment of his fellow squires is devastating.

Upon his death in 1792, Count Browne was succeeded by the reactionary Prince Repnin, who sided wholeheartedly with the Livonian-German nobility. The latter, having always enjoyed the sympathy of the German aristocrats frequenting the Russian court, now began to win increasing support both from this all-pervasive and highly influential element and from the growing conservatism of the Tsarist court itself.

During the first years of Russian rule, Riga had lost the proud tradition of administrative independence which had survived Polish and Swedish dominion. Shortly after its surrender in 1710, and contrary to the articles signed between the Russian Commander and the Swedish Governor which had guaranteed it all the privileges of an autonomous city, Russian infringements of this contract were in evidence. The Riga militia were disarmed, and the gates of the city were manned by Russian troops. In 1716, during a visit of the Tsar, the Burgomaster, Brockhausen, was deported to Siberia for refusing to billet an aide of the Tsar. Interpreting the unfortunate Brockhausen's attitude as representing the Riga Council's wilful opposition to the Russian Government, Peter the Great, in 1721, ordered the Governor-General of Livonia to assume the office of Supreme Comptroller of the Riga finances. At the same time, a Russian official was appointed President of the City Council and Chief of the Riga Police. The German Councilors and Elders of the guilds became mere officials, fully subject to the Russian chief administrator.[11]

As a consequence of this humiliation, the burgher élite, the German patricians, now disengaged themselves entirely from political life, preferring to devote their energies to money-making, high living, and resisting all manifestations of change or social progress. Their clothes were of the finest English cloth and cut, but their minds clung to obsolete political and economic fashions, stubbornly ignoring the new patterns of Western liberalism.

The Riga Germans, always quick to seize any opportunity for profit, in 1738 followed the example set by the squires in depriving the farmers of their property, by obtaining a measure ordering all Latvian house owners and landed proprietors within the city or its suburbs to sell their property within a year. But Count Browne, recognizing this as a concealed attempt to expropriate Latvian property, annulled the order of the City Council. Similarly disapproved was the Council's

[11] For details and statistics of the history of Riga under Russian rule, see J. Straubergs, *Rigas vēsture*, p. 416ff.

decree of 1749 forbidding Latvian citizens to wear so-called "German" clothes, that is, Western European fashions.

Encouraged by Count Browne's attitude in these matters, some Latvians demanded the right to membership in the guilds. The Riga Council, not without difficulty, averted this step until 1785, when a Russian law decreed that, instead of the Great Guild, three merchant guilds were to be formed, to which merchants of all nationalities must be admitted. That same year, the new Russian municipality law provided that Riga should have a lord mayor, two burgomasters, and a twelve-member council, all elected; the electorate to consist of all citizens over the age of twenty-five paying not less than fifty rubles in taxes. Thus at one blow the exclusive nature both of the guilds and the City Council was destroyed. However, this did not signify the end of German control, as the 1786 elections demonstrated by revealing that of the 119 citizens eligible to vote, the great majority were, naturally enough, wealthy Germans. In 1796, the newly crowned Tsar Paul I, of strongly German and conservative sympathies, restored the old régime not only in Riga, but throughout Livonia, where Catherine's lieutenancy system was abolished. In Riga the oligarchical rule of the Council and the guilds was resumed. Not until 1830 was the Artisans' Guild abolished by a Russian decree, and trades declared open to all citizens.

This move was thoroughly in accord with Paul's temperamental addiction to tyranny. During his five-year reign this frustrated son of the great Catherine sought to eradicate in Russia all the signs of French cultural influence which his mother had urged upon her court. His fear and hatred of the French Revolution, amounting to mania, pervaded his capricious and violent being. In 1798, he allowed the homeless "Louis XVIII" to settle in Mitau. But his admiration was reserved for Napoleon Bonaparte and his strong methods. His insanity afforded grounds enough for his assassination in 1801, with the approval of his liberal, sentimental, and fervent son, Alexander I, who came to the throne in an aura of youthful humanitarian aspirations. Alexander's excited admiration of the French Revolution had been fostered by his tutor, the Swiss philosopher and Republican La Harpe, who had had charge of the Grand Duke's early education with the full approval of Catherine. Alexander's tastes and interests were reflected in his entourage of young Russian liberals who encouraged him in his somewhat faint attempts (for the hard practice of politics alarmed him) to introduce a few reforms aimed at alleviating the lot of the Russian serfs and curtailing the property privileges of the nobles.

The young Russian liberals had their counterpart among the new generation of Livonian squires, who had accepted the ideas of the Enlightenment as introduced by Herder (living in Riga from 1764 to 1765), and found inspiration in the energies released by the French Revolution. One of the most notable of these Livonian liberals was Friedrich von Sievers, a demissioned officer of the Russian Imperial Guards who, upon his inheritance of his father's estate, had been profoundly shocked by the spectacle of the degraded Latvian peasants. Von Sievers was greatly impressed by a pamphlet entitled *Die Letten, vorzüglich in Livland, am Ende des philosophischen Jahrhunderts,* published in Leipzig in 1796, prepared by Garlieb Merkel, son of a Livonian pastor and ardent devotee of the philosophy of the Enlightenment. Merkel had been urged by General Superintendent Sonntag to write this denouncement of serfdom. At the time of von Sievers' election as Councilor of the Livonian Diet in 1797, Sonntag extended his support to this young intellectual by warmly recommending his program of peasant reforms.

Although von Sievers seemingly persuaded the majority of the Diet to restore some of the liberal measures of the Swedish régime, the more reactionary nobles called upon their influential kin at the court of St. Petersburg, who had little difficulty in persuading the tyrannical Paul to withhold his approval of the Diet's bill. But in 1802, Alexander I, also a reader of Merkel's book, which had been translated into French by the Abbé Sieyes, visited Vidzeme and made the acquaintance of von Sievers. Disturbed by a bloody insurrection of the farmers on a manor near Valmiera, the Tsar requested von Sievers to present to him personally his reform project of 1797, which Alexander promptly approved and forwarded to the Marshal of the Livonian Diet with the request that it be passed in extraordinary session.

This measure, which became the Agrarian Reform Bill of 1804, was passed reluctantly by the Diet over the angry protests of the reactionaries, among them the Russian Governor-General von Richter. It offered a certain degree of security to the serfs, though it did not grant them their coveted freedom. For this last reason it was not truly popular with the Latvian peasantry. On the other hand, the German squires bitterly resented its recognition of the farmers as hereditary lease-holders of their lands; its prohibition of the sale of a peasant apart from his land; its fixing of labor-duty and taxes in the rural registers; its prohibition of land appropriation by the manor-lords; and, to a marked degree, the provisions for the administration of the law, including a land survey to be conducted by Russian officials. A particular affront to the squires and their concept of their unlimited property rights was that part of the law which dealt with the special cases where the adjacent farmland could be condemned to the manor. The assumption that, in such qualifiedly exceptional cases, the farmer had a right to full compensation, invalidated the stubborn manorial claim that the peasant was only a usufructuary or tenant of the land.

In order to interpret and enforce the Agrarian Reform Bill of 1804, an accompanying law was passed providing for the establishment on every manor of a rural court whose three justices should be chosen among the members of the adjacent rural community (*pagasts*). These new courts divested the squires of the right of physical punishment over the farmers of the *pagasti*, though they still retained this right of "paternal correction" over the peasants on their manors.

A series of bad harvests canceled most of the benefits which might have accrued to the Latvian peasantry from the reform of 1804. Even worse were rural conditions in Kurland, where no reforms had been vouchsafed and starvation stalked the land. Here an unalleviated state of despair provided a suitable seed bed for revolutionary ardors and rumors that the Napoleonic forces were approaching with their gift of liberty and equality for the Baltic peoples. Leaflets were circulated bearing vague promises concerning the restoration of the Duchies of Kurland and Lithuania to independence.[12]

But the Treaty of Tilsit, concluded in June 1807 between the seemingly unconquerable Napoleon and the bewildered and dismayed Alexander, who was persuaded to renounce his allies England, Sweden, and Prussia, shattered the confused hopes of Poles, Lithuanians, and Latvians alike. Franco-Russian relations did not long maintain an amicable equilibrium. By 1809, Alexander, after annexing Finland, once more drew near to England. He looked sulkily upon Napoleon's creation of the Duchy of Warsaw with the King of Saxony for its puppet ruler, since he had dreamed of being himself elected hereditary King of Poland. The Treaty of Tilsit was but a memory when, in June 1812, Napoleon began his invasion of Russia by crossing the Niemen south of Kovno and capturing Vilna. The Russians now streamed out of Kurland, taking with them a large number of carts, cattle, horses, and peasants, all requisitioned without compensation.

This pellmell departure once more stimulated rumors that the

[12] A. Schwabe, *op.cit.*, p. 104ff.

French armies were coming to render justice to the oppressed farmers, who now found the courage to rise against their squires. But they knew themselves doomed as soon as they realized that, instead of the French, a Prussian corps, commanded by General York, had been dispatched to restore order. In accordance with a secret treaty, the Prussians were to occupy Kurland in return for their military assistance against Russia. For Frederick William III, unwilling and humbled ally of Napoleon, had been assuaged by the French Emperor's promise that, in case of Russia's defeat, he would be granted the Baltic Provinces.[13] Ominously, Prussia had now driven in her entering wedge.

The revolt of the peasants of Kurland was swiftly suppressed. A return to the *status quo* was heralded by a proclamation made by a French liaison officer, wherein he declared the intention of the occupying forces was to maintain order in the province by seeing to it that nothing was changed in the social system, especially regarding the relations between masters and servants, and by punishing severely those who might seek to disrupt these relations.[14] The attitude of the occupying Prussian corps in Kurland afforded an early example of that emphasis on rigid policing which was to characterize the behavior of German forces in the Baltic a century later.

The Russian Governor in Riga, General von Essen, panicked by the occupation of nearby Mitau, incontinently ordered the burning of the city's suburbs. On the night of July 12, 1812, a major conflagration caused a 17 million ruble loss and left homeless some 7,000 citizens, mostly Latvians. This hasty and unnecessary action may have been inspired by Napoleon's threat, voiced in a moment of rage over Riga's position as a center of English runners of the continental blockade, to destroy this "suburb of London."

On August 1, De Chamboudois and De Montigny were appointed by Napoleon as Regents of the Duchy of Kurland, the first receiving the southeastern districts of Jelgava and Sēlpils which constituted the province of Zemgale, the second, those of Kuldīga, Tukums, and Piltene, or Kurzeme proper. The purpose of this regency was to rally all the resources of the country to the service of supplying Napoleon's army in Russia, for which heavy contributions in money and goods were exacted.

But by the end of 1812, tattered remnants of the retreating Grand Army were once more at Kovno. General York, abandoning Kurland,

[13] H. Nicolson, *The Congress of Vienna* (New York, 1946), p. 20.
[14] H. Vitols, *La mer baltique* . . . , p. 204.

allowed himself to be captured by the Russians, with whom he concluded the Convention of Tauroggen on December 30, 1812. King
Frederick William III was then persuaded to renew his old alliance
with the Tsar, and Alexander now found himself on the verge of that
dazzling European reputation which was to gild the rest of his days.

The internal affairs of the Baltic Provinces could scarcely interest
this apotheosized Tsar as they had the younger and more impressionable Alexander. Although the Latvians, thoroughly disillusioned by
French opportunism, had turned once more to the Russian ruler for
an understanding of their plight, it was not until 1817, after repeated
peasant uprisings, that the Governor-General, insisting that the position of the peasants of Kurland be improved, offered the Kuronian
Diet a choice of the Livonian law of 1804 or the Estonian law of 1816.
The latter was a measure adopted by the Estonian Diet of nobles,
whereby the peasants were liberated from serfdom but deprived of
their farmlands, now declared to be the property of the manors. This
form of liberation was properly called "birds' freedom." The Kuronian
nobles, following the example of the Estonian squires who had immediately realized the value of additional manor land at a time when
grain prices were rising, grasped at the opportunity to adopt the
Estonian law. The new bill was confirmed by the Tsar and became
law in Kurland in 1817. The edict was read in Mitau, in the presence
of Alexander himself and the forcibly assembled "thankfully liberated"
serfs, who were ordered to demonstrate their enthusiasm.

The squires of Vidzeme now hastened to assume the highly profitable role of "benefactors" of the farmers. In 1818, Reinhold von
Samson-Himmelstjerna drafted a bill similar to the Estonian and
Kuronian measures. The Russian Government was pressed for confirmation. The argument was advanced that in granting freedom to
their serfs the manor-lords were losing contributions in charges and
labor-duty for which they should be compensated by receiving outright
the farms of the serfs. These farms, they insisted, were in any case the
legal property of the manor. The squires further reasoned that such
a bill would be in the spirit of Adam Smith's teachings about free
contracts and equal bargaining between owners and tenants. Whether
these far-fetched arguments had any effect is hard to say. In any event
the measure became law in Vidzeme in 1819. The serfs had their
freedom but they had no land, either by long lease or hereditary tenure.

The *vaka* books or rural registers, containing the fixed amounts of
taxes and labor-duty required of the peasants, were now abolished, the

relations between the squires and their prospective farmer-tenants being left to the much vaunted principle of freedom of contract. In actuality, the squires had a marked advantage over the farmers in any of the economic bargaining because of their education and virtual control of police and judiciary powers. Those peasants who refused to sign the new leases were forcibly evicted and punished by special military detachments apportioned to the more "unreliable" rural communities.

The squires further strengthened their hold on the rural economy by gaining increased control of the local administrative and judiciary offices. The manor-lord now appointed the mayor of the *pagasts* as well as the rural judge from a limited panel of candidates elected by the members of the rural community. These officials he could remove at will. In addition to being chief of police, he held the keys to the treasury, issued passports, and granted or withheld permission to leave the district. There was small opportunity of complaint, since the decisions of the rural court were subjected to approval by the squire. All the members of the *pagasts* were jointly responsible for the taxes of each individual. All public charges, for charity, education, recruiting, were incumbent upon the members of the rural community, the squire retaining discretionary powers in these matters.[15]

When the alarming fall of grain prices in the 1820's precipitated a serious economic crisis in the Baltic, the squires hastened to transform many of the farms into pasture for the more profitable raising of cattle and fodder. A large number of the peasants thus deprived of their means of livelihood became the helpless creatures of their squires, who responded to their need by increasing the corvées to the limit of endurance. The landed nobility was feeling more firmly ensconced in its powers than ever since Tsar Nicholas I (1826-1855), who possessed an order-loving military mind and an inherent distaste for social upheavals, had confirmed the privileges in 1829 of the Estonian, Livonian, and Kuronian nobles as compiled in 23 volumes by that same von Samson-Himmelstjerna who had drafted the agrarian law of 1819. The Livonian Diet proceeded to commission him to codify the administrative laws of Livonia, including the Statutes of the Diet and of the Corporation of the nobles. This code was likewise confirmed by the Tsar in 1845.

[15] A compact, if at times smug presentation of the case for the German squires under Russian rule is to be found in R. Freiherr von Engelhardt, *Die deutschen Ostseeprovinzen Russlands* (Munich, 1916), p. 37ff. One subdivision is entitled "Und dennoch deutsch."

The poor harvests in Vidzeme during the period between 1835 and 1840, together with the extravagant oppression by the squires, precipitated the explosion of hunger riots which had to be brutally quelled by Russian troops. An investigation into the causes of these uprisings by Governor-General von Pahlen and two aides of the Tsar led to the discovery that the peasants, being almost entirely landless, were without the means to grow their bread. Under governmental pressure, the Diet passed a few insignificant amendments to the law of 1819. A more radical bill, prepared by one of the liberal Councilors, Hamilcar von Völkersahm, proposing that all of the land held by the peasants in 1804 should be reallotted to them as tenancies, was quickly quashed.

Beneath the shadow-play reflecting the resistance of the Livonian landed interests, the whims of the Governor-Generalate in Riga, and the varying degrees of Tsarist nervousness or indifference, the Latvian and Estonian peasants remained remarkable for the steadfastness of their hatred. Though officially under the dominion of St. Petersburg, the object of their fixed distrust was the German squire, the symbol of injustice, the instrument of degradation, and now the cause of their starvation. In spite of the fact that the Russian poll tax of 4.6 rubles for every male and the iniquitous Russian recruiting system went far to cancel whatever benefits the Tsars had brought to the Baltic Provinces, even such a sovereign as Nicholas I continued, in contrast to the despotic Livonian gentry, to be an object of hope rather than of odium to the landless and desperate Baltic peasantry. The Greek Orthodox priests gathered a large following when it was understood that they were offering, somewhere in Central Russia, a "soul's acre" to every convert. Indeed, Riga was besieged by the starving, who had come from all corners of the Baltic Provinces to "get on the lists" for this earthly reward, which it was presumed the Tsar in his bounty would distribute.

Nicholas I, disturbed by reports that the proselytizing Greek Orthodox priests were stirring up trouble among the Baltic peasants and anxious that agrarian conditions in the Baltic Provinces should not lag behind those in Russia, where some reforms were going forward, ordered further investigations in Vidzeme. In 1846, he appointed the Committee on Baltic Affairs and charged it with an examination of Livonian agrarian laws. The soul of this committee was von Völkersahm, who had spent some years in America, where he had gained the friendship of George Washington. The committee drew up a bill which was confirmed by the Tsar on a temporary basis, to remain in

effect for a period of six years. This measure had for its main object
the creation of a class of smallholders. Although it provided that the
formerly tribute-paying farmland should remain the property of the
manor-lords, the latter, contrary to the law of 1819, were now no longer
entitled to dispose of the land otherwise than by selling or leasing it
to the members of the rural community. Once more the tax-paying
farmland of the *pagasti* was theoretically separated from the tax-
exempt manors, special land surveyors being commissioned to prepare
new maps clearly marking the boundaries between these two land
categories. Whereas the manor-lord retained freedom of action on his
demesne, certain immutable rights were granted the peasants of the
pagasts land.

Provision was also made for the stipulation in the contract for payment of the leases in money rather than through corvées, thus ending
the feudal economy based on produce tithes and labor-duty. But the
shrewd squires, by taking advantage of certain vague phases in the
law, often continued to exact the payment of leases with labor-duty.

Reassured by the growing reactionary temper of the Tsarist court,
where the German aristocratic element enjoyed ever-increasing influence, the Livonian-German nobles, as the six-year term of the law
of 1849 drew to a close, began preparing amendments to this unpopular measure. In 1856, the Diet of Vidzeme drew up a bill providing
for the renewal of labor-duty and the restriction of the sale of land to
farmers, under the pretext that such transactions were encouraging the
growth of a dangerous class of Latvian smallholders.

But the tide of Russian affairs had changed. While the Livonian
nobles fought for their despotic privileges, Russia had lost the Crimean
War. The rigid Paul I had died of disappointment, and his son, although not unsympathetic to certain aspects of his father's conservatism, stood committed to the liberation of the Russian serfs. Alexander
II (1856-1881) devoted the first years of his reign to the drafting of the
great Reform Bill of 1861, which finally effected this slowly-matured
emancipation. The Livonian nobles had small chance of restoring the
conditions of the eighteenth century in such an atmosphere, and were
forced to accept the peasant law of 1849, confirmed by the Tsar in
1856 with such favorable amendments as the reintroduction of the
vaka books and the enlargement of the lots to be sold to farmers to
one half *uncus*. The Russian agrarian law of 1861, which, in addition
to liberating the serfs, forced the Russian gentry to sell one half of
their lands to the newly emancipated peasants, was applied to the

Latvian province of Latgale. The squires of Vidzeme, fearing that their turn might be next, put a better face on selling small lots to the manorial farmsteaders. In 1863, the peasants finally attained freedom of movement by the introduction of the passport system which permitted them to settle in towns or even travel abroad. When the implications of the peasant's new freedom to leave his farm or community became clear, it was only logical that labor-duty should be abolished. In 1865, the Russian Government did just that, decreeing an end to the still existing labor-duty in the Baltic Provinces and forbidding the squires to inflict corporal punishment on their tenant farmers. In 1866, the squires' stranglehold on the government of the rural communities was terminated by the granting to the assemblies of the *pagasti* of the right to elect their own governing body, together with the judges of the rural court, and an executive mayor. This was in keeping with, though not patterned on, the Russian Reform of 1864 which introduced local self-government in the form of the *Zemstvo*, or local Council. The Livonian Diet, however, continued under the secure control of the German landed nobles, since the Latvian peasants had not yet gained the right to elect representatives to this body.

In order to facilitate the redemption of the farms, Hamilcar von Völkersahm organized a Farmers' Mortgage Bank which issued four per cent mortgages on farms to be sold by the squires. The latter, however, preferred the six per cent mortgages of the Bank of the Landed Nobles, and the farmers showed themselves willing to pay this higher interest in order to become their own masters. By 1901, the farmers of Vidzeme, that is 35 per cent of modern Latvia, had paid the squires for redeemed farms 76 million gold rubles; in addition, 17,641 farmsteads were burdened with six per cent mortgages to the amount of 31 million rubles.[16] Relatively the same situation prevailed in Kurland, which was to constitute 41 per cent of the later state of Latvia. In spite of the continued possession of two-thirds of the agricultural land of Vidzeme by 162 German noble families, a class of smallholders had emerged which was to bear the burden of the building of a modern state.

Up until the portentous year of 1881, when an anarchist's bomb ended the life of Alexander II, St. Petersburg had only sporadically taken any immediate interest in the Baltic Provinces. Russian authorities, frequently of German extraction, found it advisable to let the so-called Baltic barons in Kurland and Vidzeme continue their busy

[16] A. Schwabe, *op.cit.*, p. 116.

exploitation of the land and their iron-fisted political, social, and cultural control of the Latvians, an ignored and entirely uninfluential majority population with far less than what is understood in modern times as minority status. Peasant reform, no longer avoidable in Russia, had, logically, to be extended to Estonia, Vidzeme, and Kurland. With a painful slowness the Latvian serf regained his status as a human being. But care was taken not to shock too dangerously the susceptibilities of the squires, who boasted formidable supporters at the Tsarist court, where the Baltic barons were represented as the "backbone of the Russian throne." During the reign of Alexander II, although the German nobility constituted far less than one per cent of the Russian population, and about three per cent of the Livonian, they occupied from a third to a half of the high offices of the St. Petersburg Government.

In 1881, Alexander's bloody end brought to a disastrous term the liberal reforms and the constitutional movement which had gained momentum during that monarch's reign. Alexander III (1881-1894), equally threatened by the regicides, saw no choice but to repudiate liberalism; and many former liberals, shocked and grieved by the intransigence of the radicals, now abandoned their hope in Western democratic progress and tolerated the strengthening of the secret political police, the dreaded *Ochrana*, which extended its paralyzing powers to the Baltic Provinces. These lands now suffered an intensive Russification.[17]

But before we examine the effects of this new oppression, we must turn back to the beginnings of a movement which had gained gradual acceleration throughout the century and a half of Russia's semi-indifference to her Baltic conquest. While the Tsars signed Livonia's governmental decrees, which were more or less enforced by the German ruling class, and while the squires struggled for their economic control of the Latvian peasants, this last group, never entirely lost to the meaning of dignity and freedom, was stirring in the toils of its foreign tyrannies. Stimulating forces were being brought to bear on this uneasy awakening. The harsh brakes of Prussian and Russian conservatism were going to be hard put to it to hold before that least controllable of revolutions: a whole people's attainment of self-knowledge and self-esteem.

[17] Engelhardt is particularly bitter on the subject of the Tsarist Government's measures of Russification, *op.cit.*, pp. 155ff., 173ff.

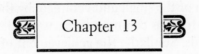

Chapter 13

The Birth of a National Consciousness*

THE nineteenth century, which saw the ripening of the stronger Powers of Western Europe into nationalistic states, brought to birth on the periphery of this maturation and under the shadow of Hapsburg or Russian dominance the national awareness of many smaller peoples. The Czechs, the Slovaks, the Poles, the South Slavs, and the Baltic peoples were all constrained to await the cataclysmic upheaval of a world war to attain the political expression of their many-sided striving for independence. The study of these various shades of national pride, embodied in the social and cultural advances of robust ethnic groups, has proved fascinating to those historians who seek an understanding of the toughly individual strands out of which modern European civilization is woven. No student of the past or scanner of the future can afford to neglect or discount any one of these particular patterns which has come, entire and undeniable, from the loom of history. Just as every citizen must be made to count in a sound polity, so every organic national entity must be reckoned with in a greater European community worthy of the name.

The denial of integrity to the least of these groups, which has found its being in a still improperly understood but natural growth, may, in essence, be compared to the denial of freedom of spirit to the individual. A people who have honored a common heritage, chosen a common destiny, and achieved the balance of true personality, may be singularly apt to martyrdom, since any striking of a balance immediately invites the attack of stronger Powers less successfully poised. And again, as in the case of the individual, such a martyrdom may become the stimulus to another victory, a return to wholeness promising a degree of ruin to those agents, those often frenzied proponents of historical error who seem constrained to attack whatever sane equilibrium opposes their creed of change by violence.

* Much of this chapter is based on two scholarly works: A. Bandrevičs, *Noti-kumi latviešu atmošanās laikmetā* (Events of the Latvian National Awakening), (Riga, 1931), and E. Arnis, *Latvju tautas politiskā atmoda* (The Political Awakening of the Latvian Nation) (Riga, 1934). Biographical details may be assumed to correspond to data collected by L. Adamovičs, see note 2, *sub nomine*.

The molestation of the small and complete by the powerful and un-integrated appears to be as common an occurrence among nations as it is among individuals. Similarly, the achievement of status by a nation which has not been befriended by history may be as slow and painful as the emergence of the underprivileged individual. Unfailingly inter-esting, like sound men from mean beginnings, such proud and rational states, whose roots go deep into centuries of oppression, claim the at-tention of all admirers of intelligent courage.

Peculiarly gratifying to the sympathetic student of emergent nation-alities is the modern history of the Baltic States, since these compact nations, in the short period of creativity granted them, manifested a highly efficient blend of sentiment and realism. This balance of sub-jective patriotism and objective politics enabled them to wrest a sense of glory from the remote past, confront the would-be destroyers of that past with potent wrath, and build their democracies on brother-hood; while at the same time refusing to ape the offensive or offended supernationalism of more grandiose Powers, to jostle one another im-moderately, or to dream of bestriding the Baltic. In the Baltic Prov-inces, what J. Holland Rose calls "the instinct of nationality,"[1] while it provided a full impulse for the emergence of a culture and the making of states, kept within the limits of this truly historical objec-tive. The necessary energy, even to the point of a degree of ruthless-ness, was forthcoming, yet not at the expense of a spirit of dedication and a belief in peaceful endeavor. The imagination, memory, love of the land, and keen response to natural pleasures of the Baltic peoples, combined with their patience, irony, independence, and practicality of born husbandmen to inspire their whole development from serfdom to a highly self-conscious citizenry within three generations.

In focusing our attention on the growth of Livonia (Vidzeme), Kurland and Latgale into united nationhood, a study which will oc-cupy us for the rest of this book, we discover certain factors which condition the national awakening and its consolidation in these prov-inces. The two facets of the oppression from which the Latvian people sought liberation were foreign dominion and oligarchical rule. The foreign domination was twofold: the Russian Government and local German administration at first superimposed their control of Livonia and Kurland, but eventually they drew apart, further wrenching the fibers of the subjugated nationality by this abrupt divergence. The role of the intelligentsia, caught as they were between German intolerance,

[1] J. Holland Rose, *Nationality in Modern History* (New York, 1916), p. 155.

Tsarist nervousness, and liberal Russian applause, was a particularly difficult one. Two versions of Christianity, the Evangelical Lutheran and the Greek Orthodox, found themselves aligned with the anti-national, antiliberal forces in an unseemly struggle to secure the Latvian converts for the German or the Russian camp. As a consequence of this spectacle, the national aspirations of the people, although markedly idealistic, bore no distinct religious imprint. Finally, although shot through with strong currents of proletarian revolt, the liberation movement in this Baltic area, especially in the cities, assumed a dominantly agrarian aspect, owing chiefly to the lingering of the feudal idea among the German-Balts. This cultural lag threw the emphasis in the struggle for self-determination upon ownership of and loyalty to the land. The peasant class, from which both the bourgeoisie and the proletariat had sprung, while allied to these latter groups by their common hatred of the Germans and a deep suspicion of the Russians, continued to furnish the leaders with the slogans and the impetus for a national liberation.

The eagerness with which the Latvian peasant class seized upon opportunities not only for advancement but for responsibility, the fact that the son of a serf may have become the father of a politically alert artist or scholar in the fields of science, journalism, or sociology, may be attributed in good part to the nature of their opponents: a foreign élite bent on depriving the peasants not only of their sense of nationality but of their very humanity. Such oppression proved a powerful stimulus and a clear rallying point, unclouded by any possible divided loyalties. There was no question here of a submerged class wresting leadership from a First Estate which, though socially obsolete and no longer serving the cause of history, might still lay claim to patriotism. The loyalty of the German-Balt nobility had been first to their own class, and then, latterly, to the Russian Tsars, towards whom those who rejoiced in the title of *Deutschrussen* evidenced a high degree of personal attachment and fidelity. Far from wishing to serve their centuries-old homeland of Livonia, the squires could not conceive of it in terms eliciting any degree of devotion. It was simply a collection of estates, individually dear to their owners, collectively apolitical and anational. For the Baltic barons the Latvian people as an entity scarcely existed. Each squire looked only to his own peasants, a valuable if mulish lot, who must not be encouraged to go straining after what could only be a ridiculous and costly sense of dignity, national or otherwise. The German masters had never considered it worth their while to police either the native tongue or the native tales of their "born" serfs. They had, of course, consistently resorted to fraud and force in their long-drawn-out conquest of the yeoman's liberty and land. Yet, in spite of their apparent success, they had been both idle and unskillful in attacking the roots of peasant pride. Upon this stubborn stock they had entirely failed to graft any degree of faith in the dominion of the master race. The descendants of the German missionaries were singularly devoid of a sense even of political mission.

Thanks to this carelessness, so unwisely coupled with cruelty, generations of peasants had been flogged for disobedience, but never seduced from remembrance of a comely past or the hope, however unformulated, of an acceptable future. At the center of this ultimate refusal of allegiance to what had come to be traditional German rule was the Latvian peasant's concept of "home," identified with woods and fields once owned and ever since relentlessly desired, and magnified by legendary prides and bitter experience of loss. This basic concept of the individual and private home—the hut, the land, and the closely gathered family—had become entrenched in the primitive and persistent rural communities, whose members held out to the starvation point against the encroachments of the manors. At the height of German oppression, little had remained to the peasants of the *pagasti* beyond their desperate sense of "ownness." Here had been fostered, under the scornful noses of the "foreigners," a sense of outrage, of differentiation and, paradoxically, of strength, since the successive generations of the enslaved were still able to teach their sons to show every respect for the beloved land and none at all for its masters. The discovery of such a heritage of loyalty and hate would have amazed the squires, who looked only for laziness and greed with which, as good policemen, they were prepared to cope.

The ruling race, snug in their oligarchical institutions and lawless on their estates, had never experienced any need to Germanize the Livs, the Latvians, or the Kurs. Beyond a modicum of Christianity, they would have considered any further civilizing, especially on the reverenced German pattern, as *infra dignitatem*. We recall the Rigan decree forbidding the Latvian citizenry to adopt Western fashions in dress. German conservative culture was not for congenital serfs, and those radicals who indulged the dangerous practice of holding the obscenities of the French Revolution before the noses of a people generally identified with dogs deserved the condemnation of the entire German élite. The clergy as a whole, being dependent upon the whim of the squires, were bound to teach their flocks that, whereas their souls belonged to God, their bodies were the indisputable property of their squires. To this dogma they added their exhortations to remain on the land and avoid the moral pitfalls of the towns.

The landed nobles, as we have seen, could not be persuaded to support primary schools for the peasants, since they held that the latter would learn all they needed from early apprenticeship to unremitting labor. With the political obtuseness of the socially ingrown and the economically satiated, the German ruling minority made no approach to the minds or the spirit of the oppressed "majority." Apparently, the sleepy manor-lords and the representatives of the quaint Diets, becalmed in the Age of Despotism, ignored the portent of the very term "majority" in the nineteenth century, and quite failed to realize the flimsiness of their feudalism in the Age of Steam. Those of their philosophers, clergy, and administrators—rare men and doubly admirable—who insisted that the spirit and works of a liberal era must be taken into account, were scoffed at and menaced. The great Russian reforms must needs be accepted, but only on the condition of continued Tsarist sympathy for the Baltic landocracy and respect for the highly-placed German-Balt administrators.

In the face of this monumental indifference of the Germans and the pronouncedly erratic interest of the Tsarist régime, the Latvian peasants toiled painfully toward the reclamation of their "home" land. They held to this single goal without ulterior aims of building themselves into a class or a nation. Their first concern was with personal dignity, liberty, and security, of which their ancient habit of independence had been compounded. The intimate relationship which enslaved peoples have always seen between freedom and knowledge had moved the Latvian peasants to further deprive themselves for the support of rural schools as soon as these were allowed them. This craving for literacy, as an aspect of the vast hunger for self-respect which gripped a whole people, provided the soil in which the still undefined national awakening put down its first feeble roots.

Chief credit for these early stirrings must go to the Moravian Brethren, a Protestant sect originating in Moravia and Saxony, bearers of the true Hussite tradition, who first appeared in Vidzeme in 1732. Among the tenets of this pietist movement were belief in the full equality of the members of a parish, where a serf might stand beside a lord in the eyes of God, free election of the ministers of the church, and compulsory primary education. The advent of these confirmed democrats to the Baltic lands brought the leaven of astonishing hope to those masses who had received little save the lessons of obedience from those timid and discouraged, or merely indifferent and obtuse, churchmen who would not even learn the language of their congregations.

The movement gained a few distinguished sponsors among the nobility, notably the Councilor of the Livonian Diet, von Kampenhausen, and the widow of General von Hallert. Both were wealthy landowners, and both were connected with the pietist Count von Zinzendorf, who had permitted the Moravian Brethren to build themselves the town of Herrnhut (whence the name "Herrnhutists") on his estate in Saxony. The support of such persons, who were known to have high connections in St. Petersburg, together with the fact that the Moravian Brethren did not wish to break with the established Evangelical Lutheran parishes but only emphasized a greater devotion to the Scriptures and the importance of education, gave neither the Evangelical Lutheran Consistory nor the squires sufficient grounds for open opposition to the movement.

In 1738, with the encouragement of Baron von Kampenhausen, a Latvian normal school was opened on the baron's estate near Valmiera, for the purpose of training preachers for the Latvian congregations of such rural communities as had no established churches. Within twenty years of this modest start the movement had proved so dynamic that the German pastors, fearing to lose their grip on their native congregations, began attacking the Brethren as dangerous agitators preaching the blasphemy of equality. The movement was then denounced in St. Petersburg by the German landed nobles as fostering a "peasant aristocracy," and in 1743 it was prohibited by the representative of the Russian Government in Vidzeme. The teachers' seminary was closed, but not before it had created the first ranks of a national intelligentsia. In a surprisingly short time the Moravian Brethren had sown the seeds of what were to be the most characteristic fruits of the Latvian national movement: a sense of brotherhood, a need for participation in the work of the community, and a dazzling hope in education. The movement now went underground, to emerge again, especially in the sphere of education, in 1764, with the consent of Catherine the Great.

The following year, as we have already learned, Count Browne ordered the opening of parish schools in Livonia. Some Latvian primers and religious works were printed, as well as almanacs and calendars. The superintendent of the Latvian congregations of the Brethren, Bishop Georg Heinrich Loskil, of Kuronian birth,[2] compiled psalters in 1790 and 1797. The Latvians, among whom illiteracy had shrunk to 37 per cent by the end of the eighteenth century, were now able to see their language, for almost five centuries relegated to the uses of the home and the field, beginning to be honored in the church, the schools, and the press. The powerful and mysterious stimulus which lies in this sort of recognition of a slighted mother tongue was to play a major part in the expansion of the Latvians' hitherto muted sense of nationality.

We must not forget, however, that through all those dark centuries the folk memory had religiously preserved by word of mouth from generation to generation those folk tales and songs, epic and lyric, which we discovered already imbedded in the imagination of the earliest known tribes. Brilliant in detail and grand in depth of meaning, such legends as the Bearslayer myth, surviving the enslavement of a whole people, had reached the dawn of an era of liberation enriched by the symbolism of betrayal and loss. The *Dainas* had come to be revered as a people's only treasure, preserved from assault by its strangeness and seeming worthlessness to the conquerors. Within the rich variety and moral elevation of their myths and legends, the Latvians had found the only scope left them for their cramped humanity. Here, unbeknownst to most of their German masters, was still an area of liberty, a broad concourse where the peasant imagination could run free, strengthening that muscular hope and courage which was to make of the serf, whom many misjudged as greedy for land alone, a citizen bound to endow that land with transcendental meaning and claim the right to express this meaning in terms of patriotism and national independence.

Yet the first to seize the beauty and power of the Latvian folksongs was a German. Johann Gottfried Herder, who lived and taught in Riga from 1764 to 1769, made the first collection and translation of Latvian and Estonian folklore and introduced it enthusiastically to Goethe and Schiller. Testifying to the oppression of what he considered an originally cultured people, he wrote, "Humanity shudders with horror at the blood which was shed there. Perhaps the time will come when they will be set free, will be established again for Humanity's sake."[3] Herder quit Riga in an atmosphere of opposition to his "radical"

---

[2] L. Adamovičs, *Dzimtenes baznīcas vēsture* (Stockholm, 1947), p. 81ff.

[3] Quoted by Schwabe, *The Story of Latvia and her Neighbors*, p. 19.

views, for thus were qualified his devotion to the philosophy of the *Aufklärung* and his admiration for folk culture.

As we have seen, some of the younger Livonian German squires also professed themselves disciples of the Enlightenment and even of the French Revolution. They found an ideal example of feudal abuses on the estates of their own fathers. Pamphlets in Latvian were distributed among the peasantry, who gained therefrom what was to prove a false hope of Napoleonic liberation. The uprisings inspired by this literature of revolt had proved costly and futile. The ideas of liberty, equality, fraternity seemed to the Baltic peoples only fine phrases for certain of their more eccentric overlords to toy with.

Not by revolution would the Baltic serfs win their freedom. Doggedly the inhabitants of the rural communities awaited the reforms which they hoped for from Alexander I, whose prestige had outlasted that of the fabulous Napoleon. In 1817, the Tsar reaffirmed the edict of Catherine tolerating the Congregation of the Brethren. By 1843, this sect claimed 92 tabernacles with a membership of some 25,000, in spite of the continued opposition of the official church. As a result of this persecution, some of the Brethren became converts to the Greek Orthodox faith, following the example of one of their leaders, David Balodis, who, finding himself severely hampered in his work in Riga by the Evangelical Lutheran Consistory, received protection from the Greek Orthodox Bishop.

The zeal of the Brethren in the educational field did induce the Evangelical Lutheran Church to make some effort to fulfill the 1765 decision of the Livonian Diet concerning the opening of parish schools. The liberation bills of 1817-1819 further provided for the founding of elementary schools in rural communities: in Vidzeme for every 500, in Kurland for every 1,000 males, and one for each parish of not less than 2,000 souls. These schools, to be supported by the parishioners, would have their teachers appointed by the squires in concurrence with the pastors. The teachers of these humble institutions were for the most part poorly educated underlings of no status or influence. Since the newly-emancipated farmers were frequently too poor to support these schools, many communities still relied on the Brethren for whatever education they received.

In 1832, a law reorganizing the official church granted the Evangelical Lutheran pastors a certain degree of independence from their squires, thus encouraging a more enlightened group of men to assume the duties of the pastorate. In 1833, the pressure of just such a group brought about the opening at Cirava in Kurzeme of the first official normal school, whose graduates became teachers in the rural elementary schools. In 1839, a normal school was founded in Valmiera and a teachers' institute at Irlava in Kurzeme. The reputation of the Valmiera institution was enhanced by the character of its first director, Jānis Cimze (1814-1881), who, with the praiseworthy support of Father Walter of the parish of Valmiera, had studied abroad, graduating from the teachers' seminary at Weissenfels. Jānis Cimze, a noted lover of Latvian folk music and tireless worker for popular education, is considered the dean of Latvian educators.

In 1840, after numberless discussions in the Diets, usually initiated by the more humanitarian pastors, a rural education law was approved by the Russian Government, to be confirmed again in 1849 and in the sixties. This decree established parish school boards consisting of the squire, the pastor, the teacher, and one farmer of the rural community. Over these rural boards was the district school board, and above that the general board of popular schools. On these higher boards the German squires and pastors predominated, since not until 1871 in Vidzeme, and 1875 in Kurland, were two representatives of the farmers admitted to the district school boards.

The important office of Provincial School Councilor was fortunately occupied, from 1844 to 1856, by the German Lutheran pastor, later bishop, K. K. Ullmann, a true friend of the Latvian rural school system, who energetically organized teachers' conferences for purposes of coordination and exchange of experience. Far less sympathetic was Ullmann's successor, R. von Klot, who promptly ordered a reduction in the curriculum of the Valmiera Normal School, to be followed by similar action at the seminary in Irlava. Von Klot agreed with the majority of the squires that there was no need for a rural teacher to be too highly educated in such subjects as the physical and natural sciences, philosophy, or mathematics. The German nobles were beginning to grow uneasy over the educational ardor of the Latvians, who might take it into their heads to study history, a dangerous subject indeed when seized upon by an oppressed majority.

When the farmers gained permission in the 1830's to live in cities, take up trades, and participate in commerce and shipping, the germ of a Latvian middle class was born. The second half of the century saw the development of this class, consisting of skilled artisans, merchants, and the intellectuals, under the pressing need of such cities as Riga, Liepāja, and Ventspils for more followers of skilled trades than the small static German population could provide. In addition, the new rural courts and self-government bodies required officials who could claim at least a secondary education and at the same time be willing to accept the low salaries which Germans refused. All these conditions of urban and governmental expansion created a demand for Latvians educated in the technical fields and sometimes even on the university level. This meant the establishment of an increasing number of normal schools, with a broadened curriculum, navigation schools, and poly-technical institutions.

Particularly remarkable was the industrial development of Riga during the nineteenth century, as well as the rapid physical and popu-lation expansion of that leading Baltic city.[4] In 1851, Riga had 63 factories producing two million rubles worth of goods. The following year, the first telegraph line in Russia was installed between Riga and Ustj-Dvinsk at the mouth of the Daugava for the transmittal of ship-ping news. In 1862, a Polytechnical Institute was opened in Riga. In 1868, the Riga-Jelgava railway was opened, and in 1872 the iron rail-way bridge over the Daugava was completed. Electricity was intro-duced for lighting purposes in 1887. The Riga-Pskov-St. Petersburg railway was opened in 1889, and a pontoon bridge over the Daugava erected in 1896. An entirely modern water supply system was installed in 1904. This progress, assuring Riga all the benefits of technical ad-vancement in utilities and transport, was unparalleled in all of Russia. It had been particularly stimulated by the Crimean War when the blockade of the Black Sea ports had drawn official attention to the strategic importance of the Baltic inlets, particularly Riga, which had always been a major port and a busy center of the export-import trade.

In 1845, the Russian Government had dispatched a special com-mission for the revision of Riga's obsolete political and social institu-tions which by now corresponded neither to her expanding population (from 28,483 in 1812, to 77,867 in 1863) nor to her important eco-nomic position. Although the report of this commission was allowed to disappear into the archives of the Russian Ministry of the Interior, Yury Samarin, one of the officials of the commission and a Slavophil publicist, began to publish in the Russian press his *Riga Letters*, which revealed the anachronisms of the German caste system operating in a modern city's government. He was imprisoned for being what the Germans at the Tsarist court called "a dangerous agitator."[5]

[4] Von Engelhardt, *Die deutschen Ostseeprovinzen*, pp. 211-220.
[5] The answer of the German-Balts was C. Schirrens' *Livländische Antwort an Herrn Juri Samarin* (Leipzig, 1869).

The Russian Municipality Law was finally extended to Riga in 1877. This measure provided for three *curia* of electors in accordance with their tax-paying capacities, both of the first two having as much representation as the lower third bracket. This curial electoral system assured the continued dominance of the wealthy German burgher element in the City Council, which retained its position as the highest court in Riga until 1889 when the Russian judicial system was introduced.

Only gradually could Latvians hope to penetrate this circle of wealth and privilege in Riga. German banks encouraged the increase of German home ownership in the city in order to maintain the proportion of the German element in the curia of the electors. Whereas by 1897 the Latvian Councilors had achieved a majority in such a provincial city as Cēsis, they were still eligible for the most part only as Councilors of the third, or minority, curia in Riga. But the Latvian burghers of Riga continued stubbornly to amass wealth, build homes, organize credit-cooperatives, and advance their economic, and *ipso facto* political, position as wholesalers, importers, shipowners, and bankers.

Throughout the nineteenth century this aggressive Latvian element in the booming port lent part of their energies to making the "pearl of the Baltic" a center of liberal culture, to which the more spirited and intellectually alert among the farmers could look for signs of continued social advancement blended with a fast ripening national pride. The press naturally assumed the lead in this democratic and progressive movement.[6]

The first newspapers and books to bear the Riga imprint were in German, although in 1632 the Riga postmaster had launched one of the oldest newspapers in Europe, the Latvian *Awihses*, containing mostly business and shipping information. During the period of the Swedish peasant reforms, the *Rigasche Novellen* appeared, and a further growth of the popular press might have been encouraged by a government which permitted the translations of the Bible and the printing of ordinances and edicts in Latvian had not the Great Northern War intervened. In 1761, the *Rigasche Anzeigen* appeared, to be followed by the *Rigasche Politische Zeitung* ("political" only in name) in 1778. The Königsberg printer Hartknoch, upon the advice of Herder, opened a subsidiary printing office in Riga in 1767, where he was soon offering

[6] M. Walters, *Lettland: seine Entwicklung zum Staat* (Rome, 1923), is perhaps more interested in German nationalism, but does not disregard the aggressive spirit of Latvian national ambitions.

the works of Herder, Kant, Klinger and other advanced German thinkers to the more discriminate German and Latvian burghers.

At the turn of the century, almanacs and calendars in the Latvian tongue were appearing both in Jelgava and Riga, the respective capitals of the two Latvian provinces which were now united under foreign rule. The time was ripe for the appearance of an all-Latvian newspaper, and the first issue of *Latweeschu Awihses* (Latvian News) came off the press of Johan Steffenhagen of Jelgava early in 1822. The editor-in-chief was Pastor Charles Watson, of Scottish origin, founder in 1815 of the Latvian Literary Society in Jelgava. The associate editor was the Latvian Matīss Stobe, who had edited Latvian almanacs and calendars. One of the features of this four-page newspaper was the report of the Riga Stock Exchange, founded in 1816.

In 1824, a Latvian newspaper was published in Limbaži, in Vidzeme; and the first Rigan gazette in Latvian appeared in 1832. This was the *Tam Latweeschu Lauschu Draugam* (The Friend of the Latvian People), published by the provost of the Latvian Church of St. John, H. Treu, who incurred the displeasure of the Russian Government by his warning addressed to Latvian Lutherans against conversion to the Greek Orthodox creed. The official suppression of *The Friend of the Latvian People* in 1846 was a bitter disappointment to those Latvian writers who had begun to gather around this lively paper as a focus for their impressive but still untutored enthusiasms.

Ten years later, one of this group, Ansis Leitans, published in Riga the weekly *Mahjas Weesis* (The House Guest), which, in its turn, immediately gathered an eager group of supporters and contributors. Conspicuous among these was J. Caunītis, who was balked in his endeavors to organize a Latvian Literary Club in Riga by Governor von Lieven's refusal to register the by-laws of such a club under the pretext that a Latvian Literary Society had been in existence since 1824. In that year, indeed, some German pastors had founded such a society with the aim of providing Latvian language courses for those Germans planning to preach in rural parishes, which were frequently considered a sort of family patrimony. The sole Latvian member of this society was Ansis Leitans, and he was eventually expelled for displaying unacceptable "Latvian tendencies." His *Mahjas Weesis* then came under attack by the German Governor for its outspoken pro-Latvian articles by such protagonists of the Latvian *risorgimento* as Juris Alunāns, the folklorist and collector of the *Dainas*.

The 1860's saw the emergence of a young and vigorous intelligentsia, possessors of a hard-won higher education, determined searchers after their people's lost culture and integrity, who were henceforth to stand unyieldingly against the dark obstinacy of the baronial idea. This entrenched prejudice, confronted by the revolutionary potential contained in the foregatherings and researches of seemingly quiet scholars, was now hitting out blindly 'at all intellectual activity, whether exclusively Latvian or sponsored by those German pastors who courageously opposed the views typical of their class. Poets, philologists, folklorists, the customary forerunners of a modern national revival, were soon joined by economists, sociologists, and scientists, who had become convinced that their people's wealth and welfare would be better served by native rather than foreign governance.

Preeminent in this early group of closely-allied Latvian cultural leaders were the aforementioned poet and philologist Juris Alunāns (1832-1864); the folklorist and collector of the *Dainas* Krišjānis Barons (1835-1923); the sociologist A. Kronvalds (1836-1875); and the economist Krišjānis Valdemārs (1825-1891). Valdemārs, who was to be known as the Father of the Latvian navy for his role in the establishment of several navigation schools and his grasp of the importance of a strong merchant marine for his people's self-reliance, soon assumed the leadership of the group. While living in St. Petersburg, he succeeded in getting himself appointed Latvian press censor, a step which opened the way for the establishment of a long-desired Latvian political newspaper in the Russian capital. On July 14, 1863, the anniversary of the fall of the Bastille, appeared the first issue of the *Peterburgas Awihses* (St. Petersburg Gazette), edited first by Valdemārs himself,[7] then by Barons, who was criticized by the Livonian Governor von Lieven in his report to the Russian Minister of the Interior wherein he demanded the suppression of the *Peterburgas Awihses*. In 1863, the paper was closed down for four months by official action on the grounds that, since it enjoyed wide circulation in Livonia and Kurland, the *Peterburgas Awihses* should be subjected to the censorship of the Governor of Riga. At this time, several of the more active contributors, especially those who were accused by the Livonian-Germans of inciting the peasants, were deported. With its resumption of publication under Barons, this gazette, while assuming a more cautious and objective tone, continued to shame the German prejudice which maintained that the Latvian was a born farmhand,

---

[7] Walters, *op.cit.*, p. 278ff. For further details in the development of Latvian nationalism see E. Blanks, *Latviešu tautiskā kustība* (Riga, 1921).

congenitally unfit for intellectual occupations. At the same time it continued to hold up to the oppressors and oppressed alike examples of the almost unknown Western European liberal way of life and industrial advancement. Nor did this judicious journal neglect to give due credit to the reforms which were going forward in Russia itself.

The reactionary Livonian-Germans were still possessed of enough influence in St. Petersburg, where naive admiration of growing German prestige and prowess was the rule, to engineer the disgrace of the "young Letts," who were represented as dangerous revolutionaries, and to obtain the final suspension of their organ, the *Peterburgas Awihses*, in June 1865. Despite this set-back, the influence of the Latvian intellectual leaders continued to grow, particularly in Riga, where the Latvian population was continually expanding and a native bourgeoisie confronted the German economic élite.

This growing population required some sort of group activity as a focus for its urgent sense of creativeness. In 1868, Ansis Leitans founded the *Rigas Latweeschu Beedriba*. At first a purely philanthropic association of Latvian Rigans, the association soon grew into a permanent cultural society and the veritable nucleus of the National Awakening, with membership in the thousands and leadership among the most prominent scientists and belletrists of the day. Various committees of this organization sponsored such ambitious projects as the publication of a Latvian encyclopedia, the founding of a national theater and lyric opera, and the encouragement of worthy literary and musical projects. In 1869, the *Rigas Latweeschu Beedriba* unveiled a monument to the German Garlieb Merkel, who had laid one of the foundation stones of Latvian liberty in his tract *Die Letten* (1796). The provinces soon founded cultural societies of their own, patterned on the Riga organization. Another example of the alert group consciousness of the Latvians was the Latvian student fraternity *Lettonia*, founded in 1868 at the Livonian-Estonian University of Dorpat. The members of *Lettonia* dueled often and well with the members of the predominating German student corporations until they gained the right to full fraternity privileges. Subsequently, some Poles, Lithuanians, Estonians, and even a Czech were admitted to *Lettonia*, which was to form the core of the future Baltic-Central European Federation.

One of the most influential achievements of the Latvian Association in Riga was the organization in 1873 of the first National Latvian Singing Festival, which was distinguished by the initial performance of the Latvian National Anthem, *Dievs Svētī Latviju* (God Bless Latvia). The words and music of this song were composed by Kārlis Baumanis, who, in addition to being a songwriter, was a professor of languages in St. Petersburg. Although similar National Singing Festivals would be permitted to convene in the future, no such repetition was allowed the Latvian School Teachers' Conference or the Conference of Agronomists which made their first and only appearance in 1873. The Russian Government, reflecting the views of the German landowners who, at this late date, were still seeking to keep the peasants on the land and the intellectuals from gathering, would not approve such national conventions.

In 1877, the first Latvian daily newspaper in Riga appeared, the *Rigas Lapa* (the Riga Newspaper), published and edited by Bernhards Dīriķis. A year later a weekly, *Balss* (The Voice) was founded, moderate in tone but of a strictly national character and destined to become the most popular organ in the country. *Balss* was the mouthpiece of the emergent national conservative opinion, while the more progressive liberal trend was represented in *Baltijas Semkopis* (The Baltic Agriculturalist), published in Jelgava. Sensing this differentiation in opinion, certain German intellectuals, notably Bishop Walter and Pastor von Klot, began propagandizing for a Latvian conservative press which would take the initial step in assimilating the Latvian and German cultural elements in Livonia and Kurland. This move won the pronounced disapproval of the squires, who had no intention of having their Latvian farmhands and tenants "assimilated," and saw to it that these two misguided churchmen offered "voluntary" retirement petitions to the General Consistory.

The assassination of Alexander II in 1881 presaged a change in that long-term equilibrium which had contrived to balance the German-Balt landed interests against the unavoidable introduction of the major Russian reforms in the Baltic Provinces. Under Alexander III (1881-1894), a strong-minded ruler convinced of the superiority of autocracy and the Russian patriarchal system over what he and his advisors considered corrupt Western democracy, the Germans, of whom the technologically backward Russians had stood in awe for over a century, lost some of their prestige in St. Petersburg.

The growing distrust in which the Russian Government began to hold its German friends and advisors was in good part the result of certain shifts on the European and Asiatic diplomatic scenes. After the humiliating Treaty of Paris which ended the disastrous Crimean

War, Russia, suspicious both of England and France, needed little persuasion to join Austria and Germany in the League of the Three Emperors of 1873. Five years later, Russia suffered a diplomatic defeat at the hands of these Powers at the Congress of Berlin, which followed the close of the Russo-Turkish War. Russia's aim of liberating the Balkan Slavs was scarcely to the liking of Austria, who was joined in 1879 by Germany in an alliance opposing Russian influence in the Balkans.[8] Only because of the mounting tension between Russia and England over the former's expansion in Central Asia was Bismarck able to renew the League of the Three Emperors in 1881 and again in 1884. Three years later, this alliance was terminated by Russia's rupture with Austria. Also about this time, German capital, in great demand at home, was less available to Russia, and the latter Power turned to France, where she succeeded in obtaining a series of loans which favored her expanding capitalistic enterprises. Germany's swelling chauvinism and sabre-rattling further alienated her former admirer, who saw her western lands menaced, so that gradually, at the turn of the century, Russian policy was oriented toward France and eventually toward England. However, Alexander's successor, the flaccid and impressionable Nicholas II (1894-1917), fully restored German influence in court and military circles.

This official alienation of affections under the Slavophil Alexander III was antedated by the antipathy which Russian liberal circles had expressed for the reactionary German element at the Tsarist Court and, to a high degree, for the intransigent and domineering Baltic barons. Both before and after the humiliating Treaty of Berlin (1878), the newspaper Den (The Day), edited by Ivan Aksakov and Yury Samarin, attacked Germanism in the Russian Empire, denounced its oppression of the Estonian and Latvian peoples, and expressed sympathy for their nationalist aspirations.

However, the overt anti-Germanism of these Russian liberals in no way influenced Alexander III, who, as a confirmed autocrat, might have been expected to sympathize with the new Prussia. Rather was it the Tsar's rabid Slavophilism which turned him against the foreign element which had swayed the Russian Court and ruled her Baltic Provinces. Nor was this disaffection compensated by any increased tolerance of the Baltic peoples themselves, who had had to bear the

[8] The classic study of this critical juncture in Eastern European politics is the brilliant work of B. H. Sumner, Russia and the Balkans, 1870-1880 (Oxford, 1937).

brunt of German obsessive oligarchy. On the contrary, these peoples, simmering as they were with a sense of nationality and seeming radicalism, were even more suspect to the new Russian police régime than the familiarly arrogant Baltic barons, who presented no undiscovered threat. These indeed, imbued as most of them were with a family tradition of service to the Tsars, could be brought to play a useful role in Russia's economic expansion, which from now on would require full cooperation from the increasingly industrialized Baltic Provinces. But the peasants, workers, and intellectuals of these lands, given the free hand they clamored for in the educational sphere, business, the press, and government, might prove dangerously divergent and a likely spearhead for the hovering revolution. The now avowedly antiliberal Tsarist régime, embarked on a two-fold program of economic expansion and political centralization, was determined to put a quietus on the democratic and nationalistic seethings of all the subject peoples on her western borders.

This policy had been initiated in Poland after the insurrection of 1863, which earned for that land, as well as for her neighbor Lithuania, the replacement of their proud names by the title Vistula Provinces. Those Lithuanians and Latgallians who had participated in the fierce Polish rebellion were further punished by such measures as the prohibition of the use of the Latin alphabet. These regions were henceforth to be divided into *guberniyas*, on the pattern of the Baltic Provinces of Estonia, Livonia, and Kurland, where these political divisions overlapped national lines with the intention of hampering the growth of national solidarity.

The Baltic Provinces, renamed the Northwest Provinces the better to dim their sense of individuality, under the last two Tsars were to suffer from a confusing policy based on opportunism and fanaticism, a characteristic Russian paradox. Voices in the German Empire crying *Kultur* and the return of the "lost provinces" of the Baltic did not ameliorate Alexander III's attitude toward the German-Balt element, whom he accused of imposing a "foreign" civilization on his valuable Baltic domains. With government support, Russian propagandists for a short term encouraged the Baltic peoples to rise against their German oppressors, and some burning of manors and forests ensued. In 1882, upon the complaint of the squires that the peasants had become subversive, a revision of governmental institutions was ordered at the hands of a commission headed by Senator Manasein. The commission immediately received thousands of complaints from the subjugated

Latvians and Estonians against the various phases of German control. The squires promptly expressed their scorn for these proceedings in their own press and their annoyance with the complaining peasants by flogging a good few of them to death. The railway car carrying the commission's documents to St. Petersburg was destroyed by a fire of unknown origin, and Manasein's report to the Tsar disappeared from Alexander's personal files. Soon the Baltic barons obtained an imperial injunction safeguarding their relations with their peasants from outside interference. The Latvians had received their token of Russian sympathy, and now other treatment was in store for them. While German pretensions would continue to be frowned upon, the knout would be brandished at any Latvian or Estonian presuming to turn his face away from Mother Russia.

In 1885, Russification burst like a thunderclap with the sudden subjection of Latvian primary and normal schools to the Ministry of Education in St. Petersburg. Teachers were given two years to learn Russian, which was henceforth to be the only acceptable language of instruction. Russian teachers, for the most part inferior in training to either the German or the Latvian instructors, soon appeared in the primary communal and district schools. The urban secondary schools, staffed with Germans, were given the choice of substituting Russian for German or losing their standing in the educational system. Their reluctance was met by the founding of a number of new state schools of inferior calibre. The Latvians who, unlike the Germans, had not the means to support private high schools, now found themselves severely crippled by the loss of their national idiom in the entire field of education. Illiteracy in the three Baltic Provinces, which was two per cent on the eve of Russification, rose to almost five per cent at the turn of the century.[9]

The University of Dorpat, although essentially German-Balt in constitution and attendance, had a fair representation of Estonians, Latvians, and Kurs. In 1895, in spite of vehement protests to Tsar Nicholas II, this institution was transformed into a colorless Russian High School and rechristened Yuriev (the ancient name for Dorpat) in order to obliterate its individualistic associations. Its native (Latvian, Estonian) enrollment dropped from 1158 students in 1890 to 389 in 1900.[10] The Russians could hope that as a rallying point for either German-Balt or pure Balt interests the University of Dorpat,

[9] Ralph Butler, The New Eastern Europe (London, 1919), p. 27.
[10] Von Engelhardt, op.cit., pp. 221-230.

which had been cooperatively supported by the Diets of Livonia and Estonia and by the municipalities of Riga and Reval, had been successfully sterilized.

In the political area Russification was carried out as radically as in the educational sphere. The governor-generalship of the three Baltic Provinces was replaced by a separate governorship for each of them, no longer subservient to the German interests. The nearly paralyzed Diets were allowed to creak along to a natural death in the World War. To have substituted popular assemblies would have opened the door to Latvian and Estonian majorities of pronouncedly anti-reactionary or at least "liberal" views. But the real rulers, impeding the Diets and replacing the German administrators, were the new bureaucrats, the Russian *tchinovniki*, who swarmed over the Latvian and Estonian lands bringing abysmal corruption and inefficiency in the place of German method and assessable intolerance. Instead of the squires' habitual and paternalistic punishments, the Baltic peoples now found themselves enmeshed in a political police system and subject to spying, denouncement, and deportation. In 1888, the Russian police system, criminal and political, manned by Russian police chiefs, constables, and secret agents, was thrown like a net over the Baltic area. The introduction of the reformed Russian judiciary system in 1889, in itself a progressive step with its ousting of the obsolete Baltic Code and its improved courts and procedure, only served to advance Russification. Here, as in the rest of the administration, Russian was declared the only official language, the higher courts were put under direct Russian control, and commissars were charged with the supervision of the affairs of the rural communities.

During the reign of Alexander III, Lutheranism, as a manifestation of Prussianism, was under open attack. The Greek Orthodox Church, increasingly the tool of Tsarist imperialism, led the assault. As early as the 1840's, the Orthodox priests had campaigned on their own against German ascendancy by welcoming peasant converts and encouraging them to migrate to Russia. The German-Balts responded to this "insurrection" with police measures. The eighties saw a different temper in the Russian Church. Demission was forbidden, and parents were ordered to raise their children in the Orthodox faith, while the conversion of Lutherans to Orthodoxy was officially rewarded. In 1888, sixty Lutheran pastors were removed for attempted reconversions.[11] Splendid gilded Byzantine domes blossomed in the larger Baltic cities.

[11] Sir Bernard Pares, A *History of Russia* (New York, 1944), p. 412.

The landless and the poor were lured into these churches with promises ranging from land allotments to exemption from military service.
Emphasis was not laid on the fact that the promised land was somewhere in Siberia.

Just as education had been high on the agenda of Russification, so
the products of education, the first flowering of the Latvian intelligentsia, received full official attention. A severe censorship of the
press was instituted, directed toward nullifying all native attempts to
instill into the popular consciousness any nationalistic ideas and idioms
or any democratic concepts. Intellectuals now found more and more
doors closed to their ambitions in their homeland. On the other hand,
many of them were offered advantageous positions in the Caucasus,
Siberia, or the Far East, on condition that they would agree to take
up permanent residence in these distant outposts. During the period
between 1891 and 1900, fifty-four per cent of the university graduates
of the Baltic Provinces could find suitable employment only in
Russia.[12] Singled out for emphatic persecution were the Jews in general
and the Jewish intelligentsia, regarded as highly radical, in particular.
This was in accordance with the strongly anti-Jewish inclinations of
the Slavophil Minister, Count Ignatyev, which led to pogroms and
segregation of the Jews for the most part in Poland and the western
provinces. This policy was to prove equally congenial to Nicholas II,
whose dislike of the Jews was proverbial.

Even more than the Latvians and Estonians the German-Balts were
astounded and shaken by this intensive program of Russification. The
loss of their beloved Dorpat, the insults to their clergy, the invasion
of the *tchinovniki*, seemed a poor return for generations of fidelity to
the Tsarist cause. They had never taken into account the growing
weight of Russian public opinion against both the Prussian idea and
the peculiar insolence, combined with often brilliant performance, of
the German-Balt element at the court of St. Petersburg. Not only to
the lower strata of Russian society, but to many of the old nobility,
German-Balt *parvenu* arrogance had become insufferable. This offended ruling class now retired before the grossness and incompetence
of the *tchinovniki*, sulked in their country houses, began to extol
German manners and morals, dropped Russian expressions from their
speech, and in general appeared, for the first time in all their ascendancy, on the defensive.[13]

[12] Schwabe, *op.cit.*, p. 23.
[13] For this rapid change in the outlook of the German-Balts, see the article

Far from sulking, the Baltic peoples, beneath this added burden of repression, now clarified their desire for self-expression and self-determination. It was borne in upon the Latvians that no ultimate help was to be looked for from the Russian colossus, once the mystique of Pan-Slavism had begun to sway even many of the liberals in their uncertain courses. The air was cleared of compromise with the realization that Germans and Russians both, though no longer on the best of terms, stood equally averse to letting the Baltic peoples raise their voices against their subjugation. The group which had a stake in self-determination had increased since a middle class and an incipient laboring class—both born of the growth of commerce and the towns and the establishment of heavy industry, now a marked feature of the Baltic cities—had ranged themselves beside the emancipated peasants. Still, no national movement could be carried forward without consulting the temper of the peasantry, whose sons were to assume a large share in both the cultural and political leadership of a rising nation.

Directly from the peasant class sprang that first wave of educated and self-conscious Latvians who found a place, however modest, in the spheres of business, commerce, navigation, education, the press, and administration. From this matrix had issued those early scholars and poets who had worked the rich vein of native legend and folklore for the larger inspiration of their people. It was the sons and grandsons of peasants, some of them incorporated into the middle classes, some of them still close to the soil, who were to carry forward both the initial Romantic tradition and the newer tenets of Realism and Positivism which countered the Russian attack on what the Latvian people, in one generation, had come to regard as indispensable liberties.

For the remainder of this chapter we shall examine more closely the texture of that native Latvian cultural renaissance now reaching its culmination. In opposition to the barbed technicalities and overt brutalities of Russia's intensified grip on her western lands, the native movement exerted the unseen, immeasurable force of a nation's difficult self-realization. A people tasting the first fruits of courage and endurance could not be effectively curbed by an alien police serving an already doomed tyranny. Such ill-advised restraint of a national effervescence resulted in two patriots cropping up where one was cut down; and in thinkers and artists stretching their powers to the utmost to meet a time of crisis.

by C. L. Lundin, "From Tsar to Kaiser" in *Journal of Central European Affairs,* x (1950), pp. 223-255.

The spirit of Romanticism, bright tincture of that mid-century crop of liberal and nationalistic aspirations which stirred certain European oppressed minorities to action, begot in others, the Latvians among them, dreams and energies which were to find their political expression in a time yet to come. No doubt this initial form of inspiration was necessary for the further awakening of a people but newly roused from the long night of serfdom. Those who have taken only this first step away from total oppression must rediscover a self-respecting past before they can aspire to a goodly future. They need to honor their humbled mother tongue and rediscover their legendary heroes. It is at this stage that the philologist, folklorist, and poet find their proper function in the formation of a nation.

The work of the philologists included the establishment of the genuine antiquity of the Latvian language, its purification from numerous Germanisms, and its enrichment by the introduction of neologisms fitting it to interpret modern civilization. Such a task was ably shouldered by A. Alunāns, whose *Little Songs*, published in classical Latvian, were a milestone in the restoration of that language.

Latvian legends and early tribal history, pregnant with epic figures and themes, became the particular preserve of those folklorists and poets who sought both comforting substance and dynamic symbols in the remote folk past. The Latvian *Dainas*, introduced in Germany by Herder and known in England through a critique by Sir Walter Scott, were repeatedly collected, edited, and even translated into Russian during the second half of the nineteenth century. The epic of "the Bearslayer," recreated by A. Pumpurs in his *Lāčplēsis*, published in 1888, became an immediate best seller and contributed a particularly robust national hero for the plaudits of the strenuous younger generation. Equally popular was the poet K. M. Auseklis' ballad *The Castle of Light* (*Gaismas Pils*), also inspired by the *Lāčplēsis* legend, and bearing the intoxicating promise of the rebirth of Latvian independence.

With the consolidation of a Latvian middle class, the wider participation of both urban and rural groups in economic and political life, the increasing materialism of the age, and the broadening philosophies of the intellectuals, the first excitement of a newborn sense of nationality settled into the firmer, and at the same time more pragmatic, sense of nationhood. A more measured approach to the expectations and risks of self-determination was now the order of the day. Youthful ardor, with its singing and its hero-worship, gave way to cool calculation, scientific studies, a reliance on common sense and its political expression in tested democratic institutions, and a general veering toward the canons of Realism, Naturalism, and Positivism, which penetrated to the remote Baltic from Western Europe. This sobered outlook, invigorated by the natural zest of a "young" people, was reflected in much of the literature of the last two decades of the nineteenth century, and persisted throughout the pre-War era. At the same time, the earlier romantic and lyrical mood, in some ways more suited to these northerners, endured in the work of those artists, musicians, and poets who, recoiling from political and social turbulence, preferred to serve their people by the enrichment of what they considered, with some justice, the true national heritage of poignancy, endurance, and poeticized hope.

The rural scene offered matter enough to those novelists and dramatists who favored the school of sombre realism. Among the works exploiting the grim aspects of farm life were *The Time of the Surveyors* (*Mērnieku laiki*) by the brothers Kaudzītes, dealing with the rise of the liberated Latvian farmers and the influence of this phenomenon upon national life; *The Homeland* (*Dzimtene*) of J. Janševskis; *The Grey Baron* (*Pelēkais Barons*) of V. Eglītis, depicting the life of the Latvian "grey" farmer in contrast to that of the German "black" baron; and, in the field of drama, the *Indrāni* of R. Baumanis, a melancholy representation of peasant family life. Removed from the gloomy tints of the rural novel was Deglavs' *Riga*, a masterful study of that capital's youthful spirit and intense activity.

Toward the end of the century, Riga had developed sufficient literary *élan* to foster schools of criticism. While E. Pīpiņš and T. Zeiferts encouraged a classical and cosmopolitan taste, the more radical group of J. Jansons and J. Asars, influenced by Darwinism and German Marxism, disparaging all forms of decadence and Romanticism, demanded political content in literature.

Neither the dictates of the positivists nor the political clamorings centering around the upheaval of 1905 could quell or pervert the naturally lyric tone of those Latvian poets whose first flights coincided with the last hectic years of the nineteenth century and the opening decade of the twentieth. Such a poet as K. Skalbe, while influenced in his youth by Jansons, developed depth of insight and the true lyric note in his verses, which place him in the front rank of poets. Jānis Rainis-Pliekšans, who was to acquire Olympian stature as a writer of classic dramas and poems and a distinguished translator of Goethe's *Faust*, began his career as a politically tendentious writer and the leader of the New Movement (*Jaunā Strahwa*), originated by the *fin de siècle* Social-Democratic intellectuals. Other lyric poets were Jānis Akurāters, F. Bārda, J. Poruks, V. Plūdonis, and E. Virza. Many of their verses were set to music and their influence among the people was thus enhanced.

Closely akin to the spirit of these poets was that of the musicians, whose melodious compositions found an immediate response among a people noted for their innate appreciation of both festive and elegiac music. The Latvians had from earliest times fostered a store of folksongs and dances, which now became the inspiration for the composers of the National Awakening. This ancient music, performed on distinctive horns, flutes, and bagpipes, which effectively rendered its sentimental and melancholy mood, was particularly congenial to the many song writers. Peculiar to the Latvians was a strong penchant for group singing which made the national singing festivals, especially under the Russian police régime, the strongest expression of national solidarity. Ballet was given whole-hearted support by a people who enjoyed a long-established tradition of folk-dancing. Introduced in Kurland in the eighteenth century, at the same time as Italian opera, the art of the ballet, established in the late nineteenth century on a more popular basis, made such rapid strides that the Riga classical ballet became second only to the Russian.

Many of the Latvian musicians and composers studied at the St. Petersburg Conservatory, where the Latvian Jāzeps Vītols initiated his famous courses in the theory of music and composition in 1886. In 1919, he was to found the Latvian Conservatory and become its first director. Such song-writers as E. Vīgners, A. Ore, A. Kalniņš, and E. Dārziņš offered their people entrancing melodies. Kalniņš entered the operatic field, as did J. Mediņš, composer of *Fire and Night*, based on the perennial *Lāčplēsis* legend.

Among the popular arts, tradition had long exercised the same ripening and preservative influence that it had in music. In their wood-, leather- and metal-work, in their ceramics, weaving, embroidery, and other decorative arts, the Latvians had evolved, through the generations, an extraordinary number of motifs, many of them dating back to the time of earliest settlement, and most of them looked upon as a treasured legacy. The leading designs are of a geometrical nature, and the color schemes, carried out in natural dyes, are both brilliant and mellow. In the folk arts, the Latvian peasant found heartening expression for his instinctive respect for tradition, his urge for creation, and his satisfying devotion to a heritage of beauty. A revival of arts and crafts was one of the features of the mid-century national revival, and led to the cult of national costumes, in which the colors red, blue, and black predominated; to the collecting of handicraft specimens; and to the imitation of ancient patterns by industrial designers and practitioners of the fine arts. An impressive collection of the products of native handicrafts, gathered by the Ethnographic Museum of the Latvian Association, was placed on exhibit during the First Baltic Archeological Congress held in Riga in 1894.

In 1907, the St. Petersburg Academy of Sciences published an authoritative treatise on Latvian wood architecture and wood utensils by A. Bielenstein,[14] a German scholar who was so impressed by his researches into the skill and taste of the early Latvian woodworkers that he placed their art above that of his own nation. The fashioning of curiously impressive simple household objects from strong woods had been a folk art from time immemorial. Woodcarvings had served as architectural ornament for all types of buildings, from the peasant's hut to the churches of the eighteenth century. The Baroque style was particularly well represented in this medium. The Church of St. Peter in Riga boasted the highest wooden spire known (440 feet), burnt more than once in wartime, but repeatedly restored.

Although the early Rigans had been knowledgeable builders, civic and ecclesiastical architecture was for the most part of German inspiration, especially in Kurland where the Dukes had indulged their tastes for both the Baroque and later eighteenth rococo styles, with their Italian flavor. Many buildings both in Kurland and Livonia had not survived the incessant wars. Furthermore, the Livonian-Germans cared little about investing in the embellishment of either their estates or the Baltic towns. Riga they considered a mere trading center for which the buildings of the old Hanseatic days must suffice. The vast fortunes accumulated by the German-Balt merchants and landlords were reinvested in trade, transferred to Germany, or lavished on high living in foreign capitals, particularly St. Petersburg. There was room for a considerable building program in Latvia employing the talents of native architects. Preeminent among these was J. Baumanis, one of the founders of the Riga Latvian Association mentioned above. He contributed greatly to the modernization of Riga, which retained the stamp of the late Middle Ages even after the introduction of heavy

[14] A. Bielenstein, *Die Holzbauten und Holzgeräte der Letten.*

industry. The buildings of the University, the Court of Appeals, and the Conservatory were monuments to Baumanis' breadth of taste and soundness of design. Distinguished among his pupils were A. Morbergs, K. Pēkšēns, and E. Laube, all of whom lent their talents to this capital city.

In addition to much of the architecture, many examples of early Latvian painting were destroyed by wars, although some church frescoes and altar paintings survived. With but scanty tradition to draw on, the two leading painters of the nineteenth century, K. Huhn and J. Fedders, became members of the St. Petersburg Academy of Arts, and produced notable historical paintings and landscapes in the classical style. Of a later generation, the landscapist V. Purvītis, also an academician, sought repeated inspiration in the tender spring scenes of his native country. He was to become the first director of the Riga Academy of Arts. Prominent in the field of portraiture were R. Tilbergs and J. Rozentals, the latter a pupil of the Swedish master Anders Zorn. Sculpture, strangely enough, was slower to mature than painting, and had to await the maturity of B. Dzenins and T. Zalkalns, both pupils of Rodin, who displayed their force and versatility in the pre-War period.

The industrious generation of writers, artists, and musicians who attained their full powers at the turn of the century had its counterpart in an energetic group of scholars and scientists inspired with a sense of urgency to gain laurels for their still unrecognized country as much as for themselves. A good number of the scientists were graduates of the Riga Polytechnic Institute, founded in 1862. Many held degrees from the University of Dorpat as well as from Russian and German institutions of higher learning. Although by their stubborn efforts to achieve status and make important contributions in their fields these men rank among the shapers of their people's developing culture, in many cases the products of their maturity belong to their nation's achieved statehood. Dean of the Latvian scientists was P. Walden, discoverer of the "Walden inversion," member of the St. Petersburg Academy of Sciences and lecturer in a number of European universities. He was the Director of the Riga Polytechnicum during the last years of its existence until 1919. In 1900, a Latvian, N. Ostwald, was awarded the Nobel prize in chemistry. B. Bīmanis, an authority in hydrography, and builder of Moscow's water-supply system, was to become president of the Latvian Power Commission; and Jēkabs

Vītols, eminent mathematician, carried out the organization of the Latvian State Electric Factory.

Internationally recognized in the field of scholarship were the philologist Jānis Endzelīns, compiler of a scientific Latvian grammar which established the close relationship of the Latvian language with ancient Sanskrit; the archeologist F. Balodis, discoverer of the "Golden Horde" near Astrakhan, and conductor of numerous Latvian excavations which brought to light the antiquity of Latvian culture; and the economist K. Balodis, author of more than fifty books in his field, professor at the University of Berlin, and organizer of Germany's rationing system during the First World War.

We have observed that many of these scholars and artists were given some recognition in St. Petersburg. There was room for talent in the Russian Empire, and the Tsarist régime had not learned that fear of thought and art which drives modern dictatorships to extreme persecution of the intellectual élite. However, those of the intelligentsia, and there were many, who associated themselves openly with the Social-Democratic or the extreme nationalist cause attracted far from favorable attention from the police of Tsarist Russia, whose worn political fabric could not tolerate stresses of radical opinion in the western lands which might add dangerous weight to the liberal and revolutionary parties clamoring for a new order in St. Petersburg. But the national tide was running strong in the first years of the opening century, and no amount of skimming-off of the intellectuals could impoverish Latvian leadership; since those who accepted Russian "hospitality" did so for the most part in order to assure their own survival and ripening against a time of decision; and, in the Latvian lands themselves, new leadership kept shooting up from a sturdy stock. Nor could reinforcement of police measures, which induced morale-building resistance, hope to divert the national resurgence from its natural course, now turning into the final political phase of self-determination. The cultural renaissance had bloomed, even in a clouded atmosphere. The dark weather of political storms, war, and revolution was to bring to maturity the hardy fruit of nationhood.

Chapter 14

Revolution, Reaction, and War: 1905-1917

THE national movement in the Baltic Provinces, aggravated by Alexander III's untoward and ill-contrived policy of Russification, came into sharper focus under Nicholas II (1894-1917). At the same time it assumed a societal orientation and political commitment more challenging and more critical than the preliminary cultural awakening which had prepared the soil for this bold growth. Forces had now to be marshaled, opinion solidified, and leadership exposed to obvious hazards. The renaissance of the sixties, which gave rise to that ebullient generation known as the New Latvians and the New Estonians, also opened the way for more acute manifestations of nationalism intimately related to the heightening class struggle. This highly combustible blend blew the breath of violence over the opening years of the new century.

One of the risks which confronted the increasingly committed Latvian intellectual leaders was the full reestablishment of the German element in the good graces of the Tsarist Court. Nicholas II did not inherit his father's coolness, born of Pan-Slav ardor, to the officious and opportunistic *Deutschrussen*. Fatalistic, irresolute, without political vision and grateful for flattery, the last of the Tsars chose to be buoyed up by those aggressive and efficient Germans who shared none of his painful weaknesses. On them Nicholas bestowed high positions in the Central Administration and in the Army Command. He suffered their encroachment on Russian industrialism. He clung to them in his personal entourage. Kaiser William II, nervous over the 1897 Franco-Russian alliance and anxious to prevent the forging of still closer bonds, held out the lure of the Far East to Nicholas' autocratic fancies and imperialistic yearnings. The Baltic barons, vaguely aware that the subject peoples, indignant over the Russian check to their national development, were studying the promises of socialism, took every occasion to point out how dangerous an outbreak of revolutionary nationalism would be for the Tsarist Government. The Latvian political thinkers and ardent writers of the nineties, like the less radical leaders of the sixties, were labeled by the Germans in St. Petersburg as revolutionaries, anarchists, nihilists, and "Young Letts," a term which comprised all the others.[1] The Germans were rewarded for their pains by receiving due consideration for their landed and industrial priorities in the Baltic area. Nicholas II, himself unfitted to take any firm stand or display even a convincing arrogance, could only admire the class loyalty and tenacity of this numerically small caste.

Coupled with the threat of closer Russian-German sympathies along the lines of vested interests and autocratic rule was the intensified chauvinism and imperialism of the Tsarist satrapy, which had received such a strong impetus from the convictions of Alexander III. Throughout the Russian Empire the Tsar, the Orthodox Church and the Great Russian element were held up as shibboleths to that hodgepodge of nationalities, many of them by now disaffected, of which the Empire was composed. The pressure of this political mysticism, with its hammering slogan of "one Tsar, one Church, one race," further irritated the subjugated peoples of the Baltic lands, where the spirit of nationalism had assumed a distinctly democratic and rational bias.

The stiffening resistance which the Baltic peoples were to offer both to the clutches of the Russian octopus and to the unrelenting grip of the German-Balt landed and industrial interests was by now profoundly rooted. The liberal-national movement, rapidly assuming the aspect of open revolt, was firmly based both on irrepressible cultural self-consciousness and on closely linked class and national unrest. Back of this lay the unbalanced social and economic conditions created by the introduction of heavy industry, which represented both the Russian economic policy and the interests of the German-Balts in Latvia and Estonia. The establishment of impressive factories in Tallinn, Riga, Liepāja, and Ventspils had resulted in the formation of a small but powerful class of German owners and managers, and a large but impotent mass of indigenous workers. A majority of the latter consisted of those peasants who, being unable to achieve land-ownership and unwilling to submit to the poor working conditions offered on the German manors, had surged into the cities in search of a livelihood. Transformed into highly skilled laborers, indispensable to German-controlled industry, they soon tipped the population balance of the larger towns to a strong Baltic majority. Nevertheless, they still enjoyed only minority representation in some of the city governments and no representation at all in the feudal Livonian and Estonian Diets. The fact that the natives had gained the ascendancy in some of the

[1] Chapter VII of Walters' *Lettland* is entitled "Das Junglettentum und die Deutschbalten."

town councils only confirmed the German-Balts in their determination to hold fast to their political prerogatives in the Baltic Provinces as a whole.

This urban proletariat was the counterpart of that still large group of landless peasants who must earn a living by accepting work on the estates on whatever terms the squires chose to dictate. Both of these groups were regarded with increasing suspicion by the German-Balt big industrialists and landowners, who even maintained private police forces to hold down, in the factories and on the estates, the rising spectre of socialism. Needless to say, the cooperation of the Russian gendarmerie was not unwelcome to these entrenched autocrats.

A sharp thorn in the flesh of both the German interests and Russian officialdom was that small but active segment of the dispossessed, the young intellectuals for whose abilities and training there was no outlet within the Russified Latvian educational and administrative systems. There was no scope for the energies and aspirations of this generation of the intelligentsia, whose education had for the most part been hard-won, other than the struggling liberal and radical press, and the newly fledged Social-Democratic party. The great Riga strike of 1898, springing from the industrial crisis of the nineties, was laid at the door of these "radicals," and resulted in the closing down of the Socialist *Deenas Lapa* (Daily News), and the deportation to central Russia of its editors Pēteris Stučka, Jānis Jansons, and Jānis Rainis-Pliekšans, together with 134 other Latvian Socialists. In accordance with the predominating spirit of the Latvian press, which responded to suppression with redoubled efforts, the *Mahjas Weesis* now came to the fore as the leading progressive newspaper with strong nationalist demands. So solidified had liberal-national opinion become under the stimulus of Russification, that a certain degree of Latvian reaction had set in, resulting in the emergence of a national-conservative party, equally bent on independence but opposing what they denounced as made-in-Germany Socialist ideas. The chief organ of this section of opinion was the *Rigas Awihses*, founded in 1902.

As a result of Tsarist intransigence, the budding Socialist movement in Latvia went underground, where it suffered a transmutation which was to make it yet more suspect to the authorities. In order to understand this development, we must consider the early modulations of Social-Democracy both in the Baltic Provinces and in Russia proper.

The prototype of Socialism in each of these areas was the German Social-Democratic party with its Marxist bias. In the Reich this party was tolerated by the ruling militarists because of its opportune emphasis on national consolidation along economic and industrial lines. In Russia, where Marxist ideas swept in after 1893 and a Social-Democratic party was founded in 1898, this insistence on unification, albeit along class lines, connoted the submission of the subjugated nationalities to the leadership of the Great Russian proletariat. Under the aegis of the Central Committee, consisting mostly of assimilated Russian Jews, the liberation of nationalities was not an issue, emphasis being laid on the international nature of the envisioned Russian Republic.[2] Dedicated to the concept of an All-Russian labor movement of international import, the Russian Workmen's Social-Democratic party condemned as divisionist the autonomous labor movements which sprang up at the turn of the century in Finland, the Baltic Provinces, Lithuania, Poland, the Ukraine, Georgia, and Armenia. The latent sense of individualism which permeated even the Marxist parties of these submerged nationalities was entirely unacceptable to Lenin. Determined to establish its ascendancy throughout the Russian dominion, the highly theoretical and uncompromising Workmen's Social-Democratic party bore down on the industrial worker everywhere with an All-Russian zeal which recalled the Pan-Slav fanaticism of its avowed enemy, Tsarist autocracy.

In 1903, the Central Committee of the Russian Social-Democratic party, dominated by Lenin and meeting in London, split into the *Bolshevik* ("men of the majority") group, vowed to revolutionary methods and aims, and a minority (*Menshevik*), group who desired to work within the framework of a democratic constitution. A comparable split occurred within the Socialist parties of the western lands, with the radical wings of the Social-Democratic parties choosing to continue in close affiliation with the Russian Bolsheviks, and the right wings adopting a national viewpoint. The Polish Socialists were the first to realize that they had nothing to gain from submission to the Russian Social-Democrats, since their eventual representation in the anticipated All-Russian Revolutionary Central Government could only be a small one. This reasoning promptly appealed to many members of the labor movement in Finland, Estonia, Latvia, and Lithuania, who now professed themselves ready to organize a common struggle for territorial political autonomy. This momentous decision was aired at the first congress of the oppressed Baltic nationalities, convened in April 1903 at Bern. Here the representatives of the subjugated Baltic

[2] E. Arnis, *Latvju tautas politiskā atmoda*, p. 95.

peoples declared their determination to make common cause against both Tsarist domination and German privilege.[3]

That same year saw the publication, also in Bern in the Latvian Socialist newspaper, "The Proletarian," of the program of the Latvian Right Wing Socialists. Prominent among them were M. Valters, the poet J. Akurāters and the economist E. Rolavs, all of whom had helped to shape the party's policies since its founding in 1900. The Right Wing Socialists' program sounded the first clear call for autonomy and a constituent assembly for the Latvian people. Its firm and uncompromising demands deserve quotation in full: "All lands inhabited by Latvians—Kurzeme or Kurland, Vidzeme or Livonia proper, and Latgale—must be united in a self-governing unity to be called Latvia, which must enjoy the right of self-determination. In Latvia the rights of self-determination belong to all citizens without distinction of birth, race or creed. The self-determination of Latvia must include an independent parliament and autonomous legislation. The parliament shall be elected by all the citizens. Latvia must have an independent executive power, autonomous judicial system and municipal self-government, both urban and rural. A Latvian Constituent Assembly should be convoked independently from the All-Russian Constituent Assembly. The Latvian Constituent Assembly should assume all administrative powers in Latvia and the project of state organization adopted by the Latvian Constituent Assembly should be submitted to a referendum."[4]

While the men who proclaimed this program were loudly denounced by the German-Balt element in St. Petersburg, their declared policies became the rallying point of Latvian political nationalism. This movement, which had taken shape under Russification and sought expression in a censored press, gained considerable impetus from the revolutionary trends in Russia leading up to the events of 1905.

This upheaval, quickly suppressed in St. Petersburg, flaring through the border provinces, and assuming a widespread and turbulent nature in the Baltic area, had long been ripening in the imbalanced Tsarist autocracy. Its explosive power had been storing up ever since the organization of the Ochrana, the secret political police, which, in 1881, had been Alexander III's answer to the assassination of his not illiberal father. This extreme measure of autocracy only served to

[3] Mitteilungen der lettischen sozialdemokratischen Arbeiter-Partei vom II. Kongress (Bern, 1905).
[4] As reprinted in Laukstrādnieks, no. 2 (1906).

deepen the discontent of the liberal forces. These consisted of the minor bureaucrats and army officers who bitterly resented German control in the Central Administration and military circles; of the intellectuals and gentry who assumed leadership in those local rural self-governing bodies established in 1864—the Zemstva; and of the progressively minded landowners; all of whom now found themselves equally suspect in the eyes of the secret police. The latter tended to lump together as "revolutionary" the leisurely liberals among the gentry who hoped only for mild reforms, the radicals among the Zemstvo officials, and the real urban revolutionaries, often Jewish.

Particularly unpalatable to the Germans in the administration were the democratic aspects and often radical opinions of the Zemstva. The German-Balts had successfully opposed the introduction of these institutions into the Baltic Provinces, since they would have admitted Estonian and Latvian smallholders, hamlets, and rural communities to representation. The Zemstvo leaders demanded a government responsible to a freely elected Duma (parliament), as well as a number of social, judicial, and economic reforms. In 1905, the All-Russian Zemstvo Congress even came out in favor of bettering the situation of national minorities.

The Russian liberals, shading from Constitutionalists to anarchists, had as their springboard the enormous mass of the destitute peasantry. Agrarian reform, as the trumpet call of the revolutionary movement, especially of the Socialist Revolutionary party, was bound to attract the interest of the underprivileged Baltic peasantry. The latter, however, differed from their Russian fellow-sufferers both in their spirit of enterprise and in their fundamental economic and social position, since their basic unit was the highly prized privately owned farm or farm tenancy, in no way comparable to the Russian mir, or rural commune. The mir was the collective owner of the lands, amounting to about fifty per cent of the manors, allotted to the liberated serfs in 1861. Since the mir's portion was to prove insufficient to support a growing peasant population, hunger revolts against the still wealthy manor-lords broke out with increasing frequency, fanned by the Social Revolutionaries with their terror tactics and their battle cry of "more land!" This revolutionary party, however, concerned itself only with the Russian peasantry proper and paid little heed to the rural conditions of the non-Slav provinces.

The Russian people as a whole, peasants, workers, minor officials, and soldiers, found further cause for disgruntlement in the war with

Japan which broke out in 1904, following the occupation of Manchuria by Russian troops after the suppression of the Boxer Rebellion. Port Arthur fell to the Japanese in January 1905. That same month violence flared in St. Petersburg.

The numerous factory workers of the industrialized suburbs of the Russian capital, many of them originally starving peasants who had accepted work under conditions of extreme exploitation, had been persuaded to appeal directly to the Tsar by the excitable Father Gapon. This Orthodox priest led the workers, unarmed and bearing ikons, to the Winter Palace. When the military chief of the capital city lost his head and ordered fire opened upon this peaceable procession, a massacre ensued. On January 13, Riga factory hands, marching in a sympathy demonstration, were also fired upon by Russian police, who killed forty and wounded some two hundred Latvians.[5] The Latvian Social-Democrats now called a general strike, on the order of the St. Petersburg strike which had been proclaimed immediately after the bloody incident before the Winter Palace. The Latvian followers of Lenin seized the occasion to make widespread propaganda for the overthrow of the Tsarist Government and the adoption of violent measures against its ally, the Baltic squirearchy.

The summer and autumn of 1905 saw the spreading of revolutionary activity throughout the Baltic Provinces and in Russia proper. The Baltic fleet had been destroyed by the Japanese. The disaffected Russian land forces, harboring the revolutionary virus, offered such poor resistance to the enemy that Russia was forced to accept a negotiated peace in September. The Russian public was quick to blame the Kaiser's encouragement of Nicholas' imperialistic vanity for the losses suffered in this costly war. It was generally felt, among all but the great landowners and the Court circles, that little was to be looked for from a Tsar who could be flattered into signing a personal "alliance" with the Kaiser in the absence of the Foreign Minister, as Nicholas did in the summer of 1905.

In August, the Tsar, responding reluctantly to cumulative liberal pressure, especially from the "Zemstvo men," granted the institution of an imperial Duma. This body, however, was to be merely consultative, and lacked the democratic basis which all the liberal parties

[5] The events of the Baltic revolution are documented in Baltische Revolutions-Chronik, 2 vols. (Riga, 1907, 1908). See also Die Revolution in den Ostseeprovinzen von 1905-1906, 3 vols. (Riga, 1907); Astaf von Transehe Roseneck, Die lettische Revolution, 2 vols. (Berlin, 1908); E. O. F. Ames, ed., The Revolution in the Baltic Provinces of Russia (London, 1907).

demanded. Socialist Revolutionaries, pointing out that such an institution could do nothing to solve the land question, and adopting the slogan "all the land to the peasants,"[6] fomented serious revolts among the hunger-maddened peasants. In several instances, after the police had given up trying to restore order, veritable local peasant republics came into being. In the Baltic Provinces, where the call of the Right Wing Socialists for moderation failed to stem the swelling tide of rebellion, violence begat violence. Armed Latvian bands broke into and looted German-Balt castles, and when the barons brought their private police forces into action, the peasants set the torch to the estates. Seventy-two castles were burned in Vidzeme, forty in Kurland. The embattled peasants fought skirmishes with Russian garrisons, especially with the Circassians imported by the landed gentry to serve as guards for their threatened estates. A number of the squires, fearing for their lives, fled to the cities. In several cities, pitched battles occurred between the Russian forces and the Latvians, almost always resulting in the withdrawal of the Russians. A general defeat of the Russian officialdom and armed forces early in the autumn paved the way for the assumption of power within Latvia by local elected revolutionary committees which now gained full control of the country. The predominance of Right Wing Socialists in these rural committees signified a defeat for the Latvian Bolsheviks, who had persistently sought to make the Baltic revolution an organic part of the Russian upheaval.

By October, Russia was in the grip of a general strike. All parties clamored for a genuinely representative constituent assembly with legislative powers, together with an extension of civil rights. In St. Petersburg the newly elected Soviet of Workers' Deputies assumed leadership of the revolutionary movement; while in Moscow the Constitutional Democratic party ("Cadets"), composed of the *Zemstvo* liberals and other moderates, was holding its first congress. Both of these groups were demanding a term to half measures. The Soviet, after calling an end to the strike, declared for a democratic republic. Nicholas, alarmed by the incessant violent uprisings, strikes, and apparent solidity of radical opinion, finally, in his manifesto of October 30, granted many of the desired civil rights as well as universal suffrage and proportional representation for a new Duma with legislative powers. At the same time, martial law was declared in Poland, where the National Democrats had profited by the revolutionary atmosphere

[6] Sir Bernard Pares, A *History of Russia*, p. 433.

to demand autonomy for their country. Subsequent strikes called by the St. Petersburg Soviet and a revolutionary outbreak in Moscow elicited a few further concessions from the Tsarist Government, but met with cooling response from the general public, who were beginning to resent the inconvenience entailed. Punitive measures against the turbulent peasantry grew more severe. Many liberals expressed the opinion that it was time to settle down and work through the new Duma. The tide had turned.

These events of the last three months of 1905 in Russia were matched in Latvia by corresponding crisis and reaction. At the end of October, the Latvian Central Federative Committee was formed in Riga, consisting of those representatives of the rural committees who had convened in Riga before the issuing of the Tsar's Manifesto. The Central Federative Committee, supported by all shades of Latvian political opinion, was solidly based on a truce concluded between the left and right wings of the Social-Democratic party. This temporary reconciliation was in large measure the work of the nationalist and socialist poet J. Rainis, who, in his many enthusiastic writings and speeches, insisted on the right of the Latvians to their own land and the free election of their government. The previously quoted program of the Right Wing Socialists (p. 262) was, he asserted, the maximum which the Latvian nation could achieve at this time. By its universal acceptance of this program, the Latvian revolution of 1905 could claim as its main accomplishment the achievement of the ideology of statehood. As the outward manifestation of this inner drive, the Central Federative Committee, not satisfied with the Tsar's promise of an All-Russian elective Duma, demanded the election of a local Latvian constituent assembly. This demand was supported by the Congress of Representatives of Rural Communities which convened in Riga at the end of December.

Congresses, indeed, were a major manifestation of the Latvian revolution, a not unnatural trend in a nation which had long since learned to find self-expression and a comforting sense of solidarity in cultural gatherings and societies on a nationwide scale. In November, Riga played host to a convention of school teachers who demanded the use of their mother tongue in the schools, favored the separation of church and state, and declared their solidarity with the Socialists.

The Latvian Lutheran pastors, sensitive to the attack on their Church from many quarters, assembled in their first synodical conference to elaborate a program of reform. During the course of the proceedings it was conceded that, of the 200 Lutheran parishes, only ten per cent were predominantly German; that 20 of the many German pastoral families within Latvia had established hereditary rights to their cures, some of which had been retained in one family for as long as nine generations; and that, of the 200 or so Latvian pastors who had finished their theological studies between 1850 and 1905, only 85 were ever ordained.

In December was held the above-mentioned congress of delegates from 600 Livonian and Kuronian rural communes. This assembly, in addition to supporting the demand of the Central Federative Committee for a national constituent assembly, favored a strong agrarian reform program which would redistribute the land of the manors among the landless. Executive committees, or peasant councils, were to take over abandoned estates; carry on local government (in the absence of the withdrawn Russian officials) until the election of the Latvian constituent assembly; and rally the defenses against the Cossacks and Dragoons which the *Landtag* had called in for the protection of the Germans.

By the end of 1905, Latvia had become self-governing. Freedom of the press and association had been established, and the Latvian language restored to the schools. The payment of taxes to the nobility was refused. Many local executive committees were functioning. A Constitutional Democratic party had been founded which, though more moderate than the Socialists, agreed in essence with the demands of the Central Federative Committee for land reforms and a constituent assembly.

The constructive cohesion of opinion and achievement which had enabled the Latvians to wrest such a large measure of autonomy from the Revolution of 1905 was all too soon marred by the defection of the few but energetic and outspoken Latvian adherents of the Russian Bolshevik party. Led by Pēteris Stučka, these followers of Lenin, heeding the directives of their master, who denounced the Manifesto of October 30 and all those who accepted it, broke with the Right Wing Socialists in December. The increasing unruliness of the peasant risings against the estates, incited by revolutionary leaders, far surpassed the program of the Central Federative Committee and the Right Wing Socialists, who still advocated a degree of moderation. The less radical elements surmised that the Russian Revolution might have been premature, and that the vociferations of the Latvian Bolsheviks together with the depredations of the peasantry against the

German barons would bring down the full wrath of the Russian Government on this tender and as yet defenseless state.

The Latvian moderates judged rightly. With the waning of revolutionary prestige in Moscow and St. Petersburg, the government assumed an increasingly intransigent position. Punitive expeditions were the order of the day in Russian rural areas where the fires of peasant desperation still burned, and in the border lands where demands for autonomy were sporadically mingled with the strikes and risings of workers and peasants. In the Baltic Provinces the Tsarist forces of suppression were to have the full benefit of German-Balt thirst for revenge.

In December, martial law was declared in Estonia, Livonia, and Kurland. That same month several Russian army detachments, consisting of Cossack cavalry and the infantry and field artillery of the Imperial Guards, began the invasion of Latvia from three directions. These forces were assisted by the German-Balts, many of whom had been enrolled as special constables as early as March. All during 1906, the enraged Germans rode with the Russian punitive expeditions through the countryside, made up part of the special execution squads, assisted in the courts-martial, denounced the farmers and the agitators, bore witness (frequently false), and urged on the executions and deportations with exemplary zeal. A reign of terror was in full swing. Hundreds of Latvian-owned farms and villages were burned, hostages shot by the score. Teachers, particularly suspect in the eyes of the German-Balts since the revolutionary manifestations at the Riga Polytechnic and the University of Dorpat in January 1905, were publicly hanged without benefit of trial. The reaction, which lasted throughout 1906, resulted in the execution of some two thousand Latvians and the deportation of an even larger number to Siberia. Several thousand sought refuge abroad, particularly in the United States, where a good proportion of the present Latvian group had its origins in this wave of emigration from slavery and death.

Following the example of the Russian Bolsheviks, after the dissolution of the Soviets, many of the Latvian revolutionaries fled abroad, a number of them to England. This exodus was received with some satisfaction by the moderates, since, though nationalist in their sentiments, these took the long view and saw their gradual gains risked by the excesses of the fire-eaters. Markedly unsympathetic towards the radicals were the growing class of Latvian landowners, the *Wirte*, who, by their prosperity and their caution, had earned from the Socialists the contemptuous title of "Grey barons," only a shade less obnoxious to the Socialist ideal than the "Black barons" or German squires.

The German-Balt squires were not without a certain sense of triumph induced by the revolution of 1905, in spite of the fact that they suffered far more than the Russian officials at the hands of the self-liberated Latvians, who hurled themselves remorselessly against their perennial oppressors. The German-Balts had always considered the policy of Russification both a personal insult and a grave political error. The flouting of their pastors, the transfiguration of their beloved University of Dorpat, the assault on their langauge, the displacement of their administrators by the unprincipled and inefficient *tchinovniki*, all these measures had caused them to fall back on their hauteur and their unassailable conviction that only a German Balticum, a veritable law of nature to the German mind, could hold what they considered the lawlessness of the Baltic peoples in check. The riotous conduct of the students in the institutions of higher learning seemed to prove their point. The fact that several Russian teachers sided with the Latvians against the exponents and supporters of the Tsarist régime further demonstrated the riskiness of the Russian policy in the Baltic Provinces, where government-appointed officials could prove unreliable in the face of revolutionary passions. Rotten as the whole Russian social and political system was in German estimation, it seemed to the Baltic barons a calamitous policy to seek to extend this administration over what, hitherto, had been the strictly controlled Baltic peoples. The Germans blamed the measures of Russification for the rise of radical opinion in both Latvia and Estonia, and even attacked the Orthodox priests for undermining the religious and moral bases of the people. Censorious, vindictive, and more confirmed than ever in their sense of superiority, the Germans stood ready to assume once again the governance of the Balticum.[7]

They stepped naturally into the void left by the disintegration of the Latvian short-lived autonomy and the indecisions of the gravely shaken Tsarist régime. There was a novel flavor to this renewed German dominance. No longer fascinated by fashionable St. Petersburg, they now oriented themselves upon Berlin and cleaved wholeheartedly to *Kultur*, which they proposed to administer as a potent

[7] See in particular for the German-Balts at this crisis, C. L. Lundin, "From Tsar to Kaiser" in *Journal of Central European Affairs*, x (1950), p. 235ff., with extensive bibliography. The conservative German position in these decades is presented by Hans Rothfels, *Reich, Staat und National im deutschbaltischen Denken* (Halle, 1930).

curative to the disturbed peoples of the Baltic Provinces. Somewhat belatedly they took stock of the local cultural renaissance to the extent of attempting to match the various Latvian and Estonian organizations and movements with similar enterprises bearing the German stamp. In Estonia, Livonia, and Kurland, German (Balt) Unions came into being for the fostering of a sense of Germandom along cultural and social lines and the edification of those among the higher native bourgeoisie who might be expected to appreciate a show of civilized advantages on the part of their ruling class.

True, the Latvian bourgeois group, now gaining an increased foothold in agriculture and industry, as well as a considerable section of the intellectuals, were relieved to see an end both to Russian bungling and radical influence. They were ready for a period of good housekeeping, of a further expansion of their economy, and a consolidation of their cultural and ideological gains. But even the "Grey barons" were not disposed to be patronized by the "Black squires," whose clanking *Kultur* had a far from liberal note. Pan-Slavism might be temporarily eclipsed by the eruptions within Russia, but Pan-Germanism, with its arrantly militaristic overtones, was in the wind. The pressure upon the new Baltic spirit of nationality had merely shifted once more.

The Latvian classes, bourgeois, labor, and peasant, were by now solidified at least to the extent of claiming their country's right to a marked degree of autonomy and to a free development of its national characteristics. Both German overlordship and Russian policing had become equally intolerable to a people who had had an intoxicating taste of self-rule and self-expression.

With the gradual reinstatement of the German-Balt régime in Latvia, a tacit acknowledgement on the part of the Russian Government that, after all, in this area the Germans certainly knew best, the use of the German language was once more permitted throughout the educational system. The Latvian tongue, on the other hand, as of April 9, 1906, was allowed only in the first two grades of the elementary schools and in private schools, of which only one was licensed in Riga by the Russian curator of schools.

The Latvians met both Russian repression and the reinvigorated German-Balt *Herrenvolk* complex with their age-old passive resistance, whose passivity was by now only nominal. Their countermeasures, though neither violent nor markedly extralegal, were possessed of a cheerful energy. Much had been already gained: self-esteem, experi-

ence in responsibility, some political practice, a degree of self-knowledge, and a talent for hope. Patience seemed a little thing for these
tested people to ask of themselves.

They saw to it that their children learned their mother tongue, and
that their students gained a knowledge of Latvian history and literature. Secret study circles abounded. They promoted a large number of
societies, cultural organizations, cooperative associations, and group
movements in all fields of activity to match the German-Balt developments along this line. Musical societies particularly, with their typically
Latvian blend of self-expression, lyricism, and national sentiment,
flourished as never before. Journalists, writers, and scholars drove their
pens to rally their people for the eventual crisis. Every effort was made
to foster farming by the establishment of agricultural schools and
associations. The peasantry moved gradually toward their goal of economic freedom by redeeming some 150,000 farms. Commercial enterprises of all kinds both created and absorbed the energies of the middle
class. Many of the politically alert moderates who had observed or
taken part in the liberation movement of 1905 pondered the risks of
imported ideologies, as well as the unsuitability of extremism, either
conservative or radical, to the body politic of a small emergent nation.

The Latvians, while maintaining their guard against the Baltic
barons once more in the saddle and dangerously stimulated by the
increasing propaganda for a German Balticum, maintained a watchful
waiting attitude toward Tsarist Russia, now at its twilight hour. It
had become apparent to all but the Bolshevik element among the
Latvians that no real sympathy for Baltic nationalistic aspirations was
to be looked for from even a liberalized Russian régime. The Baltic
Provinces were far too essential to the tottering Tsarist economy to
be indulged in their taste for autonomy. Estonia, Livonia, and Kurland
together produced a net surplus of 37.6 million rubles annually, which
was counted on to replenish the perennially exhausted Tsarist treasury.

It was also obvious to the Baltic nationalists that, although some of
the progressives, notably an element among the *Zemstvo* men, had
favored a degree of autonomy for the Baltic peoples, the Russian political party platforms did not concern themselves with this issue, even
the Bolshevik Social-Democrats revealing themselves to be far from
liberal on this score. The *Zemstvo* representatives to the Moscow
Conference of 1905 had demanded that a future constitution should
grant rights of cultural self-determination to all non-Russian nationalities within the Empire, including the use of native languages in the

local Diets and administrations.[8] But the Great Russian element (42 per cent of the entire population in 1897), predominant in every political group, regarded the notion of a united, indivisible Russia wherein the most the minority nationalities could hope for was a restricted local self-government under the firm control of whatever Russian régime might be in power, as a common and necessary basis for all shades of opinion. The Great Russians of all political creeds experienced a common desire to maintain the integrity of the Empire by holding firmly to those border provinces whose advanced economic and cultural status afforded that Empire much of its strength and prestige. Russia's position as a first-class power could not be guaranteed if her more affluent areas broke away from her hegemony. Although less concise and energetic than the German-Balts in its dominance of the Baltic Provinces, the Russian Government, in the period preceding the First World War, took due precautions against any threatening manifestations of nationalism, and against any effective representation of this "unreliable" area in the successive Dumas.

The first Duma, elected in March 1906, without the participation of the Social-Democrats, convened in May of that year. Eight elected representatives from Latvia participated. The preponderant party, by a wide margin, were the Constitutional Democrats, including many active members of the Zemstva. The opening address of the Assembly demanded equality of all citizens before the law, and some solution of the problem of individual nationalities.[9] This last issue was ignored in the Declaration of the Council of Ministers of May 13, and Article I of the Constitution of April 23 stated that "the Russian State is one and indivisible."

But the Assembly's liberal program of agrarian reform could not be so lightly dismissed. Indeed, under pressure from the reactionary landowners, the first Duma was summarily dissolved for its excesses in this regard. Jānis Čakste, Latvian representative and future first President of the Latvian Republic, together with other progressive members of the Duma signed the Viborg Manifesto protesting against the forcible dismissal of that body. For this degree of assertiveness Čakste was deprived of election rights and confined to Jelgava.

As a concession to aroused public opinion, the Tsar now appointed Stolypin Premier. Known for his progressive ideas in the field of

[8] G. A. Yevreinoff, *Natsionalniye voprosi* (St. Petersburg, 1908), p. 4.
[9] T. T. Savich, *Novy gosudarstvenny stroy Rossiyi* (St. Petersburg, 1907), pp. 137-138.

agrarian reform, Stolypin gave promise of cooperation with the majority of the second Duma. The fate of this assembly was no better than that of the first. Elected in March 1907, this time with the participation of the Socialists, it was dismissed the following June on the grounds that a radical Socialist plot against the Tsar had been uncovered. Among the fifty-five Socialist deputies deported to Siberia were two Latvian Social-Democrats. Nicholas' manifesto dissolving the second Duma insisted that the third Duma should be "Russian" in spirit. In accordance with this proclamation, the representation of all the national minorities was reduced, leaving the Latvians with only two delegates. These two, J. Goldmanis and J. Zālītis, who were also to represent their country in the fourth Duma of 1912-1917, joined forces with the few other Baltic and Polish delegates in the third Duma to continue a stalwart but vain fight for minority rights.

Although the Russian Dumas appeared to be at the mercy of Court and gentry whims, some measure of reform was introduced in the debilitated Empire, if only as a sop to increasingly concerned Western democratic opinion. Latvia profited to the extent of having a provincial council set up in Riga in 1907 by the Governor-General to work out a project of district and provincial self-government. A more ambitious plan of territorial self-government on the Zemstvo pattern was sent to St. Petersburg for approval, where it promptly disappeared in the bottomless files of the German-directed Chanceries.

Obviously, demands for autonomy were premature. The shibboleth of "Russia indivisible" afforded a common ground to those political parties who could not bring themselves to agree on such an urgent matter as agrarian reform. Whereas both the Cadets and the Socialist Revolutionaries deplored Stolypin's bold program of dividing up the lands of the mir into individual peasant farms, they united in nodding approval to his renewal of Russification in the Baltic Provinces.

This policy was heralded by Stolypin's Secret Order of 1908 for a more intensive Russification of the Baltic Provinces, and confirmed a year later by a particularly stern attitude toward Finland. The Tsar's Ukase of October 1909, concerning this latter country, contained the general statement that questions "affecting the interests of the Russian Empire" as a whole were to fall exclusively within the competence of the Imperial Duma. In Latvia, the teaching of the native tongue was forbidden once more even in the elementary schools. This repeated emphasis on the language issue was due in part to the fact that Russian gained very little hold on the common usage, failing to reach anywhere near the ascendancy of the German tongue, still the accepted idiom of business, administration, commerce, and even petty rural intercourse, facilitating as it did necessary daily relations among German-Balts, Jewish middlemen, and the Latvian population.

The Russian Government now went to the extent of fostering the emigration of Latvians to Central Russia, a move scarcely calculated to appeal to a peasant and industrial population who, for all their economic and social discontents, were still considerably advanced over their Russian equals' standard of living and level of culture. The Government also encouraged the settlement in Kurland both of Russians and of German colonists from the Volga region. This was part of the policy of strengthening the frontiers, since these colonists were planted near the East Prussian border.

Colonization, as a long-term defense measure, also appealed to the German-Balts, who, after centuries of confident dependence on a native slave class, had finally to face the fact that the Baltic peoples might be far from reliable in times of revolution or war. The Baltic barons, deprived of their serfs, had no peasantry they could call their own; and the German-Balt industrialists were without a loyal laboring class. Since there were no German-Balts who would enter the ranks of the rural or urban working classes, German colonists must be imported. A beginning was made in the period immediately preceding the First World War; especially in Kurland, where Silvio Brödrich, a German-Balt holding some 160,000 acres, succeeded in settling them with almost 14,000 Germans drawn from German minority areas in the Russian Empire. By 1914, in addition to these Kurland settlers, some 7,000 German colonists had made a start in Livonia proper. The German-Balt enthusiasm for this form of enterprise was to survive the War.[10]

These respective efforts of the Russians and the German-Balts to strengthen their hands along the Baltic were inspired by the increasing tempo of nervous diplomatic and paramilitary maneuvers throughout Europe presaging a major armed conflict. Within a relatively short period Russian-German relations had deteriorated from the solidarity of the Bismarck era to the swinging of the Tsarist Empire into the anti-German orbit by her adherence to the Triple Entente in 1907. Little significance could be attached to the Declaration of St. Petersburg of

[10] It is significant that von Engelhardt, writing in 1916 (*Die deutschen Ostseeprovinzen Russlands*, pp. vii-ix), was still appealing for a great effort of colonization of German peasantry in the area.

1908, wherein Germany and Russia agreed to respect the territorial *status quo* of the Baltic shores, thus implying a mutual recognition of their respective acquisitions in that area and of the Baltic as a *mare clausum*.[11] The concept of a German-Russian condominium was fast proving untenable.

The opening of the Kiel Canal in 1895, by facilitating the movements of the German fleet, had undermined Russia's security in the Baltic Sea. It had stimulated the Tsar's government to fortify the Baltic fleet, to increase its bases, and build strategic railways to the coast and through the borderlands to the Western frontier. Russia, secured by French capital, applied her *ad valorem* tariff to German goods, thus dealing a severe blow to German foreign trade. Thrust and counterthrust were felt in the Baltic lands like electric currents. It seemed inevitable that, wherever the conflagration might be ignited, control of the Balticum would be one of the main issues between Germany and at least one of the Allies. That body of water would assume its time-honored role as a bone of contention, and that segment of its coast which had suffered so many trampling armies would become once more a battleground, this time of a world-wide war.

Although the initial outbreak of war was in the Balkans, the Latvians felt their involvement immediately. J. Goldmanis, Latvian deputy from Kurland to the fourth Imperial Duma, in an Extraordinary Session of that body on August 7, 1914, committed his people by his statement that the Latvians and Estonians would fight "with all our heroism in the ranks of the Russian army, so that Berlin shall drown in the sea of blood which it has released."[12] The grim horror of the Teutonic threat had made service in the Russian cause seem the lesser of two evils. Nor must we forget that Russia's alliance with the Western democracies had aroused the hopes of most liberals within her boundaries that a spate of internal reforms might ensue. It also seemed likely that the shock of war would wash away much of the dry rot which permeated her body politic and bring a democratic era to birth. While the Latvian people as a whole, swayed by their centuries-long emotional conditioning against the Germans, chose spontaneously to fight openly against their oldest foe, their leaders weighed the consequences of electing to side with the Russians and found them promising. The impending crisis appeared as that awaited period of solidarity in intense suffering which many had deemed a necessary preliminary

[11] A. Schwabe, *The Story of Latvia and her Neighbors*, p. 26.
[12] *Ibid.*

to the autonomy which had become the declared goal of the Latvian people. Certainly the attainment of such a goal might be indefinitely postponed should the Baltic Provinces fall to German military might. Whereas an Allied victory might bring a degree of democratization to Russia, German conquest could only portend an iron régime of police rule and exploitation, with a possibility of the extermination of the native stock, now that German colonization had made a threatening start.[13]

Throughout the war the peoples of the Baltic Provinces remained irreproachably loyal to Russia. Mobilization in this area was completed six days ahead of Russia proper. The initial impetus of the Russian armies, reinforced by the fierce will-to-defend of the Latvians, who composed almost eighty per cent of some of the fighting units, swept them victoriously across East Prussia. But it needed little time for the extreme inefficiency of the Russian administration to bring its military machine to the point of breakdown. Between January 31 and February 8, 1915, von Hindenburg had encircled General Samsonov's divisions and begun that drastic decimation which was the first of a number of severe blood-lettings suffered by the Latvian forces. The German thrust for the Baltic Provinces was on. Lithuania was overrun. The naval base of Liepāja fell, and shortly thereafter most of Kurland was occupied.

Since, upon the insistence of the Allies, the Daugava line was to be held, the population of Vidzeme and Latgale did not bear the brunt of the war suffering, which fell upon the inhabitants of Kurzeme and Zemgale. By order of the government, and at the immediate instigation of the Cossacks who were scorching the earth before the German advance, a majority of the peasants evacuated Kurland. Most of their livestock had been requisitioned by the Russian armies. With what little was left them, some 355,000 Latvian refugees streamed into Russia in the wake of the retreating armies. Eventually about 27 per cent of the entire Latvian population were living on Russian soil, many of them under poor conditions on the uncultivated lands behind the Volga. Such a number was beyond the scope of the Refugee Committees in Petrograd and Moscow, whose funds soon proved inadequate to the emergency. One solution which suggested itself to the Committees was the absorption of the able-bodied men into Latvian battalions.

In April 1915, two Latvian reserve battalions, displaying extraor-

[13] See in general André Tibal, *L'Allemagne et la Baltique Orientale 1915-1919* (Riga, 1932); O. Gaillard, *L'Allemagne et le Baltikum* (Paris, 1919).

dinary combat qualities, had repulsed a German attack on Jelgava, thus slowing down the drive on Riga. This persistence of their people's fighting spirit, in the face of maximum losses, inspired the two Latvian representatives in the Duma to urge the creation of recognized Latvian armed forces. Goldmanis' appeal of July 19 ended with the call to "gather around the Latvian colors! Forward with the Latvian colors for the future of Latvia."

In spite of the clamorings of the *Deutschrussen* and the chauvinists against such a move, both the Tsar and his uncle, Grand Duke Nicholas, Commander-in-Chief of the Russian armies, finally consented to the creation of eight volunteer Latvian field battalions and one battalion of reserves, whose battle flags and insignia were to be allowed to bear Latvian colors, emblems, and inscriptions. Thus, by the Tsar's decree of August 1, 1915, establishing these regiments, the Latvian language, in reference to the inscriptions, was granted official recognition for the first time in seven hundred years.[14]

Shortly after the enlargement of these Latvian battalions into regiments, two brigades of four regiments each were organized. Their total strength amounted to 130,000 men. There was no dearth of Latvian officers to command all nine regiments (including the reserve), many of these officers being graduates of the highest Russian Military Academy. The Latvian regiments soon became known as the Latvian Rifles, since they were limited strictly to infantry, being specifically denied artillery or cavalry by the Russian High Command.[15]

The creation of the Latvian Rifles had been a matter of dire necessity. The Allies, disturbed by the hasty Russian retreat through East Prussia, Lithuania, and Kurland, had demanded that a serious effort be made to hold the Daugava line which defended both Petrograd and Finland. General Gourko, Commander of the weakened Twelfth Army covering Petrograd, had favored a concentrated Latvian force in this strategic position, judging correctly that their defense would be far more effective than that of any Russian divisions, since the Russian soldiers were interested only in the protection of their own villages.

The Latvian Rifles lived up to the highest expectations, holding the Daugava line for two years. Their resistance was not without repercussions on the Western Front, since they forced the German High Command to keep their Eighth and Tenth Armies on the northeastern

[14] Schwabe, *op.cit.*, p. 27.
[15] Gen. M. Peniķis, *Pasaules karš un Latvju strēlnieku pulku cīņas* (The World War and the Latvian Rifles). Hoover War Library.

front, where their every thrust was met with stubborn a costly counterthrust. Field-Marshal von Hindenburg admitted that he would have taken Riga by Easter 1916, had it not been for "the eight bright stars in its sky," by which he indicated the eight Latvian Rifle Regiments.

Russia's attitude toward these, the most vigorous and aggressive of her fighting forces, was both inefficient and treacherous. Her indifference to Latvian losses as well as her blindness to strategy were highlighted by the tragic waste of the Christmas campaign of 1916. On December 23, the Latvians, who were granted no artillery cover, began their breakthrough toward Jelgava by opening up eight kilometers of the German front, taking thirty guns and 1500 prisoners. Had they been granted support, all of Kurland might have been recaptured. But Grand Duke Nicholas had remarked "I spit upon your Kurland!" The Germans threw in two fresh divisions with artillery, and by January 5, 1917, the Latvians were back at their initial positions, having lost 32,000 out of 180,000 officers and men in an operation ordered and then deserted by the Russian High Command.

The passivity of the High Command seemed to reflect the attitude of the Russian soldiers, who felt no call to shed their blood in defense of a land not their own. It was a common remark among them that they would fight only for their own villages. The extraordinary valor of the Latvian Rifles, as well as of the Siberian Rifles, consisting mostly of descendants of Polish, Ukrainian, Lithuanian, and Latvian deportees, elicited only shrugs from the exhausted and confused Russian soldiers who wanted nothing more than to go home. The low ebb of their morale was illustrated by the frequent comment that there was little difference between a Tsar with a beard and one with a mustache, meaning the Kaiser. Indeed, they were impressed by the superior lot of the better clad, fed, armed, and commanded German fighting forces.

The defeatism of the Russian soldiers was aggravated by conditions within the Empire, where the hysterical rule of the Empress and the monk Rasputin, together with the apathy of Nicholas II, had finally brought the Tsarist régime to the brink of collapse. All classes of society were appalled by the recurring crises in finance, munitions, and transportation. Poland had fallen to the enemy. The Baltic Provinces could not hope to hold out much longer alone. The Duma wrestled unavailingly with the reactionary Court. Following the murder of Rasputin on December 30, 1916, the tempo of political, social, and military crisis was accelerated. Soldiers and workers took to the streets of Petrograd and rioted for bread. On March 12, the Petrograd Soviet of Soldiers' and Workers' Deputies held its first meeting, the same day that the harassed Duma chose a Provisional Committee to put an end to anarchy. Two days later, the ministers of the Provisional Government were appointed. On March 15, the new Government received the abdication of the Tsar.

Although the Provisional Government stood pledged to the democratic election of a constituent assembly and appeared well disposed toward a program of urgently necessary reforms, the immediate result of the "bloodless revolution" was disastrous confusion, with the Provisional Government and the Soviet fostering different political as well as military aims and issuing contradictory directives. These two powers in Petrograd, neither of which was in a position to gain full control of the Revolution, by their rivalry in a time of enormous external and internal stress, by their opposed political and social philosophies, were to accomplish the ruin of Russia's armies and entirely undermine her status as a combatant.

The Provisional Government, under the mild aegis of the Premier, Prince Lvov, was committed to continuing the war with renewed vigor. Such was not the temper of the Revolutionary Soviets, where defeatism and desertion were rewarded with vast promises of political power and distributed land. The result was bewilderment of the High Command and demoralization of the fighting forces. A measure of internal democratic reform was achieved by the new régime, but it became increasingly clear that all the good will in the world could not maintain an even liberal tenor in the midst of an impending military debacle and a growing Bolshevik threat. The Baltic peoples had hoped that a democratized Russian Government, with the ministers responsible to the Duma, would reward their loyalty and military feats with self-government. It was not so much the will of the Provisional Government as its weakness, bred of unpreparedness, compromise, devotion to European constitutionalism, and the proneness to meet menace with sweet reasonableness, which was to undermine their initial hopes of "a free Baltic in a free Russia."

While Petrograd simmered in the throes of political indigestion, and disorganization and defeatism ate the heart out of the Russian military effort, the burdens of war lay with increasing heaviness upon the Baltic Provinces. Foreign trade, so essential to the economic health of this area, had been drastically curtailed. Industry and agriculture suffered from the transportation breakdown and the lack of machinery, practically all rolling stock, machinery, and stocked raw materials having been evacuated to Russia in 1914 or having fallen into German hands. Churches, schools, hospitals, railway stations, and bridges were blown up equally ruthlessly by retreating Russians and advancing Germans. The population was bowed down by the weight of taxes, a relentless requisitioning, and inflation. Censorship went to the length of forbidding any Latvian newspaper to appear in Riga. Battle losses, together with continued mobilization and evacuation, severely depleted the human resources of all the Latvian provinces; while German occupation threw a pall over Kurland.

German looting and harsh police methods in this area alarmed all Latvians, in whose minds the continuing threat of German colonization was ever present. In July 1915, an organization of the German-Balt nobility known as the *Baltischer Vertrauensrat* had petitioned the German Chancellor to have the Baltic Provinces established as a German province at the peace settlement. In April of the following year, Chancellor Bethmann Hollweg had announced to the Reichstag that upon annexation of the Baltic region its colonial status would be maintained. The disproportionate cost of the war to the Baltic countries matched the staggering price of defeat.

Hard pressed by the enemy, uneasy over the confused shape of things to come in Russia, the Baltic peoples clung to the new gospel of self-determination, striking out hard and single-mindedly for autonomy, the only loophole through which they might hope, by joining the embattled family of Western democracies, to escape German enslavement or fatal embroilment in further revolution within the eastern Empire. Only the Left Wing Social-Democrats felt that the Latvians would have much to gain from an ultimate triumph of the Bolsheviks over the liberal Provisional Government. The majority of Latvian political thinkers believed that the chief hope of their country lay in consolidating the gains of the March Revolution by establishing, at this rare moment of democratic ascendancy, a free Latvia within what they could only hope would remain a free Russia.

At the end of March 1917, there convened in Valmiera a Congress of Representatives of Latvian Rural Communities which elected a Provincial Territorial Council for Vidzeme, which, in turn, chose as Commissioners the Socialist A. Priedkalns and the Agrarian Kārlis Ulmanis. The Provisional Government in Petrograd, recognizing a *fait accompli*, confirmed these two men as High Commissioner and Deputy

Commissioner. The Kuronian refugees meeting in Tartu elected a similar Council for Kurland with Jānis Čakste as High Commissioner; and the Latgallian Congress of Rural Communities, meeting in Rēzekne, chose the Roman Catholic prelate Jāzeps Rancans as High Commissioner of their Land Council. It was the expressed wish of all these elected land councils to form a united Latvian Land Council as the supreme repository of Latvian political power. Resolutions to this effect were passed by the Provincial Councils, municipalities, various social and political organizations, and the Latvian Army.

On July 5, Prince Lvov issued a decree promising Livonia and Kurland the Zemstvo type of self-government. But no further political, social, or economic reforms were accorded the Latvian provinces. The Corporation of the German nobles was left intact. Such a reactionary attitude in this region contrasted shockingly with the toleration of advanced revolutionary aims and measures within Russia, and the Latvian leaders realized that they must exhibit still further initiative if their country was to profit substantially from the overthrow of the Tsarist régime.

Accordingly, upon the proposal of the Provincial Land Council of Vidzeme, there convened in the castle of Riga, on July 30, 1917, a Latvian National Political Conference to discuss the legal status of Latvia. Participating in this conference were seven representatives from the Council of Social Organizations of Riga; six from the Council of Workmen's Deputies of Riga; three from the Council of Latvian Workmen, Soldiers, and Landless Peasants; eighteen from the Latvian Rifles; six from the Provincial Land Council of Vidzeme; six from the City Council of Riga; six from the Provincial Land Council of Kurland; and one from the Latvian Farmers' Union.[16]

The Political Conference unanimously adopted the following decisions: (1) that the Latvian nation, like other nations, should have the full right of self-determination, (2) that Latvia was indivisible and should include the provinces of Vidzeme, Kurzeme and Latgale, (3) that Latgale as an individual component part of Vidzeme should enjoy autonomy in local matters, (4) that Latvia was a political, autonomous unit within the Russian democratic republic, (5) that legislative, executive, judicial, and local municipal powers should be in the hands of the Latvian nation and its Constituent Assembly, to be elected by general, equal, secret and proportional vote, (6) that the Conference

---

[16] See article on this Political Conference by V. Zamuelis in *Latvijas republikas desmit pastāvēšanas gados*, ed. by A. Bilmanis (Riga, 1928), p. 22ff.

protested against annexations, and any attempt to determine the legal political status as well as the frontiers of Latvia or its constituent parts without the knowledge and acquiescence of the Latvian nation.

These resolutions of the Conference of July 30 recalled in general the program of the Latvian Right Wing Socialists of 1903, sovereign independence being the common aim of both groups. The more mature formulations of 1917 had been hammered out on the anvil of revolution, reaction, and three years of catastrophic war. Any doctrinaire flavor had been sloughed off during the course of this stern experience. The men who stood behind these resolutions were no longer Young Letts, hopeful Socialists, or revolutionary poets. They stood prepared to face still more and perhaps graver difficulties. Undemonstrative but determined, they would match their fighting forces' stubborn resistance to one enemy with a series of skilled political maneuvers calculated to release their small but irrefutably vital nation from the crushing pressure of either a Teutonic or a Slavic Empire. The Baltic peoples, Lithuanians, Latvians, and Estonians, now shared the common hope that through a show of timely courage and decision they might at last escape their common fate as mere pawns in the ever recurring struggle for dominion over the Baltic.

PART V

INDEPENDENCE

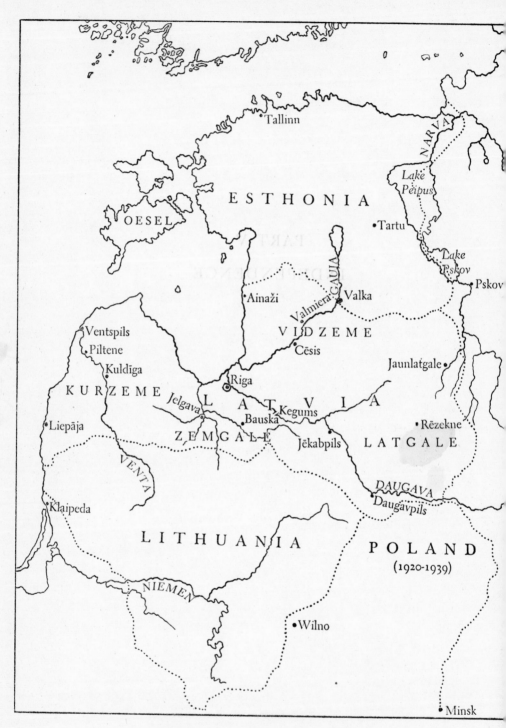

Latvia as an Independent Power

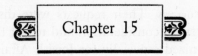

Chapter 15

The Shaping of a Modern State

LATVIA's emergence into statehood during the last year of the First World War cannot be clearly delineated without filling in the tempestuous background. Against the lowering scene of the wreck of the Russian Empire, the relatively peaceful efforts of the Baltic Provinces to liberate themselves stand out in neat relief.

Between her two revolutions, the Liberal-Socialist triumph of March 6, 1917, and the Bolshevik coup eight months later, Russia presented a dire spectacle of social and political upheaval coupled with military debacle which rejoiced her enemies and bewildered her allies. Both the Central and Western Powers were too concerned with the rapidly ripening likelihood of a separate Russian peace to notice the dignified achievement of one of the tenets of democracy, the self-determination of peoples, within the boundaries of an Empire now dramatically casting off all hope of democracy for generations to come.

It seems probable that had the Russian Provisional Government shown any firmness in its initial policy of continuing the war on the side of the Allies, or in supporting a democratic, constitutional régime, the Baltic Provinces might not have demanded complete independence. They might, instead, have remained content with some badly-needed reforms and a measure of autonomy. It was the vacillations of the government in power, together with the demoralization of the Russian soldiers, the blindness of the High Command, the rumors of understanding with the German Intelligence Service, the demogoguery stirring up the cry of "Peace, bread, land," the hysteria of Kerensky, and the complete opportunism of Lenin and his Bolsheviks—all of which could only lead to eventual dictatorship—which forced the issue on the "little peoples." They would gain nothing by passing from one tyranny to another. They must act now, decisively, if they were to emerge into the comparatively free atmosphere of Western democracy.

The gradualist policy which had inspired the leaders of the Latvian Political Conference of July 30, 1917, to elaborate a program of reforms for Latvia and present it to the Provisional Government did not meet with much success. Their requests were disregarded and the petition handed over for consideration and report to the Department of Minorities, organized especially for Jewish Affairs.

Particularly disappointing was the attitude of Kerensky, Premier since July 21, 1917. Ten years earlier, in Tukums, Kurzeme, as an attorney and a democrat, he had defended Latvian revolutionaries before the Russian military court. Now, as head of the Provisional Russian Government, he sympathized with the Cadets (Russian Constitutional Democrats) in the matter of preserving the indivisibility of the Russian Empire. One of their leaders, Foreign Minister Miljukov, in the first Duma Cabinet of Prince Gregori Lvov, had ridiculed Latvian demands for political-territorial autonomy, arguing that the Samoyedes, primitive Arctic nomads, might insist on the same rights.

Miljukov and Kerensky had stormier troubles on their hands than the peaceable demands of national minorities. The breakup of the Eastern front, hastened by both German and Russian propaganda, confronted them. The March Revolution and its creation, the Provisional Government, had been, in a sense, two-faced: promising a continuation of the war to the Allies, yet somewhat vaguely assuring the returning soldiers and the weary civilians that their eternal cry of "peace, peace" would not be disregarded.

Moreover, the Provisional Government had a rival for the loyalty of the masses in the Soviet of Workers', Soldiers', and Peasants' deputies, elected in Petrograd on March 10. This body, full of revolutionary zeal, refused to cooperate with the Provisional Government and sat independently in Petrograd, holding in its hands, besides the sympathies of the people, such actual elements of power as the troops, the railways, and postal and telegraph services. It developed its own foreign policy which, likewise, looked two ways: urging on the Provisional Government the immediate negotiation of a general democratic peace between all the belligerent governments; and appealing by propaganda directly to all the people, above the heads of these governments.[1]

It was this phantom of a separate peace, soon to achieve a grim reality, which haunted and distorted the judgment of the Provisional Government to the point of impotence. First the Liberals reassured the Allies, then they condoned the general Russian defeatism; now they desperately preached resistance on the Eastern front, now the

[1] J. W. Wheeler-Bennett, *The Forgotten Peace* (New York, 1939), p. 28f.

sought to get in touch with German Intelligence. The latter took full advantage of the chaos which ruled in Russian foreign policy. In April, they had seen to it that Lenin returned safely from exile in Zürich. Their reward, though not an intentional one on the part of the entirely opportunistic Russian revolutionist, was Lenin's ceaseless, intense, and highly successful admonishments to the Russian soldiers and workers to end the war which was started by capitalists, to fraternize with the German soldiers, to come home and seize their just due, the factories and the land. German Intelligence quickly jumped in the breach by ordering the German soldiers to meet and further demoralize the defeatist and fraternizing Russians. The call for "peace" rang up and down the lines, with the Russian peasant-soldiers deserting in masses. Russia now lay open to the German army, which only defeats on the Western front prevented from sweeping on to a total victory.

Miljukov's duplicity in foreign policy, his attempt to promise war to the Allies and peace to the Soviet, caused the latter, now strongly influenced by Lenin, to force his resignation on May 17. The following day, Prince Lvov reorganized his Cabinet. That same day, the government declared that its policy was not to seek a separate peace "but to bring about at the earliest possible moment a general peace." The basis of this peace was to be non-annexation and self-determination. Three days earlier, the Petrograd Soviet had also declared against a separate peace, in a Manifesto to the Socialists of all countries, urging them to obtain from their governments a "platform of peace without annexations or indemnities, on the basis of the self-determination of peoples."[2] Apparently, both liberals and revolutionaries thought it was wise at this time to voice the new democratic slogan of self-determination.

The Allies continued to demand the impossible of the Provisional Government: a summer offensive. The Russian middle class and intellectuals, dreading a German-Bolshevik victory, also urged the stiffening of Russian resistance. German military sources have revealed that the agents of the Provisional Government approached Erzberger in Stockholm in the spring and early summer, probably to cover up the Russian preparations for a July offensive.[3] Kerensky, fiercely opposed by Lenin and his forces, now sought to reorganize the army. General Kornilov, who favored old-fashioned discipline, was made the new Commander-in-Chief; and the offensive was under way by the first of July. On July 19, the German High Command launched a counter-

[2] op.cit., p. 48ff.
[3] Mathias Erzberger, Erlebnisse im Weltkrieg (Berlin, 1920), p. 237f.

attack. The Russian army, rotten with Bolshevik agents, murdered its officers, hesitated, then fled; thus, as Lenin said, voting for peace with its legs. The Germans, after taking Tarnopol, struck through to the Baltic in the direction of Petrograd, several divisions succeeding in crossing the Daugava and spreading to the north and south. Since only two brigades of the strongly decimated Latvian Rifle regiments remained to defend it, Riga fell to Ludendorff on September 3, after two days of severe fighting. The Germans then occupied Livonia proper. Probably only German transportation difficulties saved Petrograd, where Kerensky's government was by now in a precarious position.

In July, after the offensive had failed, the Bolsheviks had attempted an abortive coup d'état which resulted in temporary repressive measures against them and the escape of Lenin to Finland, where he remained for the next three months. Kerensky reorganized his Cabinet and once more assured the Allies that Russia was still in the war.[4] Following the fall of Riga, General Kornilov, for a brief moment, emerged into the political limelight. On September 10, he demanded of Kerensky extraordinary military powers; then, receiving no answer from the jealous Premier, assumed full military and civil powers. Kerensky, whose judgment was weakest in moments of crisis, turned to the Soviet for help against the one man whom the army still followed. True, Kornilov was defeated, since his Cossacks would not fight their comrades in arms, the bolshevized garrison of Petrograd, and even joined them in demanding immediate peace with Germany. But Kerensky, too, had lost, by restoring the Bolsheviks to favor and arming their cohorts.

The bulk of the army was by now completely undermined by Bolshevik propaganda, nor did Kerensky's proclamation of himself as supreme military commander at the end of September stem the tide. On October 3 and 8, Bolshevik majorities took control of the Moscow and Petrograd Soviets. Kerensky, realizing that the Constituent Assembly would never be called, desperately created the Council of the Russian Republic, a mere consultative assembly, which held its first session on October 20. The Bolshevik delegates, after a demonstration, noisily withdrew from participation in a "Government of treason to the people." In the first week of November, they issued a call for an All-Russian Congress of Soviets "to take over the government of Russia." But Lenin, back from Finland, preferred a coup to a Congress.

4 Wheeler-Bennett, *op.cit.*, p. 54f.

This time the situation was ripe. On the morning of November 7, the members of the Government, undefended and bewildered, were arrested at their last session. Kerensky, who had gone in search of an army, escaped.[5]

The Bolshevik leaders declared that they had obtained information that on November 8 Kerensky's representatives intended to begin secret peace negotiations with Austrian emissaries in Stockholm. This was their accusation against the Government. But the very day of their *coup de force*, the Bolsheviks, fully realizing that the political group which succeeded in offering peace to the masses would indeed become the ruling power, declared themselves ready for a general peace. The following day, Lenin was elected chairman of the revolutionary government; Trotsky, Commissar for foreign affairs; and Joseph Stalin, Commissar for National Minorities. At nine o'clock on the night of November 8, Lenin, obsessed by his conviction that a proletarian revolution in Germany only awaited a signal, appeared before the Soviet Congress now in session and presented a Decree of Peace with the assertion that "we shall offer peace to the peoples of all the belligerent countries upon the basis of the Soviet terms: no annexations, no indemnities, and the right of self-determination of peoples."

Lenin, urging immediate approval of the Peace Decree by the Congress, received wild applause.[6]

The Allied diplomats decided to ignore both the new régime and its peace proposals. Trotsky, after issuing an anonymous call to the world by wireless for an immediate armistice and receiving no response, set about preparing for the seemingly inevitable separate armistice. Lenin's promise to publish all secret treaties found in the Tsarist archives was fulfilled. The Council of Commissars ordered the cessation of hostilities on November 26. Trotsky then applied to the German High Command for the negotiation of an immediate armistice for the discussion of a democratic peace. At the same time, he informed the Allied diplomats that, although there was still hope of concluding a general settlement, Russia would have to have peace at any cost. The armistice agreement was finally signed at Brest-Litovsk on December 15, Trotsky throwing the blame for its separatism on the aloof Allies.

At last, the peace the Allies had dreaded and the Russian people cried out for was to materialize; a peace far removed from the slogans of non-annexation and self-determination which the Bolsheviks, up

[5] *op.cit.*, p. 57ff.   [6] *op.cit.*, p. 68f.

to the last moment, loudly proclaimed; a black peace indeed, which was to horrify the still fighting Western Powers by its humiliating terms to a self-defeated nation, and realize the worst fears of the Baltic Provinces.

The tempo and the cataclysmic nature of the changes taking place in revolutionary Russia from March to November 1917, both favored and at times confused the plans for independence of the submerged nationalities on the vulnerable western borders of this crumbling Empire. As the Russian armies melted away, slowly-maturing projects were quickly discarded for forthright action. By the end of November, the Ukraine, Poland, the Central Baltic States, and Finland had all seceded. On the part of Latvia, this decisive gesture had been preceded by a systematic and deliberate marshaling of political forces, and the laying of a solid basis for the democratic state which was to emerge from Russia's violence. It took what appeared to be the deliberate betrayal of Riga by the Russian Supreme Command to hasten the calm and rationalistic Latvian leaders into overt action.

Toward the end of the Tsarist régime, when a good part of the inhabitants of Kurland were refugees in Russia, there was formed in Petrograd, by Latvian deputies in the Duma and such active exiles as Jānis Čakste and Zigfrīds Meierovics, the Latvian Refugees' Committee, which worked for autonomy and reform in Latvia. On October 2, 1917, this Committee, at its headquarters, met with representatives of the Latvian Farmers' Association, the Radical Democrats, the National Democrats, the Provincial Councils of Kurzeme and Latgale, the National Union of Latvian Warriors, and the Central Association of Agriculturists. The object of this gathering was a discussion of the situation of Latvia. In order to assure more responsible action, it was decided to convoke a Latvian National Assembly in Valmiera on October 29, particularly with the view to taking steps against the planned betrayal of the Allied cause by the Bolsheviks.

Upon learning that both Russian and a few Latvian Bolsheviks had got wind of this project and planned to attack and disperse the assembly, the leaders postponed the gathering until November 16, changing the meeting place to Valka, at that time still unoccupied by the Germans. Valka, situated on the Latvian-Estonian border, had been the site of the first Constitutional Diet of the Livonian Confederation in the fifteenth century. It was now to become the cradle of Latvia's independence and, as the site of the first National Assembly, the temporary political capital of Latvia.

The appeal for Latvian unity and for the formation of a National Assembly had received an enthusiastic response in all Latvia, which yearned for a representative body similar to the Estonian parliament elected in May. To Valka hurried the Latvian representatives of the former Russian Imperial Dumas, of the Provincial Councils of Vidzeme, Latgale, and Kurzeme, and of the Latvian National Warriors' Organization; also the leaders of various political parties; members of the Petrograd Central Committee of Latvian War Refugees, of the Latgallian War Victims' Committee, and of numerous Latvian cooperative associations; as well as representatives of the Latvian National Postal and Telegraph Union, of trade unions, and of the press. Prominent poets and publicists, such as E. Virza, J. Akurāters, K. Skalbe, and E. Freivalds, were the first on the scene, just as they had been among the first to join the Latvian Rifles. Except for a few observers, no Latvian Social-Democrats participated in the proceedings of the Assembly. By and large, they were still dallying with the Bolsheviks.

However, the Latvian Social-Democrats (Leftist but not Communist), who remained in Riga after the German occupation in September, had submitted to the German Commandant of the city a petition demanding the rights of self-government for Riga. At the end of September, a Democratic Bloc, a coalition of the representatives of different Latvian parties, addressed the following petition to the German *Reichskanzler*:

"In view of the advance of the German army, the question of Latvia's future becomes an international problem, since not only its neighbors, Germany and Russia, but all Europe must be interested in the solution of this problem.

"On the basis of the decision of the Latvian Political Conference of July 30, 1917, and of the principle of self-determination of nations, and, taking also into consideration the new state of affairs, we the undersigned emphasize that the future fate of Latvia should not be made dependent upon the issue of an armed conflict. For the sake of a peaceful solution, the legal question connected with Latvia must be decided on an international level. Taking into consideration in particular the fact that the establishment of continued friendly relations between Germany and Russia is possible only if all interests around the Baltic Sea are harmonized in a spirit of mutual understanding; which in its turn is impossible if one or another country retains in its hands the most important part of this area;—we, striving for a democratic peace which must also assure the political and economic future of Latvia, propose that Latvia be neutralized in such a way as to become an autonomous state, guaranteed by international law. A republican, neutralized, indivisible Latvia, free to choose its own constitution, and to administer its territory and its neutral seacoast and harbors, is a categorical demand emanating from the decision of the Latvian Political Conference of July 30, 1917.

"The Latvian nation considers the successful cultural development of the Baltic area and the insurance of its economic progress to be the only possibility of solving this question. Hence, all efforts aimed at germanizing, russifying or colonizing the Baltic should be rejected.

"Without the slightest hatred against the German people, we decisively and firmly reject the planned annexation of Latvia or of any part of it to Germany, regardless of the legal manner in which this might be effected, since such a step would contain the germs of a new conflict, and would hinder the possibilities of Latvia's economic development."

This appeal had no effect, since Germany was fully determined to annex the Baltic Provinces.

The First Latvian National Assembly was formally convened in Valka on November 16, 1917. The session was opened by J. Goldmanis, a member of the Duma and the organizer of the Latvian Rifles, who proposed the election of a presiding body, consisting of a president, several vice-presidents, and a secretariat. To this presiding body were elected the following prominent Latvian political and social leaders: A. Klive, Z. A. Meierovics, V. Rubulis, G. Palcmanis, K. Skalbe, J. Akurāters, and A. Dobelis. On November 18, K. Skalbe proposed the proclamation of the Assembly as the Latvian Provisional National Council, whose chief task would be to convoke a Latvian Constituent Assembly, which should also have representatives from Latgale. This motion was supported by the Assembly and adopted unanimously. Independent Latvia was born. A special proclamation of the event, addressed to all Latvians, was printed and distributed throughout the land.[7]

A Supreme Board was elected to serve as the Executive of the

[7] See note 16, chap. 14. A fair if not detailed account of the Latvian moves for independence is given in H. W. V. Temperly, *History of the Peace Conference of Paris*, VI (London, 1924), 292-302. Many facts and events could obviously not be known to the author of this sketch, Prof. J. V. Simpson, so soon after the fact.

Latvian Provisional National Council (L.P.N.C.); its component departments being those of Foreign Affairs, Defense, Agrarian and Cultural Affairs, Legal Affairs, and the Department for Latvian Colonies abroad (more than 200,000 Latvian refugees were still in Russia). The *Lihdums* (Pioneer's Land), organ of the Latvian Farmers' Association, was chosen as the official gazette of the L.P.N.C., with prominent Latvian authors and publicists as contributors. V. Zamuelis, a lawyer, prominent publicist, and organizer of the Latvian Constitutional Democratic party, was elected president of the supreme board, with three vice-presidents. K. Skalbe was elected secretary.

The Latvian Provisional National Council, possessing strong moral authority, internal solidarity and cohesion, was promptly recognized by the Latvian people as the repository of Latvia's sovereign power. The American historian M. W. Graham describes the L.P.N.C. as "the principal agency for the constructive expression of Latvian nationalism."[8]

The leading role in the L.P.N.C. was to be assumed by the Foreign Department, headed by Goldmanis, whose immediate duty it became to obtain recognition for Latvia from the Allied Powers, soon to be reassured by the L.P.N.C.'s unequivocal repudiation of the Bolshevik's separatistic peace policy. In order to facilitate the establishment of relations with Allied diplomats, the Foreign Department transferred its seat to Petrograd. The L.P.N.C. also felt called upon to send telegrams of solidarity to the National Assemblies of Finland, the Ukraine, Lithuania, and Estonia. The possibility of maintaining connections with Bolshevik Russia, even in terms of a federal relationship, grew increasingly remote.

The second session of the L.P.N.C. convened in Petrograd early in January. Decisions were reached to strengthen the Latgallian department; to protest against the imminent Brest-Litovsk peace treaty; to establish the residence of the Supreme Board in Latvia, however illegally; and to empower the Foreign Department to act in the name of the L.P.N.C. abroad.

On January 5, 1918, shortly before the dissolution of the All-Russian Constituent Assembly (elected November 25, 1917) by the Bolsheviks, Goldmanis came before the Assembly to protest against the Brest-Litovsk peace treaty which violated the natural rights of Latvia. Goldmanis declared: "The Latvian problem has become inter-

[8] M. W. Graham, *Diplomatic Recognition of the Baltic States.* Part III: *Latvia* (Berkeley, 1941), p. 403.

national. It can no longer be solved here in this house. The Latvian nation will decide on its internal structure and its relations with other nations in its own Constituent Assembly."[9]

This declaration was recorded by the Secretary of the Russian Constituent Assembly. By this official pronouncement Latvia's political relations with Russia were now actually severed.

The Russian Constituent Assembly was existing in a state of limbo, and that only by the grace of the Bolsheviks, who had permitted its election only after they had planned its dissolution. It did not have much longer to live. After the Bolshevik motion to proclaim a Russian Soviet Socialist Republic was rejected by a large majority (563 votes against 140), Lenin's heavily armed sailors "invited" the representatives to leave the Tauride Palace on the morning of January 19. The alternative was death. Trotsky later testified that the decision to disperse had been taken shortly before the Assembly convened, soon after the Bolsheviks had discovered their weakness in the elections. He also refuted the insinuation of certain Russian émigrés that Latvians took part in the dispersal.[10]

Such an ending to the Russian "democratic un-bloody Revolution" came as no surprise to the Latvians, who kept on with the work of organization of their newly created state apparatus. The L.P.N.C. delegated J. Čakste, former representative in the first Duma and later first President of Latvia, Z. A. Meierovics, professor of economics, Cooperative worker, and, later, Latvian Foreign Minister, and two others to establish contacts with foreign governments.

It fell to this first Latvian Foreign Delegation to announce that the Latvians had seceded from Russia, that they continued faithful to the Allied cause, and that Latvia's future status would be decided by a Constituent Assembly freely elected after Latvia's liberation from the Germans. In January, Meierovics visited French, British, and American Ambassadors in Petrograd.

The Foreign Delegation emphasized Latvia's right to full self-determination, and outlined the Latvian plan to create an independent state, including Kurzeme, Zemgale, Vidzeme, and Latgale. The Delegation also declared that under the present circumstances the L.P.N.C. felt itself morally and politically bound to decide the fate of the Latvian people in accordance with their vital interests, which coincided

[9] J. Goldmanis, Zvaigžnu pulku atmirdza (Stockholm, 1947), p. 19.
[10] L. Trotsky, Stalin (New York, 1937), pp. 16ff., 342.

with those of the Allies. Encouraging answers were received from the Allied diplomats.

The Foreign Delegates of the L.P.N.C. were invited by Soviet emissaries to participate in the Brest-Litovsk peace negotiations. They refused, realizing that Germany held all the strings, and that the Bolsheviks, not yet securely entrenched at home, were helpless before the still powerful Reich. They also knew that many of the Bolsheviks were simply tools on the payroll of the German Intelligence Service. The correctness of their information was confirmed by documents published in the volume of the United States State Department *Papers Relating to Foreign Relations*, concerning the Russian Revolution, published in 1931.[11]

Negotiations at Brest-Litovsk, in process since December 1917, were indeed a study in cross-purposes, stalemate, false hopes, and useless gestures. Only two men emerged as cool and calculating, with an eye to the future: the German Secretary of State, Richard von Kühlmann, who for a while sought to tone down the annexation mania of Ludendorff; and Lenin, who, in the end, to save the Russian Revolution, defeated what democratic hopes Trotsky had supported at the conference table.

Early in the discussion, the Russians and the Germans had reached an impasse on the question of non-annexation and self-determination, which the Germans had agreed to accept as a basis of negotiation; always reserving the right to furnish their own interpretation of these principles. This interpretation stressed that Russia's borderland provinces had already taken matters into their own hands by seceding and electing Constituent Assemblies; hence a return of these territories to the Soviets would be a violation of the principle of self-determination. Some Germans even pointed out that the Bolsheviks could not be trusted in matters of freedom, since they had broken up the White Russian and Ukrainian Constituent Assemblies by force.

Back of this bland reasoning was the German High Command's adamant refusal to evacuate occupied territories, which it considered important sources of food, men, and war material; Ludendorff emphasizing the value of East Prussia, in these respects, in the event of another war. Lithuania and Kurland were closely embraced by all Rightist elements in the German Empire. After the fall of Riga, the Commander of the German forces of occupation had insisted on the formation of *Landesräte* representing the German baronial class, now

[11] Vol. I, 371ff.

plotting outright annexation to Germany. The Diet of Mitau, made up largely of German-Balts obviously acting under "suggestion" from occupying German commanders, had even implored the Kaiser to become Duke of Kurland; while the Diet of Vilna was instructed to vote for an "independent" Lithuania which, together with Kurland, was to enter into a personal union with the German Crown. The High Command also insisted that the Russians must promptly evacuate Livonia and Estonia, the better to allow these provinces the "right of self-determination."

Pro-German elements in the occupied Baltic territories, notably the Baltic barons, were not idle. The Kaiser was encouraged. Early in 1918, a delegation of landowners from Livonia and Estonia, still nominally part of Russia, had appeared before him to demand protection from the Bolshevik terrorists. Enraged by a Bolshevik attempt on his life in early February, the Kaiser now incontinently demanded control of all the Baltic Provinces. Kühlmann, still on the side of moderation, threatened resignation and managed to hold down German demands a little longer.

The Russian delegation had at first entertained the hope that a peace without annexations would return to them Russian Poland, Lithuania, and Kurland. But the Germans reminded the Soviets that their own Decree of November 15 on the Self-Determination of Nations naturally forbade such a step, adding that technical and administrative considerations also stood in the way. The Bolsheviks countered with a proposal to remove both Russian and German military forces from Estonia and Livonia, as well as Lithuania and Kurland, and permit plebiscites under the auspices of the local militia. Germany balked.

The intransigence of the Central Powers was further stiffened by the dissolution of the Russian Constituent Assembly by Bolshevik force, a coup which encouraged the Germans to ridicule any Bolshevik pretensions to or defense of "freedom." Confronted by a German ultimatum, Lenin, in his Twenty-one Theses, now presented his reasons for accepting an annexationist peace: "The Brest-Litovsk negotiations have made it clear by now that the war party in Germany has the upper hand. . . . The Russian Socialist Government is confronted with a question which requires an immediate solution, either to accept the annexation peace or to start at once a revolutionary war. . . . A truly revolutionary war at this moment would be a war between a Socialist Republic and the bourgeois countries. . . . For the time being, however, we cannot make this our object. In reality we should be fighting now for the liberation of Poland, Lithuania and Kurland. There is not a single Marxist who, while adhering to the foundations of Marxism and Socialism, would not say that the interests of Socialism are above the right of nations to self-determination. . . ."

But the comedy of Russian hesitation was not quite at an end. Apparently there were still elements within and without Russia which it was deemed worth while to impress with a show of resistance. On February 10, Trotsky permitted himself a dramatic gesture of refusal to sign the treaty, and departed the same day for Petrograd.

Kühlmann was left no alternative but to close the conference proceedings on February 11. The High Command was champing at the bit, with Hindenburg and Ludendorff insisting upon a denunciation of the Armistice. This time they had their way. The resumption of hostilities was announced on the 17th.

The Germans had a new slogan for this particular offensive: they were saving the non-Russian lands from Bolshevism. Prince Leopold of Bavaria issued a proclamation to the Russian people explaining that the German armies were coming to rescue them from the tyranny "which has raised its bloody hand against your best people, as well as against the Poles, Lithuanians, Letts, and Estonians."

In no real sense could the German advance be called an offensive, since the Russian opposition was nil. The old army was no more, and a new, revolutionary force had not yet been created. The Germans swept on to Daugavpils (Dvinsk) and Luck. On February 19, Lenin and Trotsky sent a telegram to German Headquarters accepting the conditions of peace which Trotsky had so pompously turned down. The Germans, demanding more formalities, continued to advance, and took Pskov. In Livonia and Estonia, not only the Baltic Germans, but even upper class Latvians and Estonians (who had had a taste of Bolshevik rule) greeted them as deliverers from Bolshevik depredations.

On the 20th, a courier returned from Germany and handed to the Soviet Central Committee Germany's new peace terms. They were Draconian. Russia had only lost by her delay. Those demands which concerned the Baltic Provinces ran as follows:

"The territories which lie west of the line communicated to the Russian representatives at Brest-Litovsk, and which belonged to the Russian Empire, will no longer be under the territorial sovereignty of Russia. In the vicinity of Dünaburg (Dvinsk) the line is to be shifted to the eastern frontier of Kurland. No obligations of any sort will arise from the former allegiance of these territories to the Russian Empire. . . . Livonia and Estonia will without delay be evacuated by Russian troops and Red Guards and occupied by a German policing force until the country's institutions guarantee security and political order is restored."

This ultimatum concluded that "the Russian plenipotentiaries must immediately proceed to Brest-Litovsk and there within three days sign the Peace Treaty, which must be ratified within a further two weeks."

This time the German delegation held all the cards. Lenin, realizing that there would be no Socialist revolution in Germany, and deeming that there had been enough "reluctance" for the Bolsheviks to save face, now recommended to the Central Soviet in Petrograd that, in view of the German "menace," the peace treaty of Brest-Litovsk be accepted. It was accordingly signed on March 3, 1918. Notwithstanding President Wilson's telegram of March 11, urging the Central Soviet to continue resistance against German militarism, this body ratified the peace treaty on March 16, 1918.[12]

By this treaty the Baltic lands were ceded to the Germans. The Baltic peoples could not do otherwise than consider this treaty as *res inter alias*, and the Bolsheviks as their enemies.

What treatment the Germans reserved for the Balts can be surmised from article 6 of the treaty, which provided that Estonia and Livonia proper (the area of Latvia north of the Daugava River, not including Latgale) should be occupied by German police forces until internal safety was secured. This portended a permanent occupation of the Baltic by the Germans, with whom would rest exclusively decisions of public safety. Kurland, together with the district and city of Riga, came directly under a German protectorate. This meant the partitioning of Latvia; with Kurland absorbed by Prussia; Livonia and Estonia subjected to the Germans, and Latgale left to Russia.

Regardless of Bolshevik persecutions, the courageous Foreign Delegation of the L.P.N.C. decided to convene in a third secret meeting in Petrograd from June 26 to 28, 1918.

This time their achievement was no less than the drafting of a solemn protest to friendly foreign Powers against the activities of Germany in the Baltic as well as against the territorial cessions at Brest-Litovsk, and the passing of a resolution demanding of the Allies

---

[12] For the above discussion of the Brest-Litovsk Peace Treaty, the author is greatly indebted to Wheeler-Bennett, *op.cit.*, chaps. III-VII.

international protection of Latvia's independence. Latvia's
the L.P.N.C. insisted, was necessary to guarantee the freedo
Baltic Sea from German or Russian imperialistic encroachm

The Foreign Delegation, charged with the delivery of all the
lutions and declarations to foreign governments friendly to the ...ic
States, finally succeeded in going abroad via Finland. Čakste and
Kreicbergs took up residence in Stockholm, while Meierovics proceeded to London, where he was well received by the group of Liberals
around Lloyd George. Eventually, the Conservatives also inclined to
give more consideration to Latvia's requests, which were in harmony
with the Baltic policy of Great Britain.

As early as May, the Provisional Government of Estonia had been
recognized *de facto* by Great Britain. On October 30, 1918, Meierovics
addressed to the British Government the appeal of the Latvian Foreign
Delegation asking for protection of Latvia's independence. The answer
was favorable. On November 11, Foreign Secretary Balfour sent the
following letter to M. Z. A. Meierovics:

Foreign Office
November 11th, 1918

Sir:

I have the honour to acknowledge with thanks your letter of
the 30th ultimo in which you enclose a copy of your appeal to
Great Britain and the Allies to give their protection to Latvia.

I am happy to take this opportunity of repeating the assurance
which I gave you on the occasion of your recent visit. His Majesty's Government have viewed with the deepest sympathy the
aspirations of the Latvian people and its desire for liberation from
the German yoke. They are glad to reaffirm their readiness to
grant provisional recognition to the Latvian National Council as
a de facto independent body until such time as the Peace Conference lays its foundations of a new era of freedom and happiness
for your people. In the meantime His Majesty's Government will
be glad to receive you as the informal diplomatic Representative
of the Latvian Provisional Government.

(Signed) A. Balfour

This was high encouragement to the new-born state. Latvia now
stood before the community of democratic nations eager for their
acceptance and for a responsible role in the future of the West.

Chapter 16

The Struggle for National Survival

THE nascent Latvian state now had to face almost two years of various, at times fantastic, but always taxing threats to its right to a free existence. This small territory, which had so often played a role disproportionate to its size in the recurrent contentions for Baltic supremacy, was to endure the huge jealousies of East and West, Slav and Teuton, far beyond the term of Brest-Litovsk. At the tag end of an exhausting World War the Latvian people found themselves involved in those apocryphal battles which raged on in areas out of the international limelight. German-Balts, Prussian militarists, White Russians, and Bolsheviks clung avidly to the ancient disputed ground; and from their greed rose offensives, both direct and oblique, against a newly born state, which stood all but undefended and often unregarded by its mightier sister democracies unable to compass the confusion of threats besetting the still unfledged small nations of the Baltic.

The German menace loomed singularly large even at a time when German military might was beginning to confront the unbelievable specter of defeat. This was in good part due to the busyness of the German-Balt landowners in the cause of that German supremacy which alone could save them from a day of reckoning, if not with the Bolsheviks, then with the Latvians. The latter, it was feared, as masters in their own house, could be counted on to sweep it fairly clean of oppressive alien interests.

We have already mentioned the *Baltischer Vertrauensrat*, a sort of Council of Trustees formed by a group of German landed nobles in Kurland immediately after the occupation of that province by the German army. On July 28, 1915, this body had addressed an appeal to the Reich requesting military protection, permission to elect the Kaiser as Duke of Kurland, and the annexation of the entire Baltic lands, comprising an area of 93,800 square kilometers, by the German Empire. It was further suggested that this region would provide suitable terrain for colonial settlement by a million and a half demobilized German soldiers of reliable peasant stock.

On September 22, 1917, after the fall of Riga and the evident collapse of the Russian war effort, this same Council of Trustees decided that the big Kuronian landowners should "donate" a third of their cultivated lands to prospective German settlers, provided the Reich engage itself to annex Kurland and to assure the German-Balt nobility of preponderance in the administration of the land reform. This project was submitted to the German occupational authorities as a basis for further negotiation on December 15. A similar proposal had been put forward in November by the "liberated" Livonian nobles of the province of Vidzeme.

On March 8, 1918, five days after the signing of the Brest-Litovsk treaty, the nobility of Kurland renewed their appeal to the Kaiser. This *démarche* was acknowledged by von Hertling in his speech before the Reichstag of March 19, recommending the ratification of the peace treaty, and mentioning an "authorized delegation" from Kurland, "the country farthest advanced in development of all the East-European countries," which had given notice of Kurland's separation from Russia and implored the German Government for close economic, military, and political attachment to the Reich. The Chancellor, by order of the Kaiser, recognized Kurland's autonomy, but reserved final decisions until "constitutionally authorized organs shall have defined their attitude." He then added that, with regard to Livland (Latvian Vidzeme) and Estonia, which were situated east of the boundary agreed upon at Brest-Litovsk, "We hope and wish that they also may come to close and friendly relations with the German Empire, but of such a nature as not to exclude peaceable and friendly relations with Russia."[1] Here was the essence of the so-called bridge theory, whereby the Baltic lands, while remaining German satellites, would serve as a bridge between the Teutonic and Slavic Empires.

By permission of the occupational authorities, a Baltic *Landesrat* was formed in Riga on April 12, 1918. This body was composed of thirty-four German-Balt landed nobles of Livland and Estonia, some German representatives of the Evangelical Lutheran General Consistory and of the cities, and a dozen Latvian and a dozen Estonian peasants, picked Elders of rural communities, entirely ignorant of the purpose for which they were ordered to appear in Riga. The intention of this *Landesrat* was to request the Kaiser to recognize Livland-Estonia as a united independent Baltic State with the *Landesrat* as the repository of its political power. The Latvian and Estonian Elders flatly refused to vote on such an issue, claiming incompetence to make a

---

[1] *Papers Relating to the Foreign Relations of the United States. The Paris Peace Conference*, 1919, XII (Washington, D.C., 1947), pp. 436-437.

decision of this kind. However, the motion was duly adopted by the German-Balt technical majority and laid "at the feet of the Kaiser."

By its decree of May 23, the German military administration in Kurland propounded a plan of colonization which capped the "patriotic" offer of the nobles to cede a third of their domains, by accepting these lands without a corresponding allocation to their proprietors of forest domain lands, which had been part of the original proposal. The German squires protested that this decree was contrary to the will and conditions of the Council of Trustees as expressed on September 22, 1917.[2] Over these objections, the German military commander of Kurland, General von Hahndorff, by virtue of an order of Marshal von Hindenburg, decreed on June 17 a colonization scheme for Kurland which was intended to remain in force until 1948.

This decree formally instituted the *Landesgesellschaft Kurlands*, already organized in January, now broadened to include nobles of tested reliability as well as a few specialists imported from Germany, including August Winnig, the Social-Democrat secretary of the German Trade Unions. The operating capital of the *Landesgesellschaft*, amounting to about fifty million marks, was subscribed by nineteen big corporations, among them Fr. Krupp A.G. in Essen, and the *Rheinisch-Westphalisches Kohlensyndikat*. Every Kuronian squire possessing not less than 360 hectares (1 hectare = 2.471 acres) was under obligation to sell a third of his land to the *Landesgesellschaft Kurlands* at 1914 prices. To paragraph 6 of the decree of June 17, providing that until 1948 the *Landesgesellschaft* was to have the right of preemption of all sales of land, the nobility of Kurland objected that "this provision bears the character of a theft of honestly acquired private property for the profit of the *Landesgesellschaft*." They further protested that the creation of new German farms of from fifteen to twenty hectares would tend to produce a crop of smallholders who, because of their petty social standing, might sympathize with Latvian tendencies, and by common interests and intermarriage bring the two nationalities into close and undesirable contact. To offset such a contingency, the squires recommended the creation of a group of reliable German agrarians with farms of from 150 to 370 hectares. Such a class might be expected to exhibit conservative tendencies while at the same time supporting German national aspirations.[3]

The German-Balt landed interests hoped, by promoting the outright

[2] A. Schwabe, *Agrarian History of Latvia*, p. 119.
[3] Schwabe, *op.cit.*, pp. 120-121.

annexation of Kurland to the Reich as well as the indirect annexation of the projected Duchy of Livonia (the rest of the Latvian provinces together with Estonia), to preserve their status as a privileged class and save at least two-thirds of their actual land holdings. While these would provide foodstuffs for industrialized Germany, their owners could be expected to strengthen the conservative party which represented big landed interests in the Reich.

It was just this last probability which aroused the suspicions of the Social-Democrats (with the exception of the Right Wing, headed by Noske and Winnig, who encouraged colonization plans in the Baltic, provided the workers might have their share), and the Catholic Center party. Both these parties objected to the strengthening of the Prussian tories by the support of the Kuronian and Livonian nobility through the annexationist plans of the Prussian militarists in the Baltic.

In order to expedite this projected annexation, the German Government put pressure on the Soviets, by threatening to occupy Petrograd, to conclude a supplementary German-Bolshevik treaty. On August 27, 1918, this treaty, signed in Berlin, traced the frontiers between Russia and Livland-Estonia along the Narev River, Lake Peipus, and the Velikaya marshes down to Daugavpils. While the province of Latgale remained to the Bolsheviks, they renounced all claims to Estonia and Livland (Latvian Vidzeme) by article 7 of the treaty of Berlin, which read: "Russia, taking account of the position at present existing in Estonia and Livland, renounces sovereignty over these regions as well as all interference in their internal affairs. The future fate of these regions shall be decided in agreement with their inhabitants. No obligation of any kind toward Russia shall accrue to Estland and Livland through the former union with Russia." Article 8 of the supplementary treaty provided for free transit for Russia over the Daugava as well as for free-port zones in Reval, Riga, and Ventspils, but not in Liepāja, which was to remain an exclusively German base.

On September 22, 1918, the Kaiser recognized the independence of the new Baltic State, combining Livland and Estonia, with the German-Balt *Landesrat* as the repository of its sovereign power. This body set about preparing the annexation to Greater Germany. In its session of October 19 in the Castle of Riga the *Landesrat* decided to invite Kurland to become part of a Baltic constitutional Grand-Duchy whose hereditary ruler would be the Kaiser. A Board was elected to elaborate the constitution for the new state, form a temporary government, and request Germany to continue to defend the Baltic State and to maintain an occupational administration until a local one should have been organized. The *Landesrat* took occasion to protest against "persons . . . assuming to represent the Baltic," evidently with reference to the Latvian and Estonian National Committees. The *Vertrauensrat* of Kurland sent representatives to the *Landesrat* in Riga, but elected no members to the Board of the projected Baltic State. Strong protestations against the self-styled German Council of the Baltic State were lodged both by the Latvian Democratic bloc of Riga, and by the Estonians.

Germany had already set a precedent in state-making by forcing the Lithuanian National Assembly and the Finnish Parliament to accept German princes as Grand Dukes. In spite of the signs of disaster on her military fronts and revolutionary chaos at home, she proceeded with her well-laid plans to annex the Baltic, in whose ports mutinies were exploding. On November 7, 1918, the Board of the Baltic State elected a Council of Regency consisting of four German-Balts, von Pilchau, von Bulmeringck, von Samson-Himmelstjerna, and E. Hepner; two Estonians, and two Latvians, all, of course, carefully picked. This Council was empowered to offer the Kaiser, as King of Prussia, the Grand Ducal Crown of the new Baltic State.

Two days later, the Kaiser abdicated, and on November 10 went into exile in the Netherlands. The Council of Regency gave way to a National Board of German-Balts headed by R. von Samson-Himmelstjerna and Baron Taube, both of whom were chiefly concerned at this point to save the privileges and estates of the big Baltic-German landholders. Baron von Stryck hurried to Sweden in the hope of placing a German-dominated Baltic State under Swedish protection. The Reich might be collapsing like a house of cards, but the Baltic barons, skilled in the art of self-protection, rallied their forces to guard their Baltic State from German demoralization, Bolshevik counter-attack, Latvian and Estonian claims, and any misplaced idealism which the Allies might conceivably contribute to the pacification of this area.

One of their defensive measures was the formation of a local German-Balt army, which had been prepared for, when, during the summer of 1918, von Sievers-Römershof and Baron Taube requested of Oberkommando VIII, that is, the Commander-in-Chief of the Eighth Army which occupied the Baltic, permission to form a *Baltische Schutztruppe* consisting of German-Balt volunteers and "others."[4]

---

[4] *Die Rückführung des Ostheeres,* I, published by the *Reichskriegsministerium* (Berlin, 1936), 135ff.

While this request was refused at the time, on November 11 Ober-kommando VIII granted permission for the formation of a *Baltische Landeswehr* of 20,000 "territorials." A German major, Scheibert, and a former Russian colonel, von Weiss, were appointed commanders of the Latvian and Estonian groups, respectively. Recruits who enlisted in Berlin for the *Baltische Landeswehr*, as well as for other German volunteer formations in the Baltic, were given to understand that they might receive land and be encouraged to settle as colonists in the rich Baltic provinces.[5]

This extraordinary military activity on the part of a defeated Power was legitimized by article 12 of the Armistice, wherein the German Government promised to keep their troops in the Baltic region until such time as the Lithuanian, Latvian, and Estonian Provisional Governments should have organized the defense of their countries against the Bolsheviks. The latter, upon conclusion of the Armistice, had denounced the Brest-Litovsk and Berlin treaties and were preparing to seize power in the Baltic Provinces.

The German Eighth Army was itself in full decomposition. Soldier soviets were organized with the aim of returning the men to their homeland as soon as possible. Supplies were seized and sold by the soldiers. On November 10, the commander-in-chief of the Eastern forces ordered the Eighth Army to retreat to Prussia. The order to halt, delivered on the following day, failed to restrain troops desperate to return home. Hence the order of November 15, establishing voluntary military formations which could continue to defend the Baltic.

These formations found a ready pretext for their "defense" activities in the prompt formation by the Kuronian Latvians of local police forces and administration. The Germans, labeling these moves as "mutinous" and Bolshevik, immediately set about "restoring order." Most active in this work was the so-called "Iron Brigade," commanded by Major Bischoff, stationed at Liepāja, and consisting of some 5,000 volunteers, wearers of the Iron Cross, all of whom had been promised Baltic land in return for their services.[6]

The proclamation of a Latvian Government in Riga on November 18 further encouraged the Latvian population to revolt against the intolerable presence of German military forces remaining after an Allied victory. That same day the *Oberbefehlshaber-Ost* reiterated the

[5] *Die Kämpfe im Baltikum nach der zweiten Einnahme von Riga*, published by the *Reichskriegsministerium* (Berlin, 1938), p. 59.
[6] *ibid.*

official order to what remained of the Eighth Army to continue its mission in the Baltic as the protector of Prussia against Bolshevism. The Germans have themselves admitted that the ulterior aim was the revival of a German army to liberate their country from the Allies, if possible with the help of a restored monarchistic Northwestern Russia which would permit Germany to retain her protectorate of the Baltic State, under the immediate domination of the local German-Balt oligarchy.[7]

To this end, the German army in the Baltic was reorganized in the form of voluntary formations headed by a sort of modern *condottieri*, among them such German-Balts as von Manteuffel, whose family had dominated Kuronian affairs for centuries. While Prussian conservative political and military leaders made a natural alliance with the German-Balts, non-German liberals may have been astonished to observe the activities of the Social-Democrat August Winnig, who, in the summer of 1918, had appeared in Kurland at the invitation of the *Reichskommissar für den Osten* to study the possibilities of colonizing the Baltic with German workers. During the revolutionary November days, Winnig had successfully quieted the mutiny of German sailors in the harbor of Liepāja. As a reward for such a show of conservatism he was appointed, after November 11, German Civil High Commissioner in the Baltic with his headquarters in Riga. In January 1919, Winnig was appointed *Landespräsident* in East Prussia, whence he continued to cooperate with the German militarists in the Baltic by actively supporting their schemes.

As German Civil Commissioner, Winnig showed no disposition to take a stand in regard to renewed Bolshevik activity, which, after the Soviet denunciation of the treaties of Brest-Litovsk and Berlin on November 13, had begun to menace the Baltic States. Puppet Bolshevik governments for these countries, as well as for Finland and Poland, had reached at least the paper stage. The heads of these governments, including the Latvian Pēteris Stučka for Latvia, were all Russian subjects and members of the Russian Bolshevik party. They had at their command trained Bolshevik cadres to organize the regiments which were to be mobilized forcibly on the territories as they were gradually reoccupied. The retreating German soldiers, influenced by the German Communists (Spartakists) in their ranks, handed over to the advancing Bolsheviks arms and munition dumps. During the first part of November, the province of Latgale had come almost entirely under Russian

[7] *Die Rückführung des Ostheeres*, I, 21ff.

occupation. In Daugavpils, Dr. Joffe, Bolshevik Brest-Litovsk ambassador to Berlin, surrounding himself with Communist members of the numerous Russian war prisoner repatriation committees, became very active on behalf of the Lithuanian, Latvian, and Estonian puppet Soviet governments.

In view of the growing Bolshevik threat, and the indifference to it of the German military forces whose commanders ignored Foch's intention that they should serve, not as occupational forces, but rather as military auxiliaries to the local Baltic governments, the latter saw every need to establish themselves as soon as possible. Regarding the situation as militarily as well as politically precarious, a committee of Latvian officers and soldiers urged the haggling members of the Democratic bloc in Riga and the Latvian Provisional National Council to form immediately a joint national council. Both these groups were suffering internal dissension over their political programs; the Socialist element insisting on attention to radical reforms, while the liberal democrats and conservatives emphasized the need for a definitive liberation of their country, whose reform program might then be left in the hands of a freely elected constituent assembly.

The urgings of the patriotic Latvian military groups acted as a needed precipitant and brought about the formulation of a political program wherein the opposing parties composed their differences in order to establish the first Latvian national government. On November 17, 1918, in the offices of the Society of Latvian Artisans in Riga, Jānis Čakste, Gustav Zemgals, and Kārlis Ulmanis were nominated respectively President, Vice-President, and Prime Minister of the Republic of Latvia. The following day, in the so-called Second City Theatre (the German occupational authorities having refused the use of the House of the Diet), a plenary session of the Latvian National Council, successor to the Latvian Provisional National Council, was assembled.

Although the Latvian Social-Democrats, as well as the national minorities, were fully represented, the non-socialist parties predominated, the largest of them being the powerful Farmers' Union, of which Kārlis Ulmanis was the leader. The first business of the assembly of the National Council was the election of the above-mentioned high officials of the new Republic. In the absence of Čakste on a diplomatic mission abroad, the declaration of Latvia's independence was read by the Vice-President, Gustav Zemgals, as follows:

1. Latvia, united in its ethnographic limits, is a self-governing, independent, democratic Republic, whose Constitution and relations with foreign states shall be in the near future specifically defined by a Constituent Assembly convoked on the basis of direct, equal, secret and proportional suffrage for both sexes.
2. The Latvian National Council has established a Provisional Government of Latvia as its supreme executive power.
3. The Latvian National Council requests the citizens of Latvia to maintain peace and order and to assist the Provisional Government with all their power in its difficult and responsible task.[8]

Following this Declaration, Kārlis Ulmanis, as Prime Minister, presented the political platform of the new Republic. In addition to emphasizing the democratic nature of the Latvian state and guaranteeing the prompt convocation of a Constituent Assembly, power was vested in the Latvian National Council to appoint the Provisional Government which should be formed on the principle of coalition, and which should be charged with full executive power until the convocation of the Constituent Assembly. Ample political privileges were accorded the national minorities, whose cultural and national rights were to be guaranteed in the Constitution. Civil liberties were to be fully guaranteed by decrees of the Provisional Government. A national militia was to be conscripted for purposes of defense, and the German military forces were to be evacuated within a definite period.

After a few days of deliberation, the Provisional Government formed a cabinet of the following men: P. Juraševskis, lawyer and former member of the Duma, as Minister of Justice; K. Kasparsons, Minister of Schools; T. Hermanovskis, Minister of Labor and Communications; J. Goldmanis, co-founder of the Latvian Rifles, as Minister of Agriculture; K. Puriņš, Professor of Economics, as Minister of Finance; S. Paegle, Minister of Commerce and Industry; and P. Blumbergs, Minister of Supplies. D. Rudzītis, a higher official of the Chancery of the former Russian Governor, was appointed Director of the Chancery. During the absence on a diplomatic mission of Zigfrīds Meierovics, Premier Ulmanis temporarily took over the portfolio of Foreign Affairs. Although offered two ministries in the Cabinet, neither the Socialists nor the national minorities were willing to assume these positions. Some recognition was accorded a liberal element

---

[8] *Latvijas likumu krājums* (Collection of Latvian Laws), no. 1, July 5, 1919.

among the German-Balts by appointing Baron Rosenberg and W. Schreiner as envoys to Vienna and Prague, respectively.

The German High Commissioner, August Winnig, on November 26, addressed to the Latvian Prime Minister a note wherein he recognized the Latvian Provisional Government as the government of Latvia pending the decision of the Peace Conference at Paris. This limited recognition Ulmanis refused to accept, on the grounds that, under paragraph 12 of the Armistice, Winnig was bound to surrender his powers to the Provisional Government unconditionally. The following day, Winnig sent a second note, recognizing the Latvian Provisional Government as the successor-power to the German occupational authorities, which were to surrender their functions to the Latvian administration by mutual agreement.

This surrender was to prove neither prompt nor entire. The German authorities held fast to telephone, telegraph, and railway facilities. Their dismantling of local industries and general looting of natural resources, as well as the expediting of requisitioned goods to East Prussia, were protested by a decree of the Provisional Government on December 2. Two days later, the Provisional Government issued a law establishing elected local rural councils as instruments of rural self-government, which was itself to be the basis of Latvia's administration. These councils were to concern themselves immediately with bettering the food situation by cooperating with special regional supply councils. On December 5, the Ministry of the Interior was empowered to create and supervise an adequate police force. The following day, Latvia's judicial system was established by law, and that same day ten million rubles worth of five per cent tax-free government bonds were issued to swell the coffers of the empty State Treasury. On December 14, laws were passed regulating postal communications, and democratizing the schools, where the mother tongue was reestablished as the language of instruction.

This spate of laws and decrees aimed at consolidating the position of the Provisional Government, democratizing the nation in detail, and building an administrative as well as a moral bulwark against the German octopus, met with unremittant scorn and obstructionism on the part of those remnants of the master race who crowded the hotels and public buildings of Riga. These, together with the majority of the German-Balts, baited the still financially and militarily weak Latvian *Kerle*, and reviled those few German-Balts who had courageously cast in their lot with the citizens of the young Republic. One of their deputies to the Latvian National Council, P. Shiemann, the editor of the *Rigasche Rundschau*, was deported to Berlin as a dangerous radical. To flaunt their opinion of the rabble who would aspire to nationhood, the Baltic barons continued to dress their *Landeswehr* contingents in increasingly fantastic uniforms and to encourage their arrogance.

None the less, with their own fighting forces still minimal, it was to the German and German-Balt troops that the Latvians must look for some sort of defense against the ever-increasing Bolshevik pressure. Russia, with her economy ruined, with her body politic enduring revolt and counterrevolt, and with her invaluable Baltic ports gone, experienced once again that ancient anxiety which had motivated Peter the Great in his thrust to the sea. The establishment of the Baltic as a free water by the Allied victory appeared intolerable to the Slavic Empire, which had lost little of its imperial urge in its conversion to a socialist state. A slogan was soon found: the Baltic, sea of social revolution. The Baltic ports must serve the new régime to the limit of their capacities, both as indispensable commercial outlets and as springboards for a further triumph of the Bolshevik order in northern lands. Latvia, as the possessor of sturdy and strategic Riga, "the key to the Baltic," was marked for swift and uncompromising regimentation.

There can be no question that the Germans knew of this purpose. Their cynicism in the matter can only be called exemplary. In their own time and on their own terms they intended to "save" the Baltic. For the moment they were concerned with achieving the status of an occupational force in the Baltic States. Let the Latvians and Estonians stew in the juice of their stubborn independence and suffer some salutary bloodletting at the hands of the wild Red Army! The Allied Powers, bewildered as is the wont of liberal, democratic nations by a vast military victory which leaves a ruptured civilization on their hands, unnerved by the jumble of political visions demanding their attention, sought to improvise as best they could on the various fronts; using what means came to hand, admitting to no master plan, and allowing their enemies, in the name of expediency, to retain some master cards. In the Baltic the Reich Germans, immutably in league with the German-Balts, were permitted a small policing duty, which they promptly translated into terms of might. They were, furthermore, at liberty to intrigue with the omnipresent White Russians, who played so skillfully on the Allies' galloping dread of the Red Menace.

Time, the German militarists felt, might well be on their side in the Baltic. The peace treaty might prove to be stillborn. The ultimate victory was not yet properly assessed. Hard-headed Prussians and hard-fisted Bolsheviks might yet shape their respective triumphs from the guesses and gropings of the democracies. The toughness of the German superiority complex is well illustrated in the aspirations of their leading commander in the Baltic, General Graf Rudiger von der Goltz, as revealed in his memoirs: "Why not revive under a new form, in agreement with the White Russians, and under the flag of an anti-Bolshevik crusade, our old eastern policy which was forgotten in August 1914? Above all, why not work for an economic and political *rapprochement* with the Russia of tomorrow? With a Russia which, having massacred its intellectuals, needs merchants, engineers and administrators, and whose frontier provinces, devastated and depopulated, might offer a fertile land for hard-working German peasants?"[9]

But the time was not yet ripe for *Realpolitik* on such a scale. The immediate concern of the Germans was, by giving the Latvians and Estonians a taste of Red terror, to exact from them concessions in return for which they would receive military assistance from the German and German-Balt forces. The Allies could spare neither the time nor the trouble to analyze this latest manifestation of German aggression in the Baltic, where their single vision saw the Bolshevik threat as paramount, both over the German machinations and the painful strivings of the Baltic peoples to keep their balance on the tightrope of independence. Indeed, the White Russian contingents forming on Estonian soil received more aid and encouragement from the Allied Powers than did the slender forces of the new nations, whose melancholy political realism fully grasped that a White Russian victory would enslave them as much as a Bolshevik triumph, since it would submerge them once more in a reactionary, "indivisible" empire. Although the British fleet did afford the Estonians some support in their effort to free their land of Bolshevik occupation, in Riga only one British cruiser stood by and the object of its concern was not immediately obvious.

In the face of the pronounced opposition of the German Command in Riga to Latvian general mobilization as provided for in the political platform adopted on November 18, 1918, the Provisional Government encouraged the formation of voluntary forces under the aegis of loyal officers. While small companies were thus being organized, the German

[9] Rudiger von der Goltz, *Als Politischer General im Osten* (Leipzig, 1936), quoted in J. Hampden Jackson, *Estonia*, p. 140.

Command categorically refused the request of the Provisional Government that they call out the Iron Brigade, which was loitering in Riga,
against the relatively weak Bolshevik troops now advancing unchallenged into Latvia, whose frontier they crossed on December 2. Orderly
retreat continued to be the tactics of the German and German-Balt so-
called defense forces. On December 7, Ulmanis, in the hope of saving
Riga, acceded to Winnig's request to organize a Latvian Defense Force
directly under German command. This regrouping of the military
forces on Latvian soil was to place under German direction not only
the German-Balt *Landeswehr*, but also a local Russian formation commanded by the White Russian Prince Lieven, and Latvian volunteer
detachments not to exceed in number the combined forces of the
German-Balt and Russian volunteers. Arms and supplies, hitherto so
crucially lacking to the Latvian military effort, were now promised to
this combined defense force by the Germans.

The latter, however, showed no immediate intention of organizing
an effective defense of the Latvian State. They preferred to prolong
the atmosphere of confusion and menace which they considered
propitious to the extension of their sojourn in the Baltic. On December 7, they had surrendered to the Bolsheviks the fortress of Daugavpils
with its considerable stock of munitions. The road to Riga lay open.
On December 20, Bolshevik Fifth Columnists in the Latvian capital
began a sniping action against wearers of the German uniform. Two
Latvian companies who revolted against the *Oberkommando* were
fired upon by the British cruiser standing in the Daugava. Word was
received that Pēteris Stučka's puppet government, recognized by Lenin
as the Latvian Soviet Government on December 22, had established
residence in Valmiera.

The Germans, indifferent to the insistence of the British Naval
Commander in the Baltic that they fulfill their obligations under
Article 12 of the Armistice, melted systematically before the Russian
advances. Their object was to receive further concessions, both from
the Allies, who were expected to accept their status as an occupational
force, and from the Latvians, from whom they hoped to extort
acquiescence in the settlement of Reich soldiers in the Balticum. On
December 29, they did succeed in obtaining from Ulmanis a promise
to grant Latvian citizenship to German volunteers in the Latvian
Defense Force. The entire text of the agreement is presented here as
evidence that the Prime Minister refused to agree even in principle to

the actual settlement of such citizens, a concession of which he was subsequently accused by the Latvian Socialists.

AGREEMENT BETWEEN THE PLENIPOTENTIARIES OF THE GERMAN REICH AND THE PROVISIONAL LATVIAN GOVERNMENT

Riga, December 29, 1918

1. The Provisional Latvian Government declares its willingness to grant Latvian citizenship, upon their request, to all voluntarily enlisted alien members of the Latvian defense forces after they have participated in the struggle for the liberation of the territory of the Latvian State from the Bolsheviks for at least four weeks.

2. German-Balt citizens of the Latvian State enjoy the right to join the volunteer associations of the German Reich.

Conversely, for the duration of the military compaign, there is no objection to the transfer of commissioned and non-commissioned officers of the army of the German Reich to the German-Balt *Landeswehr* as instructors.

3. The right granted to the German-Balts in the Agreement of December 7th to form seven national companies and two batteries in association with the Defense Forces of Latvia is expressly guaranteed by the Latvian Provisional Government, even though Article 2 of the present Agreement should result in the temporary abolition of the German-Balt associations.

If the number of Latvian companies in the Latvian Defense Forces should be increased, a proportionate increase shall be made in the number of German companies.

4. In fulfilling Article 1 the necessary lists of deserving volunteers shall be transmitted to the Latvian Provisional Government at least once a week.

It shall be established between the contracting parties on the basis of these lists which German citizens shall gain citizenship in accordance with Article 1.

> (signed) August Winnig, German Minister
> Kārlis Ulmanis, Prime Minister
> P. Paegle, Minister of Trade and Industry
> J. Sālits, Minister of War

The matter of German settlement had indeed become a *Machtfrage*,[10] the question being where would rest the power to realize the promise of the German-Balt landowners to offer a third of their estates for the use of Reich volunteers in the *Landeswehr*. However, while the German Command continued to cherish this project, the rapid course of events was to render void of actuality both the legalities of the settlement and any agreement which had been reached with the Provisional Government.

Retreat had been the Germans' forte to date; and the end was not yet. On the eve of the New Year, Prince Anatol Lieven's Russians and

---

[10] *Der Feldzug im Baltikum bis zur zweiten Einnahme von Riga, Januar bis Mai 1919*, II, published by the *Reichskriegsministerium* (Berlin, 1937), 23.

the German forces streamed out of Riga in the still open direction of Kurzeme and Lithuania. On January 3, the Red Army entered the Latvian capital. The British cruiser then weighed anchor with some prominent Latvian refugees aboard. Since Stučka was preparing to establish his puppet government in the Diet House of the Livonian nobles, the Provisional Government had no choice but to retire to Jelgava. Soviet Russia's estimate of the importance of her victory had already appeared in *Izvestiya* in the following terms: "Estonia, Latvia, and Lithuania are directly on the road from Russia to Western Europe and are therefore a hindrance to our revolution. . . . This separating wall must be destroyed. . . . The Russian red proletariat must find an opportunity to influence the revolution in Germany. The conquest of the Baltic Sea would make it possible for Soviet Russia to agitate in favor of the social revolution in the Scandinavian countries, thus transforming the Baltic Sea into the Sea of the Social Revolution."[11]

On January 5, the Provisional Government moved from Jelgava to Liepāja, which was now protected by one cruiser and six destroyers from the British Baltic Fleet. The German Command proposed to defend the Liepāja-Ventspils line and the railroad connecting Liepāja with East Prussia. At this late hour, the Latvian Government was still forbidden general mobilization. Latvian garrison commanders were arrested and their troops disarmed and left helpless in the path of the Red Army, which immediately forced them into its ranks. The German Command used this forced mobilization by the Bolsheviks, which they represented as voluntary desertion to the Reds on the part of the Latvians, as a convenient pretext to refuse the latter the arms they desperately needed. The national military leaders, whose Latvian troops now amounted to 3,500 men, felt strongly that, had they received proper cooperation from the German and German-Balt forces of the *Landeswehr*, they might at any point have successfully opposed the poorly disciplined Russian troops, especially since the unwilling Latvians in the latter's ranks were ready to desert at the first opportunity. Even unsupported, the Latvian forces acquitted themselves well. In February 1919, Colonel Kalpaks, Commander of the national forces, took Kuldīga and repulsed the Bolsheviks from Ventspils.

That same month saw the fiasco of one of the more baroque German ventures in the Baltic. The German Junker, von Stryck, whose mission

[11] *Izvestiya*, Dec. 25, 1918.

to Sweden we have already mentioned, had undertaken to prepare the ground for the transference of the *Landeswehr* to Swedish territory, where it was to be reorganized, strengthened by further volunteers, and launched as gallant liberators of the Baltic against the Bolsheviks and their alleged Latvian and Estonian coadjutors. Following upon a German victory, a neutral Baltic State was to be created on the pattern of the old Livonian Confederation, with the German-Balts restored to the unchallenged role of *Herrenvolk*, and the Baltic peoples relegated to that of workers. Sweden, it was hoped, would act as the high protector of such a state, which might recall to her the useful buffer aspect of ancient Livonia. Von Stryck, promptly arrested by Latvian police upon his return from Sweden on February 19, was freed by the commando tactics of young Hans von Manteuffel, idol of the *Landeswehr*. The documents in the case remained in Latvian hands, and were brought to the attention of the Allies, who could no longer blink at the sinister intentions of the German Command and its brothers-in-arms and in spirit, the Baltic barons.

On February 3, General Rudiger von der Goltz, fresh from victories over the Bolsheviks in Finland, had arrived in Liepāja to take command of the defense forces in the Baltic. Apparently it was now judged advisable to make a show of genuine defense activity on the Baltic front, lest the Allies, alerted by the von Stryck affair, send naval reinforcements to strengthen the hand of the Latvians. The German Minister of War, Noske, instructed General von der Goltz to repulse the Bolsheviks and restore order in the German forces. Not for Allied consumption was the third order: to establish pro-German tendencies in the Baltic States.[12]

Von der Goltz, as much power-hungry adventurer as calculating soldier, and confirmed scorner of the unsoldierly Weimar Republic, after studying the political and military mazes of the Baltic, concluded that a man of his genius might extract therefrom the royal reward of power. He delighted in the multiple challenge to his highly personal aims offered by the increasingly meddlesome Allies, the obtuseness of the German High Command, the stubbornness of the Latvians, the fanfaronade of the Baltic barons, and, obviously, the ambitions of the Bolsheviks. Certainly he would have to defeat the latter before the Latvians did it for him. To this end, he reorganized and considerably reinforced the German contingents in the region. Lieutenant Colonel Warwick Greene, the American observer in the Baltic, estimated that

12 *Der Feldzug im Baltikum* . . . , p. 140.

the German troops were brought up to a strength of 20,000 men, while the *Landeswehr* grew to 3,800 effectives. Prince Lieven's forces amounted to two companies of infantry and one squadron of cavalry.

Such a military potential, obtained in large part by further promises of Baltic land to the unemployed of Berlin, aroused the sluggish mistrust of the Allies. The British Military Commissioner in Liepāja, Major Keenan, thought it opportune to supply the Latvians with 5,000 rifles and 200 machine guns, which the Germans attempted to snatch before delivery. The odor of blackmail hung over the Balticum while the leaders of the swollen *Landeswehr* pressed the Provisional Government to reorganize itself on a parity basis with the German-Balts (who now represented even less than their pre-War three per cent of the population), General von der Goltz threatened to retreat from Kurland to the Memel-Priekule line if the Allies failed to recognize the Germans as cobelligerents against the Bolsheviks. The Allies answered on March 6 with the proclamation of a blockade of Liepāja and Ventspils for ships bound to or from Prussian ports.

On March 6, Colonel Kalpaks was killed by a stray German bullet. His command was assumed by Colonel Jānis Balodis, who achieved the recapture of Jelgava on March 20. But the *Grenzschutz Nord*, whose headquarters were in Königsberg, continued to exact, as the price of Riga's liberation, the Provisional Government's acceptance of the political demands made by the bosses of the *Landeswehr*.

The Latvian Government in Liepāja, stimulated by the pressures of General von der Goltz and his *Landeswehr*, and encouraged by the presence of an Allied naval squadron, by the manifest sympathy of Major Keenan, and by the arrival in the Baltic of a military mission headed by Lt. Col. Warwick Greene, made strenuous efforts to improve its position on the military, political, and diplomatic fronts. A keen sense of urgency possessed the Latvian statesmen, who saw their small gains increasingly menaced by Bolshevik aggression, White Russian aspirations, German-Balt rage for mastery, and the hunger of crippled but not mortally wounded German imperialism. One must add to this array of threats the confusion and procrastination of the Allies, now locked in the puzzles of the Peace Conference.

Since military effort was of prime importance for the survival of the Latvian state, the Provisional Government concerned itself unswervingly with the improvement of its forces' fighting position. In order to counter certain attempts of General von der Goltz to sunder the Estonians from their brothers-in-arms to the south, Ulmanis reached an agreement with the Estonian Foreign Minister, Piip, which assured closer cooperation between the two Bolshevik-threatened peoples along their mutual frontier. A specially appointed Latvian High Commissioner for the districts of Valka, Valmiera, Cēsis, and Riga (exclusive of the capital) organized, with the assistance of the Estonian military commander, a Latvian Northern Army which was soon to join the Estonians in their defense of the northeastern frontier.

The Provisional Government, fully realizing that German-Balt encroachments were everywhere, passed a number of measures intended to keep control of the home front. In order to counteract the German High Command's arbitrary promises of Baltic land to its volunteers, the Latvian Government passed a law making a similar guarantee to those of its own soldiers who were landless. This "bonus" was to be provided by the State Land Fund which embraced all state domains together with those German-Balt estates which had been owned by or mortgaged to the former Russian Peasant Agrarian Bank.

Other governmental measures were aimed at increasing the number and the morale of Latvian fighters and insuring order and progress in internal affairs against the day of ultimate victory. In the teeth of German opposition, general mobilization was decreed in those districts which the Latvian forces had succeeded in liberating from the Bolsheviks. A Home Guard was instituted in rural communities to guarantee order. The families of soldiers were encouraged by the provision of social security in the cities and arrangements for the cultivation of their farms in rural areas. Requisition laws were passed to procure supplies for the army. Taxation and excise measures replenished the national treasury. A State Treasury and Savings Bank was created and the emission of treasury notes begun, the exchange being fixed at one Latvian ruble for two German marks or one German "Ost-rubel."

On the diplomatic front, the Provisional Government was variously challenged in its determination to gain *de jure* recognition at the Peace Conference, where it was allowed a delegation of observers only. Certain German-Balt elements in Paris found occasions to insinuate that "agrarian radicalism" was undermining the social order in Latvia. The so-called Russian Political Conference, meeting in Paris on March 9, 1919, urged that *de jure* recognition of the Latvian Government be indefinitely postponed, since determination of the status of the Baltic States must await the restoration of a united, indivisible (and reactionary) Russia.

On March 24, the Latvian Delegation to the Paris Peace Conference, headed by Zigfrīds Meierovics, addressed a memorandum to Clemenceau reiterating a previous request for official recognition of the State of Latvia. The Memorandum insisted that further postponement of this recognition of the independence claimed by the Baltic States would only foster that anarchy from which they were so painfully emerging. The Latvian Delegation pointed out that Latvia's secession from the Russian Empire, whether Tsarist or Bolshevik, was final and irrevocable. It was further argued that the precedent of the Conference's decision on Poland, which was taken independently of Russian consent, could be applied to the Baltic nations. But these reasonings far from persuaded the Big Five, who, nursing fond hopes of reviving a non-Bolshevik Russia, turned deaf ears to this as well as to subsequent pleadings on the same issue.

The consolidation of the Latvian armed forces and administration behind the lines, together with the activities of the Delegation in Paris, further aroused the hostility of the German-Balts and their Commander-in-Chief, General von der Goltz. It was in this unfavorable atmosphere that the question of the liberation of Riga, only some twenty miles from liberated Jelgava, came to the fore. It was apparent to all that it would cost but little effort to oust the Bolsheviks from the Latvian capital. It was obvious to von der Goltz that whoever liberated Riga would acquire a useful measure of prestige. Since it would be a political error to allow the Latvians this privilege, the German commander and his *Landeswehr* colleagues decided to undermine the Provisional Government in Liepāja before proceeding to "save" Riga. They were supported in this further delay by the *Kommando Nord*, which found in the presence of Bolsheviks on Latvian territory an indispensable excuse for the maintenance of its own troops in that area. Furthermore, it was not the intention of the German High Command to restore Latvia as an independent state, the ultimate aim being rather the creation of a "neutral zone" under permanent German control and serving as a buffer against Soviet Russia.

Baron Hans von Manteuffel, by virtue of his ambition, boldness, and prestige, seemed the ideal instrument for a *coup*. Accordingly, he was withdrawn from the front; and on April 16, 1919, he gave the order to his *Landeswehr Stosstruppe* to take over all government buildings in Liepāja and arrest the Latvian Ministers. In this last he was unsuccessful, since several of the Ministers, including Ulmanis, sought refuge with the British Military Mission, whence they moved to a Latvian ship which enjoyed the protection of the Allied naval squadron.

Lieutenant Colonel Warwick Greene promptly investigated and reported on the *coup* in terms which can scarcely be considered pro-Latvian, since he had already given not unsympathetic attention to the German-Balt point of view. From this quarter he had been informed that the Latvian people were historically anti-German; that the Ulmanis government was neither representative nor constitutional; that it had failed to combat Bolshevism and might, in view of its radical measures to date, turn Socialist from within. Greene, while granting truth to some of these asseverations, none the less insisted that the Provisional Government "was a *de facto* government and the best foundation on which to have built a stable and representative government with the necessary help from outside which was essential. Its violent overturn by young soldiers is a serious reflection on General von der Goltz's responsibility under Article 12 of the Armistice, an affront to the Allies and a crime for which there should be a reckoning. . . . Lettish soldiers have been instructed not to resist and so far have shown admirable fortitude and forbearance under intense provocation and almost intolerable circumstances. For the moment people are quiet. They look westward for help from the democracies or eastward from Bolshevism. . . . They will not tolerate baron dominance and will eventually resist the new régime with bloodshed. In proportion as their hope of help from the West dies they will turn Red."[13]

Soon after the *coup* in Liepāja, which both the Latvian army and the civilian population had angrily denounced, the German-Balt *Sicherheitsausschuss* (Committee of Safety) invited Prince Lieven and Colonel Balodis to join them in forming a provisional directory. Both commanders refused, Balodis stating in writing that he and his army were responsible only to the Latvian Provisional Government and the National Council.

Meanwhile, the Latvian Delegation in Paris had repeated their request to be seated at the Peace Conference, and had been once more refused. However, at the April 19 session of the Council of Five, Mr. Lansing had recommended that it be stipulated in the preliminary draft of the Treaty that German troops should evacuate the Baltic under Allied supervision and without interfering with the civil administrations or with such defense measures as might have been adopted locally. Warwick Greene, in his report of April 23, following an unsatisfactory conversation with General von der Goltz, recommended

---

[13] Lieutenant Colonel Warwick Greene, Telegram of April 20, 1919, in *Papers Relating to the Foreign Relations . . .* , XII, 138ff.

the collective recognition of the Lithuanian, Latvian, and Estonian provisional governments, adding that these nations should be supplied forthwith with food, military equipment, and credit.[14] In response to this and a corresponding British report, the Council of Five, on April 30, created an Interallied Baltic Commission centered in Paris.

While Red terror increased in Riga and the German Command continued to hold in leash the Latvian forces, in Liepāja diplomacy ground to a stop. The correspondence between Warwick Greene and von der Goltz satisfied neither party. The German general acceded to such minor demands as the readmission of the Latvians to their barracks at the naval port and the return of von Manteuffel to the front lines. Further he would not go, insisting that "the absolutely essential condition for seriously combatting Bolshevism is peace behind the front; this is to be brought about by the creation of a government representing all national elements."[15]

General von der Goltz gained confidence from the deliberative airs of the American representative who, unlike Major Keenan, was by no means convinced of the soundness of the Ulmanis government and distrusted the Latvians' capacity for self-defense. Warwick Greene remained open to the German and German-Balt argument that, as Germanophobes, the Latvians were congenitally unfair to the German-Balt element; and that, as agrarian radicals, they might yet accept the Bolshevik program, at least to the extent of igniting a civil war within their borders.

Unimpressed either by scoldings from Paris or diplomatic conversations in Liepāja, von der Goltz was concerned only with consolidating his neatly planned and executed *coup*. As a master tactician, he seized the occasion of the presence of the German War Minister, Noske, to produce a *deus ex machina*. A certain Borkowsky, an obscure Latvian attorney available to the German-Balts, was now permitted to appoint as Prime Minister an equally obscure Germanophile Latvian pastor, Andrievs Niedra. Borkowsky then announced that the German forces constituted a bona fide army of occupation, that Latvian mobilization was undesirable, and endorsed the promises of the enlistment bureaus in Germany regarding Baltic land for German volunteers. Niedra was naive only for German benefit. On April 29, he protested to Lieutenant Colonel Greene that he was, above all, a fervent anti-Bolshevik, and that he had not consented to being nominated Prime Minister.[16] Greene appears to have been impressed. Elsewhere, Niedra

[14] *op.cit.*, p. 148.   [15] *op.cit.*, pp. 176-177.   [16] *op.cit.*, p. 177ff.

was to state that he did not consider the Latvians ready for democracy and free elections.[17] The Latvian people immediately repudiated this puppet, who, as a member of that small group of reactionaries who accepted German leadership, was held in thorough contempt by his compatriots.

Warwick Greene, cool to the demands of the Big Five that the Ulmanis government be immediately restored and allowed to proceed with general mobilization, had evolved a compromise plan. Claiming that "the hereditary hatred between Letts and Germans is now so intensified that a general arming of undisciplined Lettish levies is out of the question if serious bloodshed is to be avoided," he continued to cling to the services of the *Landeswehr*. Realizing that order must be restored, he favored a reorganization of the Ulmanis government to include four members of the old Cabinet, four from the Niedra Cabinet, and four representatives of the German-Balt minority. This solution satisfied neither the Ulmanis party nor General von der Goltz.[18] The latter, who was at last preparing to move on Riga, insisted that he could not hold the front without the cooperation of the *Landeswehr*. Since the German-Balts demanded the Niedra government, that Cabinet was installed intact on May 10.

Two days later, the hated Niedra was kidnapped by some Latvian officers and persuaded to sign his resignation. However, a substitute was hurried into office by the German-Balts and on May 15 ordered the liberation of Riga.

But once more the Germans held back. At this point von der Goltz's quite sincere desire to liberate the Baltic (in his own time and on his own terms) was hampered by German-Bolshevik machinations which as early as May 5 had resulted in the official cessation of recruitment of German volunteers for the Baltic forces. A few days later, the German War Minister recalled the First Reserve Guard Regiment to Prussia, at the same time informing von der Goltz that there was increasing hope for the creation of a neutral zone of 300 kilometers (including Riga and most of Kurzeme) between Bolshevik territory and East Prussia.[19] General von der Goltz had no alternative but to countermand the participation of German Reich troops in the liberation of Riga.

[17] Conversation with Finnish Professor Mikkola in Liepāja, May 1919, as reported to the author.
[18] *Papers Relating to the Foreign Relations* . . . , XII, 197.
[19] *Der Feldzug im Baltikum* . . . , p. 115ff.

On May 22, the *Landeswehr* took the Latvian capital by assault, the Latvian forces having been ordered to secure the mouth of the Daugava and encircle the Bolsheviks from the north. Baron Hans von Manteuffel was killed during the attack. Colonel Balodis and his troops entered the city in the evening and received an enthusiastic reception, which was promptly interrupted by orders to harry the Bolshevik rear. Niedra, who had escaped his Latvian captors, put in an appearance during the course of the victorious day but was generally ignored. The German-Balts lost no time in taking over the House of the Diet, Riga Castle, police headquarters, and communication centers. They then launched a regulation White Terror which elicited indignant protests from Lieutenant Colonel Greene and some counteraction from the British.

Von der Goltz chose to allow the *Landeswehr* a few days of unbridled bloodletting in Riga, during which thousands of real or alleged Bolsheviks were left dead in the streets as a lesson to all radically inclined Latvians. On May 29, the commander of the *Landeswehr*, in accordance with a directive from the Niedra Cabinet, issued an order to continue the war against the Reds. The advance, however, was not to the southeast, where the Bolsheviks were holding the Krustpils-Daugavpils line, but into northern Latvia, where a special army group under Colonel Zemitāns was successfully cooperating with the Estonian forces. The suspicions which the efficacy of this joint effort aroused in the German Command were enhanced when it finally established contact on May 30 with Colonel Balodis, who had been carrying the weight of the conflict in the southeast. Von der Goltz, who planned an ultimate *Landeswehr* attack upon the Estonians, now bent his energies to occupying northern Latvia, separating the Latvian and Estonian armies, and eventually turning on the Balodis forces.

On June 3, 1919, the *Landeswehr* (reinforced with some "borrowed" troops from the Iron Division) made contact with the Estonian-Latvian armies. A conference was then held in Cēsis at which the representatives of the *Landeswehr* insisted that the Estonians retreat behind their national boundaries. When this demand was stoutly refused, open warfare broke out, continuing until June 10, on which date Lieutenant Colonel Warwick Greene contrived an armistice and arranged for a further conference. After a few days of stalemate, the British Chief of the Allied Military Mission in the Baltic, General Gough, who had been sent to Reval by the Baltic Commission in Paris, presented to von der Goltz a series of demands which essentially repeated those made by Marshal Foch on May 26 and transmitted to

German representatives in Spa. These terms[20] the German general received with offended dignity. His only suggestion to the German-Balts was that they present one more ultimatum to the Estonians and, should this fail, attack Cēsis.

On June 14, the Red Army launched an offensive in Latgale which put considerable strain on the Zemitāns group. General Gough agreed to arrange a renewal of the interrupted Cēsis conference only on condition that the Landeswehr be ordered to join the fighting front in the Lake Lubana-Krustpils sector. The German answer was another ultimatum to the effect that the Estonians withdraw from Latvia or consider the armistice broken as of midnight June 19.[21] When the Estonian commander chose to abide by his agreement with the Ulmanis government, the conflict (around Cēsis) was resumed, which was to end on June 22 in a complete defeat of the Landeswehr and the borrowed Iron Division contingents.

The following day saw the German-Balt and German forces in full retreat from Cēsis, and the Latvian General Dankers taking over the command of Liepāja where the Ulmanis government had just landed. By crossing the Gauja River and sending gunboats into the mouth of the Daugava to bomb the bridges, the Estonians compelled the Landeswehr to retreat to the river Jagel and sue for an armistice.

The Treaty of Strazdmuiža, signed on the night of July 2, stipulated that Riga should be cleared of German and German-Balt occupation by July 5; that Reich Germans should be repatriated; that the fate of the Landeswehr should be decided by the Chief of the Allied Military Mission; and that, pending the arrival of the legal Latvian Government, the administration of the city would be taken over by the British Colonel Tallents.

On July 4, units of the Zemitāns and Balodis groups made their appearance in the Latvian capital, which the slightly reorganized Ulmanis government reentered four days later by sea. Niedra had disappeared immediately after the signing of the Strazdmuiža treaty. The National Council reconvened and resumed its legislative functions. While administrative matters were firmly taken in hand during the summer of 1919, the question of national defense was still to the

[20] 1. Withdrawal of German troops behind the Sigulda-Jaungulbene line; 2. immediate return to Germany of one half of Reich-German contingents; 3. Ulmanis to form a national government, mobilize troops, and organize defense forces without interference; 4. private property to be respected; etc. See *Die Kämpfe im Baltikum* . . . , pp. 9-10.

[21] *op.cit.*, p. 16.

fore, since the whole of Latvia had not yet been liberated from the Bolsheviks, who were holding out in Latgale. The Latvian army was raised to a strength of 24,000 and reorganized into three divisions for the provinces of Kurzeme-Zemgale, Vidzeme, and Latgale. On July 10, General D. Simonsons was appointed to the Ministry of War, while General P. Radziņš was made Chief of Staff.

Warwick Greene, unconvinced by the joint Estonian-Latvian victories, continued to consider the military situation in the Baltic as critical. In his report of July 5 he stated: "It is now clear that the Estonians in advancing on Riga . . . are aggressive and that all American food and help for them should cease until this internal fighting has come to an end."[22] He omitted entirely any report on the Strazd-muiža agreement, continuing to hope for a German-Balt and Latvian understanding. He opposed the withdrawal of German forces from the Baltic, while recommending the strengthening of the White Russian formations, now in full decomposition. Colonel Greene's Commission for the Baltic States was recalled to Paris on August 4.

The signing of the Treaty of Versailles by the representatives of the Reich on June 28 had confronted General von der Goltz with Article 433, which provided for the orderly evacuation of German troops from the Baltic Provinces "as soon as the Governments of the Principal Allied and Associated Powers shall think the moment suitable, having regard to the internal situation of these territories." However, pending the ratification of the Treaty, which was not to take place until January 10, 1920, "the Prussian fox," still acting under Article 12 of the Armistice, hoped to remain key man in the Baltic, commanding 40,000 troops in Lithuania and 20,000 in Latvia, where he had taken up headquarters in Kurland.

With the *Landeswehr* reduced to 2,000 men who were dispatched to the Russian front under the watchful command of a British Colonel, the Honorable H. R. L. G. Alexander, von der Goltz had to look elsewhere for means of implementing his unyielding drive for power in the Baltic. In this final fling of the dice full scope was afforded his political flair, his taste for daring adventure, and his stubborn imperialism. It was due in large measure to the inordinate ambition of this single man that the Latvians were to be kept from their peace for many more months to come.

In his determination to hold the Balticum, von der Goltz was to have the connivance of a group of German-Russian monarchists in-

[22] *Papers Relating to the Foreign Relations . . .* , XII, 215.

triguing in Berlin to restore German and Russian monarchies, which would then enter into a close military alliance directed against the Allies. On May 30, 1919, the dashing Colonel Bermondt, of Caucasian origin and gaudy fame, had arrived in Jelgava with some 300 Russians. These were promptly formed into the Corps of Count von Keller (a Russified German aristocrat), a body which expanded all through the summer as more and more German contingents found it opportune to place themselves under the Russian adventurer's flag. Far from withdrawing from the Baltic, German forces continued to receive volunteers from East Prussia, Austria, and the Sudetenland, as well as several hundred picked Russian prisoners of war with their officers. All these reinforcements moved openly in military formations on German railways. Eventually, all German troops in the Baltic, amounting to 30,000 men, had joined the Corps of Count Keller, commanded by Bermondt.

The order issued by the Government of the Reich on September 5 to the Eastern Command to clear all German troops from Kurland fell on deaf ears. It seemed probable that the merger of German and Russian forces to fight the Bolsheviks might well pass as a *fait accompli* which would not greatly shock some of the more nervous statesmen among the Allies. It was this element which the German-Balt Committee in Paris, purporting to represent the Baltic national minorities at the Peace Conference, succeeded to a degree in impressing. The representatives of the German-Balt nobility had informed Admiral Koltchak, head of the "White Government" in Siberia, that the Baltic States (i.e. the corporation of the landed nobles) had no desire to be separated from "the one and indivisible Russia." They planned, indeed, to become eventually a member of a new Russian federation, with complete political and economic autonomy and a caste society which would preserve its autocracy through its preponderance in the Diet of this future Baltic State.[23]

As late as July 1919, Sir Esme Howard, chief of the Baltic Commission of the Peace Conference, the Marchese della Torretta, and the French Commandant Aublet were all more concerned over the probable fate of the German-Balt and Russian minorities in the Baltic after the withdrawal of German forces than they were over conditions confronting the Estonians and Latvians. Sir Esme Howard's White Rus-

[23] Report of Lieutenant Commander J. A. Gade, American observer in the Baltic, May 3, 1919, in *Papers Relating to the Foreign Relations . . .* , XII, 156-157.

sian and German-Balt leanings[24] were offset by General Gough's report to the Big Five on September 18, 1919.[25] He emphasized the fact that the Baltic middle class, genuinely democratic, was both anti-German and anti-Bolshevik, but well-disposed toward the Allies. He believed the Latvians to be quite capable of defending themselves against the Bolsheviks, and he stressed the necessity for withdrawal of German forces which, under Russian disguise, were assuming a menacing aspect not only for Latvia and the rest of the Baltic, but for the demobilizing Allies themselves. The German Government, General Gough suggested, was waiting to see which would prove the stronger: the Peace Conference in Paris, or General von der Goltz in Kurland, whose increasing forces were well supplied and in direct railway connection with East Prussia.

Impressed by both the sincerity and experience of the British Chief of the Allied Mission in the Baltic, the Council of Five dispatched a strong note to the German Government demanding under threat of sanctions the complete evacuation of the Baltic by October 20, including the withdrawal of the so-called Russian Corps, which could claim only a few hundred White Russians for its 30,000 Germans. The German Government replied that on September 25 it had replaced von der Goltz by General von Eberhard who was to supervise the evacuation. It did not add that, before he received notice of his removal, von der Goltz had transferred his command to Bermondt, with the consent of the *Reichswehrministerium*.[26]

Previous to this move, the "Prussian fox" had informed the British Commander in the Baltic that he intended to give the central sector of the Bolshevik front, centering on Riga, to the Russian volunteers under his command. While the British rejected such a threat to the Latvian capital, French military representatives favored granting Riga as a base of operations to Bermondt. The latter had by now appointed his so-called Western Russian Government, headed in Jelgava by the German-Balt Count Pahlen, backed by German Jewish bankers (to whom Latvian forests had been mortgaged), and free both with its baseless currency and with promises of Baltic land to German volunteers.

[24] M. W. Graham, *The Diplomatic Recognition of the Border States*. Part III: *Latvia*, 409-433.
[25] *Papers Relating to the Foreign Relations* . . . , VIII (Washington, D.C., 1946), 258ff.
[26] *Die Kämpfe im Baltikum* . . . , p. 76.

On October 5, under strong pressure from Marshal Foch, the German Government categorically forbade Reich soldiers to join the Bermondt army, ordering home those who had already volunteered. Three days later, Bermondt announced the beginning of his campaign against the Bolsheviks, falsely declaring himself to be in full cooperation with the White Russian Commanders Yudenitch and Koltchak. Proclaiming all the Baltic to be a Russian military base, he ordered a move on Riga.

The Latvian forces promptly crossed to the north bank of the Daugava, where Balodis organized a defense of the bridgeheads which stopped the enemy on the southern bank, where a six day battle was engaged. On October 12, the Allied blockade of the Baltic Sea was declared. A squadron of four French and four British warships, under the command of the French Rear Admiral Brisson, appeared in the mouth of the Daugava. When Bermondt ignored an ultimatum to retreat from Riga, Brisson, influenced by Brigadier-General Sir Alfred Burt, British military representative, applied sanctions and ordered the bombardment of the Bermondt forces on October 15. By November 3, the decisive joint Latvian-Allied counterattack had begun, with the Latgallian Division crossing the mouth of the Daugava under Allied naval gunfire and executing a pincer movement to cut off the bulk of the Bermondt forces lingering in a suburb of Riga on the south bank of the river. The Russian commander ordered a retreat on November 10, and the following day Riga was completely relieved. When an attack on Liepāja failed, Bermondt telegraphed General von Eberhard asking for means to evacuate his forces by rail from Jelgava and Lithuania. General Eberhard ordered a counterattack on the Latvians. Defeated on November 19, he proposed an armistice, informing the Latvian commander-in-chief that he had taken the Russian Western Army under his personal command. The Latvian Government, wary of such delay tactics, severed relations with the German Government, whom it made responsible for the Bermondt aggression as organized by General von der Goltz in connivance with Berlin.

When the Latvians persisted in their advantage, von Eberhard, on November 21, ordered full retreat from Kurland. Bermondt took to his horse in unseemly haste. German mercenaries, after looting the Ducal castle of Jelgava, set it afire. By the end of November, Zemgale and Kurzeme were cleared of the Germans and Russians who had hoped for fortune under the command of the self-styled Prince, Admiral, and Imperial Aide-de-camp, Bermondt-Avalov.

Bermondt's preeminence in the Balticum during September and October 1919 was not entirely due to his extravagant character or the support of that other adventurer, General von der Goltz. Behind his crass aggression, based on false claims to being the right-hand man of General Yudenitch, lay the confused hopes of many of the Peace Conference statesmen, particularly the French, who clung to the expectation of a restored Russia capable of resuming payment on a heavy debt to the French Government. On November 7, there had arrived in Berlin the Baltic Interallied Military Mission, headed by the French General Niessel. At this late date, Niessel was still disposed to put some faith in Bermondt as an anti-Bolshevik who might yet assist Yudenitch in the recapture of Petrograd. When the White Russian General suffered a decisive defeat on November 14 and fled behind the Estonian lines, Niessel's Commission was reduced to its proper function of overseeing the German evacuation of the Baltic. The non-committal attitude toward recognition of the Baltic States revealed in the instructions of the Big Five to this Interallied Mission must be attributed to the persistent belief of the French that, if not Koltchak, Yudenitch, or Bermondt, then Denikin or Wrangel might be expected to settle the fate of those small nations whose intense efforts to defend and liberate themselves had received little understanding and only sporadic sympathy from the powers assembled in Paris.

These efforts the Latvians had now to persist in until the Bolsheviks were routed from Latgale, as they might have been months before had it not been for German-Russian machinations. During the Bermondt attack on Riga, the Bolsheviks had proposed an armistice with the intention of holding Latgale, which they hoped to proclaim a Soviet Republic. This province, however, showed no signs of separatism from the mother country of Latvia, which it had decided to rejoin in 1917, and where its special cultural and religious (Roman Catholic) interests had received satisfactory consideration. Its peasantry, in so far as it consisted of Russian Old-Believers, White Russians, and Poles, was particularly averse to the Bolsheviks, against whom they waged fierce partisan warfare.

After the signing of an armistice with Estonia on December 20, 1919, the Bolsheviks concentrated overwhelming forces on Latvia. In this precarious situation Latvia turned to her fellow-sufferer from Red aggression, Poland, whose Marshal Piłsudski promptly ordered 20,000 Polish troops to come to the aid of the 100,000 Latvians in the field. Poland was unique in her willingness to offer her small neighbor military aid without compensation. On January 3, the Polish forces stormed Daugavpils, which fell two days later. By January 20, 1920, not a Bolshevik soldier remained on Latvian territory.

Following the Latvian-Soviet armistice of February 1, a series of peace treaties was concluded between the Soviet Union and the former Baltic Provinces. The Bolshevik Government accorded *de jure* recognition to an independent Estonia by the Treaty of Tartu, February 2, 1920; to Lithuania by the Treaty of Moscow, July 12; and to Latvia by the Treaty of Riga, signed on August 11.

Article 2 of the Latvian-Soviet Union peace treaty read: "By virtue of the principle proclaimed by the Federal Socialist Republic of the Russian Soviets, which established the right of self-determination for all nations, even to the point of total separation from the States with which they have been incorporated, and in view of the desire expressed by the Latvian people to possess an independent national existence, Russia unreservedly recognizes the independence, self-subsistency and sovereignty of the Latvian State and voluntarily and for eternal times renounces all sovereign rights over the Latvian people and territory which formerly belonged to Russia under the then existing constitutional law as well as under international treaties, which, in the sense here indicated, shall in the future cease to be valid. The previous status of subjection of Latvia to Russia shall not entail any obligation towards Russia on the part of the Latvian people or territory."[27]

Thus did the Soviet Union clearly and voluntarily acknowledge the international obligation to recognize the *de jure* independence of the Latvian State. Simultaneously, this act denounced those former treaties by which Russia had gradually annexed the old Latvian provinces: the Treaty of Nystadt of 1721, whereby Livonia, or 35 per cent of modern Latvia, was taken from Sweden; the Treaty of Poland, 1772, the First Partition, annexing Latgale (24 per cent of Latvia); and the treaty of 1795 wherein Duke Peter Biron and the Diet of the landed nobles of Kurland had laid that province (41 per cent of Latvia) at the feet of Catherine the Great.

Article 3 of the Treaty of Riga fixed the historical ethnographical border separating the Latvian and the Russian peoples as the modern

[27] English text of treaty in *Latvian-Russian Relations. Documents*, ed. A. Bilmanis (Washington, 1944), pp. 70-81.

frontier between the two states. Other sections of the treaty provided for the repatriation of Latvian refugees; the restitution of deposits, personal property, and archives sent into Russia during the World War; and financial compensation to Latvia for war losses. An advance payment of four million rubles was the first and last installment on reparations which the Latvian Government was to receive from the Soviet Union.

A few final moves were needed to settle the new state peacefully within her boundaries and her long contested rights. The mediation of Colonel Tallents was instrumental in establishing, in the Convention of March 22, 1920, the Latvian-Estonian frontier by partitioning the hitherto disputed town of Valka. The delimitation of the Latvian-Lithuanian frontier, referred to a court of arbitration, was not completed till March of the following year. The peace treaty with Germany was signed on July 15, 1920. While the Reich agreed to accord *de jure* recognition to Latvia as soon as the rest of the big signatories of the Treaty of Versailles should do so, it denied all responsibility in the Bermondt affair, and refused reparations for Latvian losses in the First World War.

It remained now for the battered young state to gather up the reins of government and repair the damage not only of the First World War, but of the War of Liberation, which cost her another 5,000 lives during its 628 days' duration, called old men and school children into the trenches, reduced her army to rags, and put her under heavy debts to foreign governments for their sporadic help. The Latvian Government was to assume the obligation of £1,303,000 to Great Britain for supplies and services rendered during the war of independence; and of $5,775,000 to the United States for supplies from the AEF. The French Government, for the support and transport of two Latvian regiments of refugees mobilized in the Far East (where they had been put to use by the French High Commissioner unloading trains), presented a bill of five million francs.

The true nature of the Latvian War of Liberation, while a sore puzzle to some of the neutral observers in the Baltic, struck home to at least one representative of the most consistently helpful of the big Powers. A correspondent of the *London Times* in Riga wrote: "Eighteen months between the autumn of 1918 and the spring of 1920 were truly a heroic period. To impartial onlookers the aspirations of the men of Latvia at that time could not seem otherwise than sheer folly.

How these men could find room for hope, squeezed in as they were between the great nations of Germany and Russia, the front of whose armed forces kept sweeping to and fro over the devastated lands of Latvia, must for ever remain a thing to wonder at and admire!"[28]

[28] R. O. G. Urch, *Latvia: Country and People*, p. 90.

Chapter 17

Self-Rule: Trial and Error. 1920-1934

In the opening months of 1920 Latvia's statesmen, many of whom had borne the strain of front-line combat in the final fight for freedom, were confronted by staggering demands on their energies in the sphere of internal affairs. They faced the problems of restoring domestic order and inaugurating a long-term program of good housekeeping with an eagerness which was soon matched by general optimism among the people. The inventiveness and initiative which the Latvian people and their leaders discovered at a time of near exhaustion brought forth some error, far more progress than any outside observer would have anticipated, and a large amount of exciting first-hand experience in engineering a compact yet flexible, progressive yet responsible, self-contained though internationally-minded, democratic republic.

A spirit of new beginnings sustained these men, who might excusably have carried the weight of ancient rancors with them into public life. Instead, they realized that their small nation, still weak from the dark enslavements of the past, must lose no time in brooding on revenge, but must rather set about living up to the democratic principles for which it had poured out blood and resources in desperate measure. The treaty of peace with the Soviet Union was to be concluded in terms of the future rather than the past.

The same constructive attitude had characterized two measures passed by the Latvian National Council late in 1919. The first of these, an amnesty for those guilty of political disloyalty previous to October 8, restored to citizenship Latvians who now wished to leave the Bolshevik ranks, as well as the German-Balts who had supported the Niedra government. The statutory law of cultural autonomy passed on December 18 and based on the Declaration of Policy issued by the Latvian State Council on November 18, 1918, granted equal cultural, political, and economic rights to the national minorities, of whom the largest were the Russians, the Jews, the Germans, and the Poles. These groups were admitted to all spheres of national activity and accorded their full share of democratic privileges. They obtained permission to establish their own school departments within the National Ministry of Education, and their children were granted free and compulsory elementary education, the only restriction on their curricula being the compulsory teaching of Latvian history, geography, and language. The curator of each minority's school administration was to represent his nationality in other cultural matters and was to have the right to participate, in an advisory capacity, in Cabinet sessions concerning his nationality's cultural affairs. This Latvian law of cultural autonomy was the first piece of minority legislation of its kind passed in post-war Europe, and as such was widely acclaimed abroad.

Following the armistice with the Soviet Union on February 1, 1920, the question of the election of a Constituent Assembly came to the fore. A national census bill was passed to prepare for the elections of April 17-18. But the young nation could not wait for the convening of the Constituent Assembly on May 1 to set about repairing its war-torn fabric. Before that date, 247 laws and decrees covering every phase of national existence had been promulgated by the National Council and the Provisional Government.

Among the fiscal measures taken to bolster a tottering economy was a law providing for the issuance of 200 million Latvian rubles in treasury notes for the specific purpose of supporting economic recovery. In order to stabilize and uphold the value of these notes a state gold fund was established, for which the Treasury bought gold at a rate fixed on the Riga Exchange. After establishment of the Latvian ruble as the sole legal tender, a law was passed to permit the immediate redemption, at a fixed rate, of mortgages and other debts contracted in Russian rubles or German marks, thus enabling pre-war debtors to make a fresh start. On March 18, the government, which had already set aside five million rubles for farm reconstruction, passed a bill for the issuance of four per cent recovery bonds to the amount of 25 million rubles redeemable in fifty years.

The freely elected Latvian Constituent Assembly of 150 members convened on May 1, 1920. Jānis Čakste, until then President of the National Council, was elected President of the Assembly and of the Latvian Republic. Premier Kārlis Ulmanis, commissioned to form a Cabinet, did so on a coalition basis, choosing representatives of the leading political parties as well as of the national minorities. This Cabinet was to continue national reconstruction by issuing decrees to be confirmed later by the Constituent Assembly.

This body, which was to function at full speed from May 1, 1920, to November 7, 1922, the date of the opening of the first Parliament

(*Saeima*), saw as one of its first duties the solemn reaffirmation of Latvia's independence and sovereignty. On May 29, the Constituent Assembly proclaimed Latvia a sovereign and independent democratic republic whose sovereignty inheres in the nation. The Provisional Constitution of June 1 declared the Constituent Assembly to be the repository of the sovereign power of the Latvian State; defined its duties, chief of which was the preparation of a permanent constitution and the passing of an agricultural reform bill; assigned the executive power to the Cabinet of Ministers which was made responsible to the Constituent Assembly; established the position and duties of the President of the Assembly; and defined a number of democratic rights for Latvian citizens.

Highly anachronistic in a modern democratic state organization was the *Ritterschaft*, or corporation of the landed German nobles in Vidzeme, Kurland, and Piltene. This institution, repeatedly confirmed by successive Tsarist régimes, and tolerated even by the Russian Provisional Government, had controlled the Livonian Diets and kept a strong hold in administrative and judiciary matters until the First World War. It was legally dissolved on June 29, 1920. The German-Balt nobles then established their scroll committee in Geneva, where their representatives were determined to make a stand for the antiquated privileges of their caste. Their protests were bitterest over the Agrarian Reform Bill, keystone to Latvia's economic recovery, and *coup de grace* to the German caste system.

Before proceeding to drastic repairs of the devastated land and a ruined economy, a program and a policy were needed to set a steady course for the makers of this new nation. The consensus of opinion favored the retention of private property and enterprise as the foundations of Latvia's economy. With foreign credits currently unavailable, and a recent history of foreign control encroaching on artificially large industries, a high degree of economic self-sufficiency was now favored. This was to be attained by the fostering of a variety of local industries, though not to the point of once more encouraging economic aggression from abroad, and by maintaining the close dependence of these industries upon agriculture, which would remain the foundation stone of the nation.

On September 16, 1920, the much discussed Agrarian Reform Bill became law. It created a state land fund of almost three and a half million hectares from governmental, municipal, church, and private estates exceeding 110 hectares. Owners of confiscated estates were permitted to retain 50 hectares of land, which put them on a favorable basis with the rest of the farming population, the majority of which owned farms of from 10 to 30 hectares. From the state land fund distributions were made of not more than 22 hectares of agricultural land apiece to nearly 100,000 newly created farms and the same number of enlarged holdings.

Naturally, the chief opponents of this reform were the Baltic barons, whose 1,338 private estates in 1918 had occupied 48.1 per cent of Latvia's area, some of them attaining the size of 10,000 hectares. These big landowners were further outraged by the Latvian Government's appropriation of all forests, excluding those held by farmers, for the purpose of protection and conservation. Their accusation of illegality, as made in the League of Nations, was groundless, since the reform bill had been duly adopted by the Constituent Assembly by an overwhelming vote. Ironically, the representatives of the national minorities had sided with the parties of the Left in voting against compensation, but not for the same reasons, the German-Balt minority maintaining that the compensation would be insufficient, while the radicals opposed it on general principles.

The agricultural reform bill was accompanied by laws establishing government agricultural schools and governing cooperative organizations and associations. The beneficiaries of the reform bill, while they were required to pay the government for the land allotted them, were granted long-term contracts, and in addition received cheap credit for seed, fertilizer, and farm improvements. A period of highly intensive and scientific farming was about to begin.

While the Latvian Government eschewed centralization on the whole, certain parts of the national economy which showed a deficiency beyond the help of private capital were taken over by the state, largely in order to avoid dependence on mistrusted foreign capital. Most of the railways fell into this category, as well as the maintenance of highways, the repair of destroyed ports and harbor installations, and such public services as were not assumed by the municipalities. In order to assure the farmers a fair price, the buying and selling of crude alcohol and the buying of flax were declared state monopolies. But, in general, private initiative was encouraged in farming, building, commerce, industry, fishing, and shipping, by means of the extension of cheap state credits and long-term mortgages.

During the latter half of 1920 and all through 1921, the Constituent Assembly continued to approve a number of laws concerning administrative, economic, commercial, financial, and cultural affairs. Education received special emphasis, with the opening of a wide range of vocational and normal schools and technical institutes, the creation of public libraries, and the establishment, in addition to the already functioning State University at Riga, of a State Conservatory of Music and Academy of Fine Arts. But throughout this period of intensive legislation the Constituent Assembly held undeviatingly to its main purpose of adopting a constitution and thus establishing the pattern of normal political development.

Finally, on February 15, 1922, after some two years of serious study, the Bill of the Latvian Constitution was passed by the Constituent Assembly. In seven parts and 88 articles it provided for a democratic republic with a unicameral parliament (Saeima); a president; separation of the legislative, executive, and judicial branches of the government; freedom of the press, conscience, speech, and assembly; equal rights for all citizens together with cultural autonomy for racial minorities; and equality of opportunity.

The Latvian Constitution of 1922 provided for the election of the president of the state by a simple majority of the Saeima for a term of three years. In addition to his other duties as the head of the republic, the president was required to call upon the prime minister to form a cabinet responsible to the Saeima. This body, of a hundred members and a unicameral structure, was elected for a period of three years by direct, secret, and proportional ballot. Its duty was to pass on legislative bills introduced by the president of the republic, the cabinet of ministers, the committees of the Saeima, any group of not less than five members of the Saeima, or by one-tenth of the electorate. In addition, the Saeima adopted the budget, confirmed the cabinet, passed votes of confidence, fixed the strength of the armed forces in time of peace, and elected the president of the republic. Decisions were made by an absolute majority of members present at the session, providing not less than one-half of the membership was in attendance.

Provision was made for amendment of the constitution by two-thirds of the Saeima. One-tenth of the electorate could submit to the chief of state a full-drawn bill for the amendment of the constitution which, should it fail of ratification by the parliament, might be put to a plebiscite.

The extreme taste for egalitarianism which governed public opinion at that time resulted in the ultra-liberal election law of June 9, seen later as a major stumbling block to national unity. By this law, any group of Latvian citizens, over twenty-one years of age, could propose the list of Saeima candidates for any one of the five electoral districts of Vidzeme, Latgale, Kurzeme, Zemgale, and the city of Riga. A highly complicated proportional ballot was introduced based on the untested radical theories of French and German political mathematicians. We shall examine the ills of this system later in this chapter.*

Having passed a referendum law and chosen the dates of October 7 and 8 for the national election and of November 7 for the opening of the first Latvian parliament, the Constituent Assembly recessed the Provisional Government. One of the most important pieces of legislation of the interim period was the Financial Bill of August 3, introducing the lat as a monetary unit. The lat was fixed at one gold franc (19.3 cents), and was the equivalent of fifty Latvian paper rubles. This financial reform was among the earliest successful stabilization efforts in post-war Europe, where inflation and unstable currencies were devouring the fruits of reconstruction. An initial bout of this economic virus had inspired the Latvian Constituent Assembly to work unremittingly for the stabilization of the country's finances, without which there could be no balanced state budget and no refounding of the nation's economy.

Before considering the activities and difficulties of Latvia's first parliaments, a survey of her conduct of foreign affairs in the period between the cessation of hostilities and the opening of the Saeima on November 7, 1922, will attest her establishment in a remarkably short time as a lively yet tactful new member of the family of nations.

The final disillusionment of certain Western European Powers and of the United States in regard to the long-hoped-for end of the Bolshevik régime in Russia led to a wave of esteem for the new border

---

* The author may be permitted to refer, with reference to economic and statistical matters, for this and the following chapter, to some of his own studies in which the events and developments of these years are treated in greater detail: *La Lettonie en 1921* (Paris, 1922); *Latvia in the Making* (Riga, 1925); *La Lettonie d'aujourd'hui, son développement historique et la situation actuelle* (Riga, 1925); *Latvia in the Making, 1918-1928. Ten Years of Independence* (Riga, 1928). The Latvian Ministry of Foreign Affairs published various studies, collections of documents, laws and treaties: *Latvie. Mémoire présenté par la delegation latvienne à l'Assemblée de la Société des Nations* (Riga, 1920, 2nd ed. 1921); *La République de Lettonie: documents, traités et lois* (Riga, 1922); *Recueil des principaux traités conclus par la Lettonie avec les pays étrangers: 1918-1928*, I (Riga, 1928, 2nd ed. 1930), II (Riga, 1938).

Statistics are taken from *Latvijas Skaitļos* (Latvian Statistics), (Riga, 1938) ed. by A. Meldups, or from various *Statistical Yearbooks of Latvia* (with French translation).

nations, most of whom were so eagerly putting into action Western democratic ideals which had grown somewhat tarnished in the older democracies. Certainly the small Baltic nations had proved themselves worthy of full recognition by the diplomatic world. On January 26, 1921, Latvia was recognized *de jure* by the European Great Powers and most of the Latin American Republics. Following her admission to the League of Nations on September 22, came further recognition of her sovereign independence. On May 30, 1922, a Concordat was signed with the Holy See, reestablishing the Roman Catholic Archbishopric of Riga on condition that the Archbishop be a Latvian citizen and his appointment approved by the government. On July 28 of that same year, the United States extended to Latvia, Estonia, and Lithuania full, unrestricted, and unconditional recognition.[1] The statement publicly issued by the Department of State on this occasion left no doubt as to the attitude of the United States toward the new Baltic nations: "The Governments of Estonia, Latvia, and Lithuania have been recognized either *de jure* or *de facto* by the principal governments of Europe, and have entered into treaty relations with their neighbors.

"In extending to them recognition on its part, the Government of the United States takes cognizance of the actual existence of these governments during a considerable period of time and of the successful maintenance within their borders of political and economic stability.

"The United States has consistently maintained that the disturbed condition of Russian affairs may not be made the occasion for alienation of Russian territory, and this principle is not deemed to be impaired by the recognition at this time of the Governments of Estonia, Latvia and Lithuania, which have been set up and maintained by an indigenous population. . . ."[2]

This wide recognition of their independence, culminating in the American appreciation of their position, represented a major diplomatic triumph for the Baltic States. While relations with the West were thus stabilized, Latvia took pride in her frontier treaties,[3] out-

[1] The text of the Latvian Constitution, adopted by the Latvian Constituent Assembly February 15, 1922, is printed in English translation as Appendix I of the author's *Latvia as an Independent State* (Washington, 1947).

[2] *Papers Relating to the Foreign Relations of the United States . . .* , II, 873-874.

[3] 331 mile frontier with Lithuania: Border Treaty of Sept. 25, 1920; Protocols of March 20, 1921 and Oct. 15, 1927. 60 mile frontier with Poland: Demarcation Treaty of 1929. 230 mile frontier with Estonia: Treaty of March 22, 1920; Nov. 1, 1923; March 30, 1927. 220 mile frontier with the Soviet Union:

lined in the previous chapter, which, after being duly ratified by the signatory states, were deposited at the League of Nations. Hopes for the flowering of a good neighbor policy toward Soviet Russia followed upon the determination of frontiers in the Treaty of Riga. The fact that the natural geographic border (a system of lakes, rivers, swamps, and marshes stretching from the Narev River on the Gulf of Finland to the Pripet marshes in the south) coincided with the more than a thousand-year-old ethnographical and cultural frontier between Latvians and Slavs, led to the easy choice of a boundary by mutual consent. This natural frontier, however, had not withstood Russian invasion in the past, when eastern armies had availed themselves of the few ridges leading through this water barrier toward the Baltic, or crossed the marshes and rivers during the deep frosts of a northern winter.

Latvian leadership felt that the time had come to lessen the risk of future invasion by winning the good will of the powerful Soviet neighbor in matters where mutual interest might reasonably be expected to prevail. The economic field seemed the most promising in this regard, Latvia's fine ports and harbors, as well as her rail and waterways having served the Russian hinterland well in the past. The smaller nation saw no objection to being considered as a transit state for her own profit and the convenience of foreign commerce. Her territory was historically and geographically a natural traffic-link between Western Europe and Russia, and modern Latvia, anxious though she was to establish a national rather than a foreign-controlled economy, realized the shortsightedness of shutting off this international flux in the name of self-sufficiency or self-defense. In order to serve these transit purposes to the best of her ability she lost no time in restoring and further improving her three great ports: Riga, which was connected by rail with Central Russia; Ventspils, similarly linked with the Volga region and with Siberia; and Liepāja, connected with the Ukraine. At this last port an international quarantine was established. The Latvian railroads, heavily developed under the Tsarist régimes, continued to maintain both broad and narrow gauges to serve western and eastern systems and provide direct connection between Germany and the Soviet Union.

This desire to restore and enlarge economic relations with the Russian hinterland was implemented by the "Russian clause" which

---

Treaty of Aug. 11, 1920; Border Treaty of Aug. 1, 1921; Protocols of April 7, 1923, July 19, 1926, April 9, 1937.

Latvia had agreed by treaty to insert in future economic treaties with other nations. This clause (paralleled by a similar Baltic clause, applicable to Finland, Estonia, and Lithuania) stipulated that the special privileges accorded by Latvia to the Soviet Union (as to the above-mentioned Baltic nations) were exceptional to the "most favored nation" concept, and were therefore not subject to claim by other nations under "most favored nation" clauses. Among the special privileges accorded to Russian transit goods were lower custom tariffs, reduction in freight rates, and exemption from surtaxes. Thus did Latvia hope to maintain the delicate balance of her political independence and economic prosperity without being swallowed into the Soviet orbit. The unexpectedly meagre results from these early overtures will be considered elsewhere.

Latvia's eagerness to stabilize relations with her erstwhile sovereign loomed no larger than her desire to create a closer bond with her sister states on the Baltic, particularly the newly liberated nations. These were peculiarly sensible of the changed status of the Baltic Sea brought about by the reduction of the German Navy, the internationalization of the Kiel Canal, and the radical shrinkage of the Russian Baltic coast line. The Russian-Finnish and Russian-Estonian peace treaties had contained paragraphs concerning the neutrality of the Baltic Sea. One of Latvia's leading ideas in the field of international relations at this time was the formation of a Baltic regional bloc to guarantee this neutrality together with the independence of the riparian states. Her most ardent hope was that the question of Baltic dominium, which had repeatedly led to the ruin of her land and the enslavement of her people, might finally be put to rest. It seemed fitting that the Baltic States themselves should set an example of mutual harmony and responsibility for the preservation of peace and freedom in this area.

The first of two enlightened conferences concerning the outlook and mutual interests of the new riparian nations was held in Helsinki in January 1920. The following August at Bulduri, near Riga, a second gathering adopted resolutions which, had they been carried out, might well have led to the formation of a United States of the Baltic and a true guarantee of the freedom of that water. On this occasion the Latvian Foreign Minister, Meierovics, paved the way for close political and economic relations among Finland, Estonia, Latvia, Lithuania, and Poland by proposing the creation of a High Economic Council, and the unification of railroads, telegraph and telephone services, tariffs, and other media of communication and commerce. Uniform legislation was proposed in the field of fiscal, social, and cultural affairs. Numerous other regional projects were broached during the five-week Bulduri Conference, including a Permanent Baltic Court of Arbitration, and the establishment of a Permanent Council of Plenipotentiaries of the Baltic States, to be situated in Riga, for the execution of the decisions of the Conference.

These progressive plans foundered on the refusal of Poland and Finland to ratify the conventions adopted at Bulduri. Finland, though consistently friendly toward the Central Baltic States, did not wish to risk alienation from the Scandinavian neutrality bloc, nor possible commitments against Soviet Russia. Baltic solidarity was further threatened by the refusal of Lithuania, following the Polish *coup* in Vilna, in October 1920, to participate in any future conferences at which Poland might be represented.

Conflicting interests were also in evidence at the Warsaw Conference of March 1922, where an agreement was proposed providing for benevolent neutrality towards any of the signatory states which might be attacked without provocation, and for immediate consultation with regard to subsequent steps to be taken. When the Finnish Diet refused to ratify the Warsaw Agreement, Poland followed suit. The Latvian and Estonian parliaments were the only ones to ratify this agreement, which was then registered at the League of Nations. These two states, more defenseless than Finland or Poland in the event of Soviet aggression, and disappointed both by Sweden's unwillingness to support a Baltic bloc and the divergent views of the other riparian states, drew together in increasingly close alliance. The preliminary political and military agreement of July 1921, between Estonia and Latvia was, as a result of the failure of the Warsaw Conference, consolidated into an outright Defensive Alliance in November 1923.

Although the ground swell of mutual jealousies and independent orientations in the critical Baltic region was naturally disturbing to the small nation, which has been called the "key of the Baltic States,"[4] Latvia, on the whole, had good reason to feel satisfied with her foreign relations in the early days of her statehood. She chose to steer consistently a middle course within the framework of the League of Nations, of which she was one of the most ardent supporters. She

[4] E. W. Polson Newman, *Britain and the Baltic* (London, 1930), chap. IV. See also in chapter by S. H. Thomson on Polish "Foreign Relations" in *Poland*, ed. by B. E. Schmitt (Berkeley, 1945), p. 380f.

participated to the full in all international conventions, accepting the obligatory arbitration of the International Court and putting her signature to the Hague Conventions. Anxious neither to go counter to her obligations to the League of Nations nor to alienate Poland, she rejected any entanglement with the Soviet Union in schemes of "unrestricted" neutrality and disarmament, as proposed by the larger Power, both to Latvia and Estonia, after the collapse of the Warsaw Agreement and the Moscow Disarmament Conference.

With her foreign affairs on an even keel, and a notable start made in the reestablishment of her national economy, Latvia could give her full attention to the forthcoming parliamentary elections. To grasp the political complexity of the four Latvian Saeimas[5] of what may be called the "period of disunity" or of political tribalism (1922-1934), an analysis of the leading Latvian parties is requisite. Proportional representation, for which so much had been hoped, was to reduce the Latvian parliamentary system to an unconstructive game centered around building up politicians' rather than truly representative majorities.

As in other modern continental European democracies, there were in independent Latvia all shades of political opinion, seeking organized expression in a multitude of political parties which can be roughly grouped under the five classifications of Leftists, Left-Centrists, Agrarians, Rightists, and National Minorities. Many of the parties within these various groups had their origins in the political trends of the pre-war generation. Tables below indicate the names as well as the proportions in the first four parliaments of the forty chief political parties which won representation during this period.

POLITICAL PARTIES IN THE FIRST, SECOND, THIRD, AND FOURTH PARLIAMENTS

	1922-25 82% of voters	1925-28 74% of voters	1928-31 79% of voters	1931-34 80% of voters
Socialist Wing:				
Social-Democrats	30%	31%	25%	20%
Latgallian Social-Democrats	–	1	1	–
Socialist Jewish "Bund"	1	1	1	–
Independent Social-Democrats	–	–	1	1
Right Wing Social-Democrats	7	4	2	–
Peasant and Labor Bloc (Communistic)	–	–	6	7
Total	38%	37%	36%	28%

[5] 1. 1922-1925; 2. 1925-1928; 3. 1928-1931; 4. 1931-1934.

Left Center:

Democratic Center	6%	3%	3%	6%
Labor Union	–	–	–	1
Progressive Union	–	–	–	1
Economic Union	–	–	1	1
Radical Democrats	–	1	–	–
Democrats at large	–	–	1	–
New Settlers	3	5	–	–
Christian Labor	–	–	1	–
Latgallian Progressives	4	2	3	2
Total	**13%**	**11%**	**9%**	**11%**

Agrarian Bloc:

Farmers' Union	16%	16%	16%	14%
Small Landholders	–	3	4	9
Latgallian Christian Farmers	3	5	6	8
Latgallian Progressive Farmers	4	2	3	3
Devastated Areas (by World War I)	1	1	–	–
Latgallian Independent Farmers	–	1	–	–
Zemgallian Christian Farmers	1	–	–	–
Total	**25%**	**28%**	**29%**	**34%**

Right Wing:

Christian Union	–	–	–	6%
National Union	4	3	2	–
Christian Nationalists	4	2	4	–
House Owners	–	1	1	1
Latgallian Union	1	2	1	–
National Farmers	–	1	–	–
New Farmer Union	–	–	–	1
Total	**9%**	**9%**	**8%**	**8%**

National Minorities:

Old Believers (Russian)	1%	2%	2%	2%
Greek Orthodox Russians	–	2	2	2
Union of Russian Municipal Employees	1	1	2	1
Russian Farmer Union	–	–	–	1
Russian National Democrats	1	–	–	–
Germans	6	5	6	6
Agudas Israel	2	2	1	2
Misrachi	2	1	2	2
Ceire Zion	1	1	1	1
Poles	1	2	2	2
Total	**15%**	**16%**	**18%**	**19%**

In addition to the ultra-liberal ballot, a law was passed by the first Saeima, in July 1923, granting to a group of any five persons the right to register as a political party. This opened the way to the absurd political recognition of a battalion of soldiers or the inhabitants of an apartment building. The situation was further complicated by the special situation of the Latgallians, who paralleled the other Latvian parties with an independent structure of their own, and by the generous representation accorded national minorities. Given the unreconstructed attitude of some of these minorities, the vigilance and opportunism of the leaders of the Left, and the cynicism of politicians, political tribalism was the inevitable end-result of a constitution and an election law which had been elaborated at a time when any internal threat to that national unity so hardly won seemed unthinkable. Generosity and the optimism begotten of an almost incredible victory had clouded the political judgment even of some of those who prepared the way for Latvia's maturity.

In the first parliament of 1922, 22 political parties found representation; in the Saeima of 1925, 27; in that of 1928, 27; and in 1931, 24. We shall review the origin and the nature of only the most important of these parties. The extreme conservatives, the Christian Nationalists, represented the Lutheran Church as well as certain professional and business groups. Early adherents to this group had been the founders of the Latvian Association (*Latweeschu Beedriba*) of 1869, and the moving spirits of the early nationalistic newspapers, *Mahjas Weesis* and *Latweeshu Awihses*. More to the Center, though still basically conservative, was the strong Farmers' Union party, whose forebears might be found among those young leaders of the National Awakening gathered around K. Valdemārs and the *Peterburgas Awihses*. This group had been concerned with peasant questions in the sixties of the previous century. The Latvian Farmers' Union was officially founded and incorporated in 1917, when it could hope to represent that 65 per cent of the Latvian population which was normally engaged in agriculture. With the active support of the numerous cooperative and other agricultural associations, as well as of the farmers' press, it formed the core of the nonsocialist yet liberal political group, and was a leading force in the movement for autonomy, and in the opposition to the German-Balt landowners. This party's policy was founded on the belief that agriculture is the backbone of Latvian economic life and as such should be consistently promoted. National unity, based on the keying of other interests to those of agriculture, should be the predominant aim of the Latvian State. The Farmers' Union was a breeder of statesmen, among them Jānis Čakste, Kārlis Ulmanis, Zigfrīds Meierovics, General Balodis, and J. Goldmanis, all of whom we have already seen at their work of creating and defending the Latvian State.

Thirteen of the eighteen prime ministers in office from 1918 to 1934 were members of this tough-spirited party.

More to the Left than the Farmers' Union, but not socialistic, was the Democratic Center party, favored by the professional and middle classes, and appealing to those radical-democrats who fluctuated between the Farmers' Union and the Left Wing. Leaders of this group were Gustavs Zemgals, President of the Republic from 1927 to 1930, and two Prime Ministers, Zamuelis and Juraševskis. From this political group, as well as from the Left Wing Socialists, were to come the adherents of the Society for Cultural Rapprochement with the Soviet Union.

The most powerful antagonists of the agrarian bloc were the Social-Democrats, leading Left Wing party. Originating in a union of some of the radical nationalistic groups on the eve of the Revolution of 1905, they laid claim to that stirring event, ignoring the important role played at that time by the Right Wing nationalistic Socialists who rejected the affiliation with the Russian Social-Democratic movement of which the Latvian Social-Democrats were an autonomous section.

Like the other Latvian Left Wing parties, the Social-Democrats had never had an agrarian program, but limited themselves to promoting the interests of trade unions, the urban proletariat, and agricultural workers. They favored industrialization over agriculture, and opposed the protectionist policy of the Agrarians. While they worked for closer ties with the Soviet Union, they were averse to any strengthening of relations with Germany or Poland.

Whereas, during the period of the Constituent Assembly (1920-1922), the entire socialist wing constituted a solid bloc, this group showed symptoms of deviation in the earliest Saeima. The first to break away were the Right Wing Social-Democrats. In 1929, this group took the name "Progressive Union" and aligned themselves with the democratic Center. The leftist Trade Unionists eventually dissented from the Central Committee of the radical Socialists; while the Jewish Bund preserved a degree of autonomy which allowed it to vote sometimes with the bourgeois Jewish representatives and with other national minority representatives. In the parliamentary elections of the autumn of 1928 there appeared for the first time the Peasant and Labor party, consisting of radical trade unionists and outright Communists. This group, the farthest to the Left of the Saeima, supported the platform of the Third International.

The political temper of the national minority parties was closely allied to their economic ambitions. Their lack of interest in Latvian national unity, their desire to improve their own positon at all costs, even to the extent of fostering foreign control of part of their country's economy, led them to extend their votes in the Saeima to whichever bloc had the most to offer them in return. In order to improve their bargaining position they created their own bloc, which opposed a degree of cohesion to the continuous political dissension of the Latvians proper. Most sympathetic to their industrial rather than agricultural interests, and to their "international" outlook, were the various shades of socialism. By an unexpected alliance, the national minority parties and the Left Wing bloc gained a working majority in parliament over the agrarian group, even though the latter represented a larger segment of the population. In exchange for their support, the Latvian Socialists supported the demands of the national minorities for such concessions as economic privileges, more liberal immigration rules for Germans, and less obstacles to the acquisition of Latvian citizenship.

The unusual position of the national minorities in independent Latvia demands some consideration at this point, since their economic ascendancy and political aggressiveness helped to shape the first decade of Saeima rule in a direction neither anticipated by nor acceptable to a large body of middle class and farmer Latvians. The minority peoples, Germans, Jews, Great and White Russians, Poles, Lithuanians and Estonians formed roughly about 20 per cent of the population, the Russians 10.58 per cent, the Jews 4.54 per cent, and the Germans 2.96 per cent.

Most of the Russians were in Latgale, where they had gradually settled during the course of centuries, often for religious reasons. From 1925 to 1935, the number of Great Russians was on the increase, as refugees received good treatment and the rights of citizenship after a period of five years. In the Saeima the Great Russian representatives (the White Russians had no representation) voted with the other national minorities, generally in opposition to the Latvian agrarian bloc, although their individual interests were in close accord with those of the Latvian farmers. While a good many of the successfully settled Great Russians wanted only to enjoy quietly the peace of a democratic way of life, there was an element which took up the cause of Communism and sovietization, while another segment, that of the assimilated Russian Jews, gained control over the Russian press,

theatre, and private schools, where the restoration of a "united indivisible Russia" was preached.

The shifting of several thousand Jews to the Russian minority ac-
counted in part for the drop in the Jewish total by 1935. The figure
had risen when many of the Jews forcibly removed from Latvia by
the Russian Government during the First World War returned to
their homeland, most of them settling in Riga, then opened to unrestricted settlement, as, indeed, was all of Latvia. Whereas some of
the German-Livonian Diets (1659, 1728, 1739) sought to adopt anti-
Jewish laws, the Dukes of Kurland had refused to confirm them, and
had encouraged Jews to foster trade and commerce in the Kuronian
cities. Not until after the official census of 1835 was further Jewish
settlement forbidden in this province. In general, Jews in old Livonia,
especially in the rural areas, had been well treated as middlemen,
peddlers of goods and gossip, accepted figures in a static society.

The Jews in Latvia fell into three cultural-religious groupings: the
German, the Russian, and the Orthodox. The Germanized Jews,
mostly from Kurland and Vidzeme, had officially adopted the German
language, which was used by their representatives in the Saeima. These
Jews had always enjoyed a profitable relationship with the German-
Balts, who realized their value as middlemen and busy promoters of
German-Balt commercial and financial enterprises. We have already
mentioned the assimilated Russian Jews, most of whom settled in
Riga, where they identified themselves closely with Russian interests.
Their parliamentary representatives spoke the Russian language. The
Orthodox Jews, more numerous and less prosperous than the other
two groups, lived mostly in Latgale, whose tradition of tolerance
allowed them to preserve their ancient religion and customs. Their
Saeima representatives spoke in Latvian.

Although the Latvian Government offered the Jews facilities for
obtaining land, only seven per cent lived in the country, the rest preferring to carry on their intensive economic and intellectual interests
in the cities. They supported their own schools, press, theatre, cultural
and economic associations, sport organizations, and even a war veterans' association. Regardless of their smaller proportion of the total
population, they had as large a parliamentary representation as the
Russians.

A far more resistant minority group than the Russians or the Jews
was the slowly diminishing remnant of the German-Balts. In 1897,
there were 120,191 Germans in Latvian Livonia; in 1935, there re-

mained 62,144, of which 4,315 were not Baltic Germans. The majority of those claiming Latvian citizenship belonged to the burgher class; only 14,721 being of the peasantry. In this last group were descendants of peasants imported from Bavaria and Württemberg by Catherine II in 1766. Granted equal land rights with the rest of the Latvian citizens, the German peasants farmed successfully in small, exclusive settlements and villages where their consistent practice of endogamy lowered their birth rate and led to a degree of degeneracy.

Some misconceptions have been current as to the situation and numbers of the German-Balt nobility, whose caste was technically broken up in 1920. At that time, all titles and class distinctions were abolished by law, although the prized "von" could still be retained as an integral part of the family name, but no longer conferring any legal or other privileges. Simultaneously, the caste system governing the guilds in Riga's municipal government, and the preferential vote accorded German houseowners in the township were also abolished. Those German-Balts who could trace their lineage back to the Teutonic Knights were far fewer than is commonly assumed. The census statistics of 1839 revealed only 685 hereditary noble Livonian-German families in all the Baltic Provinces. Of these, only 177 descended from the Knights or vassals of the old Livonian Order or from the ministerials of the Archbishopric of Riga. The census of 1897 registered 8,124 nobles in Latvia, of whom only 2,293 belonged to the landed gentry. The greater part of the "exclusive" German-Balt nobility, by the end of the nineteenth century, consisted of the descendants of Germans who had received patents of nobility from the Polish, Swedish, and Russian sovereigns. The latter particularly were generous with titles and lands accorded to the *Verdienstadel* for services rendered the Tsars in the army or administration.

After the abolition of the corporation of the nobility in 1920 and the Agrarian Reform, the German-Balt landed gentry made common fortune with their fellow-Germans of the burgher class, who, together with the Germanized Jews, were gaining marked advantages in the industrial, financial, and commercial fields. Outward signs of both their continued prosperity and their sense of exclusiveness were the smartness of their social, sports, and cultural organizations, the caliber of their schools, and the affluence of their banks and other business organizations. They had a flourishing press, a veterans' society for members of the *Landeswehr*, and their own churches and cemeteries. The German Lutherans (5.48 per cent of all Latvian Lutherans), established a separate church and synod, and elected their own bishop. While, in 1935, there were, in Riga, only 38,523 Germans as against 242,731 Latvians, the former claimed the Cathedrals of St. Mary and St. Peter for their exclusive use—a situation which had to be met by a referendum.

The German-Balt middle class, like the peasantry, paid the penalty for their sense of superiority by a declining birth rate. Their biological debility made them all the more anxious to take full advantage of the liberal political situation in their homeland which enabled them to elect six representatives to the Saeima. The weakness of the election law, which failed to demand residence, literacy, or taxation requirements of the voters, was exploited to the limit by this still power-hungry minority. Owing to their inveterate respect for the aristocracy, at least one ex-baron was always elected.

Influential in the disunited parliaments, entrenched in higher industrial and commercial circles, the Germans found life in independent Latvia far more to their advantage than might have been expected after the final defeat of the *Landeswehr*. The Government was generous with pardons. It was also unable to defeat the ambition of young German-Balts, highly educated and worldly-wise, in the national service. They sought, as no more than their hereditary due, positions in the judiciary, the navy, the general staff, and the diplomatic service.

Representatives of the national minorities, particularly of the Germans and Jewish-Russians, made full use of their political bargaining power to advance the interests of their voters. Their alliance with the Left Wing was opportunistic rather than doctrinaire. Both groups favored the encouragement of large, artificial industries over small, local ones; the manipulation of credit, domestic or foreign, to suit their purposes; and the growth of the urban proletariat, with its concentrated voting power and possibilities of mass unemployment. This last contingency would give the Socialists an excuse to demand more government benefits and eventual state ownership, while it afforded cheap labor to the industrialists. Left-Wingers and unreconstructed national minorities alike opposed any heavy support for agriculture and favored even foreign credit and control rather than limited industrial development and self-sufficiency, and political chaos over national unity. The technical political majority in the successive parliaments achieved by the aggressive and supple tactics of the professional politicians of the Left, of some of the slippery Centrist parties, and of the national minorities, did not correspond to either the social consistency or the political temper of the actual majority of the Latvian nation. But it was effective in a period of political tribalism and conditioned the unstable cabinet coalitions and much of the short-sighted legislation of the decade or so of Saeima rule.

It was in the economic field that the results were most obvious of party politics running riot and special interests cutting the national cloth to suit themselves. Whereas the Left Wing parties looked upon the Latvian middle class as overconservative and the agrarian bloc as their enemies, the national minorities, particularly the Germans, considered all educated, self-reliant Latvians as their competitors in business and the professions. In the early days of the Republic, when cheap credit had been available to farmers and their various cooperative associations, hope for the development of local industries had been premised on the continuance of this policy. The Latvian State Bank and the Agrarian Bank, both founded in 1923, together with the Mortgage Bank, opened the following year, were all established with the purpose of fostering Latvian economic life. However, representatives of the leading political parties in the Saeima were usually appointed to the boards of these state banks, with the result that the farmers, who did not have a majority in Parliament, obtained only very limited credit at six per cent interest plus one per cent for expenses. The rural credit cooperatives, lacking collateral, failed to obtain from the state banks the loans which they had hoped for. The State Bank and the State Mortgage Bank were advised by their boards to extend loans, based on capital accrued from taxes, preferably to private banks. Many of these were hastily established by homeowning non-Latvians who mortgaged their properties for the purpose. They then received loans from the state banks at six per cent, which they reloaned at as high as twelve per cent. Not until 1934 was the rate of eight per cent established by law for private banks, and that was still too high for all but the most prosperous farmers.

This credit advantage, so cleverly achieved by the Germans and Jews, was further increased by the passing of the important law concerning exchange societies, of which the Riga Exchange Society (founded in 1816) was the most active. By the law of 1923, one-fifth of the members of the highly influential "Committee of the Exchange of Riga," could be of non-Latvian nationality, though of Latvian citizenship. The importance of this concession, which acknowledged the German control of this exchange in effect ever since its founding, lay in the fact that the Riga Exchange Committee was the chief advisor to the Ministry of Finance on questions of economic legislation. The export and import trade, banking, and shipping were in its hands, a control which soon tended to become once more exclusively German. No Jewish merchants were ever elected to the committee, and such Latvians as were allowed to come up for election were chosen from a group ready to compromise with German-Balt interests. The Riga Exchange Society also had its own bank, which enjoyed credit privileges from the state bank. Not until 1939 was this institution truly democratized.

The prevalence of German-Balt interests in banking and the export and import trade was partly the work of those Latvian politicians who courted public opinion abroad by exhibiting their broadmindedness toward national minorities. They were sensitive to the continued accusation of "chauvinism" directed against the Latvians in the press of both the Russian and German minorities. Foreign financial interests were offered inducements to invest in what the German-controlled big business and commercial circles hoped might prove to be a boom in heavy industry and trade. However, at this point, the unnatural political alliance of the non-Latvian financial interests with the Latvian Socialists proved awkward, scaring off any marked interest on the part of foreign capital. Of the foreign investors, the largest was Germany, with 25 million lats, the next England with 16 million lats, and the third Sweden with 11 million lats. Many of these investments were a continuation of pre-war policies. Some 25 per cent of foreign capital found its way into private banks and commerce, leaving little for the building of industry. Almost all foreign credits were in the hands of the national minorities.

Needless to say those organizations and enterprises owned or controlled by alien minority interests did not favor the employment of Latvian stock. The key positions in the Riga public utilities were in German hands, a reflection of pre-war control. Private banks, as well as many commercial establishments, offered jobs to members of national minority groups rather than to the younger Latvian generation. Tobacco manufacturers, for the most part Jewish, employed Baltic Russians almost exclusively, as did the ceramics factories, which were mostly owned by Russians enjoying Latvian citizenship.

This ascendancy of non-Latvian interests in the economic field contributed not a little to the unemployment which began to make itself felt in Latvia toward the end of the twenties. Equally detrimental to the maintenance of the sound national economy originally planned

by the members of the Constituent Assembly was the attitude of the
Latvian Social-Democrats toward the Soviet Union, a romance destined to terminate in serious disillusionment for the Left Wing vision-
aries, and in grave economic difficulties for their country, whose course
they had so naively tried to set by the Red Star in the East.

Latvian-Soviet relations, as we have seen, had early been conditioned
by the Latvian need for peace with her neighbors and for drastic
economic reconstruction after her ruinous wars. The faith of the Latvian leaders in their people's continued desire and capacity for independence and national unity had mitigated what qualms they might
have experienced in regard to possible Communist pressures. That
same incautious pride in democratic tolerance which had opened the
political and economic gates to the unpatriotic national minorities,
had hopefully welcomed the economic promises and agreements proffered by the U.S.S.R. Soviet trade representatives made ready to han-
dle a heavy quota of imports and exports in Riga. A concession was
issued for a Soviet Transit Bank. Processing plants were established
in Riga for the conversion of Soviet timber to be floated down the
Daugava. This timber constituted the bulk of Soviet transit in the
middle twenties. The grain which was to have been exported via the
largest grain elevator in the world erected at Ventspils, never materialized, nor did the other promised Soviet exports. But promises were
still forthcoming. It was suggested that the situation might be improved by evidence of a "friendlier" attitude on the part of the
Latvian Government, for instance in permitting the publication of a
pro-Soviet newspaper. This concession was granted, and a few head of
cattle or pigs were occasionally purchased by the U.S.S.R. to nurse
the expectations of the Latvian farmers.

The Leftist Latvian Cabinet of 1927 concluded with the Soviet
Union a commercial treaty wherein the U.S.S.R. agreed to purchase
certain products of Latvian heavy industry, such as refrigerator cars,
if Latvia could arrange for long-term credits and reestablish certain
export industries. By 1929, after considerable capital had gone into
the refounding of these export industries, the Soviet Trade Commissioner had ceased to buy any Latvian goods, on the excuse of "unfriendliness" in the Latvian press, and frontier police and judicial
restrictions, purportedly also unfriendly to "friends of the Soviet Red
Army." At the same time, Soviet officials were spreading rumors in
French, British, and German economic and financial circles that the
lack of Baltic port facilities was what was hampering Russian trade.

No word of the highly advantageous transit terms and port and harbor services repeatedly offered by the Latvian Government and invested in by the Latvian people was allowed to appear in the Soviet press; nor was the fact that Russia's quota of export goods was so low that her own port of Leningrad was operating at only thirty per cent capacity.

Neither the so-called "unfriendliness" of the Baltic peoples, nor a lack of transit and port facilities, nor even the serious dearth of Soviet exports were at the bottom of the falling-off of Russian commerce which proved such a disappointment to certain factions in Latvia. Even in Tsarist times, Russia's foreign trade had begun to shift from the Baltic to the Black Sea routes, so that by 1913 seven times more grain was shipped over the Black Sea than through the Baltic. In 1935, 47 per cent of the Soviet foreign trade turnover was via the Black Sea, with only 25 per cent passing through Leningrad and Archangel. A mere 200,000 odd tons, mostly timber, was in transit through the Baltic ports. Agricultural products, which had constituted the bulk of Russian export tonnage through these ports in the first decade of the twentieth century, were no longer available for export. The industrial raw materials, constituting about 60 per cent of the Soviet exports in 1937, were produced near and shipped via the Black Sea ports. The U.S.S.R.'s policy of cutting down on imports, limiting them chiefly to machinery, also adversely affected her shipping in the Baltic. Taking into consideration these facts, together with the basic reorientation of Russian commercial and industrial interest to the Middle and Far East, it becomes evident that expectations of the maintenance, let alone the increase of Soviet trade in the Baltic, were not solidly founded. Communist clamorings for more Baltic ports were to be based on strategic rather than commercial demands.

The government expenditures, and the political compromises in the divided Saeimas and unstable cabinets elicited by these mistaken hopes in Latvian-Soviet mutual benefit rapprochement had not left a hopeful impression on the Latvian people as a whole. They saw the expensive harbor installations lying idle; their agricultural produce without an eastern market; and the big artificial export industries closing down. The Left Wing politicians, still dallying with Soviet promises, demanded public works and social welfare for the increasing number of Latvian unemployed.

The situation was aggravated by the onset of the world economic crisis, which was to have its repercussions in the Baltic States. In

Latvia, overindustrialization, credit inflation, an excess of middlemen, expensive government experiments, the neglect of agrarian interests, and the lack of a truly national economic policy, all began to tell by 1928, following the costly ventures of the 1927 Cabinet.

Undeniably, the successive coalition governments had found themselves unable to promulgate any far-reaching policies. For the most part, accidental measures resulted from their attempts to balance the demands of the more vociferous party politicians. This had often led to robbing Peter to pay Paul. Public works, subsidies, and experiments in state ownership, conducted not in accordance with the will of a united nation, but haphazardly to assuage threatening special interests, entailed great expenditures for which the farmers and small business men paid with high taxes and lack of credit. The economic, and to a degree political flirtation of the Left Wing parties with the Soviet Union, instead of benefiting the Latvian working class, brought on them unemployment and high prices; while the few increments from the expanded industries went into the pockets of the alien Latvians who had organized them with government credit. The national minority merchants, rather than support the Latvian farmer, imported cheaper grain from abroad. State control was set over the export of butter, fruit, meat, and other comestibles in order to improve their quality, and a state sugar factory was planned for the processing of beets; but cheap credit to farmers and to farmer cooperatives for improvement purposes was not available. Prices for consumer goods remained high, since small local industries for home consumption had not been developed as originally planned, and Latvian agricultural products were not yet produced cheaply enough to guarantee imports of industrial products.

Although many of the promises made to the farmers in the early years of national independence had not been realized, much had been accomplished by the cooperatives and other self-help organizations. Persistent efforts had been made to obtain improved cattle, seed, fertilizers, and agricultural machinery. The centuries-old habits of good husbandry and rural pride had resulted not only in the gradual modernization of farms, but in the continued maintenance of roads, schools, churches, and public buildings. The Latvian land, faithfully served by its energetic and devoted owners, had fully recovered from the devastation of war, and continued to produce with increasing efficiency at a time when the overly-ambitious industrial program was breaking down. Beginning in 1929, when state financial reserves, called

upon to support private banks, failing industries, civic enterprises, and
the import of luxury goods, were dwindling seriously, the Farmer
Union party was gaining in prestige. Two members of this party, H.
Celmiņš and Kārlis Ulmanis, held the portfolio of Prime Minister
from 1928 to 1931.

The world-wide financial crisis which struck in 1929 caught the
Latvian economy off balance. Much of the capital in her banks was
of foreign origin. When a credit crisis broke on Germany in early
July 1931, there was a sudden withdrawal of gold and credit reserves
from Latvian banks. This became so serious that only a banking
moratorium, imposed on July 21, saved Latvia's financial structure
from collapse. The way back to stability was to be a hard one. Shaken
Leftists and national minorities offered no objection to the emergency
legislation inspired by Kārlis Ulmanis. Contingent-quotas were placed
on certain import goods, favoring such home products as textiles,
paper, sugar, etc., while at the same time import credits were shifted
from luxuries to such necessities as fertilizers, machinery, and a number of basic industrial products. Special premiums and export credits
were supplied to encourage the flagging Latvian export trade. A state
grain and flour import monopoly insured a market for the locally
grown products. Rye and wheat even began to move to foreign markets. The production of wool and flax was fostered, together with local
textile industries. The credit policy of the state bank was adjusted to
favor agricultural necessities. Private banks were forced to guarantee
their deposits by placing securities in the state bank, which then re-
guaranteed the private deposits, thus averting disastrous runs on the
banks. Overcredited industrial establishments were put in the hands of
special business administrators in order to save as much production as
possible and thus avoid further unemployment. At the same time a
number of speculative enterprises were closed down. Since no loans
could be obtained from abroad, budgetary expenses were cut, particularly the salaries of government officials.

This economic reform policy, which had averted a major financial
and industrial crisis, seemed endangered by the elections of 1931,
which once more produced twenty-four political parties for what
promised to be a Saeima on the old pattern of confusion, corruption,
and compromise. Some of the small parties believed in good faith that
their multiplicity represented the flowering of democracy. Variety as
well as freedom of opinion, they felt, produced the supple and responsive political machinery which a modern nation required. Intel-

lectuals enjoyed the voting choice offered their discriminating tastes. Many of them were more alarmed by any suggestion of enforced national unity than they were by the boundless opportunity which the present system offered to non-patriotic interests, both economic and political. Many believed sincerely that the small Latvian nation had achieved enough natural cohesion to be able to afford the luxury of a multi-party system and parliamentarianism pushed to the extreme.

It was this continued optimism, together with the hardheaded and far less diffuse interests of the Left Wing and national minority blocs, which defeated the 1933 proposal of the Farmer Union party for a moderate constitutional reform. It was the firm conviction of this party and its leader Ulmanis that without such a reform, which would have reduced the number of political parties, the economic gains of the early thirties could not be stabilized. Blocked by the indifference or confusion of the small Saeima parties, and by the categorical denouncement of the Socialists, Left-Centerists, and national minorities, the measure was crippled to the extent of eliminating any possibility of a constitutional reform at this time.

A more immediate realization of the sinister political fruits which had sprung from the soil of economic disintegration was needed before public opinion veered in favor of a simpler representative structure and a stronger executive. Like all reforms too long delayed, the measures finally adopted were to be more extreme and more offensive to the liberals than the program first proposed. National unity was to come, but with a flavor of the political realism and budding faith in authoritarianism of the thirties, rather than the experimentation and effervescence which had characterized the too elastic decade of Saeima rule.

Chapter 18

National Unity

THE wave of authoritarianism which swept over many of the Western democracies in the thirties rose from a widespread political disillusionment born of acute economic insecurity. In those nations where the multi-party ballot bred the political bloc system and weak coalition cabinets, public opinion found vent for its uneasiness in blaming the faction-ridden parliaments where the deputies of organized vested interests wrangled to obtain unstable and unrepresentative majorities. The people came to look upon themselves as grossly betrayed by their politicians, whom they had elected but over whom they had no control in ultra-liberal parliaments. Constitutions written in the early twenties had left many heads of state at the mercy of the untrammeled legislatures. These, having generally failed to curb or remedy a terrifying economic depression, were now freely, if not always fairly, blamed for the origin and spread of the crisis. An unfettered executive authority with emergency powers made a strong appeal to peoples confounded by free-for-all politics.

In all three of the Baltic States a reaction against parliamentarianism set in; early, in the case of Lithuania, with the *coup* of December 1926; eight years later, and, almost simultaneously in Estonia and Latvia, where authoritarian régimes were installed in March and May of 1934, respectively. The post-war constitutions of these republics had been primarily concerned with asserting the sovereign power of the people, and establishing a delicate system of checks on the executive by the legislatures. The close involvement of these two powers entirely prevented any strong or consistent course of action in times of national emergency.

Such a sense of emergency arose in Latvia when the Left Wing parties and those of the national minorities angrily opposed the Farmer Union proposals for a constitutional reform, which would have reduced the scope of political representation and, by strengthening the executive power, rendered it freer of party politics. National tension mounted with the bitterness of the parliamentary debate on this issue. When certain representatives spoke in the Saeima of sending armed forces into the streets, the spectre of civil war began to haunt the more pessimistic Latvians.

The dread of violence was fanned by the attitude of extremists in both the Left Wing and conservative camps. A Communist *coup* had not been considered impossible since the *Putsch* of December 1924 in Estonia, when Russian workers employed in a Soviet trading organization and Estonian Communists commingled with a number of alien agitators sought to possess themselves of official buildings in Tallinn. Mistrust of Bolshevik sympathizers had grown with the formation of the Latvian Peasants' and Labor bloc which was discovered to have prepared a Communistic overthrow of the Government, and all of whose members were accordingly impeached for high treason in the autumn of 1933. Some were arrested, while others fled abroad.

At the same time, the so-called "Organization of Labor Sport" of the Social-Democrats was suppressed on the grounds that it was a disguised politico-military organization. The increasingly revolutionary tone of the Social-Democratic party was emphasized by their erection in Riga, on the pattern of the Viennese socialist building projects, of strategically placed workers' block-houses and clubs, suitable for use as arsenals or fortresses in any eventual uprisings.

These threatening manifestations of the extreme Left had their counterpart in certain National Socialist manifestations in the German style on the Right. An offshoot of the Conservative-Nationalists were the *Pērkoņkrustieši*, or Thundercross (Swastika) nationalists, also known as the Legionnaires. Their leader was G. Celmiņš, and their membership consisted of militarists and young chauvinists. By 1934, both the "Organization of Labor Sport" and the *Pērkoņkrustieši*, as extra-legal political groups working outside the Saeima, appeared ready to seize power.

A third element of disloyalty was that of the clandestine "Hitler youth." Small groups of these Nazis were beginning to maneuver at night, with the cooperation and approval of many of the German-Balts. The latter, in close touch with the rearming Third Reich, were gleefully prepared to fish in the troubled waters of Communist plots and Saeima deadlock.

The same atmosphere of economic depression and sinister political threats which had inspired the Päts *coup* in Estonia, on March 12, 1934, brought on the Latvian constitutional crisis of May 15. On that day, acting under Article 62 of the Constitution, the Cabinet of Ministers in the persons of Premier Kārlis Ulmanis and the Minister of War,

General Jānis Balodis, issued a decree declaring a state of siege in Latvia.

The Cabinet, under Article 81 of the Constitution, assumed the right to issue regulations with the force of law. One of its first measures was the dissolution of the Saeima and of all political parties, including that of the Farmers' Union. The Government then took temporary control of public buildings, the state bank, and communication centers. A group of Leftist deputies to the Saeima were placed under protective custody, but later released. On May 16 was promulgated the Declaration of the Government of National Unity, signed by Ulmanis and countersigned by General Balodis, both leading founders of Latvia's independence.

This Declaration recognized "the necessity for declaring a state of emergency throughout the Republic and for taking extraordinary steps to protect internal order within the Republic." Reference was made to "the growing tension of the domestic political state of affairs"; to the distrust of the people in their elected representatives; to "a dangerous indifference . . . regarding the fate of the State, and a sense of insecurity about the future . . ."; and to the "disgust and indignation" felt in extensive circles, particularly among the youth, for the Saeima and its weltering political parties. The unresponsiveness of the elected deputies to the will of the whole nation was illustrated by their failure to "create a new basis for state legislation and administration." After the people's frustration in the matter of a constitutional reform, the government considered it its duty "to take the necessary steps for security before the internal tension has broken out into struggles among the citizens themselves." The government, it was asserted, was also motivated in its present action "by considerations based upon an appraisal of the present international state of affairs," there being "not the slightest doubt that anxiety and a sense of insecurity continue to grow among nations."

The Declaration wound up with the affirmation that "our action is not aimed against Latvian democracy, but wishes to prevent party strife from suppressing the sound national spirit and will of the nation. The Government desires only to create as soon as possible conditions under which this spirit and this will may be freely expressed, and to permit the rebirth of unanimity and a national consciousness which will . . . again give us a united, strong and free Latvia."

The third President of the Republic, Alberts Kviesis (1930-1936), swayed by what appeared on the whole to be an enthusiastic and sincere popular reception of the Declaration of National Unity, did not put the dissolution of the Saeima to a referendum. On May 18, the reorganized Cabinet of National Unity, with Kārlis Ulmanis as Prime Minister and Minister of Foreign Affairs, assumed the legislative functions of the Saeima until the completion of the constitutional reform. The laws adopted by this legislative cabinet, except for administrative decrees, were to be promulgated by the President of the Republic, in accordance with the presidential decision of June 8.

The political history of Latvia between the establishment of this moderate authoritarian régime and the outbreak of the Second World War was undramatic. The Army Law of January 1, 1935, appointed the President of the Republic Supreme Commander of all the armed forces. The law of March 19, 1936, provided that upon the expiration of Kviesis' second term of office in April of that year, he should be succeeded by Kārlis Ulmanis who would hold office until the termination of the constitutional reform. Many parts of the Constitution of 1922 were still in force, notably those concerning the judiciary, and the powers of the cabinet and the president. A corporative form of government came into effect with the formation, in January 1936, of a National Economic Council, made up of the elected boards of the newly created chambers of commerce, industry, agriculture, artisans, and labor. A State Cultural Council was also created, consisting of the boards of the Chamber of Professions, and the Chamber of Literature and Art. These councils were allowed to collaborate with the respective governmental departments, individually and jointly. The two National Councils constituted the Joint Economic and Cultural State Council, which was convoked by the President of the Republic, and worked in close collaboration with the Cabinet of Ministers. The Joint State Council represented all sections of the nation, including the national minorities. It passed resolutions by simple majority vote of its members.

The reorganization of the producing population on a guild basis was paralleled by a readjustment in municipal and rural self-government, where elections were now held along guild rather than political lines. A new communal law provided for an organic coordination between the various corporative chambers and the self-governing territorial administrations. It was generally conceded at the time that the direct participation of every producing socio-economic group in the governmental machinery insured that national unity which both public opinion and the men in office sought as a remedy for the current ills and a new foundation for the future security of the state.

The character of the Latvian "dictatorship" was determined by the personality and experience of the chief of state, and by the ancient national qualities of the Latvian people. The tested democratic convictions of Kārlis Ulmanis, his commitment to the increasing welfare and continued independence of the nation to which he had long devoted his best energies, furnished the Latvians with a sense of security against any greed for personal power on the part of their leadership. Although certain "old soldiers" had for a time concerned themselves with politics, bringing with them the tincture of fascism, the absence of sustained political persecution and the government's persistent appeal to youth to participate freely and without regimentation in the new order suggested that liberalism had not suffered a total eclipse. Particularly reassuring was the continued encouragement of cooperative societies, where Latvian self-reliance and non-political action had long had its most satisfactory outlet. Labor found itself strengthened against the grumblings of the Social-Democrats by the steady development of the trade union movement. While there were those who openly deplored the introduction of the corporate state, and many who could justifiably hope for the return to a rational parliamentarianism based on a modified constitution, there was little organized opposition to either the temper or the tactics of the hard-working Cabinet of National Unity. The Latvians as a whole had confidence in the men, a number of them fighters and leaders in the early days of the Republic, who conducted the authoritarian régime, as well as in their own capacity to forge a sound nation, given the proper realization of their common interests by their governors. For the time being, unity of effort and aims seemed more essential than a centrifugal degree of freedom.

If the new Constitution was not completed, and if the authoritarian rule was more enduring and more pervasive than had been expected, a large degree of blame must be placed on the mounting threats to international peace and to the continued existence of the small and vulnerable nations from the larger dynamic neighbors of Latvia, Nazi Germany, and Soviet Russia. When martial law finally lapsed in February 1938, a new Law for the Defense of the State took its place, bestowing extraordinary powers on the Minister of the Interior in matters regarding freedom of the press and person, and the rights of assembly and association. This tightening of controls, a disappointment to liberal opinion, was accepted with resignation at a time when German Fifth Column activities were agitating the Latvian nation,[1] and Soviet Russia was preparing to attack Finland. Work on remodeling the constitution went on, but before laws governing the election of the Saeima and the president and the formation of the cabinet could be promulgated, Russian troops were once more on Latvian soil.

By 1940, an impressive amount of legislation had been put into effect. In general, its emphasis was on economic recovery and stability, with particular attention to agriculture, and on a degree of government control compatible with the enduring Latvian demand for private property and enterprise, individual business initiative, and self-government.

The initial steps taken in the early thirties to check the economic depression were supplemented by a number of decrees intended to stabilize the gains and complete the reorganization of Latvia's economy. Credit inflation remained a crucial problem. The national budget, taxes, excises, loans, imports and exports, credit institutions, and commercial establishments now all came in for government consideration and, in many cases, control. Speculation was radically attacked by a law requiring the registration of all commercial and industrial enterprises and their licensing through the Ministry of Finance. In 1935, the newly created Latvian Credit Bank began the liquidation of insolvent private credit and banking institutions and of speculative and unsound industrial concerns. By the beginning of 1938, the Credit Bank had a paid up capital of forty million lats, its largest shareholders being the Ministry of Finance, the Postal Savings Bank, and several independent funds of the Finance Ministry. As the leading financial and economic institution in Latvia, whose influence reached into almost every industrial, commercial and agricultural activity, the Credit Bank was responsible for the recovery of public confidence in banking institutions.

The government, through the Latvian Credit Bank and through the licensing activities of the Ministry of Finance, launched an intensive program to foster a variety of export and a large number of home industries. This move was prompted in large measure by the growing restrictions on international trade which turned Latvia into the expensive path of self-sufficiency. By discouraging speculative export

[1] C. L. Lundin's study "The Nazification of the Baltic German Minorities" in *Journal of Central European Affairs*, VII (1947), 1-28, is based on an acute perception of the aims of the German Fifth Column.

enterprises, by backing new industrial and commercial undertakings in the form of joint-stock companies, and encouraging small, financially weak concerns to consolidate, the Credit Bank guided Latvia's industrial economy away from a precarious heavy-industry export program to a diversified system of small local industries closely related to her agricultural production. In 1937, 32.5 per cent of the 5,717 industrial enterprises in Latvia processed raw materials produced by agriculture.

Leading the export list were the foodstuff and timber industries. Centralized organization in the form of joint-stock companies, with the full participation of farmer cooperatives, governed the export of bacon, butter, cheese, eggs, seeds, hides, flax, wool, and other agricultural products. Timber and its by-products, which in some years formed about 40 per cent of the total value of Latvia's exports, furnished considerable income to the state, which, in 1939, owned 79.57 per cent of the forests. Also in the export market were the leather and textile industries. The quarry, mining, metallurgical, and chemical industries were geared rather for domestic consumption, which mounted as the nation sought to supply her own industrial machinery needs and embarked on a major building and improvement program. A marked aptitude for technical specialization came to the fore in the artisanship and industrial expansion which was soon to produce 24 per cent of the national income. Among Latvia's manufactured goods were automobiles, small airplanes, tank locomotives, streetcars, rail- and refrigerator cars, radios, refrigerators, cameras, shoes, pottery, and glassware.

Putting the national economy into high gear required an intensive development of power, for which the two prime sources were water and peat, timber being conserved for export. Swedish experts were consulted and Swedish financing solicited for the construction of a huge power station at the rapids of Kegums on the Daugava, thirty miles south of Riga. The loan extended to "Kegums" by the Swedish Bank represented the biggest participation of foreign capital in Latvian industry. Construction on the project, started in August 1936, was completed in four years. Several smaller hydro-electric plants were also built to take full advantage of Latvia's many rivers.

While industrial reorganization and development received concentrated attention from a government which had been brought into power by economic crisis, it was agriculture which could hope for the most rewards from the triumph of the Farmers' Union party. Such emphasis might well be regarded as reflecting the true will of the majority, since 63.50 per cent of Latvia's population in 1935 lived in rural areas, 60 per cent being engaged in some form of rural occupation, against the 13 per cent engaged in industry. In that year there were 237,500 farms in Latvia, with a large proportion practicing diversified farming. Closely connected with farming were a number of rural industries and crafts located in the small country towns and converting agricultural products with a minimum of intermediary services. By 1939, about 60 per cent of the land was under cultivation. Agriculture contributed 40 per cent of the national income, provided about 35 per cent of the raw materials for local industries, and constituted the major part of the export trade.

The Ministry of Agriculture, in close collaboration with the Chamber of Agriculture (whose members were directly elected by the populations of the rural districts), sponsored and directed an intensive agricultural development program in the six years of freedom which remained to the Latvian people. Government experts worked at all times in cooperation with the agricultural societies which existed in all of the 517 rural communes, and with the numerous farmer cooperatives.

Land improvement, a problem uppermost in the public mind ever since the achievement of national independence, was given additional impetus by the large-scale construction of drainage works and of river regulation by the state. Subsidies were made available for soil improvement. Much educational work was done both by government experts and by land improvement societies, of which there were 2,300 in 1939 with a membership of 70,000 farmers.

Intensification of crop production, which had already received some attention from the agricultural societies, was closely related to the production, distribution, and use of fertilizers and adequate farm machinery. The government was empowered to inspect the latter in the factories, as well as to make loans to the farmers or to their cooperative societies for the purchase of both light and heavy agricultural machinery.

Agricultural credits, both long- and short-term, were available at the State Agrarian Bank, the Bank of Latvia, and the Farmers' Credit Bank, founded in 1935. The rate of interest varied from two to four per cent per annum with small additional administrative charges. Both private individuals and agricultural associations were eligible for these advantageous loans. In 1938 agricultural indebtedness amounted altogether to 292.2 million lats, which, mainly as a result of remission effected by the State Agrarian Bank, represented a decrease of 42 million lats from the 1933 figure.

In addition to the national credit establishments, the cooperative credit societies played a large part in regularizing the rural economy. This form of credit was one of the oldest cooperative economic enterprises in Latvia. By 1937 there were 503 credit and savings cooperative associations, and the following year showed an impressive increase in membership and aggregate deposits.

Cooperatives, both cultural and economic, were a time-honored feature of Latvia's self-helpful and community-minded society. During the thirties they became highly influential in the development of a more scientific and more profitable agriculture. The year 1937, in addition to the above-mentioned loan and savings associations and 448 mutual insurance societies, numbered 184 consumer cooperatives, 258 cooperative dairies, 228 agricultural machinery cooperative associations, 54 peat-producing associations, 24 cooperative distilleries, and 18 fishermen societies. Subsequently, these figures suffered some reduction due to a movement of amalgamation. Centralized unions were favored by the government, which exercised both supervision and a degree of control over the cooperative movement by its inspection and credit policies. The services of the Ministry of Agriculture's Research Institute were available to the cooperatives as well as to the individual farmer.

The government, working through these organizations and directly with the farmers, regulated both the production and marketing of agricultural produce. The quantity, quality, and variety of crops all came in for a degree of control. The Latvian farmer, a jealous proprietor but progressive cultivator, accepted "advice" on where, when, and how much to plant. Price ceilings on chemical fertilizers, agricultural machinery, and building materials encouraged farm improvement, while guaranteed higher prices for quality produce, together with export subsidies combined with rigid government inspection, spurred on the growing of crops fit for foreign markets. Certain crops, such as cereals, flax, hemp, sugar-beets, and potatoes for alcohol production, were purchased by government authorities; while others were handled by joint-stock companies, the majority of whose shares were held by farmers or their cooperative societies. Bacon, dairy, and poultry products, honey, hides, wool, seeds, fishery products, vegetables, and fodder were all exported through these associations, which had to meet the rigid standards set by the government for all agricultural produce offered for export. Leading the list on the foodstuffs export list were butter, flax, and bacon. Present for the first time on this list were wheat and rye, in contrast to previous decades when grains had to be imported for Latvian consumption.

Particularly impressive was the improvement in horse, cattle, pig, and poultry raising, all of which had suffered drastic ravages during the war. The establishment of numerous inspection societies and breeding stations provided an exportable surplus of breeding stock, as well as the high-quality butter, bacon, and eggs which were to restore Latvia's foreign markets for these products.

The managed economy of the National Unity régime, while offensive to enthusiasts of laissez faire and unlimited competition, and disturbing to those who dreaded the trend toward state capitalism, met no organized opposition from the farmers, industrial workers, and entrepreneurs, who witnessed a rapid swing away from depression into an unparalleled prosperity. The farmer enjoyed cheap credit and, for many of his crops, a guaranteed market and government subsidies. His income was at last in favorable adjustment to the price of consumer goods, which, under an intensified program of industrialization, were beginning to be produced in quantity. Material gathered by the League of Nations indicated that, among the northern European nations, Latvia held the leading position in industrial recovery. In addition to such obvious indices as the rise in employment, the rise in prices and production, and the consequent improvement in the standard of living, the economic recovery is interpretable in terms of national income and wealth, the balance of payments, and a favorable balance of trade.[2]

The national income, which had dropped from 926 million lats in 1927 to 754 million in 1932, passed the two billion mark in 1938. The budgetary needs of the state had been adequately met, even in times of depression, since reserves were on hand. The National Unity Government practiced rigid economy in order to meet the expanding needs of the state, 54.03 per cent of whose income was provided by customs and stamp duties, excises, real estate and investment taxes; 40.21 per cent from state monopolies and enterprises; and 5.76 per

[2] There is a summary of finances and economy of the Baltic States in *The Baltic States: Estonia, Latvia, Lithuania* (Royal Institute of International Affairs, London, 1938), pp. 154-189.

cent from personal income taxes. By 1940, the total national wealth had attained the figure of 9 billion lats, or 3,000 lats per capita, with 40 per cent owned, either directly or indirectly, by the state.[3]

The Latvian National Bank's assets in gold and foreign currencies rose from 45 million lats in gold bullion and 3.2 million lats in foreign exchange in 1934, to 87.7 million in gold and 37.9 in foreign exchange in 1939. This increase was due in part to a devaluation of the lat and its pegging to the pound, in September 1936, at the rate of 25.2215. This joining of the sterling bloc was equivalent to the abandonment of the gold standard, a step which reacted favorably on the Latvian economy as a whole.

Of crucial importance to the balance of international payments was the foreign trade balance. The credit crisis, more marked in Latvia than in the other two Baltic States, was in good part attributable to the large quantity of merchandise imports which that nation required. It was in the trough of the world depression that Latvia learned the hard lesson that a nation which must import heavily and whose few exports are subject to suddenly diminishing markets, is economically oversensitive. A rigid control of foreign trade began in 1932, emphasizing a sharp curtailment of imports to save foreign exchange in the face of falling prices and the gradual exclusion of Latvian agricultural and semi-manufactured goods from France and their subjection to quotas in Great Britain and Germany. Tariff and import quotas, and the requirement of import licenses, implemented the dual policy of preserving foreign exchange and launching Latvia into the paths of self-sufficiency. In 1932 and again in 1936 and 1937, Latvia showed a favorable balance of trade. This activation of her foreign trade was closely related to the new program of diversification and intensification in both industrial and agricultural production. Timber, peat, and textiles, among other resources, were exported both in the form of raw materials and as finished goods. Foodstuffs found a renewed market, as necessities and luxuries. Together with the other two Central Baltic States, Latvia belonged to the small group of foodstuffs-surplus countries, and found herself a natural purveyor to Great Britain and continental Europe. The trade agreement concluded with the United Kingdom in 1934 assured Latvia of an unrestricted market in that area for certain agricultural products, chiefly bacon and butter; in return for these she undertook to import 70 per cent of her coal from

[3] A. Schwabe, *The Story of Latvia and her Neighbors*, p. 36.

the United Kingdom, and to reduce duties on British textiles, iron and steel goods.

Latvia's trade was Western-oriented, as the following figures for 1939 indicate: In terms of percentage of the total, Latvia imported 20.8 from and exported 41.9 to the United Kingdom; she imported 38.9 from and exported 29.5 to Germany; with the United States the relation was, imports 6.3, exports 1.4; while with the Soviet Union it was, imports 3.5, exports 3.0.[4] Latvia's share in world trade, in 1938, was 0.19 per cent, with a population of two million; about one-fifth that of Soviet Russia, whose population was 170,000,000.

A considerable proportion of Latvia's exports were carried in her own merchant fleet, which had been steadily growing all through the period of independence. By 1939, she possessed 103 ships, with a total tonnage of about 200,000. The previous year, a direct shipping line had been opened to New York, where a Latvian-American Chamber of Commerce was established. Latvia's merchant marine, together with her fully-equipped harbors, constituted a very important part of her national wealth.

The official statistics indicate that by 1939 she was essentially self-supporting, and that the limits of her industrial, commercial and agricultural expansion had not yet been attained. Complete self-sufficiency would be neither practicable nor desirable since she did not possess the raw materials requisite for heavy industry or mechanized farming. By a canny use of what resources were hers, an all-out effort to secure stable foreign markets together with a proper respect for the domestic market, she appeared to have established a resistant economy, with industry and agriculture responsive to each other's demands, and both prepared to meet the requirements of foreign trade. The farmer, still the representative Latvian, found his purchasing power underwritten by price guarantees, subsidies, and cheap credit; while his consumer potential and his standard of living were raised by every encouragement to increase and improve his yields. With the financial situation firm, employment at a maximum, foreign trade and shipping expanding, prices and real income both rising, Latvia, together with the other Baltic States, had good reason to consider herself a socially and economically stable nation, fully able to contribute her share to the European community.

Although politically she had deviated from the strictly democratic

[4] *ibid.*

pattern, and economically she had abandoned the classic doctrines of laissez faire, Latvia could nevertheless lay claim to having espoused the increasingly vaunted "middle way." A delicate balance of individual and public interest, initiative and orderliness, adjusted the nation's essentially liberal spirit to an authoritarian régime. Private property and enterprise, protected at all times by the law, before which full equality and responsibility were enjoined, were subject to regulation wherever the national welfare was involved. The sense of freedom from past prejudices, of experimental "modernity" which, after the War, had engendered sweeping social, constitutional, and agricultural reforms, was modulated by the reasoned recognition of the government as a coordinating authority perhaps indispensable to a small nation in a stormy civilization. In turn, this willingness to accept a high degree of centralization and control, born of disillusionment with unlimited individualism, was colored by a keen spirit of cooperativeness, working through the ancient, self-regarding rural communities and the innumerable economic and cultural associations, reflecting a sense of togetherness which the government might applaud but not improve. The Latvian, in his hard-won independence and relative repose, rejected the socialist creed, claimed his private property and civil rights, cherished the spirit of individual initiative, enjoyed unregimented teamwork in all fields of activity, and could be persuaded to pay a certain political price for what he looked upon as national progress. He desired peace at home and abroad, a moderate and assured plenty, and above all mastery in his own land, to the extent of actively supporting a totalitarian régime if it were Latvian and if it seemed capable of raising a bulwark against either internal dissension or the sinister phantoms beginning to walk the German and Russian earth.

While political and economic reorientation were products of the uneasy thirties, social welfare and cultural development had indicated the steady pulse of the national life in its naturally liberal health all during the period of independence. Progressive legislation in the fields of labor relations, social security, and public hygiene, initiated in the twenties, received the fullest attention from the Government of National Unity.

Labor had little to complain of under a régime which, though opposed to radical opinion, protected trade unions and promoted the establishment of favorable working conditions. In the late twenties, Latvia had ratified four Conventions of the International Labor Organization dealing with workmen's compensation. Additional legislation and the creation of the Accident Insurance Board in 1939 further enlarged accident and occupational disease benefits. Industrial inspection was assured by law. Pensions, working hours and conditions, medical care, leaves, wages, and child labor were all regulated according to progressive standards.

Latvia stood second of 23 nations in volume of employment. Indeed, as an agricultural country, she was obliged, seasonally, to import farm workers, mostly from Poland. These aliens, amounting in some years to as many as 65,000, were allowed the full benefit of the high labor standards prevalent in Latvia.

The numerous, freely organized trade unions formed the National Chamber of Labor, whose elected board constituted part of the National Economic Council, on the same footing as the chambers of industry, commerce, and agriculture. In general, disputes between labor and management were settled by the state labor inspector, with the participation of the board of the appropriate national chamber. Strikes virtually ceased, thanks to the liberal labor legislation and the favorable relation of wages to commodity prices. After the reorganization of Latvia's post-depression economy, both the wage-earner and the farmer were soon in a position to lay away savings in banks which they could once more trust.

Pension and insurance laws were extended to cover a large number of the employed in all fields, including civil servants, army and navy personnel, and most branches of the intelligentsia. In imitation of the British system, all Latvian citizens who were indigent or invalided were entitled to welfare assistance from the central government or the municipalities. Child and maternity welfare received particular attention from government, municipal, and private organizations, all of which reflected the general esteem for a healthy and growing population. Numerous private organizations cooperated with the Ministry of Public Welfare and the public health departments of the municipalities in an extensive cradle-to-the-grave service, with medical, therapeutic, pharmaceutical, and dental assistance reaching every section of the population. This happy emphasis on hygiene as everybody's business was the concern of the Latvian Red Cross (founded in 1918), the Junior Red Cross, the Boy Scouts, and the *Mazpulki* ("little troops"), corresponding to the American 4-H clubs, of which there were over a thousand in Latvia by 1939. Markets and restaurants, industrial establishments and schools were all subject to regular inspection and control by state medical officers. Laws were passed for the control of venereal diseases and tuberculosis. Hospitals, health resorts, and rest homes dotted the country, and by 1938 Latvia had 1,566 physicians, 474 of them women.

Another field in which effort and success had been continuous since the achievement of independence was that of popular education. Its reconstitution on the basis of democratic principles and the newest pedagogic discoveries had been one of the first acts of the Latvian Government. The people had thrown their undivided support behind the intensive rebuilding of ruined schools and the erection of many new institutions. There emerged from this concerted effort one of the most modern educational systems in Europe. Instruction was in the Latvian tongue. It was free and compulsory for all children between the ages of six and fourteen. On the secondary school level tuition was required, but numerous scholarships were offered. The Latvians prided themselves on the absence of discrimination with regard to sex, religion, or national origin. The Education Law of 1934 extended the secondary school term from four to five years, placed greater responsibility on the headmasters, and gave the central administration more control over school affairs. Fifteen percent of the state budget was allotted to education.

The rapid development in this field is illustrated by comparative figures. In 1914, with a total population of 2,552,000, only 67 pupils out of 1,000 inhabitants were attending some sort of school. The census of 1920 found the population reduced to 1,596,131, with 80 school children for every 1,000 inhabitants. The number had reached 110 in 1925, 130 in 1935, and 137 by 1937. Expenditures per student and per inhabitant had quadrupled. Illiteracy, from 22 per cent in 1920, had dropped to 10.15 per cent in 1937. This figure included the relatively high number of illiterates near the Soviet border where White Russians and Russians were established. The figure 7 per cent would more nearly represent the illiteracy rating of the rest of the Latvian provinces.

Upon termination of, or in lieu of the five-year secondary school curriculum, a student might attend higher institutions of learning, vocational schools, or technical institutes. Many responded to these opportunities, reflecting the Latvians' high regard for the professions of teacher, pastor, agronomist, and physician, in that order. Agricultural schools, culminating in the Academy of Agriculture at Jelgava (separated from the State University in 1937), were particularly well attended, the number of students in all 59 agricultural institutions in

1939 totaling 1,542 boys and 1,822 girls. Many of these schools were on the secondary level of instruction, while others, especially in forestry and domestic economy, were more advanced. Mostly on the secondary school level were numerous professional institutes, including normal schools, and technical, commercial, navigation, and foreign language institutes. These, together with theological seminaries, schools of nursing, drama and music institutes, were financed by the state, the municipalities, or various societies. Adult education was promoted by fourteen people's universities and their branches, all approved in every respect by the powerful Ministry of Education.

The leading institution of higher learning was the State University at Riga, opened in 1919 in lieu of the old Polytechnic Institute, which had been evacuated during the War to Moscow, where it was liquidated after the advent of the Bolsheviks to power. During the period 1919-1940, the State University had a total of 9,209 graduates. To it were attached law, medicine, and both Lutheran and Roman Catholic theological faculties. It boasted an impressive library of some 320,000 volumes.

Also in Riga were the State Academy of Arts (successor to the old Riga Academy), with a strong emphasis on the technical aspects of the applied arts, particularly in the field of ceramics, and the State Conservatory of Music. This institution trained musicians for the schools, where every teacher in the lower grades was required to know at least one instrument, for the churches, the innumerable musical organizations, and the two Grand Opera houses. In 1936, the Latvian State Historical Institute was opened for research in Latvian history and as the foundation for a future Academy of Science. We have already mentioned the remaining institution of higher education, the State Academy of Agriculture at Jelgava.

Members of the faculties of the State University and of the Academy of Arts formed the Special Government Board for the Protection of Monuments. One of its enterprises was the organization of the Historical Museum, which was housed in a wing of the Presidential Palace in Riga. Another was the preservation of folklore, in connection with which it was preparing a monumental edition of the Dainas. The government also undertook the protection and restoration of historical buildings, among them the Ducal Palace at Jelgava, which had been destroyed by fire. It was restored with the help of students from the Academy of Arts at the cost of a million dollars, and subsequently turned over to the Academy of Agriculture.

At the instigation of President Ulmanis there was created a working fund entitled "the Fund for Fostering Culture" (*Kulturas Fonds*), which was outside the regular state budget, being supported by special taxes on tobacco, alcohol, and imported motion pictures. This fund was used to promote the creation of works and monuments of national culture; to award prizes for distinguished achievements in the cultural field; to support science, the arts, and literature, and to assist their practitioners in the production of their works. It granted sums for scholarships, research, publication, exhibition, the publication of textbooks and scientific works, the extension of libraries, for study abroad, for buildings, for lectureships, for subscriptions to learned journals, and for the support of symphony orchestras.

In addition to the *Kulturas Fonds*, the government established a fund for scientific research and another for historical research. A special endowment was also made for a "Gratitude Prize of the Nation," to be bestowed annually on the oldest and most notable representatives of the national cultural life.

Riga had long enjoyed an international reputation in the field of printing, the Latvian State Printing Office being one of the finest in northern Europe. The book-buying potential both of the general public and its institutions was revealed by the fact that, in the number of books in proportion to population, Latvia stood next to Denmark among European countries. By 1939 there were 1,911 school and 912 public libraries. Among the latter, the State Library in Riga counted 549,517 volumes. In January 1935 Premier Ulmanis appealed to the Latvian people to remember their schools with a gift. Within three and a half years, 1,302,000 volumes, together with 3,672 paintings and sculptures, and half a million lats in cash were presented.

During the twenty-two years of independence, 26,754 books were published. In 1937, of the 1,333 books appearing, 1,151 were in Latvian; also in Latvian were 137 out of 154 monthlies, 30 out of 34 weeklies, and 10 out of 13 daily newspapers. Latvian translators, most of them writers of merit, were intensively occupied with rendering ancient and European classics of every kind into the Latvian tongue. The public taste proved to be eclectic, and particularly open to the offerings of Western and Scandinavian Europe and of America.

Of the 255 Latvian authors mentioned in the *Latvian Encyclopedia* of 1938,[5] many were those same poets, dramatists, and novelists, whose young voices, emerging during the excitement of the National Awaken-

---

[5] *Latviešu konversācijas vārdnīca*, XI (Riga, 1938).

ing, had given such impetus to that movement. A number of them were writing for the National Theater, the Theater of Arts, and the National Opera, all in Riga and all state supported. The Classical Ballet of the Riga Opera gave performances all over Europe, and, together with the Opera proper, enjoyed the writing and composing talent of J. Mediņš, and A. and J. Kalniņš, whose colorful musical dramas were for the most part based on Baltic legends and folklore.

In 1929, Latvia lost her master poet, Jānis Rainis-Pliekšans, mentioned at length in a previous chapter. E. Virza (1883-1939) lived another ten years, and came to be venerated as the leading pastoral poet and novelist. K. Skalbe (1879-1945), poet in the classical style and author of children's tales which established him as the Hans Andersen of Latvia, was active during the era of independence; as were the lyric poets J. Akurāters (1876-1937) and V. Plūdonis (1874-1939).

In a small, teeming nation where no intellectual allowed himself to grow far removed from practicality and where achievement in any field was readily applauded by a public which felt itself, in an immediate sense, both audience and patron, the cross-fertilization of the arts was a common occurrence. Dramatists composed music. Authors (J. Jaunsudrabiņš, V. Eglītis) illustrated their own works. Painters (J. Siliņš, Z. Vidbergs) turned editor, or, as in the case of J. Muncis, producer. The leading landscapist of the period, V. Purvītis (1872-1945) was the first director of the busy Academy of Arts, with its numerous departments and its annual enrollment of 200 students. Graduates of this institution found ready employment in the schools, where design was eagerly studied; in the factories, especially textile and ceramics factories, jealous of their international reputation; and in numerous printing offices and lithographic institutes. Portrait and landscape paintings found ready purchasers even among the lower income brackets. A new generation of artists, among them Cielavs, Tone, Strunke, Liberts, Suta, and Tidemanis, faced a promising future. Fewer in number, but equally prized by their public, were the sculptors. We have already mentioned B. Dzenins and T. Zalkalns, both pupils of Rodin. K. Zale, who died in 1939, left to the nation a notable War Heroes Memorial Cemetery and a Memorial of Liberty, both in Riga.

Architecture found a powerful stimulus in the reconstruction which was required after the First World War. Riga, though more or less intact, was badly in need of modernization, while its ancient buildings, many of them dating back to the days of the Livonian Order, had to be restored or preserved with discrimination. To assist young students in acquiring a sense of the historical trends in Baltic architecture, the government established an open air Museum of Architecture near Riga, where ancient specimens of provincial architecture were transplanted and erected intact, under the guidance of P. Kundziņš, builder of several churches, and graduate of the former Riga Polytechnicum. Also graduates of this Institute were the distinguished architects E. Laube and A. Raisters, who, together with Kundziņš, joined the faculty of the State University. Most of the buildings erected in Riga during the period 1934-1940 escaped destruction during the German and Soviet invasions. Among them, the War Museum, the Ministry of Finance, the Palace of Justice, and the Social Club remain as stimulating examples of modern Baltic architecture.

Music, always to the fore in Latvian cultural life, was given ample support by the state, the municipalities, and a host of societies and organizations. It held a strong position in the curricula of the schools. Composing for the two lyric operas, in Riga and Liepāja, as well as for symphony orchestras which were heard often over Latvia's four broadcasting stations, were the above-mentioned J. Mediņš, and the Kalniņš (father and son), as well as Wolfgang Dārziņš, son of the popular composer Emīlis Dārziņš.

While the arts satisfied the lyric temperament and national spirit of the creative Latvians, the world of learning, particularly in the field of science, attracted the earnest and diligent Latvian scholar. The generation which had received its training at the Riga Polytechnic Institute (founded in 1862) at the University of Dorpat, or at Russian and German universities, hastened to offer their services to the State University at Riga and to other Latvian institutions of higher learning, where they were promptly set the tasks of organizing courses and research projects, writing much needed textbooks, and establishing laboratories and experiment stations. It was to the following scientists and scholars, well-trained and ardently dedicated to the advancement of learning in their homeland, that the University of Riga owed its rapidly acquired reputation: The philologist J. Endzelīns, who wrote the authoritative Latvian Grammar (*Lettische Grammatik*), published in 1922 in Heidelberg, revised K. Mühlenbach's Latvian-German Dictionary, and helped compile the 1932 edition of the *Dainas*; the historian J. Krodzinieks-Krigers; the ethnographer and folklorist P. Schmits; the archeologist F. Balodis, indefatigable organizer of Latvian excavations; A. Tentelis, first Director of the Latvian Historical Institute; the economist K. Balodis; B. Bīmanis, distinguished civil engineer and president of the Latvian Power Commission; Jēkabs Vītols, mathematician, president of the Latvian State Electric Factory; P. Kreišmanis, mineralogist and geologist, and first director of the State Agricultural Academy. These, together with many other philologists, folklorists, historians, economists, scientists, and technicians, most of whom had started their studies during the National Awakening, launched the University of Riga in its distinguished development. They directed the education of a younger generation of scientists (the chemist Dravnieks; the physicists Straumanis, Ieviņš, Janeks, Slaucītājs; the biologists Zīle, Prīmanis, Krimbergs; the archeologist Ginters, and the historian Dunsdorfs), who joined ranks with the elder generation to carry forward the work of the university and the scientific reputation of the Latvian nation under the university's motto: *Scientia et Patria*.

The results of Latvian research work were generally published as monographs in the Annals of the State University (*Acta Universitatis Latviensis*). The Latvian Historical Institute also published important researches in monographic form or in its quarterly, *Latvijas Vēstures Institūta Žurnāls*. International recognition was accorded its *Les sources de l'histoire de Lettonie*, the initial volume of which (1936) was devoted to the first Latvian political newspaper, the *Peterburgas Awihses* (1862-1865); while the second volume offered an exhaustive study of the sources of Latvian medieval history. Equally important to the national culture was the Latvian Encyclopedia, edited by A. Schwabe in collaboration with a group of scientists and scholars.

Over a long period of time many of the ablest Latvian minds had been attracted to the law, generally regarded as the basis of society and of the state. In 1933, a new Criminal Code was introduced, abolishing the death sentence. On January 1, 1938, the new Latvian Civil Code came into effect. The collective work of leading judges and lawyers, it consisted of 2,500 articles and constituted one of the most progressive civil codes in Western Europe. Its elaborations conformed to the principle of one law and equal justice for all Latvian citizens, the motto engraved on the walls of the Chief Court of the Senate, which was Latvia's Supreme Court.

In the sphere of religion likewise, a liberal spirit prevailed. Church and state were separated. The Church Law of December 13, 1934, recognized full freedom of religion, any group of 50 citizens being entitled to register as a denomination, and ten of such denominational groups being sufficient to form a national religious association. No single denomination was given special privileges or protection. All came under the supervision of the Department of Religious Affairs of the Ministry of the Interior. All were accorded public rights, including those of levying voluntary dues, owning buildings, and opening seminaries and schools, the latter being academically subject to the Ministry of Education. The Criminal Code of 1933 protected legally established communities of faith against profane acts, and also forbade political propaganda in the churches by members of the clergy or others. The figures for 1938 indicate that 56.15 per cent of the population were of the Evangelical Lutheran faith; 24.45 per cent were of the Roman Catholic; the Greek Orthodox religion claimed 8.94 per cent; the Russian Old Believers, 5.50; and the Hebrew, 4.79. Other sects had smaller followings. The failure of the Greek Orthodox faith to establish a firmer hold on the Latvian conscience, in spite of ample opportunity through the ages, has been regarded by some as another clear indication of the essential western-mindedness of the Latvian people. The Greek Orthodox Church in Latvia, the majority of whose members were Great Russians, separated from the Moscow Patriarchate and submitted directly to the Patriarch of Constantinople, who came personally to Riga in 1936 to consecrate the Metropolitan Archbishop of Latvia, who was of Latvian origin. Latvian origin for archbishops and bishops was also the stipulation of the Concordat signed with the Holy See in 1922, reestablishing the Roman Catholic Metropolitan Archbishopric in Riga, restoring monastic orders, permitting the Catholic faith to be taught again in the schools and Catholic educational institutions to be opened.

Economically restored, culturally enthusiastic, nationally united and self-confident, Latvia had reason to congratulate herself on the free use of her creative forces during the first two decades of her independence. She had carried through some major experiments. She had indulged in tonic if excessive magnanimity toward disaffected elements. She had taken certain lessons to heart, made vigorous use of a new broom at a time of crisis, and consolidated her gains. By the utmost use of her resources, human and material, she had achieved, at some expense, a degree of self-sufficiency which she had not originally envisaged or even desired.

But nothing could change her position as a small, externally vulnerable nation. We have now to consider, in contrast to the brightening scene of domestic progress, the clouds gathering over her international relations and the storms which finally washed away the

treasures of freedom and enterprise, of good will and good housekeeping, so painstakingly accumulated during the short span of national existence which she was allowed. Small peoples, living profitably
and breathing freely on the shores of the Baltic, were an offensive
anomaly to the amassed Teutons and Slavs whose colossal statism was
now prepared to crush the needless flowerings of unmilitant and therefore "undynamic" minor nationalities.

PART VI

AGAIN THE PREDATORY POWERS

Chapter 19

Betrayals and Invasions

THE hectic chiaroscuro of the interval between the World Wars induced what many of the uneasy peoples of the West looked upon as a creative effort on the part of the large and the lesser Powers to elaborate a pattern of collective security on the new loom of the League of Nations. Particularly anxious for the success of this activity were the new nations who occupied, in Toynbee's words, that "vast no man's land which the peace settlement . . . had left derelict in the great open spaces between Moscow and Berlin."[1] These succession states felt that not only their organic functioning within the European community but their continued existence in any terms might ultimately depend upon the toughness of the new defensive fabric, whose warp was the collective attitude toward aggression and whose woof must be a multitude of nonaggression, conciliation, and arbitration pacts and agreements. The Baltic States, incurably nervous by reason of their exposed and strategic position, showed a marked anxiety to nest their absolute neutrality in a tightly woven tissue of bilateral and multilateral guarantees.

During the twenty-two years of her independence Latvia signed over 300 agreements with foreign Powers, many of them concerned with economic matters, some of them defensive, and none aggressive in nature. For a perspective of her clear determination to throw her small but not inconsiderable weight on the side of peace, we must review her foreign relations through the period of Saeima rule and of National Unity, down to catastrophe's appointed time. For the era was not yet when the peace-potential of hope, good will, open diplomacy, and defensive democracy could contain the octopus of modern imperialism, which, with its multiple devices of deceit and death, surprised and strangled freedom where it stood.

In their ten-year Defensive Alliance of November 1, 1923, Latvia and Estonia had undertaken to "afford each other assistance, should either of them suffer an unprovoked attack on its present frontiers," and to "follow a wholly pacific policy, directed toward maintaining and

[1] A. Toynbee, *Survey of International Affairs*, 1936 (London, 1937), p. 10.

strengthening the bonds of friendship and developing their economic relations with other nations, more particularly with the Baltic States and neighboring countries."[2] A preliminary economic agreement signed at this time was elaborated into the treaty of February 5, 1927, appointing a mixed commission for the realization of a joint Customs Union and for the uniformization of various trade and economic practices within and between the two countries.[3] These early agreements were to remain unimplemented until February 17, 1934, when Latvia and Estonia signed a convention which put into effect their Defensive Alliance by regularizing the hitherto occasional meetings between their foreign ministers, and providing for joint action at all international conferences as well as for the establishment of a joint council for the coordination of legislation and the consideration of common political and economic action.[4]

Further Baltic rapprochement was precipitated by the Communist-inspired *coup* of December 1, 1924, in Tallinn. Supported by the concentration of several Soviet divisions near the Estonian border and by a naval squadron off Tallinn, hundreds of Communists in Estonian military uniforms had attempted to unseat the Estonian Government. Although their efforts were foiled by the quick action and loyalty of Estonian police and troops, the affair caused a flurry of dismay in all Baltic capitals. As a result of this tension, a revived interest was shown in the idea of a Baltic League, especially on the part of Poland, who saw her role in such a regional bloc as a dominant one.[5]

The project for such a league had had its incipience at the Paris Peace Conference, where Estonia had taken the initiative in drawing up plans for separate groupings of all the Baltic nations along lines of economic and political cooperation, with the basic objective of establishing a common defense system and guaranteeing the newly-won freedom of the Baltic Sea. The first Baltic Conference, meeting at Helsinki in January 1920 and attended by Finland, Estonia, Latvia, Lithuania, and Poland, had promoted the discussion of the neutralization of the Baltic, of a defensive union, and of a common foreign policy. The second conference at Bulduri and its aftermath have been considered in Chapter 17. Poland, who busied herself diplomatically with the whole area from the Black Sea to the Baltic, found her efforts

[2] *League of Nations Treaty Series*, XXIII, 82. Text of the Treaty reprinted in *Latvian-Russian Relations. Documents*, p. 246f.

[3] *League of Nations Treaty Series*, LXII, 319.

[4] *op.cit.*, CL, 104.

[5] cf. S. H. Thomson, Poland's "Foreign Relations" in *Poland*, p. 380f.

to consolidate the latter region nullified both by her own actions in Vilna and by Finland's leanings toward a Scandinavian bloc.

But by 1925, her hopes for a larger Baltic Union seemed again in the ascendancy. At a January meeting in Helsinki, Finland, the Central Baltic States, and Poland, all of whom dreaded further Communist machinations, reached a degree of understanding. With the exception of Lithuania, who attended only as an observer, all adhered to the Treaty of Conciliation and Arbitration concluded on January 17 and ratified on September 7, 1925.[6] While a Permanent Conciliation Commission was provided for, disputes among the signatories might also be directly submitted to the Court at The Hague. Latvia later signed similar conventions with Denmark and Sweden, with whom she also concluded a number of agreements regulating her ever-increasing economic and cultural relations with the Scandinavian countries.

The four-Power agreement of January 1925 was to remain largely inactive, owing to the abatement of Communist propaganda in the area, and to improved relations with Germany, who had signed arbitration pacts with Finland and Estonia. By August 1926, the Latvian Foreign Minister was expressing hopes of a closer alliance of the three central states. The extension of the Latvian-Estonian Customs Union, and arbitration, defense, and trade agreements to include Lithuania, had been the subject of conferences between the three states in May 1924, July 1925, and again in 1926. The delay in the consolidation of such an entente was caused by the elaborate configurations of the diplomatic dance in which the Soviet Union's indefatigable M. Litvinov engaged the energies of Poland and the Baltic States.

Between 1925 and 1933, the U.S.S.R. displayed considerable initiative in seeking to stabilize her position in regard to the nations on her northwestern frontiers by the conclusion of trade agreements and non-aggression pacts. Determined to present herself as the guardian of the Baltic, she wooed, in the person of the comforting Litvinov, the small democracies with all the reassuring formulae of their venerated League of Nations. And the greatest of these was neutrality, by which the Baltic States meant their right to abstain from any conflict in which they were not directly involved, and by which Stalin meant their isolation from any such conflict until the Soviet Union was ready to call the turns in the Baltic.

While Poland openly opposed bilateral agreements, which might go counter to her still cherished scheme of a Greater Baltic Union,

[6] *League of Nations Document* C34.1926, p. 121.

Litvinov, encouraged by the successful negotiation of a nonaggression pact with Germany (April 25, 1926) and by Lithuania's increasing bitterness over the Vilna dispute, approached this last state separately and gained her signature to a nonaggression pact on September 28, 1926.[7] In this matter, both Kārlis Ulmanis' urgings to maintain a common Baltic diplomatic front and Poland's overtures were disregarded by Lithuania. Latvia, Estonia, and Finland proved more resistant to the Soviet suggestion of a multilateral pact of nonaggression and neutrality which would guarantee all existing frontiers. Separate negotiations with Latvia and Estonia ended in stalemate, since the U.S.S.R. stood firm against the principle of arbitration, so dear to the Baltic States. However, on March 9, 1927, the Latvian Social-Democratic Government, under the aegis of M. Skujenieks, did initial a nonaggression pact; while the following June the five-year Latvian-Soviet commercial treaty was concluded, with special clauses providing for arbitration in commercial and civil matters.[8] Estonia could but deplore this second breach in the Baltic front brought about by the unrealistic Left Wing element in Latvia.

The Soviet Union's addiction to separate dealings in the Baltic was part of her long-range strategy for the establishment of her tutelage over this critical area, whose increasing "bloc-mindedness" was not to her taste. However, when the occasion suited, she would promote multilateral agreements, as in the case of the Moscow Protocol, concluded between the U.S.S.R., Rumania, Poland, and the Baltic States in the early spring of 1929. It concerned the immediate participation of these Powers in the Kellogg-Briand Pact, outlawing war as an instrument of national policy.[9]

The Soviet Government's persistent efforts to secure nonaggression treaties with the Baltic nations were finally crowned with success early in 1932. Latvia's three-year nonaggression pact was signed in Riga on February 5,[10] a supplementary convention regarding the settlement of disputes by conciliation being signed on June 18.[11] The Soviet nonaggression pacts with Latvia, with Estonia (May 4, 1932) and with

[7] *League of Nations Treaty Series*, LV, 145.

[8] *op.cit.*, LXVIII, 321. Text reprinted in *Latvian-Russian Relations. Documents*, pp. 146-159.

[9] *League of Nations Treaty Series*, LXXIX, 369; *Latvian-Russian Relations*, pp. 166-169.

[10] *League of Nations Treaty Series*, CXLVIII, 113; *Latvian-Russian Relations*, pp. 170-172.

[11] *League of Nations Treaty Series*, CXLVIII, 130; *Latvian-Russian Relations*, pp. 172-175.

Lithuania (1926) were to be extended until the end of 1945 by the Moscow Protocols of April 4, 1934.

The sinister ascendancy of the National Socialist party in Germany was not without early repercussions in the Baltic States, where the phantom of a German Balticum once more took on substance, and German minority populations, known to be inflammable, were looked at askance. Confronted by the Third Reich's rapid rearmament and her boasts of being a bulwark against Communism, Litvinov showed less aversion to collective action in the Baltic. On July 3, 1933, in London, he obtained the signature of eight states, among them Latvia, Estonia, and Poland (Lithuania and Finland signed later) to the Geneva Draft Convention defining the aggressor.[12] In December of that year, Latvia and the U.S.S.R. concluded a commercial treaty and economic agreement which, with certain modifications, were to remain in force until 1940.

By January 1934, the U.S.S.R. was again assailing Baltic solidarity with a proposal that Poland join her in guaranteeing the security of Finland and the Baltic States, an attempt at sponsorship which the latter countries rejected on the grounds that the already existing non-aggression pacts sufficed for the purpose. These nations felt, furthermore, that Germany might very well be incensed by her exclusion from such an agreement. Their general distrustfulness seemed borne out by the German-Polish ten-year Nonaggression Declaration of January 26, 1934. The following March, the Soviet Union approached the Reich in secrecy over the question of arranging a joint tutelage for Finland and the Baltic States. The Baltic governments in question were not apprized of this *démarche* until after Berlin's rejection of the Soviet proposals late in April, when German diplomatic representatives communicated to them the negative attitude of their government.

Germany and Poland also rejected the idea of an Eastern Locarno, promulgated by the U.S.S.R. and France in the spring of 1934. This mutual assistance pact was to have included, besides Germany and Poland, Czechoslovakia, Finland, the Baltic States and the Soviet Union. In spite of Colonel Beck's cautionary visit to Tallinn and Riga in July 1934, that same month in Moscow the Foreign Ministers of Latvia and Estonia expressed approval of the general principle of an Eastern Pact, an opinion which was to be concurred in a little later by

[12] *League of Nations Treaty Series*, CXLVII, 69; *Latvian-Russian Relations*, pp. 175-178.

the Lithuanian Foreign Minister. In actuality, however, the Baltic States felt that Germany's objection to a mutual assistance clause, together with her now open defiance of the Armaments Clause of the Treaty of Versailles, could only render such a pact valueless from any practical point of view.

On the other hand, the interest of the Baltic States in a Little Baltic Union had assumed a realistic tinge following the crises of the world economic depression, the Polish-German rapprochement, the Third Reich's opposition to an Eastern security pact, and the Memel affair, which now loomed larger than the Vilna dispute. On March 15, 1934, Lithuania was invited to join the Latvian-Estonian Defensive Alliance of February 17, on condition that her cosignatories would not be required to involve themselves in either of the above-mentioned Lithuanian problems. A Treaty of Understanding and Cooperation, signed at Geneva in September, was ratified in Riga on November 3.[13] This ten-year agreement provided for semi-annual conferences on matters of common concern, particularly questions of foreign policy; for the friendly settlement of disputes among the signatories; for the mutual communication of treaties signed with other Powers; and for the possible later adherence of other states to the treaty.

At the first conference of this new Baltic Entente, held in Tallinn in December 1934, it was decided to have a single representative act for the three Baltic States at all international conferences as well as in Geneva. The international relations of the three states were coordinated in further detail. Latvia, Lithuania, and Estonia went on record as favoring, again in principle, an East European Pact of Mutual Assistance. The following January, there came into existence in Riga a Bureau for the Promotion of Cooperation between the Baltic States which was essentially an amalgamation of the various already existing Baltic cultural organizations. It was generally felt that the new Baltic bloc had received international recognition when, in October 1936, Latvia, as a representative of all three states, was unanimously elected by the Assembly to a nonpermanent seat on the Council of the League of Nations.

The League, for all its difficulties and disillusionments, continued to hold the somewhat desperate loyalty of the Baltic States, who by now realized that, in the eyes of their former exploiters, the German and Russian nations, they might once more fill the role of pawns. Poland's attitude toward the Baltic area also appeared equivocal.

[13] *League of Nations Treaty Series*, CLIV, 93f.

When, in the autumn of 1934, the Soviet Union became a member of the League of Nations, the Baltic States had hopefully acclaimed this step as a sign of good-neighborly intentions on the part of their self-styled sponsor. Following the informal visit of their Chiefs-of-Staff to Moscow in the spring of 1936, Latvia, Lithuania, and Estonia, at the fourth Baltic Conference, issued a statement offering to participate in a general system of collective security, while at the same time insisting on their continued adherence to the principles embodied in the League Covenant, within whose framework, they maintained, regional agreements must be worked out.[14]

Up until August 1939, the Baltic States had to remain delicately attuned to German threats and Soviet overtures. As German rearmament proceeded apace and talk of the *Ostland* became increasingly current, Nazi organizations stirred up subversive eddies in all three of the Baltic States. As early as 1934, the Latvian Government had had to suppress the Latvian branch of the *Baltischer Bruderschaft* for its treasonous urgings concerning the outright incorporation of the Balticum into the Third Reich. In January 1936, von Neurath pointed out in a press interview that his country's relations with the Baltic States depended directly upon the latter's attitude toward their German minorities. In this connection, he insisted that the recent Latvian law dissolving the old German guilds in order to set up the new Chambers of Commerce and Industry was a case of open discrimination unacceptable to the Reich. Ulmanis' reaction to the violent attack in the German press and to representations on the part of the German Minister in Riga was a categorical objection to German interference in Latvian domestic affairs. There followed the prompt arrest of 35 German-Balts active in a secret organization for the dissemination of Nazi propaganda.[15] Uncompromising action against undercover Nazi movements on the part of all three authoritarian régimes in the Baltic, as well as this region's remarkable economic recovery, contributed to the amelioration of official German relations with the Baltic States, with whom the Reich now entered into trade agreements. Nazism, however, continued to cast its spells on the German-Balts, whose press, by 1939, was entirely in tune with the new order in Germany. In May of that year, the Germans in Latvia staged a celebration, planned in

[14] *The Baltic States. Estonia, Latvia, Lithuania,* p. 85f.

[15] *op.cit.,* p. 36; see also C. L. Lundin "The Nazification of the Baltic German Minorities," *Journal of Central European Affairs,* VII (1947), 1-28 *passim.*

Berlin, honoring the "German" liberation of Riga from "Latvian Communism" on May 22, 1919.[16]

The Soviet Russian attitude toward her Baltic neighbors continued to be that of a singularly tactless protector. Late in 1936, at an All-Union Congress in Moscow, Zhdanov, as the new Secretary of the Russian Communist party, declared that, while the U.S.S.R. wished to live in peace with the Baltic nations, "if these tiny peoples allow big adventurers to use their territories for big adventures, we shall widen our little window onto Europe with the help of the Red Army."[17] On December 2, the Soviet Minister in Riga thought to temper this ill-judged threat by his assurance that his government harbored no aggressive intentions. Shortly thereafter, the Soviet Minister in Kaunas (Lithuania) informed the Baltic States that the only Power on which they could count for the protection of their security was the Soviet Union. In June 1937, Litvinov added his public assurance that "Latvia's geographical position is such that the U.S.S.R. cannot help being interested in the maintenance of her complete independence."

No less anxious than the Soviet Union to secure their own absolute neutrality, now that the war threat rumbled on their horizon, the nations of the Baltic Entente continued the conferences of their foreign ministers. Latvia and Estonia in December 1938, and Lithuania the following January, adopted neutrality laws based on the pattern set by Sweden in May 1938. As an indication of the interpretation she might be expected to put on Baltic neutrality, Soviet Russia, by the spring of 1939, had constructed three parallel strategic railway lines in the direction of the Latvian border.

In March of that year, following Germany's reappropriation of Memel, the U.S.S.R., announcing unilaterally that Estonia and Latvia fell in her particular zone of interest, offered these states military assistance and protection against either direct or indirect aggression, at the same time cautioning them against extending any exceptional rights or privileges to any other nation. This suggestion was rejected by the two Baltic governments on April 7, 1939, as being an infringement of their sovereignty.[18]

There are indications that as early as March of that year a rapproche-

---

[16] The Baltic States, p. 36, and Lundin, op.cit. pp. 17-26.
[17] The Baltic States, p. 86.
[18] Text in Latvian-Russian Relations, p. 188f., both of Soviet declaration and reply of the Latvian Government.

ment had occurred between Germany and the Soviet Union, who were engaged in secret conversations. By May, Foreign Commissar Litvinov, who had been well-disposed toward the Baltic States, was replaced by the nationalistic Great Russian, V. Molotov. Sensing these shifting pressures, Estonia and Latvia signed a nonaggression pact with Germany on June 7, following the example set by Lithuania in March.[19]

During the course of the summer, the U.S.S.R. sought, through protracted conferences with French and British representatives, to obtain their governments' consent to her occupation of the Baltic States for strategic purposes whenever she might deem the moment ripe, and reserved the right to her unilateral and automatic interpretation of direct or indirect aggression. It is reported that whereas the French and British representatives finally agreed to the Soviet demands without the Baltic States having been consulted, Poland rejected the French request that Soviet troops pass through her territory in case of war with Germany.[20] The U.S.S.R. used this refusal as a pretext for breaking off the conversations which had already won her Germany's disposition to come to terms.

The stage was set for the startling Treaty of Moscow, the Nonaggression and Friendship Pact concluded between Germany and the Soviet Union on August 23, 1939. At the time of the Nuremberg trials there came to light the texts of two secret Soviet-Nazi agreements, which immediately preceded the official Ribbentrop-Molotov Pact. In the first of these, spheres of influence in Eastern Europe were delimited, the northern frontier of Lithuania being established as the demarcation line between the Russian and the German zones of interest. To the Nonaggression Pact of August 23 was appended a secret protocol wherein the Reich sanctioned the occupation of the Baltic States by the Red Army whenever the U.S.S.R. considered the moment opportune.

Hitler's realization that the Soviet forces would eventually invade this terrain is indicated by his recall of the *Volksdeutsche* in the Baltic States, for whose repatriation to their "Homeland" he began negotiations soon after he had, by secret agreement, abandoned the Baltic lands to Moscow. All persons of German origin in the area were urged by the Reich to liquidate their interests as expeditiously as possible. Hitler's anxiety to move German-Balts out of the region showed his estimation of what the immediate future held for these lands—an

[19] *op.cit.*, p. 190f.
[20] G. Gafencu, *Les derniers jours de l'Europe* (Paris, 1946), pp. 219-234.

estimation revealed to the German people in his speech of June 22, 1941, when, in addition to explaining the Reich's part in ceding the Baltic nations to Soviet interests, he maintained that the *Volksdeutsche* had been evacuated "in order to escape living under another régime which sooner or later meant their complete destruction."

The Soviet Union's moves, following the Agreement of August 23, were entirely in accord with Hitler's premonitions. The General Staff printed strategic military maps for the Lithuanian, Latvian, and Estonian "Socialist Republics." Troops in Siberia were routed westwards. Maneuvers were started on the Baltic frontiers. Airfields, roads, and railways in the region were under construction.

On September 1, Latvia and her sister states proclaimed their neutrality in the conflict which had just broken out on the face of Europe. Three days later, the German Minister in Riga assured V. Munters, the Latvian Foreign Minister, that his country, in her friendship pact with the U.S.S.R., had in no way violated previous German-Latvian agreements. On September 17, the Red Army, ordered to occupy Polish territory, took Vilna. Shortly thereafter, German and Soviet commanders established a demarcation line in Poland which was to be confirmed by an agreement signed between the respective military authorities in Brest-Litovsk on September 28. The preceding day Ribbentrop and Molotov had signed another secret agreement in Moscow, modifying the secret protocol of August 23 to the extent of relegating Lithuania to the Soviet sphere of interest. Officially, on that same day, the two allies concluded another friendship pact confirming the Fourth Partition of Poland and warning off any third parties who might seek to interfere in the newly-indicated spheres of German and Russian interest. In a joint declaration, Molotov and Ribbentrop announced that they had now laid "the secure foundation for a lasting peace in Eastern Europe."

Stalin's scant faith in this "secure foundation" was revealed by his next moves in the Baltic, where he sought the guarantee of entrenchment. Seizing upon the escape of an interned Polish submarine as a pretext, the Soviet Union declared her security to be menaced by Baltic ports which were lending aid to foreign U-boats. The Estonian Foreign Minister, in Moscow for economic negotiations, found himself compelled to sign, on September 28, a mutual assistance treaty with the U.S.S.R. By this agreement the Estonian Government was forced to lease to the Soviet Union, for a ten-year period, all of the Estonian islands for military, naval, and air force bases. Twenty-five thousand Soviet troops were to be garrisoned on these islands and at Baltiski (Baltishport), with the promise of withdrawal at the end of the war.

The Latvian Foreign Minister, V. Munters, was then summoned to the Kremlin. Here, in the conversations of October 2 and 3, he was told by Stalin that "that which was determined in 1920 (Soviet-Latvian Peace Treaty) cannot remain for eternity. Peter the Great saw to it that an outlet to the sea was gained. We also wish to insure ourselves the use of ports, roads to these ports, and their defense." When Munters suggested that, in view of the establishment of two mutually friendly Powers on the Baltic Sea through the Russo-German friendship pacts, he could not understand "what additional security there could be," Stalin conjured up the possibility of Swedish and even British aggression.[21]

With British or French assistance unthinkable, with Molotov and Ribbentrop forming a mutual-admiration society, with Estonia's sovereignty already violated, and with sixteen divisions of the Red Army on her border, Latvia signed a dictated Pact of Mutual Assistance on October 5, 1939.[22] The U.S.S.R. gained control of the Gulf of Riga by obtaining ten-year leases on bases in Liepāja and Ventspils, several airfields, and the right to set up coast artillery between Ventspils and Pitrags. Thirty thousand Soviet troops were to be garrisoned on Latvian soil for the duration of the war.

Under comparable pressure, offered the alternative of being thrown to the Germans or accepting Vilna at Soviet hands, Lithuania, on October 10, signed a similar mutual assistance pact on even harder terms. All three pacts with the Baltic States specifically stipulated that the sovereignty of these nations would be wholly preserved and that the Soviet Union would in all ways refrain from interference in their internal affairs. On the day after the conclusion of the Latvian treaty, a communiqué in *Pravda* asserted that: "At the basis of the pacts of mutual assistance are irremovable principles of treaties of peace and nonaggression. The contracting parties affirm once more their unshaken desire to recognize the sovereign rights of each State as well as their firm desire not to interfere with the inner affairs of another State."

Molotov, reporting to the Extraordinary Session of the Supreme Soviet on October 31, stated: "These pacts are based on mutual re-

[21] *Latvian-Russian Relations*, pp. 192-198.
[22] Text in *Latvian-Russian Relations*, p. 198f.

spect for the political, social and economic structure of the contracting parties, and are designed to strengthen the basis for peaceful, neighborly cooperation between our peoples. We stand for scrupulous and punctilious observance of pacts on a basis of complete reciprocity, and we declare that all nonsense about sovietizing the Baltic countries is only to the interest of our common enemies and of all anti-Soviet provocateurs."

Hitler, for one, was not convinced that talk of sovietization was "nonsense." German agents were everywhere, explaining the horrors which might befall any German-Balts who chose to linger in the oncoming shadow of Soviet invasion. After protracted negotiations, repatriation agreements with the Estonian and Latvian governments were concluded on October 14 and 30 respectively. By the beginning of 1940, 49,885 German-speaking inhabitants of Latvia had left the country, and by the beginning of May, all were gone.

While the German-Balts were, not always willingly, pulling up roots, Soviet agents in the Baltic States were busily complying with the Soviet Security Police (GPU) order of October 11, demanding the preparation of lists of "anti-Soviet" persons in all ranks of society. This secretly-elaborated order contained the plans for five periodic deportations which were to replace the bulk of the Baltic populations by Russians.

As the Baltic nations absorbed the first shocks of this groundswell of aggression and Molotov inveighed against those who accused his government of a breach of its neighbors' sovereignty, Stalin could sit back and congratulate himself on the sure operation, under new techniques, of the old massive machinery of Russian imperialism which he had put into motion at the opportune time.

Only with Finland did his method of diplomatic and military coercion fail. The Finnish delegation, invited to Moscow on October 5, conceded all but the port of Hangoe, on which the U.S.S.R. demanded a 35 year lease. Subsequent to a violent press and radio anti-Finnish campaign, the Soviet Government, on November 28, denounced her 1934 nonaggression pact with Finland. Two days later, the military attack was launched. In consequence of her action, the U.S.S.R. was suspended from membership in the League of Nations on December 14. Finland, forced to her knees, signed a peace treaty on March 12, 1940.

During the Russo-Finnish war the behavior of Soviet garrisons in the Baltic States was circumspect. Even the underground workings of the illegal Communist parties were temporarily discontinued. Although as many as three parallel roads had been constructed toward the Latvian frontier during the course of the Finnish campaign, Molotov, as late as March 29, speaking before the Supreme Soviet, promised "further amelioration of relations between the U.S.S.R. and the Baltic Republics."

This conciliatory behavior, aimed at preventing the formation of an anti-Soviet bloc in the Baltic, changed abruptly upon termination of the war with Finland. April and May saw sharp attacks against the Lithuanian and Estonian governments appearing in the Soviet press, Latvia being spared for the above-mentioned reason. The wild talk of the Soviet soldiers in their cups scarcely convinced the Baltic peoples that the Russian garrisons would be temporary. Although Latvian relations with the U.S.S.R. continued officially "good," there being no disputes in existence between the two Powers, the Ulmanis government sensed disaster in the wind. Accordingly, on May 17, a secret decision was reached, providing for Latvia's political continuity. In case of an emergency, the powers of state authority abroad were to be conferred upon K. Zariņš, Latvian Minister in London. Alfred Bilmanis, Latvian Minister to Washington, was designated as his substitute.

Latvia's hour struck when Hitler occupied Paris. Stalin then judged it advisable to act before the Third Reich should become omnipotent in Europe. On June 14, 1940, Moscow, on the grounds of an alleged kidnapping of two Soviet soldiers, presented an ultimatum to Lithuania in which that nation, together with her sister states, were accused of military conspiracy against the U.S.S.R.

On that same day, frontier guards in Latvia were killed in order to create an incident. Lithuania, with Finland's fate in mind, accepted the ultimatum and on June 15 Red Army detachments invaded the country, moving toward the Lithuanian-Latvian border. The following day, twenty-four-hour ultimatums were presented to Latvia and Estonia.[23] All three Baltic States were accused of non-fulfillment of their mutual assistance pacts with the U.S.S.R. The Latvian-Estonian defensive alliances and the Treaty of Collaboration signed by the Baltic States in 1934, all registered at the League of Nations, all obviously nonaggressive, and none objected to at the time of the mutual assistance pacts, should, the Soviet Government now protested, have been abrogated upon conclusion of the "bases" treaties. In addition, the

[23] op.cit., p. 202f.

Baltic States were accused of holding secret conferences in December 1939 and March 1940 (these were the regular, open, and nonmilitary meetings of the Baltic Entente); of intensifying the relations between their military staffs *vis à vis* the U.S.S.R. (an entirely groundless complaint); and of founding in the *Revue Baltique* what Molotov qualified as a secret "special organ of the militaristic Baltic Entente." This periodical, the first number of which appeared in Tallinn in February 1940, was in reality a trilingual publication of the Societies of Friendship of the Baltic Peoples, dedicated exclusively to economic, social, and cultural affairs.

Although these baseless accusations were formally denied by the Baltic States, the Soviet ultimatums demanded the immediate entry of Soviet troops whose presence would safeguard the formation of new "friendly" governments, see to it that these governments properly fulfilled the mutual assistance pacts, and protect the already established Soviet garrisons from "unfriendly" acts. Should the ultimatums be rejected, the Baltic cities might expect bombardment. The terms were perforce accepted.

Without waiting for answers to the ultimatums, the Red Army, held in heavy concentration on the Baltic frontiers, on June 17 occupied Estonia and appeared in the streets of Riga.[24] The following day, the Russian cruiser *Marat* arrived in Riga, freighted with Soviet Communist agitators, who organized on June 19, with the assistance of local Communists emerging hourly, a stereotyped demonstration for "the Liberator, Stalin."

On June 17, Kārlis Ulmanis, under pressure of the presence of 200,000 Soviet troops accompanied by tanks and a strong air force, had released his cabinet from all its duties. The following day, he was called upon by Andrei Vishinsky, Vice President of the Council of Commissars, who then proceeded to form a new government for Latvia, selecting many of the ministers himself, but proclaiming, on June 21, that "the Secretariat of Dr. Kārlis Ulmanis announces that a new cabinet has been formed." The new Prime Minister was the elderly, malleable Professor August Kirchenšteins, and three of his Vice Ministers were Soviet subjects.

The illegal Latvian Communist party with about 150 registered members, and the Communist Youth Organization, hitherto small underground movements, now came forward to take their places

[24] For these eventful days see M. Čakste, "Latvia and the Soviet Union," *Journal of Central European Affairs*, ix (1949), pp. 31-60, 173-211.

beside the Red Army (of which there were a total of 800,000 troops in the three Baltic States) and with Soviet representatives and agents, to play their role in the destruction of the Latvian Republic. It was their part to see to it that the Ulmanis régime was made to appear as the arch foe of the Latvian people, who were dumbfounded to hear that so deep had been their degradation and insecurity that they were now ripe for revolution. The bitter accusations hurled against the Government of National Unity were scarcely borne out by the small number of political prisoners (some 250) liberated by the Soviet invasion, by the total absence of death sentences for political offenders, by the absence of strikes, or by the small number of unemployed. The dissatisfaction which had been voiced against the authoritarian régime had been centered around a demand for the return to a representative system of government, for an abatement of state capitalism, and for a restoration of full civil rights, which had indeed suffered serious diminishment as the international situation had grown more tense. The return to a more democratic system had, in more hopeful times, been foreseen by President Ulmanis himself, who informed the author personally, in October 1935, that the reformed constitution would provide for the election of both the Saeima and the Chief of State, with the executive stronger and more independent of the legislative, and more guarantees of national unity than the 1922 constitution had allowed. The Communist asseverations concerning the "reign of terror" under which the Latvians had been suffering elicited as little response as the assurances of the Red Army troops that they had come to save the Baltic peoples from the menace of war. The Latvians took the appearance of Soviet forces for what it was: an invasion. At Alūksne, in northern Vidzeme, the population had spontaneously withstood the advance of the Russian troops for three days.

In view of the disaffection of the people, the Soviet Government deemed it advisable to engineer the "voluntary" approval of its aggression in the Baltic by holding "elections." This "people's choice" of puppet parliaments in the Baltic States remains one of the early classics of Soviet manipulation of the techniques of democracy to obtain fantastically fraudulent results.

Declarations blackened the air. Kirchenšteins' government informed the nation that, whereas the former régime had failed to carry out loyally Latvia's mutual assistance pact with the U.S.S.R., that pact would now be fully complied with, and the increasing bonds of friend-

ship with the Soviet Union would be a guarantee of Latvia's independence. A new order, corresponding to the true will of the Latvian
people, was about to come into being. The Minister of Information,
Blaus, next informed his radio audience that their democratic rights,
including freedom of speech, of the press, and of assembly, would
now be restored. In actuality, the measures enacted by the Ulmanis
régime to curb political disloyalty were now enforced to the hilt by
this same Minister of Information. Unless they were of the proper
persuasion, no new publications were allowed to appear, while the
non-Communist ones already in existence were severely muzzled.
Foreign correspondents were told that they must get their information from TASS.

It was in this atmosphere of pious exhortations and relentless suppression that the elections of July 14 and 15 were staged. Regardless
of the fact that the electoral law of 1922 was still in existence, the
Kirchenšteins government, accusing the former régime of illegality in
permitting the cabinet to assume the functions of the Saeima, committed a genuine illegality in altering the electoral procedures.[25] The
new electoral law of July 5 made all members of the voting commissions government appointees and allowed only five days for the presentation of candidates, this period being subsequently further curtailed by the central commission. On July 8, the central commission
insisted that the candidates, in the brief time allotted them, must
present their entire program and proof that these programs had been
laid before the electorate. Blaus then forbade any printing establishment to print election material which did not bear his stamp of approval. The single bloc of the former democratic parties now found its
desperate efforts to get before the electorate foiled by police seizure of
all its material. The arrest and deportation of its leader followed as a
matter of course.

In the end, all five electoral districts were presented with a single
list containing only candidates of the "Union of the Toiling People."
This exclusively Communist list was drawn up by a specially empowered emissary from the Kremlin, and included twenty Soviet
citizens. In all three of the Baltic States these Unions of the Toiling
People, through their election candidates assured the voters that they
stood for democratic rights, for a foreign policy conducive to close
friendship with the U.S.S.R., and for the continued national inde-

[25] Professor Čakste, Justice of the Latvian Supreme Court from 1934, has
treated the legal questions involved in considerable detail.

pendence of the respective states. Rumors of sovietization or of incorporation into the Soviet Union were loudly attacked as malicious propaganda.

All the campaign speeches of the Workers' bloc contained threats of reprisals on those who abstained from voting. Passports of those who voted would be stamped. Absentees would lose their jobs and be regarded as enemies of the new order. The voters were marched en masse from their place of work to the polling-stations, with bands to cheer them on, Soviet troops in full battle regalia affording "military protection," and Soviet airplanes overhead. The ballots were cast openly. It was officially announced that the "labor bloc" had obtained 1,155,807, or 94.8 per cent of the 1,181,323 votes cast in Latvia, the percentage being almost identical to that claimed for the other two Baltic States. Election results for all three states appeared in the foreign press twenty-four hours before the count had been completed.

By July 18, organized street demonstrations were flourishing posters demanding "the establishment of Soviet Latvia" as the "fourteenth republic of the Soviet Union." The secretary of the Latvian Communist party proclaimed that the demands of the people would be met. The new parliament, assembling on July 21, was deluged with nearly identical telegrams urging Latvia's sovietization and her incorporation into the U.S.S.R. On July 21, Kārlis Ulmanis was arrested and deported to Soviet Russia. The deportation order for General Balodis, arrested early in July, was signed on July 31. The fate of these two builders of the Latvian nation remains unknown.

Kirchenšteins' first move, upon the opening of the Saeima, was to appoint himself Chief of State. Greetings and expressions of gratitude were then dispatched to Stalin and Molotov. Following the election of officers, tirades were delivered by Z. Spure (Secretary of the Latvian Communist party) and V. Lacis (Minister of Internal Affairs) qualifying the former régime as one of bondage, with "a small clique . . . plundering the State's resources," and "the people . . . subjected to a tyrannous and corrupt oppression" during which "the greatest misery and unemployment reigned in the land, and the people were plunged into the direst poverty." Properly warmed up, the Saeima then proclaimed the "Latvian Soviet Republic" and "requested" the Supreme Council of the Soviet Union to accept Soviet Latvia as a member republic of the Union, on the same basis as that of the Ukrainian, the White Russian Socialist Soviet Republics, and of other member republics in the past. A number of bills for the sovietization and nationalization of most of Latvia's national wealth, all elaborated by the Kremlin, were also hurried before the Saeima in its initial meeting of seven and a half hours. In this record time, the elected representatives of the Latvian people reversed themselves on the issues which had been blared out to the electorate.

On the same day, in all three of the Baltic States, sovietization laws and pleas for incorporation into the Soviet Union were passed by acclamation, with no discussion, by all-Communist parliaments elected under conditions which had made the free expression of the will of the people an impossibility. Moscow's unique *"coup d'état* in progressive stages"[26] was being run off on schedule.

On July 30, the Latvian commission chosen to submit the parliamentary resolution to the Soviet Supreme Council left for Moscow, where the Seventh Session met on August 1, 1940. Molotov, reviewing again the unfriendliness of the Baltic bourgeois cliques and their Baltic Entente, announced that "the parliaments of Lithuania, Latvia, and Estonia, elected universally, directly, equally, and secretly, have already expressed their majority views of basic policy." On August 5, the Latvian delegation, pleading for incorporation, declared that "Parliament has unanimously called for the sovietization of Latvia because every historical experience of the Soviet Union has shown the people that only soviet might is just might, true peoples' might." On that same day, the Supreme Soviet unanimously passed the law accepting "the entry into the Union of the Soviet Socialist Republic of Latvia." Estonia had already been accepted two days earlier, and Lithuania was incorporated on August 6. The official attitude of the U.S.S.R. toward this and similar incorporations was summarized in Molotov's boast that ninety-five per cent of the population of the newly acquired territories had once belonged to Russia, who had had them torn from her at a time of weakness by the imperialist powers.

The illegality of this annexation has been closely and convincingly argued. It represents only the last link in a chain of illegal acts and pressures. The June ultimatum had been an infraction of the Pact of Paris of 1928, the nonaggression pact of 1932, the Pact for the Definition of the Aggressor of 1939, and the Mutual Assistance Pact of 1939. The demand for the formation of a new government and the military occupation had been a serious breach of Latvia's sovereignty. The elections, held under coercion of a foreign occupation, had not produced a Saeima which could speak for the people. Even had the

[26] S. Schwartz in *The New Leader*, Feb. 26, 1944.

resolutions of the Saeima represented the will of the people, this body was not empowered constitutionally to represent the state internationally or to conclude the treaty which alone could have provided the legal basis for the incorporation. In addition to existing in the first place, which it never did, such a treaty would have had to be ratified. Had such a treaty been negotiated, it should, according to Article 77 of the Latvian Constitution, have been referred to a free plebiscite. No such referendum was even considered for the resolutions of the Saeima.

Fully aware that the Soviet Union's military occupation of Latvia and the incorporation law passed by the Supreme Soviet in August 1940 did not invalidate the sovereignty of the Baltic States, their representatives abroad have persistently protested the Soviet aggression to the governments to which they were accredited by the Ulmanis régime. As was the case in other diplomatic protests, the notes of July 13, 18, 23 and August 5, 1940, addressed by the Latvian Minister in Washington to the United States Government, contained proofs of the illegality of the Soviet actions in Latvia and pleas for the nonrecognition of the incorporation and of the puppet Kirchenšteins government.

The faith which the Baltic peoples, although cut off from the West and sucked down helplessly into the Soviet orbit, continued to pin on the Western democracies seemed justified by the unequivocal declaration of policy issued by the Department of State of the United States on July 23, 1940. This declaration, a further step in the United States' already established nonrecognition policy, expressed the official American reaction to the Soviet Union's breach of treaties in the following terms:

"During these past few days the devious processes whereunder the political independence and territorial integrity of the three small Baltic republics—Estonia, Latvia and Lithuania—were to be deliberately annihilated by one of their more powerful neighbors, have been rapidly drawing to their conclusion.

"From the day when the peoples of these republics first gained their independence and democratic form of government the people of the United States have watched their admirable progress in self-government with deep and sympathetic interest.

"The policy of this Government is universally known. The people of the United States are opposed to predatory activities no matter whether they are carried on by the use of force or by the threat of force. They are likewise opposed to any form of intervention on the part of one state, however powerful, in the domestic concerns of any other sovereign state, however weak.

"These principles constitute the very foundations upon which the existing relationship between the 21 sovereign republics of the New World rests.

"The United States will continue to stand by these principles, because of the conviction of the American people that unless the doctrine in which these principles are inherent once again governs the relations between nations, the rule of reason, of justice, and of law—in other words, the basis of modern civilization itself—cannot be preserved."[27]

So strong was the position of the independent Baltic States in international law that Nazi Germany alone, and quite logically in view of her previous commitments, recognized the Soviet-contrived incorporation at the time of its occurrence.

The Latvian parliamentary commission returned to Riga on August 13, when Prime Minister Kirchenšteins resumed his duties as Chief of State. On August 24, the Saeima approved the work of the commission. The following day, the draft of the new Constitution of the Latvian Soviet Republic was read and unanimously accepted. It was further decided that:

"Pending elections for the Supreme Council (Soviet) of the Latvian S.S.R., the People's Saeima, as the unanimous expression of the Latvian working people, assumes temporarily the designation of Supreme Council of the Latvian S.S.R.

"The People's Saeima directs the Presidium of the temporary Supreme Council to appoint a date for general elections for the Supreme Council of the Latvian S.S.R., in accordance with the dispositions of the Constitution of the Latvian Soviet Republic."[28]

This Presidium was appointed on August 25. It was a body of eleven members, with Kirchenšteins as President, and V. Lacis as chairman of the Council of People's Commissars. The proletarian dictatorship, proclaimed in Article 2 of the new Constitution, was officially established.

This Soviet-designed Constitution was, after its fashion, an efficient instrument of the new-model Russian imperialism. It made Latvia

[27] Published in *Department of State Bulletin*, July 27, 1940, p. 48.
[28] The integral text of the Constitution of the Latvian Soviet Republic is given in *Latvian-Russian Relations*, pp. 211-226.

economically, socially, and politically so subservient to the central organizations of the U.S.S.R. and to the Russian Communist party that she could never hope either to secede from the Soviet Union or develop an independent domestic or foreign policy. The laws of the U.S.S.R. were made mandatory in Latvia. The administration of justice was controlled by the Attorney General of the U.S.S.R. through his appointee, the Latvian Attorney General. The Soviet Union might establish special courts (such as the GPU tribunals) at will; and the All-Union Commissariat of the Interior might establish its own administrations within the local Soviets. Electoral candidates could be nominated by "social organizations," "societies of the workers," trade unions, cooperatives, youth organizations, and cultural societies, in addition to the omnipotent Communist party and its affiliates. All important branches of agriculture, industry, and commerce were subjected to the appropriate All-Union Commissariats.

Since, according to Article 11, the purpose of the new order was to increase public rather than personal wealth, the capitalistic system was categorically abolished, and private ownership of Latvia's natural resources, means of communication, and the most important forms of agricultural and industrial wealth was annulled. The property of the cooperatives was also declared to be "public."

By the end of September 1940, all large private fortunes, private industrial, commercial, and transportation enterprises, the land and its natural resources, and the banks, had been nationalized. Only small retailers were still allowed to operate in free competition. The stocks of large and small businesses alike had suffered considerably from the wholesale looting, in the early months of the "friendly" occupation, by the members of the Red Army, who shipped home whatever they could seize in the way of consumer-goods. As early as August, large amounts of cattle fodder and grain were sent to Russia, the remainder being seized for the Soviet garrisons in Latvia. Warehouses, hospitals, pharmacies were stripped. Industrial and agricultural machinery, raw materials and railway rolling stock, trucks, timber, and cattle were all removed in large quantities. The funds in the possession of the disorganized banks were converted to worthless paper, and the equally worthless Soviet paper rubles flooded the country. Ceiling prices were then established in these rubles, one ruble being declared equivalent to one lat (a rate of exchange which meant a loss of 50 million lats to the national economy), and the stores were promptly emptied by the Soviet Army and officialdom.[29]

By January 1941, when the elections were staged for the Supreme Council, the cost of living had increased tenfold while salaries had barely doubled since the Soviet occupation. Furthermore, the Latvian peasant had been attacked in his most stubborn interests and pride by the threat of the dreaded Kolkhoz system. Not only was it necessary to multiply threats and magnify the propaganda in order to get the highly disaffected people out to the polls for what the authorities were determined to present as another "plebiscite," but the reign of terror had to be constantly heightened as more and more Latvians felt that they had less and less to lose.

The elaborate patterns of Soviet terror were introduced as soon as the GPU, following close on the heels of the occupation forces, was installed in Riga. In the first stages of the mass-deportation program, 34,340 Latvians were sent to Siberia and Central Russia, where they disappeared into the slave labor camps. Of some 6,000 political prisoners deported to the northernmost part of European Russia, the majority, according to a few escapees, perished in the winter of 1941-1942. It was part of the genocide plan to scatter the deportees widely throughout the U.S.S.R., always in the most insalubrious spots, and to separate families. Between June 13 and 17, 1941, 824 railway cars of deportees were dispatched into Soviet Russia. The Soviets subsequently insisted that these people left their country voluntarily. In all, over two per cent of the Latvian population was either massacred or deported during the 12 months of Russian occupation and nine months of Soviet rule.

Especially marked for extermination were the government officials, members of the intelligentsia, and army officers. The peacetime Latvian army of 20,000 troops lost 1,084 of its officer personnel. On June 14, between 300 and 400 Latvian and Lithuanian officers were shot and buried in a mass grave near the frontier station of Vainode. Although the mutual assistance pacts which the U.S.S.R. had extorted from the Baltic States had contained Soviet promises to furnish muni-

[29] The description of conditions in Latvia under the Soviet and Nazi occupations may be assumed to rest upon reports sent to the author from Latvians who escaped from the terrors. These reports have been regularly published in the *Latvian Information Bulletin* published by the Latvian Legation in Washington. The author may be permitted to refer to his own books, *Latvia in 1939-1942* (Washington, 1942) and *Latvia under German Occupation, 1941-1943* (Washington, 1943).

tions to these nations "on favorable terms," no military equipment was ever delivered. On the contrary, by July 1940, the national armies had been disarmed, the Home Guards disbanded, and the majority of officers discharged. By the end of that year, those elements which were considered "reliable" were incorporated into the newly-organized Baltic Military District. Following the German declaration of war on Soviet Russia, numerous Latvian and Lithuanian officers discharged as politically unreliable were seized by the GPU patrols and executed without formalities.

Accorded equal attention with statesmen, army officers, teachers, and "exploiters" were the leaders in the religious field. Those Roman Catholic, Protestant, and Jewish churchmen who were not murdered, tortured, jailed, or deported, found their teaching and preaching severely inhibited, their publications suppressed, and the property of their churches and schools expropriated. Only a few churches, by paying an exorbitant tax, were allowed to continue holding divine service.

It was neither among the intellectuals nor the capitalists, however, that the Soviet régime found its most surly opponents. These were bred in the ranks of the peasants, who could no longer think of their beloved soil and their difficult toil as their own, and among the laboring classes, who found that the ruble scarcely purchased enough to sustain life and that working hours and conditions were rapidly approximating those of slavery. In spite of Soviet methods of breaking up the workers into small cadres under the surveillance of GPU men, and Soviet insistence on indoctrination courses, the passive resistance of this group became more and more overt.

Following Nazi Germany's attack upon Soviet Russia on June 22, the Baltic peoples, knowing their forces to have been disarmed by the Soviets and seeing the latter unwilling to defend their Baltic bases, rose in revolt. Even before the German troops entered Kaunas on June 23, the Lithuanians, proclaiming their country free, had formed a national government. In Riga, insurrectionists seized the radio station and occupied important buildings, while national guards came out of hiding to attack the Russians in the rural areas. On June 28, the Stockholm radio reported that a Riga broadcast had announced the overthrow of the Soviet régime and the organization of a Latvian government. The following day, the Russians, fleeing from Lithuania, reentered Riga, where they overpowered the insurrectionists and read the names of hundreds of executed partisans over the Riga station, which then went off the air.

The Soviet forces, for whom "strategic" bases had been so insistently claimed by the U.S.S.R., offered scarcely any defense against the German invaders. Indeed, Stalin's attention to the economic, social, and cultural disorganization of the Baltic States and his marked indifference to their military situation would indicate that the Soviet "strategic" demands were not yet serious, and that political and economic expansionism was the prime motive behind the occupations and annexations in the Baltic. The Russian forces retreated from the Baltic States speedily, in disorder, and with considerable loss of men and matériel. In their wake they left many of Riga's historical buildings in flames.

By July 1, German troops had entered Riga and seized the radio station. They promptly broadcast their success as liberators of the Latvian people from Soviet domination. The Rigans were permitted to sing the Latvian anthem and hold religious services. On July 28, a special decree of the German Government proclaimed the constitution of the new German province of the Ostland, to consist of the Baltic Republics and White Russia, all now occupied by German military forces.

The German occupation of the Baltic territories soon proved itself an able imitator of the Soviet régime, with a higher premium on efficiency and the curious addiction to "legality" which characterized the Nazi administrators in their termite activities. On October 17, 1941, the decrees signed by the Reichskommissar für das Ostland, H. Lohse, revealed the German intention to legalize the Soviet practices and then profit from them to the fullest extent. Far from restoring Latvian property rights in any form, they demanded that rent be paid to the German Government by the former owners of real estate, business enterprises, factories, farms, forests, etc. On October 19, the Deutsche Zeitung im Ostland, the official organ of the Reichskommissar, declared that "at the commencement of the German-Soviet War on June 22, 1941, private property did not exist in the countries under Soviet rule, so nobody can claim to be a legal proprietor. By sacrificing the blood of German soldiers, all these countries had been liberated. The German Reich, therefore, became the legal heir to the Soviet inheritance."

The Reich had entered upon its long-desired exploitation of the rich Baltic economy. The restoration of national governments was out of the question, a Berlin broadcast maintaining that "Latvia has no chance of regaining its independence" since "twenty years of Latvian independence have proved to be a succession of fatal mistakes." Germany's intention of outright annexation was confirmed by the creation of a Ministry for the Ostland in charge of Alfred Rosenberg. Puppet "Counsellors" were appointed for Lithuania, "General Directors" for Latvia, and "Directors" for Estonia.

The early advent of the Gestapo in the Ostland satrapy presaged the program of persecution for the Jews; and for Latvian patriots the confiscation of property, illegal arrests, killing of hostages, executions without trial, mass deportations, and the mass extermination of the population of certain provincial cities where German looters had been killed. It was evident that the Reich policy would be to hold the Baltic peoples in bondage, using their resources and their labor for the German war effort, until such time as these lands could be entirely Germanized.

On February 19, 1943, the Reich issued a decree mobilizing the Baltic peoples into the German armed forces, the detachments to receive the title of "Voluntary SS forces." Labor conscription followed on May 11. Severe penalties were inflicted on evaders and their relatives.

These measures were the signal for the flights of Latvian youths to the forests, where they organized guerilla groups. In August 1943, a Latvian Central Council was constituted in the form of an underground organization. This leader of the people's resistance was to make known the principles of the Atlantic Charter to the Latvian nation, insist on the latter's restoration as an independent and democratic republic, and in general follow a policy based on the presumed victory of the Allies. Latvia's leading political parties—the Agrarians, the Democrats, the Catholics, and the Social-Democrats, which together had polled two-thirds of the votes cast in the last parliamentary elections held in Latvia, were represented on the council by men who soon suffered for their leadership. P. Kalniņš (Social-Democrat), deported to Germany, died there in 1945. Bishop Rancans succeeded Kalniņš as President of the Latvian Central Council, and, though deported by the Nazis, was liberated by the Americans.

The return of the Red Army in all its violence to Latgale in the summer of 1944 prompted most of the members of the Central Council to flee abroad. Their example was followed by masses of Latvians seeking refuge in Western Europe and Scandinavia from increasing

German deportations and the renewed threat of Soviet terror. The victorious reentry of the Soviet forces into the Baltic States brought with it the full apparatus of terror, as well as conscription into the labor brigades and the Red Army. Instead of the solemnly-promised reestablishment of their freedom, the Baltic States witnessed the speedy restoration of the proletarian dictatorships.

Not until February 20, 1945, did the German Government finally consent to the formation of a provisional Latvian Government. With the German forces on the verge of collapse, the Latvian National Council, consisting of 73 nationally elected members, rallied in still Soviet-free Kurzeme to fight for the restoration of the Latvian Republic. On May 7, 1945, the National Council endorsed a Provisional Government under the premiership of Colonel Osis. The following day, the Soviets began the subjugation of Kurzeme, the last Latvian province to hold out. In accordance with the threats, broadcast from March 31 on, of severe reprisals on all who refused to recognize the incorporation of Latvia into the Soviet Union, the "capitalists" who had sought refuge in Kurzeme were now subjected to the wide scope of Soviet revenge. After May 12, all men between 16 and 65 years of age, and all women between 18 and 45 were mobilized. They had before their eyes the fate of those already conscripted Latvians who had been thrown, untrained and well nigh unarmed, against the retreating *Wehrmacht.*

Through the Iron Curtain which now shuttered the resovietized peoples of the Baltic States reports leaked out of the resumption of the mass-deportation program. In January 1945, some 40 to 50,000 Latvian peasants and their families were removed to the U.S.S.R., whence came their replacements of 50,000 Russian colonists. Between October 13, 1944 and March 5, 1945, 8,000 persons were deported from Riga alone. The Soviet Government claimed that 38,000 workers had "volunteered" for reconstruction work in Russia, whither they made their way on foot in winter weather.

Hunger, isolation, fear, helplessness, and death were all that the Latvians, whatever their occupation, could expect from the reestablishment of Soviet rule. Escape alone could promise them any future. According to information furnished by the Latvian Red Cross, there were 134,000 Latvian political refugees abroad by 1947. Those who became displaced persons in the American, British, and French zones in Germany were fortunate in the refusal of the authorities to deliver them to the Soviet Union.

This latter Power has been singularly matter-of-fact in its attempted liquidation of the Baltic States. Soviet Ambassador Maisky's adherence to the Atlantic Charter on September 24, 1941, which aroused hopes that the U.S.S.R. might reestablish relations with the Baltic States as independent Republics, was countered by Stalin's speech of November 6 wherein he declared the Soviet war aims to be the liberation of "our own territory." Within this concept he included, *expressis verbis*, the Ukraine, Bessarabia, Bukovina, White Russia, and the Baltic States.

The U.S.S.R. took the attitude that she had adhered to the Atlantic Charter after the annexation of the Baltic States, though Germany alone had recognized this incorporation and the Soviet Union had lost her control over the Baltic peoples by July 1941. Furthermore, in her treaty of July 30, 1941, with Poland, the U.S.S.R. had declared null and void the Russo-German treaty of August 23, 1939, and thereby nullified all action stemming from that treaty.

When, following the German attack of June 22, 1941, the Soviet Union became the ally of the Western democracies, her spokesmen redoubled their efforts to achieve diplomatic recognition of the annexation of the Baltic States as a *fait accompli*. To this end they employed the argument that these countries, as well as the eastern provinces of Poland, had been an integral part of the Russian Empire before the First World War. The Baltic States, they claimed, were an artificial creation of the Treaty of Versailles, a "barrier" area carved out of Russian territory in order to separate the Soviet Union from the West. They then insisted that the U.S.S.R. must have control of this region for security reasons, a claim scarcely borne out by the easy German successes in June 1941, when, in nine days, the *Wehrmacht* forced the Soviet garrisons from all their Baltic bases, trapping a good number of them in Estonia as the victors swept on to Leningrad. Had the Soviets won the confidence of the Baltic peoples and permitted them to maintain their armies, Estonians, Latvians, and Lithuanians would have fought at the side of the Red Army against the German invaders. Finally, the Soviet argument that the U.S.S.R. must have the Baltic ports for economic purposes has been disposed of elsewhere. Certainly the immediate need for political dominance of the ancient Baltic peoples lay behind the Soviet insistence on absolute control in this region; a control which she still claims was authorized by the "plebiscites" of 1940. Latvia, Lithuania, Estonia, the Soviet press drones on, attained liberty when they chose to become member Republics of the U.S.S.R. Ultimately, "strategy" on a sinister scale was to stand revealed in Russia's furious efforts to turn the Baltic Sea once more into a *mare clausum,* with secret weapons surging in and over its waters, and liberty a poor ghost on the shores of its little republics.

These republics, however, continue, through the thickening darkness, to think of themselves as democracies. It was on the side of their sister democracies of the West that they expended what small resources they had abroad in the way of ships and men. Their diplomats hastened to adhere to the Atlantic Charter and the Declaration of the United Nations, published on January 3, 1942. Lacking governments-in-exile, since their legal governments were early deported to the U.S.S.R., they have not been accepted into the United Nations, or asked to take part in international conferences. The Government of the United States continues to grant full recognition to representatives of the Baltic Republics in Washington, and to honor all treaties formerly concluded with these states.

At the present, all three natural guardians of the freedom of the Baltic Sea are in serious danger of being obliterated by Soviet terror in full deployment, with genocide for its aim. The U.S.S.R. has refused to consider the obligation to restore sovereign rights and self-government to those peoples who had been forcibly deprived of them, undertaken repeatedly in numerous international agreements, from the Atlantic Charter to Yalta, as applying to the Baltic States. This refusal has seemingly suspended Latvia and her sister nations from the domain of international law and morality. This suspension is one which they have suffered in other centuries, beneath other tyrants. And still their selfhood lasted on, and still they thought their national personality and their stubborn determination to own themselves might some day be made to count. Should this ability to drink life from rock-bottom despair survive the immense inhumanity of twentieth-century terror, the men of any democracy, large or small, may rightly judge that victory was innate in the very stuff of their material and spiritual society.

Selective Bibliography

THE following lists of titles do not pretend to be complete. Some works referred to in the text of this work may not appear here, and many titles here listed may not appear in the footnotes. Standard non-Latvian collections, such as the *Monumenta Germaniae Historica*, are not listed. A number of Latvian scientific periodicals, such as the journal of the Latvian Historical Institute, *Latvijas Vēstures Institūta Žurnāls*, are also not specifically listed. Much archival material has, since 1941, been ruthlessly destroyed, so that it would now seem pointless to speak of it as consultable. The author may be permitted to refer to the 35-page bibliography in his *Baltic Essays* (Washington, 1945), pp. 222-256.

PRIMARY SOURCES

Adam of Bremen, *Gesta Hammaburgensis ecclesiae pontificum*, in *Mon. Germ. Hist.* Hannover, 1846 and 1888, and ed. B. S. Schmeidler, Leipzig, 1917.

Akty i pisma k baltiskomu voprosu w 16 i 17 weku, ed. G. V. Forsten, St. Petersburg, 1898.

Akty otnosiashchisya k istorii zapadnoj Rossii izd. archeogr. komm. 5 vols. St. Petersburg, 1846-1853.

Alnpeke, Dittleb von, *Die Livländische Rheimchronik*. Reval, 1848.

Annuaire Statistique. Riga, 1918-1940.

Vita Anskarii auctore Rimberto, ed. G. Waitz, in *Scriptores rerum germanicarum*. Hannover, 1884.

Archiv für die Geschichte Liv-, Est- und Curlands. 12 vols. Riga, 1842, ed. F. von Bunge.

Baltische Revolutions-Chronik. 2 vols. Riga, 1907-1908.

Bienemann, F. A., *Briefe und Urkunden zur Geschichte Livlands*. Riga, 1876.

Birkel, H., *Statuta Curlandica*. Mitau, 1804.

Blomberg, K. J., *An Account of Livonia*. London and The Hague, 1701.

Bruiningk, H., and N. Busch, *Livländische Güterurkunden aus dem Jahren 1207-1545*. 2 vols. Riga, 1909, 1924.

Buddenbrock, G. von, *Sammlung der Gesetze*. 14 vols. Riga, 1821.

Bulmerincq, A., *Aktenstücke und Urkunden zur Geschichte der Stadt Riga, 1710-1740*. 3 vols. Riga, 1902-1906.

Bunge, F. G. von, *Liv-, Est- und Curländische Urkunden. Regesten bis zum Jahre 1300*. Leipzig, 1881.

Ceumern, C. von, *Theatridicum livonicum*. Riga, 1690.

Dainas, ed. K. Barons and H. Vissendorfs. 6 vols. St. Petersburg, 1906ff.

Dionysius Fabricius, *Livonicae historiae compendiosa series* in *Scriptores rerum livonicarum*, q.v.

De Lettis, Henricus, *Origines Livoniae sacrae et civilis*, also known as *Chronicon Livonicarum vetus continens res gestas trium primorum episcoporum*, in *Scriptores rerum livonicarum*, q.v.

Dogiel, P., *Codex diplomaticus regni Poloniae*. 3 vols. Vilna, 1758-1764.
Einhorn, P., *Historia Lettica* in *Scriptores rerum livonicarum*, *q.v.*
Gadebusch, F. K., *Livländische Bibliothek nach alphabetischer Ordnung*. 3 vols. Riga, 1777.
——, *Livländische Jahrbücher*. 4 vols. Riga, 1780.
Gundling, Nicolaus H., *Discours über den jetzigen Zustand der Europäischen Staaten*. Leipzig, 1733.
Hagemeister, H. von, *Materialen zu einer Geschichte der Landgüter Livlands*. Riga, 1836.
Hakluyt, R., *Principal Navigations*. . . . , London, 1589.
Helmold, *Chronica Slavorum*, ed. B. S. Schmeidler. Leipzig, 1909. English translation by F. J. Tschan. New York, 1935.
Henning, Solomon, *Liffländische-Curländische Chronica*. Leipzig, 1594.
Hildebrand, H., *Livonica in den Vatikanischen Archiven*. Riga, 1881.
Latvian-Russian Relations. Documents, ed. A. Bilmanis. Washington, 1944.
Lieffländische Landesordnungen. Riga, 1707.
Liv-, Est- und Curländisches Urkundenbuch. 12 vols. Riga, 1853.
Olaus Magnus, *De gentibus septentrionalium*. Rome, 1555.
Meldups, A., ed., *Latvijas Skaitļos*. Riga, 1938.
Monumenta Livoniae antiquae. 5 vols. Riga, 1835-1847.
Napiersky, K. E., *Index corporis historiae diplomaticae Livoniae, Esthoniae, Curoniae*. 2 vols. Riga, 1833, 1835.
——, *Russisch-Livländische Urkunden*. St. Petersburg, 1868.
Nettelbladt, C., *Anecdota Curlandiae*. Leipzig, 1736.
——, *Fasciculus rerum curlandicarum*, Rostock, 1729.
Recueil des principaux traités conclus par la Lettonie avec les pays étrangers. 2 vols. Riga, 1928, 1938.
Renner, J., *Chronica Livoniae*, ed. R. Hammann. Leipzig, 1876.
Russow, Balthasar, *Chronica der Provintz Lyffland* in *Scriptores rerum livonicarum*, *q.v.*
Saxo Grammaticus, *Gesta Danorum*, ed. A. Holder, Strassburg, 1886.
Sbornik materialov i statei po istorii pribaltyskogo kraja. 3 vols. Riga, 1881.
Schwedisches Landrecht, ed. J. Schiedemann. Riga, 1709.
Scriptores rerum livonicarum. 2 vols. Leipzig and Riga, 1848, 1853.
Scriptores rerum prussicarum, ed. Th. Hirsch, M. Töppen, and E. Strehlke. 4 vols. Leipzig, 1861-1874.
Les sources de l'histoire de Lettonie. 2 vols. Riga, 1937.
Theiner, August, *Vetera Monumenta Poloniae et Lithuaniae*. 2 vols. Rome, 1860-1861.
Valdības vēstnesis (Official Gazette). Riga, 1918ff.
Zeigenhorn, C. von, *Staatsrecht der Herzogtümer Kurland und Semigallen*. Königsberg, 1772.

MONOGRAPHIC STUDIES

Adamovičs, Ludvigs, *Dzimtenes baznīcas vēsture*. Stockholm, 1947.
Ahnlund, Nils, *Gustav Adolf the Great*. Princeton, 1940.
Ames, E. O. F., ed., *The Revolution in the Baltic Provinces of Russia*. London, 1907.
Arbusov, Leonid, *Grundriss der Geschichte Liv-, Est- und Kurlands*. 4th ed., Riga, 1918.
——, *Die Altlivländischer Bauernrechte* in *Mitteilungen aus der Livländischen Geschichte*. Riga, 1924-1926.

Arnis, A., *Latvju tautas politiskā atmoda*. Riga, 1934.

Bainville, Jacques, *La Russie et la barrière de l'Est*. Paris, 1937.

Balodis, Francis, *La Lettonie du 9me au 12me siècle*. Riga, 1936.

————, *Die Burgberge Lettlands*. Rome, 1940.

————, *Det Äldsta Lettland*. Stockholm, 1940.

————, *Jersika*, Riga, 1940.

————, "Latvia and the Latvians" in *Journal of Central European Affairs*, VI (1947), 241-284.

————, ed., *Die Letten, Schriftensammlung der Lettländischen Universität*. Riga, 1930.

The Baltic States. Estonia, Latvia, Lithuania. Published by the Royal Institute of International Affairs, London, 1938.

Bandrevičs, A., *Notikumi latviešu atmošanās laikmetā*. Riga, 1931.

Berg, Arved, *La Latvie et la Russie, considérations sur un des problèmes de la paix mondiale*. Paris, 1919.

Bielenstein, A., *Die Holzbauten und Holzgeräte der Letten*. 2 vols. St. Petersburg, 1907.

Bilmanis, Alfred, *Latvijas Werdegang*. Riga, 1925; revised and greatly expanded, Berlin, 1930, and Riga, 1934.

————, *La Lettonie d'aujourd'hui, son développement historique et la situation actuelle*. Riga, 1925; 3rd ed. 1929; German ed. *ibid.*, 1925; also English edition, Riga, 1928, and Russian edition, Riga, 1929.

————, *Latvia in 1939-42*. Washington, 1942.

————, *The Baltic States in Post-War Europe*. Washington, 1943.

————, *Latvia under German Occupation: 1941-1943*. Washington, 1943.

————, *Baltic Essays*. Washington, 1945.

————, *Latvia as an Independent State*. Washington, 1947. And see notes to Chapter 17.

Blanks, Ernests, *Latviešu tautiskā kustība*. Riga, 1921.

Bock, Woldemar von, *Die deutsche-russische Konflikt an der Ostsee*. Leipzig, 1869.

————, *Livländische Beiträge*. 2 vols. Berlin, 1868.

Böhm, Max H., *Die Letten*. Berlin, 1917.

Braatz, Kurt von, *Fürst Anatol Pavlovitch Lieven im Kampfe gegen den baltischen Separatismus, russischen Bolschewismus und die Avaloff Bermondt Affäre*. Stuttgart, 1926.

Bray, François G., *Essai critique sur l'histoire de la Livonie*. 3 vols. Dorpat, 1817.

Brenneisen, Reinhold, *Lettland: Das Werden und Wesen einer neuen Volkswirtschaft*. Berlin, 1936.

Bunge, F. G. von, *Geschichte des Gerichtswesens*. Reval, 1874.

Butler, Ralph, *The New Eastern Europe*. London, 1919.

Čakste, M., "Latvia and the Soviet Union," in *Journal of Central European Affairs*, IX (1949), 31-60, 173-211.

Carlson, F. F., *Geschichte Schwedens*. 5 vols. Gotha, 1855.

Chance, J. F., *George I and the Northern War*. London, 1909.

Chase, T. G., *The Story of Lithuania*. New York, 1946.

De Chambon, Henry, *Origines et histoire de la Lettonie*. Paris, 1933.

De Wahl, A., *Histoire de l'Ordre Teutonique*. 2 vols. Paris, 1784.

Deutsches Reichskriegsministerium, *Die Rückführung des Ostheeres*. 2 vols. Berlin, 1936, 1937.

————, *Die Kämpfe im Baltikum nach der zweiten Einnahme von Riga*. Berlin, 1938.

Doering, J., *Ueber die Herkunft der Kurländischen Liven*. Mitau, 1880.

Dominian, Leon, *The Frontiers of Language and Nationality in Europe*. New York, 1917.

Eckert, W., *Kurland unter dem Einfluss des Mercantilismus*. Riga, 1927.

Engelhardt, R. Frh. von, *Die deutschen Ostseeprovinzen Russlands*. Munich, 1916.

Endzelīns, Jānis, *Ueber die Nationalität und Sprache der Kuren*. Leipzig, 1912.

Gaillard, O., *L'Allemagne et le Baltikum*. Paris, 1919.

Geijer, E. G., *Geschichte Schwedens*. 7 vols. Hamburg and Gotha, 1832-1908.

Goldmanis, Jānis, *Zvaigžnu pulku atmirdza*. Stockholm, 1947.

Goltz, Rudiger von der, *Als politischer General im Osten*. Leipzig, 1936.

Górski, Karol, *Państwo Krzyżackie w Prusach*. Gdańsk, 1946.

Graham, M. W., *Diplomatic Recognition of the Baltic States*. Part III: *Latvia*. Berkeley, 1941.

Halecki, O., *Dzieje unii jagiellońskiej*. 2 vols. Cracow, 1919-1920.

Haumant, E., *La guerre du Nord et la paix d'Oliva*. Paris, 1893.

Hubert, W., *Wojny bałtyckie*. Warsaw, 1937.

Jackson, J. Hampden, *Estonia*. London, 1941.

Jakubowski, J., *Polska XVI wieku*, vol. III, *Inflanty*, Warsaw, 1915.

Juškevičs, J., *Hercoga Jēkaba laikmets Kurzemē*. Riga, 1931.

Koczy, Leon, *The Baltic Policy of the Teutonic Order*, Toruń, 1936.

Konopczyński, Władysław, *Dzieje Polski nowożytnej*. 2 vols. Warsaw, 1936.

————, *Kwestia bałtycka do XX w*. Gdańsk, 1947.

Korzon, Th., *Dzieje Wojen*. 2 vols. Cracow, 1912.

Kruse, Friedrich, *Ur-Geschichte des Esthnischen Volkstammes und der Kaiserlich Russichen Liv-, Est- und Curland*. Moscow, 1846.

Kutrzeba, St., *Historja zródeł dawnego prawa polskiego*. 2 vols. Warsaw, 1925-1926.

Kubala, L., *Wojna Szwecka, 1655-56*. Warsaw, 1913.

Lelewel, J., *Histoire de Pologne*. 2 vols. Paris, 1844.

Ligers, Z., *Histoire des villes de Lettonie*. Paris, 1946.

Lundin, C. L., "The Nazification of the Baltic German Minorities," in *Journal of Central European Affairs*, VII (1947), 1-28.

Meuvret, J., *Histoire des pays baltiques*. Paris, 1934.

Nash, E. G., *The Hansa*. London, 1929.

Newman, E. W. P., *Britain and the Baltic*. London, 1930.

Olins, P., *The Teutonic Knights in Latvia*. Riga, 1928.

Papée, F., *Polska i Litwa na przełomie wieków średnich*. Cracow, 1904.

Pares, Bernard, *History of Russia*. New York, 1944.

Pick, F. W., *The Baltic Nations*. London, 1945.

Pistohlkhors, H. von, *Livlands Kampf um Deutschtum und Kultur. Eine Uebersicht aller Bedeutungsvoller Ereignisse aus der Geschichte des alten Ordensgebiet Livland*. Berlin, 1918.

Plantie-Cazejus, Armand, *La Constitution de la Lettonie: Documents et Commentaires*. Toulouse, 1925.

Rolnik, Hirsch, *Die baltischen Staaten, Litauen, Lettland und Estland und ihr Verfassungsrecht*. Leipzig, 1927.

Rosenberg, E. von, *Für Deutschtum und Fortschritt in Lettland*. Riga, 1928.

Ruhl, A. B., *New Masters of the Baltic*. New York, 1921.

Ruhl, P. J., *Geschichte Ernst Biron Herzogs*. Frankfort, 1764.

Rutenberg, O. von, *Geschichte der Ostseeprovinzen*. 2 vols. Leipzig, 1859, 1860.

Schiemann, Ch., *Russland, Polen und Livland*. 2 vols. Berlin, 1887.

Schirren, Carl, *Die Recesse der Livländischen Landtage, 1681-1711.* 2 vols. Dorpat, 1865.

Schwabe (Švābe), Arveds, *Agrarian History of Latvia.* Riga, 1928. A slightly abridged edition of the following title.

————, *Grundriss der Agrargeschichte Lettlands.* Riga, 1928.

————, *Latvijas tiesību vēsture.* 2 vols. Riga, 1932.

————, *The Story of Latvia and her Neighbors.* Edinburgh, n.d.

Seraphim, E., *Grundriss der baltischen Geschichte.* Reval, 1908.

————, *Klaus Kursell und seine Zeit.* Reval, 1897.

Sobieski, W., *Der Kampf um die Ostsee.* Leipzig, 1933.

Solovyev, S. M., *Istoria Rossii.* 12 vols. St. Petersburg, 1895.

Spekke, A., "Vichinghi e Lettoni" in *Studi Baltici.* 3 vols., Rome, 1941-1942.

Sternberg, E. von, *Die livländischen Bekehrungen wie sie Herr Samarin erzählt.* Leipzig, 1872.

Strakhovsky, L. I., *The Origins of American Intervention in North Russia (1918).* Princeton, 1937.

Straubergs, J., *Rigas vēsture.* Riga, 1937.

Stryjkonski, M., *Kronika Polska, Litevska, Zmodska i Wsystkiej Rusi.* Warsaw, 1846.

Tetsch, C. L., *Curländische Kirchengeschichte.* 3 vols. Riga, 1767, and Königsberg, 1768.

Transehe-Roseneck, Astaf von, *Die lettische Revolution.* 2 vols. Berlin, 1908.

Urch, R. O. G., *Latvia. Country and People.* London, 1938.

Vernadsky, G., *Ancient Russia.* New Haven, 1943.

————, *Kievan Russia.* New Haven, 1948.

Vigrabs, J. *Die Rosensche Deklaration vom Jahre 1739, ein Beitrag zur Geschichte der Leibeigenschaft im Livland und Estland.* Tartu, 1937.

Vitols, H., *La mer baltique et les états baltes.* Paris, 1935.

Walters, Michael, *Lettland: seine Entwicklung zum Staat und die baltischen Fragen.* Riga (Rome), 1923.

————, *Le Peuple Letton.* Riga, 1926.

Wasilewski, Leon, *Die Ostprovinzen des alten Polenreichs.* Cracow, 1916.

Wheeler-Bennett, J. W., *The Forgotten Peace.* New York, 1939.

Wihksmusch, Nikolai, *Die Aufklärung und die Agrarfrage in Livland.* Riga, 1933.

Winkler, A., *Die deutsche Hanse in Russland.* Berlin, 1886.

Yevreinoff, G. A., *Natsionalniye voprosi.* St. Petersburg, 1908.

Zalts, Alberts, *Die politischen Parteien Lettlands.* Riga, 1926.

————, *Latvian Political Economy.* 2nd ed., Riga, 1931.

Zivier, E., *Neuere Geschichte Polens.* Gotha, 1915.

Schober, T. M., Die Bauten der deutschen Hanse... , 1 ... Berlin 1961.
Dargun ...
Schreiber, Arthur, Anglo-Saxon History of Latvia, Augs 1949, Knight ...
phaidroshalltop of the following 1 ...
——, Comtesse des Sammlungen der Lettland, Riga, 1932.
——, Latvijas Higher verfasz. a.voll. Riga, 1932.
——, Theodor von Chartn und der Neuphoren, Jahrbuch a.d.
Seraphim, E., Grundriss der baltischen Geschichte, Reval 1908.
——, Aus Kampf und eine Zeit, Riga, 1929.
Silberer, W., Boei Kampf um die Ostsee, Leipzig, 1933.
——, Sh., Jäecht Rigas Zustock St. Petersburg, 1914.
Spekke, A., Velmeplanu Latijot in Sinnt Balter's... voll. Bonn, 1933 ...
Stervens, P., von Oberhausische Entwicklungen im südlia Z.Journ erste...
——, Toujoncij, s.
Stankiewicz, T. Iz The Origin of American Intervention in North-East ...
——, Princeton 1955.
Strehlow, J., Mogu versunt-Kiew, 1957.
Stryphonta, M., Krumia Poeta, Lettevoli, London 1947, sparisa Russ. Warsau.
——, 1857.
Tetsch, C. L., Curlandisch-Kirchen und schulau, 3 voll. Riga, 1767 und König-berg, 1768.
Thaiden Puckburr, Adel um die lettesche Republik, 3 voll. Berlin, 1954.
Thub, R. G. D., Latvia, Country and People, London 1934.
Vorsdeus, C., Ancient Russes, New Haven, 1943.
——, Kievan Russia, NVW Haven 1928.
Vazaka, J., Une Renaissance Lxidtivation vom Anny 1905, mit Beitrag zur
——, Osten-Mittel Lahren einheit, an Livland und Estland, Lang, 1925.
Viloff, H., La monarchique et La arts balber Paris, 1952.
Wielhorn, Michael, Lettland, seine Verwaltung Entwicklung und die politischen
——, Parteien Riga (Rome), 1922.
——, La Petite Lettou, Riga, 1920.
Wielowski, J., ?90, The Untermannische dhad Folenische Cracov, 1938.
Wheeler-Bennet, J. W., The Forgotten Peace, New York, 1938.
Winhumach, Wilhelm, Die Auflösung und die Aneignung in Lettland, 1938,
——, 1939.
Winkler, A., Die Z.teupche Haare in Kurland, Berlin, 1938.
Jerenhardt, G., A., Nationalithey reform Mr. Telzthinen, 1908.
Zeihn, Albert, Die politischen Parteien Lettlands, Riga, 1926.
——, Latvian Political Economist, 2nd ed., Riga, 1931.
Zinn, E., Neuere Geschichte Europas, Gotha, 1918.

INDEX

Aa River, *see* Lielupe
Abel, Danish prince, 36
Academia Carolina (Riga), 180
Academia Gustaviana (Dorpat), 172
Academia Petrina (Mitau), 210
Acta Universitatis Latviensis, 376
Adalbert, Bishop of Prague, 71
Adam of Bremen, Bishop, 4, 36, 46
Aestii (*Aestyorum gentes*), 30ff., 48, 71
Agrarian party, *see* Farmers' Union
agrarian reform laws (1804) 222f.; (1819) 225ff.; (1849) 227f.; (1861, Russian), 228; (1920) 12, 334ff., 348. *See also* land revision
agricultural associations, 271, 335, 344, 364. *See also* cooperative societies
agricultural schools, 271, 335, 371f. *See also* Latvian State Academy of Agriculture
agriculture, 5, 11ff.; ancient, 9, 40, 42; in tribal times, 42; in Livonia, 176 (*see also* serfdom); in Latvian Republic, 335, 344, 355, 363
Ainaži, 6, 28
Aizpute, Kuronian stronghold, 81
Aksakov, Ivan, 246
Akūraters, Jānis, poet, 254, 262, 291f., 374
Albert, Bishop of Livonia, 46, 55, 57-69, 99f.
Albert Suerbeer, Archbishop of Riga, 84
Albert of Brandenburg, Grand Master of the Teutonic Order, 113, 117
Albert, Duke of East Prussia, 119
Alençon, François, Duke of, 144
Alexander I, Tsar, 221-225, 238
Alexander II, Tsar, 228ff., 245
Alexander III, Tsar, 230, 245ff., 258f., 262
Alexander, Lithuanian grand duke, King of Poland, 116
Alexander, Col. H. R. L. G., 324
Alexandra, Tsarina, 278
Alexis I Romanov, Tsar, 167ff., 197
Alfred the Great, 4
Algirdas, Grand Duke of Lithuania, 83, 105

Allied Military Mission in the Baltic (1919), 322f., 326
Allies (Western Powers), in World War I, 275ff., 285f., 288f.; recognize Latvian State, 293ff., 299; and Baltic War of Liberation (1918-1920), 304, 306, 310, 312, 315f., 318, 325ff.; in World War II, 405
Altmark, Truce of (1629), 165
Alt-Rundstadt, Treaty of (1707), 201
Alūksne (Marienburg), 18, 395
Alunāns, Juris, poet and folklorist, 242f., 252
Amartolo, Greek chronicler, 46
Amberland, 5, 26, 30ff.
American zone in Germany, 406
Ancient Prussians, 43, 53; culture of, 27ff.; conflict with Teutonic Knights, 71f., 105
Andrew, Apostle, 46
Andrussovo, Peace of (1667), 169
Anglo-Saxons, 6
Animal husbandry, 9ff., 27, 366
Anna, Grand Duchess, 193; Dowager Duchess of Kurland, 204f.; Tsarina, 206ff.
Anna Leopoldovna, Princess of Mecklenburg, 208; Duchess of Brunswick, 208; Regent of Russia, 208f.
Anna of Mecklenburg, Duchess of Kurland, 157
Anna, Jagiellonian princess, 145
Anscarius, Bishop, 35
anthropology, 16, 28ff.
Apule, ancient capital of Kurzeme, 34f., 48
Archangel, 124, 353
Archbishopric, *see* Riga Archbishopric
archeology, ix, 27ff., 38-43, 257; First Baltic Congress of (1894), 255
architecture, 255; in Duchy of Kurland, 207, 210; in Riga, 14f., 255f., 374f.; Museum of, 375
Armistice (November 1918), Article 12 of, 305, 309, 312, 319, 324
army, *see* Latvian armed forces, German armed forces, Russian armed forces
Army Law of 1935, 360
Arnold of Lübeck, chronicler, 55

arts, 20f., 254ff., 374f.; Chamber of Literature and Art, 360. *See also* architecture, crafts, painting, sculpture, Latvian State Academy of Arts

Aryans, 28

Asars, Jānis, literary critic, 253

Atlantic Charter, 405, 407f.

Aublet, Commandant, 325

Augsburg Confession (1530), 125, 149, 158

Augsburg, Peace of (1555), 119

Augustus II, Elector of Saxony, King of Poland, 192, 197-206, 210, 214

Augustus III, King of Poland, 206f., 209ff.

Auseklis, K. M., author, 252

Austria, 143, 161, 211f., 246, 325

Austrvaegr, 6, 14, 32, 40, 99

authoritarianism, 356f., 360f., 369

autonomy, movement for in Baltic Provinces, 273; Latvian, 262, 267ff., 276, 290ff.

Avignon, Livonian archbishops at, 85, 88, 102

Azov, battle of (1696), 197

Baghdad, coins of, 33

Baldwin of Aune, papal legate, 70, 72ff.

Balfour, A., 299

Balkans, 246, 275

Balke, Hermann, Master of Livonian Order, 77

ballet, in Duchy of Kurland, 14, 254; in Riga, 254, 374

Balodis, David, pastor, 238

Balodis, F. archeologist, 61, 257, 375

Balodis, Col. Jānis, 316, 319, 322f., 327; General, 344, 359, 397

Balodis, K. economist, 257, 375

Balss, weekly, 245

"Balt," origin of term, 4f.; German appropriation of, 132

"Baltia," 4f., 31

Baltic barons, *see* German-Balts

Baltic-Central European Federation, 244

Baltic Commission (Interallied), 320, 322, 325

Baltic Conferences, 340f., 382, 387; *see also* Bulduri, Helsinki

Baltic Entente (1934), 386, 388, 394, 398

Baltic Essays (A. Bilmanis), 3n, 409

Baltic Interallied Military Mission, 328

Baltic League, 382

Baltic Manifesto of Emperor Frederick II, 66, 69, 71f.

Baltic peoples, vii, ix; influence of climate on, 5f.; origins of, 26ff.; early culture of, 4, 32ff., 38-49; under Livonian Order, 131; under Poland, 137, 155f., 160; under Sweden, 178; and Great Northern War, 203; under Tsarist Russia, 216f., 227, 249; and French Revolution, 223, 238; and National Awakening, 231f., 246f., 259, 271; in World War I, 276, 280; achievement of independence, 282; and Soviet Union, 353, 378, 407; societies of friendship of, 394. *See also* Baltic tribes

Baltic Provinces (Russian), vii, 3, 24, 215, 225f., 229, 245ff., 260f., 271., 273; in World War I, 275-280; liberation of, 285, 290, 293, 295; Germany's struggle for, 292, 297f., 300-328

Baltic Sea, 3ff., freedom of, 3, 6, 23f., 180, 203, 299, 310, 340, 382, 408; *mare clausum*, 275, 408; neutrality of, 340; struggle for dominion over, ix, 13, 166, 197, 275, 282, 300, 310, 314, 408; Allied blockade of, 314; and Russian trade, 353. *See also dominium maris Baltici*

Baltic States, 232, 299; strategic position of, 24; achievement of independence, 290, 292ff., 300-328; diplomatic recognition of, vii, 318, 328, 338; mutual relations of, 340ff., 382-388; and Third Reich, 387, 389ff.; and Soviet Union, 329, 383 *passim*; in World War II, 390, 403ff.; sovietization of, 397ff. *See also* Estonia, Lithuania.

Baltic Treaty of Understanding and Cooperation (1934), 386, 393

Baltic tribes, movement of, 5, 7, 26-30, 43; cultural development of, 6, 26f., 30ff., 39-48; early wars of, 32,

34ff.; subjugation of, 57-64, 71-85
Baltic Union, 24, 383, 386
Baltic War of Liberation (1918-1920), 311-329
Balticum, 269, 271, 275, 324, 385, 387
Baltijas Semkopis, newspaper, 245
Baltischer Bruderschaft, 387
Baltische Landeswehr, 305, 310, 312ff., 318, 321ff., 348f.
Baltischer Vertrauensrat, 280, 300ff.
Baltiski, 391
Balts, ancient, 30. *See also* Baltic tribes and Baltic peoples
banks and banking, 173, 229, 241, 335, 348, 350f., 362ff.; moratorium (1931), 355; nationalization, 401
Bārda, F., poet, 254
Barons, K., folklorist, 243
Bärwalde, Peace of (1631), 165
Basilius II, Emperor, 34
Basra, coins of, 33
Bátory, *see* Stephen
Baumanis, J., architect, 255f.
Baumanis, K., composer, 245
Baumanis, R., author, 253
Bauska, Kuronian town, 164, 192
Bavaria, 348; Prince Leopold of, 297
Beck, Col. Józef, 385
Berezina River, 32
Berlin, 192, 211, 275, 325, 328, 381
Berlin, Congress of (1878), 246
Berlin, Treaty of (1878), 246
Berlin, Treaty of (1918), 303, 305
Bermondt-Avalov, "Prince," 325ff.
Bern, Congress of oppressed Baltic nationalities at (1903), 261f.
Bernard, Bishop of Selonia, 63
Bernt von Borch, Master of Livonian Order, 108f.
Berthold of Hannover, Bishop of Riga, 56f.
Besminiers, de, French Ambassador, 168
Bessarabia, 407
Bethmann-Hollweg, Theobald von, Chancellor, 280
Bible, in Latvian, 179f., 241
Bielenstein, A., German scholar, 255
Bilmanis, Alfred, viiff., 393
Bīmanis, B., engineer, 256, 375
Birin, Jānis, Latvian commander, 146

Birka, Viking trading post, 34, 36
Biron, duc de Périgord, 207
Biron, Ernst Johann, 206-210
Biron, Karl Ernst, 210
Biron, Peter, Duke of Kurland, 210ff., 329
Birži, Kuronian town, 164
Bischoff, Commander of Iron Brigade, 305
Bismarck, Prince Otto von, 246
Black Sea, 7, 27, 29, 31, 353
Blaus, Latvian Communist, 396
Blumbergs, P. statesman, 308
Bohemia, 143
Bolderaa, 191
Bolesław IV, King of Poland, 71
Bolsheviks, 261, 268, 271, 280, 285, 288f., 291, 293ff.; in Baltic States, 296, 305, 310, 317, 325; in Latvia, 312, 314, 319f., 323ff., 328f.; Latvian, 290, 306, 322. *See also* Communists
Boniface VIII, Pope, 70, 84, 100, 109
Boro-Russians (Borussians), *see* Ancient Prussians
Bourbon-Conti, Prince François of, 209
Bourgeoisie, in Riga, 220, 241, 244; in Baltic Provinces, 215, 233, 239, 251; German-Balt, 241, 348f.; Latvian, 241, 252, 270f., 350
Boxer Rebellion, 264
Boy Scouts, 370
Brandenburg, 167, 198; Margrave of, 205; Elector of, 165, 168f., 187, 191f.
Brawalla, battle of (*ca.* 750), 35
Bremen, 53, 55, 69, 97, 99, 166; Archbishop of, 56f., 67, 70
Brest-Litovsk, Armistice of, 289, 297; Peace of, 289f., 293, 295ff., 300f., 305f.; agreement of (1939), 390
Brethren of the Sword, see *Fratres Militiae Christi*
Brinken, leader in Calendar Riots, 153
Brisson, Rear Admiral, 327
British Fleet in Baltic War of Liberation, 311f., 314
British Isles, 31; trade with Kurland, 10. *See also* England
British zone in Germany, 406.

Brockhausen, Burgomaster of Riga, 220

Brödrich, Silvio, German-Balt colonizer, 274

Broemsebroe, Treaty of (1645), 166

Bronze Age, 30

Browne, Count G., Governor-General of Livonia, 217ff., 236

Brüggeney, Hermann von, Grand Master of Livonian Order, 118f.

Bruno, Bishop of Prague, 71

Brunswick, Prince Ludwig Ernst of, 208f.; Anna, Duchess of, 208; Elizabeth, Princess of, 157

Bug River, 28

Bukovina, 407

Bulduri Conference (1920), 340f., 382

Bulmeringck, von, 304

Burghers, in Livonia, 111, 132; in Baltic Provinces, 215 (see bourgeoisie); in Duchy of Kurland, 184; Rigan, 98, 100, 150ff., 220f., 241

Burt, Brig. Gen. Sir Alfred, 327

Burtnieki, 43, 48

Burtnieks, lake, 8, 43

Byzantium, early trade with, 7, 32ff., 38; relations with Lithuanian Empire, 105

Cadaster, Great Livonian, 176

"Cadets," see Constitutional Democrats (Russian)

Čakste, Jānis, statesman, 272, 281, 290, 294, 299, 344; and President of Latvian Republic, 272, 307, 333

Calendar Riots in Riga, 151ff.

capitalism, 23, 401; foreign investments and control, 335, 346, 351, 355; state, 335, 354, 368, 395

Caspar Linde, Archbishop of Riga, 117f.

Castle-mounds, 13, 39ff.

Catherine I, Tsarina, 205

Catherine II, Tsarina, 211ff., 217ff., 221, 236, 348

Catherine Jagiellonka, Polish princess, 137, 139

Catholic League, 164f.

Caunis, mythological figure, 43

Caunītis, J., publicist, 242

Cautio Radziviliana, 127, 140

Celestin III, Pope, 56f.

Celmiņš, G., nationalist, 358

Celmiņš, H., statesman, 355

Central Committee of Russian Social-Democratic party, 261

Central Council (Latvian, 1943), 405

Central Federative Committee (Latvian, 1905), 266ff.

Central Powers, 285, 296

Cēsis (Wenden), 13, 18, 83, 145f., 162, 214, 241; castle of, 170; in Baltic War of Liberation, 317, 322f.

Chamboudois, de, Regent of Kurland, 224

Charles IV, Emperor, 102

Charles V, Emperor, 118f.

Charles VI, Emperor, 207

Charles Vasa, Regent of Sweden, 161f.; and King (Charles IX), 162

Charles Gustavus X, King of Sweden, 167f., 174, 179, 190f.

Charles XI, King of Sweden, 174ff., 214, 216f.

Charles XII, King of Sweden, viii, 192, 198-203, 214

Charles I, King of England, 186, 188f.

Charles II, King of England, 190

Charles, Duke of Kurland, 209

Chodkiewicz, Voyevode, Viceroy of Livonia, 139, 149, 162

Christian IV, King of Denmark, 162, 166

Christianity, coming of, 6, 34, 45f., 49; German manipulation of, 101, 131, 234; in Lithuania, 104, 106, 128; in Baltic Provinces, 233. See also Roman Catholicism, Greek Orthodoxy, Lutheranism

Christina, Queen of Sweden, 165, 167, 174

Christopher, Prince of Mecklenburg, 119, 125f.

Chronica slavorum (Arnold of Lübeck), 55

Church, see Christianity, Greek Orthodoxy, Roman Catholicism, Lutheranism, religion

Church Law of 1934, 376

Cielavs, J., artist, 374

Cimze, J., educational leader, 239

Cirava, normal school of, 238

Circassians, in Revolution of 1905, 265

cities, see towns

Civil Code of 1938, 376

Civil Rights (Liberties), 22, 267, 308, 334, 336, 361, 369, 396

Clemenceau, Georges, 318

Clement V, Pope, 72, 102

clergy, see Lutheran pastors

climate, 5f., 11

Codex Zamoyski, 55

colonization, aim of Teutonic Knights, 86; policy of Duke Jacob, 189ff.; German aim, 129, 131, 274, 276, 280, 300-312; Latvian protest against, 292

commerce, see trade and trade agreements

Committee on Baltic Affairs (1846), 227

common law, see law

Communism, in German army, 305f.; in Estonia, 358, 382; in Latvia, 346, 358, 388, 401; in Baltic area, 383, 393

Communists, Latvian, 345, 394ff. See also Bolsheviks

conciliation and arbitration agreements, 383, 393

Concordat of 1922, 338, 377

Conference of Latvian School Teachers (1873), 245

Conference of Agronomists (1873), 245

Congress of Berlin (1878), 246

Congress of Oppressed Baltic Nationalities at Bern (1903), 261f.

Congress of Representatives of Rural Communities (1905), 266f.

Congresses of Representatives of Rural Communities (1917), 280f.

Congress of Soviets (Nov. 1917), 288f.

Conrad, Duke of Mazovia, 71f.

Conservatory of Music, see Latvian State Conservatory

Constantine VIII, Emperor, 34

Constantinople, 33; Patriarchate, 377

Constituent Assembly (All-Russian), 262, 279, 288, 294, 297

Constituent Assembly (Latvian), 262, 266f., 281, 292, 294, 308, 332, 345, 352

Constitution of April 23, 1906 (Russian), 272

Constitution of 1922 (Latvian), 334, 336, 358ff., 399

Constitution of August, 1940 (Latvian), 400f.

Constitutional Democrats (Russian), 265, 272f., 286; Latvian, 267, 293

Constitutional reform, 356f., 360ff.

Cooperative societies, 291, 344, 354, 361, 365, 401

Copenhagen, 199

Copenhagen, Treaty of (1660), 169

Corporation of the Livonian-German nobles, 2, 81, 174, 183f., 215f., 226, 281, 348. See also Ritterschaft

Corporative State, 360

Corpus juris Livonici, 173, 249

Corpus privilegiorum Stephaneum, 149

Cossacks, 202, 267f., 276

Council of the Russian Republic (1917), 288

Courland, see Kurland

courts, manorial, 96, 240; of the pagasti, 92, 95, 223, 226; archiepiscopal, 94f.; Kuronian, 188; of Livonian districts, 172; of Latvian Republic, 376

Cracow, 106, 144f., 149, 167, 200

crafts, 20, 26f., 40ff., 254f., 374

Crimean War, 228, 240, 245

Criminal Code of 1933, 376f.

Cromwell, Oliver, 188f.

cultural autonomy, law of (1919), 332f.; constitutional, 336

Cultural Council of Latvian State, 360

cultural societies, Baltic, 386; Latvian, 244, 266, 271; German-Balt, 270, 348

cultural traits, 19ff., 42ff., 131, 232, 235f., 254. See also national tradition

Curland, see Kurland

"Curonia," 18

currency, 317, 337, 367, 401

customs, 3, 6, 10ff., 20f., 41-48, 131

Czechoslovakia, 385

Czechs, 231; at battle of Tannenberg, 106

Dainas, 26f., 30, 42ff., 48, 132, 242f., 252, 373, 375
Damascus, coins of, 33
Danes, 56, 62, 103; as christianizers, 36, 46; and Livonian Order, 62ff. *See also* Denmark
Dankers, Latvian General, 323
Danzig, 28, 35, 106, 113f., 124, 144, 164, 192f.
Darwinism, 253
Dārziņš, E., composer, 375
Dārziņš, W., composer, 375
Daugava River (Düna, Dvina), 6ff., 27ff., 40, 43, 54, 60f., 142, 148ff., 192, 303; line in World War I, 276f., 288
Daugava-Lielupe canal, 7
Daugavpils (Dünaburg, Dvinsk), 14f., 18, 211, 303, 307; Germans in (1918), 297; Bolsheviks in (1918), 312; liberation of, 329
Daugmale, Zemgallian port, 33, 39ff., 56, 58
Declaration of the Government of National Unity (May, 1934), 359f.
Deenas Lapa, newspaper, 260
defensive alliance, Latvian-Estonian (1923), 341, 381f., 393
Deglavs, A., author, 253
Den, newspaper, 246
Denikin, Gen. Anton, 328
Denmark, 5, 53, 114, 137ff., 168; early Balt relations with, 33ff.; and Estonia, 62ff., 80, 103, 124f., 129, 166; and the Hansa, 97f., 103, 113f.; and Muscovy, 116, 122; trade with Livonia, 162f.; at war with Sweden, 141, 162f., 166, 168f.; and Kurland, 185, 188; in Great Northern War, 198ff., 202f., and Latvian Republic, 383
deportations, Tsarist, 249; Soviet, 392, 402, 406; Nazi, 405f.
De Potestate civili (Francisco de Vittoria), 180
Deutsche Zeitung im Ostland, 404
Deutschrussen, 233, 258, 277. *See also* Germans at St. Petersburg
Die Letten (G. Merkel), 222, 244
diets, Livonian (*Landtag, Landrat*), 8, 347, under German dominion, 13, 110f., 117, 119f., 123, 130;

under Polish suzerainty, 140, 154; under Swedish rule, 170, 173, 175, 178; under Russian rule, 214, 219, 222, 229, 235, 239, 249, 259, 267, 334; Polish, *see* Sejm; Swedish, 173ff., 179
Dignaja, castle-mound, 39
Dionysius Fabricius, 18
Diploma unionis, 140f.
diplomatic recognition of Baltic States, vii, 318, 328, 338; nonrecognition of Soviet annexation, 399ff.
Dīriķis, B., editor, 245
Dnieper River, 7, 28, 33, 169
Dniester River, 31
Dobele, town, 13, 80
Dobelis, A., 292
Dobrzyn, 107; Order of 71
Doering, J., philologist, 29
Dole, island, 33
Dolgoruky, Prince, 168
Domesnaes, Kurish settlement, 36
dominium maris Baltici, 23, 23n., 166, 197
Dorchester, Viscount, 186f.
Dorno, King of the Kurs, 35
Dorpat, bishopric of, 65, 75, 88, 94, 101, 110, 114, 127; Livonian district of, 153; tribunal of, 172f.; university of, 179, 244, 248ff., 256, 268f., 375. *See also* Tartu
Douglas, Swedish General, 191
Dravnieks, A., Chemist, 376
Dresden, 198
Ducatus ultradunensis (*transdunensis*), 127, 139ff., 153
Duma (Russian parliament), 263ff., 272f., 278, 290f.
Düna, *see* Daugava
Dünaburg, Livonian district of, 109, 120, 125, 139. *See also* Daugavpils
Dünamunde, 199, 209
Duna urbs, 15, 35, 99
Dunsdorfs, E., historian, 376
Durbe, battle of (1260), 80f.
Dvina, *see* Daugava
Dvinsk, *see* Daugavpils
Dzenins, B., sculptor, 256, 374

East Prussia, 27, 30, 116, 119, 124, 306, 314, 321, 325f.; in World

War I, 276f., 295. *See also* Prussia,
Duchy of
"Eastern Locarno," 385f.
Eberhard von Monhein, Master of
Livonian Order, 102
Eberhard, Gen. von, 326f.
economic agreements, *see* trade agreements
economic crises, 226, 351, 353ff., 357
economic controls, 362ff.
Economic and Cultural Council, 360
economic recovery of Latvian Republic, 337, 360-368
education, under German dominion,
132, 171f.; under Swedish rule, 171,
178, 180, 216; under Russian rule,
216, 218, 235ff., 238ff., 248; in
Latvian Republic, 332f., 336, 371ff.,
377. *See also* schools
Eglītis, V., author, 253, 374
Einhorn, Paul, pastor, 171
elections, 337, 342ff., 395ff.; laws,
337, 349. *See also* proportional representation
Elizabeth Petrovna, Tsarina, 209
Elizabeth, Queen of England, 123f.
Elizabeth, Swedish princess, 144
Elizabeth of Brunswick, Princess, 157
Endzelīns, Jānis, philologist, 256, 375
Engelbrecht, Canon of Riga, 67
England, 122, 161, 163f., 168, 199,
202f.; Muscovite trade with, 121,
123f.; and Kurland, 185ff., 193;
and Russia, 223, 246; Latvian exiles
in, 268. *See also* Great Britain
Engure, lake, 8
Enlightenment (*Aufklärung*), in Li-
vonia, 222, 238
Eric Gustavson, Swedish king, 122
Eric XIV, King of Sweden, 137ff.,
141
Ernemordus, Bishop of Kurland, 36
Ernest, son of Maximilian II, 144
Ernst Johann Biron, 206-210
Erzberger, Mathias, 287
Essen, Gen. von, Governor-General
of Livonia
Estonia, 3, 105, 137, 140, 166, 168,
298; tribal, 55; under Livonian Or-
der, 5, 88, 91, 110, 127; Danish
interests in, 62f., 103, 124f., 166;
Sweden in, 122, 139, 141f., 146f.,

160ff., 165, 168, 171, 175, 214;
Poland in, 156, 162; Russians in,
203; under Russian rule, 216f., 225,
230, 249; German-Balt interests in,
259; revolutionary trends in, 261,
269; liberation of, 296ff., 299, 301,
303; and Bolsheviks, 305, 307, 311,
314, 317, 322f., 328; and Soviet
Union, 329, 384-394, 407; Baltic
relations of, 340f., 381f., 386f.; and
Third Reich, 389, 405; authoritarianism in, 357; communism in, 358,
382 (*see also* Tallinn); in World
War II, 407. *See also* Estonians
Estonian islands, 62. *See also* Oesel
Estonians, 16, 35f., 43, 49, 53, 55f.,
60, 137, 169f.; conflict with Knights
of the Sword, 62f., 73; under Livonian Order, 89, 117, 130, 132;
uprising of (1343), 88, 94; in Muscovite Wars, 122f.; under Russian
rule, 226, 248; at University of
Dorpat, 244, 248; in Baltic War of
Liberation, 216f., 322f., 325; in
World War II, 407
Etruscans, 31

Farmers' Union, 281, 307, 344f.,
355ff., 359, 363
farms in tribal times, 20, 41f.; under
Russian rule, 226, 228f.; in Latvian
Republic, 11f., 16, 335, 364
Fedders, J., painter, 256
Ferdinand I, Emperor, 120, 124
Ferdinand, Regent of Kurland, 192f.,
199, 204; and Duke, 206f.
feudalism, in Livonia, 87-94, 132,
154-157, 174f., 178; in Polish Commonwealth, 154, 160; in Duchy of
Kurland, 157f.; in Baltic Provinces,
216f., 225, 228, 233, 235
finances, of Latvian Republic, 309,
317, 333, 337, 362, 366f., 366n.
See also currency
Finland, 118, 138, 166, 175, 198,
202f., 223, 261, 273, 315; in World
War I, 277; Lenin in, 288; independence of, 290, 293; and Germany, 383; and Baltic States, 340f.,
382f.; and Soviet Union, 306, 341,
362, 384f., 392f.

Finno-Ugric, language, 5, 17; racial strain, 16; tribes, 4, 30, 32

Finns, 16f., 28, 137

Flanders, medieval trade with, 53

Foch, Marshal Ferdinand, 307, 322, 327

folklore, ix, 26ff., 131, 237, 251f., 372, 374

folksongs, 17, 21, 42, 254. See also Dainas

Fontebasso, Francesco, painter, 207

Foreign Delegation (1918), 294f., 299

foreign relations of Latvian Republic, 337-342, 381 passim; diplomatic recognition of Latvian State, 299, 317ff., 338; relations with Baltic nations, 340ff., 382ff.; with Poland, 341f., 385; with Third Reich, 367f., 387, 389; with Soviet Union, 339ff., 352f., 384 passim

forestry, 10, 335

Formula Regiminis (1617), 183f.

Fort Jacob, 190

France, medieval trade with, 53; and Polish Commonwealth, 144; interests in the Baltic, 149; and Thirty Years' War, 163; and Kurland, 185, 188f., 192, 209, 212, 221, 223f., and Russia, 223, 246, 389; and Baltic War of Liberation, 328, 330; Latvia's trade with, 367. See also French diplomacy

François, duc d'Alençon, 144

François Louis Bourbon, Prince de Conti, 209

Fratres, Hospitalis Sanctae Marie Teutonicorum per Jerosolemitam, 70. See Teutonic Knights

Fratres Militiae Christi, organization of, 58f.; character of, 65f.; conquests in Baltic lands, 61ff., 72ff.; merger with Teutonic Knights, 75f.

Frederick I Barbarossa, Emperor, 96

Frederick II, Emperor, 64, 66, 69, 71f.

Frederick III, Emperor, 108

Frederick William, the Great Elector, 168f., 187, 191f.

Frederick I, King of Prussia, 193

Frederick William I, King of Prussia, 205

Frederick II, King of Prussia, 210f.

Frederick William II, King of Prussia, 212

Frederick William III, King of Prussia, 224f.

Frederick II, King of Denmark, 142, 145f.

Frederick IV, King of Denmark, 198f., 202

Frederick I, King of Sweden, 203

Frederick, Duke of Kurland, 145, 157, 182f., 185, 187

Frederick William, Duke of Kurland, 182, 192

Frederick Casimir, Duke of Kurland, 191f.

Frederick, Archbishop of Riga, 85, 102

Freivalds, E., 291

French diplomacy, 144, 165, 168, 202, 209, 212, 385, 389, 391

French influence at Court of St. Petersburg, 209, 221

French merchants and Muscovy, 124

French Revolution, 221f., 234, 238

French zone in Germany, 406

Frisians, 6, 30

frontiers, 8, 13, 43, 282, 330, 338f., 338n. See also natural boundaries

Fürstenberg, von, Grand Master of Livonian Order, 120f.

Gaisina, Mt., 8

Galen, Heinrich von, Grand Master of Livonian Order, 118ff.

Gambia, Kuronian interests in, 189f.

Gapon, Father, 264

Gardie, General de la, 168

Gauja River, 6f., 19, 27f., 32f., 54, 61, 323

Gediminas, Prince (Grand Duke) of Lithuania, 83, 104f., 115

Geer, Sten de, geographer, 9

Geneva Draft Convention, 385

Geneva, German-Balt Committee at, 334

genocide, Soviet, 402, 408; Nazi, 405

gentry, see German-Balts and Nobility

geological features, 9

George William, Elector of Brandenburg, 165

German armed forces, in World War II, 276f., 287f., 297; occupying Kurland, 304ff.; in Baltic War of

Liberation, 312, 315, 320ff.; in World War II, 404, 406. *See also* Iron Brigade, *Baltischer Landeswehr* (German-Balt), *Wehrmacht*.

German-Balt clergy, *see* Lutheran pastors

German-Balt cultural unions, 270

German-Balt historians, 38, 66, 129, 130, 217

German-Balt industrialists, 259f., 274

German-Balt pro-Germanism in World War I, 296f., 300ff.; in World War II, 358, 387, 389ff.

German-Balt squires and squirearchy, viiif., 20ff., 88, 93ff., 112, 124, 127f., 130ff.; under Polish suzerainty, 139f., 154ff.; in Duchy of Kurland, 157f.; under Swedish rule, 170-178; under Russian rule, 204, 214-220, 225-230, 233ff., 239, 243, 245ff., 255, 259f., 264, 269; relations with St. Petersburg, *see* Germans at Court of; and Russification, 248ff., 269; and Revolution of 1905, 265, 267ff.

German-Balts, in Baltic War of Liberation, 300-326; and Latvian Provisional Government, 316, 320, 324, 332; at Paris Peace Conference, 325; in Latvian Republic, 334f., 347ff.; and Nazism, 358, 387, 389; evacuation of by Hitler, 389f., 392

German Council of the Baltic State (1918), 304

German Fleet, 275

German High Command, in World War I, 277, 287, 289, 295ff.; in Baltic War of Liberation, 315, 317f.

German Intelligence Service, 285, 287, 295

German language, 141, 248, 270, 274

Germania (Tacitus), 31

Germanization, 19, 234; after 1905, 269ff., 292; under Nazis, 405

Germans, merchants, ix, 6f., 37-53ff., 63f., 116; missionaries, 7, 37f., 45, 49, 55ff., 234; *Kulturtraeger*, 24, 38; forces of Livonian Order, 58-66, 73-84, 103, 106ff., 116, 120, 122; mercenaries, see *Lansknechte*; at Court of St. Petersburg, vii, 209, 219f., 222, 228ff., 240, 244ff., 255,

258, 263, 269, (see also *Deutschrussen*); clergy, *see* Lutheran pastors; as Latvian national minority, 16, 332

Germany, medieval trade with, 53 (*see also* German merchants, Hanseatic League); and Thirty Years' War, 165; Imperial, 246, 258, 274f.; in World War I, 274-280, 287f.; and Brest-Litovsk negotiations, 295ff.; occupation of Kurland, 292, 296, 300ff.; and struggle for Baltic dominion (1918-1920), 300-331; and Bolshevik Russia, 287ff., 295ff., 301, 303, 314, 318, 321; and Latvian Republic, 345, 351. Third Reich, 361, 369, 385, 387, 393, 400; diplomacy of, 383-391, 407; in World War II, 390, 403ff.; and *Ostland*, 404ff.

Gesta Danorum, 35

Gestapo, 405

Giese, Martin, 151ff.

Ginters, A., archeologist, 376

Goethe, J. W. von, 237, 253

Golden Bull of Charles IV, 102, 110

Goldingen, *see* Kuldīga

Goldmanis, Jānis, statesman, 273, 275, 277, 292f., 308, 344

Goltz, Gen. Rudiger von der, 311, 315f., 318-328

Gordon, Patrick, English Ambassador to Poland, 186

Goths, 28; Wakia-Goths, 29; Western Goths, 28, 32

Gotland, 6f., 28, 32f., 53, 162, 166; code of, 95

Gough, Gen. Hubert, 322f., 326

Gourko, Russian general, 277

GPU, 392, 401ff.

Graham, M. W., American historian, 293

Great Britain, recognizes Latvian State, 299; and Baltic War of Liberation, 311ff., 316, 322, 330; trade with Latvia, 10, 367f., investments in Latvia, 351

Great Livonian Cadaster, 176

Great Northern War, 192f., 198-203, 214, 219, 241

Great Russians, 259, 272; national

minority in Latvia, 16, 346, 377
Greece, Baltic amber in, 30
Greek Orthodoxy, 14, 45f., 56, 60f.,
    85, 121, 163, 227, 376; in Estonia,
    171; in the Baltic Provinces, 233,
    238, 242, 249f.; in Russia, 259
Greene, Lt.-Col. Warwick, 315f., 319-
    324
Gregory IX, Pope, 70, 73, 75, 84, 91
Gregory XIII, Pope, 146
Grobina, town, 36; district of, 124,
    157, 212
Grodno, 210f.
Grotius, Hugo, 180
Grunwald, 107
Guberniyas, 18, 247
Guersike, see Jersika
guilds of Riga, 100, 149, 151ff., 180,
    221, 348, 387
Gulf of Riga, 5f., 28, 30, 37, 391
Gulf Stream, 5
Gustav Ericson, Swedish king, 176
Gustavus Adolphus, King of Sweden,
    162ff., 170ff., 179ff., 186
Gustavus Vasa, King of Sweden, 118,
    122

Hading, Danish prince, 35
Hadinga Saga, 35
Hahndorff, Gen. von, 302
Hakluyt, Richard, 15
Hallert, Countess von, 236
Hamburg, 97; statutes of, 95, 99f.
Hangoe, 392
Hanseatic League, 6f., 81, 97ff., 102,
    110, 114, 116, 124, 128f., 166,
    180; and Teutonic Knights, 98, 103,
    113f.
Hapsburgs, 161, 164, 231; Empire,
    144
harbors and ports, 10f., 185, 310, 339,
    353, 407
Hartknoch, printer, 241
Hastfehr, Governor-General of Livo-
    nia, 175f.
Hedwiga Eleanora, Swedish queen,
    174
Heiligenberg, German stronghold, 82
Heinrich von Galen, Grand Master
    of Livonian Order, 118ff.
Helsinki Conference (1920), 340,
    382f.

Henricus de Lettis, 18, 55ff., 61ff.
Henry the Lion, Duke of Saxony, 53
Henry (VII), King of the Romans,
    66f., 69
Henry VII, King of England, 110
Henry of Valois, King of Poland, 144,
    149
Hepner, E., 304
Herder, J. G., 222, 237, 241f., 252
Hermann, Bishop of Estonia, 64f.,
    69, 87
Hermann Balke, Master of Livonian
    Order, 77
Hermann von Salza, Grand Master of
    Teutonic Order, 72ff.
Hermanovskis, T., statesman, 308
Hermanric, King of Ostrogoths, 32
Herodotus, 9
Herrnhut, Saxon town, 236
Herrnhutists, 236
Hertling, Georg von, 301
Hesse-Homburg, Prince of, 205, 209
Heyking, Baron, 212
Hilchen code, 155, 173
Hilchen, David, 149, 152, 155, 173
Hiltuin, 46
Himmelstjerna,   Hermann   Samson
    von, 172
Hindenburg, Field-Marshal Paul von,
    276, 278, 297, 302
Historia Lettica (Paul Einhorn), 171
historians, see German-Balt historians
Historical Institute, see Latvian State
    Historical Institute
Historical Museum, 372
Hitler, Adolf, 389f., 392f.
Holland, medieval trade with, 53. See
    Netherlands
Holstein (Gottorp), Duke of (Fred-
    erick IV), 199
Holy Roman Empire, 66f., 108, 110,
    119, 122, 126, 128, 187
Holy See, see Papacy
Honorius III, Pope, 68ff., 72
Hospitallers, Order of, 70
Howard, Sir Esme, 325f.
Huhn, K., painter, 256
Humanism, 21, 150f.
Hungary, 143, 167f.; Teutonic Knights
    in, 71
Hupel, pastor, 218
Hussites, 235

Ice Age, 4, 9, 11, 29
Icelanders, 6
Iduma 18, 60
Ieviņš, E., physicist, 376
Ignatyev, Count, 250
illiteracy, 237, 248, 371
India, possible cradle of Baltic peoples, 26
industry, in Duchy of Kurland, 187f.; in Riga, 15, 240, 256; in Baltic Provinces, 247, 251, 256, 259f.; in Latvian Republic, 10, 349f., 352, 362f.; under Soviets, 401
Inflantes (*Inflanty*), 18, 123, 127, 211
Ingria, 163, 165f., 175, 199, 201, 203
Ingrians, 17, 137
Innocent III, Pope, 58, 68, 70
Innocent IV, Pope, 84
Innocent X, Pope, 189
intelligentsia, 23; Baltic, 232; Latvian, 236, 242ff., 250, 257f., 260, 402f.
international conventions and conferences, 342, 383, 386
International Court at The Hague, 342, 383
International Labor Organization, 369
Iran, possible cradle of Baltic peoples, 26
Iron Ages, 30, 39f., 42
Iron Brigade, 305, 312, 322f.
Iron Curtain, 406
Isarus, Archbishop of Riga, 85, 101f.
Isphagan, coins of, 33
Italy, Baltic amber in, 30
Ivan Kalita, Grand Prince of Muscovy, 115
Ivan III, Grand Prince of Muscovy, 115f.
Ivan IV the Terrible, Tsar, 29, 118-124, 138f., 141-147
Ivan VI, Tsarevitch, 208
Ivangorod, 114, 191
Izborsk, 29
Izvestiya, 314

Jacob Kettler, Duke of Kurland, 10, 146, 183, 185-191, 208
Jacob, Fort (Africa), 190
Jadwiga, bride of Jagiełło, 106
Jagel River, 323
Jagiełło, Grand Duke of Lithuania, 105ff.

James I, King of England, 186
Janeks, A., physicist, 376
Janševskis, J., author, 253
Jansons, J., literary critic, 253, 260
Japan, 14, 264
Jarl Birger, Swedish duke, 56, 77
Jaroslav, Russian grand duke, 75
Jaunā Straḫwa (New Movement), 254
Jaunsudrabiņš, J., author, 374
Jelgava (Mitau), 7, 14, 18, 82, 164, 185, 314, 316, 325ff. *See also* Mitau
Jersika, town and castle-mound, 13, 39ff., 48, 61
Jesuits, in Riga, 151f.; and Sigismund III, 161, 185
Jesusburg (Kuldīga, Goldingen), Livonian district of, 109. *See also* Kuldīga
Jews, in Livonia, 347; in Baltic Provinces, 250; in Poland, 250; in Russia, 261, 263; in Latvian Republic, 16, 274, 332, 345ff., 377; in *Ostland* satrapy, 405
Joffe, Dr. A., 307
John XXII, Pope, 102, 104
John, Duke of Finland, 137ff.; and King of Sweden (John III), 141, 144f., 147, 149, 161
John V, Archbishop of Riga, 109
John VI Habundi, Archbishop of Riga, 110
John Casimir, Cardinal, 166
Jordanes, Gothic historian, 32
judiciary system, feudal, 94ff.; in Duchy of Kurland, 183f.; Tsarist, 241, 249; Latvian, 309, 376f.; reforms of, 172f., 223. *See also* courts, law, *Mannrichter*
Juraševskis, P., statesman, 308, 345
Jurpils (Seeburg), 14. *See* Seeburg

Kalmar, Statute of (1587), 160
Kalmar, War of, 162
Kalmuks, 121, 142
Kalniņš, A., composer, 254, 374f.
Kalniņš, J., composer, 374f.
Kalniņš, P., statesman, 405
Kalpaks, Col. Oskars, 314, 316
Kampenhausen, B. von, Councilor of Livonian Diet, 236

Kant, Immanuel, 242
Kardis, Treaty of (1661), 169, 199
Karelia, 29
Karšava, Samogithian stronghold, 80
Kasparsons, K., statesman, 308
Kaudzītes, authors, 253
Kaunas, 388, 403
Keenan, Major, 316, 320
Kegums dam, 7, 363
Keksholm, 163; province of, 203
Keller, Count von, 325
Kellogg-Briand Pact, 384
Kerensky, A., 285ff.
Kestutis, Lithuanian ruler, 105
Kettler, see Ferdinand, Frederick, Frederick Casimir, Frederick William, Dukes of Kurland
Kettler, Princess Anna, 157
Kettler dynasty, 157, 159, 182, 185ff., 193, 205f.
Kettler, Gothard, 120; Grand Master of Livonian Order, 122ff., 130; Duke of Kurland, 26, 139, 142f., 145, 149, 156f., 182ff.
Kettler, Jacob, see Jacob, Duke of Kurland
Kiel Canal, 275, 340
Kiev, 201
Kirchenšteins, August, Latvian Communist Prime Minister, 394ff., 399f.
Kirchholm, Treaty of (1452), 109
Kirghiz, 121
Kiwerowa Horka, Truce of (1582), 146
Klangi, castle-mound, 39
Klapeja, town, 80
Klinger, F. M. von, 242
Klive, A., 292
Klot, R. von, Provincial School Councilor, 239, 245
Knights of the Sword, see Fratres Militiae Christi and Livonian Order
Knights Templar, see Templars
Knopken, Andreas, humanist, 150
Koknese (Kokenhusen), 13, 60, 68, 164, 167ff., 200; in the Hansa, 98; tribunal of, 172
Kolkhoz system, 402
Koltchak, Admiral A. V., 325, 328
Kornilov, Gen., 287f.
Koskinnen, philologist and historian, 29

Kovno, 200, 224; castle of Teutonic Knights, 105
Kovno, Treaty of (1562), 141
Kreicbergs, J., statesman, 299
Kreišmanis, P., geologist, 376
Krewo, Act of (1385), 106
Krimbergs, R., biologist, 376
Krodzinieks-Krigers, J., historian, 375
Kronstadt, 201
Kronvalds, A., sociologist, 243
Krupp, Fr., A.G., 302
Kufa, coins of, 33
Kühlmann, Richard von, 295ff.
Kuldīga (Jesusburg), 13, 18, 81, 185, 224, 314
Kulm, 72; Bishop of, 79
Kultur, 269f.
Kulturas Fonds, 373
Kundziņš, P., architect, 375
Kurbads, mythological hero, 43
Kurisches Haff, 5, 165
Kurland, Duchy of, 18, 47, 126ff.; under Kettler dynasty, 157ff., 162, 182-193; administration of, 184, 193, 205, 209, 213; Diets of, 182ff., 204ff., 209, 212f., 225; and Western Europe, 185, 187f., 191, 193n.; and Poland, 182ff., 191, 204ff., 210f.; in Swedish wars, 164f., 168, 185f., 191; in Great Northern War, 192, 199ff., 204; and Russia, 204ff., 209, 212f.
Kurland as a Baltic Province, 221, 223f., 229, 232, 243, 274; in World War I, 276ff., 280f.; German struggle for, 295f., 298, 300ff., 324, 327
Kurland (Curland, Courland), see Kurzeme
Kurland, Dukes of, 11, 14, 182, 184, 255, 347. See also under Kettler and Biron
Kurlyandskaya Gubernya, 18, 247
Kuronian colonies, 189ff.
Kuronian navy, 182, 187ff.
Kuronian nobility, 157ff., 182f., 190f., 205ff., 209, 212, 224, 226
Kurs, 39, 53, 61, 65, 71, 73, 187, 234; early culture of, 27ff., 34ff., 56, 70
Kurzeme, tribal kingdom of, 30, 34ff., 46, 54, 60, 185; under Livonian Order, 73ff., 78ff., 88, 110, 212; dio-

cese of, 84, 87f., 158; in Duchy of Kurland, 182ff., 224; under Russian rule, 239; in World War I, 276; province of Latvian Republic, 11, 13, 281, 294, 337; in World War II, 406

Kviesis, Alberts, President of Latvian Republic, 359ff.

Labor, in Latvian Republic, 369f. (*See also* Proletariat, Trade Unions); under Soviets, 403; under Nazis, 405

Lacis, V., Latvian Communist politician

Lāčplēsis (Bearslayer), 13, 43f., 47, 254

Lāčplēsis (A. Pumpurs), 252

Ladoga, lake, 32, 201; canal, 215

La Harpe, J.-F. de, 221

lakes, 8

Lamikis (Lammekinus), King of the Kurs, 73f.

"Land of the Blessed Virgin," see *Tarra Mariana*

land reform, see agrarian reform laws, land revision

land revision, under Stephen Bátory, 154; under Swedish dominion, 169f., 175ff.; under Russian rule, 216

Landesgesellschaft Kurlands, 302

Landesrat (German-Balt, 1918), 295, 301, 313f.

Landrats, see diets

Landtag, 110. See diets

language, see German, Latvian, Russian language, philology

Lansing, Robert, 319

Lansknechte, 120ff., 130

Lata (Late, Latve) River, 4f.

Lateran Council of 1215, 55, 67f., 70

Latgale, in tribal times, 5, 46, 48; under Livonian Order, 60f., 68f.; under Poland, 11, 127, 157, 165, 169 (see also *Inflantes*); under Russia, 211, 232, 329; in World War I, 276; under Bolshevik régime, 298, 303, 306; in Baltic War of Liberation, 323f., 328; province of Latvian Republic, 11ff., 18, 281, 294, 328, 337; Orthodox Jews in, 328

Latgallians (Latgali), 28, 33, 43, 54, 56, 73

Latin American Republics, recognize Latvian State, 338

Latupe River, 5

Latvian-American Chamber of Commerce, 368

Latvian armed forces, in Livonia, 120, 123, 130, 140, 156; in World War I, 275ff. (see also Latvian Rifles); in Baltic War of Liberation, 311f., 314, 317f., 320ff., 327; in Latvian Republic, 337, 360; under Soviets, 402f.

Latvian Association (*Latweeschu Beedriba*, 1869), 244, 255, 344

Latvian Board of Monuments, 39, 372

Latvian Central Council (1943), 405

Latvian Central Federative Committee (1905), 266ff.

Latvian Conference of Agronomists (1873), 245

Latvian Conference of School Teachers (1873), 245

Latvian Congress of Representatives of Rural Communities (1905), 266f.

Latvian Congresses of Representatives of Rural Communities (1917), 280f.

Latvian Encyclopedia (*Latviešu konversācijas vārdnica*), 244, 373, 376

Latvian Foreign Delegation (1918), 294f., 299

Latvian language, 17ff., 34, 132, 150, 236f., 249, 271, 277; early publications in, 152, 171f., 179f.; in the schools, 248, 266f., 270, 273, 371. *See also* philology

Latvian Literary Society, 242

Latvian National Anthem, 245

Latvian National Political Conference (1917), 280f., 285, 291f.

Latvian National Singing Festivals, 244

Latvian Power Commission, 256, 376

Latvian Provisional Government (1918), 305, 308-330, 333, 337

Latvian Provisional Government (1945), 406

Latvian Provisional National Council

(L.P.N.C.) (1917), 292ff., 298f., 307

Latvian Rifles, 277f., 281, 288, 291f.

Latvian State Academy of Agriculture (Jelgava), 371f., 376

Latvian State Academy of Arts (Riga), 256, 336, 372, 374

Latvian State Academy of Science (proposed), 372

Latvian State Conservatory of Music (Riga), 254, 336, 372

Latvian State Cultural Council, 360

Latvian State Historical Institute, 197n., 372, 375f., 409

Latvian State Library, 373

Latvian State Printing Office, 373

Latvian State University (Riga), 17, 336, 372, 375f.

Latvian War of Liberation, see Baltic War of Liberation

Latvijas vēstures institūta žurnāls, 376, 409

"Latviji," 4f.

Latweeschu Awihses, 242, 344

Latweeschu Beedriba, see Latvian Association

Laube, E., architect, 256

law, common, 22f., 44f., 95; Roman, 44, 87, 94f., 155, 183, 216f.; canon, 95; manorial, 94, 96, 156, 172; medieval codes, 95; Baltic Code, 173, 249; Rigan laws, 95, 99f.; laws of Latvian Republic, 309, 335f., 362, 376. See also Corpus Juris Livonici, Ritterrecht, Sachsenspiegel, courts, judiciary system

League of Nations, 2, 3, 381; German-Balt representations at, 335; and Latvian Republic, viii, 338, 341f., 386; and Baltic States, 386f.; and Soviet Union, 387, 392

League of the Three Emperors (1873), 246

Lecouvreure, Adrienne de, 205

Leftist parties and politics, 261, 280, 342ff., 349f., 352-358. See also political parties, Socialists, Social-Democrats, Communists

Leipzig, University of, 187

Leitans, Ansis, newspaper publisher, 242, 244

Lembit, King of the Estonians, 62

Lemsal, see Limbaži

Lenin, Nikolai, 261, 267, 285, 287ff., 294f., 297f.; Twenty-one Theses of, 296f.; and Latvian Bolsheviks, 312

Leningrad, 353, 407

Leopold I, Hapsburg Emperor, 168

Leopold of Bavaria, Prince, 297

Lepanto, battle of (1571), 128

Les sources de l'histoire de Lettonie, 376

Leszczyński, Stanisław, 201

"Lettia" (Lettigallia), 49

Lettische Grammatik (J. Endzelīns), 375

"Lettland," 5

Lettonia, student organization, 244

Letts (Lette, Letten), 5, 18, 49

Libau, see Liepāja

liberalism, Western European, 21f., 220, 244, 252, 273; of Catherine the Great, 217, 219; of Alexander I, 221; of Alexander II, 230; Livonian-German, 222, 235, 238; in Tsarist Russia, 244, 246, 257, 263ff., 273, 275; Latvian, 245

Liberts, L., artist, 374

libraries, 336, 373, 376; ducal library at Mitau, 205

Lichton, R., Governor-General of Livonia, 175

Lielupe (Aa) River, 7, 19, 28, 32

Lielvārde, town, 13; battle of (1261), 81

Liepāja (Libau), 6, 11, 14f., 18, 31, 185, 208, 212, 239, 259, 339; in World War I, 276; German occupation of, 313, 315f.; Latvian Provisional Government in, 314, 316, 318ff., 323; Soviets in, 391

Lieven, Prince Anatol, 312f., 316, 319

Lieven, von, Governor-General of Livonia, 243

"Lifland" (Liefland, Livland), 5, 18, 127

Liflyandskaya Gubernya, 18, 247

Lihdums, gazette, 293

Limbaži (Lemsal), 169, 242; in the Hansa, 98

linguistics, see philology

literacy, 218, 235, 237, 248, 371

Literary Society (Latvian), 242

literature, 271, 252ff., 373f.; Chamber

of Literature and Art, 360. See also *Dainas*, folksongs, folklore

Lithuania, 3, 261, 293, 296, 324, 357, 403, 405; tribal, 7, 27, 49; and Livonian Order, 77, 79ff., 83, 101, 103ff., 120ff.; united with Poland, 106f.; and Muscovy, 115f., 118f., 138, 143; and Livonia, 126, 140, 154, 156f.; in Swedish wars, 164; in Great Northern War, 200; Russians in 211f.; in Napoleonic wars, 223; rebellion in (1863), 247; in World War I, 276f., 295, 304; and Bolshevism, 305, 307, 314; Baltic policy of, 340f., 382f., 388; and Soviet Union, 329, 384-393, 407

Lithuanians, 16f.; tribal, 28, 43, 49, 56, 60f., 63, 73; magnates, 140f., 143, 154ff., 159, 167; in Kurzeme (1794), 212; at University of Dorpat, 244; and Soviets, 407

Litvinov, Maxim, 383, 385, 388f.

"Livland" (Liefland, Lifland), 5, 18

Livonia, 5, 18, 37, 55, 203; diocese of, 56, 59f., 67, 84; Mark of, 67; under the Livonian Order, 70-133; under Polish suzerainty, 139ff., 147, 153-157; "Kingdom of," 142-146; under Sweden, 169-180, 214ff.; under Russia, 203, 213 (see Baltic Provinces)

Livonian Confederation, 110f., 125, 315

Livonian nobles, 127f., 141, 145, 155f.; under Swedish rule, 170, 173, 177, 199; under Russian rule, 203ff., 212, 214ff., 222, 226, 228f., 233. *See also* diets, German-Balt squires, *Ritterschaft*, Corporation of Livonian-German nobles

Livonian Order, refounding of, 75; organization, 75ff., 89, 103, 108f.; feudal aspects of, 87-96, 112, 127; conquest of southern Livonia, 78ff.; conflict with Muscovites, 77f., 115, 121-124; relations with Papacy, 84f., 102; relations with Hansa, 96ff.; relations with Riga, 100ff., 109f.; conflict with Lithuania, 101ff.; foreign policy of, 103, 116ff., 129; growing autonomy of, 107ff., 110,

118; decay of, 118f., 124, 129ff.; dissolution of, 128

Lloyd George, D., 299

Lohse, H., German Commissioner for the *Ostland*, 404

Lokher, King of the Kurs, 35

London, Russian Social-Democrats in, 261; Latvian Foreign Delegates in, 299

London Times, quoted, 330

Loskil, G. H., Bishop, 237

"Lothavia," 18

Louis IV, Emperor, 102

Louis XIV, King of France, 188f.

Louis XVI, King of France, 212

"Louis XVIII," in Mitau, 221

Louise Charlotte, Duchess of Kurland, 187

Lübeck, 33, 53, 57, 70, 99; in the Hansa, 97, 101, 103, 118, 138, 165

Lublin, Union of, 141

Luck, German forces in (1918), 297

Ludendorff, Gen. E. von, 288, 295, 297

Ludza marshes, 8

Luther, Martin, 113, 129

Lutheran Church (Evangelical), 238, 301

Lutheran pastors, ix, 17, 171, 184, 234ff., 238, 249, 267

Lutheranism, 14, 117, 119, 171, 233, 249, 377; in Kurland, 158, 184ff.

Lutherans, 117, 242, 266f., 348f.

Lützen, battle of (1632), 165

Lvov, Prince Gregori, 279, 281, 286f.

Magnus, Duke, "King of Livonia," 142-146, 149

Mahjas Weesis, periodical, 242, 260, 344

Maisky, Soviet Ambassador, 407

Manasein, Senator, 247f.

Manchuria, 264

Manifesto of October 30, 1905 (Tsarist), 265ff.

Mannrichter, 95, 184

Manntage, 95

manor-lords, *see* German-Balt squires

manorial system, 91ff. See also feudalism, serfdom

Manteuffel, Hans von, 315, 316, 318, 320, 322

Marat, Russian cruiser, 394
Mare Balticum liberatum (treatise, 1649), 180
Margrave of Livonia, 69
Marienburg, 72, 76f., 107. *See* Alūksne
Marienwerder, 165
Marxism, 22, 253; in Germany, 260f.; in Russia, 261
Maximilian II, Emperor, 143f., 149
Mazepa, Hetman, 202
Mazovia, 71
Mazpulki, 370
Mecklenburg, 124; Anna of, 157; Christopher of, 119, 125f.
Mediņš, J., composer, 254, 374f.
Mediterranean civilization, and Baltic trade, 30ff.; and Baltic culture, 6, 27, 30ff.
Mediterranean Sea, 24, 35
Meiendorf, 64
Meierovics, Zigfrīds, statesman, 290f., 294, 299, 308, 318, 340, 344
Meinard, Bishop of Riga, 55ff.
Memel, 80, 165, 386, 388
Mensheviks, 261
Menshikov, Prince, 205
mercantilism, 21; in Duchy of Kurland, 187ff.
Mercator, Gerardus, 18
merchant marine, 11, 243, 368
Mergentheim, 114
Merkel, Garlieb, 222, 244
Mežotne, town, 13, 39ff., 63f., 68
Milyukov, Prof. Paul, 286f.
Mindaugas, King of Lithuanians, 79ff., 84, 104
Minsk, 211
Mir (Russian), 12, 263, 273
Mirabeau, Count H.-G., 212
Mitau, 82f., 191ff., 200f., 205f., 209, 225, 242, 277f.; Articles of, 206; castle of, 82, 205, 207, 210, 327, 373. *See* Jelgava
Mogilev, battle of (1564), 138
Moldavians, 71
Mollyn, Nicolas, printer, 152
Molotov, Vyacheslav, 289ff., 397f.
Mongols, 77, 84, 142
Montigny, de, Regent of Kurland, 224
Monumenta Germaniae historica, 409
Moravia, 235
Moravian Brethren, 235f., 238

Morbergs, A., architect, 256
Moscow, 142, 163, 199f., 206, 219, 256; and Revolution of 1905, 266, 268; Patriarchate, 377; diplomacy in, 390ff.
Moscow Disarmament Conference, 342
Moscow Protocol (1929), 384
Moscow, Treaty of (1920), 329
Moscow, Treaty of (1939), 389. *See also* Ribbentrop-Molotov Pact
Mstislav, 211
Mühlenbach, K., philologist, 375
Muncis, J., artist, 374
Municipality Law of 1864 (Russian), 229, 241
Munters, V., statesman, 390f.
Muscovite wars, 121ff., 132, 138-147, 154, 167ff., 174
Muscovites, 13, 24, 77, 81, 154, 168
Muscovy, viiif., 76f., 84, 114-129, 166; expansion of, 114ff., 123, 147, 181; and Poland-Lithuania, 116f., 127; and Livonia, 114-124, 129f.; and Polish Commonwealth, 138, 140f., 160, 167ff.; and Sweden, 163, 193
music, and National Awakening, 245f., 254; in Latvian Republic, 372, 374f.; musical associations, 271 (*see* Singing Festivals). *See also* Latvian State Conservatory
Mutual Assistance Treaties, Baltic States-Soviet Union (1939), 390-395, 398
mythology, 43, 46

Nameitis, King of Zemgallians, 82f.
Napoleon, Emperor, 221
Napoleonic wars, 223ff., 238
Narev River, 28, 124, 303, 339
Narva, 114, 121, 123f., 127, 139, 142, 146, 148, 198ff.
National Anthem (*Dievs svētī Latviju*), 245
National Awakening, 22, 131, 232-257, 344, 373f., 376
National Assembly (Valka, 1917), 290ff.
National Council (1918), 13, 307f., 319, 323, 332f.
National Council (1945), 406

National Cultural Council, 360
National Economic Council, 360, 370
national income, 366f.
national minorities, in Latvia, 16, 307f., 332f., 346-351, 357 (*see also* cultural autonomy); in Russian Empire, 263, 271f., 286; in revolutionary Russia, 290; in Soviet Union, 289
National Socialism, in Latvia, 358; in Germany, 385. See also *Pērkoṇkrustieši*, Nazis
national tradition, 3, 12, 19f., 23, 234f., 252ff. *See also* customs, cultural traits, *Dainas*, folklore
nationalism, in Western Europe, 85, 87, 113, 210, 231f., 237, 252; German, 246; Russian, 259, 272f., 389; in Baltic Provinces, 233, 246, 257f., 270; Latvian, 237, 252f., 262, 293
nationalization, under Soviets, 401ff.
natural boundaries, 8, 14, 17, 339
natural resources, 9ff.; in Duchy of Kurland, 182
naturalism, in National Awakening, 253
Nazis, 19, 358, 362, 387, 404ff.
Nemunas River, 28
Neolithic Age, 30
Nestor, Russian chronicler, 55
Netherlands, 161ff., 164ff., 168, 199, 202; and the Hansa, 114; and Duchy of Kurland, 188f.
Neurath, Constantin von, 387f.
Neutrality, of Duchy of Kurland, 139, 157, 188, 191; Scandinavian, 341, 388; of Baltic Sea, 340; of Baltic States, 292, 341f., 381, 383f.
Neva River, 201
Nevsky, Prince Alexander, 77f.
New York, 368
Nicholas V, Antipope, 102
Nicholas I, Tsar, 226f.
Nicholas II, Tsar, 246, 248, 250, 258f., 264ff., 272f., 277ff.
Nicholas, Grand Duke, 277f.
Nicholas, Bishop of Livonia, 70
Niedra, Andrievs, 320ff.
Niemen River, 28, 80
Niessel, General, 328
Nobel Prize in chemistry, 256
nobility, *see* Corporation of Livo-
nian-German nobles, German-Balt squires, Lithuanian magnates, Livonian nobles, Swedish nobles, *Szlachta, Ritterschaft*, Russian nobility
nonaggression pacts, Soviet-German (1926), 383f., (1939), 389; Soviet-Lithuanian (1926), 384f.; Soviet-Latvian (1932), 385, 398; Soviet-Estonian (1932), 385; Soviet-Finnish (1934), 392; Moscow Protocols (1934), 385; German-Polish (1934), 385
Northern Seven Years' War (1563-1570), 138f.
"Northwest Provinces," 247
Norway, 208
Norwegians, 6f.
Noske, Gustav, 303, 315, 320f.
Novgorod, 7, 29, 32f., 54, 77, 79, 103, 114ff., 163, 200; Slavs of, 62, 101; in the Hansa, 81, 97f.
Nuremberg trials, 389
Nystad, Peace of (1721), 203f., 208, 216, 329

Ochrana, 230, 249, 262
Oeland, island, 36
Oesel, island, 62ff., 73, 87f., 99, 124, 142, 146, 162, 203, 216
Ojars, mythological figure, 43
Oka River, 28
Olaf, King of Sweden, 35, 46
Olaf II, King of Denmark, 36
Old Believers (Russian), 328, 343, 377
Oliva, Peace of (1660), 168f., 191, 201
Opera, in Duchy of Kurland, 14, 254; in Riga, 244, 254, 372, 374f.; in Liepāja, 375
Ordinatio Livoniae (1589), 156
Ore, A., composer, 254
Orient, Baltic trade with, 6f., 30, 32ff.
Orsza, battle of (1564), 138
Osis, Col., 406
Ostermann, Count H. von, statesman, 203, 208f.
Ostland (1941-1945), 19, 387, 404ff.
Ostrogoths, *see* Goths
Ostsee, origin of term, 6
Ostwald, N., scientist, 256

Oxenstjerna, Axel, Regent of Sweden, 166, 170

Pacta conventa (1573), 144
Pacta subjectionis (1561), 126f., 140, 144, 148
Paegle, S., statesman, 308
Pagasti (rural communities), 15f., 92f., 95f., 154, 156, 223, 226, 228f., 234, 238, 369
Pahlen, von, Governor-General of Livonia, 227
painting, in Duchy of Kurland, 207; Latvian, 256, 374
Palanga, Kurish settlement, 36
Palcmanis, G., 292
Pan-Germanism, 270
Pan-Slavism, 251, 258, 261, 270
Papacy, and Livonian Order, 65f., 68f., 70ff., 84ff., 101, 109, 128, 188; Baltic policy of, 68f., 70, 72f., 86; and Latvian Republic, 338, 377
Papers Relating to the Foreign Relations of the United States, 295
Paris Peace Conference (1919), 308, 316ff., 326, 328, 382; Latvian delegation at, 317ff.; German-Balts at, 325
Paris, Treaty of (1856), 245
Parliament, *see* Saeima
parliamentarianism, 342, 356f.
Pärnu, 137, 147, 164, 200ff.
Patkul, Johann Reinhold von, 175, 178, 198-201, 214
Päts, Konstantin, 358
Paul I, Tsar, 213, 221, 228
peasants, ix, 11f.; in German Livonia, 85, 87-96, 108, 111, 117, 128, 131f., 171f.; in Polish Livonia, 154ff.; in Swedish Livonia, 170, 174, 176ff.; in Duchy of Kurland, 184, 191, 208; in Baltic Provinces, 215-219, 222, 224-230, 233ff., 237, 243, 245, 247, 249, 251, 260, 270; in Latvian Republic, 344, 354, 358, 364ff.; under Soviets, 402; revolts of, 88, 94, 211f., 219, 224f., 227, 238; German-Balt, 348; Russian, 263, 265, 268. *See also* farms, serfdom
Peipus, lake, 78, 201, 303
Pēkšēns, K., architect, 256

Pērkoņkrustieši, 358
Pernau, Livonian district of, 153. *See* Pärnu
Persia, Baltic trade with, 32f., 38
Peter I the Great, Tsar, 192f., 197-205, 208f., 213ff., 220, 310, 391
Peter II, Tsar, 206
Peter III, Tsar, 210
Peter Biron, Duke of Kurland, 210ff., 329
Peterburgas Awihses, newspaper, 243f., 344, 376
Petrograd, 276ff., 286, 288, 290, 297; Latvian statesmen in, 293f., 298
Pharaohs, 30
Philip of Suabia, King of the Romans, 60, 66, 68
Philology, ix, 17, 28ff., 252, 257; at Latvian State University, 17, 375
Phoenicians, 30f.
Piip, Ants, 317
Pilchau, von, 304
Piłsudski, Marshal, 329
Piltene, Kuronian town, 13, 36, 145; district of, 124, 142, 146, 158, 184, 224, 334
Pīpiņš, E., critic, 253
Pitrags, 391
Pleskava, *see* Pskov
Plettenberg, Walter von, Grand Master of the Livonian Order, Prince of Holy Roman Empire, 110, 116ff., 130f.
Pliny the Elder, 4, 31
Plūdonis, V., poet, 254, 374
poetry, 252ff., 274. See also *Dainas,* folksongs
Poland, union with Lithuania, 106f., 116; and Teutonic Knights, 106f., 109, 113; Baltic policy of, viii, 114, 138, 167, 340ff., 382f., 386; and Muscovy, 120-127, 137ff.; over Livonia, 126ff., 137-156, 159 (*see also* Lithuania); elections to throne of, 143f.; and Kurland, 157, 183ff., 191f., 204ff., 210f.; and Sweden, 155f., 160-165, 167f., 198; and Russia, 197, 210f., 223; First Partition, 211, 329; Second Partition, 212; under Russia, 261, 265, 296, 318; insurrection of 1863, 247; in World War I, 278; gains inde-

pendence, 290; and Latvian Republic, 328f., 345; and Soviet Union, 306, 383, 407

Poles, 71, 231; at University of Dorpat, 244; in Third Imperial Duma, 273; in Latgale, 328; as a Latvian national minority, 16, 332, 343, 346; imported laborers, 370

Polish-Swedish Livonian wars, 147, 164, 166ff.

Polizei Ordnungen (1671), 174

political parties, 342-355, 359, 405; tables of, 342f.

Polotzk, 33, 54, 56, 97, 123, 138, 142, 146, 211; Knyaz of, 56, 60f.; Slavs of, 60f.

Poltava, battle of (1709), viii, 193, 202, 215

Pomerania, 27, 77, 114, 165ff.

Poniatowski, Stanisław, 211

population, 12, 13n., 16, 364

Port Arthur, 264

ports, see harbors

Portugal, 188

Poruks, J., poet, 254

Possevino, papal nuncio, 146

positivism, in National Awakening, 251, 253

Posvol, Treaty of (1557), 120, 122

Potemkin, Prince Gregori Alexandrovitch, 211f.

Pravda, 391

press, the, 180, 237, 250, 262; Russian, 240, 260; Rigan, 241-245; in Latvian Republic, 291, 373; freedom of, 23, 267, 336

Priedkalns, A., statesman, 280

Prīmanis, J., biologist, 376

Principal Navigations (R. Hakluyt), 15

printing and publication, 152, 179f., 236f., 241, 373

Pripet marshes, 339

Pripet River, 5, 28

Privilegium Gothardianum (1570), 157f., 183

Privilegium Sigismundi (1561), 127, 215

proletariat, 233, 251, 259f., 270, 345, 349; in Russia, 261

proportional representation, 336f., 342ff.

Protestantism, 113, 128, 160ff., 178; in Duchy of Kurland, 186. See principally Lutheranism

Protestant League, 165

"Provincia Livonica," 153

Provincial Land Councils (1917), 280f., 290f.

Prussia, of the Teutonic Order, 70f., 80, 82ff., 98, 113; diocese of, 84; Duchy of, 119f., 124, 126, 159, 164ff., 168f.; West Prussia, 164f.; Kingdom of, 168, 193, 202, 204, 210, 212; in Napoleonic wars, 223ff.

Prussian forces in Kurland, 224

Prussianism, 132, 230, 249f., 303

Pskov, 29, 32f., 61f., 77ff., 101, 103; auxiliaries from, 75; trade with, 54, 95, 115f.; in Muscovite wars, 115f., 122, 146, 163; in World War I, 297

public health, 370f.

Pumpurs, A., author, 252

Purinš, K., statesman, 308

Purvītis, V., painter, 256, 374

Pytheas of Massilia, 4, 31

Quarenchi, Giacomo, architect, 210

Räd, Swedish Council, 161f.

radicalism, 22; in Baltic Provinces, 250, 258ff.

Radziņš, Gen. Pēteris, 324

Radziwiłł, Cardinal George, 152

Radziwiłł, Prince Nicholas, 125ff., 140, 148

Radziwiłł, Prince, Duke of Olyka, 157

Rainis-Pliekšans, Jānis, poet, 253, 260, 266, 274

Rancans, J., prelate and statesman, 281, 405

Rasputin, Gregori, 278

Rastrelli, Bartholomeo, architect, 207, 210

Rawa, 197

Razna, lake, 8

realism, in Latvian literature, 251, 253

Red Cross (Latvian), 370, 406

Reformation, 128, 150, 178

Refugee Committees in Petrograd, 276, 290, 291

refugees, of World War I, 276, 290; of World War II, 405f.

Reichstag, 166, 301

religion, in tribal times, 45f.; in Livonia, 150ff., 233; in Latvian Republic, 376f.; under Soviets, 403. See also Christianity, Greek Orthodoxy, Lutheranism, Protestantism, Roman Catholicism

Renaissance, 128, 178; Latvian cultural movement, 251-257, 258, 270. See also National Awakening

Repnin, Prince Vassily, Governor-General of Livonia, 220

Reval, 62, 64, 88, 142f., 145, 147, 201f., 313, 322; surrenders to Swedes, 122, 124; diocese of, 110, 124; Hanseatic komtor of, 97f., 115

Revolution of 1905, in Russia, 262-267; in Poland, 265f.; in Baltic Provinces, 253, 262, 264, 266-269

Revolution of March, 1917 (Russian), 279f., 285f.

Revolution of November (October), 1917 (Russian), 3, 285, 289

Revue baltique, 394

Rēzekne (Rositten), 18, 280

Rheinisch-Westphalisches Kohlensyndikat, 302

Rhinelanders, in Livonian Order, 108; in Teutonic Order, 90

Rhyme Chronicles of the Teutonic Order, 80, 132

Ribbentrop, J. von, 390f.

Ribbentrop-Molotov Pact (1939), 389f., 407; agreement of September, 1939, 390

Richter, von, Governor-General of Livonia, 222

Riga, 14f.; climate of, 6; port of, 11, 15, 179, 240, 339; early settlement of, 15, 29, 32, 34f., 46, 57f., 99 (see also Duna urbs); cathedral chapter of, 67f., 70; and Livonian Order, 63ff., 82f., 100ff., 109f., 112, 150; militia of, 108, 110, 220; traditional independence of, 15, 95, 99f., 125ff., 147f., 179, 220; Hansa activities of, 15, 97f.; German element in, 64, 75, 99, 153, 164, 180, 220, 241, 244, 348f.; Russian element in, 97; native element in, 64,

69, 100, 151, 153, 180, 241, 244; development of, 15, 99, 179, 240f.; Lutheranism in, 117, 150; internal affairs of, 150ff., 173f., 179f., 220f., 240f.; cultural activities in, 150ff., 180, 237, 241, 253ff.; in Muscovite wars, 123f., 145, 148, 168, 179; and Poland, 125, 147-153; and Sweden, 15, 148f., 162, 164, 168, 179; and Denmark, 162; Jews in, 347; in Great Northern War, 149f., 202, 215; in Napoleonic wars, 224; under Tsarist Russia, 15, 215, 219f., 227, 239ff., 259f.; and Revolution of 1905, 264ff.; in World War I, 14f., 277, 288, 290f.; under Germans, 298, 301, 305, 309, 311f., 314, 316, 318, 321ff., 326f.; and Soviet Union, 310; diplomatic activities in, 385f., 388, 390; under Soviets, 394, 402ff., 406; under Nazis, 404

Riga archbishopric, 15, 84f., 87f., 98, 101ff., 108ff., 120, 150, 338, 348, 377

Riga bishopric, 56ff., 65, 68, 84

Riga castle, 14, 101, 140, 150

Riga electoral district, 337

Riga Democratic Bloc, 291, 304, 307

Riga Letters (Y. Samarin), 240

Riga Polytechnic Institute, 240, 256, 268, 372, 375

Riga Stock Exchange, 242, 333

Riga, Treaty of (1920), 329f., 339, 391

Riga Tribunal (Hofgericht), 172, 174

Riga University, see Latvian State University

Rigas Awihses, 260

Rigas Lapa, 245

Rigas Latweeschu Beedriba, cultural society, 244, 255

Rigasche Anzeigen, 241

Rigasche Novellen, 241

Rigasche Politische Zeitung, 241

Rigasche Rundschau, 310

Rightist parties and politics, 265ff., 282, 324ff., 358f.

Riksdag, Swedish parliament, 172, 174f., 179

Rimbert, Archbishop of Bremen, 35f., 46

Ritterrecht, 95, 141, 173f., 226
Ritterschaft (Corporation of Livonian nobles), 111, 334
rivers, 6f., 18f., 28, 32
Rodin, August, 256, 374
Roe, Sir Thomas, special envoy to Poland, 186f.
Rolavs, E., economist, 262
Roman Catholic faith, 14, 61, 128, 171; in Riga, 150ff.; in Poland, 160; in Sweden, 161; in Latgale, 328; in Latvian Republic, 338, 376
Roman Empire, 32
Romandini, Luigi, painter, 207
Romanov, Michael, Tsar, 163
Romanticism, in Latvian National Awakening, 251ff.
Rome, early relations with, 38f., 54, 57, 74, 161. *See principally* Papacy
Romove, sacred grove, 71
Rose, J. Holland, quoted, 232
Rosen, Baron, Councilor of Livonian Diet, 216f.
Rosenberg Alfred, 405
Rosenberg, Baron, 309
Rosica-Crissa forests, 8
Rositten, *see* Rēzekne
Rotari, Pietro, painter, 207
Rozentals, J., painter, 256
Rubulis, V., 292
Rudolf of Hapsburg, 128
Rudzītis, D., statesman, 308
Rügen, island, 166
Rumania, 384
Rūno, island, 168, 191
rural communities, see *Pagasti*
Russia, Muscovite, *see* Muscovy
Russia, revolutionary, internal affairs, 279, 285-289; in World War I, 279, 285-290; separate peace movement of, 286-290, 293; and Baltic War of Liberation, 310, 318, 321ff.
Russia, Soviet, *see* Soviet Union
Russia, Tsarist, expansionism of, 193, 197, 203; claim to Livonia of, 197; in Great Northern War, 198-203; and Poland, 197ff., 210ff.; and Duchy of Kurland, 204-213; internal affairs, 208, 258-266, 271ff., 278f; and European diplomacy, 246, 258, 274f.; and Baltic Provinces, chaps. XII-XIV; revolutionary

trends in, 262-266; in World War I, 274-280
Russian armed forces, in World War I, 275ff., 288; in Baltic War of Liberation, 312, 314, 320, 323, 328f.; "Russian Western Army" (1919) 325ff.; in Baltic States (World War II), 389, 391ff.; in Latvia, 391, 393ff., 401, 403ff.
Russian fleet in the Baltic, 203, 264, 275
Russian High Command, in World War I, 258, 276, 278f., 285, 287, 290
Russian language, 248f., 273f., 347
Russian nobility, 209, 250
Russian Provisional Government, 279f., 285-289, 334
Russian Revolutions, *see* Revolution of 1905, of March, 1917, of November, 1917
Russian Workmen's Social Democratic Party, 261
Russians, in Riga, 97; Latvian national minority, 332, 343, 346f.; in Latvian industry, 351. *See also* Great Russians, Muscovites, Slavs, White Russians
Russification, 19, 230, 248-251, 258, 260, 262, 268, 273, 292
Russo-Finnish War, 392f.
Russo-Japanese War, 139, 263f.
Russo-Turkish War (1877), 246
Ruthenians, 107

Sachsenspiegel, 92, 94f., 141
Saeima (Latvian parliament), 334, 336f., 342-359, 362, 395ff.
Sagan and Preibus, Duchy of, 211, 213
St. Andrew's Island, 190
St. Petersburg, 193, 201f., 205ff., 211f., 216, 227, 229, 248, 250; Germans at the Court of, vii, 209, 219ff., 228ff., 240, 244ff., 255, 258, 263, 269 (see also *Deutschrussen*); Latvians in, 255ff.; revolution (1905) in, 262, 264ff., 268; Declaration of (1908), 274f. *See also* Petrograd
St. Petersburg Academy of Arts, 256

St. Petersburg Academy of Sciences, 205, 217, 255f.
St. Petersburg Conservatory, 254
St. Pierre, Abbé de, 193n.
Salza, Hermann von, Grand Master of Teutonic Order, 72ff.
Samarin, Yury, 240, 246
Samblandia, 66, 72
Samogithia, 70, 73, 78f., 105ff., 112
Samogithians, 28, 59, 61f., 78ff., 106
Samson-Himmelstjerna, Reinhold von, 225f.
Samson-Himmelstjerna, R. von, 304
Samsonov, Gen., 276
San River, 21
Sanskrit, 17, 28, 257
Saracen influences, 41
Saule, battle of (1236), 74ff.
Saxe, Count Maurice de, 205f., 209
Saxo Grammaticus, 35
Saxon forces in Great Northern War, 198ff.
Saxony, 198, 202, 223
Saxony and Anhalt, Duke of, 63f.
Schabe, King of Zemgallians, 80
Schiemann, P., editor, 310
Schiller, J. F. von, 237
Schmalkaldic Union, 150
schools, parish, 171f., 178, 216, 218, 236, 238f.; normal, 178, 216, 236, 239, 336, 372; technical, 240, 336, 372; agricultural, 371f.; catholic, 377; German-Balt, 348. For institutions of higher learning, see Riga Polytechnic Institute and under Academia and Latvian State
Schreiner, W., diplomat, 309
Schwabe (Švabe), Arveds, historian, 376
Schwartzenberg, G. E. von, 217
science and scientists, 241, 256, 372, 375f.
Scott, Sir Walter, 252
sculpture, 256, 374
Scytte, Johann, Viceroy of Vidzeme, 172
Seeburg (Jurpils), 14, 35f.
Sejm (Polish parliament), 127, 139ff., 144, 148f., 152, 155, 182f., 185ff., 200, 206, 211
self-determination, 257, 271, 280f.,

285, 287, 289, 294ff.; Russian decree on, 296, 329
Selonia, tribal kingdom, 63, 79, 123; diocese of, 84
Selonians (Sēliji), 28, 49, 60
Sēlpils (Selburg), 60, 224
"Semigallia," 18
serfdom and serfs, 94, 96, 111, 155, 170, 173ff., 214, 216ff., 222, 232, 234, 238. Liberation of, under Swedish rule, 175, 177; in Estonia, 225; in Kurland, 212, 225; in Latvian Livonia, 225; in Latgale and Vidzeme, 229; in Russia, 222, 228, 263
Seven Years' War, 210
Sheremetiev, Gen., 214
shipbuilding, 10, 27, 185
Siberia, 250, 325, 339, 390; Ernst Biron in, 208; deportations to, 219, 268, 273, 402
Siberian Rifles, 278
Sievers, Friedrich von, Livonian Liberal, 222
Sievers-Römershof, von, 304
Sieyes, Abbé, translator of Die Letten, 222
Sigismund I, King of Poland, 113, 119
Sigismund II Augustus, King of Poland, 120, 122f., 126f., 137-143; and Riga, 148ff.
Sigismund III Vasa, King of Poland, 144, 147, 152f., 155f., 160f., 163, 165, 183, 185ff.
Sigtuna, Viking depot, 36
Sigulda, castle, 13; Livonian district, 109
Silesia, 77
Siliņš, J., painter, editor, 374
Simonsons, Gen. D., 324
Singing Festivals, 244
Sintelin, Kuronian stronghold, 81
Sixtus IV, Pope, 109
Skalbe, K., poet, 253, 291ff., 374
Skäne district, 162, 166
Skujenieks, M., statesman, 384
Slaucītājs, L., geologist, 9, 376
Slavs, claim settlement of Baltic lands, 28f.; cultural influence of, 12, 17, 339; early westward pressure of, 7, 24, 33, 42f., 49, 73, 130; medieval

trade with, 7, 29, 54, 97, 102f., 116. *See also* Muscovites, Novgorod and Polotzk (Slavs of)

Slovaks, 231

Smith, Adam, 225

Smolensk, 54, 97, 106, 116

social classes, *see* bourgeoisie, nobility, peasants, proletariat

Social-Democracy, 257, 260f.

Social-Democrats, Latvian, 254, 260, 264, 266, 290, 307, 345, 352, 358, 384, 405; Russian, 261, 272f.; German, 303

social welfare, 21, 370f.

Socialism, 22, 260, 346, 369

Socialist Revolutionaries (Russian), 263, 265, 273

Socialists, in Poland, 261; in Baltic Provinces, 261; Latvian, 308, 313, 345f., 349f., 361; Right Wing, 262, 265ff., 282; Left Wing, 265, 267, 271, 280, 345, 353f., 356f. *See also* Social-Democrats

Sonntag, G. K., 222

Soviet Baltic trade, 339f., 352f.

Soviet Central Committee, 296f.

Soviet of Soldiers' and Workers' Deputies, Petrograd, 279, 286ff.; Moscow, 288

Soviet Supreme Council, 391, 397ff.

Soviet Union, Peace treaties with Baltic States, 329; and Latvia, 330, 339ff., 352f., 361f., 368, 384 *passim*; and Latvian Leftists, 345, 352f.; and Baltic States, 383 *passim*; and Poland, 306, 383, 390, 403, 407; and Third Reich, 384f., 389-407; in World War II, 390, 403-407

Soviet of Workers' Deputies (St. Petersburg), 265f.

sovietization of Baltic States, 397f., 406ff.

Sophie of Prussia, Princess, 157

Spa, 322

Spain, 122, 161, 166, 188

Spartakists, 306

Spilve, battle of (1700), 192

Spure, Z., Latvian Communist politician, 397

Stalin, Joseph, 390ff., 397, 404, 407;

Commissar for National Minorities, 289

Steffenhagen, Johann, printer, 242

Stephen, Bátory, King of Poland, 128, 144-154, 179, 217

Stettin, Peace of (1570), 141

Stobe, Matīss, editor, 242

Stockholm, 161, 173, 178, 287, 289; Latvian Foreign Delegates in, 299

Stolbovo, Treaty of (1617), 163f.

Stolypin, Piotr, 272f.

Straumanis, M., physicist, 376

Strazdmuiža, Treaty of (1919), 323f.

Streltsi, insurrection of, 197

Strunke, N., artist, 374

Stryck, Baron von, 304, 314f.

Stučke, Pēteris, Latvian Communist, 260, 267, 306, 312, 314

Stuarts, English kings, 10, 190

Suevi, 31

Suta, R., artist, 374

Sweden, viii, 49, 114, 118, 129, 137ff., 167; and Muscovy, 122, 124ff., 160, 163, 168f.; and Poland, 141f., 146ff., 155f., 160-165, 167f., 198; and Denmark, 162f., 164, 166, 168f.; over Livonia 170-180; and Kurland, 164f., 168, 185f., 188, 191f., 204; and Tsarist Russia, 223; German-Balt intrigues in, 304, 315; and Baltic States, 341, 388; and Latvian Republic, 351, 383

Swedes, 20, 56, 137; early cultural influences, 34; early conflicts with, 35f.

Swedish nobles, 174; in Livonia, 170, 177

Sweyn Astrittson, Danish king, 36

Szlachta (Polish nobility), 144f., 154, 159, 167, 183, 210

Tacitus, 26, 31

Tālava (Tholova), tribal kingdom, 46, 48, 55, 60f., 66

Talavians (Tālavi), 28, 33, 73

Tālivald, tribal ruler, 48, 55, 61f.

Tallents, Col. Stephen, 323, 330

Tallinn, 62f., 259, 385, 386; Communist coup in, 358, 382

Talsi, castle-mound, 13, 39f.; town, 3, 39ff.

Tam Latweeschu lauschu draugam, gazette, 242

Tannenberg, battle of (1410), 85, 107, 113f.

Tarnapol, 288

Tartars, 79, 103, 105, 114; forces in Livonia, 121, 132, 142; Crimean, 143

Tartu (Dorpat), 63, 77, 120, 122, 142, 146, 168, 201, 280; in the Hansa, 98. *See also* Dorpat

Tartu, Treaty of (1920), 329

TASS, 396

Taube, Baron, 304

Tauroggen, Convention of (1812), 225

taxation, in Swedish Livonia, 176f.; in Russian Kurland, 213; in Russian Livonia, 218f., 227; in Latvian Republic, 366f.

Tchnovniki (Russian bureaucrats), 20, 249f., 269

Tegetmeier, Sylvester, Rigan humanist, 150

Templars, 58, 70, 72, 76

Tentelis, A., historian, 375

Terra mariana, 68, 86

Tērvete, capital of ancient Zemgale, 13, 39ff., 80, 82f.

Teutonic Knights, Order of, 59, 69, 113, 118, 128; in Prussia, 70ff., 77, 80, 82, 84f., 88, 101, 104, 107f., 125, 129; in Livonia, *see* Livonian Order; in Pomerania, 86; in Lithuania, 105ff.; in Württemberg, 128; and Hansa, 96ff., 103, 114; secularization of, 113f.

theater, 244, 374

Theoderic, missionary, 56, 71

Theodoric, Ostrogoth Emperor, 32, 48

Third International, 345

Thirteen Years' War, 113

Thirty Years' War, 160, 164, 166

Tholova, 33; *see* Tālava

Thomas Schoening, Archbishop of Riga, 119

Thorn (Toruń), 113

Thorn, Treaties of (1411), 107; 14ff., 113

Thracians, 9

Three Emperors' League (1873), 246

Tilbergs, R., painter, 256

Tilsit, Treaty of (1807), 223

Tirsa, battle of (1559), 123

Tobago, island of, 189f.

Tone, V., artist, 374

Torretta, marchese della, 325

Tott, Count, Governor-General of Livonia, 174f.

towns, 12ff., 96, 185, 235, 239, 259; administration of, 13, 15, 184f., 229, 241, 259f.

Toynbee, Arnold, quoted, 381

trade, ancient, 30ff.; medieval, 7, 53ff., 96ff.; Teutonic Knights in, 96, 98, 101, 103; Livonian, 155f.; Kuronian, 187f.; Baltic, 180f.; Rigan, 179; of Latvian Republic, 339f., 351-355, 362f., 365ff. *See also* Hanseatic League, German merchants

trade agreements, Latvian-Soviet, 339f., 352f., 384f.; Latvian-British, 367f.; Latvian-Estonian, 382; Latvian-Scandinavian, 383; German-Baltic States, 387; of Baltic States, 383

trade unions, 291, 345, 361, 369f.

transportation facilities, 6, 8, 11, 24, 240, 339, 353, 401

Travendal, Treaty of (1700), 199

treaties, *see* Mutual Assistance Treaties, Nonaggression Pacts, trade agreements

Treiden, battle of (1298), 101

Treu, H., newspaper publisher, 242

tribal history, *see* Baltic tribes, Kurzeme, Latgale, Vidzeme, Zemgale

Triple Entente (1907), 274

Troiden, King of Samogithia, 82

Trotsky, Leon, 289, 294f., 297

Troya, 27

Tukums, town, 224, 286

Turkestan, Baltic amber in, 30

Turkey, 197, 199, 210

Turks, 146, 197, 199

Ukraine, 14, 105, 169, 202, 261, 290, 293, 295, 339, 397, 407

Ullmann, K. K., Bishop, 239

Ulmanis, Kārlis, Deputy Commissioner of Vidzeme, 280; Prime Minister, 307-313, 316, 318, 323n., 333, 344, 355f., 358f.; President

of Latvian Republic, 360f., 373, 384, 387, 394f., 397
Ulrich von Jungingen, Grand Master of Teutonic Order, 107
Union of Lublin, 141
universities, see Dorpat and Riga
United Nations, 408
United States, Latvian emigrants to, 268; Latvia's trade with, 368; Department of State, 295, 338; recognition of Baltic States, 336f.; non-recognition of Soviet annexations, 399f., 408
"United States of the Baltic," 340
Urban IV, Pope, 96
Urban V, Pope, 102
Usma, lake, 8
U.S.S.R., see Soviet Union
Üxküll, see Ykesküla

Vainode, mass executions at, 402
Valdai Mts., 6, 8
Valdemar II, King of Denmark, 62, 64, 69
Valdemar IV, King of Denmark, 88
Valdemārs, K., economist, 243, 344
Valka (Wolmar), 13, 162, 169; Diet of, 111, 290; cradle of Latvian independence, 290f.; district of, 317; frontier settlement in, 330
Valmiera, town, 13, 214, 280, 290, 312; district of, 171, 316; normal school of, 239
Valters, M., publicist, 262
Varangians, 33
Varute, castle of, 79
Vasa, Swedish dynasty, viii
Vassily I, Grand Prince of Muscovy, 116
Vassily Shuisky, Tsar, 162f.
Vatican, see Papacy
Velikaya River, 29; marshes, 303
Venta River, 7, 28
Ventspils (Windau), 6f., 11, 14f., 185, 187, 208, 212, 239, 303, 316; heavy industry in, 259; modern port, 339, 352; Soviets in, 391
Versailles, copied at Mitau, 14, 191
Versailles, Treaty of, vii, 319, 324, 330, 386, 407
Vetzeke, tribal ruler, 13

Viborg, 124, 202f.; Manifesto (1906), 272
Vidbergs, Z., painter, editor, 374
Videvuds, mythological figure, 43
Vidzeme, tribal kingdom, 60, 68; under Sweden, 169, 171, 173, 175f., 178f.; under Russia, 203f., 206, 213f., 217, 219, 222, 225f., 230, 232, 235f.; in World War I, 276; in Baltic War of Liberation, 301, 324; province of Latvian Republic, 11, 281, 294, 337
Vienna, 211; archives of Teutonic and Livonian Orders in, 128
Viesturs, King of Zemgale, 13, 60, 63, 65
Vīgners, E., composer, 254
Vikings, 30, 32f., 40; trade routes of, 6f. See also Austrvaegr
Vilna, 123, 126ff., 138, 140, 148, 167; Voyevode of, 125; in Napoleonic wars, 223; coup of 1920, 341, 383f., 386; in World War II, 390ff.
Vilna, Treaty of (1323), 104
Virza, E., poet, 254, 291, 374
Visby, 33f., 37, 54, 57, 99; Hansa of, 97
Vishinsky, Andrei, 394
Vissevald, tribal king, 13, 48f., 60ff., 69
"Vistula Provinces," 247
Vistula River, 5, 28f., 114
Vitebsk, 97, 123, 211
Vitenis, King of Lithuania-Samogithia, 101
Vitold (Vytautas), Lithuanian ruler, 105ff.
Vītols, J., mathematician, 257
Vittoria, Francisco de, 180
Volga Germans in Kurland, 274
Volga River, 7, 32f.
Völkersahm, Hamilcar von, 227, 229
Volksdeutsche, 389
Volquin, Master of Livonian Order, 59, 73ff., 78
Vytautas, see Vitold

Wahlstatt, battle of (1241), 77
Walden, P., scientist, 256
Waldstejn, Albrecht, 165
Wallachians, 71
Wallhof, battle of (1626), 164

Walter, Bishop, 239, 245
Walter von Plettenberg, see Plettenberg
War of Kalmar, 162f.
wars, see Baltic War of Liberation, Great Northern War, Muscovite wars, Napoleonic wars, Northern Seven Years' War, Polish-Swedish Livonian wars, Russo-Finnish War, Russo-Japanese War, Russo-Turkish War, Seven Years' War, Thirteen Years' War, Thirty Years' War, War of Kalmar, World War I, World War II
wars, devastation of, 13f., 169, 201, 214f., 280, 330
Warsaw, 146, 152, 155, 167, 183, 186f., 200, 206ff., 210f.
Warsaw Conference (1922), 341f.
Warsaw, Duchy of, 223
Wartenberg, barony of, 209f.
Washington, D.C., viii, 393, 398
Washington, George, 227
Watson, Charles, editor, 242
Wehlau, Treaty of (1657), 168
Wehrmacht, 406f.
Weimar Republic, see Germany
Weiss, von, Russian colonel, 305
Wenden, diocese of, 150; Livonian district of, 109, 139, 153, 157, 172. See also Cēsis
Western Powers, see Allies
Westphalia, Peace of (1648), 166
Westphalians in the Livonian Order, 57, 90, 98, 108, 131
White Russia, 14, 27, 202, 404, 407
White Russians, 22; cooperating with German-Balts, 300, 310ff., 316, 324, 326ff.; Latvian national minority, 16, 346, 371
White Ruthenia, 27, 105
"Whitland," 4
William II, Kaiser, 258, 264; and Kurland, 296, 300ff.; and Baltic States, 296
William of Brandenburg, Archbishop of Riga, 119f., 125f., 140
William of Modena, Bishop and papal legate, 55, 62, 65, 69, 74, 84
William, Duke of Kurzeme, 157, 164, 182f., 185ff.
Wilson, Woodrow, President, 298

Windau, see Ventspils
Winnig, August, German High Commissioner in the Baltic, 302f., 306, 309, 312f.
Wirte, Latvian landowners, 253, 268ff.
Wismar, province of, 166
witchcraft, 172
Władysław II, King of Poland, 106
Władysław, son of Sigismund III, 161ff., 165, 167
Władysław IV, 187
Wolfstan, 4
Wolmar, see Valka
women, in tribal times, 20, 41f., 47; in Livonia, 131; in modern Latvia, 21, 370
World War I, 3, 14, 16, 130, 249, 275-280, 285, 295, 330, 347, 407
World War II, 360, 390f., 403 passim
Wrangel, Gen. P. N., 328
Württemberg, 348; Teutonic Order in, 128

Yadvingi, 28
Yalta, 408
Ykeskūla (Üxküll, Ikšķile), 56ff., 82
York, Gen., 224
"Young Letts," 244, 258, 282
Yudenitch, Gen. Nikolai, 327f.

Zale, K., sculptor, 374
Zālītis, Jānis, statesman, 273
Zalkalns, T., sculptor, 256, 374
Zamoyski, Jan, 144, 147, 155, 160, 162
Zamuelis, V., statesman, 293, 345
Zapoli, 146
Zariņš, K., diplomat, 393
Zeiferts, T., literary critic, 253
Zemgale, tribal kingdom, 54, 60, 63ff., 70, 72ff., 78, 80; diocese of, 84, 87; under Livonian Order, 82f., 87f.; in Duchy of Kurland, 126, 182ff., 224; in World War I, 276; in Baltic War of Liberation, 327; province of Latvian Republic, 9, 11, 18, 294, 337
Zemgallians (Zemgali), 28, 33, 49, 56, 59, 63ff., 68, 72ff., 78, 80ff., 91, 128
Zemgals, Gustav, statesman, 307, 345

Zemitāns, Col. J., 322f.

Zemstva, 229, 263, 273, 281; "zemstvo men," 264f., 271f.; Congress (1905), 263, 271

Zhdanov, Andrei, Alexandrovitch, 388

Zīle, M., biologist, 376

Zilupe River, 8

Zinzendorf, Count von, 236

Zorn, Anders, 256

Zürich, 287